AF527066

# THE SACRED BOOKS OF THE EAST

*Translated by*

VARIOUS ORIENTAL SCHOLARS

*Edited by*

F. MAX MÜLLER

**Vol. 48**

# SACRED BOOKS OF THE EAST

**(50 VOLUMES)**

Series Editor : *F. Max-Müller*

ISBN: 978-81-208-0101-1 (Set) Rs. 20000 (Each Vol. Rs. 400)

These volumes of the Sacred Books of the East series include translations of all the most important works of the seven non-Christian religions that have exercised a profound influence on the civilisations of the continent of Asia. The Vedic Brahmanic system claims 21 volumes, Buddhism 10, and Jainism 2; 8 volumes comprise Sacred Books of the Parsis; 2 volumes represent Islam; and 6 the two main indigenous systems of China. Translated by twenty leading authorities in their respective fields, the volumes have been edited by the late F. Max Müller. The inception, publication and the compilation of these books cover almost 34 years.

**I. BUDDHISM**

**Vol. 49:** Buddhist Mahayana Texts (2 Parts)
**Vol. 11:** Buddhist Suttas
**Vol. 10:** The Dhammapada and Sutta Nipata
**Vols. 35 & 36:** The Questions of King Milinda (2 Parts)
**Vol. 21:** The Saddharma Pundarika or the Lotus of the True Law
**Vols. 13, 17 & 20:** Vinaya Texts (3 Parts)

**II. CHINESE**

**Vol. 19:** The Fo-Sho-Hing-Tsan-King
**Vols. 3, 16, 27, 28, 39 & 40:** The Sacred Books of China (6 Parts)

**III. A GENERAL INDEX**

**Vol. 50:** A General Index to the Names and Subject-matter of the Sacred Books of the East

**IV. ISLAM**

**Vols. 6 & 9:** The Qur'an (2 Parts)

**V. JAINISM**

**Vols. 22 & 45:** The Jaina Sutras (2 Parts)

**VI. PARSIS**

**Vols. 5, 18, 24, 37 & 47:** Pahlavi Texts (5 Parts)
**Vols. 4, 23 & 31:** The Zend-Avesta (3 Parts)

**VII. VEDIC-BRAHMANIC SYSTEM**

**Vol. 8:** The Bhagavadgita with the Sanatsujatiya and the Anugita
**Vols. 29 & 30:** The Grihya-Sutras: Rules of Vedic Domestic Ceremonies (2 Parts)
**Vol. 42:** Hymns of the Atharva Veda together with Extracts from the Ritual Books and the Commentaries
**Vol. 7:** The Institutes of Vishnu
**Vol. 25:** The Laws of Manu
**Vol. 33:** The Minor Law Books
**Vols. 2 & 14:** The Sacred Laws of the Aryas as Taught in the Schools of Apastamba, Gautama, Vasishtha and Baudhayana (2 Parts)
**Vols. 12, 26, 41, 43 & 44:** The Satapatha Brahmana According to the Text of the Madhyandina School (5 Parts)
**Vols. 1 & 15:** The Upanishads (2 Parts)
**Vols. 34 & 38:** The Vedanta Sutras (2 Parts)
**Vol. 48:** The Vedanta-Sutras (with the commentary by Ramanuja)
**Vols. 32 & 46:** Vedic Hymns (2 Parts)

# THE VEDÂNTA-SÛTRAS

*With the Commentary by*

RÂMÂNU*G*A

*Translated by*

GEORGE THIBAUT

PART III

MOTILAL BANARSIDASS PUBLISHERS
PRIVATE LIMITED • DELHI

*9th Reprint: Delhi, 2018*
*First Indian Edition: Delhi, 1962*
*First Published by Oxford University Press, 1904*



ISBN: 978-81-208-0149-3

MOTILAL BANARSIDASS
41 U.A. Bungalow Road, Jawahar Nagar, Delhi 110 007
1 B, Jyoti Studio Compound, Kennedy Bridge, Nana Chowk, Mumbai 400 007
203 Royapettah High Road, Mylapore, Chennai 600 004
236, 9th Main III Block, Jayanagar, Bengaluru 560 011
8 Camac Street, Kolkata 700 017
Ashok Rajpath, Patna 800 004
Chowk, Varanasi 221 001

UNESCO COLLECTION OF REPRESENTATIVE WORKS— Indian Series
*This book has been accepted in the Indian Translation Series of the UNESCO Collection of Representative Works, jointly sponsored by the United Nations Educational Scientific and Cultural Organization (UNESCO) and the Government of India*

*Printed in India*

by RP Jain at NAB Printing Unit,
A-44, Naraina Industrial Area, Phase I, New Delhi–110028
and published by JP Jain for Motilal Banarsidass Publishers (P) Ltd,
41 U.A. Bungalow Road, Jawahar Nagar, Delhi-110007

RASHTRAPATI BHAVAN,
NEW DELHI-4
June 10, 1962

I am very glad to know that the Sacred Books of the East, published years ago by the Clarendon Press, Oxford, which have been out of print for a number of years, will now be available to all students of religion and philosophy. The enterprise of the publishers is commendable and I hope the books will be widely read.

S. RADHAKRISHNAN

## PUBLISHER'S NOTE

First, the man distinguished between eternal and perishable. Later he discovered within himself the germ of the Eternal. This discovery was an epoch in the history of the human mind and the *East was the first to discover it.*

To watch in the Sacred Books of the East the dawn of this religious consciousness of man, must always remain one of the most inspiring and hallowing sights in the whole history of the world. In order to have a solid foundation for a comparative study of the Religions of the East, we must have before all things, complete and thoroughly faithful translation of their Sacred Books in which some of the ancient sayings were preserved because they were so true and so striking that they could not be forgotten. They contained eternal truths, expressed for the first time in human language.

With profoundest reverence for Dr. S. Radhakrishnan, President of India, who inspired us for the task; our deep sense of gratitude for Dr. C. D. Deshmukh & Dr. D. S. Kothari, for encouraging assistance; esteemed appreciation of UNESCO for the warm endorsement of the cause ; and finally with indebtedness to Dr. H. Rau, Director, Max Müller Bhawan, New Delhi, in procuring us the texts of the Series for reprint, we humbly conclude.

# CONTENTS.

## VEDÂNTA-SÛTRAS WITH THE COMMENTARY OF RÂMÂNUGA.

# INTRODUCTION.

In the Introduction to the first volume of the translation of the 'Vedânta-Sûtras with *S*ankara's Commentary' (vol. xxxiv of this Series) I have dwelt at some length on the interest which Râmânu*g*a's Commentary may claim—as being, on the one hand, the fullest exposition of what may be called the Theistic Vedânta, and as supplying us, on the other, with means of penetrating to the true meaning of Bâdarâya*n*a's Aphorisms. I do not wish to enter here into a fuller discussion of Râmânu*g*a's work in either of these aspects; an adequate treatment of them would, moreover, require considerably more space than is at my disposal. Some very useful material for the right understanding of Râmânu*g*a's work is to be found in the 'Analytical Outline of Contents' which Messrs. M. Rangâ*k*ârya and M. B. Varadarâ*g*a Aiyangâr have prefixed to the first volume of their scholarly translation of the *S*rîbhâshya (Madras, 1899).

The question as to what the Sûtras really teach is a critical, not a philosophical one. This distinction seems to have been imperfectly realised by several of those critics, writing in India, who have examined the views expressed in my Introduction to the translation of *S*ankara's Commentary. A writer should not be taxed with 'philosophic incompetency,' 'hopeless theistic bias due to early training,' and the like, simply because he, on the basis of a purely critical investigation, considers himself entitled to maintain that a certain ancient document sets forth one philosophical view rather than another. I have nowhere expressed an opinion as to the comparative philosophical value of the systems of *S*ankara and Râmânu*g*a; not because I have no definite opinions on this point, but because to introduce them into a critical enquiry would be purposeless if not objectionable.

The question as to the true meaning of the Sûtras is

no doubt of some interest; although the interest of problems of this kind may easily be over-estimated. Among the remarks of critics on my treatment of this problem I have found little of solid value. The main arguments which I have set forth, not so much in favour of the adequacy of Râmânu*g*a's interpretation, as against the validity of *S*aṅkarâ*k*ârya's understanding of the Sûtras, appear to me not to have been touched. I do not by any means consider the problem a hopeless one; but its solution will not be advanced, in any direction, but by those who will be at the trouble of submitting the entire body of the Sûtras to a new and detailed investigation, availing themselves to the full of the help that is to be derived from the study of all the existing Commentaries.

The present translation of the *S*rîbhâshya claims to be faithful on the whole, although I must acknowledge that I have aimed rather at making it intelligible and, in a certain sense, readable than scrupulously accurate. If I had to rewrite it, I should feel inclined to go even further in the same direction. Indian Philosophy would, in my opinion, be more readily and widely appreciated than it is at present, if the translators of philosophical works had been somewhat more concerned to throw their versions into a form less strange and repellent to the western reader than literal renderings from technical Sanskrit must needs be in many passages. I am not unaware of the peculiar dangers of the plan now advocated—among which the most obvious is the temptation it offers to the translator of deviating from the text more widely than regard for clearness would absolutely require. And I am conscious of having failed in this respect in more than one instance. In other cases I have no doubt gone astray through an imperfect understanding of the author's meaning. The fact is, that as yet the time has hardly come for fully adequate translations of comprehensive works of the type of the *S*rîbhâshya, the authors of which wrote with reference—in many cases tacit—to an immense and highly technical philosophical literature which is only just beginning to be studied, and comprehended in part, by European scholars.

It gives me great pleasure to acknowledge the help which I have received from various quarters in preparing this translation. Pa*nd*it Gaṅgâdhara *S*âstrin, C. I. E., of the Benares Sanskrit College, has, with unwearying kindness and patience, supplied me throughout with comments of his own on difficult sections of the text. Pa*nd*it Svâmin Râma Mi*s*ra *S*âstrin has rendered me frequent assistance in the earlier portion of my task. And to Mr. A. Venis, the learned Principal of the Benares Sanskrit College, I am indebted for most instructive notes on some passages of a peculiarly technical and abstruse character. Nor can I conclude without expressing my sense of obligation to Colonel G. A. Jacob, whose invaluable 'Concordance to the Principal Upanishads' lightens to an incalculable degree the task of any scholar who is engaged in work bearing on the Vedânta.

# VEDÂNTA-SÛTRAS

WITH

# RÂMANU*G*A'S *S*RÎBHÂSHYA.

## FIRST ADHYÂYA.

### FIRST PÂDA.

May my mind be filled with devotion towards the highest Brahman, the abode of Lakshmî; who is luminously revealed in the Upanishads; who in sport produces, sustains, and reabsorbs the entire Universe; whose only aim is to foster the manifold classes of beings that humbly worship him.

The nectar of the teaching of Parâ*s*ara's son (Vyâsa),—which was brought up from the middle of the milk-ocean of the Upanishads—which restores to life the souls whose vital strength had departed owing to the heat of the fire of transmigratory existence—which was well guarded by the teachers of old—which was obscured by the mutual conflict of manifold opinions,—may intelligent men daily enjoy that as it is now presented to them in my words.

The lengthy explanation (v*ri*tti) of the Brahma-sûtras which was composed by the Reverend Bodhâyana has been abridged by former teachers; according to their views the words of the Sûtras will be explained in this present work.

1. Then therefore the enquiry into Brahman.

In this Sûtra the word 'then' expresses immediate sequence; the word 'therefore' intimates that what has taken place (viz. the study of the karmakâ*nd*a of the Veda) constitutes the reason (of the enquiry into Brahman). For the fact is that the enquiry into (lit. 'the desire to know') Brahman—the fruit of which enquiry is infinite in nature and permanent—follows immediately in the case of him who, having read the Veda together with its auxiliary disciplines, has reached the knowledge that the fruit of mere works is limited and non-permanent, and hence has conceived the desire of final release.

The compound 'brahma*g*i*gñ*âsâ' is to be explained as 'the enquiry of Brahman,' the genitive case 'of Brahman' being understood to denote the object; in agreement with the special rule as to the meaning of the genitive case, Pâ*n*ini II, 3, 65. It might be said that even if we accepted the general meaning of the genitive case—which is that of connexion in general—Brahman's position (in the above compound) as an object would be established by the circumstance that the 'enquiry' demands an object; but in agreement with the principle that the direct denotation of a word is to be preferred to a meaning inferred we take the genitive case 'of Brahman' as denoting the object.

The word 'Brahman' denotes the highest Person (purushottama), who is essentially free from all imperfections and possesses numberless classes of auspicious qualities of unsurpassable excellence. The term 'Brahman' is applied to any things which possess the quality of greatness (b*ri*hattva, from the root 'b*ri*h'); but primarily denotes that which possesses greatness, of essential nature as well as of qualities, in unlimited fulness; and such is only the Lord of all. Hence the word 'Brahman' primarily denotes him alone, and in a secondary derivative sense only those things which possess some small part of the Lord's qualities; for it would be improper to assume several meanings for the word (so that it would denote primarily or directly more than one thing). The case is analogous to that of the term 'bhagavat[1].' The Lord only is enquired into, for the sake of immortality, by all those who are afflicted with the triad of pain. Hence the Lord of all is that Brahman which, according to the Sûtra, constitutes the object of enquiry. The word '*g*i*gñ*âsâ' is a desiderative formation meaning 'desire to know.' And as in the

[1] 'Bhagavat' denotes primarily the Lord, the Divinity; secondarily any holy person.

case of any desire the desired object is the chief thing, the Sûtra means to enjoin knowledge — which is the object of the desire of knowledge. The purport of the entire Sûtra then is as follows: 'Since the fruit of works known through the earlier part of the Mîmâ*m*sâ is limited and non-permanent, and since the fruit of the knowledge of Brahman—which knowledge is to be reached through the latter part of the Mîmâ*m*sâ—is unlimited and permanent; for this reason Brahman is to be known, after the knowledge of works has previously taken place.'—The same meaning is expressed by the V*ri*ttikâra when saying 'after the comprehension of works has taken place there follows the enquiry into Brahman.' And that the enquiry into works and that into Brahman constitute one body of doctrine, he (the V*ri*ttikâra) will declare later on 'this *S*ârîraka-doctrine is connected with *G*aimini's doctrine as contained in sixteen adhyâyas; this proves the two to constitute one body of doctrine.' Hence the earlier and the later Mîmâ*m*sâ are separate only in so far as there is a difference of matter to be taught by each; in the same way as the two halves of the Pûrva Mîmâ*m*sâ-sûtras, consisting of six adhyâyas each, are separate[1]; and as each adhyâya is separate. The entire Mîmâ*m*sâ-*s*âstra—which begins with the Sûtra 'Now therefore the enquiry into religious duty' and concludes with the Sûtra '(From there is) no return on account of scriptural statement'—has, owing to the special character of the contents, a definite order of internal succession. This is as follows. At first the precept 'one is to learn one's own text (svâdhyâya)' enjoins the apprehension of that aggregate of syllables which is called 'Veda,' and is here referred to as 'svâdhyâya.' Next there arises the desire to know of what nature the 'Learning' enjoined is to be, and how it is to be done. Here there come in certain injunctions such as

[1] The first six books of the Pûrva Mîmâ*m*sâ-sûtras give rules for the fundamental forms of the sacrifice; while the last six books teach how these rules are to be applied to the so-called modified forms.

'Let a Brâhma*n*a be initiated in his eighth year' and 'The teacher is to make him recite the Veda'; and certain rules about special observances and restrictions—such as 'having performed the upâkarman on the full moon of *S*râva*n*a or Praush*th*apada according to prescription, he is to study the sacred verses for four months and a half'—which enjoin all the required details.

From all these it is understood that the study enjoined has for its result the apprehension of the aggregate of syllables called Veda, on the part of a pupil who has been initiated by a teacher sprung from a good family, leading a virtuous life, and possessing purity of soul; who practises certain special observances and restrictions; and who learns by repeating what is recited by the teacher.

And this study of the Veda is of the nature of a sa*m*skâra of the text, since the form of the injunction 'the Veda is to be studied' shows that the Veda is the object (of the action of studying). By a sa*m*skâra is understood an action whereby something is fitted to produce some other effect; and that the Veda should be the object of such a sa*m*skâra is quite appropriate, since it gives rise to the knowledge of the four chief ends of human action—viz. religious duty, wealth, pleasure, and final release—and of the means to effect them; and since it helps to effect those ends by itself also, viz. by mere mechanical repetition (apart from any knowledge to which it may give rise).

The injunction as to the study of the Veda thus aims only at the apprehension of the aggregate of syllables (constituting the Veda) according to certain rules; it is in this way analogous to the recital of mantras.

It is further observed that the Veda thus apprehended through reading spontaneously gives rise to the ideas of certain things subserving certain purposes. A person, therefore, who has formed notions of those things immediately, i.e. on the mere apprehension of the text of the Veda through reading, thereupon naturally applies himself to the study of the Mîmâ*m*sâ, which consists in a methodical discussion of the sentences constituting the text of the

Veda, and has for its result the accurate determination of the nature of those things and their different modes. Through this study the student ascertains the character of the injunctions of work which form part of the Veda, and observes that all work leads only to non-permanent results; and as, on the other hand, he immediately becomes aware that the Upanishad sections—which form part of the Veda which he has apprehended through reading—refer to an infinite and permanent result, viz. immortality, he applies himself to the study of the *S*ârîraka-Mîmâ*m*sâ, which consists in a systematic discussion of the Vedânta-texts, and has for its result the accurate determination of their sense. That the fruit of mere works is transitory, while the result of the knowledge of Brahman is something permanent, the Vedânta-texts declare in many places—'And as here the world acquired by work perishes, so there the world acquired by merit perishes' (*Kh*. Up. VIII, 1, 6); 'That work of his has an end' (B*ri*. Up. III, 8, 10); 'By non-permanent works the Permanent is not obtained' (Ka. Up. I, 2, 10); 'Frail indeed are those boats, the sacrifices' (Mu. Up. I, 2, 7); 'Let a Brâhma*n*a, after he has examined all these worlds that are gained by works, acquire freedom from all desires. What is not made cannot be gained by what is made. To understand this, let the pupil, with fuel in his hand, go to a teacher who is learned and dwells entirely in Brahman. To that pupil who has approached him respectfully, whose mind is altogether calm, the wise teacher truly told that knowledge of Brahman through which he knows the imperishable true Person' (Mu. Up. I, 2, 12, 13).—'Told' here means 'he is to tell.'—On the other hand, 'He who knows Brahman attains the Highest' (Taitt. Up. II, 1, 1); 'He who sees this does not see death' (*Kh*. Up. VII, 26, 2); 'He becomes a self-ruler' (*Kh*. Up. VII, 25, 2); 'Knowing him he becomes immortal here' (Taitt. Âr. III, 12, 7); 'Having known him he passes over death; there is no other path to go' (*S*vet. Up. VI, 15); 'Having known as separate his Self and the Mover, pleased thereby he goes to immortality' (*S*vet. Up. I, 6).

But—an objection here is raised—the mere learning of the Veda with its auxiliary disciplines gives rise to the knowledge that the heavenly world and the like are the results of works, and that all such results are transitory, while immortality is the fruit of meditation on Brahman. Possessing such knowledge, a person desirous of final release may at once proceed to the enquiry into Brahman; and what need is there of a systematic consideration of religious duty (i. e. of the study of the Pûrva Mîmâ*m*sâ)?—If this reasoning were valid, we reply, the person desirous of release need not even apply himself to the study of the *S*ârîraka Mîmâ*m*sâ, since Brahman is known from the mere reading of the Veda with its auxiliary disciplines.—True. Such knowledge arises indeed immediately (without deeper enquiry). But a matter apprehended in this immediate way is not raised above doubt and mistake. Hence a systematic discussion of the Vedânta-texts must be undertaken in order that their sense may be fully ascertained.—We agree. But you will have to admit that for the very same reason we must undertake a systematic enquiry into religious duty!

## THE SMALL PÛRVAPAKSHA.

But—a further objection is urged—as that which has to precede the systematic enquiry into Brahman we should assign something which that enquiry necessarily presupposes. The enquiry into the nature of duty, however, does not form such a prerequisite, since a consideration of the Vedânta-texts may be undertaken by any one who has read those texts, even if he is not acquainted with works. —But in the Vedânta-texts there are enjoined meditations on the Udgîtha and the like which are matters auxiliary to works; and such meditations are not possible for him who is not acquainted with those works!—You who raise this objection clearly are ignorant of what kind of knowledge the *S*ârîraka Mîmâ*m*sâ is concerned with! What that *s*âstra aims at is to destroy completely that wrong knowledge which is the root of all pain, for man, liable to birth, old age, and death, and all the numberless other evils connected with transmigratory existence—evils that spring from the view, due to beginningless Nescience, that there is plurality of existence; and to that end the *s*âstra endeavours to establish the knowledge of the unity of the Self. Now to this knowledge, the knowledge of works—which is based on the assumption of plurality of existence—is not only useless but even opposed. The consideration of the Udgîtha and the like, which is supplementary to works only, finds a place in the Vedânta-texts, only because like them it is of the nature of knowledge; but it has no direct connexion with the true topic of those texts. Hence some prerequisite must be indicated which has reference to the principal topic of the *s*âstra.—Quite so; and this prerequisite is just the knowledge of works; for scripture declares that final release results from knowledge with works added. The Sûtra-writer himself says further on 'And there is need of all works, on account of the scriptural statement of sacrifices and the like' (Ve. Sû. III, 4, 26). And if the required works were not known, one could not determine which works have to be combined with knowledge and which not. Hence the knowledge of works is just the necessary prerequisite.—Not so, we reply. That which puts an end to Nescience is exclusively the knowledge of Brahman, which is pure intelligence and antagonistic to all plurality. For final release consists just in the cessation of Nescience; how then can works—to which there attach endless differences connected with caste, â*s*rama, object to be accomplished, means and mode of accomplishment, &c.—ever supply a means for the cessation of ignorance, which is essentially the cessation of the view that difference exists? That works, the results of which are transitory, are contrary to final release, and that such release can be effected through knowledge only, scripture declares in many places; compare all the passages quoted above (p. 7).

As to the assertion that knowledge requires sacrifices and other works, we remark that—as follows from the essential contrariety of knowledge and works, and as further appears from an accurate consideration of the words of scripture—pious works can contribute only towards the rise of the desire of knowledge, in so far namely as they clear the internal organ (of knowledge), but can have no influence on the production of the fruit, i. e. knowledge itself. For the scriptural passage concerned runs as follows: 'Brâhma*n*as desire to know him by the study of the Veda, by sacrifice, by gifts,' &c. (B*ri*. Up. IV, 4, 22).

According to this passage, the desire only of knowledge springs up through works; while another text teaches that calmness, self-restraint, and so on, are the direct means for the origination of knowledge itself. (Having become tranquil, calm, subdued, satisfied, patient, and collected, he is to see the Self within the Self (B*ri*. Up. IV, 4, 23).)

The process thus is as follows. After the mind of a man has been cleaned of all impurities through works performed in many preceding states of existence, without a view to special forms of reward, there arises in him the desire of knowledge, and thereupon—through knowledge itself originated by certain scriptural texts—'Being only, this was in the beginning, one only without a second' (*Kh*. Up. VI, 1, 2); 'Truth, Knowledge, the Infinite, is Brahman' (Taitt. Up. II, 1); 'Without parts, without actions, calm, without fault, without taint' (*S*vet. Up. VI, 19); 'This Self is Brahman' (B*ri*. Up. II, 5, 19); 'Thou art that' (*Kh*. Up. VI, 9, 7), Nescience comes to an end. Now, 'hearing,' 'reflection,' and 'meditation,' are helpful towards cognising the sense of these Vedic texts. 'Hearing' (*s*rava*n*a) means the apprehension of the sense of scripture, together with collateral arguments, from a teacher who possesses the true insight, viz. that the Vedânta-texts establish the doctrine of the unity of the Self. 'Reflection' (mananam) means the confirmation within oneself of the sense taught by the teacher, by means of arguments showing it alone to be suitable. 'Meditation' (nididhyâsanam) finally means the constant holding of that sense before one's mind, so as to dispel thereby the antagonistic beginningless imagination of plurality. In the case of him who through 'hearing,' 'reflection,' and meditation,' has dispelled the entire imagination of plurality, the knowledge of the sense of Vedânta-texts puts an end to Nescience; and what we therefore require is a statement of the indispensable prerequisites of such 'hearing,' 'reflection,' and so on. Now of such prerequisites there are four, viz. discrimination of what is permanent and what is non-permanent; the full possession of calmness of mind, self-restraint and similar means; the renunciation of all enjoyment of fruits here below as well as in the next world; and the desire of final release.

Without these the desire of knowledge cannot arise; and they are therefore known, from the very nature of the matter, to be necessary prerequisites. To sum up: The root of bondage is the unreal view of plurality which itself has its root in Nescience that conceals the true being of Brahman. Bondage itself thus is unreal, and is on that account cut short, together with its root, by mere knowledge. Such knowledge is originated by texts such as 'That art thou'; and work is of no help either towards its nature, or its origination, or its fruit (i. e. release). It is on the other hand helpful towards the desire of knowledge, which arises owing to an increase of the element of goodness (sattva) in the soul, due to the destruction of the elements of passion (ra*g*as) and darkness (tamas) which are the root of all moral evil. This use is referred to in the text quoted above, 'Brâhma*n*as wish to know him,' &c. As, therefore, the knowledge of works is of no use towards the knowledge of Brahman, we must acknowledge as the prerequisite of the latter knowledge the four means mentioned above.

## THE SMALL SIDDHÂNTA.

To this argumentation we make the following reply. We admit that release consists only in the cessation of Nescience, and that this cessation results entirely from the knowledge of Brahman. But a distinction has here to be made regarding the nature of this knowledge which the Vedânta-texts aim at enjoining for the purpose of putting an end to Nescience. Is it merely the knowledge of the sense of sentences which originates from the sentences? or is it knowledge in the form of meditation (upâsana) which has the knowledge just referred to as its antecedent? It cannot be knowledge of the former kind; for such knowledge springs from the mere apprehension of the sentence, apart from any special injunction, and moreover we do not observe that the cessation of Nescience is effected by such knowledge merely. Our adversary will perhaps attempt to explain things in the following way. The Vedânta-texts do not, he will say, produce that knowledge which makes an end of Nescience, so long as the imagination of plurality is not dispelled. And the fact that such knowledge, even when produced, does not at once and for every one put a stop to the view of plurality by no means subverts my opinion; for, to mention an analogous instance, the double appearance of the moon—presenting itself to a person affected with a certain weakness of vision—does not come to an end as soon as the oneness of the moon has been apprehended by reason. Moreover, even without having come to an end, the view of plurality is powerless to effect further bondage, as soon as the root, i. e. Nescience, has once been cut. But this defence we are unable to admit. It is impossible that knowledge should not arise when its means, i. e. the texts conveying knowledge, are once present. And we observe that even when there exists an antagonistic imagination (interfering with the rise of knowledge), information given by competent persons, the presence of characteristic marks (on which a correct inference may be based), and the like give rise to knowledge which sublates the erroneous imagination. Nor can we admit that even after the sense of texts has been apprehended, the view of plurality may continue owing to some small remainder of beginningless imagination. For as this imagination which constitutes the means for the view of plurality is itself false, it is necessarily put an end to by the rise of true knowledge. If this did not take place, that imagination would never come to an end, since there is no other means but knowledge to effect its cessation. To say that the view of plurality, which is the effect of that imagination, continues even after its root has been cut, is mere nonsense. The instance of some one seeing the moon double is not analogous. For in his case the non-cessation of wrong knowledge explains itself from the circumstance that the cause of wrong knowledge, viz. the real defect of the eye which does not admit of being sublated by knowledge, is not removed, although that which would sublate wrong knowledge is near. On the other hand, effects, such as fear and the like, may come to an end because they can be sublated by means of knowledge of superior force. Moreover, if it were true that knowledge arises through the dispelling of the imagination of plurality, the rise of knowledge would really never be brought about. For the imagination of plurality has through gradual growth in the course of beginningless time acquired an infinite strength, and does not therefore admit of being dispelled by the comparatively weak conception of non-duality. Hence we conclude that the knowledge which the Vedânta-texts aim at inculcating is a knowledge other than the mere knowledge of the sense of sentences, and denoted by 'dhyâna,' 'upâsanâ' (i. e. meditation), and similar terms.

With this agree scriptural texts such as 'Having known it, let him practise meditation' (B*ri*. Up. IV, 4, 21); 'He who, having searched out the Self, knows it' (*Kh*. Up. VIII, 7, 1); 'Meditate on the Self as Om' (Mu. Up. II, 2, 6); 'Having known that, he is freed from the jaws of death' (Ka. Up. I, 3, 15); 'Let a man meditate on the Self only as his world' (B*ri*. Up. I, 4, 15); 'The Self is to be seen, to be heard, to be reflected on, to be meditated on' (B*ri*. Up. IV, 5, 6); 'That we must search out, that we must try to understand' (*Kh*. Up. VIII, 7, 1).

(According to the principle of the oneness of purport of the different *s*âkhâs) all these texts must be viewed as agreeing in meaning with the injunction of meditation contained in the passage quoted from the B*ri*. Up.; and what they enjoin is therefore meditation. In the first and second passages quoted, the words 'having known' and 'having searched out' (vig*ñ*âya; anuvidya) contain a mere reference to (not injunction of) the apprehension of the meaning of texts, such apprehension subserving meditation; while the injunction of meditation (which is the true purport of the passages) is conveyed by the clauses 'let him practise meditation' (pra*g*ñâ*m* kurvîta) and 'he knows it.' In the same way the clause 'the Self is to be heard' is a mere anuvâda, i. e. a mere reference to what is already established by other means; for a person who has read the Veda observes that it contains instruction about matters connected with certain definite purposes, and then on his own account applies himself to methodical 'hearing,' in order definitely to ascertain these matters; 'hearing' thus is established already. In the same way the clause 'the Self is to be reflected upon' is a mere anuvâda of reflection which is known as a means of confirming what one has 'heard.' It is therefore meditation only which all those texts enjoin. In agreement with this a later Sûtra also says, 'Repetition more than once, on account of instruction' (Ve. Sû. IV, 1, 1). That the knowledge intended to be enjoined as the means of final release is of the nature of meditation, we conclude from the circumstance that the terms 'knowing' and 'meditating' are seen to be used in place of each other in the earlier and later parts of Vedic texts. Compare the following passages: 'Let a man meditate on mind as Brahman,' and 'he who knows this shines and warms through his celebrity, fame, and glory of countenance' (*Kh*. Up. III, 18, 1; 6). And 'He does not know him, for he is not complete,' and 'Let men meditate on him as the Self' (B*ri*. Up. I, 4, 7). And 'He who knows what he knows,' and 'Teach me the deity on which you meditate' (*Kh*. Up. IV, 1, 6; 2, 2).

'Meditation' means steady remembrance, i. e. a continuity of steady remembrance, uninterrupted like the flow of oil; in agreement with the scriptural passage which declares steady remembrance to be the means of release, 'on the attainment of remembrance all the ties are loosened' (*Kh*. Up. VII, 26, 2). Such remembrance is of the same character (form) as seeing (intuition); for the passage quoted has the same purport as the following one, 'The fetter of the heart is broken, all doubts are solved, and all the works of that man perish when he has been seen who is high and low' (Mu. Up. II, 2, 8). And this being so, we conclude that the passage 'the Self is to be seen' teaches that 'Meditation' has the character of 'seeing' or 'intuition.' And that remembrance has the character of 'seeing' is due to the element of imagination (representation) which prevails in it. All this has been set forth at length by the Vâkyakâra. 'Knowledge (vedana) means meditation (upâsana), scripture using the word in that sense'; i.e. in all Upanishads that knowledge which is enjoined as the means of final release is Meditation. The Vâkyakâra then propounds a pûrvapaksha (primâ facie view), 'Once he is to make the meditation, the matter enjoined by scripture being accomplished thereby, as in the case of the prayâgas and the like'; and then sums up against this in the words 'but (meditation) is established on account of the term meditation'; that means—knowledge repeated more than once (i.e. meditation) is determined to be the means of Release.—The Vâkyakâra then goes on 'Meditation is steady remembrance, on the ground of observation and statement.' That means—this knowledge, of the form of meditation, and repeated more than once, is of the nature of steady remembrance.

Such remembrance has been declared to be of the character of 'seeing,' and this character of seeing consists in its possessing the character of immediate presentation (pratyakshatâ). With reference to remembrance, which thus acquires the character of immediate presentation and is the means of final release, scripture makes a further determination, viz. in the passage Ka. Up. I, 2, 23, 'That Self cannot be gained by the study of the Veda ("reflection"), nor by thought ("meditation"), nor by much hearing. Whom the Self chooses, by him it may be gained; to him the Self reveals its being.' This text says at first that mere hearing, reflection, and meditation do not suffice to gain the Self, and then declares, 'Whom the Self chooses, by him it may be gained.' Now a 'chosen' one means a most beloved person; the relation being that he by whom that Self is held most dear is most dear to the Self. That the Lord (bhagavân) himself endeavours that this most beloved person should gain the Self, he himself declares in the following words, 'To those who are constantly devoted and worship with love I give that knowledge by which they reach me' (Bha. Gî. X, 10), and 'To him who has knowledge I am dear above all things, and he is dear to me' (VII, 17). Hence, he who possesses remembrance, marked by the character of immediate presentation (sâkshâtkâra), and which itself is dear above all things since the object remembered is such; he, we say, is chosen by the highest Self, and by him the highest Self is gained. Steady remembrance of this kind is designated by the word 'devotion' (bhakti); for this term has the same meaning as upâsanâ (meditation). For this reason scripture and sm*ri*ti agree in making the following declarations, 'A man knowing him passes over death' (*S*vet. Up. III, 8); 'Knowing him thus he here becomes immortal' (Taitt. Âr. III, 12,7); 'Neither by the Vedas, nor by austerities, nor by gifts, nor by sacrifice can I be so seen as thou hast seen me. But by devotion exclusive I may in this form be known and seen in truth, O Ar*g*una, and also be entered into' (Bha. Gî. XI, 53, 54); 'That highest Person, O Pârtha, may be obtained by exclusive devotion' (VIII, 22).

That of such steady remembrance sacrifices and so on are means will be declared later on (Ve. Sû. III, 4, 26). Although sacrifices and the like are enjoined with a view to the origination of knowledge (in accordance with the passage 'They desire to know,' B*ri*. Up. IV, 4, 22), it is only knowledge in the form of meditation which—being daily practised, constantly improved by repetition, and continued up to death—is the means of reaching Brahman, and hence all the works connected with the different conditions of life are to be performed throughout life only for the purpose of originating such knowledge. This the Sûtrakâra declares in Ve. Sû. IV, 1, 12; 16; III, 4, 33, and other places. The Vâkyakâra also declares that steady remembrance results only from abstention, and so on; his words being 'This (viz. steady remembrance = meditation) is obtained through abstention (viveka), freeness of mind (vimoka), repetition (abhyâsa), works (kriyâ), virtuous conduct (kalyâ*n*a), freedom from dejection (anavasâda), absence of exultation (anuddharsha); according to feasibility and scriptural statement.' The Vâkyakâra also gives definitions of all these terms. Abstention (viveka) means keeping the body clean from all food, impure either owing to species (such as the flesh of certain animals), or abode (such as food belonging to a *K*â*nd*âla or the like), or accidental cause (such as food into which a hair or the like has fallen). The scriptural passage authorising this point is *Kh.* Up. VII, 26, 'The food being pure, the mind becomes pure; the mind being pure, there results steady remembrance.' Freeness of mind (vimoka) means absence of attachment to desires. The authoritative passage here is 'Let him meditate with a calm mind' (*Kh.* Up. III, 14, 1). Repetition means continued practice. For this point the Bhâshya-kâra quotes an authoritative text from Sm*ri*ti, viz.: 'Having constantly been absorbed in the thought of that being' (sadâ tadbhâvabhâvita*h*; Bha. Gî. VIII, 6).—By 'works' (kriyâ) is understood the performance, according to one's ability, of the five great sacrifices. The authoritative passages here are 'This person who performs works is the best of those who know Brahman' (Mu. Up. III, 1, 4); and 'Him Brâhma*n*as seek to know by recitation of the Veda, by sacrifice, by gifts, by penance, by fasting' (B*ri*. Up. IV, 4, 22).—By virtuous conduct (kalyâ*n*âni) are meant truthfulness, honesty, kindness, liberality, gentleness, absence of covetousness. Confirmatory texts are 'By truth he is to be obtained' (Mu. Up. III, 1, 5). and 'to them belongs that pure Brahman-world' (Pr. Up. I, 16).—That lowness of spirit or want of cheerfulness which results from unfavourable conditions of place or time and the remembrance of causes of sorrow, is denoted by the term 'dejection'; the contrary of this is 'freedom from dejection.' The relevant scriptural passage is 'This Self cannot be obtained by one lacking in strength' (Mu. Up. III, 2, 4).

—'Exultation' is that satisfaction of mind which springs from circumstances opposite to those just mentioned; the contrary is 'absence of exultation.' Overgreat satisfaction also stands in the way (of meditation). The scriptural passage for this is 'Calm, subdued,' &c. (B*ri*. Up. IV, 4, 23).—What the Vâkyakâra means to say is therefore that knowledge is realised only through the performance of the duly prescribed works, on the part of a person fulfilling all the enumerated conditions.

Analogously another scriptural passage says 'He who knows both knowledge and non-knowledge together, overcoming death by non-knowledge reaches the Immortal through knowledge' (Î*s*. Up. 11). Here the term 'non-knowledge' denotes the works enjoined on the different castes and â*s*ramas; and the meaning of the text is that, having discarded by such works death, i. e. the previous works antagonistic to the origination of knowledge, a man reaches the Immortal, i. e. Brahman, through knowledge. The non-knowledge of which this passage speaks as being the means of overcoming death can only mean that which is other than knowledge, viz. prescribed works. The word has the same sense in the following passage: 'Firm in traditional knowledge he offered many sacrifices, leaning on the knowledge of Brahman, so as to pass beyond death by non-knowledge' (Vi. Pu. VI, 6, 12).—Antagonistic to knowledge (as said above) are all good and evil actions, and hence—as equally giving rise to an undesirable result—they may both be designated as evil. They stand in the way of the origination of knowledge in so far as they strengthen the elements of passion and darkness which are antagonistic to the element of goodness which is the cause of the rise of knowledge. That evil works stand in the way of such origination, the following scriptural text declares: 'He makes him whom he wishes to lead down from these worlds do an evil deed' (Ka. Up. III, 8). That passion and darkness veil the knowledge of truth while goodness on the other hand gives rise to it, the Divine one has declared himself, in the passage 'From goodness springs knowledge' (Bha. Gî. XIV, 17). Hence, in order that knowledge may arise, evil works have to be got rid of, and this is effected by the performance of acts of religious duty not aiming at some immediate result (such as the heavenly world and the like); according to the text 'by works of religious duty he discards all evil.' Knowledge which is the means of reaching Brahman, thus requires the works prescribed for the different âsramas; and hence the systematic enquiry into works (i. e. the Pûrva Mîmâ*m*sâ)—from which we ascertain the nature of the works required and also the transitoriness and limitation of the fruits of mere works—forms a necessary antecedent to the systematic enquiry into Brahman. Moreover the discrimination of permanent and non-permanent things, &c. (i. e. the tetrad of 'means' mentioned above, p. 11) cannot be accomplished without the study of the Mîmâ*m*sâ; for unless we ascertain all the distinctions of fruits of works, means, modes of procedure and qualification (on the part of the agent) we can hardly understand the true nature of works, their fruits, the transitoriness or non-transitoriness of the latter, the permanence of the Self, and similar matters. That those conditions (viz. nityânityavastuviveka, *s*ama, dama, &c.) are 'means' must be determined on the basis of viniyoga ('application' which determines the relation of principal and subordinate matters—aṅgin and aṅga); and this viniyoga which depends on direct scriptural statement (*s*ruti), inferential signs (liṅga), and so on, is treated of in the third book of the Pûrva Mîmâ*m*sâ-sûtras. And further we must, in this connexion, consider also the meditations on the Udgîtha and similar things—which, although aiming at the success of works, are of the nature of reflections on Brahman (which is viewed in them under various forms)—and as such have reference to knowledge of Brahman. Those works also (with which these meditations are connected) aim at no special results of their own, and produce and help to perfect the knowledge of Brahman: they are therefore particularly connected with the enquiry into Brahman. And that these meditations presuppose an understanding of the nature of works is admitted by every one.

## THE GREAT PÛRVAPAKSHA.

### The only Reality is Brahman.

Brahman, which is pure intelligence and opposed to all difference, constitutes the only reality; and everything else, i. e. the plurality of manifold knowing subjects, objects of knowledge, and acts of knowledge depending on those two, is only imagined on (or 'in') that Brahman, and is essentially false.

'In the beginning, my dear, there was that only which is, one only without a second' (*Kh.* Up. VI, 2, 1); 'The higher knowledge is that by which the Indestructible is apprehended' (Mu. Up. I, 1, 5); 'That which cannot be seen nor seized, which has no eyes nor ears, no hands nor feet, the permanent, the all-pervading, the most subtle, the imperishable which the wise regard as the source of all beings' (Mu. Up. I, 1, 6); 'The True, knowledge, the Infinite is Brahman' (Taitt. Up. II, 1); 'He who is without parts, without actions, tranquil, without fault, without taint' (*S*vet. Up. VI, 19); 'By whom it is not thought, by him it is thought; he by whom it is thought knows it not. It is not known by those who know it, known by those who do not know it' (Ke. Up. II, 3); 'Thou mayest not see the seer of sight; thou mayest not think the thinker of thought' (B*ri*. Up. III, 4, 2); 'Bliss is Brahman' (Taitt. Up. III, 6, 1); 'All this is that Self' (B*ri*. Up. IV, 5, 7); 'There is here no diversity whatever' (B*ri*. Up. IV, 4, 19); 'From death to death goes he who sees any difference here' (Ka. Up. II, 4, 10); 'For where there is duality as it were, there one sees the other'; 'but where the Self has become all of him, by what means, and whom, should he see? by what means, and whom, should he know?' (B*ri*. Up. IV, 5, 15); 'the effect is a name merely which has its origin in speech; the truth is that (the thing made of clay) is clay merely' (*Kh*. Up. VI, 1, 4); 'for if he makes but the smallest distinction in it there is fear for him' (Taitt. Up. II, 7);—the two following Vedânta-sûtras: III, 2, 11; III, 2, 3—the following passages from the Vish*n*u-purâ*n*a:

'In which all difference vanishes, which is pure Being, which is not the object of words, which is known by the Self only—that knowledge is called Brahman' (VI, 7, 53); 'Him whose essential nature is knowledge, who is stainless in reality'; 'Him who, owing to erroneous view, abides in the form of things' (I, 2, 6); 'the Reality thou art alone, there is no other, O Lord of the world!—whatever matter is seen belongs to thee whose being is knowledge; but owing to their erroneous opinion the non-devout look on it as the form of the world. This whole world has knowledge for its essential nature, but the Unwise viewing it as being of the nature of material things are driven round on the ocean of delusion. Those however who possess true knowledge and pure minds see this whole world as having knowledge for its Self, as thy form, O highest Lord!' (Vi. Pu. I, 4, 38 ff.).—'Of that Self, although it exists in one's own and in other bodies, the knowledge is of one kind, and that is Reality; those who maintain duality hold a false view' (II, 14, 31); 'If there is some other one, different from me, then it can be said, "I am this and that one is another"' (II, 13, 86); 'As owing to the difference of the holes of the flute the air equally passing through them all is called by the names of the different notes of the musical scale; so it is with the universal Self' (II, 14, 32); 'He is I; he is thou; he is all: this Universe is his form. Abandon the error of difference. The king being thus instructed, abandoned the view of difference, having gained an intuition of Reality' (II, 16, 24). 'When that view which gives rise to difference is absolutely destroyed, who then will make the untrue distinction between the individual Self and Brahman?' (VI, 7, 94).—The following passages from the Bhagavad-Gîtâ: 'I am the Self dwelling within all beings' (X, 20); 'Know me to be the soul within all bodies' (XIII, 2); 'Being there is none, movable or immovable, which is without me' (X, 39).—All these and other texts, the purport of which clearly is instruction as to the essential nature of things, declare that Brahman only, i. e. non-differenced pure intelligence is real, while everything else is false.

**The appearance of plurality is due to avidyâ.**

'Falsehood' (mithyâtva) belongs to what admits of being terminated by the cognition of the real thing—such cognition being preceded by conscious activity (not by mere absence of consciousness or knowledge). The snake, e. g. which has for its substrate a rope or the like is false; for it is due to an imperfection (dosha) that the snake is imagined in (or 'on') the rope. In the same way this entire world, with its distinctions of gods, men, animals, inanimate matter, and so on, is, owing to an imperfection, wrongly imagined in the highest Brahman whose substance is mere intelligence, and therefore is false in so far as it may be sublated by the cognition of the nature of the real Brahman. What constitutes that imperfection is beginningless Nescience (avidyâ), which, hiding the truth of things, gives rise to manifold illusions, and cannot be defined either as something that is or as something that is not.—'By the Untrue they are hidden; of them which are true the Untrue is the covering' (*Kh.* Up. VIII, 3, 1); 'Know Mâyâ to be Prak*ri*ti, and the great Lord him who is associated with Mâyâ' (*S*vet. Up. IV, 10); 'Indra appears manifold through the Mâyâs' (B*ri*. Up. II, 5, 19); 'My Mâyâ is hard to overcome' (Bha. Gî. VII, 14); 'When the soul slumbering in beginningless Mâyâ awakes' (Gau. Kâ. I, 16).—These and similar texts teach that it is through beginningless Mâyâ that to Brahman which truly is pure non-differenced intelligence its own nature hides itself, and that it sees diversity within itself. As has been said, 'Because the Holy One is essentially of the nature of intelligence, the form of all, but not material; therefore know that all particular things like rocks, oceans, hills and so on, have proceeded from intelligence[1]. But when, on

[1] In agreement with the use made of this passage by the Pûrvapakshin, vig*ñ*âna must here be understood in the sense of avidyâ. Vig*ñ*ânasabdena vividha*m* g*ñ*âyate-neneti kara*n*avyutpattyâ-vidyâ-bhidhîyate. *S*ru. Pra.

the cessation of all work, everything is only pure intelligence in its own proper form, without any imperfections; then no differences—the fruit of the tree of wishes—any longer exist between things. Therefore nothing whatever, at any place or any time, exists apart from intelligence: intelligence, which is one only, is viewed as manifold by those whose minds are distracted by the effects of their own works. Intelligence pure, free from stain, free from grief, free from all contact with desire and other affections, everlastingly one is the highest Lord—Vâsudeva apart from whom nothing exists. I have thus declared to you the lasting truth of things—that intelligence only is true and everything else untrue. And that also which is the cause of ordinary worldly existence has been declared to you' (Vi. Pu. II, 12, 39, 40, 43–45).

**Avidyâ is put an end to by true Knowledge.**

Other texts declare that this Nescience comes to an end through the cognition of the essential unity of the Self with Brahman which is nothing but non-differenced intelligence. 'He does not again go to death;' 'He sees this as one;' 'He who sees this does not see death' (*Kh.* Up. VI, 27); 'When he finds freedom from fear and rest in that which is invisible, incorporeal, undefined, unsupported, then he has obtained the fearless' (Taitt. Up. II, 7); 'The fetter of the heart is broken, all doubts are solved and all his works perish when he has been beheld who is high and low' (Mu. Up. II, 2, 8); 'He knows Brahman, he becomes Brahman only' (Mu. Up. III, 2, 9); 'Knowing him only a man passes over death; there is no other path to go' (*S*vet. Up. III, 8). In these and similar passages, the term 'death' denotes Nescience; analogously to the use of the term in the following words of Sanatsu*g*âta, 'Delusion I call death; and freedom from delusion I call immortality' (Sanatsu*g*. II, 5). The knowledge again of the essential unity and non-difference of Brahman—which is ascertained from decisive texts such as 'The True, knowledge, the Infinite is Brahman' (Taitt. Up. II, 1); 'Knowledge, bliss is

Brahman' (B*ri*. Up. III, 9, 28)—is confirmed by other passages, such as 'Now if a man meditates on another deity, thinking the deity is one and he another, he does not know' (B*ri*. Up. I, 4, 10); 'Let men meditate upon him as the Self' (B*ri*. Up. I, 4, 7); 'Thou art that' (*Kh*. Up. VI, 8, 7); 'Am I thou, O holy deity? and art thou me, O holy deity?'; 'What I am that is he; what he is that am I.'—This the Sûtrakâra himself will declare 'But as the Self (scriptural texts) acknowledge and make us apprehend (the Lord)' (Ve. Sû. IV, 1, 3). Thus the Vâkyakâra also, 'It is the Self—thus one should apprehend (everything), for everything is effected by that.' And to hold that by such cognition of the oneness of Brahman essentially false bondage, together with its cause, comes to an end, is only reasonable.

### Scripture is of greater force than Perception.

But, an objection is raised—how can knowledge, springing from the sacred texts, bring about a cessation of the view of difference, in manifest opposition to the evidence of Perception?—How then, we rejoin, can the knowledge that this thing is a rope and not a snake bring about, in opposition to actual perception, the cessation of the (idea of the) snake?—You will perhaps reply that in this latter case there is a conflict between two forms of perception, while in the case under discussion the conflict is between direct perception and Scripture which is based on perception. But against this we would ask the question how, in the case of a conflict between two equal cognitions, we decide as to which of the two is refuted (sublated) by the other. If—as is to be expected—you reply that what makes the difference between the two is that one of them is due to a defective cause while the other is not: we point out that this distinction holds good also in the case of Scripture and perception being in conflict. It is not considerations as to the equality of conflicting cognitions, as to their being dependent or independent, and so on, that determine which of the two sublates the other; if that were the case, the perception which presents to us the flame of the lamp as one only would not be sublated by the cognition arrived at by inference that there is a succession of different flames. Wherever there is a conflict between cognitions based on two different means of knowledge we assign the position of the 'sublated one' to that which admits of being accounted for in some other way; while that cognition which affords no opening for being held unauthoritative and cannot be accounted for in another way, is the 'sublating one[1].' This is the principle on which the relation between 'what sublates' and 'what is sublated' is decided everywhere. Now apprehension of Brahman—which is mere intelligence, eternal, pure, free, self-luminous—is effected by Scripture which rests on endless unbroken tradition, cannot therefore be suspected of any, even the least, imperfection, and hence cannot be non-authoritative; the state of bondage, on the other hand, with its manifold distinctions is proved by Perception, Inference, and so on, which are capable of imperfections and therefore may be non-authoritative. It is therefore reasonable to conclude that the state of bondage is put an end to by the apprehension of Brahman. And that imperfection of which Perception—through which we apprehend a world of manifold distinctions—may be assumed to be capable, is so-called Nescience, which consists in the beginningless wrong imagination of difference.—Well then—a further objection is raised—let us admit that Scripture is perfect because

[1] The distinction is illustrated by the different views Perception and Inference cause us to take of the nature of the flame of the lamp. To Perception the flame, as long as it burns, seems one and the same: but on the ground of the observation that the different particles of the wick and the oil are consumed in succession, we infer that there are many distinct flames succeeding one another. And we accept the Inference as valid, and as sublating or refuting the immediate perception, because the perceived oneness of the flame admits of being accounted for 'otherwise,' viz. on the ground of the many distinct flames originating in such rapid succession that the eye mistakes them for one. The inference on the other hand does not admit of being explained in another way.

resting on an endless unbroken tradition; but must we then not admit that texts evidently presupposing the view of duality, as e.g. 'Let him who desires the heavenly world offer the *G*yotish*t*oma-sacrifice'—are liable to refutation?—True, we reply. As in the case of the Udgât*ri* and Pratihart*ri* breaking the chain (not at the same time, but) in succession [1], so here also the earlier texts (which refer to duality and transitory rewards) are sublated by the later texts which teach final release, and are not themselves sublated by anything else.

### The texts which represent Brahman as devoid of qualities have greater force.

The same reasoning applies to those passages in the Vedânta-texts which inculcate meditation on the qualified Brahman, since the highest Brahman is without any qualities.—But consider such passages as 'He who cognises all, who knows all' (Mu. Up. I, 1, 9); 'His high power is revealed as manifold, as essential, acting as force and knowledge' (*S*vet. Up. VI, 8); 'He whose wishes are true, whose purposes are true' (*Kh.* Up. VIII, 1, 5); how can these passages, which clearly aim at defining the nature of Brahman, be liable to refutation?—Owing to the greater weight, we reply, of those texts which set forth Brahman as devoid of qualities. 'It is not coarse, not fine, not short, not long' (B*ri.* Up. III, 8, 8); 'The True, knowledge, infinite is Brahman' (Taitt. Up. II, 1); 'That which is free from qualities,' 'that which is free from stain'—these and similar texts convey the notion of Brahman being changeless, eternal intelligence devoid of all difference; while the other texts—quoted before—teach the qualified Brahman. And there being a conflict between the two sets of passages, we—according to the Mîmâ*m*sâ principle referred to above—decide that the texts referring to Brahman as devoid of qualities are of greater force, because they are later in

[1] The reference is to the point discussed Pû. Mî. Sû. VI, 5, 54 (*G*aim. Nyâ. Mâlâ Vistara, p. 285).

order[1] than those which speak of Brahman as having qualities. Thus everything is settled.

**The text Taitt. Up. II, 1 refers to Brahman as devoid of qualities.**

But—an objection is raised—even the passage 'The True, knowledge, infinite is Brahman' intimates certain qualities of Brahman, viz. true being, knowledge, infinity!—Not so, we reply. From the circumstance that all the terms of the sentence stand in co-ordination, it follows that they convey the idea of one matter (sense) only. If against this you urge that the sentence may convey the idea of one matter only, even if directly expressing a thing distinguished by several qualities; we must remark that you display an ignorance of the meaning of language which appears to point to some weakmindedness on your part. A sentence conveys the idea of one matter (sense) only when all its constitutive words denote one and the same thing; if, on the other hand, it expresses a thing possessing several attributes, the difference of these attributes necessarily leads to a difference in meaning on the part of the individual words, and then the oneness of meaning of the sentence is lost.—But from your view of the passage it would follow that the several words are mere synonyms!—Give us your attention, we reply, and learn that several words may convey one meaning without being idle synonyms. From the determination of the unity of purport of the whole sentence[2] we conclude that the several words, applied to one thing, aim at expressing what is opposite in nature to whatever is contrary to the meanings of the several words, and that thus they have meaning and unity of meaning and yet are not mere synonyms. The details

---

[1] The texts which deny all qualities of Brahman are later in order than the texts which refer to Brahman as qualified, because denial presupposes that which is to be denied.

[2] The unity of purport of the sentence is inferred from its constituent words having the same case-ending.

are as follows. Brahman is to be defined as what is contrary in nature to all other things. Now whatever is opposed to Brahman is virtually set aside by the three words (constituting the definition of Brahman in the Taittirîya-text). The word 'true' (or 'truly being') has the purport of distinguishing Brahman from whatever things have no truth, as being the abodes of change; the word 'knowledge' distinguishes Brahman from all non-sentient things whose light depends on something else (which are not self-luminous); and the word 'infinite' distinguishes it from whatever is limited in time or space or nature. Nor is this 'distinction' some positive or negative attribute of Brahman, it rather is just Brahman itself as opposed to everything else; just as the distinction of white colour from black and other colours is just the true nature of white, not an attribute of it. The three words constituting the text thus *have* a meaning, have *one* meaning, and are non-synonymous, in so far as they convey the essential distinction of one thing, viz. Brahman from everything else. The text thus declares the one Brahman which is self-luminous and free from all difference. On this interpretation of the text we discern its oneness in purport with other texts, such as 'Being only this was in the beginning, one only, without a second.' Texts such as 'That from whence these beings are born' (Taitt. Up. III, 1); 'Being only this was in the beginning' (*Kh*. Up. VI, 2, 1); 'Self alone was this in the beginning' (B*ri*. Up. I, 4, 1), &c., describe Brahman as the cause of the world; and of this Brahman the Taittirîya passage 'The True, knowledge, infinite is Brahman' gives the strict definition.

In agreement with the principle that all *s*âkhâs teach the same doctrine we have to understand that, in all the texts which speak of Brahman as cause, Brahman must be taken as being 'without a second,' i. e. without any other being of the same or a different kind; and the text which aims at defining Brahman has then to be interpreted in accordance with this characteristic of Brahman, viz. its being without a second. The statement of the *Kh*ândogya as to Brahman being without a second must also be taken to imply that Brahman is non-dual as far as qualities are concerned; otherwise it would conflict with those passages which speak of Brahman as being without qualities and without stain. We therefore conclude that the defining Taittirîya-text teaches Brahman to be an absolutely homogeneous substance.

But, the above explanation of the passage being accepted, it follows that the words 'true being,' 'knowledge,' &c., have to be viewed as abandoning their direct sense, and merely suggesting a thing distinct in nature from all that is opposite (to what the three words directly denote), and this means that we resort to so-called implication (implied meaning, laksha*n*â)!—What objection is there to such a proceeding? we reply. The force of the general purport of a sentence is greater than that of the direct denotative power of the simple terms, and it is generally admitted that the purport of grammatical co-ordination is oneness (of the matter denoted by the terms co-ordinated).—But we never observe that all words of a sentence are to be understood in an implied sense!—Is it then not observed, we reply, that *one* word is to be taken in its implied meaning if otherwise it would contradict the purport of the whole sentence? And if the purport of the sentence, which is nothing but an aggregate of words employed together, has once been ascertained, why should we not take two or three or all words in an implied sense—just as we had taken one—and thus make them fit in with the general purport? In agreement herewith those scholars who explain to us the sense of imperative sentences, teach that in imperative sentences belonging to ordinary speech all words have an implied meaning only (not their directly denotative meaning). For, they maintain, imperative forms have their primary meaning only in (Vedic) sentences which enjoin something not established by other means; and hence in ordinary speech the effect of the action is conveyed by implication only. The other words also, which form part of those imperative sentences and denote matters connected with the action, have their primary meaning only if connected with an action not established by other means; while if connected with an ordinary action they have a secondary, implied, meaning only[1].

**Perception reveals to us non-differenced substance only.**

We have so far shown that in the case of a conflict between Scripture and Perception and the other instruments of knowledge, Scripture is of greater force. The fact, however, is that no such conflict is observed to exist, since Perception itself gives rise to the apprehension of a non-differenced Brahman whose nature is pure Being.—But how can it be said that Perception, which has for its object things of various kinds—and accordingly expresses itself in judgments such as 'Here is a jar,' 'There is a piece of cloth'—causes the apprehension of mere Being? If there were no apprehension of difference, all cognitions would have one and the same object, and therefore would give rise to one judgment only—as takes place when one unbroken perceptional cognition is continued for some time.—True. We therefore have to enquire in what way,

[1] The theory here referred to is held by some of the Mîmâ*m*sakas. The imperative forms of the verb have their primary meaning, i. e. the power of originating action, only in Vedic sentences which enjoin the performance of certain actions for the bringing about of certain ends: no other means of knowledge but the Veda informing us that such ends can be accomplished by such actions. Nobody, e. g. would offer a soma sacrifice in order to obtain the heavenly world, were he not told by the Veda to do so. In ordinary life, on the other hand, no imperative possesses this entirely unique originative force, since any action which may be performed in consequence of a command may be prompted by other motives as well: it is, in technical Indian language, established already, apart from the command, by other means of knowledge. The man who, e. g. is told to milk a cow might have proceeded to do so, apart from the command, for reasons of his own. Imperatives in ordinary speech are therefore held not to have their primary meaning, and this conclusion is extended, somewhat unwarrantably one should say, to all the words entering into an imperative clause.

in the judgment 'here is a jar,' an assertion is made about being as well as some special form of being. These implied judgments cannot both be founded on perception, for they are the results of acts of cognition occupying different moments of time, while the perceptional cognition takes place in one moment (is instantaneous). We therefore must decide whether it is the essential nature of the jar, or its difference from other things, that is the object of perception. And we must adopt the former alternative, because the apprehension of difference presupposes the apprehension of the essential nature of the thing, and, in addition, the remembrance of its counterentities (i. e. the things from which the given thing differs). Hence difference is not apprehended by Perception ; and all judgments and propositions relative to difference are founded on error only.

**Difference—bheda—does not admit of logical definition.**

The Logicians, moreover, are unable to give a definition of such a thing as 'difference.' Difference cannot in the first place be the essential nature (of that which differs); for from that it would follow that on the apprehension of the essential nature of a thing there would at once arise not only the judgment as to that essential nature but also judgments as to its difference from everything else.—But, it may be objected to this, even when the essential nature of a thing is apprehended, the judgment 'this thing is different from other things' depends on the remembrance of its counterentities, and as long as this remembrance does not take place so long the judgment of difference is not formed !—Such reasoning, we reply, is inadmissible. He who maintains that 'difference' is nothing but 'essential nature' has no right to assume a dependence on counterentities since, according to him, essential nature and difference are the same, i. e. nothing but essential nature: the judgment of difference can, on his view, depend on counterentities no more than the judgment of essential nature does. His view really implies that the two words 'the jar' and 'different' (in the judgment 'the jar is different') are synonymous, just as the words 'hasta' and 'kara' are (both of which mean 'hand').

Nor, in the second place, can 'difference' be held to be an attribute (dharma). For if it were that, we should have to assume that 'difference' possesses difference (i.e. is different) from essential nature; for otherwise it would be the same as the latter. And this latter difference would have to be viewed as an attribute of the first difference, and this would lead us on to a third difference, and so in infinitum. And the view of 'difference' being an attribute would further imply that difference is apprehended on the apprehension of a thing distinguished by attributes such as generic character and so on, and at the same time that the thing thus distinguished is apprehended on the apprehension of difference; and this would constitute a logical seesaw.—'Difference' thus showing itself incapable of logical definition, we are confirmed in our view that perception reveals mere 'Being' only.

Moreover, it appears that in states of consciousness such as 'Here is a jar,' 'There is a piece of cloth,' 'The jar is perceived,' 'The piece of cloth is perceived,' that which constitutes the things is Being (existence; sattâ) and perception (or 'consciousness'; anubhûti). And we observe that it is pure Being only which persists in all states of cognition: this pure Being alone, therefore, is *real*. The differences, on the other hand, which do not persist, are unreal. The case is analogous to that of the snake-rope. The rope which persists as a substrate is real, while the non-continuous things (which by wrong imagination are superimposed on the rope) such as a snake, a cleft in the ground, a watercourse, and so on, are unreal.

But—our adversary objects—the instance is not truly analogous. In the case of the snake-rope the non-reality of the snake results from the snake's being sublated (bâdhita) by the cognition of the true nature of the substrate 'This is a rope, not a snake'; it does not result from the non-continuousness of the snake. In the same way the reality of the rope does not follow from its persistence, but from the fact of its being not sublated (by another cognition). But what, we ask, establishes the non-reality of jars and pieces of cloth?—All are agreed, we reply, that we observe, in jars and similar things, individual difference (vyâv*ri*tti, literally 'separation,' 'distinction'). The point to decide is of what nature such difference is. Does it not mean that the judgment 'This is a jar' implies the negation of pieces of cloth and other things? But this means that by this judgment pieces of cloth and other things are sublated (bâdhita). Individual difference (vyâv*ri*tti) thus means the cessation (or absence), due to sublation, of certain objects of cognition, and it proves the non-reality of whatever has non-continuous existence; while on the other hand, pure Being, like the rope, persists non-sublated. Hence everything that is additional to pure Being is non-real.—This admits of being expressed in technical form. 'Being' is real because it persists, as proved by the case of the rope in the snake-rope; jars and similar things are non-real because they are non-continuous, as proved by the case of the snake that has the rope for its substrate.

From all this it follows that persisting consciousness only has real being; it alone *is*.

**Being and Consciousness are one. Consciousness is svayam*prakâs*a.**

But, our adversary objects, as mere Being is the object of consciousness, it is different therefrom (and thus there exists after all 'difference' or 'plurality').—Not so, we reply. That there is no such thing as 'difference,' we have already shown above on the grounds that it is not the object of perception, and moreover incapable of definition. It cannot therefore be proved that 'Being' is the object of consciousness. Hence Consciousness itself is 'Being'—that which is.—This consciousness is self-proved, just because it is consciousness. Were it proved through something else, it would follow that like jars and similar things it is not consciousness. Nor can there be assumed, for consciousness, the need of another act of consciousness (through which its knowledge would be established); for it shines forth (prakâsate) through its own being. While it exists, consciousness—differing therein from jars and the like—is never observed not to shine forth, and it cannot therefore be held to depend, in its shining forth, on something else.—You (who object to the above reasoning) perhaps hold the following view:—even when consciousness has arisen, it is the object only which shines forth—a fact expressed in sentences such as: the jar is perceived. When a person forms the judgment 'This is a jar,' he is not at the time conscious of a consciousness which is not an object and is not of a definite character. Hence the existence of consciousness is the reason which brings about the 'shining forth' of jars and other objects, and thus has a similar office as the approximation of the object to the eye or the other organs of sense (which is another condition of perceptive consciousness). After this the existence of consciousness is inferred on the ground that the shining forth of the object is (not permanent, but) occasional only [1]. And should this argumentation be objected to on the ground of its implying that consciousness—which is essentially of the nature of intelligence—is something non-intelligent like material things, we ask you to define this negation of non-intelligence (which you declare to be characteristic of consciousness). Have we, perhaps, to understand by it the invariable concomitance of existence and shining forth? If so, we point out that this invariable concomitance is also found in the case of pleasure and similar affections; for when pleasure and so on exist at all, they never are non-perceived (i.e. they exist in so far only as we are conscious of them). It is thus clear that we have no consciousness of consciousness itself—just as the tip of a finger, although touching other things, is incapable of touching itself.

All this reasoning, we reply, is entirely spun out of your own fancy, without any due consideration of the power of consciousness. The fact is, that in perceiving colour and

[1] Being not permanent but occasional, it is an effect only, and as such must have a cause.

other qualities of things, we are not aware of a 'shining forth' as an attribute of those things, and as something different from consciousness; nor can the assumption of an attribute of things called 'light,' or 'shining forth,' be proved in any way, since the entire empirical world itself can be proved only through consciousness, the existence of which we both admit. Consciousness, therefore, is not something which is inferred or proved through some other act of knowledge; but while proving everything else it is proved by itself. This may be expressed in technical form as follows—Consciousness is, with regard to its attributes and to the empirical judgments concerning it, independent of any other thing, because through its connexion with other things it is the cause of their attributes and the empirical judgments concerning them. For it is a general principle that of two things that which through its connexion with the other is the cause of the attributes of—and the empirical judgments about—the latter, is itself independent of that other as to those two points. We see e.g. that colour, through its conjunction with earth and the like, produces in them the quality of visibility, but does not itself depend for its visibility on conjunction with colour. Hence consciousness is itself the cause of its own 'shining forth,' as well as of the empirically observed shining forth of objects such as jars and the like.

**Consciousness is eternal and incapable of change.**

This self-luminous consciousness, further, is eternal, for it is not capable of any form of non-existence—whether so-called antecedent non-existence or any other form. This follows from its being self-established. For the antecedent non-existence of self-established consciousness cannot be apprehended either through consciousness or anything else. If consciousness itself gave rise to the apprehension of its own non-existence, it could not do so in so far as 'being,' for that would contradict its being: if it is, i.e. if its non-existence is not, how can it give rise to the idea of its non-existence? Nor can it do so if not being; for if consciousness itself is not, how can it furnish a proof for its own non-existence? Nor can the non-existence of consciousness be apprehended through anything else; for consciousness cannot be the object of anything else. Any instrument of knowledge proving the non-existence of consciousness, could do so only by making consciousness its object—'this is consciousness'; but consciousness, as being self-established, does not admit of that objectivation which is implied in the word 'this,' and hence its previous non-existence cannot be proved by anything lying outside itself.

As consciousness thus does not admit of antecedent non-existence, it further cannot be held to originate, and hence also all those other states of being which depend on origination cannot be predicated of it.

As consciousness is beginningless, it further does not admit of any plurality within itself; for we observe in this case the presence of something which is contrary to what invariably accompanies plurality (this something being 'beginninglessness' which is contrary to the quality of having a beginning—which quality invariably accompanies plurality). For we never observe a thing characterised by plurality to be without a beginning.—And moreover difference, origination, &c., are objects of consciousness, like colour and other qualities, and hence cannot be attributes of consciousness. Therefore, consciousness being essentially consciousness only, nothing else that is an object of consciousness can be its attribute. The conclusion is that consciousness is free from difference of any kind.

**The apparent difference between Consciousness and the conscious subject is due to the unreal aha*m*kâra.**

From this it further follows that there is no substrate of consciousness—different from consciousness itself—such as people ordinarily mean when speaking of a 'knower.' It is self-luminous consciousness itself which constitutes the so-called 'knower.' This follows therefrom also that consciousness is not non-intelligent (*gad*a); for non-intelligence invariably accompanies absence of Selfhood (anâtmatva);

hence, non-intelligence being absent in consciousness, consciousness is not non-Self, that means, it is the Self.

But, our adversary again objects, the consciousness which expresses itself in the judgment '*I* know,' proves that the quality of being a 'knower' belongs to consciousness!—By no means, we reply. The attribution to consciousness of this quality rests on error, no less than the attribution, to the shell, of the quality of being silver. Consciousness cannot stand in the relation of an agent toward itself: the attribute of being a knowing agent is erroneously imputed to it—an error analogous to that expressed in the judgment 'I am a man,' which identifies the Self of a person with the outward aggregate of matter that bears the external characteristics of humanity. To be a 'knower' means to be the agent in the action of knowing; and this is something essentially changeful and non-intelligent (*gad*a), having its abode in the aha*m*kâra, which is itself a thing subject to change. How, on the other hand, could such agency possibly belong to the changeless 'witness' (of all change, i. e. consciousness) whose nature is pure Being? That agency cannot be an attribute of the Self follows therefrom also that, like colour and other qualities, agency depends, for its own proof, on seeing, i. e. consciousness.

That the Self does not fall within the sphere (is not an object of), the idea of 'I' is proved thereby also that in deep sleep, swoon, and similar states, the idea of the 'I' is absent, while the consciousness of the Self persists. Moreover, if the Self were admitted to be an agent and an object of the idea of 'I,' it would be difficult to avoid the conclusion that like the body it is non-intelligent, something merely outward ('being for others only, not for itself') and destitute of Selfhood. That from the body, which is the object of the idea of 'I,' and known to be an agent, there is different that Self which enjoys the results of the body's actions, viz. the heavenly word, and so on, is acknowledged by all who admit the validity of the instruments of knowledge; analogously, therefore, we must admit that different from the knower whom we understand by the term 'I,' is the 'witnessing' inward Self. The non-intelligent aha*m*kâra thus merely serves to manifest the nature of non-changing consciousness, and it effects this by being its abode; for it is the proper quality of manifesting agents to manifest the objects manifested, in so far as the latter abide in them. A mirror, e. g., or a sheet of water, or a certain mass of matter, manifests a face or the disc of the moon (reflected in the mirror or water) or the generic character of a cow (impressed on the mass of matter) in so far as all those things abide in them.—In this way, then, there arises the erroneous view that finds expression in the judgment 'I know.'—Nor must you, in the way of objection, raise the question how self-luminous consciousness is to be manifested by the non-intelligent aha*m*kâra, which rather is itself manifested by consciousness; for we observe that the surface of the hand, which itself is manifested by the rays of sunlight falling on it, at the same time manifests those rays. This is clearly seen in the case of rays passing through the interstices of network: the light of those rays is intensified by the hand on which they fall, and which at the same time is itself manifested by the rays.

It thus appears that the 'knowing agent,' who is denoted by the 'I,' in the judgment 'I know,' constitutes no real attribute of the Self, the nature of which is pure intelligence. This is also the reason why the consciousness of Egoity does not persist in the states of deep sleep and final release: in those states this special form of consciousness passes away, and the Self appears in its true nature, i. e. as pure consciousness. Hence a person who has risen from deep, dreamless sleep reflects, 'Just now I was unconscious of myself.'

### Summing up of the pûrvapaksha view.

As the outcome of all this, we sum up our view as follows.—Eternal, absolutely non-changing consciousness, whose nature is pure non-differenced intelligence, free from all distinction whatever, owing to error illusorily manifests itself (vivarttate) as broken up into manifold distinctions—knowing subjects, objects of knowledge, acts of knowledge.

And the purpose for which we enter on the consideration of the Vedânta-texts is utterly to destroy what is the root of that error, i. e. Nescience, and thus to obtain a firm knowledge of the oneness of Brahman, whose nature is mere intelligence—free, pure, eternal.

## THE GREAT SIDDHÂNTA.

This entire theory rests on a fictitious foundation of altogether hollow and vicious arguments, incapable of being stated in definite logical alternatives, and devised by men who are destitute of those particular qualities which cause individuals to be chosen by the Supreme Person revealed in the Upanishads; whose intellects are darkened by the impression of beginningless evil; and who thus have no insight into the nature of words and sentences, into the real purport conveyed by them, and into the procedure of sound argumentation, with all its methods depending on perception and the other instruments of right knowledge. The theory therefore must needs be rejected by all those who, through texts, perception and the other means of knowledge—assisted by sound reasoning—have an insight into the true nature of things.

### There is no proof of non-differenced substance.

To enter into details.—Those who maintain the doctrine of a substance devoid of all difference have no right to assert that this or that is a proof of such a substance; for all means of right knowledge have for their object things affected with difference.—Should any one, taking his stand on the received views of his sect, assert that the theory of a substance free from all difference (does not require any further means of proof but) is immediately established by one's own consciousness; we reply that he also is refuted by the fact, warranted by the witness of the Self, that all consciousness implies difference: all states of consciousness have for their object something that is marked by some difference, as appears in the case of judgments like 'I saw this.' And should a state of consciousness—although directly apprehended as implying difference—be determined by some fallacious reasoning to be devoid of difference, this determination could be effected only by means of some special attributes additional to the quality of mere Being; and owing to these special qualities on which the determination depends, that state of consciousness would clearly again be characterised by difference. The meaning of the mentioned determination could thus only be that of a thing affected with certain differences some other differences are denied; but manifestly this would not prove the existence of a thing free from all difference. To thought there at any rate belongs the quality of being thought and self-illuminatedness, for the knowing principle is observed to have for its essential nature the illumining (making to shine forth) of objects. And that also in the states of deep sleep, swoon, &c., consciousness is affected with difference we shall prove, in its proper place, in greater detail. Moreover you yourself admit that to consciousness there actually belong different attributes such as permanency (oneness, self-luminousness, &c.), and of these it cannot be shown that they are only Being in general. And even if the latter point were admitted, we observe that there takes place a discussion of different views, and you yourself attempt to prove your theory by means of the differences between those views and your own. It therefore must be admitted that reality is affected with difference well established by valid means of proof.

**Sabda proves difference.**

As to sound (speech; sabda) it is specially apparent that it possesses the power of denoting only such things as are affected with difference. Speech operates with words and sentences. Now a word (pada) originates from the combination of a radical element and a suffix, and as these two elements have different meanings it necessarily follows that the word itself can convey only a sense affected with difference. And further, the plurality of words is based on plurality of meanings; the sentence therefore which is an aggregate of words expresses some special combination of things (meanings of words), and hence has no power to denote a thing devoid of all difference.—The conclusion is that sound cannot be a means of knowledge for a thing devoid of all difference.

**Pratyaksha—even of the nirvikalpaka kind—proves difference.**

Perception in the next place—with its two subdivisions of non-determinate (nirvikalpaka) and determinate (savikalpaka) perception—also cannot be a means of knowledge for things devoid of difference. Determinate perception clearly has for its object things affected with difference; for it relates to that which is distinguished by generic difference and so on. But also non-determinate perception has for its object only what is marked with difference; for it is on the basis of non-determinate perception that the object distinguished by generic character and so on is recognised in the act of determinate perception. Non-determinate perception is the apprehension of the object in so far as destitute of some differences but not of all difference. Apprehension of the latter kind is in the first place not observed ever to take place, and is in the second place impossible: for all apprehension by consciousness takes place by means of some distinction 'This is such and such.' Nothing can be apprehended apart from some special feature of make or structure, as e.g. the triangularly shaped dewlap in the case of cows. The true distinction between non-determinate and determinate perception is that the former is the apprehension of the first individual among a number of things belonging to the same class, while the latter is the apprehension of the second, third, and so on, individuals. On the apprehension of the first individual cow the perceiving person is not conscious of the fact that the special shape which constitutes the generic character of the class 'cows' extends to the present individual also; while this special consciousness arises in the case of the perception of the second and third cow. The perception of the second individual thus is 'determinate' in so far as it is determined by a special attribute, viz. the extension, to the perception, of the generic character of a class—manifested in a certain outward shape—which connects this act of perception with the earlier perception (of the first individual); such determination being ascertained only on the apprehension of the second individual. Such extension or continuance of a certain generic character is, on the other hand, not apprehended on the apprehension of the first individual, and perception of the latter kind thence is 'non-determinate.' That it is such is not due to non-apprehension of structure, colour, generic character and so on, for all these attributes are equally objects of sensuous perception (and hence perceived as belonging to the first individual also). Moreover that which possesses structure cannot be perceived apart from the structure, and hence in the case of the apprehension of the first individual there is already perception of structure, giving rise to the judgment 'The thing is such and such.' In the case of the second, third, &c., individuals, on the other hand, we apprehend, in addition to the thing possessing structure and to the structure itself, the special attribute of the persistence of the generic character, and hence the perception is 'determinate.' From all this it follows that perception never has for its object that which is devoid of all difference.

**The bhedâbheda view is untenable.**

The same arguments tend to refute the view that there is difference and absence of difference at the same time (the so-called bhedâbheda view). Take the judgment 'This is such and such'; how can we realise here the non-difference of 'being this' and 'being such and such'? The 'such and such' denotes a peculiar make characterised, e.g. by a dewlap, the 'this' denotes the thing distinguished by that peculiar make; the non-difference of these two is thus contradicted by immediate consciousness. At the outset the thing perceived is perceived as separate from all other things, and this separation is founded on the fact that the thing is distinguished by a special constitution, let us say the generic characteristics of a cow, expressed by the term 'such and such.' In general, wherever we cognise the relation of distinguishing attribute and thing distinguished thereby, the two clearly present themselves to our mind as absolutely different. Some things—e.g. staffs and bracelets—appear sometimes as having a separate, independent existence of their own; at other times they present themselves as distinguishing attributes of other things or beings (i.e. of the persons carrying staffs or wearing bracelets). Other entities—e.g. the generic character of cows—have a being only in so far as they constitute the form of substances, and thus always present themselves as distinguishing attributes of those substances. In both cases there is the same relation of distinguishing attribute and thing distinguished thereby, and these two are apprehended as absolutely different. The difference between the two classes of entities is only that staffs, bracelets, and similar things are capable of being apprehended in separation from other things, while the generic characteristics of a species are absolutely incapable thereof. The assertion, therefore, that the difference of things is refuted by immediate consciousness, is based on the plain denial of a certain form of consciousness, the one namely—admitted by every one—which is expressed in the judgment 'This thing is such and such.'—This same point is clearly expounded by the Sûtrakâra in II, 2, 33.

**Inference also teaches difference.**

Perception thus having for its object only what is marked by difference, inference also is in the same case; for its object is only what is distinguished by connexion with things known through perception and other means of knowledge. And thus, even in the case of disagreement as to the number of the different instruments of knowledge, a thing devoid of difference could not be established by any of them since the instruments of knowledge acknowledged by all have only one and the same object, viz. what is marked by difference. And a person who maintains the existence of a thing devoid of difference on the ground of differences affecting that very thing simply contradicts himself without knowing what he does; he is in fact no better than a man who asserts that his own mother never had any children.

**Perception does not reveal mere Being.**

In reply to the assertion that perception causes the apprehension of pure Being only, and therefore cannot have difference for its object; and that 'difference' cannot be defined because it does not admit of being set forth in definite alternatives; we point out that these charges are completely refuted by the fact that the only objects of perception are things distinguished by generic character and so on, and that generic character and so on—as being relative things—give at once rise to the judgment as to the distinction between themselves and the things in which they inhere. You yourself admit that in the case of knowledge and in that of colour and other qualities this relation holds good, viz. that something which gives rise to a judgment about another thing at the same time gives rise to a judgment about itself; the same may therefore be admitted with regard to difference[1].

For this reason the charge of a regressus in infinitum and a logical seesaw (see above, p. 32) cannot be upheld. For even if perceptive cognition takes place within one moment, we apprehend within that moment the generic character which constitutes on the one hand the difference of the thing from others, and on the other hand the peculiar character of the thing itself; and thus there remains nothing to be apprehended in a second moment.

Moreover, if perception made us apprehend only pure Being, judgments clearly referring to different objects—such as 'Here is a jar,' 'There is a piece of cloth'—would be devoid of all meaning. And if through perception we did not apprehend difference—as marked by generic character, &c., constituting the structure or make of a thing—why should a man searching for a horse not be satisfied with finding a buffalo? And if mere Being only were the object of all our cognitions, why should we not remember,

[1] Colour reveals itself as well as the thing that has colour; knowledge reveals itself as well as the object known; so difference manifests itself as well as the things that differ.

in the case of each particular cognition, all the words which are connected with all our cognitions? And further, if the cognition of a horse and that of an elephant had one object only, the later cognition would cause us to apprehend only what was apprehended before, and there being thus no difference (of object of cognition) there would be nothing to distinguish the later state of cognition from remembrance. If on the other hand a difference is admitted for each state of consciousness, we admit thereby that perception has for its objects things affected with difference.

If all acts of cognition had one and the same object only, everything would be apprehended by one act of cognition; and from this it would follow that there are no persons either deaf or blind!

Nor does, as a matter of fact, the eye apprehend mere Being only; for what it does apprehend is colour and the coloured thing, and those other qualities (viz. extension, &c.), which inhere in the thing together with colour. Nor does feeling do so; for it has for its objects things palpable. Nor have the ear and the other senses mere Being for their object; but they relate to what is distinguished by a special sound or taste or smell. Hence there is not any source of knowledge causing us to apprehend mere Being. If moreover the senses had for their object mere Being free from all difference, it would follow that Scripture which has the same object would (not be originative of knowledge but) perform the function of a mere anuvâda, i. e. it would merely make statements about something, the knowledge of which is already established by some other means. And further, according to your own doctrine, mere Being, i. e. Brahman, would hold the position of an object with regard to the instruments of knowledge; and thus there would cling to it all the imperfections indicated by yourself—non-intelligent nature, perishableness and so on.—From all this we conclude that perception has for its object only what is distinguished by difference manifesting itself in generic character and so on, which constitute the make or structure of a thing. (That the generic character of a thing is nothing else but its particular structure follows) from the fact that we do not perceive anything, different from structure, which could be claimed as constituting the object of the cognition that several individuals possess one and the same general form. And as our theory sufficiently accounts for the ordinary notions as to generic character, and as moreover even those who hold generic character to be something different from structure admit that there is such a thing as (common) structure, we adhere to the conclusion that generic character is nothing but structure. By 'structure' we understand special or distinctive form; and we acknowledge different forms of that kind according to the different classes of things. And as the current judgments as to things being different from one another can be explained on the basis of the apprehension of generic character, and as no additional entity is observed to exist, and as even those who maintain the existence of such an additional thing admit the existence of generic character, we further conclude that difference (bheda) is nothing but generic character (*g*âti).—But if this were so, the judgment as to difference would immediately follow from the judgment as to generic character, as soon as the latter is apprehended!—Quite true, we reply. As a matter of fact the judgment of difference is immediately formulated on the basis of the judgment as to generic character. For 'the generic character' of a cow, e.g., means just the exclusion of everything else: as soon as that character is apprehended all thought and speech referring to other creatures belonging to the same wider genus (which includes buffaloes and so on also) come to an end. It is through the apprehension of difference only that the idea of non-difference comes to an end.

## Plurality is not unreal.

Next as to the assertion that all difference presented in our cognition—as of jars, pieces of cloth and the like—is unreal because such difference does not persist. This view, we maintain, is altogether erroneous, springs in fact from the neglect of distinguishing between persistence and non-persistence on the one hand, and the relation between what sublates and what is sublated on the other hand. Where two cognitions are mutually contradictory, there the latter relation holds good, and there is non-persistence of what is sublated. But jars, pieces of cloth and the like, do not contradict one another, since they are separate in place and time. If on the other hand the non-existence of a thing is cognised at the same time and the same place where and when its existence is cognised, we have a mutual contradiction of two cognitions, and then the stronger one sublates the other cognition which thus comes to an end. But when of a thing that is perceived in connexion with some place and time, the non-existence is perceived in connexion with some other place and time, there arises no contradiction; how then should the one cognition sublate the other? or how can it be said that of a thing absent at one time and place there is absence at other times and places also? In the case of the snake-rope, there arises a cognition of non-existence in connexion with the given place and time; hence there is contradiction, one judgment sublates the other and the sublated cognition comes to an end. But the circumstance of something which is seen at one time and in one place not persisting at another time and in another place is not observed to be invariably accompanied by falsehood, and hence mere non-persistence of this kind does not constitute a reason for unreality. To say, on the other hand, that what is is real because it persists, is to prove what is proved already, and requires no further proof.

### Being and Consciousness are not one.

Hence mere Being does not alone constitute reality. And as the distinction between consciousness and its objects —which rests just on this relation of object and that for which the object is—is proved by perception, the assertion that only consciousness has real existence is also disposed of.

### The true meaning of Svaya*m*prakâ*s*atva.

We next take up the point as to the self-luminousness of consciousness (above, p. 33). The contention that consciousness is not an object holds good for the knowing Self at the time when it illumines (i. e. constitutes as its objects) other things; but there is no absolute rule as to all consciousness never being anything but self-luminous. For common observation shows that the consciousness of one person may become the object of the cognition of another, viz. of an inference founded on the person's friendly or unfriendly appearance and the like, and again that a person's own past states of consciousness become the object of his own cognition—as appears from judgments such as 'At one time I knew.' It cannot therefore be said 'If it is consciousness it is self-proved' (above, p. 33), nor that consciousness if becoming an object of consciousness would no longer be consciousness; for from this it would follow that one's own past states, and the conscious states of others—because being objects of consciousness—are not themselves consciousness. Moreover, unless it were admitted that there is inferential knowledge of the thoughts of others, there would be no apprehension of the connexion of words and meaning, and this would imply the absolute termination of all human intercourse depending on speech. Nor also would it be possible for pupils to attach themselves to a teacher of sacred lore, for the reason that they had become aware of his wisdom and learning. The general proposition that consciousness does not admit of being an object is in fact quite untenable. The essential nature of consciousness—or knowledge — consists therein that it shines forth, or manifests itself, through its own being to its own substrate at the present moment; or (to give another definition) that it is instrumental in proving its own object by its own being[1].

[1] The comment of the *S*ru. Pra. on the above definitions runs, with a few additional explanations, as follows: The term 'anubhûti' here denotes knowledge in general, not only such knowledge as is not remembrance (which limited meaning the term has sometimes). With reference to the 'shining forth' it might be said that in this way jars also and similar things know or are conscious because they also 'shine forth' (viz. in so far as they are known); to exclude jars and the like the text therefore adds 'to its own substrate' (the jar 'shines forth,' not to itself, but to the

Now these two characteristics are established by a person's own state of consciousness and do not vanish when that consciousness becomes the object of another state of consciousness; consciousness remains also in the latter case what it is. Jars and similar things, on the other hand, do not possess consciousness, not because they are objects of consciousness but because they lack the two characteristics stated above. If we made the presence of consciousness dependent on the absence of its being an object of consciousness, we should arrive at the conclusion

knowing person). There are other attributes of the Self, such as atomic extension, eternity, and so on, which are revealed (not through themselves) but through an act of knowledge different from them; to exclude those the text adds 'through its own being.' In order to exclude past states of consciousness or acts of knowledge, the text adds 'at the present moment.' A past state of consciousness is indeed not revealed without another act of knowledge (representing it), and would thus by itself be excluded; but the text adds this specification (viz. 'at the present moment') on purpose, in order to intimate that a past state of consciousness can be represented by another state—a point denied by the opponent. 'At the present moment' means 'the connexion with the object of knowledge belonging to the present time.' Without the addition of 'to its own substrate' the definition might imply that a state of consciousness is manifest to another person also; to exclude this the clause is added. This first definition might be objected to as acceptable only to those who maintain the svaya*m*-prakâ*s*atva-theory (which need not be discussed here); hence a second definition is given. The two clauses 'to its own substrate' and 'at the present moment' have to be supplied in this second definition also. 'Instrumental in bringing about' would apply to staffs, wheels, and such like implements also; hence the text adds 'its own object.' (Staffs, wheels, &c. have no 'objects.') Knowledge depending on sight does not bring about an object depending on hearing; to exclude this notion of universal instrumentality the text specifies the object by the words 'its own.' The clause 'through its own being' excludes the sense organs, which reveal objects not by their own being, but in so far as they give rise to knowledge. The two clauses 'at the present moment' and 'to its own substrate' have the same office in the second definition as in the first.

that consciousness is not consciousness; for there are things —e. g. sky-flowers—which are not objects of consciousness and at the same time are not consciousness. You will perhaps reply to this that a sky-flower's not being consciousness is due not to its not being an object of consciousness, but to its non-existence!—Well then, we rejoin, let us say analogously that the reason of jars and the like not being contradictory to Nescience (i. e. of their being *gada*), is their not being of the nature of consciousness, and let us not have recourse to their being objects of consciousness!—But if consciousness is an object of consciousness, we conclude that it also is non-contradictory of Nescience, like a jar!—At this conclusion, we rejoin, you may arrive even on the opposite assumption, reasoning as follows: 'Consciousness is non-contradictory of Nescience, because it is not an object of consciousness, like a sky-flower! All which shows that to maintain as a general principle that something which is an object of consciousness cannot itself be consciousness is simply ridiculous.'

**Consciousness is not eternal.**

It was further maintained by the pûrvapakshin that as consciousness is self-established it has no antecedent non-existence and so on, and that this disproves its having an origin. But this is an attempt to prove something not proved by something else that is equally unproved; comparable to a man blind from birth undertaking to guide another blind man! You have no right to maintain the non-existence of the antecedent non-existence of consciousness on the ground that there is nothing to make us apprehend that non-existence; for there is something to make us apprehend it, viz. consciousness itself!—But how can consciousness at the time when it is, make us apprehend its own previous non-existence which is contradictorily opposed to it?—Consciousness, we rejoin, does not necessarily constitute as its objects only what occupies the same time with itself; were it so it would follow that neither the past nor the future can be the object of consciousness. Or do you mean that there is an absolute rule that the antecedent non-existence of consciousness, if proved, must be contemporaneous with consciousness? Have you then, we ask, ever observed this so as to be able to assert an absolute rule? And if it were observed, that would prove the existence of previous non-existence, not its negation!—The fact, however, is that no person in his senses will maintain the contemporaneous existence of consciousness and its own antecedent non-existence. In the case of perceptive knowledge originating from sensation, there is indeed this limitation, that it causes the apprehension of such things only as are actually present at the same time. But this limitation does not extend to cognitions of all kinds, nor to all instruments of knowledge; for we observe that remembrance, inference, and the magical perception of Yogis apprehend such things also as are not present at the time of apprehension. On this very point there rests the relation connecting the means of knowledge with their objects, viz. that the former are not without the latter. This does not mean that the instrument of knowledge is connected with its object in that way that it is not without something that is present at the time of cognition; but rather that the instrument of knowledge is opposed to the falsehood of that special form in which the object presents itself as connected with some place and time.—This disposes also of the contention that remembrance has no external object; for it is observed that remembrance is related to such things also as have perished.—Possibly you will now argue as follows. The antecedent non-existence of consciousness cannot be ascertained by perception, for it is not something present at the time of perception. It further cannot be ascertained by the other means of knowledge, since there is no characteristic mark (liṅga) on which an inference could be based: for we do not observe any characteristic mark invariably accompanied by the antecedent non-existence of consciousness. Nor do we meet with any scriptural text referring to this antecedent non-existence. Hence, in the absence of any valid instrument of knowledge, the antecedent non-existence of consciousness cannot be established at all.—If, we reply, you thus, altogether setting aside the force of self-provedness (on which you had relied hitherto), take your stand on the absence of valid means of knowledge, we again must request you to give in; for there is a valid means of knowledge whereby to prove the antecedent non-existence of consciousness, viz. valid non-perception (anupalabdhi).

Moreover, we observe that perceptional knowledge proves its object, be it a jar or something else, to exist only as long as it exists itself, not at all times; we do not, through it, apprehend the antecedent or subsequent existence of the jar. Now this absence of apprehension is due to the fact that consciousness itself is limited in time. If that consciousness which has a jar for its object were itself apprehended as non-limited in time, the object also—the jar—would be apprehended under the same form, i. e. it would be eternal. And if self-established consciousness were eternal, it would be immediately cognised as eternal; but this is not the case. Analogously, if inferential consciousness and other forms of consciousness were apprehended as non-limited in time, they would all of them reveal their objects also as non-limited, and these objects would thus be eternal; for the objects are conform in nature to their respective forms of consciousness.

**There is no Consciousness without object.**

Nor is there any consciousness devoid of objects; for nothing of this kind is ever known. Moreover, the self-luminousness of consciousness has, by our opponent himself, been proved on the ground that its essential nature consists in illumining (revealing) objects; the self-luminousness of consciousness not admitting of proof apart from its essential nature which consists in the lighting up of objects. And as moreover, according to our opponent, consciousness cannot be the object of another consciousness, it would follow that (having neither an object nor itself being an object) it is something altogether unreal, imaginary.

Nor are you justified in maintaining that in deep sleep, swoon, senselessness and similar states, pure consciousness, devoid of any object, manifests itself. This view is negatived by 'valid non-perception' (see above, p. 52). If consciousness were present in those states also, there would be remembrance of it at the time of waking from sleep or recovery from swoon; but as a matter of fact there is no such remembrance.—But it is not an absolute rule that something of which we were conscious must be remembered; how then can the absence of remembrance prove the absence of previous consciousness?—Unless, we reply, there be some cause of overpowering strength which quite obliterates all impressions—as e.g. the dissolution of the body—the absence of remembrance does necessarily prove the absence of previous consciousness. And, moreover, in the present case the absence of consciousness does not only follow from absence of remembrance; it is also proved by the thought presenting itself to the person risen from sleep, 'For so long a time I was not conscious of anything.'—Nor may it be said that even if there was consciousness, absence of remembrance would necessarily follow from the absence (during deep sleep) of the distinction of objects, and from the extinction of the consciousness of the 'I'; for the non-consciousness of some one thing, and the absence of some one thing cannot be the cause of the non-remembrance of some other thing, of which there had been consciousness. And that in the states in question the consciousness of the 'I' does persist, will moreover be shown further on.

But, our opponent urges, have you not said yourself that even in deep sleep and similar states there is consciousness marked by difference?—True, we have said so. But that consciousness is consciousness of the Self, and that this is affected by difference will be proved further on. At present we are only interested in denying the existence of your pure consciousness, devoid of all objects and without a substrate. Nor can we admit that your pure consciousness could constitute what we call the consciousness of the Self; for we shall prove that the latter has a substrate.

It thus cannot be maintained that the antecedent non-existence of consciousness does not admit of being proved, because consciousness itself does not prove it. And as we have shown that consciousness itself may be an object of consciousness, we have thereby disproved the alleged impossibility of antecedent non-existence being proved by other means. Herewith falls the assertion that the non-origination of consciousness can be proved.

**Consciousness is capable of change.**

Against the assertion that the alleged non-origination of consciousness at the same time proves that consciousness is not capable of any other changes (p. 36), we remark that the general proposition on which this conclusion rests is too wide: it would extend to antecedent non-existence itself, of which it is evident that it comes to an end, although it does not originate. In qualifying the changes as changes of 'Being,' you manifest great logical acumen indeed! For according to your own view Nescience also (which is not 'Being') does not originate, is the substrate of manifold changes, and comes to an end through the rise of knowledge! Perhaps you will say that the changes of Nescience are all unreal. But, do you then, we ask in reply, admit that any change is real? You do not; and yet it is only this admission which would give a sense to the distinction expressed by the word 'Being [1].'

Nor is it true that consciousness does not admit of any division within itself, because it has no beginning (p. 36). For the non-originated Self is divided from the body, the senses, &c., and Nescience also, which is avowedly without a beginning, must needs be admitted to be divided from the Self. And if you say that the latter division is unreal, we ask whether you have ever observed a real division invariably connected with origination! Moreover, if the distinction of Nescience from the Self is not real, it follows that Nescience and the Self are essentially one. You further have yourself proved the difference of views by means of the difference of the objects of knowledge as established by non-refuted knowledge; an analogous case

[1] The *S*âṅkara is not entitled to refer to a distinction of real and unreal division, because according to his theory all distinction is unreal.

being furnished by the difference of acts of cleaving, which results from the difference of objects to be cleft. And if you assert that of this knowing—which is essentially knowing only—nothing that is an object of knowledge can be an attribute, and that these objects—just because they are objects of knowledge—cannot be attributes of knowing; we point out that both these remarks would apply also to eternity, self-luminousness, and the other attributes of 'knowing,' which are acknowledged by yourself, and established by valid means of proof. Nor may you urge against this that all these alleged attributes are in reality mere 'consciousness' or 'knowing'; for they are essentially distinct. By 'being conscious' or 'knowing,' we understand the illumining or manifesting of some object to its own substrate (i. e. the substrate of knowledge), by its own existence (i. e. the existence of knowledge) merely; by self-luminousness (or 'self-illuminatedness') we understand the shining forth or being manifest by its own existence merely to its own substrate; the terms 'shining forth,' 'illumining,' 'being manifest' in both these definitions meaning the capability of becoming an object of thought and speech which is common to all things, whether intelligent or non-intelligent. Eternity again means 'being present in all time'; oneness means 'being defined by the number one.' Even if you say that these attributes are only negative ones, i. e. equal to the absence of non-intelligence and so on, you still cannot avoid the admission that they are attributes of consciousness. If, on the other hand, being of a nature opposite to non-intelligence and so on, be not admitted as attributes of consciousness—whether of a positive or a negative kind—in addition to its essential nature; it is an altogether unmeaning proceeding to deny to it such qualities, as non-intelligence and the like.

We moreover must admit the following alternative: consciousness is either proved (established) or not. If it is proved it follows that it possesses attributes; if it is not, it is something absolutely nugatory, like a sky-flower, and similar purely imaginary things.

### Consciousness is the attribute of a permanent Conscious Self.

Let it then be said that consciousness is proof (siddhi*h*) itself. Proof of what, we ask in reply, and to whom? If no definite answer can be given to these two questions, consciousness cannot be defined as 'proof'; for 'proof' is a relative notion, like 'son.' You will perhaps reply 'Proof to the Self'; and if we go on asking 'But what is that Self'? you will say, 'Just consciousness as already said by us before.' True, we reply, you said so; but it certainly was not well said. For if it is the nature of consciousness to be 'proof' ('light,' 'enlightenment') on the part of a person with regard to something, how can this consciousness which is thus connected with the person and the thing be itself conscious of itself? To explain: the essential character of consciousness or knowledge is that by its very existence it renders things capable of becoming objects, to its own substrate, of thought and speech. This consciousness (anubhûti), which is also termed *gñ*âna, avagati, sa*m*vid, is a particular attribute belonging to a conscious Self and related to an object: as such it is known to every one on the testimony of his own Self—as appears from ordinary judgments such as 'I know the jar,' 'I understand this matter,' 'I am conscious of (the presence of) this piece of cloth.' That such is the essential nature of consciousness you yourself admit; for you have proved thereby its self-luminousness. Of this consciousness which thus clearly presents itself as the attribute of an agent and as related to an object, it would be difficult indeed to prove that at the same time it is itself the agent; as difficult as it would be to prove that the object of action is the agent.

For we clearly see that this agent (the subject of consciousness) is permanent (constant), while its attribute, i. e. consciousness, not differing herein from joy, grief, and the like, rises, persists for some time, and then comes to an end. The permanency of the conscious subject is proved by the fact of recognition, 'This very same thing was formerly apprehended by me.' The non-permanency of consciousness, on the other hand, is proved by thought expressing itself in the following forms, 'I know at present,' 'I knew at a time,' 'I, the knowing subject, no longer have knowledge of this thing.' How then should consciousness and the conscious subject be one? If consciousness which changes every moment were admitted to constitute the conscious subject, it would be impossible for us to recognise the thing seen to-day as the one we saw yesterday; for what has been perceived by one cannot be recognised by another. And even if consciousness were identified with the conscious subject and acknowledged as permanent, this would no better account for the fact of recognition. For recognition implies a conscious subject persisting from the earlier to the later moment, and not merely consciousness. Its expression is '*I* myself perceived this thing on a former occasion.' According to your view the quality of being a conscious agent cannot at all belong to consciousness; for consciousness, you say, is just consciousness and nothing more. And that there exists a pure consciousness devoid of substrate and objects alike, we have already refuted on the ground that of a thing of this kind we have absolutely no knowledge. And that the consciousness admitted by both of us should be the Self is refuted by immediate consciousness itself. And we have also refuted the fallacious arguments brought forward to prove that mere consciousness is the only reality.—But, another objection is raised, should the relation of the Self and the 'I' not rather be conceived as follows:—In self-consciousness which expresses itself in the judgment 'I know,' that intelligent something which constitutes the absolutely non-objective element, and is pure homogeneous light, is the Self; the objective element (yushmad-artha) on the other hand, which is established through its being illumined (revealed) by the Self is the *I*—in 'I know'—and this is something different from pure intelligence, something objective or external?

By no means, we reply; for this view contradicts the relation of attribute and substrate of attribute of which we are directly conscious, as implied in the thought 'I know.'

Consider also what follows.—'If the *I* were not the Self, the inwardness of the Self would not exist; for it is just the consciousness of the *I* which separates the inward from the outward.

'"May I, freeing myself from all pain, enter on free possession of endless delight?" This is the thought which prompts the man desirous of release to apply himself to the study of the sacred texts. Were it a settled matter that release consists in the annihilation of the I, the same man would move away as soon as release were only hinted at. "When I myself have perished, there still persists some consciousness different from me;" to bring this about nobody truly will exert himself.

'Moreover the very existence of consciousness, its being a consciousness at all, and its being self-luminous, depend on its connexion with a Self; when that connexion is dissolved, consciousness itself cannot be established, not any more than the act of cutting can take place when there is no person to cut and nothing to be cut. Hence it is certain that the I, i.e. the knowing subject, is the inward Self.'

This scripture confirms when saying 'By what should he know the knower?' (B*ri*. Up. II, 4, 15); and Sm*ri*ti also, 'Him who knows this they call the knower of the body' (Bha. Gî. XIII, 1). And the Sûtrakâra also, in the section beginning with 'Not the Self on account of scriptural statement' (II, 3, 17), will say 'For this very reason (it is) a knower' (II, 3, 18); and from this it follows that the Self is not mere consciousness.

What is established by consciousness of the 'I' is the I itself, while the not-I is given in the consciousness of the not-I; hence to say that the knowing subject, which is established by the state of consciousness, 'I know,' is the not-I, is no better than to maintain that one's own mother is a barren woman. Nor can it be said that this 'I,' the knowing subject, is dependent on its light for something else. It rather is self-luminous; for to be self-luminous means to have consciousness for one's essential nature. And that which has light for its essential nature does not depend for its light on something else. The case is analogous to that of the flame of a lamp or candle. From the circumstance that the lamp illumines with its light other things, it does not follow either that it is not luminous, or that its luminousness depends on something else; the fact rather is that the lamp being of luminous nature shines itself and illumines with its light other things also. To explain.—The one substance te*g*as, i. e. fire or heat, subsists in a double form, viz. as light (prabhâ), and as luminous matter. Although light is a quality of luminous substantial things, it is in itself nothing but the substance te*g*as, not a mere quality like e. g. whiteness; for it exists also apart from its substrates, and possesses colour (which is a quality). Having thus attributes different from those of qualities such as whiteness and so on, and possessing illumining power, it is the substance te*g*as, not anything else (e. g. a quality). Illumining power belongs to it, because it lights up itself and other things. At the same time it is practically treated as a quality because it always has the substance te*g*as for its substrate, and depends on it. This must not be objected to on the ground that what is called light is really nothing but dissolving particles of matter which proceed from the substance te*g*as; for if this were so, shining gems and the sun would in the end consume themselves completely. Moreover, if the flame of a lamp consisted of dissolving particles of matter, it would never be apprehended as a whole; for no reason can be stated why those particles should regularly rise in an agglomerated form to the height of four fingers' breadth, and after that simultaneously disperse themselves uniformly in all directions—upwards, sideways, and downwards. The fact is that the flame of the lamp together with its light is produced anew every moment and again vanishes every moment; as we may infer from the successive combination of sufficient causes (viz. particles of oil and wick) and from its coming to an end when those causes are completely consumed.

Analogously to the lamp, the Self is essentially intelligent (*k*id-rûpa), and has intelligence (*k*aitanya) for its quality. And to be essentially intelligent means to be self-luminous. There are many scriptural texts declaring this, compare e. g. 'As a mass of salt has neither inside nor outside but is altogether a mass of taste, thus indeed that Self has neither inside nor outside but is altogether a mass of knowledge' (B*ri*. Up. IV, 5, 13); 'There that person becomes self-luminous, there is no destruction of the knowing of the knower' (B*ri*. Up. IV, 3, 14; 30); 'He who knows, let me smell this, he is the Self' (*Kh*. Up. VIII, 12, 4); 'Who is that Self? That one who is made of knowledge, among the prâ*n*as, within the heart, the light, the person' (B*ri*. Up. IV, 3, 7); 'For it is he who sees, hears, smells, tastes, thinks, considers, acts, the person whose Self is knowledge' (Pr. Up. IV, 9); 'Whereby should one know the knower' (B*ri*. Up. IV, 5, 15). 'This person knows,' 'The seer does not see death nor illness nor pain' (*Kh*. Up. VII, 26, 2); 'That highest person not remembering this body into which he was born' (*Kh*. Up. VIII, 12, 3); 'Thus these sixteen parts of the spectator that go towards the person; when they have reached the person, sink into him' (Pr. Up. VI, 5); 'From this consisting of mind, there is different an interior Self consisting of knowledge' (Taitt. Up. II, 4). And the Sûtrakâra also will refer to the Self as a 'knower' in II, 3, 18. All which shows that the self-luminous Self is a knower, i. e. a knowing subject, and not pure light (non-personal intelligence). In general we may say that where there is light it must belong to something, as shown by the light of a lamp. The Self thus cannot be mere consciousness. The grammarians moreover tell us that words such as 'consciousness,' 'knowledge,' &c., are relative; neither ordinary nor Vedic language uses expressions such as 'he knows' without reference to an object known and an agent who knows.

With reference to the assertion that consciousness constitutes the Self, because it (consciousness) is not non-intelligent (*g*a*d*a), we ask what you understand by this 'absence of non-intelligence.' If you reply 'luminousness due to the being of the thing itself (i. e. of the thing which is a*g*a*d*a)'; we point out that this definition would wrongly include lamps also, and similar things; and it would moreover give rise to a contradiction, since you do not admit light as an attribute, different from consciousness itself. Nor can we allow you to define a*g*a*d*atva as 'being of that nature that light is always present, without any exception,' for this definition would extend also to pleasure, pain, and similar states. Should you maintain that pleasure and so on, although being throughout of the nature of light, are non-intelligent for the reason that, like jars, &c., they shine forth (appear) to something else and hence belong to the sphere of the not-Self; we ask in reply: Do you mean then to say that knowledge appears to itself? Knowledge no less than pleasure appears to some one else, viz. the 'I': there is, in that respect, no difference between the judgment 'I know,' and the judgment 'I am pleased.' Non-intelligence in the sense of appearingness-to-itself is thus not proved for consciousness; and hence it follows that what constitutes the Self is the non-*g*a*d*a 'I' which is proved to itself by its very Being. That knowledge is of the nature of light depends altogether on its connexion with the knowing 'I': it is due to the latter, that knowledge, like pleasure, manifests itself to that conscious person who is its substrate, and not to anybody else. The Self is thus not mere knowledge, but is the knowing 'I.'

**The view that the conscious subject is something unreal, due to the aha*m*kâra, cannot be maintained.**

We turn to a further point. You maintain that consciousness which is in reality devoid alike of objects and substrate presents itself, owing to error, in the form of a knowing subject, just as mother o' pearl appears as silver; (consciousness itself being viewed as a real substrate of an erroneous imputation), because an erroneous imputation cannot take place apart from a substrate. But this theory is indefensible. If things were as you describe them, the conscious 'I' would be cognised as co-ordinate with the state of consciousness 'I am consciousness,' just as the shining thing presenting itself to our eyes is judged to be silver. But the fact is that the state of consciousness presents itself as something apart, constituting a distinguishing attribute of the I, just as the stick is an attribute of Devadatta who carries it. The judgment 'I am conscious' reveals an 'I' distinguished by consciousness; and to declare that it refers only to a state of consciousness—which is a mere attribute—is no better than to say that the judgment 'Devadatta carries a stick' is about the stick only. Nor are you right in saying that the idea of the Self being a knowing agent, presents itself to the mind of him only who erroneously identifies the Self and the body, an error expressing itself in judgments such as 'I am stout,' and is on that account false; for from this it would follow that the consciousness which is erroneously imagined as a Self is also false; for it presents itself to the mind of the same person. You will perhaps rejoin that consciousness is not false because it (alone) is not sublated by that cognition which sublates everything else. Well, we reply, then the knowership of the Self also is not false; for that also is not sublated. You further maintain that the character of being a knower, i. e. the agent in the action of knowing, does not become the non-changing Self; that being a knower is something implying change, of a non-intelligent kind (*gad*a), and residing in the aha*m*kâra which is the abode of change and a mere effect of the Unevolved (the Prak*ri*ti); that being an agent and so on is like colour and other qualities, an attribute of what is objective; and that if we admit the Self to be an agent and the object of the notion of the 'I,' it also follows that the Self is, like the body, not a real Self but something external and non-intelligent. But all this is unfounded, since the internal organ is, like the body, non-intelligent, an effect of Prak*ri*ti, an object of knowledge, something outward and for the sake of others merely; while being a knowing subject constitutes the special essential nature of intelligent beings. To explain. Just as the body, through its objectiveness, outwardness, and similar causes, is distinguished from what possesses the opposite attributes of subjectiveness, inwardness, and so on; for the same reason the aha*m*kâra also—which is of the same substantial nature as the body—is similarly distinguished. Hence the aha*m*kâra is no more a knower than it is something subjective; otherwise there would be an evident contradiction. As knowing cannot be attributed to the aha*m*kâra, which is an object of knowledge, so knowership also cannot be ascribed to it; for of that also it is the object. Nor can it be maintained that to be a knower is something essentially changing. For to be a knower is to be the substrate of the quality of knowledge, and as the knowing Self is eternal, knowledge which is an essential quality of the Self is also eternal. That the Self is eternal will be declared in the Sûtra, II, 3, 17; and in II, 3, 18 the term '*gñ*a' (knower) will show that it is an essential quality of the Self to be the abode of knowledge. That a Self whose essential nature is knowledge should be the substrate of the (quality of) knowledge—just as gems and the like are the substrate of light—gives rise to no contradiction whatever.

Knowledge (the quality) which is in itself unlimited, is capable of contraction and expansion, as we shall show later on. In the so-called kshetra*gñ*a-condition of the Self, knowledge is, owing to the influence of work (karman), of a contracted nature, as it more or less adapts itself to work of different kinds, and is variously determined by the different senses. With reference to this various flow of knowledge as due to the senses, it is spoken of as rising and setting, and the Self possesses the quality of an agent. As this quality is not, however, essential, but originated by action, the Self is essentially unchanging. This changeful quality of being a knower can belong only to the Self whose essential nature is knowledge; not possibly to the non-intelligent aha*m*kâra. But, you will perhaps say, the aha*m*kâra, although of non-intelligent nature, may become a knower in so far as by approximation to intelligence it becomes a reflection of the latter. How, we ask in return, is this becoming a reflection of intelligence imagined to take place? Does consciousness become a reflection of the aha*m*kâra, or does the aha*m*kâra become a reflection of consciousness? The former alternative is inadmissible, since you will not allow to consciousness the quality of being a knower; and so is the latter since, as explained above, the non-intelligent aha*m*kâra can never become a knower. Moreover, neither consciousness nor the aha*m*kâra are objects of visual perception. Only things seen by the eye have reflections.—Let it then be said that as an iron ball is heated by contact with fire, so the consciousness of being a knower is imparted to the aha*m*kâra through its contact with Intelligence.—This view too is inadmissible; for as you do not allow real knowership to Intelligence, knowership or the consciousness of knowership cannot be imparted to the aha*m*kâra by contact with Intelligence; and much less even can knowership or the consciousness of it be imparted to Intelligence by contact with the essentially non-intelligent aha*m*kâra. Nor can we accept what you say about 'manifestation.' Neither the aha*m*kâra, you say, nor Intelligence is really a knowing subject, but the aha*m*kâra manifests consciousness abiding within itself (within the aha*m*kâra), as the mirror manifests the image abiding within it. But the essentially non-intelligent aha*m*kâra evidently cannot 'manifest' the self-luminous Self. As has been said 'That the non-intelligent aha*m*kâra should manifest the self-luminous Self, has no more sense than to say that a spent coal manifests the Sun.' The truth is that all things depend for their proof on self-luminous consciousness; and now you maintain that one of these things, viz. the non-intelligent aha*m*kâra—which itself depends for its light on consciousness—manifests consciousness, whose essential light never rises or sets, and which is the cause that proves everything! Whoever knows the nature of the Self will justly deride such a view! The relation of 'manifestation' cannot hold good between consciousness and the aha*m*kâra for the further reason also that there is a contradiction in nature between the two, and because it would imply consciousness not to be consciousness. As has been said, 'One cannot manifest the other, owing to contradictoriness; and if the Self were something to be manifested, that would imply its being non-intelligent like a jar.' Nor is the matter improved by your introducing the hand and the sunbeams (above, p. 38), and to say that as the sunbeams, while manifesting the hand, are at the same time manifested by the hand, so consciousness, while manifesting the aha*m*kâra, is at the same time itself manifested by the latter. The sunbeams are in reality not manifested by the hand at all. What takes place is that the motion of the sunbeams is reversed (reflected) by the opposed hand; they thus become more numerous, and hence are perceived more clearly; but this is due altogether to the multitude of beams, not to any manifesting power on the part of the hand.

What could, moreover, be the nature of that 'manifestation' of the Self consisting of Intelligence, which would be effected through the aha*m*kâra? It cannot be origination; for you acknowledge that what is self-established cannot be originated by anything else. Nor can it be 'illumination' (making to shine forth), since consciousness cannot—according to you—be the object of another consciousness. For the same reason it cannot be any action assisting the means of being conscious of consciousness. For such helpful action could be of two kinds only. It would either be such as to cause the connexion of the object to be known with the sense-organs; as e.g. any action which, in the case of the apprehension of a species or of one's own face, causes connexion between the organ of sight and an individual of the species, or a looking-glass. Or it would be such as to remove some obstructive impurity in the mind of the knowing person; of this kind is the action of calmness and self-restraint with reference to scripture which is the means of apprehending the highest reality. Moreover, even if it were admitted that consciousness may be an object of consciousness, it could not be maintained that the 'I' assists the means whereby that consciousness is effected. For if it did so, it could only be in the way of removing any obstacles impeding the origination of such consciousness; analogous to the way in which a lamp assists the eye by dispelling the darkness which impedes the origination of the apprehension of colour. But in the case under discussion we are unable to imagine such obstacles. There is nothing pertaining to consciousness which obstructs the origination of the knowledge of consciousness and which could be removed by the aha*m*kâra.—There is something, you will perhaps reply, viz. Nescience! Not so, we reply. That Nescience is removed by the aha*m*kâra cannot be admitted; knowledge alone can put an end to Nescience. Nor can consciousness be the abode of Nescience, because in that case Nescience would have the same abode and the same object as knowledge.

In pure knowledge where there is no knowing subject and no object of knowledge—the so-called 'witnessing' principle (sâkshin)—Nescience cannot exist. Jars and similar things cannot be the abode of Nescience because there is no possibility of their being the abode of knowledge, and for the same reason pure knowledge also cannot be the abode of Nescience. And even if consciousness were admitted to be the abode of Nescience, it could not be the object of knowledge; for consciousness being viewed as the Self cannot be the object of knowledge, and hence knowledge cannot terminate the Nescience abiding within consciousness. For knowledge puts an end to Nescience only with regard to its own objects, as in the case of the snake-rope. And the consequence of this would be that the Nescience attached to consciousness could never be destroyed by any one.—If Nescience, we further remark, is viewed as that which can be defined neither as Being nor non-Being, we shall show later on that such Nescience is something quite incomprehensible.—On the other hand, Nescience, if understood to be the antecedent non-existence of knowledge, is not opposed in nature to the origination of knowledge, and hence the dispelling of Nescience cannot be viewed as promoting the means of the knowledge of the Self.—From all this it follows that the aha*m*kâra cannot effect in any way 'manifestation of consciousness.'

Nor (to finish up this point) can it be said that it is the essential nature of manifesting agents to manifest things in so far as the latter have their abode in the former; for such a relation is not observed in the case of lamps and the like (which manifest what lies outside them). The essential nature of manifesting agents rather lies therein that they promote the knowledge of things as they really are, and this is also the nature of whatever promotes knowledge and the means thereof. Nor is it even true that the mirror manifests the face. The mirror is only the cause of a certain irregularity, viz. the reversion of the ocular rays of light, and to this irregularity there is due the appearance of the face within the mirror; but the manifesting agent is the light only. And it is evident that the aha*m*kâra is not capable of producing an irregularity (analogous to that produced by the mirror) in consciousness which is self-luminous.—And—with regard to the second analogous instance alleged by you—the fact is that the species is known through the individual because the latter is its substrate (as expressed in the general principle, 'the species is the form of the individual'), but not because the individual 'manifests' the species. Thus there is no reason, either real or springing from some imperfection, why the consciousness of consciousness should be brought about by its abiding in the aha*m*kâra, and the attribute of being the knowing agent or the consciousness of that cannot therefore belong to the aha*m*kâra. Hence, what constitutes the inward Self is not pure consciousness but the 'I' which proves itself as the knowing subject. In the absence of egoity, 'inwardness' could not be established for consciousness.

**The conscious subject persists in deep sleep.**

We now come to the question as to the nature of deep sleep. In deep sleep the quality of darkness prevails in the mind and there is no consciousness of outward things, and thus there is no distinct and clear presentation of the 'I'; but all the same the Self somehow presents itself up to the time of waking in the one form of the 'I,' and the latter cannot therefore be said to be absent. Pure consciousness assumed by you (to manifest itself in deep sleep) is really in no better case; for a person risen from deep sleep never represents to himself his state of consciousness during sleep in the form, 'I was pure consciousness free from all egoity and opposed in nature to everything else, witnessing Nescience'; what he thinks is only 'I slept well.' From this form of reflection it appears that even during sleep the Self, i. e. the 'I,' was a knowing subject and perceptive of pleasure. Nor must you urge against this that the reflection has the following form: 'As now I feel pleasure, so I slept then also'; for the reflection is distinctly *not* of that kind[1]. Nor must you say that owing to the non-permanency of the 'I' its perception of pleasure during sleep cannot connect itself with the waking state. For (the 'I' is permanent as appears from the fact that) the person who has risen from sleep recalls things of which he was conscious before his sleep, 'I did such and such a thing,' 'I observed this or that,' 'I said so or so.'—But, you will perhaps say, he also reflects, 'For such and such a time I was conscious of nothing!'—'And what does this imply?' we ask. —'It implies a negation of everything!'—By no means, we rejoin. The words 'I was conscious' show that the knowing 'I' persisted, and that hence what is negated is only the objects of knowledge. If the negation implied in 'of nothing' included everything, it would also negative the pure consciousness which you hold to persist in deep sleep. In the judgment 'I was conscious of nothing,' the word 'I' clearly refers to the 'I,' i. e. the knowing Self which persists even during deep sleep, while the words 'was conscious of nothing' negative all knowledge on the part of that 'I'; if, now, in the face of this, you undertake to prove by means of this very judgment that knowledge—which is expressly denied—existed at the time, and that the persisting knowing Self did not exist, you may address your proof to the patient gods who give no reply!—But—our opponent goes on to urge—I form the following judgment also: 'I then was not conscious of myself,' and from this I understand that the 'I' did not persist during deep sleep! —You do not know, we rejoin, that this denial of the per-

[1] I. e. the reflection as to the perception of pleasure refers to the past state of sleep only, not to the present moment of reflection.

sistence of the 'I' flatly contradicts the state of consciousness expressed in the judgment 'I was not conscious of myself' and the verbal form of the judgment itself!—But what then is denied by the words 'of myself'?—This, we admit, is a reasonable question. Let us consider the point. What is negatived in that judgment is not the knowing 'I' itself, but merely the distinctions of caste, condition of life, &c. which belong to the 'I' at the time of waking. We must distinguish the objects of the several parts of the judgment under discussion. The object of the '(me) myself' is the 'I' distinguished by class characteristics as it presents itself in the waking state; the object of the word 'I' (in the judgment) is that 'I' which consists of a uniform flow of self-consciousness which persists in sleep also, but is then not quite distinct. The judgment 'I did not know myself' therefore means that the sleeper was not conscious of the place where he slept, of his special characteristics, and so on.—It is, moreover, your own view that in deep sleep the Self occupies the position of a witnessing principle with regard to Nescience. But by a witness (sâkshin) we understand some one who knows about something by personal observation (sâkshât); a person who does not know cannot be a witness. Accordingly, in scripture as well as in ordinary language a knowing subject only, not mere knowledge, is spoken of as a witness; and with this the Reverend Pâ*n*ini also agrees when teaching that the word 'sâkshin' means one who knows in person (Pâ. Sû. V, 2, 91). Now this witness is nothing else but the 'I' which is apprehended in the judgment 'I know'; and how then should this 'I' not be apprehended in the state of sleep? That which itself appears to the Self appears as the 'I,' and it thus follows that also in deep sleep and similar states the Self which then shines forth appears as the 'I.'

**The conscious subject persists in the state of release.**

To maintain that the consciousness of the 'I' does not persist in the state of final release is again altogether inappropriate. It in fact amounts to the doctrine—only expressed in somewhat different words—that final release is the annihilation of the Self. The 'I' is not a mere attribute of the Self so that even after its destruction the essential nature of the Self might persist—as it persists on the cessation of ignorance; but it constitutes the very nature of the Self. Such judgments as 'I know,' 'Knowledge has arisen in me,' show, on the other hand, that we are conscious of knowledge as a mere attribute of the Self.—Moreover, a man who suffering pain, mental or of other kind—whether such pain be real or due to error only—puts himself in relation to pain—'I am suffering pain'—naturally begins to reflect how he may once for all free himself from all these manifold afflictions and enjoy a state of untroubled ease; the desire of final release thus having arisen in him he at once sets to work to accomplish it. If, on the other hand, he were to realise that the effect of such activity would be the loss of personal existence, he surely would turn away as soon as somebody began to tell him about 'release.' And the result of this would be that, in the absence of willing and qualified pupils, the whole scriptural teaching as to final release would lose its authoritative character.—Nor must you maintain against this that even in the state of release there persists pure consciousness; for this by no means improves your case. No sensible person exerts himself under the influence of the idea that after he himself has perished there will remain some entity termed 'pure light!'—What constitutes the 'inward' Self thus is the 'I,' the knowing subject.

This 'inward' Self shines forth in the state of final release also as an 'I'; for it appears to itself. The general principle is that whatever being appears to itself appears as an 'I'; both parties in the present dispute establish the existence of the transmigrating Self on such appearance. On the contrary, whatever does not appear as an 'I,' does not appear to itself; as jars and the like. Now the emancipated Self does thus appear to itself, and therefore it appears as an 'I.' Nor does this appearance as an 'I' imply in any way that the released Self is subject to

Nescience and implicated in the Sa*m*sâra; for this would contradict the nature of final release, and moreover the consciousness of the 'I' cannot be the cause of Nescience and so on. Nescience (ignorance) is either ignorance as to essential nature, or the cognition of something under an aspect different from the real one (as when a person suffering from jaundice sees all things yellow); or cognition of what is altogether opposite in nature (as when mother o' pearl is mistaken for silver). Now the 'I' constitutes the essential nature of the Self; how then can the consciousness of the 'I,' i.e. the consciousness of its own true nature, implicate the released Self in Nescience, or, in the Sa*m*sâra? The fact rather is that such consciousness destroys Nescience, and so on, because it is essentially opposed to them. In agreement with this we observe that persons like the *ri*shi Vâmadeva, in whom the intuition of their identity with Brahman had totally destroyed all Nescience, enjoyed the consciousness of the personal 'I'; for scripture says, 'Seeing this the *ri*shi Vâmadeva understood, *I* was Manu and the Sun' (B*ri*. Up. I, 4, 10). And the highest Brahman also, which is opposed to all other forms of Nescience and denoted and conceived as pure Being, is spoken of in an analogous way; cp. 'Let me make each of these three deities,' &c. (*Kh*. Up. VI, 3, 3); 'May I be many, may I grow forth' (*Kh*. Up. VI, 2, 3); 'He thought, shall I send forth worlds?' (Ait. Âr. II, 4, 1, 1); and again, 'Since I transcend the Destructible, and am higher also than the Indestructible, therefore I am proclaimed in the world and in the Veda as the highest Person' (Bha. Gî. XV, 18); 'I am the Self, O Gû*d*âke*s*a' (Bha. Gî. X, 20); 'Never was I not' (Bha. Gî. II, 12); 'I am the source and the destruction of the whole world' (Bha. Gî. VII, 6); 'I am the source of all; from me proceeds everything' (Bha. Gî. X, 8); 'I am he who raises them from the ocean of the world of death' (Bha. Gî. XII, 7); 'I am the giver of seed, the father' (Bha. Gî. XIV, 4); 'I know the things past' (Bha. Gî. VII, 26).—But if the 'I' (aham) constitutes the essential nature of the Self, how is it that the Holy One teaches the principle of egoity (aha*m*kâra) to belong to the sphere of objects, 'The great elements, the aha*m*kâra, the understanding (buddhi), and the Unevolved' (Bha. Gî. XIII, 5)?—As in all passages, we reply, which give information about the true nature of the Self it is spoken of as the 'I,' we conclude that the 'I' constitutes the essential nature of the inward Self. Where, on the other hand, the Holy One declares the aha*m*kâra—a special effect of the Unevolved—to be comprised within the sphere of the Objective, he means that principle which is called aha*m*kâra, because it causes the assumption of Egoity on the part of the body which belongs to the Not-self. Such egoity constitutes the aha*m*kâra also designated as pride or arrogance, which causes men to slight persons superior to themselves, and is referred to by scripture in many places as something evil. Such consciousness of the 'I' therefore as is not sublated by anything else has the Self for its object; while, on the other hand, such consciousness of the 'I' as has the body for its object is mere Nescience. In agreement with this the Reverend Parâ*s*ara has said, 'Hear from me the essential nature of Nescience; it is the attribution of Selfhood to what is not the Self.' If the Self were pure consciousness then pure consciousness only, and not the quality of being a knowing subject, would present itself in the body also, which is a Not-self wrongly imagined to be a Self. The conclusion therefore remains that the Self is nothing but the knowing 'I.' Thus it has been said, 'As is proved by perception, and as also results from reasoning and tradition, and from its connexion with ignorance, the Self presents itself as a knowing 'I.' And again, 'That which is different from body, senses, mind, and vital airs; which does not depend on other means; which is permanent, pervading, divided according to bodies—that is the Self blessed in itself.' Here 'not dependent on other means' means 'self-luminous'; and 'pervading' means 'being of such a nature as to enter, owing to excessive minuteness, into all non-sentient things.'

**In cases of Scripture conflicting with Perception, Scripture is not stronger. The True cannot be known through the Untrue.**

With reference to the assertion (p. 24 ff.) that Perception, which depends on the view of plurality, is based on some defect and hence admits of being otherwise accounted for —whence it follows that it is sublated by Scripture; we ask you to point out what defect it is on which Perception is based and may hence be accounted for otherwise.—'The beginningless imagination of difference' we expect you to reply.—But, we ask in return, have you then come to know by some other means that this beginningless imagination of difference, acting in a manner analogous to that of certain defects of vision, is really the cause of an altogether perverse view of things?—If you reply that this is known just from the fact that Perception is in conflict with Scripture, we point out that you are reasoning in a circle: you prove the defectiveness of the imagination of plurality through the fact that Scripture tells us about a substance devoid of all difference; and at the same time you prove the latter point through the former. Moreover, if Perception gives rise to perverse cognition because it is based on the imagination of plurality, Scripture also is in no better case—for it is based on the very same view.—If against this you urge that Scripture, although based on a defect, yet sublates Perception in so far as it is the cause of a cognition which dispels all plurality apprehended through Perception, and thus is later in order than Perception; we rejoin that the defectiveness of the foundation of Scripture having once been recognised, the circumstance of its being later is of no avail. For if a man is afraid of a rope which he mistakes for a snake his fear does not come to an end because another man, whom he considers to be in error himself, tells him 'This is no snake, do not be afraid.' And that Scripture *is* founded on something defective is known at the very time of hearing Scripture, for the reflection (which follows on hearing) consists in repeated attempts to cognise the oneness of Brahman —a cognition which is destructive of all the plurality apprehended through the first hearing of the Veda.—We further ask, 'By what means do you arrive at the conclusion that Scripture cannot possibly be assumed to be defective in any way, while defects may be ascribed to Perception'? It is certainly not Consciousness—self-proved and absolutely devoid of all difference—which enlightens you on this point; for such Consciousness is unrelated to any objects whatever, and incapable of partiality to Scripture. Nor can sense-perception be the source of your conviction; for as it is founded on what is defective it gives perverse information. Nor again the other sources of knowledge; for they are all based on sense-perception. As thus there are no acknowledged means of knowledge to prove your view, you must give it up.—But, you will perhaps say, we proceed by means of the ordinary empirical means and objects of knowledge!—What, we ask in reply, do you understand by 'empirical'?—What rests on immediate unreflective knowledge, but is found not to hold good when tested by logical reasoning!—But what is the use, we ask, of knowledge of this kind? If logical reasoning refutes something known through some means of knowledge, that means of knowledge is no longer authoritative!—Now you will possibly argue as follows: 'Scripture as well as Perception is founded on Nescience; but all the same Perception is sublated by Scripture. For as the object of Scripture, i.e. Brahman, which is one and without a second, is not seen to be sublated by any ulterior cognition, Brahman, i.e. pure non-differenced Consciousness, remains as the sole Reality.'—But here too you are wrong, since we must decide that something which rests on a defect is unreal, although it may remain unrefuted. We will illustrate this point by an analogous instance. Let us imagine a race of men afflicted with a certain special defect of vision, without being aware of this their defect, dwelling in some remote mountain caves inaccessible to all other men provided with sound eyes. As we assume all of these cave dwellers to be afflicted with the same defect of vision, they, all of them, will equally see and judge bright things, e.g. the moon, to be double. Now in the case of these people there never arises a subsequent cognition sublating their primitive cognition; but the latter is false all the same, and its object, viz. the doubleness of the moon, is false likewise; the defect of vision being the cause of a cognition not corresponding to reality.—And so it is with the cognition of Brahman also. This cognition is based on Nescience, and therefore is false, together with its object, viz. Brahman, although no sublating cognition presents itself.—This conclusion admits of various expressions in logical form. 'The Brahman under dispute is false because it is the object of knowledge which has sprung from what is affected with Nescience; as the phenomenal world is.' 'Brahman is false because it is the object of knowledge; as the world is.' 'Brahman is false because it is the object of knowledge, the rise of which has the Untrue for its cause; as the world is.'

You will now perhaps set forth the following analogy. States of dreaming consciousness—such as the perception of elephants and the like in one's dreams—are unreal, and yet they are the cause of the knowledge of real things, viz. good or ill fortune (portended by those dreams). Hence there is no reason why Scripture—although unreal in so far as based on Nescience—should not likewise be the cause of the cognition of what is real, viz. Brahman.—The two cases are not parallel, we reply. The conscious states experienced in dreams are *not* unreal; it is only their objects that are false; these objects only, not the conscious states, are sublated by the waking consciousness. Nobody thinks 'the cognitions of which I was conscious in my dream are unreal'; what men actually think is 'the cognitions are real, but the things are not real.' In the same way the illusive state of consciousness which the magician produces in the minds of other men by means of mantras, drugs, &c., is true, and hence the cause of love and fear; for such states of consciousness also are not sublated. The cognition which, owing to some defect in the object, the sense organ, &c., apprehends a rope as a snake is real, and hence the cause of fear and other emotions. True also is the imagination which, owing to the nearness of a snake, arises in the mind of a man though not actually bitten, viz. that he has been bitten; true also is the representation of the imagined poison, for it may be the cause of actual death. In the same way the reflection of the face in the water is real, and hence enables us to ascertain details belonging to the real face. All these states of consciousness are real, as we conclude from their having a beginning and actual effects.—Nor would it avail you to object that in the absence of real elephants, and so on, the ideas of them cannot be real. For ideas require only *some* substrate in general; the mere appearance of a thing is a sufficient substrate, and such an appearance is present in the case in question, owing to a certain defect. The thing we determine to be unreal because it is sublated; the idea is non-sublated, and therefore real.

Nor can you quote in favour of your view—of the real being known through the unreal—the instance of the stroke and the letter. The letter being apprehended through the stroke (i.e. the written character) does not furnish a case of the real being apprehended through the unreal; for the stroke itself is real.—But the stroke causes the idea of the letter only in so far as it is apprehended as being a letter, and this 'being a letter' is untrue!—Not so, we rejoin. If this 'being a letter' were unreal it could not be a means of the apprehension of the letter; for we neither observe nor can prove that what is non-existent and indefinable constitutes a means.—Let then the idea of the letter constitute the means!—In that case, we rejoin, the apprehension of the real does not spring from the unreal; and besides, it would follow therefrom that the means and what is to be effected thereby would be one, i.e. both would be, without any distinction, the idea of the letter only. Moreover, if the means were constituted by the stroke in so far as it is *not* the letter, the apprehension of all letters would result from the sight of one stroke; for one stroke may easily be conceived as *not* being *any* letter.—But, in the same way as the word 'Devadatta' conventionally denotes some particular man, so some particular stroke apprehended by the eye may conventionally symbolise some particular letter to be apprehended by the ear, and thus a particular stroke may be the cause of the idea of a particular letter!—Quite so, we reply, but on this explanation the real is known through the real; for both stroke and conventional power of symbolisation are real. The case is analogous to that of the idea of a buffalo being caused by the picture of a buffalo; that idea rests on the similarity of picture and thing depicted, and that similarity is something real. Nor can it be said (with a view to proving the pûrvapaksha by another analogous instance) that we meet with a cognition of the real by means of the unreal in the case of sound (*s*abda) which is essentially uniform, but causes the apprehension of different things by means of difference of tone (nâda). For sound is the cause of the apprehension of different things in so far only as we apprehend the connexion of sound manifesting itself in various tones, with the different things indicated by those various tones [1]. And, moreover, it is not correct to argue on the ground of the uniformity of sound; for only particular significant sounds such as 'ga,' which can be apprehended by the ear, are really 'sound.'—All this proves that it is difficult indeed to show that the knowledge of a true thing, viz. Brahman, can be derived from Scripture, if Scripture—as based on Nescience—is itself untrue.

Our opponent may finally argue as follows:—Scripture is not unreal in the same sense as a sky-flower is unreal; for antecedently to the cognition of universal non-duality Scripture is viewed as something that *is*, and only on the rise of that knowledge it is seen to be unreal. At this latter time Scripture no longer is a means of cognising Brahman, devoid of all difference, consisting of pure Intelligence; as long on the other hand as it is such a means, Scripture *is*; for then we judge 'Scripture is.'—But to this we reply that if Scripture is not (true), the judgment 'Scripture is' is false, and hence the knowledge resting on false Scripture being false likewise, the object of that knowledge, i.e. Brahman itself, is false. If the cognition of fire which rests on mist being mistaken for smoke is false, it

[1] And those manifestations of sound by means of various tones are themselves something real.

follows that the object of that cognition, viz. fire itself, is likewise unreal. Nor can it be shown that (in the case of Brahman) there is no possibility of ulterior sublative cognition; for there may be such sublative cognition, viz. the one expressed in the judgment 'the Reality is a Void.' And if you say that this latter judgment rests on error, we point out that according to yourself the knowledge of Brahman is also based on error. And of our judgment (viz. 'the Reality is a Void') it may truly be said that all further negation is impossible.—But there is no need to continue this demolition of an altogether baseless theory.

### No scriptural texts teach a Brahman devoid of all difference.

We now turn to the assertion that certain scriptural texts, as e.g. 'Being only was this in the beginning,' are meant to teach that there truly exists only one homogeneous substance, viz. Intelligence free from all difference.—This we cannot allow. For the section in which the quoted text occurs, in order to make good the initial declaration that by the knowledge of one thing all things are known, shows that the highest Brahman which is denoted by the term 'Being' is the substantial and also the operative cause of the world; that it is all-knowing, endowed with all powers; that its purposes come true; that it is the inward principle, the support and the ruler of everything; and that distinguished by these and other good qualities it constitutes the Self of the entire world; and then finally proceeds to instruct *S*vetaketu that this Brahman constitutes his Self also ('Thou art that'). We have fully set forth this point in the Vedârtha-sa*m*graha, and shall establish it in greater detail in the present work also, in the so-called ârambha*n*a-adhikara*n*a.—In the same way the passage 'the higher knowledge is that by which the Indestructible is apprehended, &c.' (Mu. Up. I, 1, 5) first denies of Brahman all the evil qualities connected with Prak*ri*ti, and then teaches that to it there belong eternity, all-pervadingness, subtilty, omnipresence, omniscience, imperishableness, creativeness with regard to all beings, and other auspicious qualities. Now we maintain that also the text 'True, knowledge, infinite is Brahman,' does not prove a substance devoid of all difference, for the reason that the co-ordination of the terms of which it consists explains itself in so far only as denoting one thing distinguished by several attributes. For 'co-ordination' (sâmânâdhikara*n*ya, lit. 'the abiding of several things in a common substrate') means the reference (of several terms) to one thing, there being a difference of reason for the application (of several terms to one thing). Now whether we take the several terms, 'True,' 'Knowledge,' 'Infinite,' in their primary sense, i.e. as denoting qualities, or as denoting modes of being opposed to whatever is contrary to those qualities; in either case we must needs admit a plurality of causes for the application of those several terms to one thing. There is however that difference between the two alternatives that in the former case the terms preserve their primary meaning, while in the latter case their denotative power depends on so-called 'implication' (laksha*n*â). Nor can it be said that the opposition in nature to non-knowledge, &c. (which is the purport of the terms on the hypothesis of laksha*n*â), constitutes nothing more than the essential nature (of one non-differenced substance; the three terms thus having one purport only); for as such essential nature would be sufficiently apprehended through one term, the employment of further terms would be purposeless. This view would moreover be in conflict with co-ordination, as it would not allow of difference of motive for several terms applied to one thing. On the other hand it cannot be urged against the former alternative that the distinction of several attributes predicated of one thing implies a distinction in the thing to which the attributes belong, and that from this it follows that the several terms denote several things—a result which also could not be reconciled with 'co-ordination'; for what 'co-ordination' aims at is just to convey the idea of one thing being qualified by several attributes. For the grammarians define 'co-ordination' as the application, to one thing, of several words, for the application of each of which there is a different motive.

You have further maintained the following view:—In the text 'one only without a second,' the phrase 'without a second' negatives all duality on Brahman's part even in so far as qualities are concerned. We must therefore, according to the principle that all *S*âkhâs convey the same doctrine, assume that all texts which speak of Brahman as cause, aim at setting forth an absolutely non-dual substance. Of Brahman thus indirectly defined as a cause, the text 'The True, knowledge, infinite is Brahman,' contains a direct definition; the Brahman here meant to be defined must thus be devoid of all qualities. Otherwise, moreover, the text would be in conflict with those other texts which declare Brahman to be without qualities and blemish.—But this also cannot be admitted. What the phrase 'without a second' really aims at intimating is that Brahman possesses manifold powers, and this it does by denying the existence of another ruling principle different from Brahman. That Brahman actually possesses manifold powers the text shows further on, 'It thought, may I be many, may I grow forth,' and 'it sent forth fire,' and so on.—But how are we to know that the mere phrase 'without a second' is meant to negative the existence of all other causes in general?—As follows, we reply. The clause 'Being only this was in the beginning, one only,' teaches that Brahman when about to create constitutes the substantial cause of the world. Here the idea of some further operative cause capable of giving rise to the effect naturally presents itself to the mind, and hence we understand that the added clause 'without a second' is meant to negative such an additional cause. If it were meant absolutely to deny all duality, it would deny also the eternity and other attributes of Brahman which you yourself assume. You in this case make just the wrong use of the principle of all the *S*âkhâs containing the same doctrine; what this principle demands is that the qualities attributed in all *S*âkhâs to Brahman as cause should be taken over into the passage under discussion also. The same consideration teaches us that also the text 'True, knowledge,' &c., teaches Brahman to possess attributes; for this passage has to be interpreted in agreement with the texts referring to Brahman as a cause. Nor does this imply a conflict with the texts which declare Brahman to be without qualities; for those texts are meant to negative the evil qualities depending on Prak*ri*ti. —Those texts again which refer to mere knowledge declare indeed that knowledge is the essential nature of Brahman, but this does not mean that mere knowledge constitutes the fundamental reality. For knowledge constitutes the essential nature of a knowing subject only which is the substrate of knowledge, in the same way as the sun, lamps, and gems are the substrate of Light. That Brahman is a knowing subject all scriptural texts declare; cp. 'He who is all knowing' (Mu. Up. I, 1, 9); 'It thought' (*Kh.* Up. VI, 2, 3); 'This divine being thought' (*Kh.* Up. VI, 3, 2); 'He thought, let me send forth the worlds' (Ait. Âr. II, 4, 1, 2); 'He who arranges the wishes—as eternal of those who are not eternal, as thinker of (other) thinkers, as one of many' (Ka. Up. II, 5, 13); 'There are two unborn ones—one who knows, one who does not know—one strong, the other weak' (*S*vet. Up. I, 9); 'Let us know Him, the highest of Lords, the great Lord, the highest deity of deities, the master of masters, the highest above the god, the lord of the world, the adorable one' (*S*vet. Up. VI, 7); 'Of him there is known no effect (body) or instrument; no one is seen like unto him or better; his high power is revealed as manifold, forming his essential nature, as knowledge, strength, and action' (*S*vet. Up. VI, 8); 'That is the Self, free from sin, ageless, deathless, griefless, free from hunger and thirst, whose wishes are true, whose purposes are true' (*Kh.* Up. VIII, 1, 5). These and other texts declare that to Brahman, whose essential nature is knowledge, there belong many excellent qualities—among which that of being a knowing subject stands first, and that Brahman is free from all evil qualities. That the texts referring to Brahman as free from qualities, and those which speak of it as possessing qualities, have really one and the same object may be inferred from the last of the passages quoted above; the earlier part of which—'free from sin,' up to 'free from thirst'—denies of Brahman all evil qualities, while its latter part—'whose wishes are true,' and so on—asserts of its certain excellent qualities. As thus there is no contradiction between the two classes of texts, there is no reason whatever to assume that either of them has for its object something that is false.—With regard to the concluding passage of the Taittirîya-text, 'from whence all speech, together with the mind, turns away, unable to reach it [1],' we point out that with the passage 'From terror of it the wind blows,' there begins a declaration of the qualities of Brahman, and that the next section 'one hundred times that human bliss,' &c., makes statements as to the relative bliss enjoyed by the different classes of embodied souls; the concluding passage 'He who knows the bliss of that Brahman from whence all speech, together with the mind, turns away unable to reach it,' hence must be taken as proclaiming with emphasis the infinite nature of Brahman's auspicious qualities. Moreover, a clause in the chapter under discussion—viz. 'he obtains all desires, together with Brahman the all-wise' (II, 1)—which gives information as to the fruit of the knowledge of Brahman clearly declares the infinite nature of the qualities of the highest all-wise Brahman. The desires are the auspicious qualities of Brahman which are the objects of desire; the man who knows Brahman obtains, together with Brahman, all qualities of it. The expression 'together with' is meant to bring out the primary importance of the qualities; as also described in the so-called dahara-vidyâ (*Kh*. Up. VIII, 1). And that fruit and meditation are of the same character (i.e. that in meditations on Brahman its qualities are the chief matter of meditation, just as these qualities are the principal point in Brahman reached by the Devotee) is proved by the text 'According to what a man's thought is in this world, so will he be after he has

[1] Which passage appears to refer to a nirgu*n*a brahman, whence it might be inferred that the connected initial passage—'Satyam *gñ*ânam,' &c.—has a similar purport.

departed this life' (*Kh.* Up. III, 14, 1). If it be said that the passage 'By whom it is not thought by him it is thought,' 'not understood by those who understand' (Ke. Up. II, 3), declares Brahman not to be an object of knowledge; we deny this, because were it so, certain other texts would not teach that final Release results from knowledge; cp. 'He who knows Brahman obtains the Highest' (Taitt. Up. II, 1, 1); 'He knows Brahman, he becomes Brahman.' And, moreover, the text 'He who knows Brahman as non-existing becomes himself non-existing; he who knows Brahman as existing, him we know himself as existing' (Taitt. Up. II, 6, 1), makes the existence and non-existence of the Self dependent on the existence and non-existence of knowledge which has Brahman for its object. We thus conclude that all scriptural texts enjoin just the knowledge of Brahman for the sake of final Release. This knowledge is, as we already know, of the nature of meditation, and what is to be meditated on is Brahman as possessing qualities. (The text from the Ke. Up. then explains itself as follows:—) We are informed by the passage 'from whence speech together with mind turns away, being unable to reach it,' that the infinite Brahman with its unlimited excellences cannot be defined either by mind or speech as being so or so much, and from this we conclude the Kena text to mean that Brahman is not thought and not understood by those who understand it to be of a definitely limited nature; Brahman in truth being unlimited. If the text did not mean this, it would be self-contradictory, parts of it saying that Brahman is *not* thought and *not* understood, and other parts, that it *is* thought and *is* understood.

Now as regards the assertion that the text 'Thou mayest not see the seer of seeing; thou mayest not think the thinker of thinking' (B*ri*. Up. III, 5, 2), denies the existence of a seeing and thinking subject different from mere seeing and thinking—This view is refuted by the following interpretation. The text addresses itself to a person who has formed the erroneous opinion that the quality of consciousness or knowledge does not constitute the essential nature of the knower, but belongs to it only as an adventitious attribute, and tells him 'Do not view or think the Self to be such, but consider the seeing and thinking Self to have seeing and thinking for its essential nature.'—Or else this text may mean that the embodied Self which is the seer of seeing and the thinker of thinking should be set aside, and that only the highest Self—the inner Self of all beings—should be meditated upon.—Otherwise a conflict would arise with texts declaring the knowership of the Self, such as 'whereby should he know the knower?' (B*ri*. Up. IV, 5, 15).

Your assertion that the text 'Bliss is Brahman' (Taitt. Up. III, 6, 1) proves pure Bliss to constitute the essential nature of Brahman is already disposed of by the refutation of the view that knowledge (consciousness) constitutes the essential nature of Brahman; Brahman being in reality the substrate only of knowledge. For by bliss we understand a pleasing state of consciousness. Such passages as 'consciousness, bliss is Brahman,' therefore mean 'consciousness—the essential character of which is bliss—is Brahman.' On this identity of the two things there rests that homogeneous character of Brahman, so much insisted upon by yourself. And in the same way as numerous passages teach that Brahman, while having knowledge for its essential nature, is at the same time a knowing subject; so other passages, speaking of Brahman as something separate from mere bliss, show it to be not mere bliss but a subject enjoying bliss; cp. 'That is one bliss of Brahman' (Taitt. Up. II, 8, 4); 'he knowing the bliss of Brahman' (Taitt. Up. II, 9, 1). To be a subject enjoying bliss is in fact the same as to be a conscious subject.

We now turn to the numerous texts which, according to the view of our opponent, negative the existence of plurality.—'Where there is duality as it were' (B*ri*. Up. IV, 5, 15); 'There is not any plurality here; from death to death goes he who sees here any plurality' (B*ri*. Up. IV, 4, 19); 'But when for him the Self alone has become all, by what means, and whom, should he see?' (B*ri*. Up. IV, 5, 15) &c.—But what all these texts deny is only plurality in so far as contradicting that unity of the world which depends on its being in its entirety an effect of Brahman, and having Brahman for its inward ruling principle and its true Self. They do not, on the other hand, deny that plurality on Brahman's part which depends on its intention to become manifold—a plurality proved by the text 'May I be many, may I grow forth' (*Kh.* Up. VI, 2, 3). Nor can our opponent urge against this that, owing to the denial of plurality contained in other passages this last text refers to something not real; for it is an altogether laughable assertion that Scripture should at first teach the doctrine, difficult to comprehend, that plurality as suggested by Perception and the other means of Knowledge belongs to Brahman also, and should afterwards negative this very doctrine!

Nor is it true that the text 'If he makes but the smallest "antaram" (i.e. difference, interval, break) in it there is fear for him' (Taitt. Up. II, 7) implies that he who sees plurality within Brahman encounters fear. For the other text 'All this is Brahman; let a man meditate with calm mind on all this as beginning, ending and breathing in it, i.e. Brahman' (*Kh.* Up. III, 14, 1) teaches directly that reflection on the plurality of Brahman is the cause of peace of mind. For this passage declares that peace of mind is produced by a reflection on the entire world as springing from, abiding within, and being absorbed into Brahman, and thus having Brahman for its Self; and as thus the view of Brahman constituting the Self of the world with all its manifold distinctions of gods, men, animals, inanimate matter and so on, is said to be the cause of peace of mind, and, consequently, of absence of fear, that same view surely cannot be a *cause* of fear!—But how then is it that the Taitt. text declares that 'there is fear for him'?—That text, we reply, declares in its earlier part that rest in Brahman is the cause of fearlessness ('when he finds freedom from fear, rest, in that which is invisible, incorporeal, undefined, unsupported; then he has obtained fearlessness'); its latter part therefore means that fear takes place when there is an interval, a break, in this resting in Brahman. As the great *Ri*shi says 'When Vâsudeva is not meditated on for an hour or even a moment only; that is loss, that is great calamity, that is error, that is change.'

The Sûtra III, 2, 11 does not, as our opponent alleges, refer to a Brahman free from all difference, but to Brahman as possessing attributes—as we shall show in its place. And the Sûtra IV, 2, 3 declares that the things seen in dreams are mere 'Mâyâ' because they differ in character from the things perceived in the waking state; from which it follows that the latter things are real.

**Nor do Sm*ri*ti and Purâ*n*a teach such a doctrine.**

Nor is it true that also according to Sm*ri*ti and Purâ*n*as only non-differenced consciousness is real and everything else unreal.—'He who knows me as unborn and without a beginning, the supreme Lord of the worlds' (Bha. Gî. X, 3); 'All beings abide in me, I abide not in them. Nay, the beings abide not in me—behold my lordly power. My Self bringing forth the beings supports them but does not abide in them' (Bha. Gî. IX, 4, 5); 'I am the origin and the dissolution of the entire world; higher than I there is nothing else: on me all this is strung as pearls on a thread' (Bha. Gî. VII, 6, 7); 'Pervading this entire Universe by a portion (of mine) I abide' (Bha. Gî. X, 42); 'But another, the highest Person, is called the highest Self who, pervading the three worlds supports them, the eternal Lord. Because I transcend the Perishable and am higher than the Imperishable even, I am among the people and in the Veda celebrated as the supreme Person' (Bha. Gî. XV, 17, 18).

'He transcends the fundamental matter of all beings, its modifications, properties and imperfections; he transcends all investing (obscuring) influences, he who is the Self of all. Whatever (room) there is in the interstices of the world is filled by him; all auspicious qualities constitute his nature. The whole creation of beings is taken out of a small part of his power. Assuming at will whatever form he desires he bestows benefits on the whole world effected by him. Glory, strength, dominion, wisdom, energy, power and other attributes are collected in him, Supreme of the supreme in whom no troubles abide, ruler over high and low, lord in collective and distributive form, non-manifest and manifest, universal lord, all-seeing, all-knowing, all-powerful, highest Lord. The knowledge by which that perfect, pure, highest, stainless homogeneous (Brahman) is known or perceived or comprehended—that is knowledge: all else is ignorance' (Vishnu Purâna VI, 5, 82–87).—'To that pure one of mighty power, the highest Brahman to which no term is applicable, the cause of all causes, the name "Bhagavat" is suitable. The letter bha implies both the cherisher and supporter; the letter ga the leader, mover and creator. The two syllables bhaga indicate the six attributes—dominion, strength, glory, splendour, wisdom, dispassion. That in him—the universal Self, the Self of the beings—all beings dwell and that he dwells in all, this is the meaning of the letter va. Wisdom, might, strength, dominion, glory, without any evil qualities, are all denoted by the word bhagavat. This great word bhagavat is the name of Vâsudeva who is the highest Brahman—and of no one else. This word which denotes persons worthy of reverence in general is used in its primary sense with reference to Vâsudeva only; in a derived sense with regard to other persons' (Vi. Pu. VI, 5, 72 ff.); 'Where all these powers abide, that is the form of him who is the universal form: that is the great form of Hari. That form produces in its sport forms endowed with all powers, whether of gods or men or animals. For the purpose of benefitting the worlds, not springing from work (karman) is this action of the unfathomable one; all-pervading, irresistible' (Vi. Pu. VI, 7, 69–71); 'Him who is of this kind, stainless, eternal, all-pervading, imperishable, free from all evil, named Vishnu, the highest abode' (Vi. Pu. I, 22, 53); 'He who is the highest of the high, the Person, the highest Self, founded on himself; who is devoid of all the distinguishing characteristics of colour, caste and the like; who is exempt from birth, change, increase, decay and death; of whom it can only be said that he ever is. He is everywhere and in him everything abides; hence he is called Vâsudeva by those who know. He is Brahman, eternal, supreme, imperishable, undecaying; of one essential nature and ever pure, as free from all defects. This whole world is Brahman, comprising within its nature the Evolved and the Unevolved; and also existing in the form of the Person and in that of time' (Vi. Pu. I, 2, 10–14); 'The Prakriti about which I told and which is Evolved as well as Unevolved, and the Person—both these are merged in the highest Self. The highest Self is the support of all, the highest Lord; as Vishnu he is praised in the Vedas and the Vedânta-texts' (Vi. Pu. VI, 4, 38, 39). 'Two forms are there of that Brahman, one material, the other immaterial. These two forms, perishable and imperishable, are within all things: the imperishable one is the highest Brahman, the perishable one this whole world. As the light of a fire burning in one place spreads all around, so the energy of the highest Brahman constitutes this entire world' (Vi. Pu. I, 23, 53–55). 'The energy of Vishnu is the highest, that which is called the embodied soul is inferior; and there is another third energy called karman or Nescience, actuated by which the omnipresent energy of the embodied soul perpetually undergoes the afflictions of worldly existence. Obscured by Nescience the energy of the embodied soul is characterised in the different beings by different degrees of perfection' (Vi. Pu. VI, 7, 61–63).

These and other texts teach that the highest Brahman is essentially free from all imperfection whatsoever, comprises within itself all auspicious qualities, and finds its pastime in originating, preserving, reabsorbing, pervading, and ruling the universe; that the entire complex of intelligent and non-intelligent beings (souls and matter) in all their different estates is real, and constitutes the form, i.e. the body of the highest Brahman, as appears from those passages which co-ordinate it with Brahman by means of terms such as sarîra (body), rûpa (form), tanu (body), amsa (part), sakti (power), vibhûti (manifestation of power), and so on;—that the souls which are a manifestation of Brahman's power exist in their own essential nature, and also, through their connexion with matter, in the form of embodied souls (kshetragña);—and that the embodied souls, being engrossed by Nescience in the form of good and evil works, do not recognise their essential nature, which is knowledge, but view themselves as having the character of material things.—The outcome of all this is that we have to cognise Brahman as carrying plurality within itself, and the world, which is the manifestation of his power, as something real.

When now the text, in the *s*loka 'where all difference has vanished' (Vi. Pu. VI, 7, 53), declares that the Self, although connected with the different effects of Prak*ri*ti, such as divine, human bodies, and so on, yet is essentially free from all such distinctions, and therefore not the object of the words denoting those different classes of beings, but to be defined as mere knowledge and Being; to be known by the Self and not to be reached by the mind of the practitioner of Yoga (yogayu*g*); this must in no way be understood as denying the reality of the world.—But how is this known?—As follows, we reply. The chapter of the Purâ*n*a in which that *s*loka occurs at first declares concentration (Yoga) to be the remedy of all the afflictions of the Sa*m*sâra; thereupon explains the different stages of Yoga up to the so-called pratyâhâra (complete restraining of the senses from receiving external impressions); then, in order to teach the attainment of the 'perfect object' (*s*ubhâ*s*raya) required for dhâra*n*â, declares that the highest Brahman, i. e. Vish*n*u, possesses two forms, called powers (*s*akti), viz. a defined one (mûrta) and an undefined one (amûrta); and then teaches that a portion of the 'defined' form, viz. the embodied soul (kshetra*gñ*a), which is distinguished by its connexion with matter and involved in Nescience—that is termed 'action,' and constitutes a third power—is not perfect. The chapter further teaches that a portion of the undefined form which is free from Nescience called action, separated from all matter, and possessing the character of pure knowledge, is also not the 'perfect object,' since it is destitute of essential purity; and, finally, declares that the 'perfect object' is to be found in that defined form which is special to Bhagavat, and which is the abode of the three powers, viz. that non-defined form which is the highest power, that non-defined form which is termed embodied soul, and constitutes the secondary (apara) power, and

Nescience in the form of work—which is called the third power, and is the cause of the Self, which is of the essence of the highest power, passing into the state of embodied soul. This defined form (which is the 'perfect object') is proved by certain Vedânta-texts, such as 'that great person of sun-like lustre' (*S*vet. Up. III, 8). We hence must take the *s*loka, 'in which all differences vanish,' &c., to mean that the pure Self (the Self in so far as knowledge only) is not capable of constituting the 'perfect object.' Analogously two other passages declare 'Because this cannot be reflected upon by the beginner in Yoga, the second (form) of Vish*n*u is to be meditated upon by Yogins—the highest abode.' 'That in which all these powers have their abode, that is the other great form of Hari, different from the (material) Vi*s*va form.'

In an analogous manner, Parâ*s*ara declares that Brahmâ, *K*aturmukha, Sanaka, and similar mighty beings which dwell within this world, cannot constitute the 'perfect object' because they are involved in Nescience; after that goes on to say that the beings found in the Sa*m*sâra are in the same condition—for they are essentially devoid of purity since they reach their true nature only later on, when through Yoga knowledge has arisen in them—; and finally teaches that the essential individual nature of the highest Brahman, i.e. Vish*n*u, constitutes the 'perfect object.' 'From Brahmâ down to a blade of grass, all living beings that dwell within this world are in the power of the Sa*m*sâra due to works, and hence no profit can be derived by the devout from making them objects of their meditation. They are all implicated in Nescience, and stand within the sphere of the Sa*m*sâra; knowledge arises in them only later on, and they are thus of no use in meditation. Their knowledge does not belong to them by essential nature, for it comes to them through something else. Therefore the stainless Brahman which possesses essential knowledge,' &c. &c.—All this proves that the passage 'in which all difference vanishes' does not mean to deny the reality of the world.

Nor, again, does the passage 'that which has knowledge

for its essential nature' (Vi. Pu. I, 2, 6) imply that the whole complex of things different from knowledge is false; for it declares only that the appearance of the Self—the essential nature of which is knowledge—*as* gods, men, and so on, is erroneous. A declaration that the appearance of mother o' pearl *as* silver is founded on error surely does not imply that all the silver in the world is unreal!—But if, on the ground of an insight into the oneness of Brahman and the world—as expressed in texts where the two appear in co-ordination—a text declares that it is an error to view Brahman, whose essential nature is knowledge, under the form of material things, this after all implies that the whole aggregate of things is false!—By no means, we rejoin. As our *s*âstra distinctly teaches that the highest Brahman, i. e. Vish*n*u, is free from all imperfections whatsoever, comprises within himself all auspicious qualities, and reveals his power in mighty manifestations, the view of the world's reality cannot possibly be erroneous. That information as to the oneness of two things by means of co-ordination does not allow of sublation (of either of the two), and is non-contradictory, we shall prove further on. Hence also the *s*loka last referred to does not sublate the reality of the world.

'That from whence these beings are born, by which, when born, they live, into which they enter when they die, endeavour to know that; that is Brahman' (Taitt. Up. III, 1). From this scriptural text we ascertain that Brahman is the cause of the origination, and so on, of the world. After this we learn from a Purâ*n*a text ('He should make the Veda grow by means of Itihâsa and Purâ*n*a; the Veda fears that a man of little reading may do it harm') that the Veda should be made to grow by Itihâsa and Purâ*n*a. By this 'making to grow' we have to understand the elucidation of the sense of the Vedic texts studied by means of other texts, promulgated by men who had mastered the entire Veda and its contents, and by the strength of their devotion had gained full intuition of Vedic truth. Such 'making to grow' must needs be undertaken, since the purport of the entire Veda with all its *S*âkhâs cannot be fathomed by one who has studied a small part only, and since without knowing that purport we cannot arrive at any certitude.

The Vish*n*u Purâ*n*a relates how Maitreya, wishing to have his knowledge of Vedic matters strengthened by the holy Parâ*s*ara, who through the favour of Pulastya and Vasish*th*a had obtained an insight into the true nature of the highest divinity, began to question Parâ*s*ara, 'I am desirous to hear from thee how this world originated, and how it will again originate in future, and of what it consists, and whence proceed animate and inanimate things; how and into what it has been resolved, and into what it will in future be resolved?' &c. (Vi. Pu. I, 1). The questions asked refer to the essential nature of Brahman, the different modes of the manifestation of its power, and the different results of propitiating it. Among the questions belonging to the first category, the question 'whence proceed animate and inanimate things?' relates to the efficient and the material cause of the world, and hence the clause 'of what the world consists' is to be taken as implying a question as to what constitutes the Self of this world, which is the object of creation, sustentation, and dissolution. The reply to this question is given in the words 'and the world is He.' Now the identity expressed by this clause is founded thereon that he (i.e. Brahman or Vish*n*u) pervades the world as its Self in the character of its inward Ruler; and is not founded on unity of substance of the pervading principle and the world pervaded. The phrase 'consists of' (-maya) does not refer to an effect (so that the question asked would be as to the causal substance of which this world is an effect), for a separate question on this point would be needless. Nor does the -maya express, as it sometimes does—e.g. in the case of prâ*n*a-maya [1], the own sense of the word to which it is attached; for in that case the form of the reply 'and the world is He' (which implies a distinction between the world and Vish*n*u) would be inappropriate; the reply would in that case rather be 'Vish*n*u only.' What 'maya' actually denotes here is

[1] 'Prâ*n*amaya' is explained as meaning 'prâ*n*a' only.

abundance, prevailingness, in agreement with Pâ*n*ini, V, 4, 21, and the meaning is that Brahman prevails in the world in so far as the entire world constitutes its body. The co-ordination of the two words 'the world' and 'He' thus rests on that relation between the two, owing to which the world is the body of Brahman, and Brahman the Self of the world. If, on the other hand, we maintained that the *s*âstra aims only at inculcating the doctrine of one substance free from all difference, there would be no sense in all those questions and answers, and no sense in an entire *s*âstra devoted to the explanation of that one thing. In that case there would be room for one question only, viz. 'what is the substrate of the erroneous imagination of a world?' and for one answer to this question, viz. 'pure consciousness devoid of all distinction!'—And if the co-ordination expressed in the clause 'and the world is he' was meant to set forth the absolute oneness of the world and Brahman, then it could not be held that Brahman possesses all kinds of auspicious qualities, and is opposed to all evil; Brahman would rather become the abode of all that is impure. All this confirms the conclusion that the co-ordination expressed in that clause is to be understood as directly teaching the relation between a Self and its body.—The *s*loka, 'From Vish*n*u the world has sprung: in him he exists: he is the cause of the subsistence and dissolution of this world: and the world is he' (Vi. Pu. I, 1, 35), states succinctly what a subsequent passage—beginning with 'the highest of the high' (Vi. Pu. I, 2, 10)—sets forth in detail. Now there the *s*loka, 'to the unchangeable one' (I, 2, 1), renders homage to the holy Vish*n*u, who is the highest Brahman in so far as abiding within his own nature, and then the text proceeds to glorify him in his threefold form as Hira*n*yagarbha, Hari, and *S*aṅkara, as Pradhâna, Time, and as the totality of embodied souls in their combined and distributed form. Here the *s*loka, 'Him whose essential nature is knowledge' (I, 2, 6), describes the aspect of the highest Self in so far as abiding in the state of discrete embodied souls; the passage cannot therefore be understood as referring to a substance free from all difference. If the *s*âstra aimed at teaching that the erroneous conception of a manifold world has for its substrate a Brahman consisting of non-differenced intelligence, there would be room neither for the objection raised in I, 3, 1 ('How can we attribute agency creative and otherwise to Brahman which is without qualities, unlimited, pure, stainless?') nor for the refutation of that objection, 'Because the powers of all things are the objects of (true) knowledge excluding all (bad) reasoning, therefore there belong to Brahman also such essential powers as the power of creating, preserving, and so on, the world; just as heat essentially belongs to fire[1].' In that case the objection would rather be made in the following form: 'How can Brahman, which is without qualities, be the agent in the creation, preservation, and so on, of the world?' and the answer would be, 'Creation by Brahman is not something real, but something erroneously imagined.' —The purport of the objection as it stands in the text is as follows: 'We observe that action creative and otherwise belongs to beings endowed with qualities such as goodness, and so on, not perfect, and subject to the influence of karman; how then can agency creative, and so on, be attributed to Brahman which is devoid of qualities, perfect, not under the influence of karman, and incapable of any connexion with action?' And the reply is, 'There is nothing unreasonable in holding that Brahman as being of the nature described above, and different in kind from all things perceived, should possess manifold powers; just as fire, which is different in kind from water and all other material substances, possesses the quality of heat and other qualities.' The *s*lokas also, which begin with the words 'Thou alone art real' (Vi. Pu. I, 4, 38 ff.), do not assert that the whole world is unreal, but only that, as Brahman is the Self of the world, the latter viewed apart from Brahman is not real. This the text proceeds to confirm,

[1] The sense in which this *s*loka has to be taken is 'As in ordinary life we ascribe to certain things (e.g. gems, mantras) certain special powers because otherwise the effects they produce could not be accounted for; so to Brahman also,' &c.

'thy greatness it is by which all movable and immovable things are pervaded.' This means—because all things movable and immovable are pervaded by thee, therefore all this world has thee for its Self, and hence 'there is none other than thee,' and thus thou being the Self of all art alone real. Such being the doctrine intended to be set forth, the text rightly says, 'this all-pervasiveness of thine is thy greatness'; otherwise it would have to say, 'it is thy error.' Were this latter view intended, words such as 'Lord of the world,' 'thou,' &c., could not, moreover, be taken in their direct sense, and there would arise a contradiction with the subject-matter of the entire chapter, viz. the praise of the Holy one who in the form of a mighty boar had uplifted in play the entire earth.—Because this entire world is thy form in so far as it is pervaded as its Self by thee whose true nature is knowledge; therefore those who do not possess that devotion which enables men to view thee as the Self of all, erroneously view this world as consisting only of gods, men, and other beings; this is the purport of the next *s*loka, 'this which is seen.'—And it is an error not only to view the world which has its real Self in thee as consisting of gods, men, and so on, but also to consider the Selfs whose true nature is knowledge as being of the nature of material beings such as gods, men, and the like; this is the meaning of the next *s*loka, 'this world whose true nature is knowledge.'—Those wise men, on the other hand, who have an insight into the essentially intelligent Self, and whose minds are cleared by devotion—the means of apprehending the Holy one as the universal Self—, they view this entire world with all its manifold bodies—the effects of primeval matter—as thy body—a body the Self of which is constituted by knowledge abiding apart from its world-body; this is the meaning of the following *s*loka: 'But those who possess knowledge,' &c.—If the different *s*lokas were not interpreted in this way, they would be mere unmeaning reiterations; their constitutive words could not be taken in their primary sense; and we should come into conflict with the sense of the passages, the subject-matter of the chapter, and the purport of the entire *s*âstra. The passage, further, 'Of that Self although it exists in one's own and in other bodies, the knowledge is of one kind' (Vi. Pu. II, 14, 31 ff.), refers to that view of duality according to which the different Selfs—although equal in so far as they are all of the essence of knowledge—are constituted into separate beings, gods, men, &c., by their connexion with different portions of matter all of which are modifications of primary matter, and declares that view to be false. But this does not imply a denial of the duality which holds good between matter on the one hand and Self on the other: what the passage means is that the Self which dwells in the different material bodies of gods, men, and so on, is of one and the same kind. So the Holy one himself has said, 'In the dog and the low man eating dog's flesh the wise see the same'; 'Brahman, without any imperfection, is the same' (Bha. Gî. V, 18, 19). And, moreover, the clause 'Of the Self although existing in one's own and in other bodies' directly declares that a thing different from the body is distributed among one's own and other bodies.

Nor does the passage 'If there is some other (para) different (anya) from me,' &c. (Vi. Pu. II, 13, 86) intimate the oneness of the Self; for in that case the two words 'para' and 'anya' would express one meaning only (viz. 'other' in the sense of 'distinct from'). The word 'para' there denotes a Self distinct from that of one's own Self, and the word 'anya' is introduced to negative a character different from that of pure intelligence: the sense of the passage thus is 'If there is some Self distinct from mine, and of a character different from mine which is pure knowledge, then it can be said that I am of such a character and he of a different character'; but this is not the case, because all Selfs are equal in as far as their nature consists of pure knowledge.—Also the *s*loka beginning 'Owing to the difference of the holes of the flute' (Vi. Pu. II, 14, 32) only declares that the inequality of the different Selfs is owing not to their essential nature, but to their dwelling in different material bodies; and does not teach the oneness of all Selfs. The different portions of air, again, passing through the different holes of the flute—to which the many Selfs are compared—are not said to be one but only to be equal in character; they are one in character in so far as all of them are of the nature of air, while the different names of the successive notes of the musical scale are applied to them because they pass out by the different holes of the instrument. For an analogous reason the several Selfs are denominated by different names, viz. gods and so on. Those material things also which are parts of the substance fire, or water, or earth, are one in so far only as they consist of one kind of substance; but are not absolutely one; those different portions of air, therefore, which constitute the notes of the scale are likewise not absolutely one. Where the Purâ*n*a further says 'He (or "that") I am and thou art He (or "that"); all this universe that has Self for its true nature is He (or "that"); abandon the error of distinction' (Vi. Pu. II, 16, 23); the word 'that' refers to the intelligent character mentioned previously which is common to all Selfs, and the co-ordination stated in the two clauses therefore intimates that intelligence is the character of the beings denoted 'I' and 'Thou'; 'abandon therefore,' the text goes on to say, 'the illusion that the difference of outward form, divine and so on, causes a corresponding difference in the Selfs.' If this explanation were not accepted (but absolute non-difference insisted upon) there would be no room for the references to difference which the passages quoted manifestly contain.

Accordingly the text goes on to say that the king acted on the instruction he had received, 'he abandoned the view of difference, having recognised the Real.'—But on what ground do we arrive at this decision (viz. that the passage under discussion is not meant to teach absolute non-duality)?—On the ground, we reply, that the proper topic of the whole section is to teach the distinction of the Self and the body—for this is evident from what is said in an early part of the section, 'as the body of man, characterised by hands, feet, and the like,' &c. (Vi. Pu. II, 13, 85).—For analogous reasons the *s*loka 'When that knowledge which gives rise to distinction' &c. (Vi. Pu. VI, 7, 94) teaches neither the essential unity of all Selfs nor the oneness of the individual Self and the highest Self. And that the embodied soul and the highest Self should be essentially one, is no more possible than that the body and the Self should be one. In agreement herewith Scripture says, 'Two birds, inseparable friends, cling to the same tree. One of them eats the sweet fruit, the other looks on without eating' (Mu. Up. III, 1, 1). 'There are two drinking their reward in the world of their own works, entered into the cave, dwelling on the highest summit. Those who know Brahman call them shade and light,' &c. (Ka. Up. I, 3, 1). And in this *s*âstra also (i. e. the Vish*n*u Purâ*n*a) there are passages of analogous import; cp. the stanzas quoted above, 'He transcends the causal matter, all effects, all imperfections such as the gu*n*as' &c.

The Sûtras also maintain the same doctrine, cp. I, 1, 17; I, 2, 21; II, 1, 22; and others. They therein follow Scripture, which in several places refers to the highest and the individual soul as standing over against each other, cp. e. g. 'He who dwells in the Self and within the Self, whom the Self does not know, whose body the Self is, who rules the Self from within' (B*ri*. Up. III, 7, 22); 'Embraced by the intelligent Self' (B*ri*. Up. IV, 3, 21); 'Mounted by the intelligent Self' (IV, 3, 35). Nor can the individual Self become one with the highest Self by freeing itself from Nescience, with the help of the means of final Release; for that which admits of being the abode of Nescience can never become quite incapable of it. So the Purâ*n*a says, 'It is false to maintain that the individual Self and the highest Self enter into real union; for one substance cannot pass over into the nature of another substance.' Accordingly the Bhagavad Gîtâ declares that the released soul attains only the same attributes as the highest Self. 'Abiding by this knowledge, they, attaining to an equality of attributes with me, do neither come forth at the time of creation, nor are troubled at the time of general destruction' (XIV, 2). Similarly our Purâ*n*a says, 'That Brahman leads him who meditates on it, and who is capable of change, towards its own being (âtmabhâva), in the same way as the magnet attracts the iron' (Vi. Pu. VI, 7, 30). Here the phrase 'leads him towards his own being' means 'imparts to him a nature like his own' (not 'completely identifies him with itself'); for the attracted body does not become essentially one with the body attracting.

The same view will be set forth by the Sûtrakâra in IV, 4, 17; 21, and I, 3, 2. The V*ri*tti also says (with reference to Sû. IV, 4, 17) 'with the exception of the business of the world (the individual soul in the state of release) is equal (to the highest Self) through light'; and the author of the Drami*d*abhâshya says, 'Owing to its equality (sâyu*g*ya) with the divinity the disembodied soul effects all things, like the divinity.' The following scriptural texts establish the same view, 'Those who depart from hence, after having known the Self and those true desires, for them there is freedom in all the worlds' (*Kh.* Up. VIII, 1, 6); 'He who knows Brahman reaches the Highest' (Taitt. Up. II, 1); 'He obtains all desires together with the intelligent Brahman' (Taitt. Up. II, 1, 1); 'Having reached the Self which consists of bliss, he wanders about in these worlds having as much food and assuming as many forms as he likes' (Taitt. Up. III, 10, 5); 'There he moves about' (*Kh.* Up. VIII, 12, 3); 'For he is flavour; for only after having perceived a flavour can any one perceive pleasure' (Taitt. Up. II, 7); 'As the flowing rivers go to their setting in the sea, losing name and form; thus he who knows, freed from name and form, goes to the divine Person who is higher than the high' (Mu. Up. III, 2, 8); 'He who knows, shaking off good and evil, reaches the highest oneness, free from stain' (Mu. Up. III, 1, 3).

The objects of meditation in all the vidyâs which refer to the highest Brahman, are Brahman viewed as having qualities, and the fruit of all those meditations. For this reason the author of the Sûtras declares that there is option among the different vidyâs—cp. Ve. Sû. III, 3, 11; III, 3, 59. In the same way the Vâkyakâra teaches that the qualified Brahman only is the object of meditation, and that there is option of vidyâs; where he says '(Brahman) connected (with qualities), since the meditation refers to its qualities.' The same view is expressed by the Bhâshyakâra in the passage beginning 'Although he who bases himself on the knowledge of Being.'—Texts such as 'He knows Brahman, he becomes Brahman' (Mu. Up. III, 2, 9) have the same purport, for they must be taken in connexion with the other texts (referring to the fate of him who knows) such as 'Freed from name and form he goes to the divine Person who is higher than the high'; 'Free from stain he reaches the highest oneness' (Mu. Up. III, 2, 8; III, 1, 3); 'Having approached the highest light he manifests himself in his own shape' (Kh. Up. VIII, 3, 4). Of him who has freed himself from his ordinary name and form, and all the distinctions founded thereon, and has assumed the uniform character of intelligence, it may be said that he is of the character of Brahman.—Our Purâ*n*a also propounds the same view. The *s*loka (VI, 7, 91), 'Knowledge is the means to obtain what is to be obtained, viz. the highest Brahman: the Self is to be obtained, freed from all kinds of imagination,' states that that Self which through meditation on Brahman, is freed from all imagination so as to be like Brahman, is the object to be attained. (The three forms of imagination to be got rid of are so-called karma-bhâvanâ, brahma-bhâvanâ and a combination of the two. See Vi. Pu. VI, 7.) The text then goes on, 'The embodied Self is the user of the instrument, knowledge is its instrument; having accomplished Release—whereby his object is attained—he may leave off.' This means that the Devotee is to practise meditation on the highest Brahman until it has accomplished its end, viz. the attainment of the Self free from all imagination.—The text continues, 'Having attained the being of its being, then he is non-different from the highest Self; his difference is founded on Nescience only.' This *s*loka describes the state of the released soul. 'Its being' is the being, viz. the character or nature, of Brahman; but this does not mean absolute oneness of nature; because in this latter case the second 'being' would be out of place and the *s*loka would contradict what had been said before. The meaning is: when the soul has attained the nature of

Brahman, i. e. when it has freed itself from all false imagination, then it is non-different from the highest Self. This non-difference is due to the soul, as well as the highest Self, having the essential nature of uniform intelligence. The difference of the soul—presenting itself as the soul of a god, a man, &c.—from the highest Self is not due to its essential nature, but rests on the basis of Nescience in the form of work: when through meditation on Brahman this basis is destroyed, the difference due to it comes to an end, and the soul no longer differs from the highest Self. So another text says, 'The difference of things of one nature is due to the investing agency of outward works; when the difference of gods, men, &c., is destroyed, it has no longer any investing power' (Vi. Pu. II, 14, 33).—The text then adds a further explanation, 'when the knowledge which gives rise to manifold difference is completely destroyed, who then will produce difference that has no real existence?' The manifold difference is the distinction of gods, men, animals, and inanimate things: compare the saying of *S*aunaka: 'this fourfold distinction is founded on false knowledge.' The Self has knowledge for its essential nature; when Nescience called work—which is the cause of the manifold distinctions of gods, men, &c.—has been completely destroyed through meditation on the highest Brahman, who then will bring about the distinction of gods, &c., from the highest Self—a distinction which in the absence of a cause cannot truly exist.—That Nescience is called karman (work) is stated in the same chapter of the Purâ*n*a (st. 61—avidyâ karmasa*m*g*ñ*â).

The passage in the Bhagavad Gîtâ, 'Know me to be the kshetra*g**ñ*a' (XIII, 2), teaches the oneness of all in so far as the highest Self is the inward ruler of all; taken in any other sense it would be in conflict with other texts, such as 'All creatures are the Perishable, the unchanging soul is the Imperishable; but another is the highest Person' (Bha. Gî. XV, 16). In other places the Divine one declares that as inward Ruler he is the Self of all: 'The Lord dwells in the heart of all creatures' (XVIII, 61), and 'I dwell within the heart of all' (XV, 15), and 'I am the

Self which has its abode within all creatures' (X, 20). The term 'creature' in these passages denotes the entire aggregate of body, &c., up to the Self.—Because he is the Self of all, the text expressly denies that among all the things constituting his body there is any one separate from him, 'There is not anything which is without me' (X, 39). The place where this text occurs is the winding up of a glorification of the Divine one, and the text has to be understood accordingly. The passage immediately following is 'Whatever being there is, powerful, beautiful, or glorious, even that know thou to have sprung from a portion of my glory; pervading this entire Universe by a portion of mine I do abide' (X, 41; 42).

All this clearly proves that the authoritative books do *not* teach the doctrine of one non-differenced substance; that they do *not* teach that the universe of things is false; and that they do *not* deny the essential distinction of intelligent beings, non-intelligent things, and the Lord.

### The theory of Nescience cannot be proved.

We now proceed to the consideration of Nescience.—According to the view of our opponent, this entire world, with all its endless distinctions of Ruler, creatures ruled, and so on, is, owing to a certain defect, fictitiously superimposed upon the non-differenced, self-luminous Reality; and what constitutes that defect is beginningless Nescience, which invests the Reality, gives rise to manifold illusions, and cannot be defined either as being or non-being. Such Nescience, he says, must necessarily be admitted, firstly on the ground of scriptural texts, such as 'Hidden by what is untrue' (*Kh.* Up. VIII, 3, 2), and secondly because otherwise the oneness of the individual souls with Brahman—which is taught by texts such as 'Thou are that'—cannot be established. This Nescience is neither 'being,' because in that case it could not be the object of erroneous cognition (bhrama) and sublation (bâdha); nor is it 'non-being,' because in that case it could not be the object of apprehension and sublation[1]. Hence orthodox Philosophers declare

[1] 'Nescience' is sublated (refuted) by the cognition of Brahman,

that this Nescience falls under neither of these two opposite categories.

Now this theory of Nescience is altogether untenable. In the first place we ask, 'What is the substrate of this Nescience which gives rise to the great error of plurality of existence?' You cannot reply 'the individual soul'; for the individual soul itself exists in so far only as it is fictitiously imagined through Nescience. Nor can you say 'Brahman'; for Brahman is nothing but self-luminous intelligence, and hence contradictory in nature to Nescience, which is avowedly sublated by knowledge.

'The highest Brahman has knowledge for its essential nature: if Nescience, which is essentially false and to be terminated by knowledge, invests Brahman, who then will be strong enough to put an end to it?'

'What puts an end to Nescience is the knowledge that Brahman is pure knowledge!'—'Not so, for that knowledge also is, like Brahman, of the nature of light, and hence has no power to put an end to Nescience.—And if there exists the knowledge that Brahman is knowledge, then Brahman is an object of knowledge, and that, according to your own teaching, implies that Brahman is not of the nature of consciousness.'

To explain the second of these *s*lokas.—If you maintain that what sublates Nescience is not that knowledge which constitutes Brahman's essential nature, but rather that knowledge which has for its object the truth of Brahman being of such a nature, we demur; for as both these kinds of knowledge are of the same nature, viz. the nature of light, which is just that which constitutes Brahman's nature, there is no reason for making a distinction and saying that one knowledge is contradictory of Nescience, and the other is not. Or, to put it otherwise—that essential nature of Brahman which is apprehended through the cognition

---

and thereby shown to have been the object of erroneous cognition: it thus cannot be 'being,' i.e. real. Nor can it be altogether unreal, 'non-being,' because in that case it could not be the object either of mental apprehension or of sublation.

that Brahman is knowledge, itself shines forth in consequence of the self-luminous nature of Brahman, and hence we have no right to make a distinction between that knowledge which constitutes Brahman's nature, and that of which that nature is the object, and to maintain that the latter only is antagonistic to Nescience.—Moreover (and this explains the third *s*loka), according to your own view Brahman, which is mere consciousness, cannot be the object of another consciousness, and hence there is no knowledge which has Brahman for its object. If, therefore, knowledge is contradictory to non-knowledge (Nescience), Brahman itself must be contradictory to it, and hence cannot be its substrate. Shells (mistaken for silver) and the like which by themselves are incapable of throwing light upon their own true nature are not contradictory to non-knowledge of themselves, and depend, for the termination of that non-knowledge, on another knowledge (viz. on the knowledge of an intelligent being); Brahman, on the other hand, whose essential nature is established by its own consciousness, is contradictorily opposed to non-knowledge of itself, and hence does not depend, for the termination of that non-knowledge, on some other knowledge.—If our opponent should argue that the knowledge of the falsity of whatever is other than Brahman is contradictory to non-knowledge, we ask whether this knowledge of the falsity of what is other than Brahman is contradictory to the non-knowledge of the true nature of Brahman, or to that non-knowledge which consists in the view of the reality of the apparent world. The former alternative is inadmissible; because the cognition of the falsity of what is other than Brahman has a different object (from the non-knowledge of Brahman's true nature) and therefore cannot be contradictory to it; for knowledge and non-knowledge are contradictory in so far only as they refer to one and the same object. And with regard to the latter alternative we point out that the knowledge of the falsity of the world is contradictory to the non-knowledge which consists in the view of the reality of the world; the former knowledge therefore sublates the latter non-knowledge only, while the non-knowledge of the true nature of Brahman is not touched by it.—Against this it will perhaps be urged that what is here called the non-knowledge of the true nature of Brahman, really is the view of Brahman being dual in nature, and that this view is put an end to by the cognition of the falsity of whatever is other than Brahman; while the true nature of Brahman itself is established by its own consciousness.—But this too we refuse to admit. If non-duality constitutes the true nature of Brahman, and is proved by Brahman's own consciousness, there is room neither for what is contradictory to it, viz. that non-knowledge which consists in the view of duality, nor for the sublation of that non-knowledge.—Let then non-duality be taken for an attribute (not the essential nature) of Brahman! —This too we refuse to admit; for you yourself have proved that Brahman, which is pure Consciousness, is free from attributes which are objects of Consciousness.—From all this it follows that Brahman, whose essential nature is knowledge, cannot be the substrate of Nescience: the theory, in fact, involves a flat contradiction.

When, in the next place, you maintain that Brahman, whose nature is homogeneous intelligence, is invested and hidden by Nescience, you thereby assert the destruction of Brahman's essential nature. Causing light to disappear means either obstructing the origination of light, or else destroying light that exists. And as you teach that light (consciousness) cannot originate, the 'hiding' or 'making to disappear' of light can only mean its destruction.—Consider the following point also. Your theory is that self-luminous consciousness, which is without object and without substrate, becomes, through the influence of an imperfection residing within itself, conscious of itself as connected with innumerous substrata and innumerous objects.—Is then, we ask, that imperfection residing within consciousness something real or something unreal?—The former alternative is excluded, as not being admitted by yourself. Nor can we accept the latter alternative; for if we did we should have to view that imperfection as being either a knowing subject, or an object of knowledge, or Knowing itself. Now it cannot be 'Knowing,' as you deny that there is any distinction in the nature of knowing; and that 'Knowing,' which is the substrate of the imperfection, cannot be held to be unreal, because that would involve the acceptance of the Mâdhyamika doctrine, viz. of a general void [1].

And if knowers, objects of knowledge and knowing as determined by those two are fictitious, i. e. unreal, we have to assume another fundamental imperfection, and are thus driven into a *regressus in infinitum.*—To avoid this difficulty, it might now be said that real consciousness itself, which constitutes Brahman's nature, is that imperfection.—But if Brahman itself constitutes the imperfection, then Brahman is the basis of the appearance of a world, and it is gratuitous to assume an additional avidyâ to account for the world. Moreover, as Brahman is eternal, it would follow from this hypothesis that no release could ever take place. Unless, therefore, you admit a real imperfection apart from Brahman, you are unable to account for the great world-error.

What, to come to the next point, do you understand by the inexplicability (anirva*k*aniyatâ) of Nescience?—Its difference in nature from that which *is*, as well as that which *is not!*—A thing of such kind would be inexplicable indeed; for none of the means of knowledge apply to it. That is to say—the whole world of objects must be ordered according to our states of consciousness, and every state of consciousness presents itself in the form, either of something existing or of something non-existing. If, therefore, we should assume that of states of consciousness which are limited to this double form, the object can be something which is neither existing nor non-existing, then anything

[1] If the imperfection inhering in Consciousness is itself of the nature of consciousness, and at the same time unreal, we should have to distinguish two kinds of Consciousness—which is contrary to the fundamental doctrine of the oneness of Consciousness. And if, on the other hand, we should say that the Consciousness in which the imperfection inheres is of the same nature as the latter, i. e. unreal, we are landed in the view of universal unreality.

whatever might be the object of any state of consciousness whatever.

Against this our opponent may now argue as follows:—There is, after all, something, called avidyâ, or a*gñ*âna, or by some other name, which is a positive entity (bhâva), different from the antecedent non-existence of knowledge; which effects the obscuration of the Real; which is the material cause of the erroneous superimposition on the Real, of manifold external and internal things; and which is terminated by the cognition of the true nature of the one substance which constitutes Reality. For this avidyâ is apprehended through Perception as well as Inference. Brahman, in so far as limited by this avidyâ, is the material cause of the erroneous superimposition—upon the inward Self, which in itself is changeless pure intelligence, but has its true nature obscured by this superimposition—of that plurality which comprises the aha*m*kâra, all acts of knowledge and all objects of knowledge. Through special forms of this defect (i. e. avidyâ) there are produced, in this world superimposed upon Reality, the manifold special superimpositions presenting themselves in the form of things and cognitions of things—such as snakes (superimposed upon ropes), silver (superimposed on shells), and the like. Avidyâ constitutes the material cause of this entire false world; since for a false thing we must needs infer a false cause. That this avidyâ or a*gñ*âna (non-knowledge) is an object of internal Perception, follows from the fact that judgments such as 'I do not know,' 'I do not know either myself or others,' directly present themselves to the mind. A mental state of this kind has for its object not that non-knowledge which is the antecedent non-existence of knowledge—for such absence of knowledge is ascertained by the sixth means of proof (anupalabdhi); it rather is a state which presents its object directly, and thus is of the same kind as the state expressed in the judgment 'I am experiencing pleasure.' Even if we admit that 'absence of something' (abhâva) can be the object of perception, the state of consciousness under discussion cannot have absence of knowledge in the Self for its object. For at the very moment of such consciousness knowledge exists; or if it does not exist there can be no consciousness of the absence of knowledge. To explain. When I am conscious that I am non-knowing, is there or is there not apprehension of the Self as having non-existence of knowledge for its attribute, and of knowledge as the counterentity of non-knowledge? In the former case there can be no consciousness of the absence of knowledge, for that would imply a contradiction. In the latter case, such consciousness can all the less exist, for it presupposes knowledge of that to which absence of knowledge belongs as an attribute (viz. the Self) and of its own counterentity, viz. knowledge. The same difficulty arises if we view the absence of knowledge as either the object of Inference, or as the object of the special means of proof called 'abhâva' (i. e. anupalabdhi). If, on the other hand, non-knowledge is viewed (not as a merely negative, but) as a positive entity, there arises no contradiction even if there is (as there is in fact) at the same time knowledge of the Self as qualified by non-knowledge, and of knowledge as the counterentity of non-knowledge; and we therefore must accept the conclusion that the state of consciousness expressed by 'I am non-knowing,' has for its object a non-knowledge which is a positive entity.—But, a Nescience which is a positive entity, contradicts the witnessing consciousness, whose nature consists in the lighting up of the truth of things!—Not so, we reply. Witnessing consciousness has for its object not the true nature of things, but Nescience; for otherwise the lighting up (i.e. the consciousness) of false things could not take place. Knowledge which has for its object non-knowledge (Nescience), does not put an end to that non-knowledge. Hence there is no contradiction (between *k*aitanya and a*gñ*âna).—But, a new objection is raised, this positive entity, Nescience, becomes an object of witnessing Consciousness, only in so far as it (Nescience) is defined by some particular object (viz. the particular thing which is not known), and such objects depend for their proof on the different means of knowledge. How then can that Nescience, which is defined by the 'I' (as expressed e.g. in the judgment, 'I do not know myself'), become the object of witnessing Consciousness?—There is no difficulty here, we reply. All things whatsoever are objects of Consciousness, either as things known or as things not known. But while the mediation of the means of knowledge is required in the case of all those things which, as being non-intelligent (*gada*), can be proved only in so far as being objects known (through some means of knowledge), such mediation is not required in the case of the intelligent (a*gada*) inner Self which proves itself. Consciousness of Nescience is thus possible in all cases (including the case 'I do not know myself'), since witnessing Consciousness always gives definition to Nescience.—From all this it follows that, through Perception confirmed by Reasoning, we apprehend Nescience as a positive entity. This Nescience, viewed as a positive entity, is also proved by Inference—viz. in the following form: All knowledge established by one of the different means of proof is preceded by something else, which is different from the mere antecedent non-existence of knowledge; which hides the object of knowledge; which is terminated by knowledge; and which exists in the same place as knowledge;—because knowledge possesses the property of illumining things not illumined before;—just as the light of a lamp lit in the dark illumines things.—Nor must you object to this inference on the ground that darkness is not a substance, but rather the mere absence of light, or else the absence of visual perception of form and colour, and that hence darkness cannot be brought forward as a similar instance proving Nescience to be a positive entity. For that Darkness must be considered a positive substance follows, firstly, from its being more or less dense, and secondly, from its being perceived as having colour.

To all this we make the following reply. Neither Perception alone, nor Perception aided by Reasoning, reveals to us a positive entity, Nescience, as implied in judgments such as 'I am non-knowing,' 'I know neither myself nor others.' The contradiction which was urged above against the view of non-knowledge being the antecedent non-existence of knowledge, presents itself equally in connexion with non-knowledge viewed as a positive entity. For here the following alternative presents itself—the inner Reality is either known or not known as that which gives definition to Nescience by being either its object or its substrate. If it be thus known, then there is in it no room for Nescience which is said to be that which is put an end to by the cognition of the true nature of the Inner Reality. If, on the other hand, it be not thus known, how should there be a consciousness of Nescience in the absence of that which defines it, viz. knowledge of the substrate or of the object of Nescience?—Let it then be said that what is contradictory to non-knowledge is the clear presentation of the nature of the inner Self, and that (while there is consciousness of a*g\~n*âna) we have only an obscure presentation of the nature of the Self; things being thus, there is no contradiction between the cognition of the substrate and object of Nescience on the one side, and the consciousness of a*g\~n*âna on the other.—Well, we reply, all this holds good on our side also. Even if a*g\~n*âna means antecedent non-existence of knowledge, we can say that knowledge of the substrate and object of non-knowledge has for its object the Self presented obscurely only; and thus there is no difference between our views—unless you choose to be obstinate!

Whether we view non-knowledge as a positive entity or as the antecedent non-existence of knowledge, in either case it comes out as what the word indicates, viz. non-knowledge. Non-knowledge means either absence of knowledge, or that which is other than knowledge, or that which is contradictory to knowledge; and in any of these cases we have to admit that non-knowledge presupposes the cognition of the nature of knowledge. Even though the cognition of the nature of darkness should not require the knowledge of the nature of light, yet when darkness is considered under the aspect of being contrary to light, this presupposes the cognition of light. And the non-knowledge held by you is never known in its own nature but merely as 'non-knowledge,' and it therefore presupposes the cognition of knowledge no less than our view does, according to which non-knowledge is simply the negation of knowledge. Now antecedent non-existence of knowledge is admitted by you also, and is an undoubted object of consciousness; the right conclusion therefore is that what we are conscious of in such judgments as 'I am non-knowing,' &c., is this very antecedent non-existence of knowledge which we both admit.

It, moreover, is impossible to ascribe to Brahman, whose nature is constituted by eternal free self-luminous intelligence, the consciousness of Nescience; for what constitutes its essence is consciousness of itself. If against this you urge that Brahman, although having consciousness of Self for its essential nature, yet is conscious of non-knowledge in so far as its (Brahman's) nature is hidden; we ask in return what we have to understand by Brahman's nature being hidden. You will perhaps say 'the fact of its not being illumined.' But how, we ask, can there be absence of illumination of the nature of that whose very nature consists in consciousness of Self, i. e. self-illumination? If you reply that even that whose nature is consciousness of Self may be in the state of its nature not being illumined by an outside agency, we point out that as according to you light cannot be considered as an attribute, but constitutes the very nature of Brahman, it would—illumination coming from an external agency—follow that the very nature of Brahman can be destroyed from the outside. This we have already remarked.—Further, your view implies on the one hand that this non-knowledge which is the cause of the concealment of Brahman's nature hides Brahman in so far as Brahman is conscious of it, and on the other hand that having hidden Brahman, it becomes the object of consciousness on the part of Brahman; and this evidently constitutes a logical see-saw. You will perhaps say[1] that it hides Brahman in so far only as Brahman is conscious of it. But, we point out, if the consciousness of a*gñ*âna takes place on the part of a Brahman whose nature is not hidden, the whole hypothesis of the 'hiding' of Brahman's nature

[1] Allowing the former view of the question only.

loses its purport, and with it the fundamental hypothesis as to the nature of a*gñ*âna; for if Brahman may be conscious of a*gñ*âna (without a previous obscuration of its nature by a*gñ*âna) it may as well be held to be in the same way conscious of the world, which, by you, is considered to be an effect of a*gñ*âna.

How, further, do you conceive this consciousness of a*gñ*âna on Brahman's part? Is it due to Brahman itself, or to something else? In the former case this consciousness would result from Brahman's essential nature, and hence there would never be any Release. Or else, consciousness of a*gñ*âna constituting the nature of Brahman, which is admittedly pure consciousness, in the same way as the consciousness of false silver is terminated by that cognition which sublates the silver, so some terminating act of cognition would eventually put an end to Brahman's essential nature itself.—On the second alternative we ask what that something else should be. If you reply 'another a*gñ*âna,' we are led into a *regressus in infinitum*.—Let it then be said[1] that a*gñ*âna having first hidden Brahman then becomes the object of its consciousness.—This, we rejoin, would imply that a*gñ*âna—acting like a defect of the eye—by its very essential being hides Brahman, and then a*gñ*âna could not be sublated by knowledge.—Let us then put the case as follows:—A*gñ*âna, which is by itself beginningless, at the very same time effects Brahman's witnessing it (being conscious of it), and Brahman's nature being hidden; in this way the *regressus in infinitum* and other difficulties will be avoided.—But this also we cannot admit; for Brahman is essentially consciousness of Self, and cannot become a witnessing principle unless its nature be previously hidden.—Let then Brahman be hidden by some other cause!—This, we rejoin, would take away from a*gñ*âna its alleged beginninglessness, and further would also lead to an infinite regress. And if Brahman were assumed to become a witness, without its essential nature being hidden, it could not possess—what yet it is main-

[1] Adopting the latter view only; see preceding note.

tained to possess—the uniform character of consciousness of Self.—If, moreover, Brahman is hidden by avidyâ, does it then not shine forth at all, or does it shine forth to some extent? On the former alternative the not shining forth of Brahman—whose nature is mere light—reduces it to an absolute non-entity. Regarding the latter alternative we ask, 'of Brahman, which is of an absolutely homogeneous nature, which part do you consider to be concealed, and which to shine forth?' To that substance which is pure light, free from all division and distinction, there cannot belong two modes of being, and hence obscuration and light cannot abide in it together.—Let us then say that Brahman, which is homogeneous being, intelligence, bliss, has its nature obscured by avidyâ, and hence is seen indistinctly as it were.—But how, we ask, are we to conceive the distinctness or indistinctness of that whose nature is pure light? When an object of light which has parts and distinguishing attributes appears in its totality, we say that it appears distinctly; while we say that its appearance is indistinct when some of its attributes do not appear. Now in those aspects of the thing which do not appear, light (illumination) is absent altogether, and hence we cannot there speak of indistinctness of light; in those parts on the other hand which do appear, the light of which they are the object is distinct. Indistinctness is thus not possible at all where there is light. In the case of such things as are apprehended as objects, indistinctness may take place, viz. in so far as some of their distinguishing attributes are not apprehended. But in Brahman, which is not an object, without any distinguishing attributes, pure light, the essential nature of which it is to shine forth, indistinctness which consists in the non-apprehension of certain attributes can in no way be conceived, and hence not be explained as the effect of avidyâ.

We, moreover, must ask the following question: 'Is this indistinctness which you consider an effect of avidyâ put an end to by the rise of true knowledge or not?' On the latter alternative there would be no final release. In the former case we have to ask of what nature Reality is. 'It is of an essentially clear and distinct nature.' Does this nature then exist previously (to the cessation of indistinctness), or not? If it does, there is no room whatever either for indistinctness the effect of avidyâ, or for its cessation. If it does not previously exist, then Release discloses itself as something to be effected, and therefore non-eternal.—And that such non-knowledge is impossible because there is no definable substrate for it we have shown above.—He, moreover, who holds the theory of error resting on a non-real defect, will find it difficult to prove the impossibility of error being without any substrate; for, if the cause of error may be unreal, error may be supposed to take place even in case of its substrate being unreal. And the consequence of this would be the theory of a general Void.

The assertion, again, that non-knowledge as a positive entity is proved by Inference, also is groundless. But the inference was actually set forth!—True; but it was set forth badly. For the reason you employed for proving a*gñ*âna is a so-called contradictory one (i. e. it proves the contrary of what it is meant to prove), in so far as it proves what is not desired and what is different from a*gñ*âna (for what it proves is that there is a certain *knowledge*, viz. that all knowledge resting on valid means of proof has non-knowledge for its antecedent). (And with regard to this knowledge again we must ask whether it also has non-knowledge for its antecedent.) If the reason (relied on in all this argumentation) does not prove, in this case also, the antecedent existence of positive non-knowledge, it is too general (and hence not to be trusted in any case). If, on the other hand, it does prove antecedent non-knowledge, then this latter non-knowledge stands in the way of the non-knowledge (which you try to prove by inference) being an object of consciousness, and thus the whole supposition of a*gñ*âna as an entity becomes useless.

The proving instance, moreover, adduced by our opponent, has no proving power; for the light of a lamp does not possess the property of illumining things not illumined before. Everywhere illumining power belongs to knowledge only; there may be light, but if there is not also knowledge there is no lighting up of objects. The senses also are only causes of the origination of knowledge, and possess no illumining power. The function of the light of the lamp on the other hand is a merely auxiliary one, in so far as it dispels the darkness antagonistic to the organ of sight which gives rise to knowledge; and it is only with a view to this auxiliary action that illumining power is conventionally ascribed to the lamp.—But in using the light of the lamp as a proving instance, we did not mean to maintain that it possesses illumining power equal to that of light; we introduced it merely with reference to the illumining power of knowledge, in so far as preceded by the removal of what obscures its object!—We refuse to accept this explanation. Illumining power does not only mean the dispelling of what is antagonistic to it, but also the defining of things, i.e. the rendering them capable of being objects of empirical thought and speech; and this belongs to knowledge only (not to the light of the lamp). If you allow the power of illumining what was not illumined, to auxiliary factors also, you must first of all allow it to the senses which are the most eminent factors of that kind; and as in their case there exists no different thing to be terminated by their activity, (i.e. nothing analogous to the a*gñ*âna to be terminated by knowledge), this whole argumentation is beside the point.

There are also formal inferences, opposed to the conclusion of the pûrvapakshin.—Of the a*gñ*âna under discussion, Brahman, which is mere knowledge, is not the substrate, just because it is a*gñ*âna; as shown by the case of the non-knowledge of the shell (mistaken for silver) and similar cases; for such non-knowledge abides within the knowing subject.—The a*gñ*âna under discussion does not obscure knowledge, just because it is a*gñ*âna; as shown by the cases of the shell, &c.; for such non-knowledge hides the object.—A*gñ*âna is not terminated by knowledge, because it does not hide the object of knowledge; whatever non-knowledge is terminated by knowledge, is such as to hide the object of knowledge; as e.g. the non-knowledge of the shell.—Brahman is not the substrate of a*gñ*âna, because it is devoid of the character of knowing subject; like jars and similar things.—Brahman is not hidden by a*gñ*âna, because it is not the object of knowledge; whatever is hidden by non-knowledge is the object of knowledge; so e.g. shells and similar things.—Brahman is not connected with non-knowledge to be terminated by knowledge, because it is not the object of knowledge; whatever is connected with non-knowledge to be terminated by knowledge is an object of knowledge; as e.g. shells and the like.—Knowledge based on valid means of proof, has not for its antecedent, non-knowledge other than the antecedent non-existence of knowledge; just because it is knowledge based on valid proof; like that valid knowledge which proves the a*gñ*âna maintained by you.—Knowledge does not destroy a real thing, because it is knowledge in the absence of some specific power strengthening it; whatever is capable of destroying things is—whether it be knowledge or a*gñ*âna—strengthened by some specific power; as e.g. the knowledge of the Lord and of Yogins; and as the a*gñ*âna consisting in a pestle (the blow of which destroys the pot).—A*gñ*âna which has the character of a positive entity cannot be destroyed by knowledge; just because it is a positive entity, like jars and similar things.

But, it now may be said, we observe that fear and other affections, which are positive entities and produced by previous cognitions, are destroyed by sublative acts of cognition!—Not so, we reply. Those affections are not destroyed by knowledge; they rather pass away by themselves, being of a momentary (temporary) nature only, and on the cessation of their cause they do not arise again. That they are of a momentary nature only, follows from their being observed only in immediate connexion with the causes of their origination, and not otherwise. If they were not of a temporary nature, each element of the stream of cognitions, which are the cause of fear and the like, would give rise to a separate feeling of fear, and the result would be that there would be consciousness of many distinct feelings of fear (and this we know not to be the case).—In conclusion we remark that in defining right knowledge as 'that which has for its antecedent another entity, different from its own antecedent non-existence,' you do not give proof of very eminent logical acuteness; for what sense has it to predicate of an entity that it is different from non-entity?—For all these reasons Inference also does not prove an a*gñ*âna which is a positive entity. And that it is not proved by Scripture and arthâpatti, will be shown later on. And the reasoning under Sû. II, 1, 4, will dispose of the argument which maintains that of a false thing the substantial cause also must be false.

We thus see that there is no cognition of any kind which has for its object a Nescience of 'inexplicable' nature.—Nor can such an inexplicable entity be admitted on the ground of apprehension, erroneous apprehension and sublation (cp. above, p. 102). For that only which is actually apprehended, can be the object of apprehension, error and sublation, and we have no right to assume, as an object of these states of consciousness, something which is apprehended neither by them nor any other state of consciousness.—'But in the case of the shell, &c., silver is actually apprehended, and at the same time there arises the sublating consciousness "this silver is not real," and it is not possible that one thing should appear as another; we therefore are driven to the hypothesis that owing to some defect, we actually apprehend silver of an altogether peculiar kind, viz. such as can be defined neither as real nor as unreal.'—This also we cannot allow, since this very assumption necessarily implies that one thing appears as another. For apprehension, activity, sublation, and erroneous cognition, all result only from one thing appearing as another, and it is not reasonable to assume something altogether non-perceived and groundless. The silver, when apprehended, is not apprehended as something 'inexplicable,' but as something real; were it apprehended under the former aspect it could be the object neither of erroneous nor of sublative cognition, nor would the apprehending person endeavour to seize it. For these reasons you (the anirva-

*k*anîyatva-vâdin) also must admit that the actual process is that of one thing appearing as another.

Those also who hold other theories as to the kind of cognition under discussion (of which the shell, mistaken for silver, is an instance) must—whatsoever effort they may make to avoid it—admit that their theory finally implies the appearing of one thing as another. The so-called asatkhyâti-view implies that the non-existing appears as existing; the âtmakhyâti-view, that the Self—which here means 'cognition'—appears as a thing; and the akhyâti-view, that the attribute of one thing appears as that of another, that two acts of cognition appear as one, and—on the view of the non-existence of the object—that the non-existing appears as existing[1].

Moreover, if you say that there is originated silver of a totally new inexplicable kind, you are bound to assign the cause of this origination. This cause cannot be the perception of the silver; for the perception has the silver for its object, and hence has no existence before the origination of the silver. And should you say that the perception, having arisen without an object, produces the silver and thereupon makes it its object, we truly do not know what to say to such excellent reasoning!—Let it then be said that the cause is some defect in the sense-organ.—This, too, is inadmissible; for a defect abiding in the percipient person cannot produce an objective effect.—Nor can the organs of sense (apart from defects) give rise to the silver; for they are causes of cognitions only (not of things cognised). Nor, again, the sense-organs in so far as modified by some defect; for they also can only produce modifications in what is effected by them, i. e. cognition.—And the hypothesis of a beginningless, false a*gñ*âna constituting the general material cause of all erroneous cognitions has been refuted above.

How is it, moreover, that this new and inexplicable thing

---

[1] For a full explanation of the nature of these 'khyâtis,' see A. Venis' translation of the Vedânta Siddhânta Muktâvali (Reprint from the Pandit, p. 130 ff.).

(which you assume to account for the silver perceived on the shell) becomes to us the object of the idea and word 'silver,' and not of some other idea and term, e.g. of a jar?—If you reply that this is due to its similarity to silver, we point out that in that case the idea and the word presenting themselves to our mind should be that of 'something resembling silver.' Should you, on the other hand, say that we apprehend the thing as silver because it possesses the generic characteristics of silver, we ask whether these generic characteristics are real or unreal. The former alternative is impossible, because something real cannot belong to what is unreal; and the latter is impossible because something unreal cannot belong to what is real.

But we need not extend any further this refutation of an altogether ill-founded theory.

### All knowledge is of the Real.

'Those who understand the Veda hold that all cognition has for its object what is real; for *S*ruti and Sm*ri*ti alike teach that everything participates in the nature of everything else. In the scriptural account of creation preceded by intention on the part of the Creator it is said that each of these elements was made tripartite; and this tripartite constitution of all things is apprehended by Perception as well. The red colour in burning fire comes from (primal elementary) fire, the white colour from water, the black colour from earth—in this way Scripture explains the threefold nature of burning fire. In the same way all things are composed of elements of all things. The Vish*n*u Purâ*n*a, in its account of creation, makes a similar statement: "The elements possessing various powers and being unconnected could not, without combination, produce living beings, not having mingled in any way. Having combined, therefore, with one another, and entering into mutual associations—beginning with the principle called Mahat, and extending down to the gross elements—they formed an egg," &c. (Vi. Pu. I, 2, 50; 52). This tripartiteness of the elements the Sûtrakâra also declares (Ve. Sû. III, 1, 3). For the same reason *S*ruti enjoins the use of Putîka sprouts when no Soma can be procured; for, as the Mîmâ*m*sakas explain, there are in the Putîka plant some parts of the Soma plant (Pû. Mî. Sû.); and for the same reason nîvâra grains may be used as a substitute for rice grains. That thing is similar to another which contains within itself some part of that other thing; and Scripture itself has thus stated that in shells, &c., there is contained some silver, and so on. That one thing is called "silver" and another "shell" has its reason in the relative preponderance of one or the other element. We observe that shells are similar to silver; thus perception itself informs us that some elements of the latter actually exist in the former. Sometimes it happens that owing to a defect of the eye the silver-element only is apprehended, not the shell-element, and then the percipient person, desirous of silver, moves to pick up the shell. If, on the other hand, his eye is free from such defect, he apprehends the shell-element and then refrains from action. Hence the cognition of silver in the shell is a true one. In the same way the relation of one cognition being sublated by another explains itself through the preponderant element, according as the preponderance of the shell-element is apprehended partially or in its totality, and does not therefore depend on one cognition having for its object the false thing and another the true thing. The distinctions made in the practical thought and business of life thus explain themselves on the basis of everything participating in the nature of everything else.'

In dreams, again, the divinity creates, in accordance with the merit or demerit of living beings, things of a special nature, subsisting for a certain time only, and perceived only by the individual soul for which they are meant. In agreement herewith Scripture says, with reference to the state of dreaming, 'There are no chariots in that state, no horses, no roads; then he creates chariots, horses, and roads. There are no delights, no joys, no bliss; then he creates delights, joys, and bliss. There are no tanks, no lakes, no rivers; then he creates tanks, lakes, and rivers.

For he is the maker' (Bri. Up. IV, 3, 10). The meaning of this is, that although there are then no chariots, &c., to be perceived by other persons, the Lord creates such things to be perceived by the dreaming person only. 'For he is the maker'; for such creative agency belongs to him who possesses the wonderful power of making all his wishes and plans to come true. Similarly another passage, 'That person who is awake in those who are asleep, shaping one lovely sight after another, that indeed is the Bright, that is Brahman, that alone is called the Immortal. All worlds are contained in it, and no one goes beyond it' (Ka. Up. II, 5, 8).—The Sûtrakâra also, after having in two Sûtras (III, 2, 1; 2) stated the hypothesis of the individual soul creating the objects appearing in dreams, finally decides that that wonderful creation is produced by the Lord for the benefit of the individual dreamer; for the reason that as long as the individual soul is in the samsâra state, its true nature—comprising the power of making its wishes to come true—is not fully manifested, and hence it cannot practically exercise that power. The last clause of the Katha text ('all worlds are contained in it,' &c.) clearly shows that the highest Self only is the creator meant. That the dreaming person who lies in his chamber should go in his body to other countries and experience various results of his merit or demerit—being at one time crowned a king, having at another time his head cut off, and so on—is possible in so far as there is created for him another body in every way resembling the body resting on the bed.

The case of the white shell being seen as yellow, explains itself as follows. The visual rays issuing from the eye are in contact with the bile contained in the eye, and thereupon enter into conjunction with the shell; the result is that the whiteness belonging to the shell is overpowered by the yellowness of the bile, and hence not apprehended; the shell thus appears yellow, just as if it were gilt. The bile and its yellowness is, owing to its exceeding tenuity, not perceived by the bystanders; but thin though it be it is apprehended by the person suffering from jaundice, to whom it is very near, in so far as it issues from his own eye, and through the mediation of the visual rays, aided by the action of the impression produced on the mind by that apprehension, it is apprehended even in the distant object, viz. the shell.—In an analogous way the crystal which is placed near the rose is apprehended as red, for it is overpowered by the brilliant colour of the rose; the brilliancy of the rose is perceived in a more distinct way owing to its close conjunction with the transparent substance of the crystal.—In the same way the cognition of water in the mirage is true. There always exists water in connexion with light and earth; but owing to some defect of the eye of the perceiving person, and to the mysterious influence of merit and demerit, the light and the earth are not apprehended, while the water *is* apprehended.—In the case again of the firebrand swung round rapidly, its appearance as a fiery wheel explains itself through the circumstance that moving very rapidly it is in conjunction with all points of the circle described without our being able to apprehend the intervals. The case is analogous to that of the perception of a real wheel; but there is the difference that in the case of the wheel no intervals are apprehended, because there are none; while in the case of the firebrand none are apprehended owing to the rapidity of the movement. But in the latter case also the cognition is true.—Again, in the case of mirrors and similar reflecting surfaces the perception of one's own face is likewise true. The fact is that the motion of the visual rays (proceeding from the eye towards the mirror) is reversed (reflected) by the mirror, and that thus those rays apprehend the person's own face, subsequently to the apprehension of the surface of the mirror; and as in this case also, owing to the rapidity of the process, there is no apprehension of any interval (between the mirror and the face), the face presents itself as being in the mirror.—In the case of one direction being mistaken for another (as when a person thinks the south to be where the north is), the fact is that, owing to the unseen principle (i. e. merit or demerit), the direction which actually exists in the other direction (for a point which is to the north of me is to the south of another point) is apprehended by itself, apart from the other elements of direction; the apprehension which actually takes place is thus likewise true.—Similar is the case of the double moon. Here, either through pressure of the finger upon the eye, or owing to some abnormal affection of the eye, the visual rays are divided (split), and the double, mutually independent apparatus of vision thus originating, becomes the cause of a double apprehension of the moon. One apparatus apprehends the moon in her proper place; the other which moves somewhat obliquely, apprehends at first a place close by the moon, and then the moon herself, which thus appears somewhat removed from her proper place. Although, therefore, what is apprehended is the one moon distinguished by connexion with two places at the same time—an apprehension due to the double apparatus of vision—yet, owing to the difference of apprehensions, there is a difference in the character of the object apprehended, and an absence of the apprehension of unity, and thus a double moon presents itself to perception. That the second spot is viewed as qualifying the moon, is due to the circumstance that the apprehension of that spot, and that of the moon which is not apprehended in her proper place, are simultaneous. Now here the doubleness of the apparatus is real, and hence the apprehension of the moon distinguished by connexion with two places is real also, and owing to this doubleness of apprehension, the doubleness of aspect of the object apprehended, i.e. the moon, is likewise real. That there is only one moon constituting the true object of the double apprehension, this is a matter for which ocular perception by itself does not suffice, and hence what is actually seen is a double moon. That, although the two eyes together constitute one visual apparatus only, the visual rays being divided through some defect of the eyes, give rise to a double apparatus—this we infer from the effect actually observed. When that defect is removed there takes place only one apprehension of the moon as connected with her proper place, and thus the idea of one moon only arises. It is at the same time quite clear how the defect of the eye gives rise to a double visual apparatus, the latter to a double apprehension, and the latter again to a doubleness of the object of apprehension.

We have thus proved that all cognition is true. The shortcomings of other views as to the nature of cognition have been set forth at length by other philosophers, and we therefore do not enter on that topic. What need is there, in fact, of lengthy proofs? Those who acknowledge the validity of the different means of knowledge, perception, and so on, and—what is vouched for by sacred tradition—the existence of a highest Brahman—free from all shadow of imperfection, of measureless excellence, comprising within itself numberless auspicious qualities, all-knowing, immediately realising all its purposes—, what should they not be able to prove? That holy highest Brahman—while producing the entire world as an object of fruition for the individual souls, in agreement with their respective good and ill deserts —creates certain things of such a nature as to become common objects of consciousness, either pleasant or unpleasant, to all souls together, while certain other things are created in such a way as to be perceived only by particular persons, and to persist for a limited time only. And it is this distinction—viz. of things that are objects of general consciousness, and of things that are not so—which makes the difference between what is called 'things sublating' and 'things sublated.'—Everything is explained hereby.

### Neither Scripture nor Sm*ri*ti and Purâ*n*a teach Nescience.

The assertion that Nescience—to be defined neither as that which is nor as that which is not—rests on the authority of Scripture is untrue. In passages such as 'hidden by the untrue' (*Kh.* Up. VIII, 3, 2), the word 'untrue' does not denote the Undefinable; it rather means that which is different from '*ri*ta,' and this latter word—as we see from the passage 'enjoying the *ri*ta' (Ka. Up. I, 3, 1)—denotes such actions as aim at no worldly end, but only at the propitiation of the highest Person, and thus enable the devotee to reach him. The word 'an*ri*ta' therefore denotes actions of a different kind, i.e. such as aim at worldly results and thus stand in the way of the soul reaching Brahman; in agreement with the passage 'they do not find that Brahma-world, for they are carried away by an*ri*ta' (*Kh.* Up. VIII, 3, 2).—Again, in the text 'Then there was neither non-Being nor Being' (*Ri.* Sa*m*h. X, 129, 1), the terms 'being' and 'non-being' denote intelligent and non-intelligent beings in their distributive state. What that text aims at stating is that intelligent and non-intelligent beings, which at the time of the origination of the world are called 'sat' and 'tyat' (Taitt. Up. II, 6), are, during the period of reabsorption, merged in the collective totality of non-intelligent matter which the text denotes by the term 'darkness' (*Ri.* Sa*m*h. X, 129, 3). There is thus no reference whatever to something 'not definable either as being or non-being': the terms 'being' and 'non-being' are applied to different modes of being at different times. That the term 'darkness' denotes the collective totality of non-intelligent matter appears from another scriptural passage, viz. 'The Non-evolved (avyaktam) is merged in the Imperishable (akshara), the Imperishable in darkness (tamas), darkness becomes one with the highest divinity.'—True, the word 'darkness' denotes the subtle condition of primeval matter (prak*ri*ti), which forms the totality of non-intelligent things; but this very Prak*ri*ti is called Mâyâ—in the text 'Know Prak*ri*ti to be Mâyâ,' and this proves it be something 'undefinable'!—Not so, we reply; we meet with no passages where the word 'Mâyâ' denotes that which is undefinable!—But the word 'Mâyâ' is synonymous with 'mithyâ,' i.e. falsehood, and hence denotes the Undefinable also!—This, too, we cannot admit; for the word 'Mâyâ' does not in all places refer to what is false; we see it applied e.g. to such things as the weapons of Asuras and Râkshasas, which are not 'false' but real. 'Mâyâ,' in such passages, really denotes that which produces various wonderful effects, and it is in this sense that Prak*ri*ti is called Mâyâ. This appears from the passage (*S*vet. Up. IV, 9) 'From that the "mâyin" creates all this, and in that the other one is bound up by mâyâ.' For this text declares that Prak*ri*ti—there called Mâyâ—produces manifold wonderful creations, and the highest Person is there called 'mâyin' because he possesses that power of mâyâ; not on account of any ignorance or nescience on his part. The latter part of the text expressly says that (not the Lord but) another one, i. e. the individual soul is bound up by mâyâ; and therewith agrees another text, viz. 'When the soul slumbering in beginningless Mâyâ awakes' (Gau*d*. Kâ.). Again, in the text 'Indra goes multiform through the Mâyâs' (*Ri*. Sa*m*h. VI, 47, 18), the manifold powers of Indra are spoken of, and with this agrees what the next verse says, 'he shines greatly as Tvash*tri*': for an unreal being does not shine. And where the text says 'my Mâyâ is hard to overcome' (Bha. Gî. VII, 14), the qualification given there to Mâyâ, viz. 'consisting of the gu*n*as,' shows that what is meant is Prak*ri*ti consisting of the three gu*n*as.—All this shows that Scripture does not teach the existence of a 'principle called Nescience, not to be defined either as that which is or that which is not.'

Nor again is such Nescience to be assumed for the reason that otherwise the scriptural statements of the unity of all being would be unmeaning. For if the text 'Thou art that,' be viewed as teaching the unity of the individual soul and the highest Self, there is certainly no reason, founded on unmeaningness, to ascribe to Brahman, intimated by the word 'that'—which is all-knowing, &c.—Nescience, which is contradictory to Brahman's nature.—Itihâsa and Purâ*n*a also do not anywhere teach that to Brahman there belongs Nescience.

But, an objection is raised, the Vish*n*u Purâ*n*a, in the *s*loka, 'The stars are Vish*n*u,' &c. (II, 12, 38), first refers to Brahman as one only, and comprising all things within itself; thereupon states in the next *s*loka that this entire world, with all its distinctions of hills, oceans, &c., is sprung out of the 'a*gñ*âna' of Brahman, which in itself is pure '*gñ*âna,' i. e. knowledge; thereupon confirms the view of the world having sprung from a*gñ*âna by referring to the fact that Brahman, while abiding in its own nature, is free from all difference (*s*l. 40); proves in the next two *s*lokas the non-reality of plurality by a consideration of the things of this world; sums up, in the following *s*loka, the unreality of all that is different from Brahman; then (43) explains that action is the root of that a*gñ*âna which causes us to view the one uniform Brahman as manifold; thereupon declares the intelligence constituting Brahman's nature to be free from all distinction and imperfection (44); and finally teaches (45) that Brahman so constituted, alone is truly real, while the so-called reality of the world is merely conventional.—This is not, we reply, a true representation of the drift of the passage. The passage at the outset states that, in addition to the detailed description of the world given before, there will now be given a succinct account of another aspect of the world not yet touched upon. This account has to be understood as follows. Of this universe, comprising intelligent and non-intelligent beings, the intelligent part—which is not to be reached by mind and speech, to be known in its essential nature by the Self only, and, owing to its purely intelligential character, not touched by the differences due to Prak*ri*ti—is, owing to its imperishable nature, denoted as that which is; while the non-intelligent, material, part which, in consequence of the actions of the intelligent beings undergoes manifold changes, and thus is perishable, is denoted as that which is not. Both parts, however, form the body of Vâsudeva, i. e. Brahman, and hence have Brahman for their Self. The text therefore says (37), 'From the waters which form the body of Vish*n*u was produced the lotus-shaped earth, with its seas and mountains': what is meant is that the entire Brahma-egg which has arisen from water constitutes the body of which Vish*n*u is the soul. This relation of soul and body forms the basis of the statements of co-ordination made in the next *s*loka (38), 'The stars are Vish*n*u,' &c.; the same relation had been already declared in numerous previous passages of the Purâ*n*a ('all this is the body of Hari,' &c.). All things in the world, whether they are or are not, are Vish*n*u's body, and he is their soul. Of the next *s*loka, 'Because the Lord has knowledge for his essential nature,' the meaning is 'Because of the Lord who abides as the Self of all individual souls, the essential nature is knowledge only—while bodies divine, human, &c., have no part in it—, therefore all non-intelligent things, bodies human and divine, hills, oceans, &c., spring from his knowledge, i. e. have their root in the actions springing from the volitions of men, gods, &c., in whose various forms the fundamental intelligence manifests itself. And since non-intelligent matter is subject to changes corresponding to the actions of the individual souls, it may be called 'non-being,' while the souls are 'being.'—This the next *s*loka further explains 'when knowledge is pure,' &c. The meaning is 'when the works which are the cause of the distinction of things are destroyed, then all the distinctions of bodies, human or divine, hills, oceans, &c.—all which are objects of fruition for the different individual souls—pass away.' Non-intelligent matter, as entering into various states of a non-permanent nature, is called 'non-being'; while souls, the nature of which consists in permanent knowledge, are called 'being.' On this difference the next *s*loka insists (41). We say 'it is' of that thing which is of a permanently uniform nature, not connected with the idea of beginning, middle and end, and which hence never becomes the object of the notion of non-existence; while we say 'it is not' of non-intelligent matter which constantly passes over into different states, each later state being out of connexion with the earlier state. The constant changes to which non-intelligent matter is liable are illustrated in the next *s*loka, 'Earth is made into a jar,' &c. And for this reason, the subsequent *s*loka goes on to say that there *is* nothing but knowledge. This fundamental knowledge or intelligence is, however, variously connected with manifold individual forms of being due to karman, and hence the text adds: 'The one intelligence is in many ways connected with beings whose minds differ, owing to the difference of their own acts' (*s*l. 43, second half). Intelligence, pure, free from stain and grief, &c., which constitutes the intelligent element of the world, and unintelligent matter—these two together constitute the world, and the world is the body of Vâsudeva; such is the purport of *s*loka 44.—The next *s*loka sums up the whole doctrine; the words 'true and untrue' there denote what in the preceding verses had been called 'being' and 'non-being'; the second half of the *s*loka refers to the practical plurality of the world as due to karman.

Now all these *s*lokas do not contain a single word supporting the doctrine of a Brahman free from all difference; of a principle called Nescience abiding within Brahman and to be defined neither as that which is nor as that which is not; and of the world being wrongly imagined, owing to Nescience. The expressions 'that which is' and 'that which is not' (*s*l. 35), and 'satya' (true) and 'asatya' (untrue; *s*l. 45), can in no way denote something not to be defined either as being or non-being. By 'that which is not' or 'which is untrue,' we have to understand not what is undefinable, but that which has no true being, in so far as it is changeable and perishable. Of this character is all non-intelligent matter. This also appears from the instance adduced in *s*l. 42: the jar is something perishable, but not a thing devoid of proof or to be sublated by true knowledge. 'Non-being' we may call it, in so far as while it is observed at a certain moment in a certain form it is at some other moment observed in a different condition. But there is no contradiction between two different conditions of a thing which are perceived at different times; and hence there is no reason to call it something futile (tu*kh*k*h*a) or false (mithyâ), &c.

**Scripture does not teach that Release is due to the knowledge of a non-qualified Brahman.—The meaning of 'tat tvam asi.'**

Nor can we admit the assertion that Scripture teaches the cessation of avidyâ to spring only from the cognition of a Brahman devoid of all difference. Such a view is clearly negatived by passages such as the following: 'I know that great person of sun-like lustre beyond darkness; knowing him a man becomes immortal, there is no other path to go' (*S*vet. Up. III, 8); 'All moments sprang from lightning, the Person—none is lord over him, his name is great glory—they who know him become immortal' (Mahânâ. Up. I, 8–11). For the reason that Brahman is characterised by difference all Vedic texts declare that final release results from the cognition of a qualified Brahman. And that even those texts which describe Brahman by means of negations really aim at setting forth a Brahman possessing attributes, we have already shown above.

In texts, again, such as 'Thou art that,' the co-ordination of the constituent parts is not meant to convey the idea of the absolute unity of a non-differenced substance: on the contrary, the words 'that' and 'thou' denote a Brahman distinguished by difference. The word 'that' refers to Brahman omniscient, &c., which had been introduced as the general topic of consideration in previous passages of the same section, such as 'It thought, may I be many'; the word 'thou,' which stands in co-ordination to 'that,' conveys the idea of Brahman in so far as having for its body the individual souls connected with non-intelligent matter. This is in accordance with the general principle that co-ordination is meant to express one thing subsisting in a twofold form. If such doubleness of form (or character) were abandoned, there could be no difference of aspects giving rise to the application of different terms, and the entire principle of co-ordination would thus be given up. And it would further follow that the two words co-ordinated would have to be taken in an implied sense (instead of their primary direct meaning). Nor is there any need of our assuming implication (laksha*n*â) in sentences[1] such as 'this person is that Devadatta (known to me from former occasions)'; for there is no contradiction in the cognition of the oneness of a thing connected with the past on the one hand, and the present on the other, the contradiction that arises from difference of place being removed

[1] Which are alleged to prove that sâmânâdhikara*n*ya is to be explained on the basis of laksha*n*â.

by the accompanying difference of time. If the text 'Thou art that' were meant to express absolute oneness, it would, moreover, conflict with a previous statement in the same section, viz. 'It thought, may I be many'; and, further, the promise (also made in the same section) that by the knowledge of one thing all things are to be known could not be considered as fulfilled. It, moreover, is not possible (while, however, it would result from the absolute oneness of 'tat' and 'tvam') that to Brahman, whose essential nature is knowledge, which is free from all imperfections, omniscient, comprising within itself all auspicious qualities, there should belong Nescience; and that it should be the substrate of all those defects and afflictions which spring from Nescience. If, further, the statement of co-ordination ('thou art that') were meant to sublate (the previously existing wrong notion of plurality), we should have to admit that the two terms 'that' and 'thou' have an implied meaning, viz. in so far as denoting, on the one hand, one substrate only, and, on the other, the cessation of the different attributes (directly expressed by the two terms); and thus implication and the other shortcomings mentioned above would cling to this interpretation as well. And there would be even further difficulties. When we form the sublative judgment 'this is not silver,' the sublation is founded on an independent positive judgment, viz. 'this is a shell'; in the case under discussion, however, the sublation would not be known (through an independent positive judgment), but would be assumed merely on the ground that it cannot be helped. And, further, there is really no possibility of sublation, since the word 'that' does not convey the idea of an attribute in addition to the mere substrate. To this it must not be objected that the substrate was previously concealed, and that hence it is the special function of the word 'that' to present the substrate in its non-concealed aspect; for if, previously to the sublative judgment, the substrate was not evident (as an object of consciousness), there is no possibility of its becoming the object either of an error or its sublation.—Nor can we allow you to say that, previously to sublation, the substrate was non-concealed in so far as (i.e. was known as) the object of error, for in its 'non-concealed' aspect the substrate is opposed to all error, and when that aspect shines forth there is no room either for error or sublation.—The outcome of this is that as long as you do not admit that there is a real attribute in addition to the mere substrate, and that this attribute is for a time hidden, you cannot show the possibility either of error or sublation. We add an illustrative instance. That with regard to a man there should arise the error that he is a mere low-caste hunter is only possible on condition of a real additional attribute—e.g. the man's princely birth—being hidden at the time; and the cessation of that error is brought about by the declaration of this attribute of princely birth, not by a mere declaration of the person being a man: this latter fact being evident need not be declared at all, and if it is declared it sublates no error.—If, on the other hand, the text is understood to refer to Brahman as having the individual souls for its body, both words ('that' and 'thou') keep their primary denotation; and, the text thus making a declaration about one substance distinguished by two aspects, the fundamental principle of 'co-ordination' is preserved. On this interpretation the text further intimates that Brahman—free from all imperfection and comprising within itself all auspicious qualities—is the internal ruler of the individual souls and possesses lordly power. It moreover satisfies the demand of agreement with the teaching of the previous part of the section, and it also fulfils the promise as to all things being known through one thing, viz. in so far as Brahman having for its body all intelligent and non-intelligent beings in their gross state is the effect of Brahman having for its body the same things in their subtle state. And this interpretation finally avoids all conflict with other scriptural passages, such as 'Him the great Lord, the highest of Lords' (*S*vet. Up. VI, 7); 'His high power is revealed as manifold' (ibid. VI, 8); 'He that is free from sin, whose wishes are true, whose purposes are true' (*Kh*. Up. VIII, 7, 1), and so on.

But how, a question may be asked, can we decide, on

your interpretation of the text, which of the two terms is meant to make an original assertion with regard to the other?—The question does not arise, we reply; for the text does not mean to make an original assertion at all, the truth which it states having already been established by the preceding clause, 'In that all this world has its Self.' This clause does make an original statement—in agreement with the principle that 'Scripture has a purport with regard to what is not established by other means'—that is, it predicates of 'all this,' i.e. this entire world together with all individual souls, that 'that,' i.e. Brahman is the Self of it. The reason of this the text states in a previous passage, 'All these creatures have their root in that which is, their dwelling and their rest in that which is'; a statement which is illustrated by an earlier one (belonging to a different section), viz. 'All this is Brahman; let a man meditate with calm mind on this world as beginning, ending, and breathing in Brahman' (*Kh.* Up. III, 14, 1). Similarly other texts also teach that the world has its Self in Brahman, in so far as the whole aggregate of intelligent and non-intelligent beings constitutes Brahman's body. Compare 'Abiding within, the ruler of beings, the Self of all'; 'He who dwells in the earth, different from the earth, whom the earth does not know, whose body the earth is, who rules the earth within—he is thy Self, the ruler within, the immortal.—He who dwells in the Self,' &c. (B*ri*. Up. III, 7, 3; 22); 'He who moving within the earth, and so on—whose body is death, whom death does not know, he is the Self of all beings, free from sin, divine, the one God, Nârâya*n*a' (Subâl. Up. VII, 1); 'Having created that he entered into it; having entered it he became sat and tyat' (Taitt. Up. II, 6). And also in the section under discussion the passage 'Having entered into them with this living Self let me evolve names and forms,' shows that it is only through the entering into them of the living soul whose Self is Brahman, that all things possess their substantiality and their connexion with the words denoting them. And as this passage must be understood in connexion with Taitt. Up. II, 6 (where the 'sat' denotes the individual soul) it follows that the individual soul also has Brahman for its Self, owing to the fact of Brahman having entered into it.—From all this it follows that the entire aggregate of things, intelligent and non-intelligent, has its Self in Brahman in so far as it constitutes Brahman's body. And as, thus, the whole world different from Brahman derives its substantial being only from constituting Brahman's body, any term denoting the world or something in it conveys a meaning which has its proper consummation in Brahman only: in other words all terms whatsoever denote Brahman in so far as distinguished by the different things which we associate with those terms on the basis of ordinary use of speech and etymology.—The text 'that art thou' we therefore understand merely as a special expression of the truth already propounded in the clause 'in that all this has its Self.'

This being so, it appears that those as well who hold the theory of the absolute unity of one non-differenced substance, as those who teach the doctrine of bhedâbheda (co-existing difference and non-difference), and those who teach the absolute difference of several substances, give up all those scriptural texts which teach that Brahman is the universal Self. With regard to the first-mentioned doctrine, we ask 'if there is only one substance; to what can the doctrine of universal identity refer?'—The reply will perhaps be 'to that very same substance.'—But, we reply, this point is settled already by the texts defining the nature of Brahman[1], and there is nothing left to be determined by the passages declaring the identity of everything with Brahman.—But those texts serve to dispel the idea of fictitious difference!—This, we reply, cannot, as has been shown above, be effected by texts stating universal identity in the way of co-ordination; and statements of co-ordination, moreover, introduce into Brahman a doubleness of aspect, and thus contradict the theory of absolute oneness.—The bhedâbheda view implies that owing to Brahman's connexion with limiting adjuncts (upâdhi) all the imperfections

[1] Such as 'The True, knowledge,' &c.

resulting therefrom—and which avowedly belong to the individual soul—would manifest themselves in Brahman itself; and as this contradicts the doctrine that the Self of all is constituted by a Brahman free from all imperfection and comprising within itself all auspicious qualities, the texts conveying that doctrine would have to be disregarded. If, on the other hand, the theory be held in that form that 'bhedâbheda' belongs to Brahman by its own nature (not only owing to an upâdhi), the view that Brahman by its essential nature appears as individual soul, implies that imperfections no less than perfections are essential to Brahman, and this is in conflict with the texts teaching that everything is identical with Brahman free from all imperfections.—For those finally who maintain absolute difference, the doctrine of Brahman being the Self of all has no meaning whatsoever—for things absolutely different can in no way be one—and this implies the abandonment of all Vedânta-texts together.

Those, on the other hand, who take their stand on the doctrine, proclaimed by all Upanishads, that the entire world forms the body of Brahman, may accept in their fulness all the texts teaching the identity of the world with Brahman. For as genus (*g*âti) and quality (gu*n*a), so substances (dravya) also may occupy the position of determining attributes (vi*s*esha*n*a), in so far namely as they constitute the body of something else. Enunciations such as 'the Self (soul) is, according to its works, born either (as) a god, or a man, or a horse, or a bull,' show that in ordinary speech as well as in the Veda co-ordination has to be taken in a real primary (not implied) sense. In the same way it is also in the case of generic character and of qualities the relation of 'mode' only (in which generic character and qualities stand to substances) which determines statements of co-ordination, such as 'the ox is broken-horned,' 'the cloth is white.' And as material bodies bearing the generic marks of humanity are definite things, in so far only as they are modes of a Self or soul, enunciations of co-ordination such as 'the soul has been born as a man, or a eunuch, or a woman,' are in every way appropriate. What determines statements of co-ordination is thus only the relation of 'mode' in which one thing stands to another, not the relation of generic character, quality, and so on, which are of an exclusive nature (and cannot therefore be exhibited in co-ordination with substances). Such words indeed as denote substances capable of subsisting by themselves occasionally take suffixes, indicating that those substances form the distinguishing attributes of other substances—as when from da*nd*a, 'staff,' we form da*nd*in, 'staff-bearer'; in the case, on the other hand, of substances not capable of subsisting and being apprehended apart from others, the fact of their holding the position of attributes is ascertained only from their appearing in grammatical co-ordination.—But, an objection is raised, if it is supposed that in sentences such as 'the Self is born, as god, man, animal,' &c., the body of a man, god, &c., stands towards the Self in the relation of a mode, in the same way as in sentences such as 'the ox is broken-horned,' 'the cloth is white,' the generic characteristic and the quality stand in the relation of modes to the substances ('cow,' 'cloth') to which they are grammatically co-ordinated; then there would necessarily be simultaneous cognition of the mode, and that to which the mode belongs, i. e. of the body and the Self; just as there is simultaneous cognition of the generic character and the individual. But as a matter of fact this is not the case; we do not necessarily observe a human, divine, or animal body together with the Self. The co-ordination expressed in the form 'the Self is a man,' is therefore an 'implied' one only (the statement not admitting of being taken in its primary literal sense).—This is not so, we reply. The relation of bodies to the Self is strictly analogous to that of class characteristics and qualities to the substances in which they inhere; for it is the Self only which is their substrate and their final cause (prayo*g*ana), and they are modes of the Self. That the Self only is their substrate, appears from the fact that when the Self separates itself from the body the latter perishes; that the Self alone is their final cause, appears from the fact that they exist to the end that the fruits of the actions of the Self may be enjoyed; and that they are modes of the Self, appears from the fact that they are mere attributes of the Self manifesting itself as god, man, or the like. These are just the circumstances on account of which words like 'cow' extend in their meaning (beyond the class characteristics) so as to comprise the individual also. Where those circumstances are absent, as in the case of staffs, earrings, and the like, the attributive position is expressed (not by co-ordination but) by means of special derivative forms—such as da*nd*in (staff-bearer), ku*nd*alin (adorned with earrings). In the case of bodies divine, human, &c., on the other hand, the essential nature of which it is to be mere modes of the Self which constitutes their substrate and final cause, both ordinary and Vedic language express the relation subsisting between the two, in the form of co-ordination, 'This Self is a god, or a man,' &c. That class characteristics and individuals are invariably observed together, is due to the fact of both being objects of visual perception; the Self, on the other hand, is not such, and hence is not apprehended by the eye, while the body is so apprehended. Nor must you raise the objection that it is hard to understand how that which is capable of being apprehended by itself can be a mere mode of something else: for that the body's essential nature actually consists in being a mere mode of the Self is proved—just as in the case of class characteristics and so on—by its having the Self only for its substrate and final cause, and standing to it in the relation of a distinguishing attribute. That two things are invariably perceived together, depends, as already observed, on their being apprehended by means of the same apparatus, visual or otherwise. Earth is naturally connected with smell, taste, and so on, and yet these qualities are not perceived by the eye; in the same way the eye which perceives the body does not perceive that essential characteristic of the body which consists in its being a mere mode of the Self; the reason of the difference being that the eye has no capacity to apprehend the Self. But this does not imply that the body does not possess that essential nature: it rather is just the possession of that essential nature on which the judgment of co-ordination ('the Self is a man, god,' &c.) is based. And as words have the power of denoting the relation of something being a mode of the Self, they denote things together with this relation.—But in ordinary speech the word 'body' is understood to mean the mere body; it does not therefore extend in its denotation up to the Self!—Not so, we reply. The body is, in reality, nothing but a mode of the Self; but, for the purpose of showing the distinction of things, the word 'body' is used in a limited sense. Analogously words such as 'whiteness,' 'generic character of a cow,' 'species,' 'quality,' are used in a distinctive sense (although 'whiteness' is not found apart from a white thing, of which it is the prakâra, and so on). Words such as 'god,' 'man,' &c., therefore do extend in their connotation up to the Self. And as the individual souls, distinguished by their connexion with aggregates of matter bearing the characteristic marks of humanity, divine nature, and so on, constitute the body of the highest Self, and hence are modes of it, the words denoting those individual souls extend in their connotation up to the very highest Self. And as all intelligent and non-intelligent beings are thus mere modes of the highest Brahman, and have reality thereby only, the words denoting them are used in co-ordination with the terms denoting Brahman.—This point has been demonstrated by me in the Vedârthasa*m*graha. A Sûtra also (IV, 1, 3) will declare the identity of the world and Brahman to consist in the relation of body and Self; and the Vâkyakâra too says 'It is the Self—thus everything should be apprehended.'

### Summary statement as to the way in which different scriptural texts are to be reconciled.

The whole matter may be summarily stated as follows. Some texts declare a distinction of nature between non-intelligent matter, intelligent beings, and Brahman, in so far as matter is the object of enjoyment, the souls the enjoying subjects, and Brahman the ruling principle. 'From that the Lord of Mâyâ creates all this; in that the other one is bound up through that Mâyâ' (*S*vet. Up. IV, 9); 'Know Prak*ri*ti to be Mâyâ, and the great Lord the ruler of Mâyâ' (10); 'What is perishable is the Pradhâna, the immortal and imperishable is Hara: the one God rules the Perishable and the Self' (*S*vet. Up. I, 10)—In this last passage the clause 'the immortal and imperishable is Hara,' refers to the enjoying individual soul, which is called 'Hara,' because it draws (harati) towards itself the pradhâna as the object of its enjoyment.—'He is the cause, the lord of the lords of the organs, and there is of him neither parent nor lord' (*S*vet. Up. VI, 9); 'The master of the pradhâna and of the individual souls' (*S*vet. Up. VI, 16); 'The ruler of all, the lord of the Selfs, the eternal, blessed, undecaying one' (Mahânâr. Up. XI, 3); 'There are two unborn ones, one knowing, the other not knowing, one a ruler, the other not a ruler' (*S*vet. Up. I, 9); 'The eternal among the non-eternal, the intelligent one among the intelligent, who though one fulfils the desires of many' (*S*vet. Up. VI, 13); 'Knowing the enjoyer, the object of enjoyment and the Mover' (*S*vet. Up. I, 12); 'One of them eats the sweet fruit, the other looks on without eating' (*S*vet. Up. IV, 6); 'Thinking that the Self is different from the Mover, blessed by him he reaches Immortality' (*S*vet. Up. I, 6); 'There is one unborn female being, red, white, and black, uniform but producing manifold offspring. There is one unborn male being who loves her and lies by her; there is another who leaves her after he has enjoyed her' (*S*vet. Up. IV, 5). 'On the same tree man, immersed, bewildered, grieves on account of his impotence; but when he sees the other Lord contented and knows his glory, then his grief passes away' (*S*vet. Up. IV, 9).—Sm*ri*ti expresses itself similarly.—'Thus eightfold is my nature divided. Lower is this Nature; other than this and higher know that Nature of mine which constitutes the individual soul, by which this world is supported' (Bha. Gî. VII, 4, 5). 'All beings at the end of a Kalpa return into my Nature, and again at the beginning of a Kalpa do I send them forth. Resting on my own Nature again and again do I send forth this entire body of beings, which has no power of its own, being subject to the power of nature' (Bha. Gî. IX, 7, 8); 'With me as supervisor Nature brings forth the movable and the immovable, and for this reason the world ever moves round' (Bha. Gî. IX, 10); 'Know thou both Nature and the Soul to be without beginning' (XIII, 19); 'The great Brahman is my womb, in which I place the embryo, and thence there is the origin of all beings' (XIV, 3). This last passage means—the womb of the world is the great Brahman, i.e. non-intelligent matter in its subtle state, commonly called Prak*ri*ti; with this I connect the embryo, i.e. the intelligent principle. From this contact of the non-intelligent and the intelligent, due to my will, there ensues the origination of all beings from gods down to lifeless things.

Non-intelligent matter and intelligent beings—holding the relative positions of objects of enjoyment and enjoying subjects, and appearing in multifarious forms—other scriptural texts declare to be permanently connected with the highest Person in so far as they constitute his body, and thus are controlled by him; the highest Person thus constituting their Self. Compare the following passages: 'He who dwells in the earth and within the earth, whom the earth does not know, whose body the earth is, and who rules the earth within, he is thy Self, the ruler within, the immortal,' &c. (B*ri*. Up. III, 7, 3–23); 'He who moves within the earth, whose body the earth is, &c.; he who moves within death, whose body death is,' &c. (Subâla Up. VII, 1). In this latter passage the word 'death' denotes what is also called 'darkness,' viz. non-intelligent matter in its subtle state; as appears from another passage in the same Upanishad, 'the Imperishable is merged in darkness.' And compare also 'Entered within, the ruler of creatures, the Self of all' (Taitt. Âr. III, 24).

Other texts, again, aim at teaching that the highest Self to whom non-intelligent and intelligent beings stand in the relation of body, and hence of modes, subsists in the form of the world, in its causal as well as in its effected aspect, and hence speak of the world in this its double aspect as that which is (the Real); so e.g. 'Being only this was in the beginning, one only without a second—it desired, may

I be many, may I grow forth—it sent forth fire,' &c., up to 'all these creatures have their root in that which is,' &c., up to 'that art thou, O *S*vetaketu' (*Kh.* Up. VI, 2–8); 'He wished, may I be many,' &c., up to 'it became the true and the untrue' (Taitt. Up. II, 6). These sections also refer to the essential distinction of nature between non-intelligent matter, intelligent beings, and the highest Self which is established by other scriptural texts; so in the *Kh*ândogya passage, 'Let me enter those three divine beings with this living Self, and let me then evolve names and forms'; and in the Taitt. passage, 'Having sent forth that he entered into it; having entered it he became sat and tyat, knowledge and (what is) without knowledge, the true and the untrue,' &c. These two passages evidently have the same purport, and hence the soul's having its Self in Brahman—which view is implied in the *Kh.* passage—must be understood as resting thereon that the souls (together with matter) constitute the body of Brahman as asserted in the Taitt. passage ('it became knowledge and that which is without knowledge,' i. e. souls and matter). The same process of evolution of names and forms is described elsewhere also, 'All this was then unevolved; it became evolved by form and name' (B*ri*. Up. I, 4, 7). The fact is that the highest Self is in its causal or in its 'effected' condition, according as it has for its body intelligent and non-intelligent beings either in their subtle or their gross state; the effect, then, being non-different from the cause, and hence being cognised through the cognition of the cause, the result is that the desired 'cognition of all things through one' can on our view be well established. In the clause 'I will enter into these three divine beings with this living Self,' &c., the term 'the three divine beings' denotes the entire aggregate of non-sentient matter, and as the text declares that the highest Self evolved names and forms by entering into matter by means of the living souls of which he is the Self, it follows that all terms whatsoever denote the highest Self as qualified by individual Selfs, the latter again being qualified by non-sentient matter. A term which denotes the highest Self in its causal condition may therefore be exhibited in co-ordination with another term denoting the highest Self in its 'effected' state, both terms being used in their primary senses. Brahman, having for its modes intelligent and non-intelligent things in their gross and subtle states, thus constitutes effect and cause, and the world thus has Brahman for its material cause (upâdâna). Nor does this give rise to any confusion of the essential constituent elements of the great aggregate of things. Of some parti-coloured piece of cloth the material cause is threads white, red, black, &c.; all the same, each definite spot of the cloth is connected with one colour only white e.g., and thus there is no confusion of colours even in the 'effected' condition of the cloth. Analogously the combination of non-sentient matter, sentient beings, and the Lord constitutes the material cause of the world, but this does not imply any confusion of the essential characteristics of enjoying souls, objects of enjoyment, and the universal ruler, even in the world's 'effected' state. There is indeed a difference between the two cases, in so far as the threads are capable of existing apart from one another, and are only occasionally combined according to the volition of men, so that the web sometimes exists in its causal, sometimes in its effected state; while non-sentient matter and sentient beings in all their states form the body of the highest Self, and thus have a being only as the modes of that—on which account the highest Self may, in all cases, be denoted by any term whatsoever. But the two cases are analogous, in so far as there persists a distinction and absence of all confusion, on the part of the constituent elements of the aggregate. This being thus, it follows that the highest Brahman, although entering into the 'effected' condition, remains unchanged—for its essential nature does not become different—and we also understand what constitutes its 'effected' condition, viz. its abiding as the Self of non-intelligent and intelligent beings in their gross condition, distinguished by name and form. For becoming an effect means entering into another state of being.

Those texts, again, which speak of Brahman as devoid of

qualities, explain themselves on the ground of Brahman being free from all touch of evil. For the passage, *Kh.* Up. VIII, 1, 5—which at first negatives all evil qualities 'free from sin, from old age, from death, from grief, from hunger and thirst,' and after that affirms auspicious qualities 'whose wishes and purposes come true'—enables us to decide that in other places also the general denial of qualities really refers to evil qualities only.—Passages which declare knowledge to constitute the essential nature of Brahman explain themselves on the ground that of Brahman—which is all-knowing, all-powerful, antagonistic to all evil, a mass of auspicious qualities—the essential nature can be defined as knowledge (intelligence) only—which also follows from the 'self-luminousness' predicated of it. Texts, on the other hand, such as 'He who is all-knowing' (Mu. Up. I, 1, 9); 'His high power is revealed as manifold, as essential, acting as force and knowledge' (*S*vet. Up. VI, 8); ; 'Whereby should he know the knower' (B*ri*. Up. II, 4, 14), teach the highest Self to be a knowing subject. Other texts, again, such as 'The True, knowledge, infinite is Brahman' (Taitt. Up. II, 1, 1), declare knowledge to constitute its nature, as it can be defined through knowledge only, and is self-luminous. And texts such as 'He desired, may I be many' (Taitt. Up. II, 6); 'It thought, may I be many; it evolved itself through name and form' (*Kh.* Up. VI, 2), teach that Brahman, through its mere wish, appears in manifold modes. Other texts, again, negative the opposite view, viz. that there is a plurality of things not having their Self in Brahman. 'From death to death goes he who sees here any plurality'; 'There is here not any plurality' (B*ri*. Up. IV, 4, 19); 'For where there is duality as it were' (B*ri*. Up. II, 4, 14). But these texts in no way negative that plurality of modes—declared in passages such as 'May I be many, may I grow forth'—which springs from Brahman's will, and appears in the distinction of names and forms. This is proved by clauses in those 'negativing' texts themselves, 'Whosoever looks for anything elsewhere than in the Self,' 'from that great Being there has been breathed forth the *Ri*g-veda,' &c. (B*ri*. Up. II, 4, 6, 10).—

On this method of interpretation we find that the texts declaring the essential distinction and separation of non-sentient matter, sentient beings, and the Lord, and those declaring him to be the cause and the world to be the effect, and cause and effect to be identical, do not in any way conflict with other texts declaring that matter and souls form the body of the Lord, and that matter and souls in their causal condition are in a subtle state, not admitting of the distinction of names and forms while in their 'effected' gross state they are subject to that distinction. On the other hand, we do not see how there is any opening for theories maintaining the connexion of Brahman with Nescience, or distinctions in Brahman due to limiting adjuncts (upâdhi)—such and similar doctrines rest on fallacious reasoning, and flatly contradict Scripture.

There is nothing contradictory in allowing that certain texts declare the essential distinction of matter, souls, and the Lord, and their mutual relation as modes and that to which the modes belong, and that other texts again represent them as standing in the relation of cause and effect, and teach cause and effect to be one. We may illustrate this by an analogous case from the Karmakâ*nd*a. There six separate oblations to Agni, and so on, are enjoined by separate so-called originative injunctions; these are thereupon combined into two groups (viz. the new moon and the full-moon sacrifices) by a double clause referring to those groups, and finally a so-called injunction of qualification enjoins the entire sacrifice as something to be performed by persons entertaining a certain wish. In a similar way certain Vedânta-texts give instruction about matter, souls, and the Lord as separate entities ('Perishable is the pradhâna, imperishable and immortal Hara,' &c., *S*vet. Up. I, 10; and others); then other texts teach that matter and souls in all their different states constitute the body of the highest Person, while the latter is their Self ('Whose body the earth is,' &c.); and finally another group of texts teaches—by means of words such as 'Being,' 'Brahman,' 'Self,' denoting the highest Self to which the body belongs—that the one highest Self in its causal and effected states comprises within itself the triad of entities which had been taught in separation ('Being only this was in the beginning'; 'In that all this has its Self'; 'All this is Brahman').—That the highest Self with matter and souls for its body should be simply called the highest Self, is no more objectionable than that that particular form of Self which is invested with a human body should simply be spoken of as Self or soul—as when we say 'This is a happy soul.'

**Nescience cannot be terminated by the simple act of cognising Brahman as the Universal Self.**

The doctrine, again, that Nescience is put an end to by the cognition of Brahman being the Self of all can in no way be upheld; for as bondage is something real it cannot be put an end to by knowledge. How, we ask, can any one assert that bondage—which consists in the experience of pleasure and pain caused by the connexion of souls with bodies of various kind, a connexion springing from good or evil actions—is something false, unreal? And that the cessation of such bondage is to be obtained only through the grace of the highest Self pleased by the devout meditation of the worshipper, we have already explained. As the cognition of universal oneness which you assume rests on a view of things directly contrary to reality, and therefore is false, the only effect it can have is to strengthen the ties of bondage. Moreover, texts such as 'But different is the highest Person' (Bha. Gî. XV, 17), and 'Having known the Self and the Mover as separate' (*S*vet. Up. I, 6), teach that it is the cognition of Brahman as the inward ruler different from the individual soul, that effects the highest aim of man, i. e. final release. And, further, as that 'bondage-terminating' knowledge which you assume is itself unreal, we should have to look out for another act of cognition to put an end to it.—But may it not be said that this terminating cognition, after having put an end to the whole aggregate of distinctions antagonistic to it, immediately passes away itself, because being of a merely instantaneous nature?—No, we reply. Since its nature, its origination, and its destruction are all alike fictitious, we have clearly to search for another agency capable of destroying that avidyâ which is the cause of the fiction of its destruction!—Let us then say that the essential nature of Brahman itself is the destruction of that cognition!—From this it would follow, we reply, that such 'terminating' knowledge would not arise at all; for that the destruction of what is something permanent can clearly not originate!—Who moreover should, according to you, be the cognising subject in a cognition which has for its object the negation of everything that is different from Brahman?—That cognising subject is himself something fictitiously superimposed on Brahman!—This may not be, we reply: he himself would in that case be something to be negatived, and hence an object of the 'terminating' cognition; he could not therefore be the subject of cognition!—Well, then, let us assume that the essential nature of Brahman itself is the cognising subject!—Do you mean, we ask in reply, that Brahman's being the knowing subject in that 'terminating' cognition belongs to Brahman's essential nature, or that it is something fictitiously superimposed on Brahman? In the latter case that superimposition and the Nescience founded on it would persist, because they would not be objects of the terminating cognition, and if a further terminating act of knowledge were assumed, that also would possess a triple aspect (viz. knowledge, object known, and subject knowing), and we thus should be led to assume an infinite series of knowing subjects. If, on the other hand, the essential nature of Brahman itself constitutes the knowing subject, your view really coincides with the one held by us[1]. And if you should say that the terminating knowledge itself and the knowing subject in it are things separate from Brahman and themselves contained in the sphere of what is to be terminated by that knowledge, your statement would be no less absurd than if you were to say 'everything on the surface of the earth has been cut

[1] According to which Brahman is not *gñânam*, but *gñâtri*.

down by Devadatta with one stroke'—meaning thereby that Devadatta himself and the action of cutting down are comprised among the things cut down!—The second alternative, on the other hand—according to which the knowing subject is not Brahman itself, but a knower superimposed upon it—would imply that that subject is the agent in an act of knowledge resulting in his own destruction; and this is impossible since no person aims at destroying himself. And should it be said that the destruction of the knowing agent belongs to the very nature of Brahman itself[1], it would follow that we can assume neither plurality nor the erroneous view of plurality, nor avidyâ as the root of that erroneous view.—All this confirms our theory, viz. that since bondage springs from a*gñ*âna in the form of an eternal stream of karman, it can be destroyed only through knowledge of the kind maintained by us. Such knowledge is to be attained only through the due daily performance of religious duties as prescribed for a man's caste and â*s*rama, such performance being sanctified by the accompanying thought of the true nature of the Self, and having the character of propitiation of the highest Person. Now, that mere works produce limited and non-permanent results only, and that on the other hand works not aiming at an immediate result but meant to please the highest Person, bring about knowledge of the character of devout meditation, and thereby the unlimited and permanent result of the intuition of Brahman being the Self of all—these are points not to be known without an insight into the nature of works, and hence, without this, the attitude described—which is preceded by the abandonment of mere works—cannot be reached. For these reasons the enquiry into Brahman has to be entered upon *after* the enquiry into the nature of works.

[1] And, on that account, belongs to what constitutes man's highest aim.

**The Vedântin aiming to ascertain the nature of Brahman from Scripture, need not be disconcerted by the Mîmâ*m*sâ-theory of all speech having informing power with regard to actions only.**

Here another primâ facie view[1] finally presents itself. The power of words to denote things cannot be ascertained in any way but by observing the speech and actions of experienced people. Now as such speech and action always implies the idea of something to be done (kârya), words are means of knowledge only with reference to things to be done; and hence the matter inculcated by the Veda also is only things to be done. From this it follows that the Vedânta-texts cannot claim the position of authoritative means of knowledge with regard to Brahman, which is (not a thing to be done but) an accomplished fact.—Against this view it must not be urged that in the case of sentences expressive of accomplished facts—as e.g. that a son is born to somebody—the idea of a particular thing may with certainty be inferred as the cause of certain outward signs—such as e.g. a pleased expression of countenance—which are generally due to the attainment of a desired object; for the possible causes of joy, past, present, and future, are infinite in number, and in the given case other causes of joy, as e.g. the birth having taken place in an auspicious moment, or having been an easy one, &c., may easily be imagined. Nor, again, can it be maintained that the denotative power of words with regard to accomplished things may be ascertained in the way of our inferring either the meaning of one word from the known meaning of other words, or the meaning of the radical part of a word from the known meaning of a formative element; for the fact is that we are only able to infer on the basis of a group of words known to denote a certain thing to be done, what the meaning of some particular constituent of that group may be.—Nor, again, when a person, afraid of what he thinks to be a snake, is ob-

[1] This view is held by the Prâbhâkara Mîmâ*m*sakas.

served to dismiss his fear on being told that the thing is not a snake but only a rope, can we determine thereby that what terminates his fear is the idea of the non-existence of a snake. For there are many other ideas which may account for the cessation of his fear—he may think, e.g., 'this is a thing incapable of moving, devoid of poison, without consciousness'—the particular idea present to his mind we are therefore not able to determine.—The truth is that from the fact of all activity being invariably dependent on the idea of something to be done, we learn that the meaning which words convey is something prompting activity. All words thus denoting something to be done, the several words of a sentence express only some particular action to be performed, and hence it is not possible to determine that they possess the power of denoting their own meaning only, in connexion with the meaning of the other words of the sentence.—(Nor must it be said that what moves to action is not the idea of the thing to be done, but the idea of the means to do it; for) the idea of the means to bring about the desired end causes action only through the idea of the thing to be done, not through itself; as is evident from the fact that the idea of means past, future, and even present (when divorced from the idea of an end to be accomplished), does not prompt to action. As long as a man does not reflect 'the means towards the desired end are not to be accomplished without an effort of mine; it must therefore be accomplished through my activity'; so long he does not begin to act. What causes activity is thus only the idea of things to be done; and as hence words denote such things only, the Veda also can tell us only about things to be done, and is not therefore in a position to give information about the attainment of an infinite and permanent result, such result being constituted by Brahman, which is (not a thing to be done, but) an accomplished entity. The Veda does, on the other hand, actually teach that mere works have a permanent result ('Imperishable is the merit of him who offers the *k*âturmâsya-sacrifices,' and so on); and hence it follows that to enter on an enquiry into Brahman for the reason that the knowledge of Brahman has an infinite and permanent result, while the result of works is limited and non-permanent, is an altogether unjustified proceeding.

To this we make the following reply.—To set aside the universally known mode of ascertaining the connexion of words and their meanings, and to assert that all words express only one non-worldly meaning (viz. those things to be done which the Veda inculcates), is a proceeding for which men paying due attention to the means of proof can have only a slight regard. A child avowedly learns the connexion of words and meanings in the following way. The father and mother and other people about him point with the finger at the child's mother, father, uncle, &c., as well as at various domestic and wild animals, birds, snakes, and so on, to the end that the child may at the same time pay attention to the terms they use and to the beings denoted thereby, and thus again and again make him understand that such and such words refer to such and such things. The child thus observing in course of time that these words of themselves give rise to certain ideas in his mind, and at the same time observing neither any different connexion of words and things, nor any person arbitrarily establishing such connexion, comes to the conclusion that the application of such and such words to such and such things is based on the denotative power of the words. And being taught later on by his elders that other words also, in addition to those learned first, have their definite meaning, he in the end becomes acquainted with the meanings of all words, and freely forms sentences conveying certain meanings for the purpose of imparting those meanings to other persons.

And there is another way also in which the connexion of words and things can easily be ascertained. Some person orders another, by means of some expressive gesture, to go and inform Devadatta that his father is doing well, and the man ordered goes and tells Devadatta 'Your father is doing well.' A by-stander who is acquainted with the meaning of various gestures, and thus knows on what errand the messenger is sent, follows him and hears the words employed by him to deliver his message: he therefore readily infers that such and such words have such and such a meaning.—We thus see that the theory of words having a meaning only in relation to things to be done is baseless. The Vedânta-texts tell us about Brahman, which is an accomplished entity, and about meditation on Brahman as having an unlimited result, and hence it behoves us to undertake an enquiry into Brahman so as fully to ascertain its nature.

We further maintain that even on the supposition of the Veda relating only to things to be done, an enquiry into Brahman must be undertaken. For 'The Self is to be seen, to be heard, to be reflected on, to be meditated on' (B*ri*. Up. II, 4, 5); 'He is to be searched out, him we must try to understand' (*Kh*. Up. VIII, 7, 1); 'Let a Brâhma*n*a having known him practise wisdom' (B*ri*. Up. IV, 4, 21); 'What is within that small ether, that is to be sought for, that is to be understood' (*Kh*. Up. VIII, 1, 1); 'What is in that small ether, that is to be meditated upon' (Mahânâr. Up. X, 7)—these and similar texts enjoin a certain action, viz. meditation on Brahman, and when we then read 'He who knows Brahman attains the highest,' we understand that the attainment of Brahman is meant as a reward for him who is qualified for and enters on such meditation. Brahman itself and its attributes are thus established thereby only—that they subserve a certain action, viz. meditation. There are analogous instances in the Karmakâ*nd*a of the Veda. When an arthavâda-passage describes the heavenly world as a place where there is no heat, no frost, no grief, &c., this is done merely with a view to those texts which enjoin certain sacrifices on those who are desirous of the heavenly world. Where another arthavâda says that 'those who perform certain sattra-sacrifices are firmly established,' such 'firm establishment' is referred to only because it is meant as the reward for those acting on the text which enjoins those sattras, 'Let him perform the râtri-sattras' (Pû. Mî. Sû. IV, 3, 17). And where a text says that a person threatening a Brâhma*n*a is to be punished with a fine of one hundred gold pieces, this statement is made merely with reference to the prohibitory passage, 'Let him not threaten a Brâhma*n*a' (Pû. Mî. Sû. III, 4, 17).

We, however, really object to the whole theory of the meaning of words depending on their connexion with 'things to be done,' since this is not even the case in imperative clauses such as 'bring the cow.' For you are quite unable to give a satisfactory definition of your 'thing to be done' (kârya). You understand by 'kârya' that which follows on the existence of action (k*ri*ti) and is aimed at by action. Now to be aimed at by action is to be the object (karman) of action, and to be the object of action is to be that which it is most desired to obtain by action (according to the grammarian's definition). But what one desires most to obtain is pleasure or the cessation of pain. When a person desirous of some pleasure or cessation of pain is aware that his object is not to be accomplished without effort on his part, he resolves on effort and begins to act: in no case we observe an object of desire to be aimed at by action in any other sense than that of its accomplishment depending on activity. The prompting quality (prerakatva) also, which belongs to objects of desire, is nothing but the attribute of their accomplishment depending on activity; for it is this which moves to action.—Nor can it be said that 'to be aimed at by action' means to be that which is 'agreeable' (anukûla) to man; for it is pleasure only that is agreeable to man. The cessation of pain, on the other hand, is not what is 'agreeable' to man. The essential distinction between pleasure and pain is that the former is agreeable to man, and the latter disagreeable (pratikûla), and the cessation of pain is desired not because it is agreeable, but because pain is disagreeable: absence of pain means that a person is in his normal condition, affected neither with pain nor pleasure. Apart from pleasure, action cannot possibly be agreeable, nor does it become so by being subservient to pleasure; for its essential nature is pain. Its being helpful to pleasure merely causes the resolve of undertaking it.—Nor, again, can we define that which is aimed at by action as that to which action is auxiliary or supplementary (*s*esha), while itself it holds the position of something principal to be subserved by other things (*s*eshin); for of the *s*esha and *s*eshin also no proper definition can be given. It cannot be said that a *s*esha is that which is invariably accompanied by an activity proceeding with a view to something else, and that the correlate of such a *s*esha is the *s*eshin; for on this definition the action is not a *s*esha, and hence that which is to be effected by the action cannot be the correlative *s*eshin. And moreover a *s*eshin may not be defined as what is correlative to an action proceeding with a view to—i. e. aiming at—something else; for it is just this 'being aimed at' of which we require a definition, and moreover we observe that also the *s*eshin (or 'pradhâna') is capable of action proceeding with a view to the *s*esha, as when e. g. a master does something for—let us say, keeps or feeds—his servant. This last criticism you must not attempt to ward off by maintaining that the master in keeping his servant acts with a view to himself (to his own advantage); for the servant in serving the master likewise acts with a view to himself. —And as, further, we have no adequate definition of 'kârya,' it would be inappropriate to define *s*esha as that which is correlative to kârya, and *s*eshin as that which is correlative to *s*esha.—Nor, finally, may we define 'that which is aimed at by action' as that which is the final end (prayo*g*ana) of action; for by the final end of an action we could only understand the end for which the agent undertakes the action, and this end is no other than the desired object. As thus 'what is aimed at by action' cannot be defined otherwise than what is desired, kârya cannot be defined as what is to be effected by action and stands to action in the relation of principal matter (pradhâna or *s*eshin).

(Let it then be said that the 'niyoga,' i. e. what is commonly called the apûrva—the supersensuous result of an action which later on produces the sensible result—constitutes the prayo*g*ana—the final purpose—of the action.—But) the apûrva also can, as it is something different from the direct objects of desire, viz. pleasure and the cessation of pain, be viewed only as a means of bringing about these direct objects, and as something itself to be effected by the action; it is for this very reason that it is something different from the action, otherwise the action itself would be that which is effected by the action. The thing to be effected by the action—which is expressed by means of optative and imperative verbal forms such as yageta, 'let him sacrifice'—is, in accordance with the fact of its being connected with words such as svargakâmah, 'he who is desirous of heaven,' understood to be the means of bringing about (the enjoyment of) the heavenly world; and as the (sacrificial) action itself is transitory, there is assumed an altogether 'new' or 'unprecedented' (apûrva) effect of it which (later on) is to bring about the enjoyment of heaven. This so-called 'apûrva' can therefore be understood only with regard to its capability of bringing about the heavenly world. Now it certainly is ludicrous to assert that the apûrva, which is assumed to the end of firmly establishing the independent character of the effect of the action first recognised as such (i. e. independent), later on becomes the means of realising the heavenly world; for as the word expressing the result of the action (yageta) appears in syntactical connexion with 'svargakâmah' (desirous of heaven), it does not, from the very beginning, denote an independent object of action, and moreover it is impossible to recognise an independent result of action other than either pleasure or cessation of pain, or the means to bring about these two results.—What, moreover, do you understand by the apûrva being a final end (prayogana)?—You will perhaps reply, 'its being agreeable like pleasure.'—Is then the apûrva a pleasure? It is pleasure alone which is agreeable!—Well, let us then define the apûrva as a kind of pleasure of a special nature, called by that name!—But what proof, we ask, have you for this? You will, in the first place, admit yourself that you do not directly experience any pleasure springing from consciousness of your apûrva, which could in any way be compared to the pleasure caused by the consciousness of the objects of the senses.—Well, let us say then that as authoritative doctrine gives us the notion of an apûrva as something beneficial to man, we conclude that it will be enjoyed later on.—But, we ask, what is the authoritative doctrine establishing such an apûrva beneficial to man? Not, in the first place, ordinary, i. e. non-Vedic doctrine; for such has for its object action only which always is essentially painful. Nor, in the next place, Vedic texts; for those also enjoin action only as the means to bring about certain results such as the heavenly world. Nor again the Smriti texts enjoining works of either permanent or occasional obligation; for those texts always convey the notion of an apûrva only on the basis of an antecedent knowledge of the apûrva as intimated by Vedic texts containing terms such as svargakâmah. And we, moreover, do not observe that in the case of works having a definite result in this life, there is enjoyment of any special pleasure called apûrva, in addition to those advantages which constitute the special result of the work and are enjoyed here below, as e.g. abundance of food or freedom from sickness. Thus there is not any proof of the apûrva being a pleasure. The arthavâda-passages of the Veda also, while glorifying certain pleasurable results of works, as e.g. the heavenly world, do not anywhere exhibit a similar glorification of a pleasure called apûrva.

From all this we conclude that also in injunctory sentences that which is expressed by imperative and similar forms is only the idea that the meaning of the root—as known from grammar—is to be effected by the effort of the agent. And that what constitutes the meaning of roots, viz. the action of sacrificing and the like, possesses the quality of pleasing the highest Person, who is the inner ruler of Agni and other divinities (to whom the sacrifices are ostensibly offered), and that through the highest Person thus pleased the result of the sacrifice is accomplished, we shall show later on, under Sû. III, 2, 37.—It is thus finally proved that the Vedânta-texts give information about an accomplished entity, viz. Brahman, and that the fruit of meditation on Brahman is something infinite and permanent. Where, on the other hand, Scripture refers to the fruit of mere works, such as the *k*âturmâsya-sacrifices, as something imperishable, we have to understand this imperishableness in a merely relative sense, for Scripture definitely teaches that the fruit of all works is perishable.

We thus arrive at the settled conclusion that, since the fruit of mere works is limited and perishable, while that of the cognition of Brahman is infinite and permanent, there is good reason for entering on an enquiry into Brahman—the result of which enquiry will be the accurate determination of Brahman's nature.—Here terminates the adhikara*n*a of 'Enquiry.'

What then is that Brahman which is here said to be an object that should be enquired into?—To this question the second Sûtra gives a reply.

2. (Brahman is that) from which the origin, &c., of this (world proceed).

The expression 'the origin,' &c., means 'creation, subsistence, and reabsorption.' The 'this' (in 'of this') denotes this entire world with its manifold wonderful arrangements, not to be fathomed by thought, and comprising within itself the aggregate of living souls from Brahmâ down to blades of grass, all of which experience the fruits (of their former actions) in definite places and at definite times. 'That from which,' i.e. that highest Person who is the ruler of all; whose nature is antagonistic to all evil; whose purposes come true; who possesses infinite auspicious qualities, such as knowledge, blessedness, and so on; who is omniscient, omnipotent, supremely merciful; from whom the creation, subsistence, and reabsorption of this world proceed—he is Brahman: such is the meaning of the Sûtra.—The definition here given of Brahman is founded on the text Taitt. Up. III, 1, 'Bh*ri*gu Vâru*n*i went to his father Varu*n*a, saying, Sir, teach me Brahman,' &c., up to 'That from which these beings are born, that by which when born they live, that into which they enter at their death, try to know that: that is Brahman.'

A doubt arises here. Is it possible, or not, to gain a knowledge of Brahman from the characteristic marks stated in this passage?—It is not possible, the Pûrvapakshin contends. The attributes stated in that passage—viz. being that from which the world originates, and so on—do not properly indicate Brahman; for as the essence of an attribute lies in its separative or distinctive function, there would result from the plurality of distinctive attributes plurality on the part of Brahman itself.—But when we say 'Devadatta is of a dark complexion, is young, has reddish eyes,' &c., we also make a statement as to several attributes, and yet we are understood to refer to one Devadatta only; similarly we understand in the case under discussion also that there is one Brahman only!—Not so, we reply. In Devadatta's case we connect all attributes with one person, because we know his unity through other means of knowledge; otherwise the distinctive power of several attributes would lead us, in this case also, to the assumption of several substances to which the several attributes belong. In the case under discussion, on the other hand, we do not, apart from the statement as to attributes, know anything about the unity of Brahman, and the distinctive power of the attributes thus necessarily urges upon us the idea of several Brahmans.—But we maintain that the unity of the term 'Brahman' intimates the unity of the thing 'Brahman'!—By no means, we reply. If a man who knows nothing about cows, but wishes to know about them, is told 'a cow is that which has either entire horns, or mutilated horns, or no horns,' the mutally exclusive ideas of the possession of entire horns, and so on, raise in his mind the ideas of several individual cows, although the term 'cow' is one only; and in the same way we are led to the idea of several distinct Brahmans. For this reason, even the different attributes combined are incapable of defining the thing, the definition of which is desired.—Nor again are the characteristics enumerated in the Taitt. passage (viz. creation of the world, &c.) capable of defining Brahman in the way of secondary marks (upalakshana), because the thing to be defined by them is not previously known in a different aspect. So-called secondary marks are the cause of something already known from a certain point of view, being known in a different aspect—as when it is said 'Where that crane is standing, that is the irrigated field of Devadatta.'—But may we not say that from the text 'The True, knowledge, the Infinite is Brahman,' we already have an idea of Brahman, and that hence its being the cause of the origin, &c., of the world may be taken as collateral indications (pointing to something already known in a certain way)?—Not so, we reply; either of these two defining texts has a meaning only with reference to an aspect of Brahman already known from the other one, and this mutual dependence deprives both of their force.—Brahman cannot therefore be known through the characteristic marks mentioned in the text under discussion.

To this primâ facie view we make the following reply. Brahman can be known on the basis of the origination, subsistence, and reabsorption of the world—these characteristics occupying the position of collateral marks. No objection can be raised against this view, on the ground that, apart from what these collateral marks point to, no other aspect of Brahman is known; for as a matter of fact they point to that which is known to us as possessing supreme greatness (b*ri*hattva) and power of growth (b*rim*hana)—this being the meaning of the root b*rim*h (from which 'Brahman' is derived). Of this Brahman, thus already known (on the basis of etymology), the origination, sustentation, and reabsorption of the world are collateral marks. Moreover, in the Taitt. text under discussion, the relative pronoun—which appears in three forms, (that) 'from whence,' (that) 'by which,' (that) 'into which' —refers to something which is already known as the cause of the origin, and so on, of the world. This previous knowledge rests on the *Kh.* passage, 'Being only this was in the beginning,' &c., up to 'it sent forth fire'—which declares that the one principle denoted as 'being' is the universal material, and instrumental cause. There the clause 'Being only this was in the beginning, one only,' establishes that one being as the general material cause; the word 'without a second' negatives the existence of a second operative cause; and the clauses 'it thought, may I be many, may

I grow forth,' and 'it sent forth fire,' establish that one being (as the cause and substance of everything). If, then, it is said that Brahman is that which is the root of the world's origination, subsistence, and reabsorption, those three processes sufficiently indicate Brahman as that entity which is their material and operative cause; and as being the material and the operative cause implies greatness (b*ri*hattva) manifesting itself in various powers, such as omniscience, and so on, Brahman thus is something already known; and as hence origination, &c., of the world are marks of something already known, the objection founded above on the absence of knowledge of another aspect of Brahman is seen to be invalid.—Nor is there really any objection to the origination, &c., of the world being taken as characteristic marks of Brahman in so far as they are distinctive attributes. For taken as attributes they indicate Brahman as something different from what is opposed to those attributes. Several attributes which do not contradict each other may serve quite well as characteristic marks defining one thing, the nature of which is not otherwise known, without the plurality of the attributes in any way involving plurality of the thing defined; for as those attributes are at once understood to belong to one substrate, we naturally combine them within that one substrate. Such attributes, of course, as the possession of mutilated horns (mentioned above), which are contradictorily opposed to each other, necessarily lead to the assumption of several individual cows to which they severally belong; but the origination, &c., of the world are processes separated from each other by difference of time only, and may therefore, without contradiction, be connected with one Brahman in succession.—The text 'from whence these beings,' &c., teaches us that Brahman is the cause of the origination, &c., of the world, and of this Brahman thus known the other text 'The True, knowledge, the Infinite is Brahman,' tells us that its essential nature marks it off from everything else. The term 'True' expresses Brahman in so far as possessing absolutely non-conditioned existence, and thus distinguishes it from non-intelligent matter, the abode of change, and the souls implicated in matter; for as both of these enter into different states of existence called by different names, they do not enjoy unconditioned being. The term 'knowledge' expresses the characteristic of permanently non-contracted intelligence, and thus distinguishes Brahman from the released souls whose intelligence is sometimes in a contracted state. And the term 'Infinite' denotes that, whose nature is free from all limitation of place, time, and particular substantial nature; and as Brahman's essential nature possesses attributes, infinity belongs both to the essential nature and to the attributes. The qualification of Infinity excludes all those individual souls whose essential nature and attributes are not unsurpassable, and who are distinct from the two classes of beings already excluded by the two former terms (viz. 'true being' and 'knowledge').—The entire text therefore defines Brahman—which is already known to be the cause of the origination, &c., of the world—as that which is in kind different from all other things; and it is therefore not true that the two texts under discussion have no force because mutually depending on each other. And from this it follows that a knowledge of Brahman may be gained on the ground of its characteristic marks—such as its being the cause of the origination, &c., of the world, free from all evil, omniscient, all-powerful, and so on.

To those, on the other hand, who maintain that the object of enquiry is a substance devoid of all difference, neither the first nor the second Sûtra can be acceptable; for the Brahman, the enquiry into which the first Sûtra proposes, is, according to authoritative etymology, something of supreme greatness; and according to the second Sûtra it is the cause of the origin, subsistence, and final destruction of the world. The same remark holds good with regard to all following Sûtras, and the scriptural texts on which they are based—none of them confirm the theory of a substance devoid of all difference. Nor, again, does Reasoning prove such a theory; for Reasoning has for its object things possessing a 'proving' attribute which constantly goes together with an attribute 'to be proved.'

And even if, in agreement with your view, we explained the second Sûtra as meaning 'Brahman is that whence proceeds the error of the origination, &c., of the world,' we should not thereby advance your theory of a substance devoid of all difference. For, as you teach, the root of all error is Nescience, and Brahman is that which witnesses (is conscious of) Nescience, and the essence of witnessing consciousness consists in being pure light (intelligence), and the essence of pure light or intelligence is that, distinguishing itself from the Non-intelligent, it renders itself, as well as what is different from it, capable of becoming the object of empiric thought and speech (vyavahâra). All this implies the presence of difference—if there were no difference, light or intelligence could not be what it is, it would be something altogether void, without any meaning.—Here terminates the adhikara*n*a of 'origination and so on.'

An objection to the purport of the preceding Sûtras here presents itself.—The assertion that Brahman, as the cause of the origination, &c., of the world, must be known through the Vedânta-texts is unfounded; for as Brahman may be inferred as the cause of the world through ordinary reasoning, it is not something requiring to be taught by authoritative texts.—To this objection the next Sûtra replies.

3. Because Scripture is the source (of the knowledge of Brahman).

Because Brahman, being raised above all contact with the senses, is not an object of perception and the other means of proof, but to be known through Scripture only; therefore the text 'Whence these creatures are born,' &c., has to be accepted as instructing us regarding the true nature of Brahman.—But, our opponent points out, Scripture cannot be the source of our knowledge of Brahman, because Brahman is to be known through other means. For it is an acknowledged principle that Scripture has a meaning only with regard to what is not established by other sources of knowledge.—But what, to raise a primâ facie counter objection, are those other sources of knowledge? It cannot, in the first place, be Perception. Perception is twofold, being based either on the sense-organs or on extraordinary concentration of mind (yoga). Of Perception of the former kind there are again two sub-species, according as Perception takes place either through the outer sense-organs or the internal organ (manas). Now the outer sense-organs produce knowledge of their respective objects, in so far as the latter are in actual contact with the organs, but are quite unable to give rise to the knowledge of the special object constituted by a supreme Self that is capable of being conscious of and creating the whole aggregate of things. Nor can internal perception give rise to such knowledge; for only purely internal things, such as pleasure and pain, fall within its cognisance, and it is incapable of relating itself to external objects apart from the outer sense-organs. Nor, again, perception based on Yoga; for although such perception—which springs from intense imagination—implies a vivid presentation of things, it is, after all, nothing more than a reproduction of objects perceived previously, and does not therefore rank as an instrument of knowledge; for it has no means of applying itself to objects other than those perceived previously. And if, after all, it does so, it is (not a means of knowledge but) a source of error.—Nor also inference either of the kind which proceeds on the observation of special cases or of the kind which rests on generalizations (cp. Nyâya Sû. I, 1, 5). Not inference of the former kind, because such inference is not known to relate to anything lying beyond the reach of the senses. Nor inference of the latter kind, because we do not observe any characteristic feature that is invariably accompanied by the presence of a supreme Self capable of being conscious of, and constructing, the universe of things.—But there *is* such a feature, viz. the world's being an effected thing; it being a matter of common experience that whatever is an effect or product, is due to an agent who possesses a knowledge of the material cause, the instrumental cause, the final end, and the person meant to make use of the thing produced. It further is matter of experience that whatever consists of non-sentient matter is dependent on, or ruled by, a single intelligent principle. The former generalization is exemplified by the case of jars and similar things, and the latter by a living body in good health, which consists of non-intelligent matter dependent on an intelligent principle. And that the body is an effected thing follows from its consisting of parts.—Against this argumentation also objections may be raised. What, it must be asked, do you understand by this dependence on an intelligent principle? Not, we suppose, that the origination and subsistence of the non-intelligent thing should be dependent on the intelligent principle; for in that case your example would not help to prove your contention. Neither the origin nor the subsistence of a person's healthy body depends on the intelligent soul of that person alone; they rather are brought about by the merit and demerit of all those souls which in any way share the fruition of that body—the wife, e. g. of that person, and others. Moreover, the existence of a body made up of parts means that body's being connected with its parts in the way of so-called intimate relation (samavâya), and this requires a certain combination of the parts but not a presiding intelligent principle. The existence of animated bodies, moreover, has for its characteristic mark the process of breathing, which is absent in the case of the earth, sea, mountains, &c.—all of which are included in the class of things concerning which you wish to prove something—, and we therefore miss a uniform kind of existence common to all those things.—Let us then understand by the dependence of a non-intelligent thing on an intelligent principle, the fact of the motion of the former depending on the latter!—This definition, we rejoin, would comprehend also those cases in which heavy things, such as carriages, masses of stone, trees, &c., are set in motion by several intelligent beings (while what you want to prove is the dependence of a moving thing on one intelligent principle). If, on the other hand, you mean to say that all motion depends on intelligence in general, you only prove what requires no proof.—Another alternative, moreover, here presents itself. As we both admit the existence of individual souls, it will be the more economical hypothesis to ascribe to them the agency implied in the construction of the world. Nor must you object to this view on the ground that such agency cannot belong to the individual souls because they do not possess the knowledge of material causes, &c., as specified above; for all intelligent beings are capable of direct knowledge of material causes, such as earth and so on, and instrumental causes, such as sacrifices and the like. Earth and other material substances, as well as sacrifices and the like, are directly perceived by individual intelligent beings at the present time (and were no doubt equally perceived so at a former time when this world had to be planned and constructed). Nor does the fact that intelligent beings are not capable of direct insight into the unseen principle—called 'apûrva,' or by similar names—which resides in the form of a power in sacrifices and other instrumental causes, in any way preclude their being agents in the construction of the world. Direct insight into powers is nowhere required for undertaking work: what *is* required for that purpose is only direct presentative knowledge of the things endowed with power, while of power itself it suffices to have some kind of knowledge. Potters apply themselves to the task of making pots and jars on the strength of the direct knowledge they possess of the implements of their work—the wheel, the staff, &c.—without troubling about a similar knowledge of the powers inherent in those implements; and in the same way intelligent beings may apply themselves to their work (to be effected by means of sacrifices, &c.), if only they are assured by sacred tradition of the existence of the various powers possessed by sacrifices and the like.—Moreover, experience teaches that agents having a knowledge of the material and other causes must be inferred only in the case of those effects which can be produced, and the material and other causes of which can be known: such things, on the other hand, as the earth, mountains, and oceans, can neither be produced, nor can their material and other causes ever be known; we therefore have no right to infer for them intelligent producers. Hence the quality of being an effected thing can be used as an argument for proving the existence of an intelligent causal agent, only where that quality is found in things, the production of which, and the knowledge of the causes of which, is possible at all.—Experience further teaches that earthen pots and similar things are produced by intelligent agents possessing material bodies, using implements, not endowed with the power of a Supreme Lord, limited in knowledge and so on; the quality of being an effect therefore supplies a reason for inferring an intelligent agent of the kind described only, and thus is opposed to the inference of attributes of a contrary nature, viz. omniscience, omnipotence, and those other attributes that belong to the highest Soul, whose existence you wish to establish.—Nor does this (as might be objected) imply an abandonment of all inference. Where the thing to be inferred is known through other means of proof also, any qualities of an opposite nature which may be suggested by the inferential mark (liṅga) are opposed by those other means of proof, and therefore must be dropped. In the case under discussion, however, the thing to be inferred is something not guaranteed by any other means of proof, viz. a person capable of constructing the entire universe: here there is nothing to interfere with the ascription to such a person of all those qualities which, on the basis of methodical inference, necessarily belong to it. —The conclusion from all this is that, apart from Scripture, the existence of a Lord does not admit of proof.

Against all this the Pûrvapakshin now restates his case as follows:—It cannot be gainsaid that the world is something effected, for it is made up of parts. We may state this argument in various technical forms. 'The earth, mountains, &c., are things effected, because they consist of parts; in the same way as jars and similar things.' 'The earth, seas, mountains, &c., are effects, because, while being big (i. e. non-atomic), they are capable of motion; just as jars and the like.' 'Bodies, the world, &c., are effects, because, while being big, they are solid (mûrtta); just as jars and the like.'—But, an objection is raised, in the case of things made up of parts we do not, in addition to this attribute of consisting of parts, observe any other aspect determining that the thing is an effect—so as to enable us to say 'this thing is effected, and that thing is not'; and, on the other hand, we do observe it as an indispensable condition of something being an effect, that there should be the possibility of such an effect being brought about, and of the existence of such knowledge of material causes, &c. (as the bringing about of the effect presupposes).—Not so, we reply. In the case of a cause being inferred on the ground of an effect, the knowledge and power of the cause must be inferred in accordance with the nature of the effect. From the circumstance of a thing consisting of parts we know it to be an effect, and on this basis we judge of the power and knowledge of the cause. A person recognises pots, jars and the like, as things produced, and therefrom infers the constructive skill and knowledge of their maker; when, after this, he sees for the first time a kingly palace with all its various wonderful parts and structures, he concludes from the special way in which the parts are joined that this also is an effected thing, and then makes an inference as to the architect's manifold knowledge and skill. Analogously, when a living body and the world have once been recognised to be effects, we infer—as their maker—some special intelligent being, possessing direct insight into their nature and skill to construct them.—Pleasure and pain, moreover, by which men are requited for their merit and demerit, are themselves of a non-intelligent nature, and hence cannot bring about their results unless they are controlled by an intelligent principle, and this also compels us to assume a being capable of allotting to each individual soul a fate corresponding to its deserts. For we do not observe that non-intelligent implements, such as axes and the like, however much they may be favoured by circumstances of time, place, and so on, are capable of producing posts and pillars unless they be handled by a carpenter. And to quote against the generalization on which we rely the instance of the seed and sprout and the like can only spring from an ignorance and stupidity which may be called truly demoniac. The same remark would apply to pleasure and pain if used as a counter instance. (For in all these cases the action which produces an effect must necessarily be guided by an intelligent principle.)—Nor may we assume, as a 'less complicated hypothesis,' that the guiding principle in the construction of the world is the individual souls, whose existence is acknowledged by both parties. For on the testimony of observation we must deny to those souls the power of seeing what is extremely subtle or remote in time or place (while such power must necessarily be ascribed to a world-constructing intelligence). On the other hand, we have no ground for concluding that the Lord is, like the individual souls, destitute of such power; hence it cannot be said that other means of knowledge make it impossible to infer such a Lord. The fact rather is that as his existence is proved by the argument that any definite effect presupposes a causal agent competent to produce that effect, he is proved at the same time as possessing the essential power of intuitively knowing and ruling all things in the universe.—The contention that from the world being an effect it follows that its maker does not possess lordly power and so on, so that the proving reason would prove something contrary to the special attributes (belonging to a supreme agent, viz. omnipotence, omniscience, &c.), is founded on evident ignorance of the nature of the inferential process. For the inference clearly does not prove that there exist in the thing inferred all the attributes belonging to the proving collateral instances, including even those attributes which stand in no causal relation to the effect. A certain effect which is produced by some agent presupposes just so much power and knowledge on the part of that agent as is requisite for the production of the effect, but in no way presupposes any incapability or ignorance on the part of that agent with regard to things other than the particular effect; for such incapability and ignorance do not stand towards that effect in any causal relation. If the origination of the effect can be accounted for on the basis of the agent's capability of bringing it about, and of his knowledge of the special material and instrumental causes, it would be unreasonable to ascribe causal agency to his (altogether irrelevant) incapabilities and ignorance with regard to other things, only because those incapabilities, &c., are observed to exist together with his special capability and knowledge. The question would arise moreover whether such want of capability and knowledge (with regard to things other than the one actually effected) would be helpful towards the bringing about of that one effect, in so far as extending to all other things or to some other things. The former alternative is excluded because no agent, a potter e.g., is quite ignorant of all other things but his own special work; and the second alternative is inadmissible because there is no definite rule indicating that there should be certain definite kinds of want of knowledge and skill in the case of all agents [1], and hence exceptions would arise with regard to every special case of want of knowledge and skill. From this it follows that the absence of lordly power and similar qualities which (indeed is observed in the case of ordinary agents but) in no way contributes towards the production of the effects (to which such agents give rise) is not proved in the case of that which we wish to prove (i.e. a Lord, creator of the world), and that hence Inference does not establish qualities contrary (to the qualities characteristic of a Lord).

A further objection will perhaps be raised, viz. that as experience teaches that potters and so on direct their implements through the mediation of their own bodies, we are not justified in holding that a bodiless Supreme Lord directs the material and instrumental causes of the universe. —But in reply to this we appeal to the fact of experience, that evil demons possessing men's bodies, and also venom, are driven or drawn out of those bodies by mere will power. Nor must you ask in what way the volition of a bodiless

[1] A certain potter may not possess the skill and knowledge required to make chairs and beds; but some other potter may possess both, and so on. We cannot therefore point to any definite want of skill and knowledge as invariably accompanying the capability of producing effects of some other kind.

Lord can put other bodies in motion; for volition is not dependent on a body. The cause of volitions is not the body but the internal organ (manas), and such an organ we ascribe to the Lord also, since what proves the presence of an internal organ endowed with power and knowledge is just the presence of effects.—But volitions, even if directly springing from the internal organ, can belong to embodied beings only, such only possessing internal organs!—This objection also is founded on a mistaken generalization: the fact rather is that the internal organ is permanent, and exists also in separation from the body. The conclusion, therefore, is that—as the individual souls with their limited capacities and knowledge, and their dependence on merit and demerit, are incapable of giving rise to things so variously and wonderfully made as worlds and animated bodies are—inference directly leads us to the theory that there is a supreme intelligent agent, called the Lord, who possesses unfathomable, unlimited powers and wisdom, is capable of constructing the entire world, is without a body, and through his mere volition brings about the infinite expanse of this entire universe so variously and wonderfully planned. As Brahman may thus be ascertained by means of knowledge other than revelation, the text quoted under the preceding Sûtra cannot be taken to convey instruction as to Brahman. Since, moreover, experience demonstrates that material and instrumental causes always are things absolutely distinct from each other, as e.g. the clay and the potter with his implements; and since, further, there are substances not made up of parts, as e.g. ether, which therefore cannot be viewed as effects; we must object on these grounds also to any attempt to represent the one Brahman as the universal material and instrumental cause of the entire world.

Against all this we now argue as follows:—The Vedânta-text declaring the origination, &c., of the world does teach that there is a Brahman possessing the characteristics mentioned; since Scripture alone is a means for the knowledge of Brahman. That the world is an effected thing because it consists of parts; and that, as all effects are observed to have for their antecedents certain appropriate agents competent to produce them, we must infer a causal agent competent to plan and construct the universe, and standing towards it in the relation of material and operative cause—this would be a conclusion altogether unjustified. There is no proof to show that the earth, oceans, &c., although things produced, were created at one time by one creator. Nor can it be pleaded in favour of such a conclusion that all those things have one uniform character of being effects, and thus are analogous to one single jar; for we observe that various effects are distinguished by difference of time of production, and difference of producers. Nor again may you maintain the oneness of the creator on the ground that individual souls are incapable of the creation of this wonderful universe, and that if an additional principle be assumed to account for the world—which manifestly is a product—it would be illegitimate to assume more than one such principle. For we observe that individual beings acquire more and more extraordinary powers in consequence of an increase of religious merit; and as we may assume that through an eventual supreme degree of merit they may in the end qualify themselves for producing quite extraordinary effects, we have no right to assume a highest soul of infinite merit, different from all individual souls. Nor also can it be proved that all things are destroyed and produced all at once; for no such thing is observed to take place, while it is, on the other hand, observed that things are produced and destroyed in succession; and if we infer that all things are produced and destroyed because they are effects, there is no reason why this production and destruction should not take place in a way agreeing with ordinary experience. If, therefore, what it is desired to prove is the agency of one intelligent being, we are met by the difficulty that the proving reason (viz. the circumstance of something being an effect) is not invariably connected with what it is desired to prove; there, further, is the fault of qualities not met with in experience being attributed to the subject about which something has to be proved; and lastly there is the fault of the proving collateral instances being destitute of what has to be proved—for experience does not exhibit to us one agent capable of producing everything. If, on the other hand, what you wish to prove is merely the existence of an intelligent creative agent, you prove only what is proved already (not contested by any one).—Moreover, if you use the attribute of being an effect (which belongs to the totality of things) as a means to prove the existence of one omniscient and omnipotent creator, do you view this attribute as belonging to all things in so far as produced together, or in so far as produced in succession? In the former case the attribute of being an effect is not established (for experience does not show that all things are produced together); and in the latter case the attribute would really prove what is contrary to the hypothèsis of one creator (for experience shows that things produced in succession have different causes). In attempting to prove the agency of one intelligent creative being only, we thus enter into conflict with Perception and Inference, and we moreover contradict Scripture, which says that 'the potter is born' and 'the cartwright is born' (and thus declares a plurality of intelligent agents). Moreover, as we observe that all effected things, such as living bodies and so on, are connected with pleasure and the like, which are the effects of sattva (goodness) and the other primary constituents of matter, we must conclude that effected things have sattva and so on for their causes. Sattva and so on—which constitute the distinctive elements of the causal substance—are the causes of the various nature of the effects. Now those effects can be connected with their causes only in so far as the internal organ of a person possessing sattva and so on undergoes modifications. And that a person possesses those qualities is due to karman. Thus, in order to account for the origination of different effects we must necessarily assume the connexion of an intelligent agent with karman, whereby alone he can become the cause of effects; and moreover the various character of knowledge and power (which the various effects presuppose) has its reason in karman. And if it be said that it is (not the various knowledge, &c., but) the mere wish of the agent that causes the origination of effects, we point out that the wish, as being specialised by its particular object, must be based on sattva and so on, and hence is necessarily connected with karman. From all this it follows that individual souls only can be causal agents: no legitimate inference leads to a Lord different from them in nature.—This admits of various expressions in technical form. 'Bodies, worlds, &c., are effects due to the causal energy of individual souls, just as pots are'; 'the Lord is not a causal agent, because he has no aims; just as the released souls have none'; 'the Lord is not an agent, because he has no body; just as the released souls have none.' (This last argumentation cannot be objected to on the ground that individual souls take possession of bodies; for in their case there exists a beginningless subtle body by means of which they enter into gross bodies).—'Time is never devoid of created worlds; because it is time, just like the present time (which has its created world).'

Consider the following point also. Does the Lord produce his effects, with his body or apart from his body? Not the latter; for we do not observe causal agency on the part of any bodiless being: even the activities of the internal organ are found only in beings having a body, and although the internal organ be eternal we do not know of its producing any effects in the case of released disembodied souls. Nor again is the former alternative admissible; for in that case the Lord's body would either be permanent or non-permanent. The former alternative would imply that something made up of parts is eternal; and if we once admit this we may as well admit that the world itself is eternal, and then there is no reason to infer a Lord. And the latter alternative is inadmissible because in that case there would be no cause of the body, different from it (which would account for the origination of the body). Nor could the Lord himself be assumed as the cause of the body, since a bodiless being cannot be the cause of a body. Nor could it be maintained that the Lord can be assumed to be 'embodied' by means of some other body; for this leads us into a *regressus in infinitum*.—Should we, moreover, represent to ourselves the Lord (when productive) as engaged in effort or not?—The former is inadmissible, because he is without a body. And the latter alternative is excluded because a being not making an effort does not produce effects. And if it be said that the effect, i. e. the world, has for its causal agent one whose activity consists in mere desire, this would be to ascribe to the subject of the conclusion (i. e. the world) qualities not known from experience; and moreover the attribute to be proved would be absent in the case of the proving instances (such as jars, &c., which are not the work of agents engaged in mere wishing). Thus the inference of a creative Lord which claims to be in agreement with observation is refuted by reasoning which itself is in agreement with observation, and we hence conclude that Scripture is the only source of knowledge with regard to a supreme soul that is the Lord of all and constitutes the highest Brahman. What Scripture tells us of is a being which comprehends within itself infinite, altogether unsurpassable excellences such as omnipotence and so on, is antagonistic to all evil, and totally different in character from whatever is cognised by the other means of knowledge: that to such a being there should attach even the slightest imperfection due to its similarity in nature to the things known by the ordinary means of knowledge, is thus altogether excluded.—The Pûrvapakshin had remarked that the oneness of the instrumental and the material cause is neither matter of observation nor capable of proof, and that the same holds good with regard to the theory that certain non-composite substances such as ether are created things; that these points also are in no way contrary to reason, we shall show later on under Sû. I, 4, 23, and Sû. II, 3, 1.

The conclusion meanwhile is that, since Brahman does not fall within the sphere of the other means of knowledge, and is the topic of Scripture only, the text 'from whence these creatures,' &c., *does* give authoritative information as to a Brahman possessing the characteristic qualities so often enumerated. Here terminates the adhikara*n*a of 'Scripture being the source.'

A new objection here presents itself.—Brahman does not indeed fall within the province of the other means of knowledge; but all the same Scripture does not give authoritative information regarding it: for Brahman is not something that has for its purport activity or cessation from activity, but is something fully established and accomplished within itself.—To this objection the following Sûtra replies.

4. But that (i. e. the authoritativeness of Scripture with regard to Brahman) exists on account of the connexion (of Scripture with the highest aim of man).

The word 'but' is meant to rebut the objection raised. *That*, i.e. the authoritativeness of Scripture with regard to Brahman, is possible, on account of samanvaya, i. e. connexion with the highest aim of man—that is to say because the scriptural texts are connected with, i. e. have for their subject, Brahman, which constitutes the highest aim of man. For such is the connected meaning of the whole aggregate of words which constitutes the Upanishads—'That from whence these beings are born' (Taitt. Up. III, 1, 1). 'Being only this was in the beginning, one, without a second' (*Kh.* Up. VI, 2), &c. &c. And of aggregates of words which are capable of giving information about accomplished things known through the ordinary means of ascertaining the meaning of words, and which connectedly refer to a Brahman which is the cause of the origination, subsistence, and destruction of the entire world, is antagonistic to all imperfection and so on, we have no right to say that, owing to the absence of a purport in the form of activity or cessation of activity, they really refer to something other than Brahman.

For all instruments of knowledge have their end in determining the knowledge of their own special objects: their action does not adapt itself to a final purpose, but the latter rather adapts itself to the means of knowledge. Nor is it true that where there is no connexion with activity or cessation of activity all aim is absent; for in such cases we observe connexion with what constitutes the general aim, i. e.

the benefit of man. Statements of accomplished matter of fact—such as 'a son is born to thee.' 'This is no snake'—evidently have an aim, viz. in so far as they either give rise to joy or remove pain and fear.

Against this view the Pûrvapakshin now argues as follows. The Vedânta-texts do not impart knowledge of Brahman; for unless related to activity or the cessation of activity, Scripture would be unmeaning, devoid of all purpose. Perception and the other means of knowledge indeed have their aim and end in supplying knowledge of the nature of accomplished things and facts; Scripture, on the other hand, must be supposed to aim at some practical purpose. For neither in ordinary speech nor in the Veda do we ever observe the employment of sentences devoid of a practical purpose: the employment of sentences not having such a purpose is in fact impossible. And what constitutes such purpose is the attainment of a desired, or the avoidance of a non-desired object, to be effected by some action or abstention from action. 'Let a man desirous of wealth attach himself to the court of a prince'; 'a man with a weak digestion must not drink much water'; 'let him who is desirous of the heavenly world offer sacrifices'; and so on. With regard to the assertion that such sentences also as refer to accomplished things—'a son is born to thee' and so on—are connected with certain aims of man, viz. joy or the cessation of fear, we ask whether in such cases the attainment of man's purpose results from the thing or fact itself, as e.g. the birth of a son, or from the knowledge of that thing or fact.—You will reply that as a thing although actually existing is of no use to man as long as it is not known to him, man's purpose is accomplished by his knowledge of the thing.—It then appears, we rejoin, that man's purpose is effected through mere knowledge, even if there is no actual thing; and from this it follows that Scripture, although connected with certain aims, is not a means of knowledge for the actual existence of things. In all cases, therefore, sentences have a practical purpose; they determine either some form of activity or cessation from activity, or else some form of knowledge. No sentence, therefore, can have for its purport an accomplished thing, and hence the Vedânta-texts do not convey the knowledge of Brahman as such an accomplished entity.

At this point somebody propounds the following view. The Vedânta-texts *are* an authoritative means for the cognition of Brahman, because as a matter of fact they also aim at something to be done. What they really mean to teach is that Brahman, which in itself is pure homogeneous knowledge, without a second, not connected with a world, but is, owing to beginningless Nescience, viewed as connected with a world, should be freed from this connexion. And it is through this process of dissolution of the world that Brahman becomes the object of an injunction.—But which texts embody this injunction, according to which Brahman in its pure form is to be realised through the dissolution of this apparent world with its distinction of knowing subjects and objects of knowledge?—Texts such as the following: 'One should not see (i.e. represent to oneself) the seer of seeing, one should not think the thinker of thinking' (B*ri*. Up. III, 4, 2); for this means that we should realise Brahman in the form of pure Seeing (knowledge), free from the distinction of seeing agents and objects of sight. Brahman is indeed accomplished through itself, but all the same it may constitute an object to be accomplished, viz. in so far as it is being disengaged from the apparent world.

This view (the Mîmâ*m*saka rejoins) is unfounded. He who maintains that injunction constitutes the meaning of sentences must be able to assign the injunction itself, the qualification of the person to whom the injunction is addressed, the object of the injunction, the means to carry it out, the special mode of the procedure, and the person carrying out the injunction. Among these things the qualification of the person to whom the injunction addresses itself is something not to be enjoined (but existing previously to the injunction), and is of the nature either of cause (nimitta) or a result aimed at (phala). We then have to decide what, in the case under discussion (i.e. the alleged injunction set forth by the antagonist), constitutes the qualification of the person to whom the injunction addresses itself, and whether it be of the nature of a cause or of a result.—Let it then be said that what constitutes the qualification in our case is the intuition of the true nature of Brahman (on the part of the person to whom the injunction is addressed).—This, we rejoin, cannot be a cause, as it is not something previously established; while in other cases the nimitta is something so established, as e.g. 'life' is in the case of a person to whom the following injunction is addressed, 'As long as his life lasts he is to make the Agnihotra-oblation.' And if, after all, it were admitted to be a cause, it would follow that, as the intuition of the true nature of Brahman is something permanent, the object of the injunction would have to be accomplished even subsequently to final release, in the same way as the Agnihotra has to be performed permanently as long as life lasts.—Nor again can the intuition of Brahman's true nature be a result; for then, being the result of an action enjoined, it would be something non-permanent, like the heavenly world.—What, in the next place, would be the 'object to be accomplished' of the injunction? You may not reply 'Brahman'; for as Brahman is something permanent it is not something that can be realised, and moreover it is not denoted by a verbal form (such as denote actions that can be accomplished, as e.g. yâga, sacrifice).—Let it then be said that what is to be realised is Brahman, in so far as free from the world!—But, we rejoin, even if this be accepted as a thing to be realised, it is not the object (vishaya) of the injunction—that it cannot be for the second reason just stated—but its final result (phala). What moreover is, on this last assumption, the thing to be realised—Brahman, or the cessation of the apparent world?—Not Brahman; for Brahman is something accomplished, and from your assumption it would follow that it is not eternal.—Well then, the dissolution of the world!—Not so, we reply; for then it would not be Brahman that is realised.—Let it then be said that the dissolution of the world only is the object of the injunction!—This, too, cannot be, we rejoin; that dissolution is the result (phala) and cannot therefore be the object of the injunction. For the dissolution of the world means final release; and that is the result aimed at. Moreover, if the dissolution of the world is taken as the object of the injunction, that dissolution would follow from the injunction, and the injunction would be carried out by the dissolution of the world; and this would be a case of vicious mutual dependence.—We further ask—is the world, which is to be put an end to, false or real?—If it is false, it is put an end to by knowledge alone, and then the injunction is needless. Should you reply to this that the injunction puts an end to the world in so far as it gives rise to knowledge, we reply that knowledge springs of itself from the texts which declare the highest truth: hence there is no need of additional injunctions. As knowledge of the meaning of those texts sublates the entire false world distinct from Brahman, the injunction itself with all its adjuncts is seen to be something baseless.—If, on the other hand, the world is true, we ask—is the injunction, which puts an end to the world, Brahman itself or something different from Brahman? If the former, the world cannot exist at all: for what terminates it, viz. Brahman, is something eternal; and the injunction thus being eternal itself cannot be accomplished by means of certain actions.—Let then the latter alternative be accepted!—But in that case, the niyoga being something which is accomplished by a set of performances the function of which it is to put an end to the entire world, the performing person himself perishes (with the rest of the world), and the niyoga thus remains without a substrate. And if everything apart from Brahman is put an end to by a performance the function of which it is to put an end to the world, there remains no result to be effected by the niyoga, consequently there is no release.

Further, the dissolution of the world cannot constitute the instrument (kara*n*a) in the action enjoined, because no mode of procedure (itikartavyatâ) can be assigned for the instrument of the niyoga, and unless assisted by a mode of procedure an instrument cannot operate.—But why is there no 'mode of procedure'?—For the following reasons.

A mode of procedure is either of a positive or a negative kind. If positive, it may be of two kinds, viz. either such as to bring about the instrument or to assist it. Now in our case there is no room for either of these alternatives. Not for the former; for there exists in our case nothing analogous to the stroke of the pestle (which has the manifest effect of separating the rice grains from the husks), whereby the visible effect of the dissolution of the whole world could be brought about. Nor, secondly, is there the possibility of anything assisting the instrument, already existing independently, to bring about its effect; for owing to the existence of such an assisting factor the instrument itself, i.e. the cessation of the apparent world, cannot be established. Nor must you say that it is the cognition of the non-duality of Brahman that brings about the means for the dissolution of the world; for, as we have already explained above, this cognition directly brings about final Release, which is the same as the dissolution of the world, and thus there is nothing left to be effected by special means.—And if finally the mode of procedure is something purely negative, it can, owing to this its nature, neither bring about nor in any way assist the instrumental cause. From all this it follows that there is no possibility of injunctions having for their object the realisation of Brahman, in so far as free from the world.

Here another primâ facie view of the question is set forth.—It must be admitted that the Vedânta-texts are not means of authoritative knowledge, since they refer to Brahman, which is an accomplished thing (not a thing 'to be accomplished'); nevertheless Brahman itself is established, viz. by means of those passages which enjoin meditation (as something 'to be done'). This is the purport of texts such as the following: 'The Self is to be seen, to be heard, to be reflected on, to be meditated upon' (B*ri*. Up. II, 4, 5); 'The Self which is free from sin must be searched out' (*Kh*. Up. VIII, 7, 1); 'Let a man meditate upon him as the Self' (B*ri*. Up. I, 4, 7); 'Let a man meditate upon the Self as his world' (B*ri*. Up. I, 4, 15).—These injunctions have meditation for their object, and meditation again is defined by its own object only, so that the injunctive word immediately suggests an object of meditation; and as such an object there presents itself, the 'Self' mentioned in the same sentence. Now there arises the question, What are the characteristics of that Self? and in reply to it there come in texts such as 'The True, knowledge, infinite is Brahman'; 'Being only this was in the beginning, one without a second.' As these texts give the required special information, they stand in a supplementary relation to the injunctions, and hence are means of right knowledge; and in this way the purport of the Vedânta-texts includes Brahman—as having a definite place in meditation which is the object of injunction. Texts such as 'One only without a second' (*Kh.* Up. VI, 2, 1); 'That is the true, that is the Self' (*Kh.* Up. VI, 8, 7); 'There is here not any plurality' (B*ri*. Up. IV, 4, 19), teach that there is one Reality only, viz. Brahman, and that everything else is false. And as Perception and the other means of proof, as well as that part of Scripture which refers to action and is based on the view of plurality, convey the notion of plurality, and as there is contradiction between plurality and absolute Unity, we form the conclusion that the idea of plurality arises through beginningless avidyâ, while absolute Unity alone is real. And thus it is through the injunction of meditation on Brahman—which has for its result the intuition of Brahman—that man reaches final release, i.e. becomes one with Brahman, which consists of non-dual intelligence free of all the manifold distinctions that spring from Nescience. Nor is this becoming one with Brahman to be accomplished by the mere cognition of the sense of certain Vedânta-texts; for this is not observed—the fact rather being that the view of plurality persists even after the cognition of the sense of those texts—, and, moreover, if it were so, the injunction by Scripture of hearing, reflecting, &c., would be purposeless.

To this reasoning the following objection might be raised.—We observe that when a man is told that what he is afraid of is not a snake, but only a rope, his fear comes to an end; and as bondage is as unreal as the snake imagined in the rope it also admits of being sublated by knowledge, and may therefore, apart from all injunction, be put an end to by the simple comprehension of the sense of certain texts. If final release were to be brought about by injunctions, it would follow that it is not eternal—not any more than the heavenly world and the like; while yet its eternity is admitted by every one. Acts of religious merit, moreover (such as are prescribed by injunctions), can only be the causes of certain results in so far as they give rise to a body capable of experiencing those results, and thus necessarily produce the so-called sa*m*sâra-state (which is opposed to final release, and) which consists in the connexion of the soul with some sort of body, high or low. Release, therefore, is not something to be brought about by acts of religious merit. In agreement herewith Scripture says, 'For the soul as long as it is in the body, there is no release from pleasure and pain; when it is free from the body, then neither pleasure nor pain touch it' (*Kh*. Up. VIII, 12, 1). This passage declares that in the state of release, when the soul is freed from the body, it is not touched by either pleasure or pain—the effects of acts of religious merit or demerit; and from this it follows that the disembodied state is not to be accomplished by acts of religious merit. Nor may it be said that, as other special results are accomplished by special injunctions, so the disembodied state is to be accomplished by the injunction of meditation; for that state is essentially something *not* to be effected. Thus scriptural texts say, 'The wise man who knows the Self as bodiless among the bodies, as persisting among non-persisting things, as great and all-pervading; he does not grieve' (Ka. Up. I, 2, 22); 'That person is without breath, without internal organ, pure, without contact' (Mu. Up. II, 1, 2).—Release which is a bodiless state is eternal, and cannot therefore be accomplished through meritorious acts.

In agreement herewith Scripture says, 'That which thou seest apart from merit (dharma) and non-merit, from what is done and not done, from what exists and what has to be accomplished—tell me that' (Ka. Up. I, 2, 14).—Consider what follows also. When we speak of something being accomplished (effected—sâdhya) we mean one of four things, viz. its being originated (utpatti), or obtained (prâpti), or modified (vi*kri*ti), or in some way or other (often purely ceremonial) made ready or fit (sa*m*sk*ri*ti). Now in neither of these four senses can final Release be said to be accomplished. It cannot be originated, for being Brahman itself it is eternal. It cannot be attained; for Brahman, being the Self, is something eternally attained. It cannot be modified; for that would imply that like sour milk and similar things (which are capable of change) it is non-eternal. Nor finally can it be made 'ready' or 'fit.' A thing is made ready or fit either by the removal of some imperfection or by the addition of some perfection. Now Brahman cannot be freed from any imperfection, for it is eternally faultless; nor can a perfection be added to it, for it is absolutely perfect. Nor can it be improved in the sense in which we speak of improving a mirror, viz. by polishing it; for as it is absolutely changeless it cannot become the object of any action, either of its own or of an outside agent. And, again, actions affecting the body, such as bathing, do not 'purify' the Self (as might possibly be maintained) but only the organ of Egoity (aha*m*kart*ri*) which is the product of avidyâ, and connected with the body; it is this same aha*m*kart*ri* also that enjoys the fruits springing from any action upon the body. Nor must it be said that the Self *is* the aha*m*kart*ri*; for the Self rather is that which is conscious of the aha*m*kart*ri*. This is the teaching of the mantras: 'One of them eats the sweet fruit, the other looks on without eating' (Mu. Up. III, 1, 1); 'When he is in union with the body, the senses, and the mind, then wise men call him the Enjoyer' (Ka. Up. I, 3, 4); 'The one God, hidden in all beings, all-pervading, the Self within all beings, watching over all works, dwelling in all beings, the witness, the perceiver, the only one, free from qualities' (*S*vet. Up. VI, 11); 'He encircled all, bright, bodiless, scatheless, without muscles, pure, untouched by evil' (Î*s*a Up. 8).—All these texts distinguish from the aha*m*kart*ri* due to Nescience, the true Self, absolutely perfect and pure, free from all change. Release therefore

—which *is* the Self—cannot be brought about in any way.—But, if this is so, what then is the use of the comprehension of the texts?—It is of use, we reply, in so far as it puts an end to the obstacles in the way of Release. This scriptural texts declare: 'You indeed are our father, you who carry us from our ignorance to the other shore' (Pra. Up. VI, 8); 'I have heard from men like you that he who knows the Self overcomes grief. I am in grief. Do, Sir, help me over this grief of mine' (*Kh.* Up. VII, 1, 3); 'To him whose faults had thus been rubbed out Sanatkumâra showed the other bank of Darkness' (*Kh.* Up. VII, 26, 2). This shows that what is effected by the comprehension of the meaning of texts is merely the cessation of impediments in the way of Release. This cessation itself, although something effected, is of the nature of that kind of non-existence which results from the destruction of something existent, and as such does not pass away.—Texts such as 'He knows Brahman, he becomes Brahman' (Mu. Up. III, 2, 9); 'Having known him he passes beyond death' (*S*vet. Up. III, 8), declare that Release follows immediately on the cognition of Brahman, and thus negative the intervention of injunctions.—Nor can it be maintained that Brahman is related to action in so far as constituting the object of the action either of knowledge or of meditation; for scriptural texts deny its being an object in either of these senses. Compare 'Different is this from what is known, and from what is unknown' (Ke. Up. I, 3); 'By whom he knows all this, whereby should he know him?' (B*ri*. Up. IV, 5, 15); 'That do thou know as Brahman, not that on which they meditate as being this' (Ke. Up. II, 4). Nor does this view imply that the sacred texts have no object at all; for it is their object to put an end to the view of difference springing from avidyâ. Scripture does not objectivise Brahman in any definite form, but rather teaches that its true nature is to be non-object, and thereby puts an end to the distinction, fictitiously suggested by Nescience, of knowing subjects, acts of knowledge, and objects of knowledge. Compare the text 'You should not see a seer of seeing, you should not think a thinker of thought,' &c. (B*ri*. Up. III, 4, 2).—Nor, again, must it be said that, if knowledge alone puts an end to bondage, the injunctions of hearing and so on are purposeless; for their function is to cause the origination of the comprehension of the texts, in so far as they divert from all other alternatives the student who is naturally inclined to yield to distractions.—Nor, again, can it be maintained that a cessation of bondage through mere knowledge is never observed to take place; for as bondage is something false (unreal) it cannot possibly persist after the rise of knowledge. For the same reason it is a mistake to maintain that the cessation of bondage takes place only after the death of the body. In order that the fear inspired by the imagined snake should come to an end, it is required only that the rope should be recognised as what it is, not that a snake should be destroyed. If the body were something real, its destruction would be necessary; but being apart from Brahman it is unreal. He whose bondage does not come to an end, in him true knowledge has not arisen; this we infer from the effect of such knowledge not being observed in him. Whether the body persist or not, he who has reached true knowledge is released from that very moment. —The general conclusion of all this is that, as Release is not something to be accomplished by injunctions of meditation, Brahman is not proved to be something standing in a supplementary relation to such injunctions; but is rather proved by (non-injunctory) texts, such as 'Thou art that'; 'The True, knowledge, infinite is Brahman'; 'This Self is Brahman.'

This view (the holder of the dhyâna-vidhi theory rejoins) is untenable; since the cessation of bondage cannot possibly spring from the mere comprehension of the meaning of texts. Even if bondage were something unreal, and therefore capable of sublation by knowledge, yet being something direct, immediate, it could not be sublated by the indirect comprehension of the sense of texts. When a man directly conscious of a snake before him is told by a competent by-stander that it is not a snake but merely a rope, his fear is not dispelled by a mere cognition contrary to that of a snake, and due to the information received; but the information brings about the cessation of his fear in that way that it rouses him to an activity aiming at the direct perception, by means of his senses, of what the thing before him really is. Having at first started back in fear of the imagined snake, he now proceeds to ascertain by means of ocular perception the true nature of the thing, and having accomplished this is freed from fear. It would not be correct to say that in this case words (viz. of the person informing) produce this perceptional knowledge; for words are not a sense-organ, and among the means of knowledge it is the sense-organs only that give rise to direct knowledge. Nor, again, can it be pleaded that in the special case of Vedic texts sentences may give rise to direct knowledge, owing to the fact that the person concerned has cleansed himself of all imperfection through the performance of actions not aiming at immediate results, and has been withdrawn from all outward objects by hearing, reflection, and meditation; for in other cases also, where special impediments in the way of knowledge are being removed, we never observe that the special means of knowledge, such as the sense-organs and so on, operate outside their proper limited sphere.—Nor, again, can it be maintained that meditation acts as a means helpful towards the comprehension of texts; for this leads to vicious reciprocal dependence—when the meaning of the texts has been comprehended it becomes the object of meditation; and when meditation has taken place there arises comprehension of the meaning of the texts!—Nor can it be said that meditation and the comprehension of the meaning of texts have different objects; for if this were so the comprehension of the texts could not be a means helpful towards meditation: meditation on one thing does not give rise to eagerness with regard to another thing!—For meditation which consists in uninterrupted remembrance of a thing cognised, the cognition of the sense of texts, moreover, forms an indispensable prerequisite; for knowledge of Brahman—the object of meditation—cannot originate from any other source.—Nor can it be said that

that knowledge on which meditation is based is produced by one set of texts, while that knowledge which puts an end to the world is produced by such texts as 'thou art that,' and the like. For, we ask, has the former knowledge the same object as the latter, or a different one? On the former alternative we are led to the same vicious reciprocal dependence which we noted above; and on the latter alternative it cannot be shown that meditation gives rise to eagerness with regard to the latter kind of knowledge. Moreover, as meditation presupposes plurality comprising an object of meditation, a meditating subject and so on, it really cannot in any perceptible way be helpful towards the origination of the comprehension of the sense of texts, the object of which is the oneness of a Brahman free from all plurality: he, therefore, who maintains that Nescience comes to an end through the mere comprehension of the meaning of texts really implies that the injunctions of hearing, reflection, and meditation are purposeless.

The conclusion that, since direct knowledge cannot spring from texts, Nescience is not terminated by the comprehension of the meaning of texts, disposes at the same time of the hypothesis of the so-called 'Release in this life' (*g*îvanmukti). For what definition, we ask, can be given of this 'Release in this life'?—'Release of a soul while yet joined to a body'!—You might as well say, we reply, that your mother never had any children! You have yourself proved by scriptural passages that 'bondage' means the being joined to a body, and 'release' being free from a body!—Let us then define *g*îvanmukti as the cessation of embodiedness, in that sense that a person, while the appearance of embodiedness persists, is conscious of the unreality of that appearance.—But, we rejoin, if the consciousness of the unreality of the body puts an end to embodiedness, how can you say that *g*îvanmukti means release of a soul while joined to a body? On this explanation there remains no difference whatsoever between 'Release in this life' and Release after death; for the latter also can only be defined as cessation of the false appearance of embodiedness.—Let us then say that a person is '*g*îvanmukta' when the appearance of embodiedness, although sublated by true knowledge, yet persists in the same way as the appearance of the moon being double persists (even after it has been recognised as false).—This too we cannot allow. As the sublating act of cognition on which Release depends extends to everything with the exception of Brahman, it sublates the general defect due to causal Nescience, inclusive of the particular erroneous appearance of embodiedness: the latter being sublated in this way cannot persist. In the case of the double moon, on the other hand, the defect of vision on which the erroneous appearance depends is *not* the object of the sublative art of cognition, i.e. the cognition of the oneness of the moon, and it therefore remains non-sublated; hence the false appearance of a double moon may persist.—Moreover, the text 'For him there is delay only as long as he is not freed from the body; then he will be released' (*Kh.* Up. VI, 14, 2), teaches that he who takes his stand on the knowledge of the Real requires for his Release the putting off of the body only: the text thus negatives *g*îvanmukti. Âpastamba also rejects the view of *g*îvanmukti, 'Abandoning the Vedas, this world and the next, he (the Sa*m*nyâsin) is to seek the Self. (Some say that) he obtains salvation when he knows (the Self). This opinion is contradicted by the *s*âstras. (For) if Salvation were obtained when the Self is known, he should not feel any pain even in this world. Hereby that which follows is explained' (Dh. Sû. II, 9, 13–17).—This refutes also the view that Release is obtained through mere knowledge.—The conclusion to be drawn from all this is that Release, which consists in the cessation of all Plurality, cannot take place as long as a man lives. And we therefore adhere to our view that Bondage is to be terminated only by means of the injunctions of meditation, the result of which is direct knowledge of Brahman. Nor must this be objected to on the ground that Release, if brought about by injunctions, must therefore be something non-eternal; for what is effected is not Release itself, but only the cessation of what impedes it. Moreover, the injunction does not directly produce the cessation of

Bondage, but only through the mediation of the direct cognition of Brahman as consisting of pure knowledge, and not connected with a world. It is this knowledge only which the injunction produces.—But how can an injunction cause the origination of knowledge?—How, we ask in return, can, on your view, works not aiming at some immediate result cause the origination of knowledge?—You will perhaps reply 'by means of purifying the mind' (manas); but this reply may be given by me also.—But (the objector resumes) there is a difference. On my view Scripture produces knowledge in the mind purified by works; while on your view we must assume that in the purified mind the means of knowledge are produced by injunction.—The mind itself, we reply, purified by knowledge, constitutes this means.—How do you know this? our opponent questions. —How, we ask in return, do *you* know that the mind is purified by works, and that, in the mind so purified of a person withdrawn from all other objects by hearing, reflection and meditation, Scripture produces that knowledge which destroys bondage?—Through certain texts such as the following: 'They seek to know him by sacrifice, by gifts, by penance, by fasting' (B*ri*. Up. IV, 4, 22); 'He is to be heard, to be reflected on, to be meditated on' (B*ri*. Up. II, 4, 5); 'He knows Brahman, he becomes Brahman' (Mu. Up. III, 2, 9).—Well, we reply, in the same way our view—viz. that through the injunction of meditation the mind is cleared, and that a clear mind gives rise to direct knowledge of Brahman—is confirmed by scriptural texts such as 'He is to be heard, to be reflected on, to be meditated on' (B*ri*. Up. II, 4, 5); 'He who knows Brahman reaches the highest' (Taitt. Up. II, 1, 1); 'He is not apprehended by the eye nor by speech' (Mu. Up. III, 1, 8); 'But by a pure mind' (?); 'He is apprehended by the heart, by wisdom, by the mind' (Ka. Up. II, 6, 9). Nor can it be said that the text 'not that which they meditate upon as this' (Ke. Up. I, 4) negatives meditation; it does not forbid meditation on Brahman, but merely declares that Brahman is different from the world. The mantra is to be explained as follows: 'What men meditate upon as this world, that is not Brahman; know Brahman to be that which is not uttered by speech, but through which speech is uttered.' On a different explanation the clause 'know that to be Brahman' would be irrational, and the injunctions of meditation on the Self would be meaningless.—The outcome of all this is that unreal Bondage which appears in the form of a plurality of knowing subjects, objects of knowledge, &c., is put an end to by the injunctions of meditation, the fruit of which is direct intuitive knowledge of Brahman.

Nor can we approve of the doctrine held by some that there is no contradiction between difference and non-difference; for difference and non-difference cannot co-exist in one thing, any more than coldness and heat, or light and darkness.—Let us first hear in detail what the holder of this so-called bhedâbheda view has to say. The whole universe of things must be ordered in agreement with our cognitions. Now we are conscious of all things as different and non-different at the same time: they are non-different in their causal and generic aspects, and different in so far as viewed as effects and individuals. There indeed is a contradiction between light and darkness and so on; for these cannot possibly exist together, and they are actually met with in different abodes. Such contradictoriness is not, on the other hand, observed in the case of cause and effect, and genus and individual; on the contrary we here distinctly apprehend one thing as having two aspects—'this jar is clay,' 'this cow is short-horned.' The fact is that experience does not show us anything that has one aspect only. Nor can it be said that in these cases there is absence of contradiction because as fire consumes grass so non-difference absorbs difference; for the same thing which exists as clay, or gold, or cow, or horse, &c., at the same time exists as jar or diadem, or short-horned cow or mare. There is no command of the Lord to the effect that one aspect only should belong to each thing, non-difference to what is non-different, and difference to what is different.—But one aspect only belongs to each thing, because it is thus that things are perceived!—On the contrary, we reply, things have twofold aspects, just because it is *thus* that they are perceived. No man, however wide he may open his eyes, is able to distinguish in an object—e. g. a jar or a cow—placed before him which part is the clay and which the jar, or which part is the generic character of the cow and which the individual cow. On the contrary, his thought finds its true expression in the following judgments: 'this jar is clay'; 'this cow is short-horned.' Nor can it be maintained that he makes a distinction between the cause and genus as objects of the idea of persistence, and the effect and individual as objects of the idea of discontinuance (difference); for as a matter of fact there is no perception of these two elements in separation. A man may look ever so close at a thing placed before him, he will not be able to perceive a difference of aspect and to point out 'this is the persisting, general, element in the thing, and that the non-persistent, individual, element.' Just as an effect and an individual give rise to the idea of one thing, so the effect *plus* cause, and the individual *plus* generic character, also give rise to the idea of one thing only. This very circumstance makes it possible for us to recognise each individual thing, placed as it is among a multitude of things differing in place, time, and character.—Each thing thus being cognised as endowed with a twofold aspect, the theory of cause and effect, and generic character and individual, being absolutely different, is clearly refuted by perception.

But, an objection is raised, if on account of grammatical co-ordination and the resulting idea of oneness, the judgment 'this pot is clay' is taken to express the relation of difference *plus* non-difference, we shall have analogously to infer from judgments such as 'I am a man,' 'I am a divine being' that the Self and the body also stand in the bhedâbheda-relation; the theory of the co-existence of difference and non-difference will thus act like a fire which a man has lit on his hearth, and which in the end consumes the entire house!—This, we reply, is the baseless idea of a person who has not duly considered the true nature of co-ordination as establishing the bhedâbheda-relation. The correct principle is that all reality is determined by states of consciousness not sublated by valid means of proof. The imagination, however, of the identity of the Self and the body *is* sublated by all the means of proof which apply to the Self: it is in fact no more valid than the imagination of the snake in the rope, and does not therefore prove the non-difference of the two. The co-ordination, on the other hand, which is expressed in the judgment 'the cow is short-horned' is never observed to be refuted in any way, and hence establishes the bhedâbheda-relation.

For the same reasons the individual soul (*g*îva) is not absolutely different from Brahman, but stands to it in the bhedâbheda-relation in so far as it is a part (a*ms*a) of Brahman. Its non-difference from Brahman is essential (svâbhâvika); its difference is due to limiting adjuncts (aupâdhika). This we know, in the first place, from those scriptural texts which declare non-difference—such as 'Thou art that' (*Kh.* Up. VI); 'There is no other seer but he' (B*ri.* Up. III, 7, 23); 'This Self is Brahman' (B*ri.* Up. II, 5, 19); and the passage from the Brahmasûkta in the Sa*m*hitopanishad of the Âtharva*n*as which, after having said that Brahman is Heaven and Earth, continues, 'The fishermen are Brahman, the slaves are Brahman, Brahman are these gamblers; man and woman are born from Brahman; women are Brahman and so are men.' And, in the second place, from those texts which declare difference: 'He who, one, eternal, intelligent, fulfils the desires of many non-eternal intelligent beings' (Ka. Up. II, 5, 13); 'There are two unborn, one knowing, the other not-knowing; one strong, the other weak' (*S*vet. Up. I, 9); 'Being the cause of their connexion with him, through the qualities of action and the qualities of the Self, he is seen as another' (*S*vet. Up. V, 12); 'The Lord of nature and the souls, the ruler of the qualities, the cause of the bondage, the existence and the release of the sa*m*sâra' (*S*vet. Up. VI, 16); 'He is the cause, the lord of the lords of the organs' (*S*vet. Up. VI, 9); 'One of the two eats the sweet fruit, without eating the other looks on' (*S*vet. Up. IV, 6); 'He who dwelling in the Self' (B*ri.* Up. III, 7, 22);

'Embraced by the intelligent Self he knows nothing that is without, nothing that is within' (B*ri*. Up. IV, 3, 21); 'Mounted by the intelligent Self he goes groaning' (B*ri*. Up. IV, 3, 35); 'Having known him he passes beyond death' (*S*vet. Up. III, 8).—On the ground of these two sets of passages the individual and the highest Self must needs be assumed to stand in the bhedâbheda-relation. And texts such as 'He knows Brahman, he becomes Brahman' (Mu. Up. III, 2, 9), which teach that in the state of Release the individual soul enters into Brahman itself; and again texts such as 'But when the Self has become all for him, whereby should he see another' (B*ri*. Up. II, 4, 13), which forbid us to view, in the state of Release, the Lord as something different (from the individual soul), show that non-difference is essential (while difference is merely aupâdhika).

But, an objection is raised, the text 'He reaches all desires together in the wise Brahman,' in using the word 'together' shows that even in the state of Release the soul is different from Brahman, and the same view is expressed in two of the Sûtras, viz. IV, 4, 17; 21.—This is not so, we reply; for the text, 'There is no other seer but he' (B*ri*. Up. III, 7, 23), and many similar texts distinctly negative all plurality in the Self. The Taittirîya-text quoted by you means that man reaches Brahman with all desires, i.e. Brahman comprising within itself all objects of desire; if it were understood differently, it would follow that Brahman holds a subordinate position only. And if the Sûtra IV, 4, 17 meant that the released soul is separate from Brahman it would follow that it is deficient in lordly power; and if this were so the Sûtra would be in conflict with other Sûtras such as IV, 4, 1.—For these reasons, non-difference is the essential condition; while the distinction of the souls from Brahman and from each other is due to their limiting adjuncts, i.e. the internal organ, the sense-organs, and the body. Brahman indeed is without parts and omnipresent; but through its adjuncts it becomes capable of division just as ether is divided by jars and the like. Nor must it be said that this leads to a reprehensible mutual dependence—Brahman in so far as divided entering into conjunction with its adjuncts, and again the division in Brahman being caused by its conjunction with its adjuncts; for these adjuncts and Brahman's connexion with them are due to action (karman), and the stream of action is without a beginning. The limiting adjuncts to which a soul is joined spring from the soul as connected with previous works, and work again springs from the soul as joined to its adjuncts: and as this connexion with works and adjuncts is without a beginning in time, no fault can be found with our theory.—The non-difference of the souls from each other and Brahman is thus essential, while their difference is due to the Upâdhis. These Upâdhis, on the other hand, are at the same time essentially non-distinct and essentially distinct from each other and Brahman; for there are no other Upâdhis (to account for their distinction if non-essential), and if we admitted such, we should again have to assume further Upâdhis, and so on *in infinitum*. We therefore hold that the Upâdhis are produced, in accordance with the actions of the individual souls, as essentially non-different and different from Brahman.

To this bhedâbheda view the Pûrvapakshin now objects on the following grounds:—The whole aggregate of Vedânta-texts aims at enjoining meditation on a non-dual Brahman whose essence is reality, intelligence, and bliss, and thus sets forth the view of non-difference; while on the other hand the karma-section of the Veda, and likewise perception and the other means of knowledge, intimate the view of the difference of things. Now, as difference and non-difference are contradictory, and as the view of difference may be accounted for as resting on beginningless Nescience, we conclude that universal non-difference is what is real.—The tenet that difference and non-difference are not contradictory because both are proved by our consciousness, cannot be upheld. If one thing has different characteristics from another there is distinction (bheda) of the two; the contrary condition of things constitutes non-distinction (abheda); who in his senses then would maintain that these two—suchness and non-suchness—can be found together? You have maintained that non-difference belongs to a thing viewed as cause and genus, and difference to the same viewed as effect and individual; and that, owing to this twofold aspect of things, non-difference and difference are not irreconcileable. But that this view also is untenable, a presentation of the question in definite alternatives will show. Do you mean to say that the difference lies in one aspect of the thing and the non-difference in the other? or that difference *and* non-difference belong to the thing possessing two aspects?—On the former alternative the difference belongs to the individual and the non-difference to the genus; and this implies that there is no one thing with a double aspect. And should you say that the genus and individual together constitute one thing only, you abandon the view that it is difference of aspect which takes away the contradictoriness of difference and non-difference. We have moreover remarked already that difference in characteristics and its opposite are absolutely contradictory.—On the second alternative we have two aspects of different kind and an unknown thing supposed to be the substrate of those aspects; but this assumption of a triad of entities proves only their mutual difference of character, not their non-difference. Should you say that the non-contradictoriness of two aspects constitutes simultaneous difference and non-difference in the thing which is their substrate, we ask in return—How can two aspects which have a thing for their substrate, and thus are different from the thing, introduce into that thing a combination of two contradictory attributes (viz. difference and non-difference)? And much less even are they able to do so if they are viewed as non-different from the thing which is their substrate. If, moreover, the two aspects on the one hand, and the thing in which they inhere on the other, be admitted to be distinct entities, there will be required a further factor to bring about their difference and non-difference, and we shall thus be led into a *regressus in infinitum*.—Nor is it a fact that the idea of a thing inclusive of its generic character bears the character of unity, in the same way as the admittedly uniform idea of an individual; for wherever a state of consciousness expresses itself in the form 'this is such and such' it implies the distinction of an attribute or mode, and that to which the attribute or mode belongs. In the case under discussion the genus constitutes the mode, and the individual that to which the mode belongs: the idea does not therefore possess the character of unity.

For these very reasons the individual soul cannot stand to Brahman in the bhedâbheda-relation. And as the view of non-difference is founded on Scripture, we assume that the view of difference rests on beginningless Nescience.—But on this view want of knowledge and all the imperfections springing therefrom, such as birth, death, &c., would cling to Brahman itself, and this would contradict scriptural texts such as 'He who is all-knowing' (Mu. Up. I, 1, 9); 'That Self free from all evil' (*Kh.* Up. VIII, 1, 5). Not so, we reply. For all those imperfections we consider to be unreal. On your view on the other hand, which admits nothing but Brahman and its limiting adjuncts, all the imperfections which spring from contact with those adjuncts must really belong to Brahman. For as Brahman is without parts, indivisible, the upâdhis cannot divide or split it so as to connect themselves with a part only; but necessarily connect themselves with Brahman itself and produce their effects on it.—Here the following explanation may possibly be attempted. Brahman determined by an upâdhi constitutes the individual soul. This soul is of atomic size since what determines it, viz. the internal organ, is itself of atomic size; and the limitation itself is without beginning. All the imperfections therefore connect themselves only with that special place that is determined by the upâdhi, and do not affect the highest Brahman which is not limited by the upâdhi.—In reply to this we ask—Do you mean to say that what constitutes the atomic individual soul is a part of Brahman which is limited and cut off by the limiting adjunct; or some particular part of Brahman which, without being thereby divided off, is connected with an atomic upâdhi; or Brahman in its totality as connected with an upâdhi; or some other intelligent being connected with an upâdhi, or finally the upâdhi itself?—The first alternative is not possible, because Brahman cannot be divided; it would moreover imply that the individual soul has a beginning, for division means the making of one thing into two.—On the second alternative it would follow that, as a part of Brahman would be connected with the upâdhi, all the imperfections due to the upâdhis would adhere to that part. And further, if the upâdhi would not possess the power of attracting to itself the particular part of Brahman with which it is connected, it would follow that when the upâdhi moves the part with which it is connected would constantly change; in other words, bondage and release would take place at every moment. If, on the contrary, the upâdhi possessed the power of attraction, the whole Brahman—as not being capable of division—would be attracted and move with the upâdhi. And should it be said that what is all-pervading and without parts cannot be attracted and move, well then the upâdhi only moves, and we are again met by the difficulties stated above. Moreover, if all the upâdhis were connected with the parts of Brahman viewed as one and undivided, all individual souls, being nothing but parts of Brahman, would be considered as non-distinct. And should it be said that they are not thus cognised as one because they are constituted by different parts of Brahman, it would follow that as soon as the upâdhi of one individual soul is moving, the identity of that soul would be lost (for it would, in successive moments, be constituted by different parts of Brahman).—On the third alternative (the whole of) Brahman itself being connected with the upâdhi enters into the condition of individual soul, and there remains no non-conditioned Brahman. And, moreover, the soul in all bodies will then be one only.—On the fourth alternative the individual soul is something altogether different from Brahman, and the difference of the soul from Brahman thus ceases to depend on the upâdhis of Brahman.—And the fifth alternative means the embracing of the view of the *K*ârvâka (who makes no distinction between soul and matter).—The conclusion from all this is that on the strength of the texts declaring non-difference we must admit that all difference is based on Nescience only. Hence, Scripture being an authoritative instrument of knowledge in so far only as it has for its end action and the cessation of action, the Vedânta-texts must be allowed to be a valid means of knowledge with regard to Brahman's nature, in so far as they stand in a supplementary relation to the injunctions of meditation.

This view is finally combated by the Mîmâ*m*saka. Even if, he says, we allow the Vedânta-texts to have a purport in so far as they are supplementary to injunctions of meditation, they cannot be viewed as valid means of knowledge with regard to Brahman. Do the texts referring to Brahman, we ask, occupy the position of valid means of knowledge in so far as they form a syntactic whole with the injunctions of meditation, or as independent sentences? In the former case the purport of the syntactic whole is simply to enjoin meditation, and it cannot therefore aim at giving instruction about Brahman. If, on the other hand, the texts about Brahman are separate independent sentences, they cannot have the purport of prompting to action and are therefore devoid of instructive power. Nor must it be said that meditation is a kind of continued remembrance, and as such requires to be defined by the object remembered; and that the demand of the injunction of meditation for something to be remembered is satisfied by texts such as 'All this is that Self,' 'the True, knowledge, infinite is Brahman,' &c., which set forth the nature and attributes of Brahman and—forming a syntactic whole with the injunctions—are a valid means of knowledge with regard to the existence of the matter they convey. For the fact is that the demand on the part of an injunction of meditation for an object to be remembered may be satisfied even by something unreal (not true), as in the case of injunctions such as 'Let him meditate upon mind as Brahman' (*Kh*. Up. III, 18, 1): the real existence of the object of meditation is therefore not demanded.—The final conclusion arrived at in this pûrvapaksha is therefore as follows. As the Vedânta-texts do not aim at prompting to action or the cessation of action; as, even on the supposition of their being supplementary to injunctions of meditation, the only thing they effect is to set forth the nature of the object of meditation; and as, even if they are viewed as independent sentences, they accomplish the end of man (i.e. please, gratify) by knowledge merely—being thus comparable to tales with which we soothe children or sick persons; it does not lie within their province to establish the reality of an accomplished thing, and hence Scripture cannot be viewed as a valid means for the cognition of Brahman.

To this primâ facie view the Sûtrakâra replies, 'But this on account of connexion.' 'Connexion' is here to be taken in an eminent sense, as 'connexion with the end of man.' That Brahman, which is measureless bliss and therefore constitutes the highest end of man, is connected with the texts as the topic set forth by them, proves Scripture to be a valid means for the cognition of Brahman. To maintain that the whole body of Vedânta-texts—which teach us that Brahman is the highest object to be attained, since it consists of supreme bliss free of all blemish whatsoever—is devoid of all use and purpose merely because it does not aim at action or the cessation of action; is no better than to say that a youth of royal descent is of no use because he does not belong to a community of low wretches living on the flesh of dogs!

The relation of the different texts is as follows. There are individual souls of numberless kinds—gods, Asuras, Gandharvas, Siddhas, Vidyâdharas, Kinnaras, Ki*m*purushas, Yakshas, Râkshasas, Pisâ*k*as, men, beasts, birds, creeping animals, trees, bushes, creepers, grasses and so on—distinguished as male, female, or sexless, and having different sources of nourishment and support and different objects of enjoyment. Now all these souls are deficient in insight into the true nature of the highest reality, their understandings being obscured by Nescience operating in the form of beginningless karman; and hence those texts only are fully useful to them which teach that there exists a highest Brahman—which the souls in the state of release may cognise as non-different from themselves, and which then, through its own essential nature, qualities, power and energies, imparts to those souls bliss infinite and unsurpassable. When now the question arises—as it must arise—, as to how this Brahman is to be attained, there step in certain other Vedânta-texts — such as 'He who knows Brahman reaches the highest' (B*ri*. Up. II, 1, 1), and 'Let a man meditate on the Self as his world' (B*ri*. Up. I, 4, 15) —and, by means of terms denoting 'knowing' and so on, enjoin meditation as the means of attaining Brahman. (We may illustrate this relation existing between the texts setting forth the nature of Brahman and those enjoining meditation by two comparisons.) The case is like that of a man who has been told 'There is a treasure hidden in your house.' He learns through this sentence the existence of the treasure, is satisfied, and then takes active steps to find it and make it his own.—Or take the case of a young prince who, intent on some boyish play, leaves his father's palace and, losing his way, does not return. The king thinks his son is lost; the boy himself is received by some good Brahman who brings him up and teaches him without knowing who the boy's father is. When the boy has reached his sixteenth year and is accomplished in every way, some fully trustworthy person tells him, 'Your father is the ruler of all these lands, famous for the possession of all noble qualities, wisdom, generosity, kindness, courage, valour and so on, and he stays in his capital, longing to see you, his lost child. Hearing that his father is alive and a man so high and noble, the boy's heart is filled with supreme joy; and the king also, understanding that his son is alive, in good health, handsome and well instructed, considers himself to have attained all a man can wish for. He then takes steps to recover his son, and finally the two are reunited.

The assertion again that a statement referring to some accomplished thing gratifies men merely by imparting a knowledge of the thing, without being a means of knowledge with regard to its real existence—so that it would be comparable to the tales we tell to children and sick people—, can in no way be upheld. When it is ascertained that a thing has no real existence, the mere knowledge or idea of the thing does not gratify. The pleasure which stories give to children and sick people is due to the fact that they erroneously believe them to be true; if they were to find out that the matter present to their thought is untrue their pleasure would come to an end that very moment. And thus in the case of the texts of the Upanishads also. If we thought that these texts do not mean to intimate the real existence of Brahman, the mere idea of Brahman to which they give rise would not satisfy us in any way.

The conclusion therefore is that texts such as 'That from whence these beings are born' &c. do convey valid instruction as to the existence of Brahman, i. e. that being which is the sole cause of the world, is free from all shadow of imperfection, comprises within itself all auspicious qualities, such as omniscience and so on, and is of the nature of supreme bliss.—Here terminates the adhikara*n*a of 'connexion.'

5. On account of seeing (i. e. thinking) that which is not founded on Scripture (i. e. the Pradhâna) is not (what is taught by the texts referring to the origination of the world).

We have maintained that what is taught by the texts relative to the origination of the world is Brahman, omniscient, and so on. The present Sûtra and the following Sûtras now add that those texts can in no way refer to the Pradhâna and similar entities which rest on Inference only.

We read in the *Kh*ândogya, 'Being only was this in the beginning, one only, without a second.—It thought, may I be many, may I grow forth.—It sent forth fire' (VI, 2, 1 ff.)—Here a doubt arises whether the cause of the world denoted by the term 'Being' is the Pradhâna, assumed by others, which rests on Inference, or Brahman as defined by us.

The Pûrvapakshin maintains that the Pradhâna is meant. For he says, the *Kh*ândogya text quoted expresses the causal state of what is denoted by the word 'this,' viz. the aggregate of things comprising manifold effects, such as ether, &c., consisting of the three elements of Goodness,

Passion and Darkness, and forming the sphere of fruition of intelligent beings. By the 'effected' state we understand the assuming, on the part of the causal substance, of a different condition; whatever therefore constitutes the essential nature of a thing in its effected state the same constitutes its essential nature in the causal state also. Now the effect, in our case, is made up of the three elements Goodness, Passion and Darkness; hence the cause is the Pradhâna which consists in an equipoise of those three elements. And as in this Pradhâna all distinctions are merged, so that it is pure Being, the *Kh*ândogya text refers to it as 'Being, one only, without a second.' This establishes the non-difference of effect and cause, and in this way the promise that through the knowledge of one thing all things are to be known admits of being fulfilled. Otherwise, moreover, there would be no analogy between the instance of the lump of clay and the things made of it, and the matter to be illustrated thereby. The texts speaking of the origination of the world therefore intimate the Pradhâna taught by the great Sage Kapila. And as the *Kh*ândogya passage has, owing to the presence of an initial statement (prati*gñ*â) and a proving instance, the form of an inference, the term 'Being' means just that which rests on inference, viz. the Pradhâna.

This primâ facie view is set aside by the words of the Sûtra. That which does not rest on Scripture, i. e. the Pradhâna, which rests on Inference only, is not what is intimated by the texts referring to the origination of the world; for the text exhibits the root 'îksh'—which means 'to think'—as denoting a special activity on the part of what is termed 'Being.' 'It thought, may I be many, may I grow forth.' 'Thinking' cannot possibly belong to the non-sentient Pradhânà: the term 'Being' can therefore denote only the all-knowing highest Person who is capable of thought. In agreement with this we find that, in all sections which refer to creation, the act of creation is stated to be preceded by thought. 'He thought, shall I send forth worlds. He sent forth these worlds' (Ait. Âr. II, 4, 1, 2); 'He thought he sent forth Prâ*n*a' (Pr. Up. VI, 3);

and others.—But it is a rule that as a cause we must assume only what corresponds to the effect!—Just so; and what corresponds to the total aggregate of effects is the highest Person, all-knowing, all-powerful, whose purposes realise themselves, who has minds and matter in their subtle state for his body. Compare the texts 'His high power is revealed as manifold, as inherent, acting as force and knowledge' (*S*vet. Up. VI, 8); 'He who is all-knowing, all-perceiving' (Mu. Up. I, 1, 9); 'He of whom the Unevolved is the body, of whom the Imperishable is the body, of whom Death is the body, he is the inner Self of all things' (Subâl. Up. VII).—This point (viz. as to the body of the highest Person) will be established under Sû. II, 1, 4. The present Sûtra declares that the texts treating of creation cannot refer to the Pradhâna; the Sûtra just mentioned will dispose of objections. Nor is the Pûrvapakshin right in maintaining that the *Kh*ândogya passage is of the nature of an Inference; for it does not state a reason (hetu—which is the essential thing in an Inference). The illustrative instance (of the lump of clay) is introduced merely in order to convince him who considers it impossible that all things should be known through one thing—as maintained in the passage 'through which that is heard which was not heard,' &c.,—that this *is* possible after all. And the mention made in the text of 'seeing' clearly shows that there is absolutely no intention of setting forth an Inference.

Let us assume, then, the Pûrvapakshin resumes, that the 'seeing' of the text denotes not 'seeing' in its primary, direct sense—such as belongs to intelligent beings only; but 'seeing' in a secondary, figurative sense which there is ascribed to the Pradhâna in the same way as in passages immediately following it is ascribed to fire and water—'the fire saw'; 'the water saw' (*Kh*. Up. VI, 2, 3). The transference, to non-existent things, of attributes properly belonging to sentient beings is quite common; as when we say 'the rice-fields look out for rain'; 'the rain delighted the seeds.'—This view is set aside by the next Sûtra.

6. If it be said that (the word 'seeing') has a secondary (figurative) meaning; we deny this, on account of the word 'Self' (being applied to the cause of the world).

The contention that, because, in passages standing close by, the word 'seeing' is used in a secondary sense, the 'seeing' predicated of the Sat ('Being') is also to be taken in a secondary sense, viz. as denoting (not real thought but) a certain condition previous to creation, cannot be upheld; for in other texts met with in the same section (viz. 'All this has that for its Self; that is the True, that is the Self,' *Kh.* Up. VI, 8, 7), that which first had been spoken of as Sat is called the 'Self.' The designation 'Self' which in this passage is applied to the Sat in its relation to the entire world, sentient or non-sentient, is in no way appropriate to the Pradhâna. We therefore conclude that, as the highest Self is the Self of fire, water, and earth also, the words fire, &c. (in the passages stating that fire, &c. thought) denote the highest Self only. This conclusion agrees with the text 'Let me enter into these three beings with this living Self, and evolve names and forms,' for this text implies that fire, water, &c. possess substantial being and definite names only through the highest Self having entered into them. The thought ascribed in the text to fire, water, &c. hence is thought in the proper sense, and the hypothesis that, owing to its connexion with these latter texts, the thought predicated of 'Being' ('*it* thought,' &c.) should be thought in a figurative sense only thus lapses altogether.

The next following Sûtra confirms the same view.

7. Because release is taught of him who takes his stand on it.

*S*vetaketu, who is desirous of final release, is at first—by means of the clause 'Thou art that'—instructed to meditate on himself as having his Self in that which truly is; and thereupon the passage 'for him there is delay' only as long as 'I shall not be released, then I shall be united' teaches that for a man taking his stand upon that teaching there will be Release, i.e. union with Brahman—which is delayed only until this mortal body falls away. If, on the other hand, the text would teach that the non-intelligent Pradhâna is the general cause, it could not possibly teach that meditation on this Pradhâna being a man's Self is the means towards his Release. A man taking his stand on such meditation rather would on death be united with a non-sentient principle, according to the scriptural saying, 'According as his thought is in this world, so will he be when he has departed this life' (*Kh.* Up. III, 14, 1). And Scripture, which is more loving than even a thousand parents, cannot possibly teach such union with the Non-sentient, which is acknowledged to be the cause of all the assaults of suffering in its threefold form. Moreover, those who hold the theory of the Pradhâna being the cause of the world do not themselves maintain that he who takes his stand upon the Pradhâna attains final release.

The Pradhâna is not the cause of the world for the following reason also:

8. And because there is no statement of its having to be set aside.

If the word 'Sat' denoted the Pradhâna as the cause of the world, we should expect the text to teach that the idea of having his Self in that 'Sat' should be set aside by *S*vetaketu as desirous of Release; for that idea would be contrary to Release. So far from teaching this, the text, however, directly inculcates that notion in the words 'Thou art that.'—The next Sûtra adds a further reason.

9. And on account of the contradiction of the initial statement.

The Pradhâna's being the cause of the world would imply a contradiction of the initial statement, viz. that through the knowledge of one thing all things are to be known. Now, on the principle of the non-difference of cause and effect, this initial statement can only be fulfilled in that way that through the knowledge of the 'Sat,' which is the cause, there is known the entire world, whether sentient or non-sentient, which constitutes the effect. But if the Pradhâna were the cause, the aggregate of sentient beings could not be known through it—for sentient beings are not the effect of a non-sentient principle, and there would thus arise a contradiction.—The next Sûtra supplies a further reason.

10. On account of (the individual soul) going to the Self.

With reference to the 'Sat' the text says, 'Learn from me the true nature of sleep. When a man sleeps here, he becomes united with the Sat, he is gone to his own (Self). Therefore they say he sleeps (svapiti), because he is gone to his own (sva-apîta)' (*Kh.* Up. VI, 8, 1). This text designates the soul in the state of deep sleep as having entered into, or being merged or reabsorbed in, the Self. By reabsorption we understand something being merged in its cause. Now the non-intelligent Pradhâna cannot be the cause of the intelligent soul; hence the soul's going to its Self can only mean its going to *the*, i.e. the universal, Self. The term 'individual soul' (*g*îva) denotes Brahman in so far as having an intelligent substance for its body, Brahman itself constituting the Self; as we learn from the text referring to the distinction of names and forms. This Brahman, thus called *g*îva, is in the state of deep sleep, no less than in that of a general pralaya, free from the investment of names and forms, and is then designated as mere 'Being' (sat); as the text says, 'he is then united with the Sat.' As the soul is in the state of deep sleep free from the investment of name and form, and invested by the intelligent Self only, another text says with reference to the same state, 'Embraced by the intelligent Self he knows nothing that is without, nothing that is within' (B*ri*. Up. IV, 3, 21). Up to the time of final release there arise in the soul invested by name and form the cognitions of objects different from itself. During deep sleep the souls divest themselves of names and forms, and are embraced by the 'Sat' only; but in the waking state they again invest themselves with names and forms, and thus bear corresponding distinctive names and forms. This, other scriptural texts also distinctly declare, 'When a man lying in deep sleep sees no dream whatever, he becomes one with that prâ*n*a alone;—from that Self the prâ*n*as proceed, each towards its place' (**Kau. Up. III, 3**); 'Whatever these creatures are here, whether a lion or a wolf or a boar or a gnat or a mosquito, that they become again' (*Kh.* Up. VI, 9, 3).—Hence the term 'Sat' denotes the highest Brahman, the all-knowing highest Lord, the highest Person. Thus the V*ri*ttikâra also says, 'Then he becomes united with the Sat—this is proved by (all creatures) entering into it and coming back out of it.' And Scripture also says, 'Embraced by the intelligent Self.'—The next Sûtra gives an additional reason.

11. On account of the uniformity of view.

'In the beginning the Self was all this; there was nothing else whatsoever thinking. He thought, shall I send forth worlds? He sent forth these worlds' (Ait. Âr. II, 4, 1, 1); 'From that Self sprang ether, from ether air, from air fire, from fire water, from water earth' (Taitt. Up. II, 1); 'From this great Being were breathed forth the *Ri*g-veda,' &c.—These and similar texts referring to the creation have all the same purport: they all teach us that the Supreme Lord is the cause of the world. We therefore conclude that in the *Kh.* passage also the Sat, which is said to be the cause of the world, is the Supreme Lord.

12. And because it is directly stated in Scripture.

The text of the same Upanishad directly declares that the being denoted by the word 'Sat' evolves, as the universal Self, names and forms; is all-knowing, all-powerful, all-embracing; is free from all evil, &c.; realises all its wishes and purposes. 'Let me, entering those beings with this living Self, evolve names and forms' (*Kh.* Up. VI, 3, 2); 'All these creatures have their root in the Sat, they dwell in the Sat, they rest in the Sat' (VI, 8, 4); 'All this has that for its Self; it is the True, it is the Self' (VI, 8, 7);

'Whatever there is of him here in the world, and whatever is not, all that is contained within it' (VIII, 1, 3); 'In it all desires are contained. It is the Self free from sin, free from old age, from death and grief, from hunger and thirst, whose wishes come true, whose purposes come true' (VIII, 1, 5).—And analogously other scriptural texts, 'Of him there is no master in the world, no ruler; not even a sign of him. He is the cause, the lord of the lords of the organs, and there is of him neither parent nor lord' (*S*vet. Up. VI, 9). 'The wise one who, having created all forms and having given them names, is calling them by those names' (Taitt. Âr. III, 12, 7); 'He who entered within is the ruler of all beings, the Self of all' (Taitt. Âr. III, 24); 'The Self of all, the refuge, the ruler of all, the Lord of the souls' (Mahânâr. Up. XI); 'Whatsoever is seen or heard in this world, inside or outside, pervading that all Nârâya*n*a abides' (Mahânâr. Up. XI); 'He is the inner Self of all beings, free from all evil, the divine, the only god Nârâya*n*a.'—These and other texts which declare the world to have sprung from the highest Lord, can in no way be taken as establishing the Pradhâna. Hence it remains a settled conclusion that the highest Person, Nârâya*n*a, free from all shadow of imperfection, &c., is the single cause of the whole Universe, and is that Brahman which these Sûtras point out as the object of enquiry.

For the same reasons the theory of a Brahman, which is nothing but non-differenced intelligence, must also be considered as refuted by the Sûtrakâra, with the help of the scriptural texts quoted; for those texts prove that the Brahman, which forms the object of enquiry, possesses attributes such as thinking, and so on, in their real literal sense. On the theory, on the other hand, of a Brahman that is nothing but distinctionless intelligence even the witnessing function of consciousness would be unreal. The Sûtras propose as the object of enquiry Brahman as known from the Vedânta-texts, and thereupon teach that Brahman is intelligent (Sû. I, 1, 5 ff.) To be intelligent means to possess the quality of intelligence: a being devoid of the quality of thought would not differ in nature from the

Pradhâna. Further, on the theory of Brahman being mere non-differenced light it would be difficult to prove that Brahman is self-luminous. For by light we understand that particular thing which renders itself, as well as other things, capable of becoming the object of ordinary thought and speech; but as a thing devoid of all difference does not, of course, possess these two characteristics it follows that it is as devoid of intelligence as a pot may be.—Let it then be assumed that although a thing devoid of all distinction does not actually possess these characteristics, yet it has the potentiality of possessing them!—But if it possesses the attribute of potentiality, it is clear that you abandon your entire theory of a substance devoid of all distinction!—Let us then admit, on the authority of Scripture, that the universal substance possesses this one distinguishing attribute of self-luminousness.—Well, in that case you must of course admit, on the same authority, all those other qualities also which Scripture vouches for, such as all-knowingness, the possession of all powers, and so on.—Moreover,. potentiality means capability to produce certain special effects, and hence can be determined on the ground of those special effects only. But if there are no means of knowing these particular effects, there are also no means of cognising potentiality.—And those who hold the theory of a substance devoid of all difference, have not even means of proof for their substance; for as we have shown before, Perception, Inference, Scripture, and one's own consciousness, are all alike in so far as having for their objects things marked by difference.—It therefore remains a settled conclusion that the Brahman to be known is nothing else but the highest Person capable of the thought 'of becoming many' by manifesting himself in a world comprising manifold sentient and non-sentient creatures.—Here terminates the adhikara*n*a of 'seeing.'

So far the Sûtras have declared that the Brahman which forms the object of enquiry is different from the non-intelligent Pradhâna, which is merely an object of fruition for intelligent beings. They now proceed to show that Brahman—which is antagonistic to all evil and constituted by supreme bliss—is different from the individual soul, which is subject to karman, whether that soul be in its purified state or in the impure state that is due to its immersion in the ocean of manifold and endless sufferings, springing from the soul's contact with Prak*ri*ti (Pradhâna).

13. The Self consisting of Bliss (is the highest Self) on account of multiplication.

We read in the text of the Taittirîyas, 'Different from this Self, which consists of Understanding, is the other inner Self which consists of bliss' (Taitt. Up. II, 5).—Here the doubt arises whether the Self consisting of bliss be the highest Self, which is different from the inner Self subject to bondage and release, and termed '*g*îva' (i. e. living self or individual soul), or whether it be that very inner Self, i. e. the *g*îva.—It *is* that inner Self, the Pûrvapakshin contends. For the text says 'of that this, i. e. the Self consisting of bliss, is the *s*ârîra Self'; and *s*ârîra means that which is joined to a body, in other words, the so-called *g*îva.—But, an objection is raised, the text enumerates the different Selfs, beginning with the Self consisting of bliss, to the end that man may obtain the bliss of Brahman. which was, at the outset, stated to be the cause of the world (II, 1), and in the end teaches that the Self consisting of bliss is the cause of the world (II, 6). And that the cause of the world is the all-knowing Lord, since Scripture says of him that 'he thought,' we have already explained.—That cause of the world, the Pûrvapakshin rejoins, is not different from the *g*îva; for in the text of the *Kh*ândogyas that Being which first is described as the creator of the world is exhibited, in two passages, in co-ordination with the *g*îva ('having entered into them with that living Self' and 'Thou art that, O *S*vetaketu'). And the purport of co-ordination is to express oneness of being, as when we say, 'This person here is that Devadatta we knew before.' And creation preceded by thought can very well be ascribed to an intelligent *g*îva. The connexion of the whole Taittirîya-text then is as follows. In the introductory clause, 'He who knows Brahman attains the

Highest,' the true nature of the *g*îva, free from all connexion with matter, is referred to as something to be attained; and of this nature a definition is given in the words, 'The True, knowledge, the Infinite is Brahman.' The attainment of the *g*îva in this form is what constitutes Release, in agreement with the text, 'So long as he is in the body he cannot get free from pleasure and pain; but when he is free from the body then neither pleasure nor pain touches him' (*Kh.* Up. VIII, 12, 1). This true nature of the Self, free from all avidyâ, which the text begins by presenting as an object to be attained, is thereupon declared to be the Self consisting of bliss. In order to lead up to this—just as a man points out to another the moon by first pointing out the branch of a tree near which the moon is to be seen—the text at first refers to the body ('Man consists of food'); next to the vital breath with its five modifications which is within the body and supports it; then to the manas within the vital breath; then to the buddhi within the manas—'the Self consisting of breath'; 'the Self consisting of mind' (manas); 'the Self consisting of understanding' (vi*gñ*âna). Having thus gradually led up to the *g*îva, the text finally points out the latter, which is the innermost of all ('Different from that is the inner Self which consists of bliss'), and thus completes the series of Selfs one inside the other. We hence conclude that the Self consisting of bliss is that same *g*îva-self which was at the outset pointed out as the Brahman to be attained.—But the clause immediately following, 'Brahman is the tail, the support (of the Self of bliss'), indicates that Brahman is something different from the Self of bliss!—By no means (the Pûrvapakshin rejoins). Brahman is, owing to its different characteristics, there compared to an animal body, and head, wings, and tail are ascribed to it, just as in a preceding clause the body consisting of food had also been imagined as having head, wings, and tail—these members not being something different from the body, but the body itself. Joy, satisfaction, great satisfaction, bliss, are imagined as the members, non-different from it, of Brahman consisting of bliss, and of them all the unmixed bliss-constituted

Brahman is said to be the tail or support. If Brahman were something different from the Self consisting of bliss, the text would have continued, 'Different from this Self consisting of bliss is the other inner Self—Brahman.' But there is no such continuation. The connexion of the different clauses stands as follows: After Brahman has been introduced as the topic of the section ('He who knows Brahman attains the Highest'), and defined as different in nature from everything else ('The True, knowledge'), the text designates it by the term 'Self,' &c. ('From that Self sprang ether'), and then, in order to make it clear that Brahman is the innermost Self of all, enumerates the prâ*n*a-maya and so on—designating them in succession as more and more inward Selfs—, and finally leads up to the ânandamaya as the innermost Self('Different from this, &c., is the Self consisting of bliss'). From all which it appears that the term 'Self' up to the end denotes the Brahman mentioned at the beginning.—But, in immediate continuation of the clause, 'Brahman is the tail, the support,' the text exhibits the following *s*loka: 'Non-existing becomes he who views Brahman as non-existing; who knows Brahman as existing, him we know as himself existing.' Here the existence and non-existence of the Self are declared to depend on the knowledge and non-knowledge of Brahman, not of the Self consisting of bliss. Now no doubt can possibly arise as to the existence or non-existence of this latter Self, which, in the form of joy, satisfaction, &c., is known to every one. Hence the *s*loka cannot refer to that Self, and hence Brahman is different from that Self.—This objection, the Pûrvapakshin rejoins, is unfounded. In the earlier parts of the chapter we have corresponding *s*lokas, each of them following on a preceding clause that refers to the tail or support of a particular Self: in the case, e.g. of the Self consisting of food, we read, 'This is the tail, the support,' and then comes the *s*loka, 'From food are produced all creatures,' &c. Now it is evident that all these *s*lokas are meant to set forth not only what had been called 'tail,' but the entire Self concerned (Self of food, Self of breath, &c.); and from this it follows that also the *s*loka, 'Non-existing becomes he,' does not refer to the 'tail' only as something other than the Self of bliss, but to the entire Self of bliss. And there may very well be a doubt with regard to the knowledge or non-knowledge of the existence of that Self consisting of unlimited bliss. On your view also the circumstance of Brahman which forms the tail not being known is due to its being of the nature of limitless bliss. And should it be said that the Self of bliss cannot be Brahman because Brahman does not possess a head and other members; the answer is that Brahman also does not possess the quality of being a tail or support, and that hence Brahman cannot be a tail.—Let it then be said that the expression, 'Brahman is the tail,' is merely figurative, in so far as Brahman is the substrate of all things imagined through avidyâ!—But, the Pûrvapakshin rejoins, we may as well assume that the ascription to Brahman of joy, as its head and so on, is also merely figurative, meant to illustrate the nature of Brahman, i.e. the Self of bliss as free from all pain. To speak of Brahman or the Self as consisting of bliss has thus the purpose of separating from all pain and grief that which in a preceding clause ('The True, knowledge, the Infinite is Brahman') had already been separated from all changeful material things. As applied to Brahman (or the Self), whose nature is nothing but absolute bliss, the term 'ânandamaya' therefore has to be interpreted as meaning nothing more than 'ânanda'; just as prâ*n*amaya means prâ*n*a.

The outcome of all this is that the term 'ânandamaya' denotes the true essential nature—which is nothing but absolute uniform bliss—of the *g*îva that appears as distinguished by all the manifold individualising forms which are the figments of Nescience. The Self of bliss is the *g*îva or pratyag-âtman, i. e. the individual soul.

Against this primâ facie view the Sûtrakâra contends that the Self consisting of bliss is the highest Self 'on account of multiplication.'—The section which begins with the words, 'This is an examination of bliss,' and terminates with the *s*loka, 'from whence all speech turns back' (Taitt. Up. II, 8), arrives at bliss, supreme and not to be surpassed, by successively multiplying inferior stages of bliss by a hundred; now such supreme bliss cannot possibly belong to the individual soul which enjoys only a small share of very limited happiness, mixed with endless pain and grief; and therefore clearly indicates, as its abode, the highest Self, which differs from all other Selfs in so far as being radically opposed to all evil and of an unmixed blessed nature. The text says, 'Different from this Self consisting of understanding (vig*ñ*âna) there is the inner Self consisting of bliss.' Now that which consists of understanding (vig*ñ*âna) is the individual soul (*g*îva), not the internal organ (buddhi) only; for the formative element, 'maya,' ('consisting of'; in vig*ñ*ânamaya) indicates a difference (between vig*ñ*âna and vig*ñ*ânamaya). The term 'prâ*n*amaya' ('consisting of breath') we explain to mean 'prâ*n*a' only, because no other explanation is possible; but as vig*ñ*ânamaya may be explained as *g*îva, we have no right to neglect 'maya' as unmeaning. And this interpretation is quite suitable, as the soul in the states of bondage and release alike is a 'knowing' subject. That moreover even in 'prâ*n*amaya,' and so on, the affix 'maya' may be taken as having a meaning will be shown further on.—But how is it then that in the *s*loka which refers to the vig*ñ*ânamaya, 'Understanding (vig*ñ*âna) performs the sacrifice,' the term 'vig*ñ*âna' only is used?—The essential nature, we reply, of the knowing subject is suitably called 'knowledge,' and this term is transferred to the knowing subject itself which is defined as possessing that nature. For we generally see that words which denote attributes defining the essential nature of a thing also convey the notion of the essential nature of the thing itself. This also accounts for the fact that the *s*loka ('Vig*ñ*âna performs the sacrifice, it performs all sacred acts') speaks of vig*ñ*âna as being the agent in sacrifices and so on; the buddhi alone could not be called an agent. For this reason the text does not ascribe agency to the other Selfs (the prâ*n*amaya and so on) which are mentioned before the vig*ñ*ânamaya; for they are non-intelligent instruments of intelligence, and the latter only can be an agent. With the same view the text further on (II, 6), distinguishing the intelligent and the non-intelligent by means of their different characteristic attributes, says in the end 'knowledge and non-knowledge,' meaning thereby that which possesses the attribute of knowledge and that which does not. An analogous case is met with in the so-called antaryâmi-brâhma*n*a (B*ri*. Up. III, 7). There the Kâ*n*vas read, 'He who dwells in knowledge' (vi*gñ*âna; III, 7, 16), but instead of this the Mâdhyandinas read 'he who dwells in the Self,' and so make clear that what the Kâ*n*vas designate as 'knowledge' really is the knowing Self.—That the word vi*gñ*âna, although denoting the knowing Self, yet has a neuter termination, is meant to denote it as something substantial. We hence conclude that he who is different from the Self consisting of knowledge, i. e. the individual Self, is the highest Self which consists of bliss.

It is true indeed that the *s*loka, 'Knowledge performs the sacrifice,' directly mentions knowledge only, not the knowing Self; all the same we have to understand that what is meant is the latter, who is referred to in the clause, 'different from this is the inner Self which consists of knowledge.' This conclusion is supported by the *s*loka referring to the Self which consists of food (II, 2); for that *s*loka refers to food only, 'From food are produced all creatures,' &c., all the same the preceding clause 'this man consists of the essence of food' does not refer to food, but to an effect of it which consists of food. Considering all this the Sûtrakâra himself in a subsequent Sûtra (I, 1, 18) bases his view on the declaration, in the scriptural text, of difference.—We now turn to the assertion, made by the Pûrvapakshin, that the cause of the world is not different from the individual soul because in two *Kh*ândogya passages it is exhibited in co-ordination with the latter ('having entered into them with this living Self,' 'Thou art that'); and that hence the introductory clause of the Taitt. passage ('He who knows Brahman reaches the Highest') refers to the individual soul—which further on is called 'consisting of bliss,' because it is free from all that is not pleasure.—This view cannot be upheld; for although the individual soul is intelligent, it is incapable of producing through its volition this infinite and wonderful Universe—a process described in texts such as 'It thought, may I be many, may I grow forth.—It sent forth fire,' &c. That even the released soul is unequal to such 'world business' as creation, two later Sûtras will expressly declare. But, if you deny that Brahman, the cause of the world, is identical with the individual soul, how then do you account for the co-ordination in which the two appear in the *Kh*ândogya texts?—How, we ask in return, can Brahman, the cause of all, free from all shadow of imperfection, omniscient, omnipotent, &c. &c., be one with the individual soul, all whose activities—whether it be thinking, or winking of an eye, or anything else—depend on karman, which implies endless suffering of various kind? —If you reply that this is possible if one of two things is unreal, we ask—which then do you mean to be unreal? Brahman's connexion with what is evil?—or its essential nature, owing to which it is absolutely good and antagonistic to all evil?—You will perhaps reply that, owing to the fact of Brahman, which is absolutely good and antagonistic to all evil, being the substrate of beginningless Nescience, there presents itself the false appearance of its being connected with evil. But there you maintain what is contradictory. On the one side there is Brahman's absolute perfection and antagonism to all evil; on the other it is the substrate of Nescience, and thereby the substrate of a false appearance which is involved in endless pain; for to be connected with evil means to be the substrate of Nescience and the appearance of suffering which is produced thereby. Now it is a contradiction to say that Brahman is connected with all this and at the same time antagonistic to it!—Nor can we allow you to say that there is no real contradiction because that appearance is something false. For whatever is false belongs to that group of things contrary to man's true interest, for the destruction of which the Vedânta-texts are studied. To be connected with what is hurtful to man, and to be absolutely perfect and antagonistic to all evil is self-contradictory.—But, our adversary now rejoins, what after all are we to do? The holy text at first clearly promises that through the cognition of one thing everything will be known ('by which that which is not heard *is* heard,' &c., *Kh.* Up. VI, 1, 3); thereupon declares that Brahman is the sole cause of the world ('Being only this was in the beginning'), and possesses exalted qualities such as the power of realising its intentions ('it thought, may I be many'); and then finally, by means of the co-ordination, 'Thou art that,' intimates that Brahman is one with the individual soul, which we know to be subject to endless suffering! Nothing therefore is left to us but the hypothesis that Brahman is the substrate of Nescience and all that springs from it!—Not even for the purpose, we reply, of making sense of Scripture may we assume what in itself is senseless and contradictory!—Let us then say that Brahman's connexion with evil is real, and its absolute perfection unreal!—Scripture, we reply, aims at comforting the soul afflicted by the assaults of threefold pain, and now, according to you, it teaches that the assaults of suffering are real, while its essential perfection and happiness are unreal figments, due to error! This is excellent comfort indeed!—To avoid these difficulties let us then assume that both aspects of Brahman—viz. on the one hand its entering into the distressful condition of individual souls other than non-differenced intelligence, and on the other its being the cause of the world, endowed with all perfections, &c.—are alike unreal!—Well, we reply, we do not exactly admire the depth of your insight into the connected meaning of texts. The promise that through the knowledge of one thing everything will be known can certainly not be fulfilled if everything is false, for in that case there exists nothing that could be known. In so far as the cognition of one thing has something real for its object, and the cognition of all things is of the same kind, and moreover is comprised in the cognition of one thing; in so far it can be said that everything is known through one thing being known. Through the cognition of the real shell we do not cognise the unreal silver of which the shell is the substrate.—Well, our adversary resumes, let it then be said that the meaning of the declaration that through the cognition of one thing everything is to be known is that only non-differenced Being is real, while everything else is unreal.—If this were so, we rejoin, the text would not say, 'by which the non-heard is heard—, the non-known is known'; for the meaning of this is, 'by which when heard and known' (*not* 'known as false') 'the non-heard is heard,' &c. Moreover, if the meaning were that only the one non-differenced substance understood to be the cause of the world is real, the illustrative instance, 'As by one lump of clay everything made of clay is known,' would not be suitable; for what is meant there is that through the cognition of the (real) lump of clay its (real) effects are known. Nor must you say that in the illustrative instance also the unreality of the effect is set forth; for as the person to be informed is not in any way convinced at the outset that things made of clay are unreal, like the snake imagined in the rope, it is impossible that such unreality should be referred to as if it were something well known (and the clause, 'as by one lump of clay,' &c., undoubtedly *does* refer to something well known), in order to render the initial assertion plausible. And we are not aware of any means of knowledge—assisted or non-assisted by ratiocination—that would prove the non-reality of things effected, previous to the cognition produced by texts such as 'That art thou'; a point which will be discussed at length under II, 1.—'Being only this was in the beginning, one, without a second'; 'it thought, may I be many, may I grow forth; it sent forth fire'; 'Let me now enter those three beings with this living Self and evolve names and forms'; 'All these creatures, my son, have their root in the True, they dwell in the True, they rest in the True,' &c.; these passages declare in succession that that which really is is the Self of this world; that previous to creation there is no distinction of names and forms; that for the creation of the world Brahman, termed 'the True' (or 'Real'), requires no other operative cause but itself; that at the time of creation it forms a resolution, possible to itself only, of making itself manifold in the form of endless movable and immovable things; that in accordance with this resolution there takes place a creation, proceeding in a particular order, of an infinite number of manifold beings; that by Brahman entering into all non-intelligent beings with the living soul—which has its Self in Brahman—there takes place an evolution, infinite in extent, of all their particular names and forms; and that everything different from Brahman has its root and abode in that, is moved by that, lives by that, rests on that. All the different points—to be learned from Scripture only—which are here set forth agree with what numerous other scriptural texts teach about Brahman, viz. that it is free from all evil, devoid of all imperfection, all-knowing, all-powerful; that all its wishes and purposes realise themselves; that it is the cause of all bliss; that it enjoys bliss not to be surpassed. To maintain then that the word 'that,' which refers back to the Brahman mentioned before, i.e. a Brahman possessing infinite attributes, should aim at conveying instruction about a substance devoid of all attributes, is as unmeaning as the incoherent talk of a madman.

The word 'thou' again denotes the individual soul as distinguished by its implication in the course of transmigratory existence, and the proper sense of this term also would have to be abandoned if it were meant to suggest a substance devoid of all distinctions. And that, in the case of a being consisting of non-differenced light, obscuration by Nescience would be tantamount to complete destruction, we have already explained above.—All this being thus, your interpretation would involve that the proper meaning of the two words 'that' and 'thou'—which refer to one thing—would have to be abandoned, and both words would have to be taken in an implied sense only.

Against this the Pûrvapakshin now may argue as follows. Several words which are applied to one thing are meant to express one sense, and as this is not possible in so far as the words connote different attributes, this part of their connotation becomes inoperative, and they denote only the unity of one substance; implication (laksha*n*â), therefore, does not take place. When we say 'blue (is) (the) lotus' we employ two words with the intention of expressing the unity of one thing, and hence do not aim at expressing a duality of attributes, viz. the quality of blueness and the generic character of a lotus. If this latter point was aimed at, it would follow that the sentence would convey the oneness of the two aspects of the thing, viz. its being blue and its being a lotus; but this is not possible, for the thing (denoted by the two terms) is not characterised by (the denotation of) the word 'lotus,' in so far as itself characterised by blueness; for this would imply a reciprocal inherence (samavâya) of class-characteristics and quality [1]. What the co-ordination of the two words conveys is, therefore, only the oneness of a substance characterised by the quality of blueness, and at the same time by the class attributes of a lotus. In the same way, when we say 'this (person is) that Devadatta' the co-ordination of the words cannot possibly mean that Devadatta in so far as distinguished by his connexion with a past time and a distant place is one with Devadatta in so far as distinguished by his connexion with the present time and a near place; what it means to express is only that there is oneness on the part of a personal substance—which substance is characterised by connexion with both places and moments of time. It is true indeed that when we at first hear the one word 'blue' we form the idea of the attribute of blueness, while, after having apprehended the relation of co-ordination (expressed in 'blue is the lotus'), this idea no longer presents itself, for this would imply a contradiction; but all the same 'implication' does not take place. The essence of co-ordination consists, in all cases, therein that it suppresses the distinguishing elements in the words co-ordinated. And as thus our explanation cannot be charged with 'implication,' it cannot be objected to.

All this, we rejoin, is unfounded. What the words in all sentences whatsoever aim at conveying is only a particular connexion of the things known to be denoted by those words. Words such as 'blue,' standing in co-ordination with others, express that some matter possessing the attri-

[1] I. e. we should not in that case be able to decide whether the quality (i. e., here, the blueness) inheres in the class (i. e., here, the lotus), or vice versâ.

bute of blueness, &c., as known from the ordinary use of language, is connected with some other matter. When, e.g., somebody says 'bring the blue lotus,' a thing is brought which possesses the attribute of blueness. And when we are told that 'a herd of elephants excited with passion lives in the Vindhya-forest,' we again understand that what is meant is something possessing several attributes denoted by several words. Analogously we have to understand, as the thing intimated by Vedânta-texts in the form of co-ordination, Brahman as possessing such and such attributes. —It is an error to assume that, where a sentence aims at setting forth attributes, one attribute is to be taken as qualifying the thing in so far as qualified by another attribute; the case rather is that the thing itself is equally qualified by all attributes. For co-ordination means the application, to one thing, of several words having different reasons of application; and the effect of co-ordination is that one and the same thing, because being connected—positively or negatively—with some attribute other than that which is conveyed by one word, is also known through other words. As e.g. when it is said that 'Devadatta (is) dark-complexioned, young, reddish-eyed, not stupid, not poor, of irreproachable character.' Where two co-ordinate words express two attributes which cannot exist combined in one thing, one of the two words is to be taken in a secondary sense, while the other retains its primary meaning, as e.g. in the case of the sentence, 'The Vâhîka man is an ox.' But in the case of the 'blue lotus' and the like, where there is nothing contradictory in the connexion of the two attributes with one thing, co-ordination expresses the fact of one thing being characterised by two attributes. —Possibly our opponent will here make the following remark. A thing in so far as defined by its correlation to some one attribute is something different from the thing in so far as defined by its correlation to some second attribute; hence, even if there is equality of case affixes (as in 'nîlam utpalam'), the words co-ordinated are incapable of expressing oneness, and cannot, therefore, express the oneness of a thing qualified by several attributes; not any more than the juxtaposition of two words such as 'jar' and 'cloth'—both having the same case-ending—can prove that these two things are one. A statement of co-ordination, therefore, rather aims at expressing the oneness of a thing in that way that it presents to the mind the essential nature of the thing by means of (words denoting) its attributes.—This would be so, we reply, if it were only the fact of a thing's standing in correlation to two attributes that is in the way of its unity. But this is not the case; for what stands in the way of such unity is the fact of there being several attributes which are not capable of being combined in one thing. Such incapability is, in the case of the generic character of a jar and that of a piece of cloth, proved by other means of knowledge; but there is no contradiction between a thing being blue and its being a lotus; not any more than there is between a man and the stick or the earrings he wears, or than there is between the colour, taste, smell, &c., of one and the same thing. Not only is there no contradiction, but it is this very fact of one thing possessing two attributes which makes possible co-ordination—the essence of which is that, owing to a difference of causes of application, several words express one and the same thing. For if there were nothing but essential unity of being, what reason would there be for the employment of several words? If the purport of the attributes were, not to intimate their connexion with the thing, but merely to suggest the thing itself, one attribute would suffice for such suggestion, and anything further would be meaningless. If, on the other hand, it were assumed that the use of a further 'suggestive' attribute is to bring out a difference of aspect in the thing suggested, such difference of aspect would imply differentiation in the thing (which you maintain to be free from all difference).—Nor is there any shade even of 'implication' in the judgment, 'This person is that Devadatta'; for there is absolutely no contradiction between the past Devadatta, who was connected with some distant place, and the present Devadatta, who is connected with the place before us. For this very reason those who maintain the permanency of things prove the oneness of a thing related to two moments of time on the basis of the judgment of recognition ('this is that'); if there really were a contradiction between the two representations it would follow that all things are (not permanent but) momentary only. The fact is that the contradiction involved in one thing being connected with two places is removed by the difference of the correlative moments of time. We therefore hold to the conclusion that co-ordinated words denote one thing qualified by the possession of several attributes.

For this very reason the Vedic passage, 'He buys the Soma by means of a cow one year old, of a tawny colour, with reddish-brown eyes' (aru*n*ayâ, ekahâyanyâ, piṅgâkshyâ), must be understood to enjoin that the purchase is to be effected by means of a cow one year old, possessing the attributes of tawny colour, &c. This point is discussed Pû. Mî. Sû. III, 1, 12.—The Pûrvapakshin there argues as follows: We admit that the word 'aru*n*ayâ' ('by means of a tawny one') denotes the quality of tawniness inclusive of the thing possessing that quality; for qualities as well as generic character exist only in so far as being modes of substances. But it is not possible to restrict tawny colour to connexion with a cow one year old, for the injunction of two different things (which would result from such restriction; and which would necessitate the sentence to be construed as—) 'He buys by means of a cow one year old, and that a red one' is not permissible [1]. We must therefore break up the sentence into two, one of which is constituted by the one word 'aru*n*ayâ'—this word expressing that tawny colour extends equally to all the substances enjoined in that section (as instrumental towards the end of the sacrifice). And the use of the feminine case-termination of the word is merely meant to suggest a special instance (viz. the cow) of all the things, of whatever gender, which are enjoined in that section. Tawniness must not therefore

[1] For it would imply so-called vâkyabheda, 'split of the sentence,' which arises when one injunctory clause is made to enjoin two different things.

be restricted to the cow one year old only.—Of this pûrvapaksha the Sûtra disposes in the following words: 'There being oneness of sense, and hence connexion of substance and quality with one action, there is restriction.'—The fact that the two words 'aru*n*ayâ' and 'ekahâyanyâ' —which denote a substance, viz. a cow one year old, distinguished by the quality of possessing tawny colour—stand in co-ordination establishes that they have one sense; and as the substance, viz. the cow, and the quality, viz. tawny colour—which the word 'aru*n*ayâ' denotes as standing in the relation of distinguishing attribute and thing distinguished thereby—can thus, without any contradiction, be connected with the one action called 'the buying of the Soma,' tawny colour *is* restricted to the cow one year old which is instrumental with regard to the purchase. If the connexion of tawniness with the action of buying were to be determined from syntactical connexion—in the same way as there is made out the connexion of the cow one year old with that action—then the injunctory sentence would indeed enjoin two matters (and this would be objectionable). But such is not the case; for the one word 'aru*n*ayâ' denotes a substance characterised by the quality of tawniness, and the co-ordination in which 'aru*n*ayâ' stands to 'ekahâyanyâ' makes us apprehend merely that the thing characterised by tawniness also is one year old, but does not make a special statement as to the connexion of that quality with the thing. For the purport of co-ordination is the unity of a thing distinguished by attributes; according to the definition that the application to one thing of several words possessing different reasons of application, constitutes co-ordination. For the same reason, the syntactical unity (ekavâkyatvam) of sentences such as 'the cloth is red' follows from all the words referring to one thing. The function of the syntactical collocation is to express the connexion of the cloth with the action of being; the connexion of the red colour (with the cloth) on the other hand is denoted by the word 'red' only. And what is ascertained from co-ordination (sâmânâdhikara*n*ya) is only that the cloth is a substance to which a certain colour belongs.

The whole matter may, without any contradiction, be conceived as follows. Several words—having either the affixes of the oblique cases or that of the nominative case—which denote one or two or several qualities, present to the mind the idea of that which is characterised by those qualities, and their co-ordination intimates that the thing characterised by all those attributes is one only; and the entire sentence finally expresses the connexion in which the thing with its attributes stands to the action denoted by the verb. This may be illustrated by various sentences exhibiting the co-ordination of words possessing different case-endings, as e.g. 'There stands Devadatta, a young man of a darkish complexion, with red eyes, wearing earrings and carrying a stick' (where all the words standing in apposition to Devadatta have the nominative termination); 'Let him make a stage curtain by means of a white cloth' (where 'white' and 'cloth' have instrumental case-endings), &c. &c. We may further illustrate the entire relation of co-ordinated words to the action by means of the following two examples: 'Let him boil rice in the cooking-pot by means of firewood': here we take in simultaneously the idea of an action distinguished by its connexion with several things. If we now consider the following amplified sentence, 'Let a skilful cook prepare, in a vessel of even shape, boiled rice mixed with milk, by means of sticks of dry khâdira wood,' we find that each thing connected with the action is denoted by an aggregate of co-ordinated words; but as soon as each thing is apprehended, it is at one and the same moment conceived as something distinguished by several attributes, and as such connects itself with the action expressed by the verb. In all this there is no contradiction whatever.—We must further object to the assertion that a word denoting a quality which stands in a sentence that has already mentioned a substance denotes the quality only (exclusive of the substance so qualified), and that hence the word 'aru*n*ayâ' also denotes a quality only. The fact is that neither in ordinary nor in Vedic language we ever meet with a word which—denoting a quality and at the same time standing in co-ordination with a word denoting a substance—denotes a *mere* quality. Nor is it correct to say that a quality-word occurring in a sentence which has already mentioned a substance denotes a mere quality: for in a sentence such as 'the cloth (is) white,' where a substance is mentioned in the first place, the quality-word clearly denotes (not mere whiteness but) something which possesses the quality of whiteness. When, on the other hand, we have a collocation of words such as 'pa*t*asya *s*ukla*h*' ('of the cloth'—gen.; 'white' nom.), the idea of a cloth distinguished by whiteness does not arise; but this is due not to the fact of the substance being mentioned first, but to the fact of the two words exhibiting different case-terminations. As soon as we add to those two words an appropriate third one, e.g. 'bhâga*h*' (so that the whole means 'The white part of a cloth'), the co-ordination of two words with the same case-termination gives rise to the idea of a thing distinguished by the attribute of whiteness.—Nor can we agree to the contention that, as the buying of the Soma is exclusively concluded by the cow one year old (as instrumental in the purchase), the quality of tawniness (denoted by the word 'aru*n*ayâ') cannot connect itself with the action expressed by the verb; for a word that denotes a quality and stands in co-ordination with a word denoting a substance which has no qualities opposed in nature to that quality, denotes a quality abiding in that substance, and thus naturally connects itself with the action expressed by the verb. And since, as shown, the quality of tawniness connects itself with its substance (the cow) on the mere basis of the form of the words, it is wrong (on the part of the Pûrvapakshin to abandon this natural connexion and) to establish their connexion on the ground of their being otherwise incapable of serving as means of the purchase.

All this confirms our contention, viz. that the co-ordination of 'thou' and 'that' must be understood to express oneness, without, at the same time, there being given up the different attributes denoted by the two words. This however is not feasible for those who do not admit a highest Self free from all imperfection and endowed with all perfections, and different from that intelligent soul which is conditioned by Nescience, involved in endless suffering and undergoing alternate states of purity and impurity.—But, an objection is raised, even if such a highest Self be acknowledged, it would have to be admitted that the sentence aims at conveying the oneness of that which is distinguished by the different attributes denoted by the words co-ordinated, and from this it follows that the highest Self participates in all the suffering expressed by the word 'thou'!—This is not so, we reply; since the word 'thou' also denotes the highest Self, viz. in so far as it is the inner Ruler (antaryâmin) of all souls.—The connected meaning of the text is as follows. That which is denoted as 'Being,' i.e. the highest Brahman which is the cause of all, free from all shadow of imperfection, &c., resolved 'to be many'; it thereupon sent forth the entire world, consisting of fire, water, &c.; introduced, in this world so sent forth, the whole mass of individual souls into different bodies divine, human, &c., corresponding to the desert of each soul—the souls thus constituting the Self of the bodies; and finally, itself entering according to its wish into these souls—so as to constitute their inner Self—evolved in all these aggregates, names and forms, i.e. rendered each aggregate something substantial (vastu) and capable of being denoted by a word. 'Let me enter into these beings with this living Self' (*g*îvena âtmana) means 'with this living *me*,' and this shows the living Self, i.e. the individual soul to have Brahman for its Self. And that this having Brahman for its Self means Brahman's being the inner Self of the soul (i.e. the Self inside the soul, but not identical with it), Scripture declares by saying that Brahman entered into it. This is clearly stated in the passage Taitt. Up. II, 6, 'He sent forth all this, whatever there is. Having sent forth he entered into it. Having entered it he became *sat* and *tyat*.' For here 'all this' comprises beings intelligent as well as non-intelligent, which afterwards are distinguished as *sat* and *tyat*, as knowledge (vig*ñ*âna) and non-knowledge. Brahman is thus said to enter into intelligent beings also. Hence, owing to this evolution of names and forms, all words denote the highest Self distinguished by non-intelligent matter and intelligent souls.—Another text, viz. *Kh.* Up. VI, 8, 7, 'All this has its Self in that,' denotes by 'all this' the entire world inclusive of intelligent souls, and says that of this world that (i.e. Brahman) is the Self. Brahman thus being the Self with regard to the whole universe of matter and souls, the universe inclusive of intelligent souls is the body of Brahman.—Other scriptural texts teach the same doctrine; cp. 'Entered within, the ruler of beings, the Self of all' (Taitt. Âr. III, 24); 'He who dwelling in the earth is within the earth—whose body is the earth,' &c., up to 'he who dwelling within the Self is within the Self, whom the Self does not know, of whom the Self is the body, who rules the Self from within, he is thy Self, the Ruler within, the Immortal' (B*ri*. Up. III, 7, 3–22; Mâdhyand. *S*â.); 'He who moves within the earth, of whom the earth is the body, &c.—who moves within the Imperishable, of whom the Imperishable is the body, whom the Imperishable does not know; he the inward ruler of all beings, free from evil, the divine, the one god, Nâraya*n*a' (Subâ. Up. VII). All these texts declare that the world inclusive of intelligent souls is the body of the highest Self, and the latter the Self of everything. Hence those words also that denote intelligent souls designate the highest Self as having intelligent souls for his body and constituting the Self of them; in the same way as words denoting non-sentient masses of matter, such as the bodies of gods, men, &c., designate the individual souls to which those bodies belong. For the body stands towards the embodied soul in the relation of a mode (prakâra); and as words denoting a mode accomplish their full function only in denoting the thing to which the mode belongs, we must admit an analogous comprehensiveness of meaning for those words which denote a body. For, when a thing is apprehended under the form 'this is such,' the element apprehended as 'such' is what constitutes a mode; now as this element is relative to the thing, the idea of it is also relative to the thing, and finds its accomplishment in the thing only; hence the word also which expresses the mode finds its accomplishment in the thing. Hence words such as 'cow,' 'horse,' 'man,' which denote a mode, viz. a species, comprise in their meaning also that mass of matter which exhibits the characteristics of the species, and as that mass of matter constitutes the body and therefore is a mode of a soul, and as that soul again, so embodied, is a mode of the highest Self; it follows that all these words extend in their signification up to the highest Self. The meaning of all words then is the highest Self, and hence their co-ordination with words directly denoting that highest Self is a primary (not merely 'implied') one.

But, an objection is raised, we indeed observe that words denoting species or qualities stand in co-ordination to words denoting substances, 'the ox is short-horned,' 'the sugar is white'; but where substances appear as the modes of other substances we find that formative affixes are used, 'the man is da*nd*in, ku*nd*alin' (bearing a stick; wearing earrings).—This is not so, we reply. There is nothing to single out either species, or quality, or substance, as what determines co-ordination: co-ordination disregards such limitations. Whenever a *thing* (whether species, or quality, or substance) has existence as a *mode* only—owing to its proof, existence and conception being inseparably connected with something else—the words denoting it, as they designate a substance characterised by the attribute denoted by them, appropriately enter into co-ordination with other words denoting the same substance as characterised by other attributes. Where, on the other hand, a substance which is established in separation from other things and rests on itself, is assumed to stand occasionally in the relation of mode to another substance, this is appropriately expressed by the use of derived forms such as 'da*nd*in, ku*nd*alin.' Hence such words as 'I,' 'thou,' &c., which are different forms of appellation of the individual soul, at bottom denote the highest Self only; for the individual souls together with non-sentient matter are the body—and hence modes—of the highest Self. This entire view is condensed in the co-ordination 'Thou art that.' The individual soul being thus connected with the highest Self as its body, its attributes do not touch the highest

Self, not any more than infancy, youth, and other attributes of the material body touch the individual soul. Hence, in the co-ordination 'Thou art that,' the word 'that' denotes the highest Brahman which is the cause of the world, whose purposes come true, which comprises within itself all blessed qualities, which is free from all shadow of evil; while the word 'thou' denotes the same highest Self in so far as having for its body the individual souls together with their bodies. The terms co-ordinated may thus be taken in their primary senses; there is no contradiction either with the subject-matter of the section, or with scripture in general; and not a shadow of imperfection such as Nescience, and so on, attaches to Brahman, the blameless, the absolutely blessed. The co-ordination with the individual soul thus proves only the difference of Brahman from the soul, which is a mere mode of Brahman; and hence we hold that different from the Self consisting of knowledge, i. e. the individual soul, is the Self consisting of bliss, i. e. the highest Self.

Nor is there any force in the objection that as the Self of bliss is said to be '*s*ârîra,' i. e. embodied—viz. in the clause 'of him the embodied Self is the same' (Taitt. Up. II, 5, 6)—it cannot be different from the individual soul. For throughout this section the recurring clause 'of him the embodied Self is the same as of the preceding one,' refers to the highest Self, calling that the 'embodied' one. The clause 'From that same Self sprang ether' (II, 1) designates the highest Brahman—which is different from the individual soul and is introduced as the highest cause of all things created—as the 'Self'; whence we conclude that all things different from it—from ether up to the Self of food—constitute its body. The Subâla-upanishad moreover states quite directly that all beings constitute the body of the highest Self: 'He of whom the earth is the body, of whom water is the body, of whom fire is the body, of whom wind is the body, of whom ether is the body, of whom the Imperishable is the body, of whom Death is the body, he the inner Self of all, the divine one, the one god Nârâya*n*a.' From this it follows that what constitutes the embodied Self of the Self of food is nothing else but the highest Self referred to in the clause 'From that same Self sprang ether.' When, then, the text further on says with regard to the Self of breath, 'of him the embodied Self is the same as of the preceding one' (II, 3), the meaning can only be that what constitutes the embodied Self of the 'preceding' Self of food, viz. the highest Self which is the universal cause, is also the embodied Self of the Self consisting of breath. The same reasoning holds good with regard to the Self consisting of mind and the Self consisting of knowledge. In the case, finally, of the Self consisting of bliss, the expression 'the same' (esha eva) is meant to convey that that Self has its Self in nothing different from itself. For when, after having understood that the highest Self is the embodied Self of the vi*gñ*ânamaya also, we are told that the embodied Self of that vi*gñ*ânamaya is also the embodied Self of the ânandamaya, we understand that of the ânandamaya—which we know to be the highest Self on the ground of 'multiplication'—its own Self is the Self. The final purport of the whole section thus is that everything different from the highest Self, whether of intelligent or non-intelligent nature, constitutes its body, while that Self alone is the non-conditioned embodied Self. For this very reason competent persons designate this doctrine which has the highest Brahman for its subject-matter as the '*s*ârîraka,' i. e. the doctrine of the 'embodied' Self.—We have thus arrived at the conclusion that the Self of bliss is something different from the individual Self, viz. the highest Self.

Here the Pûrvapakshin raises the following objection.—The Self consisting of bliss (ânandamaya) is not something different from the individual soul, because the formative element -maya denotes something made, a thing effected. That this is the meaning of -maya in ânandamaya we know from Pâ*n*ini IV, 3, 144.—But according to Pâ. V, 4, 21, -maya has also the sense of 'abounding in'; as when we say 'the sacrifice is annamaya,' i. e. abounds in food. And this may be its sense in 'ânandamaya' also!—Not so, the Pûrvapakshin replies. In 'annamaya,' in an earlier part of the chapter, -maya has the sense of 'made of,' 'consisting of'; and for the sake of consistency, we must hence ascribe the same sense to it in 'ânandamaya.' And even if, in the latter word, it denoted abundance, this would not prove that the ânandamaya is other than the individual soul. For if we say that a Self 'abounds' in bliss, this implies that with all this bliss there is mixed some small part of pain; and to be 'mixed with pain' is what constitutes the character of the individual soul. It is therefore proper to assume, in agreement with its previous use, that 'ânandamaya' means 'consisting of bliss.' In ordinary speech as well as in Vedic language (cp. common words such as 'm*ri*nmaya,' 'hira*n*maya'; and Vedic clauses such as 'par*n*amayî *g*uhû*h*') -maya as a rule means 'consisting of,' and this meaning hence presents itself to the mind first. And the individual soul *may* be denoted as 'made of bliss'; for in itself it is of the essence of bliss, and its Sa*m*sâra state therefore is something 'made of bliss.' The conclusion therefore is that, owing to the received meaning of -maya, the ânandamaya is none other than the individual soul.—To this primâ facie view the next Sûtra refers and refutes it.

14. If, on account of its being a word denoting an effect, (ânandamaya be said) not (to denote the highest Self); (we say) no, on account of abundance.

We deny the conclusion of the Pûrvapakshin, on the ground of there being abundance of bliss in the highest Brahman, and 'abundance' being one of the possible meanings of -maya.—Since bliss such as described in the Taitt. Up.—bliss which is reached by successively multiplying by hundred all inferior kinds of bliss—cannot belong to the individual soul, we conclude that it belongs to Brahman; and as Brahman cannot be an effect, and as -maya may have the sense of 'abounding in,' we conclude that the ânandamaya is Brahman itself; inner contradiction obliging us to set aside that sense of -maya which is recommended by regard to 'consequence' and frequency of usage. The regard for consistency, moreover, already has to be set aside in the case of the 'prâ*n*amaya'; for in that term

-maya cannot denote 'made of.' The 'prâ*n*amaya' Self can only be called by that name in so far as air with its five modifications has (among others) the modification called prâ*n*a, i. e. breathing out, or because among the five modifications or functions of air prâ*n*a is the 'abounding,' i. e. prevailing one.—Nor can it be truly said that -maya is but rarely used in the sense of 'abounding in': expressions such as 'a sacrifice abounding in food' (annamaya), 'a procession with many carriages' (*s*aka*t*amayî), are by no means uncommon.—Nor can we admit that to call something 'abounding in bliss' implies the presence of *some* pain. For 'abundance' precludes paucity on the part of that which is said to abound, but does not imply the presence of what is contrary. The presence or absence of what is contrary has to be ascertained by other means of proof; and in our case we do ascertain the absence of what is contrary to bliss by such means, viz. the clause 'free from evil,' &c. Abundance of bliss on the part of Brahman certainly implies a relation to paucity on the part of some other bliss; and in accordance with this demand the text says 'That is one measure of human bliss,' &c. (II, 8, 1). The bliss of Brahman is of measureless abundance, compared to the bliss of the individual soul.—Nor can it be maintained that the individual soul may be viewed as being an effect of bliss. For that a soul whose essential nature is knowledge and bliss should in any way be changed into something else, as a lump of clay is made into a pot, is an assumption contradicted by all scripture, sacred tradition, and reasoning. That in the Sa*m*sâra state the soul's bliss and knowledge are contracted owing to karman will be shown later on.—The Self of bliss therefore is other than the individual soul; it is Brahman itself.

A further reason for this conclusion is supplied by the next Sûtra.

15. And because he is declared to be the cause of that.

'For who could breathe, who could breathe forth, if that bliss existed not in the ether? He alone causes bliss'

(Taitt. Up. II, 7). This means—He alone is the cause of bliss on the part of the individual souls.—Some one is here designated as the cause of bliss enjoyed by the souls; and we thus conclude that the causer of bliss, who must be other than the souls to which bliss is imparted, is the highest Self abounding in bliss.

In the passage quoted the term 'bliss' denotes him who abounds in bliss, as will be shown later on.—A further reason is given in the next Sûtra.

16. And because that (Brahman) which is referred to in the mantra is declared (to be the ânandamaya).

That Brahman which is described in the mantra, 'True Being, knowledge, infinite is Brahman,' is proclaimed as the Self abounding in bliss. And that Brahman is the highest Brahman, other than the individual soul; for the passage 'He who knows Brahman attains the Highest' refers to Brahman as something to be obtained by the individual soul, and the words 'On this the following verse is recorded' show that the verse is related to that same Brahman. The mantra thus is meant to render clear the meaning of the Brâhma*n*a passage. Now the Brahman to be reached by the meditating Devotee must be something different from him. The same point is rendered clear by all the following Brâhma*n*a passages and mantras: 'from that same Self sprang ether,' and so on. The Self abounding in bliss therefore is other than the individual soul.

Here an opponent argues as follows:—We indeed must acknowledge that the object to be reached is something different from the meditating Devotee; but the fact is that the Brahman described in the mantra does not substantially differ from the individual soul; that Brahman is nothing but the soul of the Devotee in its pure state, consisting of mere non-differenced intelligence, free from all shade of Nescience. To this pure condition it is reduced in the mantra describing it as true Being, knowledge, infinite. A subsequent passage, 'that from which all speech, with the mind, turns away, unable to reach it' (II, 9), expresses this same state of non-differentiation, describing it as lying beyond mind and speech. It is this therefore to which the mantra refers, and the Self of bliss is identical with it.—To this view the next Sûtra replies.

17. Not the other, on account of impossibility.

The other than the highest Self, i. e. the one called *g*îva, even in the state of release, is not that Self which the mantra describes; for this is not possible. For to a Self of that kind unconditioned intelligence (such as is, in the mantra, ascribed to Brahman; cp. the term 'vipa*sk*itâ') cannot belong. Unconditioned intelligence is illustrated by the power of all one's purposes realising themselves; as expressed in the text 'He desired, may I be many, may I grow forth.' Intelligence (vipa*sk*ittvam, i. e. power of insight into various things) does indeed belong to the soul in the state of release; but as in the Sa*m*sâra state the same soul is devoid of such insight, we cannot ascribe to it non-conditioned intelligence. And if the released soul is viewed as being mere non-differenced intelligence, it does not possess the capacity of seeing different things, and hence cannot of course possess vipa*sk*ittva in the sense stated above. That, however, the existence of a substance devoid of all difference cannot be proved by any means of knowledge, we have already shown before. Again, if the clause 'from whence speech returns,' &c., were meant to express that speech and mind return from Brahman, this could not mean that the Real is devoid of all difference, but only that mind and speech are not means for the knowledge of Brahman. And from this it would follow that Brahman is something altogether empty, futile. Let us examine the context. The whole section, beginning with 'He who knows Brahman reaches Brahman,' declares that Brahman is all-knowing, the cause of the world, consisting of pure bliss, the cause of bliss in others; that through its mere wish it creates the whole universe comprising matter and souls; that entering into the universe of created things it constitutes their Self; that it is the cause of fear and fearlessness; that it rules Vâyu

Âditya and other divine beings; that its bliss is ever so much superior to all other bliss; and many other points. Now, all at once, the clause 'from whence speech returns' is said to mean that neither speech nor mind applies to Brahman, and that thus there are no means whatever of knowing Brahman! This is idle talk indeed! In the clause '(that) from which speech returns,' the relative pronoun 'from which' denotes bliss; this bliss is again explicitly referred to in the clause 'knowing the bliss of Brahman'—the genitive 'of Brahman' intimating that the bliss belongs to Brahman; what then could be the meaning of this clause which distinctly speaks of a knowledge of Brahman, if Brahman had at the same time to be conceived as transcending all thought and speech? What the clause really means rather is that if one undertakes to state the definite amount of the bliss of Brahman—the superabundance of which is illustrated by the successive multiplications with hundred—mind and speech have to turn back powerless, since no such definite amount can be assigned. He who knows the bliss of Brahman as not to be defined by any definite amount, does not fear anything. —That, moreover, the all-wise being referred to in the mantra is other than the individual soul in the state of release, is rendered perfectly clear by what—in passages such as 'it desired,' &c.—is said about its effecting, through its mere volition, the origination and subsistence of the world, its being the inner Self of the world, and so on.

18. And on account of the declaration of difference.

The part of the chapter—beginning with the words 'From that same Self there sprang ether'—which sets forth the nature of the Brahman referred to in the mantra, declares its difference from the individual soul, no less than from the Selfs consisting of food, breath, and mind, viz. in the clause 'different from this which consists of knowledge, is the other inner Self which consists of bliss.'—Through this declaration of difference from the individual soul we know that the Self of bliss referred to in the mantra is other than the individual soul.

19. And on account of desire, there is no regard to what is inferred (i. e. matter).

In order that the individual soul which is enthralled by Nescience may operate as the cause of the world, it must needs be connected with non-sentient matter, called by such names as pradhâna, or ânumânika (that which is inferred). For such is the condition for the creative energy of Brahmâ and similar beings. Our text, on the other hand, teaches that the creation of the aggregate of sentient and non-sentient things results from the mere wish of a being free from all connexion with non-sentient matter, 'He desired, may I be many, may I grow forth;' 'He sent forth all, whatever there is' (Taitt. Up. II, 6). We thus understand that that Self of bliss which sends forth the world does not require connexion with non-sentient matter called ânumânika, and hence conclude that it is other than the individual soul.—A further reason is stated in the next Sûtra.

20. And Scripture teaches the joining of this (i. e. the individual soul) with that (i. e. bliss) in that (i. e. the ânandamaya).

'A flavour he is indeed; having obtained a flavour this one enjoys bliss' (Taitt. Up. II, 7). This text declares that this one, i. e. the so-called individual soul, enjoys bliss through obtaining the ânandamaya, here called 'flavour.' Now to say that any one is identical with that by obtaining which he enjoys bliss, would be madness indeed.—It being thus ascertained that the Self of bliss is the highest Brahman, we conclude that in passages such as 'if that bliss were not in the ether' (Taitt. Up. II, 7), and 'knowledge, bliss is Brahman' (B*ri*. Up. III, 9, 28), the word 'ânanda' denotes the 'ânandamaya'; just as vi*gñ*âna means the vi*gñ*ânamaya. It is for the same reason (viz. of ânanda meaning the same as ânandamaya) that the clause 'he who knows the bliss of Brahman' exhibits Brahman as being connected with ânanda, and that the further clause 'he who knows this reaches the Self of bliss,' declares the reaching of the Self of bliss to be the fruit of the knowledge of bliss. In the subsequent anuvâka also, in the clauses 'he perceived that food is Brahman,' 'he perceived that breath is Brahman,' &c. (III, 1; 2, &c.), the words 'food,' 'breath,' and so on, are meant to suggest the Self made of food, the Self made of breath, &c., mentioned in the preceding anuvâka; and hence also in the clause 'he perceived that bliss is Brahman,' the word 'bliss' must be understood to denote the Self of bliss. Hence, in the same anuvâka, the account of the fate after death of the man who knows concludes with the words 'having reached the Self of bliss' (III, 10, 5). It is thus finally proved that the highest Brahman—which in the previous adhikara*n*a had to be shown to be other than the so-called Pradhâna—is also other than the being called individual soul.—This concludes the topic of the ânandamaya.

A new doubt here presents itself.—It must indeed be admitted that such individual souls as possess only a moderate degree of merit are unable to accomplish the creation of the world by their mere wish, to enjoy supreme bliss, to be the cause of fearlessness, and so on; but why should not beings like Âditya and Pra*g*âpati, whose merit is extraordinarily great, be capable of all this?—Of this suggestion the next Sûtra disposes.

21. The one within (the sun and the eye); on account of his qualities being declared.

It is said in the *Kh*ândogya: 'Now that person bright as gold, who is seen within the sun, with beard bright as gold and hair bright as gold, golden altogether to the very tips of his nails, whose eyes are like blue lotus; his name is Ut, for he has risen (udita) above all evil. He also who knows this rises above all evil. *Ri*k and Sâman are his joints.—So much with reference to the devas.—Now with reference to the body.—Now that person who is seen within the eye, he is *Ri*k, he is Sâman, Uktha, Ya*g*us, Brahman. The form of this person (in the eye) is the same as of that person yonder (in the sun), the joints of the one are the joints of the other, the name of the one is the name of the other' (*Kh.* Up. I, 7).—Here there arises the doubt whether that person dwelling within the eye and the sun be the individual soul called Âditya, who through accumulation of religious merit possesses lordly power, or the highest Self other than that soul.

That individual soul of high merit, the Pûrvapakshin maintains. For the text states that that person has a body, and connexion with a body belongs to individual souls only, for it is meant to bring the soul into contact with pleasure and pain, according to its deserts. It is for this reason that Scripture describes final Release where there is no connexion with works as a state of disembodiedness. 'So long as he is in the body he cannot get free from pleasure and pain. But when he is free from the body, then neither pleasure nor pain touches him' (*Kh.* Up. VIII, 12, 1). And a soul of transcendent merit may possess surpassing wisdom and power, and thus be capable of being lord of the worlds and the wishes (I, 6, 8). For the same reason such a soul may be the object of devout meditation, bestow rewards, and by being instrumental in destroying evil, be helpful towards final release. Even among men some are seen to be of superior knowledge and power, owing to superior religious merit; and this holds good with regard to the Siddhas and Gandharvas also; then with regard to the devas; then with regard to the divine beings, beginning with Indra. Hence, also, one among the divine beings, beginning with Brahmâ, may in each kalpa reach, through a particularly high degree of merit, vast lordly power and thus effect the creation of the world, and so on. On this supposition the texts about that which constitutes the cause of the world and the inward Self of the world must also be understood to refer to some such soul which, owing to superiority of merit, has become all-knowing and all-powerful. A so-called highest Self, different from the individual souls, does not therefore exist. Where the texts speak of that which is neither coarse nor fine nor short, &c., they only mean to characterise the individual soul; and those texts also which refer to final

Release aim only at setting forth the essential nature of the individual soul and the means of attaining that essential nature.

This primâ facie view is set aside by the Sûtra. The person who is perceived within the sun and within the eye, is something different from the individual soul, viz. the highest Self; because there are declared qualities belonging to that. The text ascribes to him the quality of having risen above, i. e. being free from all evil, and this can belong to the highest Self only, not to the individual soul. For to be free from all evil means to be free from all influence of karman, and this quality can belong to the highest Self only, differing from all individual souls which, as is shown by their experience of pleasure and pain, are in the bonds of karman. Those essential qualities also which presuppose freedom from all evil (and which are mentioned in other Vedic passages), such as mastery over all worlds and wishes, capability of realising one's purposes, being the inner Self of all, &c., belong to the highest Self alone. Compare passages such as 'It is the Self free from evil, free from old age, from death and grief, from hunger and thirst, whose wishes come true, whose purposes come true' (*Kh.* Up. VIII, 1, 5); and 'He is the inner Self of all, free from evil, the divine one, the one god Nârâya*n*a' (Subâ. Up.). Attributes such as the attribute of being the creator of the whole universe—which presupposes the power of realising one's wishes—(cp. the passage 'it desired, may I be many'); the attribute of being the cause of fear and fearlessness; the attribute of enjoying transcending bliss not limited by the capabilities of thought and speech and the like, are essential characteristics of that only which is not touched by karman, and they cannot therefore belong to the individual soul.—Nor is there any truth in the contention that the person within the sun, &c., cannot be a being different from individual souls because it possesses a body. For since a being which possesses the power of realising all its desires can assume a body through its mere wish, it is not generally true that embodiedness proves dependence on karman.—But, it may be said, by a body we understand a certain combination of matter which springs from the primal substance (prak*ri*ti) with its three constituents. Now connexion with such a body cannot possibly be brought about by the wish of such souls even as are free from all evil and capable of realising their desires; for such connexion would not be to the soul's benefit. In the case, on the other hand, of a soul subject to karman and not knowing its own essential nature, such connexion with a body necessarily takes place in order that the soul may enjoy the fruit of its actions—quite apart from the soul's desire.—Your objection would be well founded, we reply, if the body of the highest Self were an effect of Prak*ri*ti with its three constituents; but it is not so, it rather is a body suitable to the nature and intentions of that Self. The highest Brahman, whose nature is fundamentally antagonistic to all evil and essentially composed of infinite knowledge and bliss—whereby it differs from all other souls—possesses an infinite number of qualities of unimaginable excellence, and, analogously, a divine form suitable to its nature and intentions, i. e. adorned with infinite, supremely excellent and wonderful qualities—splendour, beauty, fragrance, tenderness, loveliness, youthfulness, and so on. And in order to gratify his devotees he individualises that form so as to render it suitable to their apprehension—he who is a boundless ocean as it were of compassion, kindness and lordly power, whom no shadow of evil may touch—he who is the highest Self, the highest Brahman, the supreme soul, Nârâya*n*a!—Certain texts tell us that the highest Brahman is the sole cause of the entire world: 'From which these beings originate' (Taitt. Up.); 'Being only was this in the beginning' (*Kh.* Up. VI, 2, 1); 'The Self only was this in the beginning' (Ai. Up. I, 1); 'Nârâya*n*a alone existed, not Brahmâ nor *S*iva.' Other texts define his nature: 'The True, knowledge, infinite is Brahman' (Taitt. Up. II, 1, 1); 'Knowledge, bliss is Brahman' (B*ri*. Up. III, 9, 28); and others again deny of Brahman all connexion with evil qualities and inferior bodies sprung from Prak*ri*ti, and all dependence on karman, and proclaim his glorious qualities and glorious forms: 'Free from qualities' (?); 'Free from taint' (*S*vet. Up. VI, 19); 'Free from old age, from death and grief, from hunger and thirst, realising his wishes and purposes' (*Kh.* Up. VIII, 1, 5); 'There is no effect and no cause known of him, no one is seen like to him or superior: his high power is revealed as manifold, as inherent action of force and knowledge' (*S*vet. Up. VI, 8); 'That highest great lord of lords, the highest deity of deities' (*S*vet. Up. VI, 7); 'He is the cause, the lord of the lords of the organs, and there is of him neither parent nor lord' (*S*vet. Up. VI, 9); 'Having created all forms and given names to them the wise one goes on calling them by those names' (Taitt. Âr. III, 12, 7); 'I know that great Person of sunlike lustre beyond the darkness' (*S*vet. Up. III, 8); 'All moments originated from the Person shining like lightning' (Mahânâr. Up. I, 6).—This essential form of his the most compassionate Lord by his mere will individualises as a shape human or divine or otherwise, so as to render it suitable to the apprehension of the devotee and thus satisfy him. This the following scriptural passage declares, 'Unborn he is born in many ways' (Gau. Kâ. III, 24); and likewise Sm*ri*ti, 'Though unborn I, the imperishable Self, the Lord of the beings, presiding over my Nature, manifest myself by my Mâyâ for the protection of the Good and the destruction of the evil doers' (Bha. Gî. IV, 6, 8). The 'Good' here are the Devotees; and by 'Mâyâ' is meant the purpose, the knowledge of the Divine Being; in agreement with the Naigha*nt*ukas who register 'Mâyâ' as a synonym of *gñ*âna (knowledge). In the Mahâbhârata also the form assumed by the highest Person in his avatâras is said not to consist of Prak*ri*ti, 'the body of the highest Self does not consist of a combination of material elements.'—For these reasons the Person within the Sun and the eye is the highest Self which is different from the individual soul of the Sun, &c.

22. And on account of the declaration of difference (the highest Self is) other (than the individual souls of the sun, &c.).

There are texts which clearly state that the highest

Self is different from Âditya and the other individual souls: 'He who, dwelling within Âditya (the sun), is different from Âditya, whom Âditya does not know, of whom Âditya is the body, who rules Âditya from within; who dwelling within the Self is different from the Self,' &c. (B*ri*. Up. III, 7, 9 ff.); 'Of whom the Imperishable is the body, whom the Imperishable does not know; who moves within Death, of whom Death is the body, whom Death does not know; he is the inner self of all beings, free from evil, divine, the one God Nârâya*n*a' (Sub. Up. VII). These texts declare all individual souls to be the body of the sinless highest Self which is said to be the inward principle of all of them.—It is thereby completely proved that the highest Self is something different from all individual souls such as Âditya, and so on.—Here terminates the adhikara*n*a of the 'one within.'

The text, 'That from which these beings are born,' teaches that Brahman is the cause of the world; to the question thence arising of what nature that cause of the world is, certain other texts give a reply in general terms ('Being only this was in the beginning'; 'It sent forth fire'; 'The Self only this was in the beginning,' &c.); and thereupon it is shown on the basis of the special nature of that cause as proved by the attributes of 'thought' and 'bliss,' that Brahman is different from the pradhâna and the individual souls. The remaining part of this Pâda now is devoted to the task of proving that where such special terms as Ether and the like are used in sections setting forth the creation and government of the world, they designate not the thing—sentient or non-sentient—which is known from ordinary experience, but Brahman as proved so far.

23. Ether (is Brahman), on account of the characteristic marks.

We read in the *Kh*ândogya (I, 9), 'What is the origin of this world?' 'Ether,' he replied. 'For all these beings spring from the ether only, and return into the ether. Ether is greater than these; ether is their rest.' Here there arises the doubt whether the word 'ether' denotes the well-known element or Brahman.—The Pûrvapakshin maintains the former alternative. For, he says, in the case of things to be apprehended through words we must accept that sense of the word which, proved by etymology, is immediately suggested by the word. We therefore conclude from the passage that the well-known Ether is the cause of the entire aggregate of things, moving or non-moving, and that hence Brahman is the same as Ether.—But has it not been shown that Brahman is something different from non-sentient things because its creative activity is preceded by thought?—This has been asserted indeed, but by no means proved. For the proper way to combine the different texts is as follows. Having been told that 'that from which these beings are born is Brahman,' we desire to know more especially what that source of all beings is, and this desire is satisfied by the special information given by the text, 'All these things spring from the ether.' It thus being ascertained that the ether only is the cause of the origin, and so on, of the world, we conclude that also such general terms as 'Being' ('Being only was this in the beginning') denote the particular substance called 'ether.' And we further conclude that in passages such as 'the Self only was all this in the beginning,' the word 'Self' (âtman) also denotes the ether; for that word is by no means limited to non-sentient things—cp., e. g., the phrase, 'Clay constitutes the Self of the jar'—, and its etymology also (âtman from âp, to reach) shows that it may very well be applied to the ether. It having thus been ascertained that the ether is the general cause or Brahman, we must interpret such words as 'thinking' (which we meet with in connexion with the creative activity of the general cause) in a suitable, i. e. secondary, or metaphorical sense. If the texts denoted the general cause by general terms only, such as 'Being,' we should, in agreement with the primary sense of 'thinking,' and similar terms, decide that that cause is an intelligent being; but since, as a matter of fact, we ascertain a particular cause on the basis of the word 'ether,' our decision cannot be formed on general considerations of what would suit the sense.—But what then about the passage, 'From the Self there sprang the ether' (Taitt. Up. II, 1, 1), from which it appears that the ether itself is something created?—All elementary substances, we reply, such as ether, air, and so on, have two different states, a gross material one, and a subtle one. The ether, in its subtle state, is the universal cause; in its gross state it is an effect of the primal cause; in its gross state it thus springs from itself, i. e. ether in the subtle state. The text, 'All these beings spring from ether only' (*Kh.* Up. I, 9, 1), declares that the whole world originates from ether only, and from this it follows that ether is none other than the general cause of the world, i. e. Brahman. This non-difference of Brahman from the empirically known ether also gives a satisfactory sense to texts such as the following: 'If this ether were not bliss' (Taitt. Up. II, 7, 1); 'Ether, indeed, is the evolver of names and forms' (*Kh.* Up. VIII, 14, 1, and so on).—It thus appears that Brahman is none other than the well-known elemental ether.

This primâ facie view is set aside by the Sûtra. The word 'ether' in the text under discussion denotes the highest Self with its previously established characteristics—which is something quite different from the non-sentient elemental ether. For the qualities which the passage attributes to ether, viz. its being the one cause of the entire world, its being greater than all, and the rest of all, clearly indicate the highest Self. The non-intelligent elemental ether cannot be called the cause of all, since intelligent beings clearly cannot be its effects; nor can it be called the 'rest' of intelligent beings, for non-sentient things are evil and antagonistic to the true aim of man; nor can it be called 'greater' than all, for it is impossible that a non-sentient element should possess all excellent qualities whatever and thus be absolutely superior to everything else.—Nor is the Pûrvapakshin right when maintaining that, as the word 'ether' satisfies the demand for a special cause of the world, all other texts are to be interpreted in accordance herewith. The words, 'All these beings indeed spring from the ether only,' merely give expression to something generally known, and statements of this nature presuppose other means of knowledge to prove them. Now these other means required are, in our case, supplied by such texts as 'Being only was this in the beginning,' and these, as we have shown, establish the existence of Brahman. To Brahman thus established, the text mentioning the ether merely refers as to something well known. Brahman may suitably be called 'ether' (âkâ*s*a), because being of the nature of light it shines (âkâ*s*ate) itself, and makes other things shine forth (âkâ*s*ayati). Moreover, the word 'ether' is indeed capable of conveying the idea of a special being (as cause), but as it denotes a special non-intelligent thing which cannot be admitted as the cause of the intelligent part of the world we must deny all authoritativeness to the attempt to tamper, in the interest of that one word, with the sense of other texts which have the power of giving instruction as to an entirely new thing (viz. Brahman), distinguished by the possession of omniscience, the power of realising its purposes and similar attributes, which we ascertain from certain complementary texts—such as 'it thought, may I be many, may I grow forth,' and 'it desired, may I be many, may I grow forth.' We also point out that the agreement in purport of a number of texts capable of establishing the existence of a wonderful being possessing infinite wonderful attributes is not lightly to be disregarded in favour of one single text which moreover (has not the power of intimating something not known before, but) only makes a reference to what is already established by other texts.—As to the averment that the word 'Self' is not exclusively limited to sentient beings, we remark that that word is indeed applied occasionally to non-sentient things, but prevailingly to that which is the correlative of a body, i.e. the soul or spirit; in texts such as 'the Self only was this in the beginning,' and 'from the Self there sprang the ether,' we must therefore understand by the 'Self,' the universal spirit. The denotative power of the term 'âtman,' which is thus proved by itself, is moreover confirmed by the complementary passages 'it desired, may I send forth the worlds,' 'it desired, may I be many, may I grow forth.'—We thus arrive at the following conclusion: Brahman, which—by the passage 'Being only this was in the beginning'—is established as the sole cause of the world, possessing all those manifold wonderful attributes which are ascertained from the complementary passages, is, in the text under discussion, referred to as something already known, by means of the term 'ether.'—Here terminates the adhikara*n*a of 'ether.'

24. For the same reason breath (is Brahman).

We read in the *Kh*ândogya (I, 10; 11), 'Prastot*ri*, that deity which belongs to the Prastâva,' &c.; and further on, 'which then is that deity? He said—Breath. For all these beings merge into breath alone, and from breath they arise. This is the deity belonging to the Prastâva. If without knowing that deity you had sung forth, your head would have fallen off.' Here the word 'breath,' analogously to the word 'ether,' denotes the highest Brahman, which is different from what is commonly called breath; we infer this from the fact that special characteristics of Brahman, viz. the whole world's entering into and rising from it, are in that text referred to as well-known things. There indeed here arises a further doubt; for as it is a matter of observation that the existence, activity, &c., of the whole aggregate of creatures depend on breath, breath—in its ordinary acceptation—may be called the cause of the world. This doubt is, however, disposed of by the consideration that breath is not present in things such as stones and wood, nor in intelligence itself, and that hence of breath in the ordinary sense it cannot be said that 'all beings enter into it,' &c. We therefore conclude that Brahman is here called 'breath' in so far as he bestows the breath of life on all beings. And the general result of the discussion carried on in connexion with the last two Sûtras thus is that the words 'ether' and 'breath' denote something other than what is ordinarily denoted by those terms, viz. the highest Brahman, the sole cause of this entire world, free from all evil, &c. &c.—Here terminates the adhikara*n*a of 'breath.'

The subsequent Sûtras up to the end of the Pâda demonstrate that the being which the texts refer to as 'Light or 'Indra'—terms which in ordinary language are applied to certain other well-known beings—, and which is represented as possessing some one or other supremely exalted quality that is invariably connected with world-creative power, is no other than the highest Brahman.

25. The light (is Brahman), on account of the mention of feet.

We read in the *Kh*ândogya (III, 13, 7), 'Now that light which shines above this heaven, higher than everything, in the highest worlds beyond which there are no other worlds, that is the same light which is within man.'—Here a doubt arises, viz. whether the brightly shining thing here called 'light' is the well-known light of the sun and so on, viewed as a causal universal principle (Brahman); or the all-knowing, &c., highest Person of infinite splendour, who is different in nature from all sentient and non-sentient beings, and is the highest cause.—The Pûrvapakshin maintains that the reference is to ordinary light. For, he says, the passage does not mention a particular characteristic attribute which can belong to the highest Self only—while such attributes *were* met with in the texts referring to Ether and Breath—, and as thus there is no opening for a recognition of the highest Self, and as at the same time the text identifies 'light' with the intestinal heat of living beings, we conclude that the text represents the well-known ordinary light as Brahman, the cause of the world—which is possible as causal agency is connected with extreme light and heat.—This primâ facie view the Sûtra sets aside. The light which the text states to be connected with heaven and possessing supreme splendour can be the highest Person only, since a preceding passage in the same section—'All the beings are one foot of it, three feet are the Immortal in heaven'—refers to all beings as being a foot of that same being which is connected with heaven. Although the passage, 'That light which shines above,' &c., does not mention a special attribute of the highest Person, yet the passage previously quoted refers to the highest Person as connected with heaven, and we therefore recognise that Person as the light connected with heaven, mentioned in the subsequent passage.

Nor does the identification, made in a clause of the text, of light with the intestinal heat give rise to any difficulty; for that clause is meant to enjoin meditation on the highest Brahman in the form of intestinal heat, such meditation having a special result of its own. Moreover, the Lord himself declares that he constitutes the Self of the intestinal fire, 'Becoming the Vai*s*vânara-fire I abide in the body of living creatures' (Bha. Gî. XV, 14).

26. If it be objected that (Brahman is) not (denoted) on account of the metre being denoted; (we reply) not so, because thus the direction of the mind (on Brahman) is declared; for thus it is seen.

The previous section at first refers to the metre called Gâyatrî, 'The Gâyatrî indeed is everything' (III, 12, 1), and then introduces—with the words 'this is also declared by a *Rik* verse'—the verse, 'Such is the greatness of it (viz. the Gâyatrî),' &c. Now, as this verse also refers to the metre, there is not any reference to the highest Person. —To this objection the second part of the Sûtra replies. The word 'Gâyatrî' does not here denote the metre only, since this cannot possibly be the Self of all; but the text declares the application of the idea of Gâyatrî to Brahman, i.e. teaches, to the end of a certain result being obtained, meditation on Brahman in so far as similar to Gâyatrî. For Brahman having four feet, in the sense indicated by the *rik*, may be compared to the Gâyatrî with its four (metrical) feet. The Gâyatrî (indeed has as a rule three feet, but) occasionally a Gâyatrî with four feet is met with; so, e.g., 'Indra*s* sa*k*îpati*h* | valena pî*d*ita*h* | du*sk*yavano v*ri*shâ | samitsu sâsahi*h*.' We see that in other passages also words primarily denoting metres are employed in other senses; thus, e.g., in the sa*m*vargavidyâ (*Kh*. Up. IV, 3, 8), where Virâ*g* (the name of a metre of ten syllables) denotes a group of ten divine beings.

For this conclusion the next Sûtra supplies a further argument.

27. And thus also, because (thus only) the designation of the beings, and so on, being the (four) feet is possible.

The text, moreover, designates the Gâyatrî as having four feet, after having referred to the beings, the earth, the body, and the heart; now this has a sense only if it is Brahman, which here is called Gâyatrî.

28. If it be said that (Brahman is) not (recognised) on account of the difference of designation; (we say) not so, on account of there being no contradiction in either (designation).

In the former passage, 'three feet of it are what is immortal in heaven,' heaven is referred to as the abode of the being under discussion; while in the latter passage, 'that light which shines above this heaven,' heaven is mentioned as marking its boundary. Owing to this discrepancy, the Brahman referred to in the former text is not recognised in the latter.—This objection the Sûtra disposes of by pointing out that owing to the essential agreement of the two statements, nothing stands in the way of the required recognition. When we say, 'The hawk is on the top of the tree,' and 'the hawk is above the top of the tree,' we mean one and the same thing.—The 'light,' therefore, is nothing else but the most glorious and luminous highest Person. Him who in the former passage is called four-footed, we know to have an extraordinarily beautiful shape and colour—(cp., e.g., 'I know that great Person of sunlike colour beyond the darkness' (*S*vet. Up. III, 9)—, and as hence his brilliancy also must be extraordinary, he is, in the text under discussion, quite appropriately called 'light.'—Here terminates the adhikara*n*a of 'light.'

It has been shown that the being endowed with supreme brilliance, called 'Light,' which the text mentions as something well known, is the highest Person. The Sûtrakâra will now show that the being designated as Indra and

Prâ*n*a, which the text enjoins as an object of meditation, for the reason that it is the means for attaining immortality—a power which is inseparable from causal power—, is likewise the highest Person.

29. Prâ*n*a is Brahman, on account of connexion.

We read in the Pratardana-vidyâ in the Kaushîtaki-brâhma*n*a that 'Pratardana, the son of Divodâsa, came, by fighting and strength, to the beloved abode of Indra.' Being asked by Indra to choose a boon he requests the God to bestow on him that boon which he himself considers most beneficial to man; whereupon Indra says, 'I am prâ*n*a (breath), the intelligent Self, meditate on me as Life, as Immortality.' Here the doubt arises whether the being called Prâ*n*a and Indra, and designating itself as the object of a meditation most beneficial to man, is an individual soul, or the highest Self.—An individual soul, the Pûrvapakshin maintains. For, he says, the word 'Indra' is known to denote an individual God, and the word 'Prâ*n*a,' which stands in grammatical co-ordination with Indra, also applies to individual souls. This individual being, called Indra, instructs Pratardana that meditation on himself is most beneficial to man. But what is most beneficial to man is only the means to attain immortality, and such a means is found in meditation on the causal principle of the world, as we know from the text, 'For him there is delay only so long as he is not delivered; then he will be perfect' (*Kh.* Up. VI, 14, 2). We hence conclude that Indra, who is known as an individual soul, is the causal principle, Brahman.

This view is rejected by the Sûtra. The being called Indra and Prâ*n*a is not a mere individual soul, but the highest Brahman, which is other than all individual souls. For on this supposition only it is appropriate that the being introduced as Indra and Prâ*n*a should, in the way of grammatical co-ordination, be connected with such terms as 'blessed,' 'non-ageing,' 'immortal.' ('That prâ*n*a indeed is the intelligent Self, blessed, non-ageing, immortal,' Kau. Up. III, 9.)

30. If it be said that (Brahman is) not (denoted) on account of the speaker denoting himself; (we say, not so), because the multitude of connexions with the inner Self (is possible only) in that (speaker if viewed as Brahman).

An objection is raised.—That the being introduced as Indra and Prâ*n*a should be the highest Brahman, for the reason that it is identical with him who, later on, is called 'blessed,' 'non-ageing, 'immortal'—this we cannot admit. 'Know me only, I am prâ*n*a, meditate on me as the intelligent Self, as life, as immortality'—the speaker of these words is Indra, and this Indra enjoins on Pratardana meditation on his own person only, the individual character of which is brought out by reference to certain deeds of strength such as the slaying of the son of Tvash*tri* ('I slew the three-headed son of Tvash*tri*,' &c.). As thus the initial part of the section clearly refers to an individual being, the terms occurring in the concluding part ('blessed,' 'non-ageing,' 'immortal') must be interpreted so as to make them agree with what precedes.—This objection the Sûtra disposes of. 'For the multitude of connexions with the Self'—i. e. the multitude of things connected with the Self as its attributes—is possible only 'in that,' i. e. in that speaker viewed as the highest Brahman. 'For, as in a car, the circumference of the wheel is placed on the spokes, and the spokes on the nave, thus are these objects placed on the subjects, and the subjects on the prâ*n*a. That prâ*n*a indeed is the intelligent Self, blessed, non-ageing, immortal.' The 'objects' (bhûtamâtrâ*h*) here are the aggregate of non-sentient things; the 'subjects' (pra*gñ*âmâtrâ*h*) are the sentient beings in which the objects are said to abide; when thereupon the texts says that of these subjects the being called Indra and Prâ*n*a is the abode, and that he is blessed, non-ageing, immortal; this qualification of being the abode of this Universe, with all its non-sentient and sentient beings, can belong to the highest Self only, which is other than all individual souls.

The Sûtra may also be explained in a somewhat different way, viz. 'there is a multitude of connexions belonging to the highest Self, i. e. of attributes special to the highest Self, in that, viz. section.' The text at first says, 'Choose thou that boon for me which thou deemest most beneficial to man'—to which the reply is, 'Meditate on me.' Here Indra-prâ*n*a is represented as the object of a meditation which is to bring about Release; the object of such meditation can be none but the highest Self.—'He makes him whom he wishes to lead up from these worlds do a good deed; and him whom he wishes to lead down from these worlds he makes do a bad deed.' The causality with regard to all actions which is here described is again a special attribute of the highest Self.—The same has to be said with regard to the attribute of being the abode of all, in the passage about the wheel and spokes, quoted above; and with regard to the attributes of bliss, absence of old age and immortality, referred to in another passage quoted before. Also the attributes of being 'the ruler of the worlds, the lord of all,' can belong to the highest Self only.—The conclusion therefore is that the being called Indra and Prâ*n*a is none other but the highest Self.—But how then can Indra, who is known to be an individual person only, enjoin meditation on himself?—To this question the next Sûtra replies.

31. The instruction (given by Indra about himself) (is possible) through insight based on Scripture, as in the case of Vâmadeva.

The instruction which, in the passages quoted, Indra gives as to the object of meditation, i. e. Brahman constituting his Self, is not based on such an insight into his own nature as is established by other means of proof, but on an intuition of his own Self, mediated by Scripture. 'Having entered into them with this living Self let me evolve names and forms' (*Kh*. Up. VI, 3, 2); 'In it all that exists has its Self' (*Kh*. Up. VI, 8, 7); 'Entered within, the ruler of creatures, the Self of all' (Taitt. Âr. III, 21); 'He who dwelling in the Self is different from the Self,' &c. (B*ri*. Up.

III, 7, 22)—from these and similar texts Indra has learned that the highest Self has the individual souls for its body, and that hence words such as 'I' and 'thou,' which denote individual beings, extend in their connotation up to the highest Self; when, therefore, he says, 'Know me only,' and 'Meditate on me,' he really means to teach that the highest Self, of which his own individual person is the body, is the proper object of meditation. 'As in the case of Vâmadeva.' As the *Ri*shi Vâmadeva perceiving that Brahman is the inner Self of all, that all things constitute its body, and that the meaning of words denoting a body extends up to the principle embodied, denotes with the word 'I' the highest Brahman to which he himself stands in the relation of a body, and then predicates of this 'I' Manu Sûrya and other beings—'Seeing this the *Ri*shi. Vâmadeva understood, I am Manu, I am Sûrya' (B*ri*. Up. I, 4, 10). Similarly Prahlâda says, 'As the Infinite one abides within all, he constitutes my "I" also; all is from me, I am all, within me is all.' (Vi. Pu. I, 19, 85.) The next Sûtra states, in reply to an objection, the reason why, in the section under discussion, terms denoting the individual soul, and others denoting non-sentient things are applied to Brahman.

32. If it be said (that Brahman is not meant) on account of characteristic marks of the individual soul and the chief vital air; we say no, on account of the threefoldness of meditation; on account of (such threefold meditation) being met (in other texts also); and on account of (such threefold meditation) being appropriate here (also).

An objection is raised. 'Let none try to find out what speech is, let him know the speaker'; 'I slew the three-headed son of Tvash*tri*; I delivered the Arunmukhas, the devotees, to the wolves'; these passages state characteristic marks of an individual soul (viz. the god Indra).—'As long as Prâ*n*a dwells in this body, so long there is life'; 'Prâ*n*a alone is the conscious Self, and having laid hold of this body, it makes it rise up.'—These passages again mention characteristic attributes of the chief vital air. Hence there is here no 'multitude of attributes belonging to the Self.'—The latter part of the Sûtra refutes this objection. The highest Self is called by these different terms in order to teach threefoldness of devout meditation; viz. meditation on Brahman in itself as the cause of the entire world; on Brahman as having for its body the totality of enjoying (individual) souls; and on Brahman as having for its body the objects and means of enjoyment.—This threefold meditation on Brahman, moreover, is met with also in other chapters of the sacred text. Passages such as 'The True, knowledge, infinite is Brahman,' 'Bliss is Brahman,' dwell on Brahman in itself. Passages again such as 'Having created that he entered into it. Having entered it he became *sat* and *tyat*, defined and undefined,' &c. (Taitt. Up. II, 6), represent Brahman as having for its body the individual souls and inanimate nature. Hence, in the chapter under discussion also, this threefold view of Brahman is quite appropriate. Where to particular individual beings such as Hira*n*yagarbha, and so on, or to particular inanimate things such as prak*ri*ti, and so on, there are attributed qualities especially belonging to the highest Self; or where with words denoting such persons and things there are co-ordinated terms denoting the highest Self, the intention of the texts is to convey the idea of the highest Self being the inner Self of all such persons and things.—The settled conclusion, therefore, is that the being designated as Indra and Prâ*n*a is other than an individual soul, viz. the highest Self.

## SECOND PÂDA.

THE contents of the first Pâda may be summed up as follows:—It has been shown that a person who has read the text of the Veda; who further, through the study of the Karma-Mîmâ*m*sâ, has acquired a full knowledge of the nature of (sacrificial and similar) works, and has recognised that the fruits of such works are limited and non-permanent; in whom there has arisen the desire for the highest aim of man, i. e. Release, which, as he has come to know in the course of reading the Vedânta portions of scripture, is effected by meditation on the nature of Brahman—such meditation having an infinite and permanent result; who has convinced himself that words are capable of conveying information about accomplished things (not only about things to be done), and has arrived at the conclusion that the Vedânta-texts are an authoritative means of knowledge with regard to the highest Brahman;—that such a person, we say, should begin the study of the *S*ârîraka-Mîmâ*m*sâ which indicates the method how Brahman is to be known through the Vedânta-texts.

We next have shown that the text 'That from which these creatures are born,' &c., conveys the idea of the highest Brahman as that being which in sport, as it were, creates, sustains, and finally reabsorbs this entire universe, comprising within itself infinite numbers of variously constituted animated beings—moving and non-moving—, of objects of enjoyment for those beings, of means of enjoyment, and of abodes of enjoyment; and which is the sole cause of all bliss. We have established that this highest Brahman, which is the sole cause of the world, cannot be the object of the other means of knowledge, and hence is to be known through scripture only. We have pointed out that the position of scripture as an authoritative means of knowledge is established by the fact that all the Vedânta-texts connectedly refer to the highest Brahman, which, although not related to any injunctions of action or abstention from action, by its own essential nature constitutes the highest end of man. We have proved that Brahman, which the Vedânta-texts teach to be the sole cause of the world, must be an intelligent principle other than the non-sentient pradhâna, since Brahman is said to think. We have declared that this intelligent principle is other than the so-called individual soul, whether in the state of bondage or that of release; since the texts describe it as in the enjoyment of supreme bliss, all-wise, the cause of fear or fearlessness on the part of intelligent beings, the inner Self of all created things, whether intelligent or non-intelligent, possessing the power of realising all its purposes, and so on.—We have maintained that this highest Being has a divine form, peculiar to itself, not made of the stuff of Prak*ri*ti, and not due to karman.—We have explained that the being which some texts refer to as a well-known cause of the world—designating it by terms such as ether or breath, which generally denote a special non-sentient being—is that same highest Self which is different from all beings, sentient or non-sentient.—We have declared that, owing to its connexion with heaven, this same highest Self is to be recognised in what the text calls a 'light,' said to possess supreme splendour, such as forms a special characteristic of the highest Being. We have stated that, as we recognise through insight derived from scripture, that same highest Person is denoted by terms such as Indra, and so on; as the text ascribes to that 'Indra' qualities exclusively belonging to the highest Self, such, e. g., as being the cause of the attainment of immortality.—And the general result arrived at was that the Vedânta-texts help us to the knowledge of one being only, viz. Brahman, or the highest Person, or Nârâya*n*a—of whom it is shown that he cannot possibly be the object of the other means of knowledge, and whom the possession of an unlimited number of glorious qualities proves to differ totally from all other beings whatsoever.

Now, although Brahman is the only object of the teaching of the Vedânta-texts, yet some of these texts might give rise to the notion that they aim at setting forth (not

Brahman), but some particular being comprised within either the pradhâna or the aggregate of individual souls. The remaining Pâdas of the first Adhyâya therefore apply themselves to the task of dispelling this notion and proving that what the texts in question aim at is to set forth certain glorious qualities of Brahman. The second Pâda discusses those texts which contain somewhat obscure references to the individual soul; the third Pâda those which contain clear references to the same; and the fourth Pâda finally those texts which appear to contain even clearer intimations of the individual soul, and so on.

1. Everywhere; because there is taught what is known.

We read in the *Kh*ândogya, 'Man is made of thought; according to what his thought is in this world, so will he be when he has departed this life. Let him form this thought: he who consists of mind, whose body is breath, whose form is light,' &c. (III, 14). We here understand that of the meditation enjoined by the clause 'let him form this thought' the object is the being said to consist of mind, to have breath for its body, &c. A doubt, however, arises whether the being possessing these attributes be the individual soul or the highest Self.—The Pûrvapakshin maintains the former alternative. For, he says, mind and breath are instruments of the individual soul; while the text 'without breath, without mind,' distinctly denies them to the highest Self. Nor can the Brahman mentioned in a previous clause of the same section ('All this indeed is Brahman') be connected as an object with the meditation enjoined in the passage under discussion; for Brahman is there referred to in order to suggest the idea of its being the Self of all—which idea constitutes a means for bringing about that calmness of mind which is helpful towards the act of meditation enjoined in the clause 'Let a man meditate with calm mind,' &c. Nor, again, can it be said that as the meditation conveyed by the clause 'let him form this thought' demands an object, Brahman, although mentioned in another passage, only admits of being connected with the passage under discussion; for the demand for an object is fully satisfied by the being made of mind, &c., which is mentioned in that very passage itself; in order to supply the object we have merely to change the case-terminations of the words 'manomaya*h* prâ*n*a*s*arîra*h*,' &c. It having thus been determined that the being made of mind is the individual soul, we further conclude that the Brahman mentioned in the concluding passage of the section ('That is Brahman') is also the individual soul, there called Brahman in order to glorify it.

This primâ facie view is set aside by the Sûtra. The being made of mind is the highest Self; for the text states certain qualities, such as being made of mind, &c., which are well known to denote, in all Vedânta-texts, Brahman only. Passages such as 'He who is made of mind, the guide of the body of breath' (Mu. Up. II, 2, 7); 'There is the ether within the heart, and in it there is the Person, consisting of mind, immortal, golden' (Taitt. Up. I, 6, 1); 'He is conceived by the heart, by wisdom, by the mind. Those who know him are immortal' (Ka. Up. II, 6, 9); 'He is not apprehended by the eye nor by speech, but by a purified mind' (Mu. Up. III, 1, 8); 'The breath of breath' (B*ri*. Up. IV, 4, 18?); 'Breath alone is the conscious Self, and having laid hold of this body it makes it rise up' (Kau. Up. III, 3); 'All these beings merge into breath alone, and from breath they arise' (*Kh*. Up. I, 11, 5)—these and similar texts refer to Brahman as consisting of mind, to be apprehended by a purified mind, having breath for its body, and being the abode and ruler of breath. This being so, we decide that in the concluding passage, 'my Self within the heart, that is Brahman,' the word 'Brahman' has to be taken in its primary sense (and does not denote the individual soul). The text which declares Brahman to be without mind and breath, merely means to deny that the thought of Brahman depends on a mind (internal organ), and that its life depends on breath.

Or else we may interpret the Vedic text and the Sûtra as follows. The passage 'All this is Brahman; let a man meditate with a calm mind on this world as originating, ending, and breathing in Brahman,' conveys the imagination of meditation on Brahman as the Self of all. The subsequent clause 'Let him form the thought,' &c., forms an additional statement to that injunction, the purport of which is to suggest certain attributes of Brahman, such as being made of mind. So that the meaning of the whole section is 'Let a man meditate on Brahman, which is made of mind, has breath for its body, &c., as the Self of the whole world.'—Here a doubt presents itself. Does the term 'Brahman' in this section denote the individual soul or the highest Self?—The individual soul, the Pûrvapakshin maintains, for that only admits of being exhibited in co-ordination with the word 'all.' For the word 'all' denotes the entire world from Brahmâ down to a blade of grass; and the existence of Brahmâ and other individual beings is determined by special forms of karman, the root of which is the beginningless Nescience of the individual soul. The highest Brahman, on the other hand, which is all-knowing, all-powerful, free from all evil and all shadow of Nescience and similar imperfections, cannot possibly exist as the 'All' which comprises within itself everything that is bad. Moreover we find that occasionally the term 'Brahman' is applied to the individual soul also; just as the highest Lord (parame*s*vara) may be called 'the highest Self' (paramâtman) or 'the highest Brahman.' That 'greatness' (b*ri*hattva; which is the essential characteristic of 'brahman') belongs to the individual soul when it has freed itself from its limiting conditions, is moreover attested by scripture: 'That (soul) is fit for infinity' (*S*vet. Up.V, 9). And as the soul's Nescience is due to karman (only), the text may very well designate it—as it does by means of the term 'ta*gg*alân'—as the cause of the origin, subsistence, and reabsorption of the world. That is to say—the individual soul which, in its essential nature, is non-limited, and therefore of the nature of Brahman, owing to the influence of Nescience enters into the state of a god, or a man, or an animal, or a plant.

This view is rejected by the Sûtra. 'Everywhere,' i. e.

in the whole world which is referred to in the clause 'All this is Brahman' we have to understand the highest Brahman—which the term 'Brahman' denotes as the Self of the world—, and not the individual soul; 'because there is taught what is known,' i. e. because the clause 'All this is Brahman'—for which clause the term 'ta*gg*alân' supplies the reason—refers to Brahman as something generally known. Since the world springs from Brahman, is merged in Brahman, and depends on Brahman for its life, therefore —as the text says—'All this has its Self in Brahman'; and this shows to us that what the text understands by Brahman is that being from which, as generally known from the Vedânta-texts, there proceed the creation, and so on, of the world. That the highest Brahman only, all-wise and supremely blessed, is the cause of the origin, &c., of the world, is declared in the section which begins, 'That from which these beings are born,' &c., and which says further on, 'he knew that Bliss is Brahman, for from bliss these beings are born' (Taitt. Up. III, 6); and analogously the text 'He is the cause, the lord of lords of the organs,' &c. (*S*vet. Up. VI, 9), declares the highest Bra*h*man to be the cause of the individual soul. Everywhere, in fact, the texts proclaim the causality of the highest Self only. As thus the world which springs from Brahman, is merged in it, and breathes through it, has its Self in Brahman, the identity of the two may properly be asserted; and hence the text—the meaning of which is 'Let a man meditate with calm mind on the highest Brahman of which the world is a mode, which has the world for its body, and which is the Self of the world'—first proves Brahman's being the universal Self, and then enjoins meditation on it. The highest Brahman, in its causal condition as well as in its so-called 'effected' state, constitutes the Self of the world, for in the former it has for its body all sentient and non-sentient beings in their subtle form, and in the latter the same beings in their gross condition. Nor is there any contradiction between such identity with the world on Brahman's part, and the fact that Brahman treasures within itself glorious qualities antagonistic to all evil; for the imperfections adhering to the bodies, which are mere modes of Brahman, do not affect Brahman itself to which the modes belong. Such identity rather proves for Brahman supreme lordly power, and thus adds to its excellences. Nor, again, can it rightly be maintained that of the individual soul also identity with the world can be predicated; for the souls being separate according to the bodies with which they are joined cannot be identical with each other. Even in the state of release, when the individual soul is not in any way limited, it does not possess that identity with the world on which there depends causality with regard to the world's creation, sustentation, and reabsorption; as will be declared in Sûtra IV, 4, 17. Nor, finally, does the Pûrvapakshin improve his case by contending that the individual soul may be the cause of the creation, &c., of the world because it (viz. the soul) is due to karman; for although the fact given as reason is true, all the same the Lord alone is the cause of the Universe.—All this proves that the being to which the text refers as Brahman is none other than the highest Self.

This second alternative interpretation of the Sûtra is preferred by most competent persons. The V*ri*ttikâra, e.g. says, 'That Brahman which the clause "All this is Brahman" declares to be the Self of all is the Lord.'

2. And because the qualities meant to be stated are possible (in Brahman).

The qualities about to be stated can belong to the highest Self only. 'Made of mind, having breath for its body,' &c. 'Made of mind' means to be apprehended by a purified mind only. The highest Self can be apprehended only by a mind purified by meditation on that Self, such meditation being assisted by the seven means, viz. abstention, &c. (see above, p. 17). This intimates that the highest Self is of pure goodness, precluding all evil, and therefore different in nature from everything else; for by the impure minded impure objects only can be apprehended.—'Having the vital breath for its body' means—being the supporter of all life in the world. To stand in the relation of a body to something else, means to abide in that other thing, to be dependent on it, and to subserve it in a subordinate capacity, as we shall fully show later on. And all 'vital breath' or 'life' stands in that relation to the highest Self. 'Whose form is light'; i.e. who is of supreme splendour, his form being a divine one of supreme excellence peculiar to him, and not consisting of the stuff of Prak*ri*ti.—'Whose purposes are true'; i.e. whose purposes realise themselves without any obstruction. 'Who is the (or "of the") Self of ether'; i.e. who is of a delicate and transparent nature, like ether; or who himself is the Self of ether, which is the causal substance of everything else; or who shines forth himself and makes other things shine forth.—'To whom all works belong'; i.e. he of whom the whole world is the work; or he to whom all activities belong.—'To whom all wishes belong'; i.e. he to whom all pure objects and means of desire and enjoyment belong. 'He to whom all odours and tastes belong'; i.e. he to whom there belong, as objects of enjoyment, all kinds of uncommon, special, perfect, supremely excellent odours and tastes; ordinary smells and tastes being negatived by another text, viz. 'That which is without sound, without touch, without taste,' &c. (**Ka. Up. I, 3, 15**).—'He who embraces all this'; i.e. he who makes his own the whole group of glorious qualities enumerated.—'He who does not speak,' because, being in possession of all he could desire, he 'has no regard for anything'; i.e. he who, in full possession of lordly power, esteems this whole world with all its creatures no higher than a blade of grass, and hence abides in silence.—All these qualities stated in the text can belong to the highest Self only.

3. But, on account of impossibility, not the embodied soul.

Those who fully consider this infinite multitude of exalted qualities will recognise that not even a shadow of them can belong to the individual soul—whether in the state of bondage or that of release—which is a thing as insignificant as a glow-worm and, through its connexion with a body, liable to the attacks of endless suffering. It is not possible therefore to hold that the section under discussion should refer to the individual soul.

4. And because there is (separate) denotation of the object and the agent.

The clause 'When I shall have departed from hence I shall obtain him' denotes the highest Brahman as the object to be obtained, and the individual soul as that which obtains it. This shows that the soul which obtains is the person meditating, and the highest Brahman that is to be obtained, the object of meditation: Brahman, therefore, is something different from the attaining soul.

5. On account of the difference of words.

The clause 'That is the Self of me, within the heart' designates the embodied soul by means of a genitive form, while the object of meditation is exhibited in the nominative case. Similarly, a text of the Vâ*g*asaneyins, which treats of the same topic, applies different terms to the embodied and the highest Self, 'Like a rice grain, or a barley grain, or a canary seed, or the kernel of a canary seed, thus that golden Person is within the Self' (*S*at. Br. X, 6, 3, 2). Here the locative form, 'within the Self,' denotes the embodied Self, and the nominative, 'that golden Person,' the object to be meditated on.—All this proves the highest Self to be the object of meditation.

6. And on account of Sm*ri*ti.

'I dwell within the hearts of all, from me come memory and knowledge, as well as their loss'; 'He who free from delusion knows me to be the highest Person'; 'The Lord, O Ar*g*una, is seated in the heart of all Beings, driving round by his mysterious power all beings as if mounted on a machine; to him fly for refuge' (Bha. Gî. XV, 15, 19; XVIII, 61). These Sm*ri*ti-texts show the embodied soul to be the meditating subject, and the highest Self the object of meditation.

7. Should it be said that (the passage does) no

(refer to Brahman) on account of the smallness of the abode, and on account of the denotation of that (viz. minuteness of the being meditated on); we say no, because (Brahman) has thus to be meditated upon, and because (in the same passage) it is said to be like ether.

It might be contended that, as the text 'he is my Self within the heart' declares the being meditated on to dwell within a minute abode, viz. the heart; and as moreover another text—'smaller than a grain of rice,' &c., declares it to be itself of minute size, that being cannot be the highest Self, but only the embodied soul. For other passages speak of the highest Self as unlimited, and of the embodied soul as having the size of the point of a goad (cp. e.g. Mu. Up. I, 1, 6, and *S*vet. Up. V, 8).—This objection the Sûtra rebuts by declaring that the highest Self is spoken of as such, i.e. minute, on account of its having to be meditated upon as such. Such minuteness does not, however, belong to its true nature; for in the same section it is distinctly declared to be infinite like ether—'greater than the earth, greater than the sky, greater than heaven, greater than all these worlds' (*Kh*. Up. III, 14, 3). This shows that the designation of the highest Self as minute is for the purpose of meditation only.—The connexion of the whole section then is as follows. The clause 'All this is Brahman; let a man meditate with calm mind on this world as beginning, ending, and breathing in Brahman,' enjoins meditation on Brahman as being the Self of all, in so far as it is the cause of the origin and destruction of all, and entering into all beings as their soul gives life to them. The next clause, 'Man is made of thought; according as his thought is in this world, so will he be when he has departed this life,' declares the attainment of the desired object to depend on the nature of the meditation; and the following clause, 'Let him therefore form the following thought,' thereupon repeats the injunction with a view to the declaration of details. The clause 'He who consists of mind,' &c., up to 'who is never surprised,' then states the nature and qualities, of the being to be meditated upon, which are to be comprised in the meditation. Next, the clause 'He is my Self,' up to 'the kernel of a canary seed,' declares that the highest Person, for the purpose of meditation, abides in the heart of the meditating devotee; representing it as being itself minute, since the heart is minute. After this the clause 'He also is my Self,' up to 'who is never surprised,' describes those aspects of the being meditated upon as within the heart, which are to be attained by the devotee. Next, the words 'this my Self within the heart is that Brahman' enjoins the reflection that the highest Brahman, as described before, is, owing to its supreme kindness, present in our hearts in order thereby to refresh and inspirit us. Then the clause 'When I shall have departed from hence I shall obtain him' suggests the idea that there is a certainty of obtaining him on the basis of devout meditation; and finally the clause 'He who has this faith has no doubt' declares that the devotee who is firmly convinced of his aim being attainable in the way described, will attain it beyond any doubt.—From all this it appears that the 'limitation of abode,' and the 'minuteness' ascribed to Brahman, are merely for the purpose of meditation.

8. Should it be said that there is attainment of fruition (of pleasure and pain); we reply, not so, on account of difference.

But, if the highest Brahman is assumed to dwell within bodies, like the individual soul, it follows that, like the latter, it is subject to the experience of pleasure and pain, such experience springing from connexion with bodies!—Of this objection the Sûtra disposes by remarking 'not so, on account of difference (of reason).' For what is the cause of experiences, pleasurable or painful, is not the mere dwelling within a body, but rather the subjection to the influence of good and evil deeds; and such subjection is impossible in the case of the highest Self to which all evil is foreign. Compare the scriptural text 'One of the two eats the sweet fruit, the other one looks on without eating'

(Mu. Up. III, 1, 1).—Here finishes the adhikara*n*a of 'what is known everywhere.'

Well then, if the highest Self is not an enjoyer, we must conclude that wherever fruition is referred to, the embodied soul only is meant!—Of this view the next adhikara*n*a disposes.

9. The eater (is the highest Self) on account of there being taken all that is movable and immovable.

We read in the Ka*th*avallî (I, 2, 25), 'Who then knows where he is to whom the Brahmans and Kshattriyas are but food, and death itself a condiment?' A doubt here arises whether the 'eater,' suggested by the words 'food' and 'condiment,' is the individual soul or the highest Self. —The individual soul, the Pûrvapakshin maintains; for all enjoyment presupposes works, and works belong to the individual soul only.—Of this view the Sûtra disposes. The 'eater' can be the highest Self only, because the taking, i. e. eating, of the whole aggregate of movable and immovable things can be predicated of that Self only. 'Eating' does not here mean fruition dependent on work, but rather the act of reabsorption of the world on the part of the highest Brahman, i. e. Vish*n*u, who is the cause of the origination, subsistence, and final destruction of the universe. This appears from the fact that Vish*n*u is mentioned in the same section, 'He reaches the end of his journey, and that is the highest place of Vish*n*u' (Ka. Up. I, 3, 9). Moreover the clause 'to whom death is a condiment' shows that by the Brahmans and Kshattriyas, mentioned in the text, we have to understand the whole universe of moving and non-moving things, viewed as things to be consumed by the highest Self. For a condiment is a thing which, while itself being eaten, causes other things to be eaten; the meaning of the passage, therefore, is that while death itself is consumed, being a condiment as it were, there is at the same time eaten whatever is flavoured or made palatable by death, and that is the entire world of beings in which the Brahmans and Kshattriyas hold the foremost place. Now such eating of course is destruction or reabsorption, and hence such enjoyment—meaning general reabsorption—can belong to the highest Self only.

10. And on account of the topic of the whole section.

Moreover the highest Brahman constitutes the topic of the entire section. Cp. 'The wise who knows the Self as great and omnipresent does not grieve' (Ka. Up. I, 2, 22); 'That Self cannot be gained by the Veda, nor by understanding, nor by much learning. He whom the Self chooses, by him the Self can be gained; the Self chooses him as his own' (I, 2, 23).—Moreover, the clause (forming part of the text under discussion), 'Who knows him (i. e. the being which constitutes the topic of the section) where he is?' clearly shows that we have to recognise here the Self of which it had previously been said that it is hard to know unless it assists us with its grace.

To this conclusion a new objection presents itself.—Further on in the same Upanishad (I, 3, 1) we meet with the following text: 'There are two, drinking their reward in the world of their own works, entered into the cave, dwelling on the highest summit; those who know Brahman call them shade and light, likewise those householders who perform the Tri*n*a*k*iketa-sacrifice.' Now this text clearly refers to the individual soul which enjoys the reward of its works, together with an associate coupled to it. And this associate is either the vital breath, or the organ of knowledge (buddhi). For the drinking of '*ri*ta' is the enjoyment of the fruit of works, and such enjoyment does not suit the highest Self. The buddhi, or the vital breath, on the other hand, which are instruments of the enjoying embodied soul, may somehow be brought into connexion with the enjoyment of the fruit of works. As the text is thus seen to refer to the embodied soul coupled with some associate, we infer, on the ground of the two texts belonging to one section, that also the 'eater' described in the former text is none other than the individual soul.—To this objection the next Sûtra replies.

11. The 'two entered into the cave' are the two Selfs; on account of this being seen.

The two, entered into the cave and drinking their reward, are neither the embodied soul together with the vital breath, nor the embodied soul together with the buddhi; it is rather the embodied Self and the highest Self which are designated by those terms. For this is seen, i. e. it is seen that in that section the individual Self and the highest Self only are spoken of as entered into the cave. To the highest Self there refers I, 2, 12, 'The wise who by meditation on his Self recognises the Ancient who is difficult to see, who has entered into the dark, who is hidden in the cave, who dwells in the abyss, as God, he indeed leaves joy and sorrow far behind.' And to the individual soul there refers **II, 4, 7**, 'Who is together with the vital breath, who is Aditi, who is made of the deities, who entering into the cave abides therein, who was born variously through the elements.' Aditi here means the individual soul which enjoys (atti) the fruits of its works; which is associated with the vital breath; which is made of the deities, i. e. whose enjoyment is dependent on the different sense-organs; which abides in the hollow of the heart; and which, being connected with the elementary substances, earth, and so on, is born in various forms—human, divine, &c.—That the text speaks of the two Selfs as drinking their reward (while actually the individual soul only does so) is to be understood in the same way as the phrase 'there go the umbrella-bearers' (one of whom only carries the umbrella). Or else we may account for this on the ground that both are agents with regard to the drinking, in so far as the 'drinking' individual soul is caused to drink by the highest Self.

12. And on account of distinctive qualities.

Everywhere in that section we meet with statements of distinctive attributes of the two Selfs, the highest Self being represented as the object of meditation and attainment, and the individual Self as the meditating and attaining subject. The passage 'When he has known and understood that which is born from Brahman, the intelligent, to be divine and venerable, then he obtains everlasting peace' (I, 1, 17) refers to the meditating individual soul which recognises itself as being of the nature of Brahman. On the other hand, I, 3, 2, 'That which is a bridge for sacrificers, the highest imperishable Brahman for those who wish to cross over to the fearless shore, the Nâkiketa, may we be able to know that,' refers to the highest Self as the object of meditation; 'Nâkiketa' here meaning that which is to be reached through the Nâkiketa-rite. Again, the passage 'Know the Self to be sitting in the chariot and the body to be the chariot' (I, 3, 3) refers to the meditating individual soul; and the verse, I, 3, 9, 'But he who has understanding for his charioteer, and holds the reins of the mind, he reaches the end of his journey, and that is the highest place of Vishnu,' refers to the embodied and the highest Selfs as that which attains and that which is to be attained. And in the text under discussion also (I, 3, 1), the two Selfs are distinctly designated as light and shade, the one being all-knowing, the other devoid of knowledge.

But, a new objection is raised, the initial passage, I, 1, 20, 'That doubt which there is when a man is dead—some saying, he is; others, he is not,' clearly asks a question as to the true nature of the individual soul, and we hence conclude that that soul forms the topic of the whole chapter.—Not so, we reply. That question docs not spring from any doubt as to the existence or non-existence of the soul apart from the body; for if this were so the two first boons chosen by Nakiketas would be unsuitable. For the story runs as follows: When the sacrifice offered by the father of Nakiketas—at which all the possessions of the sacrificer were to be given to the priests—is drawing towards its close, the boy, feeling afraid that some deficiency on the part of the gifts might render the sacrifice unavailing, and dutifully wishing to render his father's sacrifice complete by giving his own person also, repeatedly asks his father, 'And to whom will you give me'? The father, irritated by the boy's persistent questioning, gives an angry reply, and in consequence of this the boy goes to the palace of Yama, and Yama being absent, stays there for three days without eating. Yama on his return is alarmed at this neglect of hospitality, and wishing to make up for it allows him to choose three boons. Na*k*iketas, thereupon, full of faith and piety, chooses as his first boon that his father should forgive him. Now it is clear that conduct of this kind would not be possible in the case of one not convinced of the soul having an existence independent of the body. For his second boon, again, he chooses the knowledge of a sacrificial fire, which has a result to be experienced only by a soul that has departed from the body; and this choice also can clearly be made only by one who knows that the soul is something different from the body. When, therefore, he chooses for his third boon the clearing up of his doubt as to the existence of the soul after death (as stated in v. 20), it is evident that his question is prompted by the desire to acquire knowledge of the true nature of the highest Self—which knowledge has the form of meditation on the highest Self—, and by means thereof, knowledge of the true nature of final Release which consists in obtaining the highest Brahman. The passage, therefore, is not concerned merely with the problem as to the separation of the soul from the body, but rather with the problem of the Self freeing itself from all bondage whatever—the same problem, in fact, with which another scriptural passage also is concerned, viz. 'When he has departed there is no more knowledge' (B*ri*. Up. II, 4, 12). The full purport of Na*k*iketas' question, therefore, is as follows: When a man qualified for Release has died and thus freed himself from all bondage, there arises a doubt as to his existence or non-existence—a doubt due to the disagreement of philosophers as to the true nature of Release; in order to clear up this doubt I wish to learn from thee the true nature of the state of Release.—Philosophers, indeed, hold many widely differing opinions as to what constitutes Release. Some hold that the Self is constituted by consciousness only, and that Release consists in the total destruction of this essential nature of the Self. Others, while holding the same opinion as to the nature of the Self, define Release as the passing away of Nescience (avidyâ). Others hold that the Self is in itself non-sentient, like a stone, but possesses, in the state of bondage, certain distinctive qualities, such as knowledge, and so on. Release then consists in the total removal of all these qualities, the Self remaining in a state of pure isolation (kaivalya). Others, again, who acknowledge a highest Self free from all imperfection, maintain that through connexion with limiting adjuncts that Self enters on the condition of an individual soul; Release then means the pure existence of the highest Self, consequent on the passing away of the limiting adjuncts. Those, however, who understand the Vedânta, teach as follows: There is a highest Brahman which is the sole cause of the entire universe, which is antagonistic to all evil, whose essential nature is infinite knowledge and blessedness, which comprises within itself numberless auspicious qualities of supreme excellence, which is different in nature from all other beings, and which constitutes the inner Self of all. Of this Brahman, the individual souls—whose true nature is unlimited knowledge, and whose only essential attribute is the intuition of the supreme Self—are modes, in so far, namely, as they constitute its body. The true nature of these souls is, however, obscured by Nescience, i. e. the influence of the beginningless chain of works; and by *Release* then we have to understand that intuition of the highest Self, which is the natural state of the individual souls, and which follows on the destruction of Nescience.—When Na*k*iketas desires Yama graciously to teach him the true nature of Release and the means to attain it, Yama at first tests him by dwelling on the difficulty of comprehending Release, and by tempting him with various worldly enjoyments. But having in this way recognised the boy's thorough fitness, he in the end instructs him as to the kind of meditation on the highest Self which constitutes knowledge of the highest Reality, as to the nature of Release—which consists in reaching the abode of the highest Self—, and as to all the required details. This instruction begins, I, 2, 12, 'The Ancient one who is difficult to see,' &c., and extends up to I, 3, 9, 'and that is the highest place of Vish*n*u.'—It thus is an established conclusion that the 'eater' is no other than the highest Self.—Here terminates the adhikara*n*a of 'the eater.'

13. (The Person) within the eye (is the highest Self) on account of suitability.

The *Kh*andogas have the following text: 'The Person that is seen within the eye, that is the Self. This is the immortal, the fearless, this is Brahman' (*Kh.* Up. IV, 15, 1). The doubt here arises whether the person that is here spoken of as abiding within the eye is the reflected Self, or some divine being presiding over the sense of sight, or the embodied Self, or the highest Self.—It is the reflected Self, the Pûrvapakshin maintains; for the text refers to the person seen as something well known, and the expression, 'is seen,' clearly refers to something directly perceived. Or it may be the individual soul, for that also may be referred to as something well known, as it is in special connexion with the eye: people, by looking into the open eye of a person, determine whether the living soul remains in him or is departing. Or else we may assume that the Person seen within the eye is some particular divine being, on the strength of the scriptural text, B*ri*. Up. V, 5, 2, 'He (the person seen within the sun) rests with his rays in him (the person within the eye).' Any of these beings may quite suitably be referred to as something well known.—Of these alternatives the Sûtra disposes by declaring that the Person within the eye is the highest Self. For the text goes on to say about the Person seen within the eye, 'They call him Sa*m*yadvâma, for all blessings go towards him. He is also Vâmanî, for he leads all blessings. He is also Bhâmanî, for he shines in all worlds.' And all these attributes can be reconciled with the highest Self only.

14. And on account of the statement as to abode, and so on.

Abiding within the eye, ruling the eye, and so on are predicated by scripture of the highest Self only, viz. in B*ri*. Up. III, 7, 18, 'He who dwells within the eye, who rules the eye within.' We therefore recognise that highest Self in the text, 'That Person which is seen within the eye.' The argument founded on reference to 'something well known' thus suits the highest Self very well; and also the clause which denotes immediate perception ('is seen') appears quite suitable, since the highest Self is directly intuited by persons practising mystic concentration of mind (Yoga).

15. And on account of the text referring only to what is characterised by pleasure.

The Person abiding within the eye is the highest Person, for the following reason also. The topic of the whole section is Brahman characterised by delight, as indicated in the passage 'Ka (pleasure) is Brahman, Kha (ether) is Brahman' (*Kh*. Up. IV, 10, 5). To that same Brahman the passage under discussion ('The Person that is seen in the eye') refers for the purpose of enjoining first a place with which Brahman is to be connected in meditation, and secondly some special qualities—such as comprising and leading all blessings—to be attributed to Brahman in meditation.—The word 'only' in the Sûtra indicates the independence of the argument set forth.

But—an objection is raised—between the Brahman introduced in the passage 'Ka is Brahman,' &c., and the text under discussion there intervenes the vidyâ of the Fires (*Kh*. Up. IV, 11–13), and hence Brahman does not readily connect itself with our passage. For the text says that after the Fires had taught Upako*s*ala the knowledge of Brahman ('Breath is Brahman, Ka is Brahman,' &c.), they taught him a meditation on themselves ('After that the Gârhapatya fire taught him,' &c., *Kh*. Up. IV, 11, 1). And this knowledge of the Fires cannot be considered a mere subordinate part of the knowledge of Brahman, for the text declares that it has special fruits of its own—viz. the attainment of a ripe old age and prosperous descendants, &c.—which are not comprised in the results of the knowledge of Brahman, but rather opposed to them in nature.—To this we make the following reply. As both passages (viz. IV, 10, 5, 'Breath is Brahman,' &c.; and IV, 15, 1, 'this is Brahman') contain the word Brahman, and as from the words of the Fires, 'the teacher will tell you the way,' it follows that the knowledge of Brahman is not complete before that way has been taught, we determine that the knowledge of the Fires which stands between the two sections of the knowledge of Brahman is a mere subordinate member of the latter. This also appears from the fact that the Gârhapatya fire begins to instruct Upako*s*ala only after he has been introduced into the knowledge of Brahman. Upako*s*ala moreover complains that he is full of sorrows (I, 10, 3), and thus shows himself to be conscious of all the sufferings incidental to human life—birth, old age, death, &c.—which result from man being troubled by manifold desires for objects other than the attainment of Brahman; when therefore the Fires conclude their instruction by combining in saying, 'This, O friend, is the knowledge of us and the knowledge of the Self which we impart to thee,' it is evident that the vidyâ of the Fires has to be taken as a subordinate member of the knowledge of the Self whose only fruit is Release. And from this it follows that the statement of the results of the Agnividyâ has to be taken (not as an injunction of results—phalavidhi —but) merely as an arthavâda (cp. Pû. Mî. Sû. IV, 3, 1). It, moreover, is by no means true that the text mentions such fruits of the Agnividyâ as would be opposed to final Release; all the fruits mentioned suit very well the case of a person qualified for Release. 'He destroys sin' (*Kh*. Up. IV, 11, 2; 12, 2; 13, 2), i.e. he destroys all evil works standing in the way of the attainment of Brahman. 'He obtains the world,' i.e. all impeding evil works having been destroyed he obtains the world of Brahman. 'He reaches his full age,' i.e. he fully reaches that age which is required for the completion of meditation on Brahman. 'He lives long,' i.e. he lives unassailed by afflictions until he reaches Brahman. 'His descendants do not perish,'

i. e. his pupils, and their pupils, as well as his sons, grandsons, &c., do not perish; i. e. they are all knowers of Brahman, in agreement with what another text declares to be the reward of knowledge of Brahman—'In his family no one is born ignorant of Brahman' (Mu. Up. III, 2, 9). 'We guard him in this world and the other,' i. e. we Fires guard him from all troubles until he reaches Brahman.—The Agnividyâ thus being a member of the Brahmavidyâ, there is no reason why the Brahman introduced in the earlier part of the Brahmavidyâ should not be connected with the latter part—the function of this latter part being to enjoin a place of meditation (Brahman being meditated on as the Person within the eye), and some special qualities of Brahman to be included in the meditation.—But (an objection is raised) as the Fires tell Upakosala 'the teacher will tell you the way,' we conclude that the teacher has to give information as to the way to Brahman only; how then can his teaching refer to the place of meditation and the special qualities of Brahman?—We have to consider, we reply, in what connexion the Fires address those words to Upakosala. His teacher having gone on a journey without having imparted to him the knowledge of Brahman, and Upakosala being dejected on that account, the sacred fires of his teacher, well pleased with the way in which Upakosala had tended them, and wishing to cheer him up, impart to him the general knowledge of the nature of Brahman and the subsidiary knowledge of the Fires. But remembering that, as scripture says, 'the knowledge acquired from a teacher is best,' and hence considering it advisable that the teacher himself should instruct Upakosala as to the attributes of the highest Brahman, the place with which it is to be connected in meditation and the way leading to it, they tell him 'the teacher will tell you the way,' the 'way' connoting everything that remains to be taught by the teacher. In agreement herewith the teacher—having first said, 'I will tell you this; and as water does not cling to a lotus leaf, so no evil clings to one who knows it'—instructs him about Brahman as possessing certain auspicious attributes, and to be meditated upon as abiding within the eye, and about the way leading to Brahman.—It is thus a settled conclusion that the text under discussion refers to that Brahman which was introduced in the passage 'Ka is Brahman,' and that hence the Person abiding within the eye is the highest Self.

But—an objection is raised—how do you know that the passage 'Ka (pleasure) is Brahman, Kha (ether) is Brahman' really refers to the highest Brahman, so as to be able to interpret on that basis the text about the Person within the eye? It is a more obvious interpretation to take the passage about Ka and Kha as enjoining a meditation on Brahman viewed under the form of elemental ether and of ordinary worldly pleasure. This interpretation would, moreover, be in agreement with other similarly worded texts (which are generally understood to enjoin meditation on Brahman in a definite form), such as 'Name is Brahman,' 'Mind is Brahman.'

16. For that very reason that (ether) is Brahman.

Because the clause 'What is Ka the same is Kha' speaks of ether as characterised by pleasure, the ether which is denoted by 'Kha' is no other than the highest Brahman. To explain. On the Fires declaring 'Breath is Brahman, Ka is Brahman, Kha is Brahman,' Upako*s*ala says, 'I understand that breath is Brahman, but I do not understand Ka and Kha.' The meaning of this is as follows. The Fires cannot speak of meditation on Brahman under the form of breath and so on, because they are engaged in giving instruction to me, who am afraid of birth, old age, death, &c., and desirous of final Release. What they declare to me therefore is meditation on Brahman itself. Now here Brahman is exhibited in co-ordination with certain well-known things, breath and so on. That Brahman should be qualified by co-ordination with breath is suitable, either from the point of view of Brahman having the attribute of supporting the world, or on account of Brahman being the ruler of breath, which stands to it in the relation of a body. Hence Upako*s*ala says, 'I understand that breath is Brahman.' With regard to pleasure and ether, on the other hand, there arises the question whether they are exhibited in the relation of qualifying attributes of Brahman on the ground of their forming the body of Brahman, and hence being ruled by it, or whether the two terms are meant to determine each other, and thus to convey a notion of the true nature of Brahman being constituted by supreme delight. On the former alternative the declaration of the Fires would only state that Brahman is the ruler of the elemental ether and of all delight depending on the sense-organs, and this would give no notion of Brahman's true nature; on the latter alternative the Fires would declare that unlimited delight constitutes Brahman's true nature. In order to ascertain which of the two meanings has to be taken, Upakosala therefore says, 'I do not understand Ka and Kha.' The Fires, comprehending what is in his mind, thereupon reply, 'What is Ka the same is Kha, what is Kha the same is Ka,' which means that the bliss which constitutes Brahman's nature is unlimited. The same Brahman therefore which has breath for its attribute because breath constitutes its body, is of the nature of unlimited bliss; the text therefore adds, 'They taught him that (viz. Brahman) as breath and as ether.' What the text, 'Ka is Brahman, Kha is Brahman,' teaches thus is Brahman as consisting of unlimited bliss, and this Brahman is resumed in the subsequent text about the Person seen within the eye. That Person therefore is the highest Self.

17. And on account of the statement of the way of him who has heard the Upanishads.

Other scriptural texts give an account of the way—the first station of which is light—that leads up to the highest Person, without any subsequent return, the soul of him who has read the Upanishads, and has thus acquired a knowledge of the true nature of the highest Self. Now this same way is described by the teacher to Upakosala in connexion with the instruction as to the Person in the eye, 'They go to light, from light to day,' &c. This also proves that the Person within the eye is the highest Self.

18. Not any other, on account of non-permanency of abode, and of impossibility.

As the reflected Self and the other Selfs mentioned by the Pûrvapakshin do not necessarily abide within the eye, and as conditionless immortality and the other qualities (ascribed in the text to the Person within the eye) cannot possibly belong to them, the Person within the eye cannot be any Self other than the highest Self. Of the reflected Self it cannot be said that it permanently abides within the eye, for its presence there depends on the nearness to the eye of another person. The embodied Self again has its seat within the heart, which is the root of all sense-organs, so as to assist thereby the activities of the different senses; it cannot therefore abide within the eye. And with regard to the divinity the text says that 'he rests with his rays in him, i. e. the eye': this implies that the divine being may preside over the organ of sight although itself abiding in another place; it does not therefore abide in the eye. Moreover, non-conditioned immortality and similar qualities cannot belong to any of these three Selfs. The Person seen within the eye therefore is the highest Self.

We have, under Sû. I, 2, 14, assumed as proved that the abiding within the eye and ruling the eye, which is referred to in B*ri*. Up. III, 7, 18 ('He who dwells in the eye,' &c.), can belong to the highest Self only, and have on that basis proved that the Self within the eye is the highest Self. —Here terminates the adhikara*n*a of that 'within.'—The next Sûtra now proceeds to prove that assumption.

19. The internal Ruler (referred to) in the clauses with respect to the gods, with respect to the worlds, &c. (is the highest Self), because the attributes of that are designated.

The Vâ*g*asaneyins, of the Kâ*n*va as well as the Mâdhyandina branch, have the following text: 'He who dwelling in the earth is within the earth, whom the earth does not know, whose body the earth is, who rules the earth within, he is thy Self, the ruler within, the Immortal.' The text thereupon extends this teaching as to a being that dwells in things, is within them, is not known by them, has them for its body and rules them; in the first place to all divine beings, viz. water, fire, sky, air, sun, the regions, moon, stars, ether, darkness, light; and next to all material beings, viz. breath, speech, eye, ear, mind, skin, knowledge, seed—closing each section with the words, 'He is thy Self, the ruler within, the Immortal.' The Mâdhyandinas, however, have three additional sections, viz. 'He who dwells in all worlds,' &c.; 'He who dwells in all Vedas,' &c.; 'He who dwells in all sacrifices'; and, moreover, in place of 'He who dwells in knowledge' (vi*gñ*âna) they read 'He who dwells in the Self.'—A doubt here arises whether the inward Ruler of these texts be the individual Self or the highest Self.

The individual Self, the Pûrvapakshin maintains. For in the supplementary passage (which follows upon the text considered so far) the internal Ruler is called the 'seer' and 'hearer,' i.e. his knowledge is said to depend on the sense-organs, and this implies the view that the 'seer' only (i.e. the individual soul only) is the inward Ruler; and further the clause 'There is no other seer but he' negatives any other seer.

This view is set aside by the Sûtra. The Ruler within, who is spoken of in the clauses marked in the text by the terms 'with respect of the gods,' 'with respect of the worlds,' &c., is the highest Self free from all evil, Nârâya*n*a. The Sûtra purposely joins the two terms 'with respect to the gods' and 'with respect to the worlds' in order to intimate that, in addition to the clauses referring to the gods and beings (bhûta) exhibited by the Kâ*n*va-text, the Mâdhyandina-text contains additional clauses referring to the worlds, Vedas, &c. The inward Ruler spoken of in both these sets of passages is the highest Self; for attributes of that Self are declared in the text. For it is a clear attribute of the highest Self that being one only it rules all worlds, all Vedas, all divine beings, and so on. Uddâlaka asks, 'Dost thou know that Ruler within who within rules this world and the other world and all beings? &c.—tell now that Ruler within'; and Yâ*gñ*avalkya replies with the long passus, 'He who dwells in the earth,' &c., describing the Ruler within as him who, abiding within all worlds, all beings, all divinities, all Vedas, and all sacrifices, rules them from within and constitutes their Self, they in turn constituting his body. Now this is a position which can belong to none else but the highest Person, who is all-knowing, and all whose purposes immediately realise themselves. That it is the highest Self only which rules over all and is the Self of all, other Upanishad-texts also declare; cp. e.g. 'Entered within, the ruler of creatures, the Self of all'; 'Having sent forth this he entered into it. Having entered it he became sat and tyat,' &c. (Taitt. Up. II, 6). Similarly the text from the Subâla-Up., which begins, 'there was not anything here in the beginning,' and extends up to 'the one God, Nârâya*n*a,' shows that it is the highest Brahman only which rules all, is the Self of all, and has all beings for its body. Moreover, essential immortality (which the text ascribes to the Ruler within) is an attribute of the highest Self only.—Nor must it be thought that the power of seeing and so on that belongs to the highest Self is dependent on sense-organs; it rather results immediately from its essential nature, since its omniscience and power to realise its purposes are due to its own being only. In agreement herewith scripture says, 'He sees without eyes, he hears without ears, without hands and feet he grasps and hastes' (*S*vet. Up. III, 19). What terms such as 'seeing' and 'hearing' really denote is not knowledge in so far as produced by the eye and ear, but the intuitive presentation of colour and sound. In the case of the individual soul, whose essentially intelligising nature is obscured by karman, such intuitive knowledge arises only through the mediation of the sense-organs; in the case of the highest Self, on the other hand, it springs from its own nature.—Again, the clause 'there is no other seer but he' means that there is no seer other than the seer and ruler described in the preceding clauses. To explain. The clauses 'whom the earth does not know,' &c., up to 'whom the Self does not know' mean to say that the Ruler within rules without being perceived by the earth, Self, and the other beings which he rules. This is confirmed by the subsequent clauses, 'unseen but a seer,' 'unheard but a hearer,' &c. And the next clauses, 'there is no other seer but he,' &c., then mean to negative that there is any other being which could be viewed as the ruler of that Ruler. Moreover, the clauses 'that is the Self of thee,' 'He is the Self of thee' exhibit the individual Self in the genitive form ('of thee'), and thus distinguish it from the Ruler within, who is declared to be their Self.

20. And not that which Sm*ri*ti assumes, on account of the declaration of qualities not belonging to that; nor the embodied one.

'That which Sm*ri*ti assumes' is the Pradhâna; the 'embodied one' is the individual soul. Neither of these can be the Ruler within, since the text states attributes which cannot possibly belong to either. For there is not even the shadow of a possibility that essential capability of seeing and ruling all things, and being the Self of all, and immortality should belong either to the non-sentient Pradhâna or to the individual soul.—The last two Sûtras have declared that the mentioned qualities belong to the highest Self, while they do not belong to the individual soul. The next Sûtra supplies a new, independent argument.

21. For both also speak of it as something different.

Both, i.e. the Mâdhyandinas as well as the Kâ*n*vas, distinguish in their texts the embodied soul, together with speech and other non-intelligent things, from the Ruler within, representing it as an object of his rule. The Mâdhyandinas read, 'He who dwells in the Self, whom the Self does not know,' &c.; the Kâ*n*vas, 'He who dwells within understanding,' &c. The declaration of the individual Self being ruled by the Ruler within implies of course the declaration of the former being different from the latter.

The conclusion from all this is that the Ruler within is a being different from the individual soul, viz. the highest Self free from all evil, Nârâya*n*a.—Here terminates the adhikara*n*a of 'the internal Ruler.'

22. That which possesses the qualities of invisibility, &c., on account of the declaration of attributes.

The Âtharva*n*ikas read in their text, 'The higher knowledge is that by which that Indestructible is apprehended. That which is invisible, unseizable, without origin and qualities, &c., that it is which the wise regard as the source of all beings'; and further on, 'That which is higher than the high Imperishable' (Mu. Up. I, 1, 5, 6; II, 1, 2). The doubt here arises whether the Indestructible, possessing the qualities of imperceptibility, &c., and that which is higher than the Indestructible, should be taken to denote the Pradhâna and the soul of the Sâṅkhyas, or whether both denote the highest Self.—The Pûrvapakshin maintains the former alternative. For, he says, while in the text last discussed there is mentioned a special attribute of an intelligent being, viz. in the clause 'unseen but a seer,' no similar attribute is stated in the former of the two texts under discussion, and the latter text clearly describes the collective individual soul, which is higher than the imperishable Pradhâna, which itself is higher than all its effects. The reasons for this decision are as follows:—Colour and so on reside in the gross forms of non-intelligent matter, viz. the elements, earth, and so on. When, therefore, visibility and so on are expressly negatived, such negation suggests a non-sentient thing cognate to earth, &c., but of a subtle kind, and such a thing is no other than the Pradhâna. And as something higher than this Pradhâna there are known the collective souls only, under whose guidance the Pradhâna gives birth to all its effects, from the so-called Mahat downwards to individual things. This interpretation is confirmed by the comparisons set forth in the next *s*loka, 'As the spider sends forth and draws in its threads, as plants spring from the earth, as hair grows on the head and body of the living man, thus does everything arise here from the Indestructible.' The section therefore is concerned only with the Pradhâna and the individual soul.

This primâ facie view is set aside by the Sûtra. That which possesses invisibility and the other qualities stated in the text, and that which is higher than the high Indestructible, is no other than the highest Self. For the text declares attributes which belong to the highest Self only, viz. in I, 1, 9, 'He who knows all, cognises all,' &c. Let us shortly consider the connexion of the text. The passage beginning 'the higher knowledge is that by which the Indestructible is apprehended' declares an indestructible being possessing the attributes of invisibility and so on. The clause 'everything arises here from the Indestructible' next declares that from that being all things originate. Next the *s*loka, 'He who knows all and cognises all,' predicates of that Indestructible which is the source of all beings, omniscience, and similar qualities. And finally the text, 'That which is higher than the high Indestructible,' characterises that same being—which previously had been called invisible, the source of beings, indestructible, all-knowing, &c.—as the highest of all. Hence it is evident that in the text 'higher than the high Indestructible' the term 'Indestructible' does not denote the invisible, &c. Indestructible, which is the chief topic of the entire section; for there can of course be nothing higher than that which, as being all-knowing, the source of all, &c., is itself higher than anything else. The 'Indestructible' in that text therefore denotes the elements in their subtle condition.

23. Not the two others, on account of distinction and statement of difference.

The section distinguishes the indestructible being, which is the source of all, &c., from the Pradhâna as well as the individual soul, in so far, namely, as it undertakes to prove that by the cognition of one thing everything is known; and it moreover, in passages such as 'higher than the high Indestructible,' explicitly states the difference of the indestructible being from those other two.—The text first relates that Brahmâ told the knowledge of Brahman, which is the foundation of the knowledge of all, to his eldest son Atharvan: this introduces the knowledge of Brahman as the topic of the section. Then, the text proceeds, in order to obtain this knowledge of Brahman, which had been handed down through a succession of teachers to Aṅgiras, *S*auṇaka approached Aṅgiras respectfully and asked him: 'What is that through which, if known, all this is known?' i. e. since all knowledge is founded on the knowledge of Brahman, he enquires after the nature of Brahman. Aṅgiras replies that he who wishes to attain Brahman must acquire two kinds of knowledge, both of them having Brahman for their object: an indirect one which springs from the study of the *s*âstras, viz. the Veda, *S*ikshâ, Kalpa, and so on, and a direct one which springs from concentrated meditation (yoga). The latter kind of knowledge is the means of obtaining Brahman, and it is of the nature of devout meditation (bhakti), as characterised in the text 'He whom the Self chooses, by him the Self can be gained' (III, 2, 3). The means again towards this kind of knowledge is such knowledge as is gained from sacred tradition, assisted by abstention and the other six auxiliary means (see above, p. 17); in agreement with the text, 'Him the Brâhma*n*as seek to know by the study of the Veda, by sacrifice, by gifts, by penance, by fasting' (B*ri*. Up. IV, 4, 22).—Thus the Reverend Parâ*s*ara also says, 'The cause of attaining him is knowledge and work, and knowledge is twofold, according as it is based on sacred tradition or springs from discrimination.' The Mu*nd*aka-text refers to the inferior kind of knowledge in the passage 'the lower knowledge is the *Ri*g-veda,' &c., up to 'and the dharma*s*âstras'; this knowledge is the means towards the intuition of Brahman; while the higher kind of knowledge, which is called 'upâsanâ,' has the character of devout meditation (bhakti), and consists in direct intuition of Brahman, is referred to in the clause 'the higher knowledge is that by which the Indestructible is apprehended.' The text next following, 'That which is invisible,' &c., then sets forth the nature of the highest Brahman, which is the object of the two kinds of knowledge previously described. After this the passage 'As the spider sends forth and draws in its thread' declares that from that indestructible highest Brahman, as characterised before, there originates the whole universe of things, sentient and non-sentient. The next *s*loka (tapasâ *k*îyate, &c.) states particulars about this origination of the universe from Brahman. 'Brahman swells through brooding'; through brooding, i.e. thought—in agreement with a later text, 'brooding consists of thought'—Brahman swells, i.e. through thought in the form of an intention, viz. 'may I become many,' Brahman becomes ready for creation. From it there springs first 'anna,' i.e. that which is the object of fruition on the part of all enjoying agents, viz. the non-evolved subtle principles of all elements. From this 'anna' there spring successively breath, mind, and all other effected things up to work, which is the means of producing reward in the form of the heavenly world, and Release. The last *s*loka of the first chapter thereupon first states the qualities, such as omniscience and so on, which capacitate the highest Brahman for creation, and then declares that from the indestructible highest Brahman there springs the effected (kârya) Brahman, distinguished by name and form, and comprising all enjoying subjects and objects of enjoyment.—The first *s*loka of the second chapter declares first that the highest Brahman is absolutely real ('That is true'), and then admonishes those who desire to reach the indestructible highest Self, which possesses all the blessed qualities stated before and exists through itself, to turn away from other rewards and to perform all those sacrificial works depending on the three sacred fires which were seen and revealed by poets in the four Vedas and are incumbent on men according to caste and â*s*rama. The section 'this is your path' (I, 2, 1) up to 'this is the holy Brahma-world gained by your good works' (I, 2, 6) next states the particular mode of performing those works, and declares that an omission of one of the successive works enjoined in *S*ruti and Sm*ri*ti involves fruitlessness of the works actually performed, and that something not performed in the proper way is as good as not performed at all. Stanzas 7 and ff. ('But frail in truth are those boats') declare that those who perform this lower class of works have to return again and again into the Sa*m*sâra, because they aim at worldly results and are deficient in true knowledge. Stanza 8 ('but those who practise penance and faith') then proclaims that works performed by a man possessing true knowledge, and hence not aiming at worldly rewards, result in the attainment of Brahman; and stanzas 12 a, 13 ('having examined all these worlds') enjoin knowledge, strengthened by due works, on the part of a man who has turned away from *mere* works, as the means of reaching Brahman; and due recourse to a teacher on the part of him who is desirous of such knowledge.—The first chapter of the second section of the Upanishad (II, 1) then clearly teaches how the imperishable highest Brahman, i.e. the highest Self—as constituting the Self of all things and having all things for its body—has all things for its outward form and emits all things from itself. The remainder of the Upanishad ('Manifest, near,' &c.) teaches how this highest Brahman, which is imperishable and higher than the soul, which itself is higher than the Unevolved; which dwells in the highest Heaven; and which is of the nature of supreme bliss, is to be meditated upon as within the hollow of the heart; how this meditation has the character of devout faith (bhakti); and how the devotee, freeing himself from Nescience, obtains for his reward intuition of Brahman, which renders him like Brahman.

It thus clearly appears that 'on account of distinction and statement of difference' the Upanishad does not treat of the Pradhâna and the soul. For that the highest Brahman is different from those two is declared in passages such as 'That heavenly Person is without body; he is both without and within, not produced, without breath and without mind, pure, higher than what is higher than the

Imperishable' (II, 1, 2); for the last words mean 'that imperishable highest Self possessing invisibility and similar qualities, which is higher than the aggregate of individual souls, which itself is higher than the non-evolved subtle elements.' The term 'akshara' (imperishable) is to be etymologically explained either as that which pervades (a*s*nute) or that which does not pass away (a-ksharati), and is on either of these explanations applicable to the highest Self, either because that Self pervades all its effects or because it is like the so-called Mahat (which is also called akshara), free from all passing away or decaying.—Here terminates the adhikara*n*a of 'invisibility and so on.'

24. And on account of the description of its form.

'Fire is his head, his eyes the sun and the moon, the regions his ears, his speech the Vedas disclosed, the wind his breath, his heart the universe; from his feet came the earth; he is indeed the inner Self of all things' (II, 1, 4)—the outward form here described can belong to none but the highest Self; that is, the inner Self of all beings. The section therefore treats of the highest Self.

25. Vai*s*vânara (is the highest Self), on account of the distinctions qualifying the common term.

The *Kh*andogas read in their text, 'You know at present that Vai*s*vânara Self, tell us that,' &c., and further on, 'But he who meditates on the Vai*s*vânara Self as a span long,' &c. (*Kh*. Up. V, 11, 6; 18, 1). The doubt here arises whether that Vai*s*vânara Self can be made out to be the highest Self or not. The Pûrvapakshin maintains the latter alternative. For, he says, the word Vai*s*vânara is used in the sacred texts in four different senses. It denotes in the first place the intestinal fire, so in B*ri*. Up. V, 9, 'That is the Vai*s*vânara fire by which the food that is eaten is cooked, i.e. digested. Its noise is that which one hears when one covers one's ears. When man is on the point of departing this life he does not hear that noise.'—It next denotes the third of the elements, so in *Ri*. Sa*m*h. X, 88, 12, 'For the whole world the gods have made the Agni Vai*s*vânara a sign of the days.'—It also denotes a divinity, so *Ri*. Sa*m*h. I, 98, 1, 'May we be in the favour of Vai*s*vânara, for he is the king of the kings,' &c. And finally it denotes the highest Self, as in the passage, 'He offered it in the Self, in the heart, in Agni Vai*s*vânara'; and in Pra. Up. I, 7, 'Thus he rises as Vai*s*vânara, assuming all forms, as breath of life, as fire.'—And the characteristic marks mentioned in the introductory clauses of the *Kh*ândogya-text under discussion admit of interpretations agreeing with every one of these meanings of the word Vai*s*vânara.

Against this primâ facie view the Sûtra declares itself. The term 'Vai*s*vânara' in the *Kh*ândogya-text denotes the highest Self, because the 'common' term is there qualified by attributes specially belonging to the highest Self. For the passage tells us how Aupamanyava and four other great *Ri*shis, having met and discussed the question as to what was their Self and Brahman, come to the conclusion to go to Uddâlaka because he is reputed to know the Vai*s*vânara Self. Uddâlaka, recognising their anxiety to know the Vai*s*vânara Self, and deeming himself not to be fully informed on this point, refers them to A*s*vapati Kaikeya as thoroughly knowing the Vai*s*vânara Self; and they thereupon, together with Uddâlaka, approach A*s*vapati. The king duly honours them with presents, and as they appear unwilling to receive them, explains that they may suitably do so, he himself being engaged in the performance of a religious vow; and at the same time instructs them that even men knowing Brahman must avoid what is forbidden and do what is prescribed. When thereupon he adds that he will give them as much wealth as to the priests engaged in his sacrifice, they, desirous of Release and of knowing the Vai*s*vânara Self, request him to explain that Self to them. Now it clearly appears that as the *Ri*shis are said to be desirous of knowing that Brahman which is the Self of the individual souls ('what is our Self, what is Brahman'), and therefore search for some one to instruct them on that point, the Vai*s*vânara Self—to a person acquainted with which they address themselves—

can be the highest Self only. In the earlier clauses the terms used are 'Self' and 'Brahman,' in the later 'Self' and 'Vais*v*ânara'; from this it appears also that the term 'Vais*v*ânara,' which takes the place of 'Brahman,' denotes none other but the highest Self. The results, moreover, of the knowledge of the Vais*v*ânara Self, which are stated in subsequent passages, show that the Vais*v*ânara Self is the highest Brahman. 'He eats food in all worlds, in all beings, in all Selfs'; 'as the fibres of the Ishîkâ reed when thrown into the fire are burnt, thus all his sins are burned' (V, 18, 1; 24, 3).

The next Sûtra supplies a further reason for the same conclusion.

26. That which the text refers to is an inferential mark—thus.

The text describes the shape of Vais*v*ânara, of whom heaven, &c., down to earth constitute the several limbs; and it is known from Scripture and Sm*ri*ti that such is the shape of the highest Self. When, therefore, we recognise that shape as referred to in the text, this supplies an inferential mark of Vais*v*ânara being the highest Self.—The 'thus' (iti) in the Sûtra denotes a certain mode, that is to say, 'a shape of such a kind being recognised in the text enables us to infer that Vais*v*ânara is the highest Self.' For in Scripture and Sm*ri*ti alike the highest Person is declared to have such a shape. Cp. e.g. the text of the Âtharva*n*as. 'Agni is his head, the sun and moon his eyes, the regions his ears, his speech the Vedas disclosed, the wind his breath, his heart the Universe; from his feet came the earth; he is indeed the inner Self of all things' (Mu. Up. II, 1, 4). 'Agni' in this passage denotes the heavenly world, in agreement with the text 'that world indeed is Agni.' And the following Sm*ri*ti texts: 'He of whom the wise declare the heavenly world to be the head, the ether the navel, sun and moon the eyes, the regions the ears, the earth the feet; he whose Self is unfathomable is the leader of all beings'; and 'of whom Agni is the mouth, heaven the head, the ether the navel, the earth the feet, the sun the eye, the regions the ear; worship to him, the Self of the Universe!'—Now our text declares the heavenly world and so on to constitute the head and the other limbs of Vai*s*vânara. For Kaikeya on being asked by the *Ri*shis to instruct them as to the Vai*s*vânara Self recognises that they all know something about the Vai*s*vânara Self while something they do not know (for thus only we can explain his special questions), and then in order to ascertain what each knows and what not, questions them separately. When thereupon Aupamanyava replies that he meditates on heaven only as the Self, Kaikeya, in order to disabuse him from the notion that heaven is the whole Vai*s*vânara Self, teaches him that heaven is the head of Vai*s*vânara, and that of heaven which thus is a part only of Vai*s*vânara, Sute*g*as is the special name. Similarly he is thereupon told by the other *Ri*shis that they meditate only on sun, air, ether, and earth, and informs them in return that the special names of these beings are 'the omniform,' 'he who moves in various ways,' 'the full one,' 'wealth,' and 'firm rest,' and that these all are mere members of the Vai*s*vânara Self, viz. its eyes, breath, trunk, bladder, and feet. The shape thus described in detail can belong to the highest Self only, and hence Vai*s*vânara is none other but the highest Self.

The next Sûtra meets a further doubt as to this decision not yet being well established.

27. Should it be said that it is not so, on account of the word, &c., and on account of the abiding within; we say, no; on account of meditation being taught thus, on account of impossibility; and because they read of him as person.

An objection is raised. Vai*s*vânara cannot be ascertained to be the highest Self, because, on the account of the text and of the abiding within, we can understand by the Vai*s*vânara in our text the intestinal fire also. The text to which we refer occurs in the Vai*s*vânara-vidyâ of the Vâ*g*asaneyins, 'This one is the Agni Vai*s*vânara,' where the two words 'Agni' and 'Vai*s*vânara' are exhibited in co-ordination. And in the section under discussion the passage, 'the heart is the Gârhapatya fire, the mind the Anvâhârya-pa*k*ana fire, the mouth the Âhavanîya fire' (*Kh*. Up. V, 18, 2), represents the Vai*s*vânara in so far as abiding within the heart and so on as constituting the triad of sacred fires. Moreover the text, 'The first food which a man may take is in the place of Soma. And he who offers that first oblation should offer it to Prâ*n*a' (V, 19, 1), intimates that Vai*s*vânara is the abode of the offering to Prâ*n*a. In the same way the Vâ*g*asaneyins declare that Vai*s*vânara abides within man, viz. in the passage 'He who knows this Agni Vai*s*vânara shaped like a man abiding within man.' As thus Vai*s*vânara appears in co-ordination with the word 'Agni,' is represented as the triad of sacred fires, is said to be the abode of the oblation to Breath, and to abide within man, he must be viewed as the intestinal fire, and it is therefore not true that he can be identified with the highest Self only.

This objection is set aside by the Sûtra. It is not so 'on account of meditation (on the highest Self) being taught thus,' i.e. as the text means to teach that the highest Brahman which, in the manner described before, has the three worlds for its body should be meditated upon as qualified by the intestinal fire which (like other beings) constitutes Brahman's body. For the word 'Agni' denotes not only the intestinal fire, but also the highest Self in so far as qualified by the intestinal fire.—But how is this to be known?—'On account of impossibility,' i.e. because it is impossible that the mere intestinal fire should have the three worlds for its body. The true state of the case therefore is that the word Agni, which is understood to denote the intestinal fire, when appearing in co-ordination with the term Vai*s*vânara represented as having the three worlds for his body, denotes (not the intestinal fire, but) the highest Self as qualified by that fire viewed as forming the body of the Self. Thus the Lord also says, 'As Vai*s*vânara fire I abide in the body of living creatures and, being assisted by breath inspired and expired, digest the four-fold food' (Bha Gî. XIV, 15). 'As Vai*s*vânara fire' here means 'embodied in the intestinal fire.'—The *Kh*ândogya text under discussion enjoins meditation on the highest Self embodied in the Vai*s*vânara fire.—Moreover the Vâ*g*asaneyins read of him, viz. the Vai*s*vânara, as man or person, viz. in the passage 'That Agni Vai*s*vânara is the person' (*S*a. Brâ. X, 6, 1, 11). The intestinal fire by itself cannot be called a person; unconditioned personality belongs to the highest Self only. Compare 'the thousand-headed person' (*Ri.* Sa*m*h.), and 'the Person is all this' (*S*ve. Up. III, 15).

28. For the same reasons not the divinity and the element.

For the reasons stated Vai*s*vânara can be neither the deity Fire, nor the elemental fire which holds the third place among the gross elements.

29. *G*aimini thinks that there is no objection to (the word 'Agni') directly (denoting the highest Self).

So far it has been maintained that the word 'Agni,' which stands in co-ordination with the term 'Vai*s*vânara,' denotes the highest Self in so far as qualified by the intestinal fire constituting its body; and that hence the text under discussion enjoins meditation on the highest Self. *G*aimini, on the other hand, is of opinion that there is no reasonable objection to the term 'Agni,' no less than the term 'Vai*s*vânara,' being taken *directly* to denote the highest Self. That is to say—in the same way as the term 'Vai*s*vânara,' although a common term, yet when qualified by attributes especially belonging to the highest Self is known to denote the latter only as possessing the quality of ruling all men; so the word 'Agni' also when appearing in connexion with special attributes belonging to the highest Self denotes that Self only. For any quality on the ground of which 'Agni' may be etymologically explained to denote ordinary fire—as when e.g. we explain 'agni' as he who 'agre nayati'—may also, in its highest non-conditioned degree, be ascribed to the supreme Self. Another difficulty remains. The passage (V, 18, 1) 'yas tv etam evam prâdesamâtram abhivimânam,' &c. declares that the non-limited highest Brahman is limited by the measure of the pradesas, i.e. of the different spaces—heaven, ether, earth, &c.—which had previously been said to constitute the limbs of Vaisvânara. How is this possible?

30. On account of definiteness; thus Âsmarathya opines.

The teacher Âsmarathya is of opinion that the text represents the highest Self as possessing a definite extent, to the end of rendering the thought of the meditating devotee more definite. That is to say—the limitation due to the limited extent of heaven, sun, &c. has the purpose of rendering definite to thought him who pervades (abhi) all this Universe and in reality transcends all measure (vimâna).—A further difficulty remains. For what purpose is the highest Brahman here represented like a man, having a head and limbs?—This point the next Sûtra elucidates.

31. On account of meditation, Bâdari thinks.

The teacher Bâdari thinks that the representation in the text of the supreme Self in the form of a man is for the purpose of devout meditation. 'He who in this way meditates on that Vaisvânara Self as "prâdesamâtra" and "abhivimâna," he eats food in all worlds, in all beings, in all Selfs.' What this text enjoins is devout meditation for the purpose of reaching Brahman. 'In this way' means 'as having a human form.' And 'the eating' of food in all worlds, &c. means the gaining of intuitional knowledge of Brahman which abides everywhere and is in itself of the nature of supreme bliss. The special kind of food, i.e. the special objects of enjoyment which belong to the different Selfs standing under the influence of karman cannot be meant here; for those limited objects have to be shunned by those who desire final release. A further question arises. If Vaisvânara is the highest Self, how can the text say that the altar is its chest, the grass on the altar its hairs, and so on? (V, 18, 2.) Such a statement has a sense only if we understand by Vaisvânara the intestinal fire.—This difficulty the next Sûtra elucidates.

32. On account of imaginative identification, thus *G*aimini thinks; for thus the text declares.

The teacher *G*aimini is of opinion that the altar is stated to be the chest of Vaisvânara, and so on, in order to effect an imaginative identification of the offering to Prâ*n*a which is daily performed by the meditating devotees and is the means of pleasing Vaisvânara, having the heaven and so on for his body, i.e. the highest Self, with the Agnihotra-offering. For the fruit due to meditation on the highest Self, as well as the identity of the offering to breath with the Agnihotra, is declared in the following text, 'He who without knowing this offers the Agnihotra—that would be as if removing the live coals he were to pour his libation on dead ashes. But he who offers this Agnihotra with a full knowledge of its purport, he offers it in all worlds, in all beings, in all Selfs. As the fibres of the Ishîkâ reed when thrown into the fire are burnt, thus all his sins are burnt.' (V, 24, 1–3.)

33. Moreover, they record him in that.

They (i.e. the Vâ*g*asaneyins) speak of him, viz. Vaisvânara who has heaven for his head, &c.—i.e. the highest Self—as within that, i.e. the body of the devotee, so as to form the abode of the oblation to Prâ*n*a; viz. in the text, 'Of that Vaisvânara Self the head is Sute*g*as,' and so on. The context is as follows. The clause 'He who meditates on the Vaisvânara Self as prâdesamâtra,' &c. enjoins meditation on the highest Self having the three worlds for its body, i.e. on Vaisvânara. The following clause 'he eats food in all worlds' teaches that the attaining of Brahman is the reward of such meditation. And then the text proceeds to teach the Agnihotra offered to Prâ*n*a, which is something subsidiary to the meditation taught. The text here establishes an identity between the members—fire, sun, &c.—of the Vaisvânara enjoined as object of meditation (which members are called Sute*g*as, Vi*s*varûpa, &c.), and parts—viz. head, eye, breath, trunk, bladder, feet—of the worshipper's body. 'The head is Sute*g*as'—that means: the head of the devotee is (identical with) heaven, which is the head of the highest Self; and so on up to 'the feet,' i.e. the feet of the devotee are identical with the earth, which constitutes the feet of the highest Self. The devotee having thus reflected on the highest Self, which has the three worlds for its body, as present within his own body, thereupon is told to view his own chest, hair, heart, mind and mouth as identical with the altar, grass and the other things which are required for the Agnihotra; further to identify the oblation to Prâ*n*a with the Agnihotra, and by means of this Prâ*n*a-agnihotra to win the favour of Vai*s*vânara, i.e. the highest Self. The final conclusion then remains that Vai*s*vânara is none other than the highest Self, the supreme Person.—Here terminates the adhikara*n*a of 'Vai*s*vânara.'

## THIRD PÂDA.

1. The abode of heaven, earth, &c. (is the highest Self), on account of terms which are its own.

The followers of the Atharva-veda have the following text, 'He in whom the heaven, the earth and the sky are woven, the mind also, with all the vital airs, know him alone as the Self, and leave off other words; he is the bank (setu) of the Immortal' (Mu. Up. II, 2, 5). The doubt here arises whether the being spoken of as the abode of heaven, earth, and so on, is the individual soul or the highest Self.

The Pûrvapakshin maintains the former alternative. For, he remarks, in the next *s*loka, 'where like spokes in the nave of a wheel the arteries meet, he moves about within, becoming manifold,' the word 'where' refers back to the being which in the preceding *s*loka had been called the abode of heaven, earth, and so on, the clause beginning with 'where' thus declaring that that being is the basis of the arteries; and the next clause declares that same being to become manifold or to be born in many ways. Now, connexion with the arteries is clearly characteristic of the individual soul; and so is being born in many forms, divine and so on. Moreover, in the very *s*loka under discussion it is said that that being is the abode of the mind and the five vital airs, and this also is a characteristic attribute of the individual soul. It being, on these grounds, ascertained that the text refers to the individual soul we must attempt to reconcile therewith, as well as we can, what is said about its being the abode of heaven, earth, &c.

This primâ facie view is set aside by the Sûtra. That which is described as the abode of heaven, earth, &c. is none other than the highest Brahman, on account of a term which is 'its own,' i. e. which specially belongs to it. The clause we have in view is 'he is the bank of the Immortal.' This description applies to the highest Brahman only, which alone is, in all Upanishads, termed the cause of the attainment of Immortality; cp. e. g. 'Knowing him thus a man becomes immortal; there is no other path to go' (*S*ve. Up. III, 8). The term 'setu' is derived from *si*, which means to bind, and therefore means that which binds, i. e. makes one to attain immortality; or else it may be understood to mean that which leads towards immortality that lies beyond the ocean of sa*m*sâra, in the same way as a bank or bridge (setu) leads to the further side of a river.—Moreover the word 'Self' (âtman) (which, in the text under discussion, is also applied to that which is the abode of heaven, earth, &c.), without any further qualification, primarily denotes Brahman only; for 'âtman' comes from *âp*, to reach, and means that which 'reaches' all other things in so far as it rules them. And further on (II, 2, 7) there are other terms, 'all knowing,' 'all cognising,' which also specially belong to the highest Brahman only. This Brahman may also be represented as the abode of the arteries; as proved e. g. by Mahânâr. Up. (XI, 8-12), 'Surrounded by the arteries he hangs . . . in the middle of this pointed flame there dwells the highest Self.' Of that Self it may also be said that it is born in many ways; in accordance with texts such as 'not born, he is born in many ways; the wise know the place of his birth.' For in order to fit himself to be a refuge for gods, men, &c. the supreme Person, without however putting aside his true nature, associates himself with the shape, make, qualities and works of the different classes of beings, and thus is born in many ways. Sm*ri*ti says the same: 'Though being unborn, of non-perishable nature, the Lord of all beings, yet presiding over my Prak*ri*ti I am born by my own mysterious power' (Bha. Gî. IV, 6). Of the mind also and the other organs of the individual soul the highest Self is strictly the abode; for it is the abode of everything.—The next Sûtra supplies a further reason.

2. And on account of its being declared that to which the released have to resort.

The Person who is the abode of heaven, earth, and so

on, is also declared by the text to be what is to be reached by those who are released from the bondage of Sa*m*sâra existence. 'When the seer sees the brilliant maker and Lord as the Person who has his source in Brahman, then possessing true knowledge he shakes off good and evil, and, free from passion, reaches the highest oneness' (Mu. Up. III, 1, 3). 'As the flowing rivers disappear in the sea, losing their name and form, thus a wise man freed from name and form goes to the divine Person who is higher than the high' (III, 2, 8). For it is only those freed from the bondage of Sa*m*sâra who shake off good and evil, are free from passion, and freed from name and form.

For the Sa*m*sâra state consists in the possession of name and form, which is due to connexion with non-sentient matter, such connexion springing from good and evil works. The Person therefore who is the abode of heaven, earth, &c., and whom the text declares to be the aim to be reached by those who, having freed themselves from good and evil, and hence from all contact with matter, attain supreme oneness with the highest Brahman, can be none other than this highest Brahman itself.

This conclusion, based on terms exclusively applicable to the highest Brahman, is now confirmed by reference to the absence of terms specially applicable to the individual soul.

3. Not that which is inferred, on account of the absence of terms denoting it, and (so also not) the bearer of the Prâ*n*as (i.e. the individual soul).

As the section under discussion does not treat of the Pradhâna, there being no terms referring to that, so it is with regard to the individual soul also. In the text of the Sûtra we have to read either anumânam, i.e. 'inference,' in the sense of 'object of inference,' or else ânumânam, 'object of inference'; what is meant being in both cases the Pradhâna inferred to exist by the Sâṅkhyas.

4. On account of the declaration of difference.

'On the same tree man sits immersed in grief, bewildered by "anîsâ"; but when he sees the other one, the Lord, contented, and his glory; then his grief passes away' (Mu. Up. III, 1, 2). This, and similar texts, speak of that one, i.e. the one previously described as the abode of heaven, earth, &c., as different from the individual soul.—The text means—the individual soul grieves, being bewildered by her who is not 'îsa,' i.e. Prak*ri*ti, the object of fruition. But its grief passes away when it sees him who is other than itself, i.e. the beloved Lord of all, and his greatness which consists in his ruling the entire world.

5. On account of the subject-matter.

It has been already shown, viz. under I, 2, 21, that the highest Brahman constitutes the initial topic of the Upanishad. And by the arguments set forth in the previous Sûtras of the present Pâda, we have removed all suspicion as to the topic started being dropped in the body of the Upanishad.

6. And on account of abiding and eating.

'Two birds, inseparable friends, cling to the same tree. One of them eats the sweet fruit; without eating, the other looks on' (Mu. Up. III, 1, 1). This text declares that one enjoys the fruit of works while the other, without enjoying, shining abides within the body. Now this shining being which does not enjoy the fruit of works can only be the being previously described as the abode of heaven, earth, &c., and characterised as all knowing, the bridge of immortality, the Self of all; it can in no way be the individual Self which, lamenting, experiences the results of its works. The settled conclusion, therefore, is that the abode of heaven, earth, and so on, is none other than the highest Self.—Here terminates the adhikara*n*a of 'heaven, earth, and so on.'

7. The bhûman (is the highest Self), as the instruction about it is additional to that about serenity.

The *Kh*andogas read as follows: 'Where one sees nothing

else, hears nothing else, knows nothing else, that is fulness (bhûman). Where one sees something else, hears something else, knows something else, that is the Little' (*Kh.* Up. VII, 23, 24).

The term 'bhûman' is derived from *bahu* (much, many), and primarily signifies 'muchness.' By 'much' in this connexion, we have however to understand, not what is numerous, but what is large, for the text uses the term in contrast with the 'Little' (alpa), i.e. the 'Small.' And the being qualified as 'large,' we conclude from the context to be the Self; for this section of the Upanishad at the outset states that he who knows the Self overcomes grief (VII, 1, 3), then teaches the knowledge of the bhûman, and concludes by saying that 'the Self is all this' (VII, 25, 2).

The question now arises whether the Self called bhûman is the individual Self or the highest Self.—The Pûrvapakshin maintains the former view. For, he says, to Nârada who had approached Sanatkumâra with the desire to be instructed about the Self, a series of beings, beginning with 'name' and ending with 'breath,' are enumerated as objects of devout meditation; Nârada asks each time whether there be anything greater than name, and so on, and each time receives an affirmative reply ('speech is greater than name,' &c.); when, however, the series has advanced as far as Breath, there is no such question and reply. This shows that the instruction about the Self terminates with Breath, and hence we conclude that breath in this place means the individual soul which is associated with breath, not a mere modification of air. Also the clauses 'Breath is father, breath is mother,' &c. (VII, 15, 1), show that breath here is something intelligent. And this is further proved by the clause 'Slayer of thy father, slayer of thy mother,' &c. (VII, 15, 2; 3), which declares that he who offends a father, a mother, &c., as long as there is breath in them, really hurts them, and therefore deserves reproach; while no blame attaches to him who offers even the grossest violence to them after their breath has departed. For a conscious being only is capable of being hurt, and hence the word 'breath' here denotes such a being only. Moreover, as it is observed that also in the case of such living beings as have no vital breath (viz. plants), suffering results, or does not result, according as injury is inflicted or not, we must for this reason also decide that the breath spoken of in the text as something susceptible of injury is the individual soul. It consequently would be an error to suppose, on the ground of the comparison of Prâ*n*a to the nave of a wheel in which the spokes are set, that Prâ*n*a here denotes the highest Self; for the highest Self is incapable of being injured. That comparison, on the other hand, is quite in its place, if we understand by Prâ*n*a the individual soul, for the whole aggregate of non-sentient matter which stands to the individual soul in the relation of object or instrument of enjoyment, has an existence dependent on the individual soul. And this soul, there called Prâ*n*a, is what the text later on calls Bhûman; for as there is no question and reply as to something greater than Prâ*n*a, Prâ*n*a continues, without break, to be the subject-matter up to the mention of bhûman. The paragraphs intervening between the section on Prâ*n*a (VII, 15) and the section on the Bhûman (VII, 23 ff.) are to be understood as follows. The Prâ*n*a section closes with the remark that he who fully knows Prâ*n*a is an ativâdin, i. e. one who makes a final supreme declaration. In the next sentence then, 'But this one in truth is an ativâdin who makes a supreme statement by means of the True,' the clause 'But this one is an ativâdin' refers back to the previously mentioned person who knows the Prâ*n*a, and the relative clause 'who makes,' &c., enjoins on him the speaking of the truth as an auxiliary element in the meditation on Prâ*n*a. The next paragraph, 'When one understands the truth then one declares the truth,' intimates that speaking the truth stands in a supplementary relation towards the cognition of the true nature of the Prâ*n*a as described before. For the accomplishment of such cognition the subsequent four paragraphs enjoin reflection, faith, attendance on a spiritual guide, and the due performance of sacred duties. In order that such duties may be undertaken, the next paragraphs then teach that bliss constitutes the nature of the individual soul, previously called Prâ*n*a, and finally that the Bhûman, i.e. the supreme fulness of such bliss, is the proper object of inquiry. The final purport of the teaching, therefore, is that the true nature of the individual soul, freed from Nescience, is abundant bliss—a conclusion which perfectly agrees with the initial statement that he who knows the Self passes beyond sorrow. That being, therefore, which has the attribute of being 'bhûman,' is the individual Self. This being so, it is also intelligible why, further on, when the text describes the glory and power of the individual Self, it uses the term 'I'; for 'I' denotes just the individual Self: 'I am below, I am above, &c., I am all this' (VII, 25, 1). This conclusion having been settled, all remaining clauses must be explained so as to agree with it.

This primâ facie view is set aside by the Sûtra. The being characterised in the text as 'bhûman' is not the individual Self, but the highest Self, since instruction is given about the bhûman in addition to 'serenity' (sa*m*prasâda). 'Sa*m*prasâda' denotes the individual soul, as we know from the following text, 'Now that "serenity," having risen from out this body, and having reached the highest light, appears in its true form' (*Kh*. Up. VIII, 3, 4). Now in the text under discussion instruction is given about a being called 'the True,' and possessing the attribute of 'bhûman,' as being something additional to the individual soul; and this being called 'the True' is none other than the highest Brahman. Just as in the series of beings beginning with name and ending with breath, each successive being is mentioned in addition to the preceding one—wherefrom we conclude that it is something really different from what precedes; so that being also which is called 'the True,' and which is mentioned in addition to the individual Self called Prâ*n*a, is something different from the individual Self, and this being called 'the True' is the same as the Bhûman; in other words, the text teaches that the Bhûman is the highest Brahman called 'the True.' This the V*ri*ttikâra also declares: 'But the Bhûman only. The Bhûman is Brahman, because in the series beginning with name instruction is given about it subsequently to the individual Self.'

But how do we know that the instruction as to 'the True' is in addition to, and refers to something different from, the being called Prâna?—The text, after having declared that he who knows the Prâna is an ativâdin, goes on, 'But really that one is an ativâdin who makes a supreme declaration by means of the True.' The 'but' here clearly separates him who is an ativâdin by means of the True from the previous ativâdin, and the clause thus does not cause us to recognise him who is ativâdin by means of Prâna; hence 'the True' which is the cause of the latter ativâdin being what he is must be something different from the Prâna which is the cause of the former ativâdin's quality.—But we have maintained above that the text enjoins the speaking of 'the True' merely as an auxiliary duty for him who knows Prâna; and that hence the Prâna continues to be the general subject-matter!—This contention is untenable, we reply. The conjunction 'but' shows that the section gives instruction about a new ativâdin, and does not merely declare that the ativâdin previously mentioned has to speak the truth. It is different with texts such as 'But that one indeed is an Agnihotrin who speaks the truth'; there we have no knowledge of any further Agnihotrin, and therefore must interpret the text as enjoining truthfulness as an obligation incumbent on the ordinary Agnihotrin. In the text under discussion, on the other hand, we have the term 'the True,' which makes us apprehend that there is a further ativâdin different from the preceding one; and we know that that term is used to denote the highest Brahman, as e.g. in the text, 'The True, knowledge, the Infinite is Brahman.' The ativâdin who takes his stand on this Brahman, therefore, must be viewed as different from the preceding ativâdin; and a difference thus established on the basis of the meaning and connexion of the different sentences cannot be set aside. An ativâdin ('one who in his declaration goes beyond') is one who maintains, as object of his devotion, something which, as being more beneficial to man, surpasses other objects of devotion. The text at first declares that he who knows Prâ*n*a, i.e. the individual soul, is an ativâdin, in so far as the object of his devout meditation surpasses the objects from name up to hope; and then goes on to say that, as that object also is not of *supreme* benefit to man, an ativâdin in the full sense of the term is he only who proclaims as the object of his devotion the highest Brahman, which alone is of supreme unsurpassable benefit to man. 'He who is an ativâdin by the True,' i.e. he who is an ativâdin characterised by the highest Brahman as the object of his meditation. For the same reason the pupil entreats, 'Sir, may I be an ativâdin with the True!' and the teacher replies, 'But we must desire to know the True!'—Moreover, the text, VII, 26, 1, 'Prâ*n*a springs from the Self,' declares the origination from the Self of the being called Prâ*n*a; and from this we infer that the Self which is introduced as the general subject-matter of the section, in the clause 'He who knows the Self passes beyond death,' is different from the being called Prâ*n*a.—The contention that, because there is no question and answer as to something greater than Prâ*n*a, the instruction about the Self must be supposed to come to an end with the instruction about Prâ*n*a, is by no means legitimate. For that a new subject is introduced is proved, not only by those questions and answers; it may be proved by other means also, and we have already explained such means. The following is the reason why the pupil does not ask the question whether there is anything greater than Prâ*n*a. With regard to the non-sentient objects extending from name to hope—each of which surpasses the preceding one in so far as it is more beneficial to man—the teacher does not declare that he who knows them is an ativâdin; when, however, he comes to the individual soul, there called Prâ*n*a, the knowledge of whose true nature he considers highly beneficial, he expressly says that 'he who sees this, notes this, understands this is an ativâdin' (VII, 15, 4). The pupil therefore imagines that the instruction about the Self is now completed, and hence asks no further question. The teacher on the other hand, holding that even that knowledge is not the highest, spontaneously continues his teaching, and tells the pupil that truly he only is an ativâdin who proclaims the supremely and absolutely beneficial being which is called 'the True,' i. e. the highest Brahman. On this suggestion of the highest Brahman the pupil, desirous to learn its true nature and true worship, entreats the teacher, 'Sir, may I become an ativâdin by the True!' Thereupon the teacher—in order to help the pupil to become an ativâdin,—a position which requires previous intuition of Brahman—enjoins on him meditation on Brahman which is the means to attain intuition ('You must desire to know the True!'); next recommends to him reflection (manana) which is the means towards meditation ('You must desire to understand reflection'); then—taking it for granted that the injunction of reflection implies the injunction of 'hearing' the sacred texts which is the preliminary for reflecting—advises him to cherish faith in Brahman which is the preliminary means towards hearing ('You must desire to understand faith'); after that tells him to practise, as a preliminary towards faith, reliance on Brahman ('You must desire to understand reliance'); next admonishes him, to apply himself to 'action,' i. e. to make the effort which is a preliminary requisite for all the activities enumerated ('You must desire to understand action'). Finally, in order to encourage the pupil to enter on all this, the teacher tells him to recognise that bliss constitutes the nature of that Brahman which is the aim of all his effort ('You must desire to understand bliss'); and bids him to realise that the bliss which constitutes Brahman's nature is supremely large and full ('You must endeavour to understand the "bhûman," i. e. the supreme fulness of bliss'). And of this Brahman, whose nature is absolute bliss, a definition is then given as follows, 'Where one sees nothing else, hears nothing else, knows nothing else, that is bhûman.' This means—when the meditating devotee realises the intuition of this Brahman, which consists of absolute bliss, he does not see anything apart from it, since the whole aggregate of things is contained within the essence and outward manifestation (vibhûti) of Brahman. He, therefore, who has an intuitive knowledge of Brahman as qualified by its attributes and its vibhûti—which also is called ais*v*arya, i. e. lordly power—and consisting of supreme bliss, sees nothing else since there *is* nothing apart from Brahman; and sees, i. e. feels no pain since all possible objects of perception and feeling are of the nature of bliss or pleasure; for pleasure is just that which, being experienced, is agreeable to man's nature.—But an objection is raised, it is an actual fact that this very world is perceived as something different from Brahman, and as being of the nature of pain, or at the best, limited pleasure; how then can it be perceived as being a manifestation of Brahman, as having Brahman for its Self, and hence consisting of bliss?—The individual souls, we reply, which are under the influence of karman, are conscious of this world as different from Brahman, and, according to their individual karman, as either made up of pain or limited pleasure. But as this view depends altogether on karman, to him who has freed himself from Nescience in the form of karman, this same world presents itself as lying within the intuition of Brahman, together with its qualities and vibhûti, and hence as essentially blissful. To a man troubled with excess of bile the water he drinks has a taste either downright unpleasant or moderately pleasant, according to the degree to which his health is affected; while the same water has an unmixedly pleasant taste for a man in good health. As long as a boy is not aware that some plaything is meant to amuse him, he does not care for it; when on the other hand he apprehends it as meant to give him delight, the thing becomes very dear to him. In the same way the world becomes an object of supreme love to him who recognises it as having Brahman for its Self, and being a mere plaything of Brahman—of Brahman, whose essential nature is supreme bliss, and which is a treasure-house, as it were, of numberless auspicious qualities of supreme excellence. He who has reached such intuition of Brahman, sees nothing apart from it and feels no pain. This the concluding passages of the text set forth in detail, 'He who sees, perceives and understands this, loves the Self, delights in the Self, revels in the Self, rejoices in the Self; he becomes a Self ruler, he moves and rules in all worlds according to his pleasure. But those who have a different knowledge from this, they are ruled by others, they live in perishable worlds, they do not move in all the worlds according to their liking.' 'They are ruled by others,' means 'they are in the power of karman.' And further on, 'He who sees this does not see death, nor illness, nor pain; he who sees this sees everything and obtains everything everywhere.'

That Brahman is of the nature of supreme bliss has been shown in detail under I, 1, 12 ff.—The conclusion from all this is that, as the text applies the term 'bhûman' to what was previously called the Real or True, and which is different from the individual soul there called Prâ*n*a, the bhûman is the highest Brahman.

8. And on account of the suitability of the attributes.

The attributes also which the text ascribes to the bhûman suit the highest Self only. So immortality ('The Bhûman is immortal,' VII, 24, 1); not being based on something else ('it rests in its own greatness'); being the Self of all ('the bhûman is below,' &c., 'it is all this'); being that which produces all ('from the Self there springs breath,' &c.). All these attributes can be reconciled with the highest Self only.—The Pûrvapakshin has pointed to the text which declares the 'I' to be the Self of all (VII, 25, 1); but what that text really teaches is meditation on Brahman under the aspect of the 'I.' This appears from the introductory clause 'Now follows the instruction with regard to the I.' That of the 'I,' i. e. the individual Self, also the highest Self is the true Self, scripture declares in several places, so e. g. in the text about the inward Ruler (B*ri*. Up. III, 7). As therefore the individual soul finds its completion in the highest Self only, the word 'I' also extends in its connotation up to the highest Self; and the instruction about the 'I' which is given in the text has thus for its object meditation on the highest Self in so far as having the individual Self for its body. As the highest Self has all beings for its body and thus is the Self of all, it is the Self of the individual soul also; and this the text declares in the passage beginning 'Now follows the instruction about the Self,' and ending 'Self is all this.' In order to prove this the text declares that everything originates from the highest Self which forms the Self of the individual soul also, viz. in the passage 'From the Self of him who sees this, perceives this, knows this, there springs breath,' &c.—that means: breath and all other beings spring from the highest Self which abides within the Self of the meditating devotee as its inner ruler. Hence, the text means to intimate, meditation should be performed on the 'I,' in order thus firmly to establish the cognition that the highest Self has the 'I,' i. e. the individual soul for its body.

It is thus an established conclusion that the bhûman is the highest Self. Here terminates the adhikara*n*a of 'fulness.'

9. The Imperishable (is Brahman), on account of its supporting that which is the end of ether.

The Vâ*g*asaneyins, in the chapter recording the questions asked by Gârgî, read as follows: 'He said, O Gârgî, the Brâhma*n*as call that the Imperishable. It is neither coarse nor fine, neither short nor long, it is not red, not fluid, it is without a shadow,' &c. (B*ri*. Up. III, 8, 8). A doubt here arises whether that Imperishable be the Pradhâna, or the individual soul, or the highest Self.—The Pradhâna, it may be maintained in the first place. For we see that in passages such as 'higher than that which is higher than the Imperishable' the term 'Imperishable' actually denotes the Pradhâna; and moreover the qualities enumerated, viz. not being either coarse or fine, &c., are characteristic of the Pradhâna.—But, an objection is raised, in texts such as 'That knowledge by which the Imperishable is apprehended' (Mu. Up. I, 1, 5), the word 'Imperishable' is seen to denote the highest Brahman!—In cases, we reply, where the meaning of a word may be determined on the basis either of some other means of proof or of Scripture, the former meaning presents itself to the mind first, and hence there is no reason why such meaning should not be accepted.—But how do you know that the ether of the text is not ether in the ordinary sense?—From the description, we reply, given of it in the text, 'That above the heavens,' &c. There it is said that all created things past, present and future rest on ether as their basis; ether cannot therefore be taken as that elementary substance which itself is comprised in the sphere of things created. We therefore must understand by 'ether' matter in its subtle state, i. e. the Pradhâna; and the Imperishable which thereupon is declared to be the support of that Pradhâna, hence cannot itself be the Pradhâna.—Nor is there any force in the argument that a sense established by some other means of proof presents itself to the mind more immediately than a sense established by Scripture; for as the word 'akshara' (i. e. the non-perishable) intimates its sense directly through the meaning of its constituent elements other means of proof need not be regarded at all.

Moreover Yâ*gñ*avalkya had said previously that the ether is the cause and abode of all things past, present and future, and when Gârgî thereupon asks him in what that ether 'is woven,' i. e. what is the causal substance and abode of ether, he replies 'the Imperishable.' Now this also proves that by the 'Imperishable' we have to understand the Pradhâna which from other sources is known to be the causal substance, and hence the abode, of all effected things whatsoever.

This primâ facie view is set aside by the Sûtra. The 'Imperishable' is the highest Brahman, because the text declares it to support that which is the end, i. e. that which lies beyond ether, viz. unevolved matter (avyâk*ri*tam). The ether referred to in Gârgî's question is not ether in the ordinary sense, but what lies beyond ether, viz. unevolved matter, and hence the 'Imperishable' which is said to be the support of that 'unevolved' cannot itself be the 'unevolved,' i. e. cannot be the Pradhâna. Let us, then, the Pûrvapakshin resumes, understand by the 'Imperishable,' the individual soul; for this may be viewed as the support of the entire aggregate of non-sentient matter, inclusive of the elements in their subtle condition; and the qualities of non-coarseness, &c., are characteristic of that soul also. Moreover there are several texts in which the term 'Imperishable' is actually seen to denote the individual soul; so e. g. 'the non-evolved' is merged in the 'Imperishable'; 'That of which the non-evolved is the body; that of which the Imperishable is the body'; 'All the creatures are the Perishable, the non-changing Self is called the Imperishable' (Bha. Gî. XV, 16).

To this alternative primâ facie view the next Sûtra replies.

10. And this (supporting) (springs) from command.

The text declares that this supporting of ether and all other things proceeds from command. 'In the command of that Imperishable sun and moon stand, held apart; in the command of that Imperishable heaven and earth stand, held apart,' &c. Now such supreme command, through which all things in the universe are held apart, cannot possibly belong to the individual soul in the state either of bondage or of release. The commanding 'Imperishable' therefore is none other than the supreme Person.

11. And on account of the exclusion of (what is of) another nature (than Brahman).

Another nature, i. e. the nature of the Pradhâna, and so on. A supplementary passage excludes difference on the part of the Imperishable from the supreme Person. 'That Imperishable, O Gârgî, is unseen but seeing; unheard but hearing; unthought but thinking; unknown but knowing. There is nothing that sees but it, nothing that hears but it, nothing that thinks but it, nothing that knows but it. In that Imperishable, O Gârgî, the ether is woven, warp and woof.' Here the declaration as to the Imperishable being what sees, hears, &c. excludes the non-intelligent Pradhâna; and the declaration as to its being all-seeing, &c. while not seen by any one excludes the individual soul. This exclusion of what has a nature other than that of the highest Self thus confirms the view of that Self being meant.—Or else the Sûtra may be explained in a different way, viz. 'On account of the exclusion of the existence of another.' On this alternative the text 'There is nothing that sees but it,' &c., is to be understood as follows: 'while this Imperishable, not seen by others but seeing all others, forms the basis of all things different from itself; there is no other principle which, unseen by the Imperishable but seeing it, could form *its* basis,' i. e. the text would exclude the existence of any other thing but the Imperishable, and thus implicitly deny that the Imperishable is either the Pradhâna or the individual Self.—Moreover the text 'By the command of that Imperishable men praise those who give, the gods follow the Sacrificer, the fathers the Darvî-offering,' declares the Imperishable to be that on the command of which there proceed all works enjoined by Scripture and Sm*ri*ti, such as sacrificing, giving, &c., and this again shows that the Imperishable must be Brahman, the supreme Person. Again, the subsequent *passus*, 'Whosoever without knowing that Imperishable,' &c., declares that ignorance of the Imperishable leads to the Sa*m*sâra, while knowledge of it helps to reach Immortality: this also proves that the Imperishable is the highest Brahman.—Here terminates the adhikara*n*a of 'the Imperishable.'

12. On account of his being designated as the object of seeing, he (i. e. the highest Self) (is that object).

The followers of the Atharva-veda, in the section containing the question asked by Satyakâma, read as follows: 'He again who meditates with this syllable Aum of three Mâtrâs on the highest Person, he comes to light and to the sun. As a snake frees itself from its skin, so he frees himself from evil. He is led up by the Sâman verses to the Brahma-world; he sees the person dwelling in the castle who is higher than the individual souls concreted with bodies and higher (than those)' (Pra. Up. V, 2). Here the terms 'he meditates' and 'he sees' have the same sense, 'seeing' being the result of devout meditation; for according to the principle expressed in the text (*Kh*. Up. III, 14) 'According as man's thought is in this world,' what is reached by the devotee is the object of meditation; and moreover the text exhibits the same object, viz. 'the highest Person' in connexion with both verbs.

The doubt here presents itself whether the highest Person in this text be the so-called four-faced Brahmâ, the Lord of the mundane egg who represents the individual souls in their collective aspect, or the supreme Person who is the Lord of all.—The Pûrvapakshin maintains the former view. For, he argues, on the introductory question, 'He who here among men should meditate until death on the syllable Om, what would he obtain by it?' The text first declares that he who meditates on that syllable as having one Mâtrâ, obtains the world of men; and next, that he who meditates on it as having two Mâtrâs obtains the world of the atmosphere. Hence the Brahma-world, which the text after that represents as the object reached by him who meditates on Om as having three syllables, must be the world of Brahmâ *K*aturmukha who is constituted by the aggregate of the individual souls. What the soul having reached that world sees, therefore is the same Brahmâ *K*aturmukha; and thus only the attribute 'etasmâ*g* *g*îvaghanât parât param' is suitable; for the collective soul, i.e. Brahmâ *K*aturmukha, residing in the Brahma-world is higher (para) than the distributive or discrete soul (*g*îva) which is concreted (ghanî-bhûta) with the body and sense-organs, and at the same time is higher (para) than these. The highest Person mentioned in the text, therefore, is Brahmâ *K*aturmukha; and the qualities mentioned further on, such as absence of decay, &c., must be taken in such a way as to agree with that Brahmâ.

To this primâ facie view the Sûtra replies that the object of seeing is He, i.e. the highest Self, on account of designation. The text clearly designates the object of seeing as the highest Self. For the concluding *s*loka, which refers to that object of seeing, declares that 'by means of the O*m*kâra he who knows reaches that which is tranquil, free from decay, immortal, fearless, the highest'—all which attributes properly belong to the highest Self only, as we know from texts such as 'that is the Immortal, that is the fearless, that is Brahman' (*Kh.* Up. IV, 15, 1). The qualification expressed in the clause 'etasmâ*g* *g*îva-ghanât,' &c. may also refer to the highest Self only, not to Brahmâ *K*aturmukha; for the latter is himself comprehended by the term '*g*îvaghana.' For that term denotes all souls which are embodied owing to karman; and that *K*aturmukha is one of those we know from texts such as 'He who first creates Brahmâ' (*S*vet. Up. VI, 18). Nor is there any strength in the argument that, since the Brahma-world mentioned in the text is known to be the world of *K*aturmukha, as it follows next on the world of the atmosphere, the being abiding there must needs be *K*aturmukha. We rather argue as follows—as from the concluding clause 'that which is tranquil, free from decay,' &c., we ascertain that the object of intuition is the highest Brahman, the Brahma-world spoken of as the abode of the seeing devotee can*not* be the perishable world of Brahmâ *K*aturmukha. A further reason for this conclusion is supplied by what the text says about 'him who is freed from all evil being led up by the Sâman verses to the world of Brahman'; for the place reached by him who is freed from all evil cannot be the mere abode of *K*aturmukha. Hence also the concluding *s*loka says with reference to that Brahma-world 'that which the wise teach': what the wise see and teach is the abode of the highest, of Vish*n*u; cp. the text 'the wise ever see that highest abode of Vish*n*u.' Nor is it even strictly true that the world of Brahmâ follows on the atmosphere, for the svarga-world and several others lie between the two.

We therefore shortly explain the drift of the whole chapter as follows. At the outset of the reply given to Satyakâma there is mentioned, in addition to the highest (para) Brahman, a lower (apara) Brahman. This lower or effected (kârya) Brahman is distinguished as twofold, being connected either with this terrestrial world or yonder, non-terrestrial, world. Him who meditates on the Pra*n*ava as having one syllable, the text declares to obtain a reward in this world—he reaches the world of men. He, on the other hand, who meditates on the Pra*n*ava as having two syllables is said to obtain his reward in a super-terrestrial sphere—he reaches the world of the atmosphere. And he finally who, by means of the trisyllabic Pra*n*ava which denotes the highest Brahman, meditates on this very highest Brahman, is said to reach that Brahman, i. e. the supreme Person.—The object of seeing is thus none other than the highest Self.—Here terminates the adhikara*n*a of the 'object of seeing.'

13. The small (ether) (is Brahman), on account of the subsequent (arguments).

The *Kh*andogas have the following text, 'Now in that city of Brahman there is the palace, the small lotus, and in it that small ether. Now what is within that small ether that is to be sought for, that is to be understood' (*Kh.* Up. VIII, 1, 1).—The question here arises whether that small ether (space) within the lotus of the heart be the material element called ether, or the individual Self, or the highest Self.—The first view presenting itself is that the element is meant, for the reason that the word 'ether' is generally used in that sense; and because the clause 'what is within that small ether' shows that the ether mentioned constitutes the abode of something else that is to be enquired into.—This view is set aside by the Sûtra. The small ether within the heart is the highest Brahman, on account of the subsequent reasons, contained in clauses of the same section. The passage 'That Self which is free from evil, free from old age, free from death, free from grief, free from hunger and thirst, whose wishes and purposes come true' (VIII, 7, 1) ascribes to that small ether qualities—such as unconditioned Selfhood, freedom from evil, &c.—which clearly show that ether to be the highest Brahman. And this conclusion is confirmed by what other texts say about him who knows the small ether attaining the power of realising his own wishes, 'Those who depart from hence having come to know the Self and those real wishes, for them there is freedom in all worlds'; and 'whatever object he desires, by his mere will it comes to him; having obtained it he is happy' (*Kh.* Up. VIII, 1, 6; 2, 9). If moreover the ether within the heart were the elemental ether, the comparison instituted in the passage 'As large as that (elemental) ether is, so large is this ether within the heart' would be wholly inappropriate. Nor must it be said that that comparison rests on the limitation of the ether within the heart (so that the two terms compared would be the limited elemental ether within the heart, and the universal elemental ether); for there still would remain the inappropriate assertion that the ether within the heart is the abode of heaven, earth and all other things.—But, an objection is raised, also on the alternative of the small ether being the highest Brahman, the comparison to the universal elemental ether is unsuitable; for scripture explicitly states that the highest Self is (not as large but) larger than everything else, 'larger than the earth, larger than the sky,' &c. (*Kh.* Up. III, 14, 3). Not so, we reply; what the text says as to the ether within the heart being as large as the universal ether is meant (not to make a conclusive statement as to its extent but only) to negative that smallness of the ether which is established by its abiding within the heart. Similarly we say 'the sun moves with the speed of an arrow'; the sun indeed moves much faster than an arrow, but what our assertion means is merely that he does not move slowly.—But, a further doubt is started, the passage 'That Self which is free from sin,' &c. does not appear to refer back to the small ether within the heart. For the text makes a distinction between that ether and that within that ether which it declares to be the due object of search and enquiry. This latter object therefore is the topic of discussion, and when the text says later on 'That Self, free from sin, &c. is to be searched out' we must understand it to refer to the same object of search.—This would be so, we reply, if the text did not distinguish the small ether and that which abides within it; but as a matter of fact it does distinguish the two. The connexion is as follows. The text at first refers to the body of the devotee as the city of Brahman, the idea being that Brahman is present therein as object of meditation; and then designates an organ of that body, viz. the small lotus-shaped heart as the palace of Brahman. It then further refers to Brahman—the all knowing, all powerful, whose love towards his devotees is boundless like the ocean—as the small ether within the heart, meaning thereby that Brahman who for the benefit of his devotees is present within that palace should be meditated upon as of minute size, and finally—in the clause 'that is to be searched out'—enjoins as the object of meditation that which abides in that Brahman, i.e. on the one hand, its essential freedom from all evil qualities, and on the other the whole treasure of its auspicious qualities, its power of realising its wishes and so on. The 'that' (in 'that is to be searched out') enjoins as objects of search the small ether, i.e. Brahman itself as well as the qualities abiding within it.—But how, it may be asked, do you know that the word 'that' really refers to both, viz. the highest Brahman, there called 'small ether,' and the qualities abiding in it, and that hence the clause enjoins an enquiry into both these entities?—Listen, attentively, we reply, to our explanation! The clause 'As large as this ether is, so large is this ether within the heart' declares the exceeding greatness of the small ether; the clause 'Both heaven and earth are contained within it' up to 'lightning and stars' declares that same small ether to be the abode of the entire world; and the clause 'And whatever there is for him in this world, and whatever there is not, all that is contained within it' declares that whatever objects of enjoyment there are for the devotee in this world, and whatever other objects there are not for him, i.e. are merely wishes but not obtained by him, all those objects are contained within that same small ether. The text next declares that that small ether, although dwelling within the heart which is a part of the body, is not affected by the body's old age and decay, for being extremely minute it is not capable of change; and adds 'that true being is the Brahman-city,' i. e. that Reality which is the cause of all is the city called Brahman, i. e. the abode of the entire Universe. The following clause 'in it all desires are contained' again referring to the small ether ('in it') declares that in it all desires, i. e. all desirable qualities are contained. The text next proceeds to set forth that the small ether possesses Selfhood and certain desirable auspicious qualities—this is done in the passage 'It is the Self free from sin' &c. up to 'whose purposes realise themselves.' The following section—'And as here on earth' down to 'for them there is freedom in all the worlds'—declares that those who do not know those eight qualities and the Self, called 'small ether,' which is characterised by them, and who perform actions aiming at objects of enjoyment different from that Self, obtain perishable results only, and do not attain the power of realising their wishes; while those on the other hand who know the Self called 'small ether' and the qualities abiding within it, through the grace of that very same highest Self, obtain all their wishes and the power of realising their purposes. On the ground of this connected consideration of the whole chapter we are able to decide that the text enjoins as the object of search and enquiry both the highest Brahman and the whole body of auspicious qualities abiding within it. This the Vâkyakâra also renders clear in the passage beginning 'In the text "what is within that" there is designation of wishes (i. e. desirable qualities).'—For all these reasons the small ether is the highest Brahman.

14. On account of the going and of the word; for thus it is seen; and (there is) an inferential sign.

'As people who do not know the country walk again and again over a gold treasure' &c., 'thus do all these creatures day after day go into *that* Brahma-world' (*Kh.* Up. VIII, 3, 2). The circumstance, here stated, of all individual souls going to a place which the qualification '*that*' connects with the subject-matter of the whole chapter, i. e. the small ether; and the further circumstance of the goal of their going being called the Brahma-world, also prove that the small ether is none other than the highest Brahman.—But in what way do these two points prove what they are claimed to prove?—'For thus it is seen'; the Sûtra adds. For we see it stated in other texts, that all individual souls go daily to Brahman, viz. in the state of deep sleep, 'All these creatures having become united with the True do not know that they are united with the True'; 'Having come back from the True they know not that they have come back from the True' (*Kh.* Up. VI, 9, 2; 10, 2). And in the same way we see that the word 'Brahma-world' denotes the highest Brahman; so e.g. 'this is the Brahma-world, O King' (B*ri*. Up. IV, 3, 32).—The Sûtra subjoins a further reason. Even if the going of the souls to Brahman were not seen in other texts, the fact that the text under discussion declares the individual souls to abide in Brahman in the state of deep sleep, enjoying freedom from all pain and trouble just as if they were merged in the pralaya state, is a sufficient 'inferential sign' to prove that the 'small ether' is the highest Brahman. And similarly the term 'Brahma-world' as exhibited in the text under discussion, if understood as denoting co-ordination (i.e. 'that world which is Brahman'), is sufficient to prove by itself that the 'small ether'—to which that term is applied—is the highest Brahman; it therefore is needless to appeal to other passages. That this explanation of 'Brahma-world' is preferable to the one which understands by Brahma-world 'the world *of* Brahman' is proved by considerations similar to those by which the Pû. Mî. Sûtras prove that 'Nishâda-sthapati' means a headman who at the same time is a Nishâda.—Another explanation of the passage under discussion may also be given. What is said there about all these creatures daily 'going into the Brahma-world,' may not refer at all to the state of deep sleep, but rather mean that although 'daily going into the Brahman-world,' i.e. although at all time moving above the small ether, i.e. Brahman which as the universal Self is everywhere, yet all these creatures not knowing Brahman do not find, i.e. obtain it; just as men not knowing the place where a treasure is hidden do not find it, although they constantly pass over it. This constant moving about on the part of ignorant creatures on the surface, as it were, of the small ether abiding within as their inward Ruler, proves that small ether to be the highest Brahman. That the highest Brahman abides within as the inner Self of creatures which dwell in it and are ruled by it, we are told in other texts also, so e.g. in the Antaryâmin-brâhma*n*a. 'He who dwells in the Self, within the Self, whom the Self does not know, of whom the Self is the body, who rules the Self within; unseen but seeing, unheard but hearing' (B*ri*. Up. III, 7, 22; 23).—On this interpretation we explain the last part of the Sûtra as follows. Even if other texts did not refer to it, this daily moving about on the part of ignorant creatures, on the ether within the heart—which the comparison with the treasure of gold shows to be the supreme good of man—, is in itself a sufficient proof for the small ether being Brahman.

15. And on account of there being observed in that (small ether), supporting which is a greatness of that (i.e. Brahman).

In continuation of the passage 'It is the Self free from Sin,' &c., which refers to the small ether, the text says: 'it is a bank, a limitary support, that these worlds may not be confounded.' What the text here says about the small ether supporting the world proves it to be the highest Brahman; for to support the world is the glory of Brahman. Compare 'He is the Lord of all, the king of all things, the protector of all things. He is a bank and a boundary, so that these worlds may not be confounded' (B*ri*. Up. IV, 4, 22); 'By the command of that Imperishable, O Gârgî, heaven and earth stand, held apart' (B*ri*. Up. III, 8, 9). Now this specific greatness of the highest Brahman, which consists in its supporting the world, is also observed in the small ether—which proves the latter to be none other than Brahman.

16. And on account of the settled meaning.

The word 'ether,' moreover, is known to have, among

other meanings, that of Brahman. Compare 'For who could breathe, who could breathe forth, if that ether were not bliss?' (Taitt. Up. II, 7); 'All these beings take their rise from the ether' (*Kh*. Up. I, 9, 1). It has to be kept in view that in the text under discussion the meaning 'Brahman' is supported by what is said about the qualities of the small ether—viz. freedom from sin, &c.—and hence is stronger than the other meaning, according to which âkâ*s*a signifies the elemental ether.

So far the Sûtras have refuted the view of the small ether being the element. They now enter on combating the notion that the small ether may possibly be the individual soul.

17. If it be said that on account of reference to the other one he is meant; we say no, on account of impossibility.

An objection is raised to the argumentation that, on account of complementary passages, the small ether must be explained to mean the highest Self.

For, the objector says, a clear reference to him who is 'other' than the highest Self, i.e. to the individual soul, is contained in the following passage (VIII, 12, 3): 'Thus does that serenity (samprasâda), having risen from this body and approached the highest light, appear in its own form.' 'That is the Self,' he said. 'That is the immortal, the fearless, this is Brahman' (VIII, 7, 3?). We admit that for the different reasons stated above the ether within the heart cannot be the elemental ether; but owing to the force of the intimations conveyed by the complementary passages just quoted, we must adopt the view that what is meant is the individual soul. And as the word 'âkâ*s*a' may be connected with prakâ*s*a (light), it may be applied to the individual soul also.—This view is set aside by the Sûtra. The small ether cannot be the individual soul because the qualities attributed in the text to the former, viz. freedom from sin, &c., cannot possibly belong to the individual soul.

18. Should it be said that from a subsequent passage (it appears that the individual Soul is meant); rather (the soul) in so far as its true nature has become manifest.

The Pûrvapakshin now maintains that we ascertain from a subsequent declaration made by Pra*g*âpati that it is just the individual Soul that possesses freedom from sin and the other qualities enumerated. The whole teaching of Pra*g*âpati, he says, refers to the individual Soul only. Indra having heard that Pra*g*âpati had spoken about a Self free from sin, old age, &c., the enquiry into which enables the soul to obtain all worlds and desires, approaches Pra*g*âpati with the wish to learn the true nature of that Self which should be enquired into. Pra*g*âpati thereupon, wishing to test the capacity of his pupil for receiving true instruction, gives him successive information about the embodied soul in the state of waking, dream and dreamless sleep. When he finds that Indra sees no good in instruction of this kind and thus shows himself fit to receive instruction about the true nature of the disembodied Self, he explains to him that the body is a mere abode for a ruling Self; that that bodiless Self is essentially immortal; and that the soul, as long as it is joined to a body due to karman, is compelled to experience pleasure and pain corresponding to its embodied state, while it rises above all this when it has freed itself from the body (VIII, 12, 1). He then continues: 'Thus that serenity having risen from this body and approached the highest light, appears in its own form'; thus teaching him the true nature, free from a body, of the individual soul. He next informs him that the 'highest light' which the soul reaches is the supreme Person ('That is the supreme Person'), and that the soul having reached that highest light and freed itself from what obscured its own true nature, obtains in the world of Brahman whatever enjoyments it desires, and is no longer connected with a body springing from karman and inseparable from pain and pleasure, or with anything else that causes distress. ('He moves about there laughing,' &c.). He next illustrates the connexion with a body, of the soul in the Sa*m*sâra state, by means of a comparison: 'Like as a horse attached to a cart,' &c. After that he explains that the eye and the other sense-organs are instruments of knowledge, colour, and so on, the objects of knowledge, and the individual Self the knowing subject; and that hence that Self is different from the body and the sense-organs ('Now where the sight has entered' up to 'the mind is his divine eye'). Next he declares that, after having divested itself of the body and the senses, the Self perceives all the objects of its desire by means of its 'divine eye,' i.e. the power of cognition which constitutes its essential nature ('He by means of the divine eye,' &c.). He further declares that those who have true knowledge know the Self as such ('on that Self the devas meditate'); and in conclusion teaches that he who has that true knowledge of the Self obtains for his reward the intuition of Brahman—which is suggested by what the text says about the obtaining of all worlds and all desires ('He obtains all worlds and all desires,' &c., up to the end of the chapter).—It thus appears that the entire chapter proposes as the object of cognition the individual soul free from sin, and so on. The qualities, viz. freedom from guilt, &c., may thus belong to the individual Self, and on this ground we conclude that the small ether is the individual Self.

This view the second half of the Sûtra sets aside. The two sections, that which treats of the small ether and that which contains the teaching of Pra*g*âpati, have different topics. Pra*g*âpati's teaching refers to the individual soul, whose true nature, with its qualities such as freedom from evil, &c., is at first hidden by untruth, while later on, when it has freed itself from the bondage of karman, risen from the body, and approached the highest light, it manifests itself in its true form and then is characterised by freedom from all evil and by other auspicious qualities. In the section treating of the small ether, on the other hand, we have to do with the small ether, i.e. the highest Brahman, whose true nature is never hidden, and which therefore is unconditionally characterised by freedom from evil, and so on.—

Moreover, the daharâkâsa-section ascribes to the small ether other attributes which cannot belong to the individual Self even 'when its true nature has manifested itself.' The small ether is there called a bank and support of all worlds; and one of its names, 'satyam,' is explained to imply that it governs all sentient and non-sentient beings. All this also proves that the small ether is none other than the highest Self. That the individual soul, 'even when its true nature is manifest,' cannot be viewed as a bank and support of the worlds, &c., we shall show under IV, 4.

But if this is so, what then is the meaning of the reference to the individual soul which is made in the section treating of the small ether, viz. in the passage, 'Now that serene being, which after having risen from this body,' &c. (VIII, 3, 4)?

To this question the next Sûtra replies.

19. And the reference has a different meaning.

The text in question declares that the released individual soul when reaching the highest light, i.e. Brahman, which is free from all sin, and so on, attains its true nature, which is characterised by similar freedom from sin, and so on. Now this reference to the individual soul, as described in the teaching of Pragâpati, has the purpose of giving instruction (not about the qualities of the individual soul, but) about the nature of that which is the cause of the qualities of the individual soul, i.e. the qualities specially belonging to the supreme Person. The reason why, in the section containing the teaching of Pragâpati, information is given as to the true nature of the released individual soul is that such knowledge assists the doctrine referring to the small ether. For the individual Self which wishes to reach Brahman must know his own true nature also, so as to realise that he, as being himself endowed with auspicious qualities, will finally arrive at an intuition of the highest Brahman, which is a mass of auspicious qualities raised to the highest degree of excellence. The cognition of the soul's own true nature is itself comprised in the result of the meditation on Brahman, and the results which are proclaimed in the teaching of Pra*g*âpati ('He obtains all worlds and all wishes'; 'He moves about there laughing,' &c.) thus really are results of the knowledge of the small ether.

20. If it be said, owing to the scriptural declaration of smallness; that has been explained.

The text describes the ether within the heart as being of small compass, and this agrees indeed with the individual soul which elsewhere is compared to the point of an awl, but not with Brahman, which is greater than everything.—The reply to this objection has virtually been given before, viz. under I, 2, 7, where it is said that Brahman may be viewed as of small size, for the purpose of devout meditation.

It thus remains a settled conclusion that the small ether is none other but the highest Person who is untouched by even a shadow of imperfection, and is an ocean of infinite, supremely exalted, qualities—knowledge, strength, lordly power, &c. The being, on the other hand, which in the teaching of Pra*g*âpati is described as first having a body due to karman—as we see from passages such as 'they strike it as it were, they cut it as it were'—and as afterwards approaching the highest light, and then manifesting its essential qualities, viz. freedom from sin, &c., is the individual soul; not the small ether (or Brahman).

The next Sûtra supplies a further reason for this conclusion.

21. And on account of the imitation of that.

The individual soul, free from bondage, and thus possessing the qualities of freedom from sin, &c., cannot be the small ether, i. e. the highest Brahman, because it is stated to 'imitate,' i. e. to be equal to that Brahman. The text making that statement is Mu. Up. III, 1, 3, 'When the seer (i. e. the individual soul) sees the brilliant maker, the Lord, the Person who has his source in Brahman; then becoming wise and shaking off good and evil, he reaches the highest equality, free from passions.' The being to which the teaching of Pra*g*âpati refers is the 'imitator,' i.e. the individual soul; the Brahman which is 'imitated' is the small ether.

22. The same is declared by Sm*ri*ti also.

Sm*ri*ti also declares that the transmigrating soul when reaching the state of Release 'imitates,' i.e. attains supreme equality of attributes with the highest Brahman. 'Abiding by this knowledge they, attaining to equality of attributes with me, are not born again at the time of creation, nor are they affected by the general dissolution of the world' (Bha. Gî. XIV, 2).

Some maintain that the last two Sûtras constitute a separate adhikara*n*a (head of discussion), meant to prove that the text Mu. Up. II, 2, 10 ('After him the shining one, everything shines; by the light of him all this is lighted'), refers to the highest Brahman. This view is, however, inadmissible, for the reason that with regard to the text quoted no pûrvapaksha can arise, it having been proved under I, 2, 21 ff., and I, 3, 1 ff., that the whole section of which that text forms part is concerned with Brahman; and it further having been shown under I, 1, 24 ff., that Brahman is apprehended under the form of light.—The interpretation moreover does not fit in with the wording of the Sûtras.—Here terminates the adhikara*n*a of the 'small one.'

23. On account of the term, the one measured.

We read in the Ka*th*avallî 'The Person of the size of a thumb stands in the middle of the Self, as lord of the past and the future, and henceforward fears no more'; 'That Person of the size of a thumb is like a light without smoke,' &c. (Ka. Up. II, 4, 12; 13). And 'The Person not larger than a thumb, the inner Self, is always settled in the heart of men' (Ka. Up. II, 6, 17). A doubt here arises whether the being measured by the extent of a span be the individual soul or the highest Self.—The Pûrvapakshin maintains the former view; for, he says, another scriptural text also declares the individual soul to have that measure, 'the ruler of the vital airs moves through his own works, of the size of a thumb, brilliant like the sun, endowed with purposes and egoity' (*S*vet. Up. V, 7; 8). Moreover, the highest Self is not anywhere else, not even for the purpose of meditation, represented as having the size of a thumb. It thus being determined that the being of the length of a thumb is the individual Self, we understand the term 'Lord,' which is applied to it, as meaning that it is the Lord of the body, the sense-organs, the objects and the instruments of fruition.—Of this view the Sûtra disposes, maintaining that the being a thumb long can be none but the highest Self, just on account of that term. For lordship over all things past and future cannot possibly belong to the individual Self, which is under the power of karman.—But how can the highest Self be said to have the measure of a thumb?—On this point the next Sûtra satisfies us.

24. But with reference to the heart, men being qualified.

In so far as the highest Self abides, for the purpose of devout meditation, in the heart of the devotee—which heart is of the measure of a thumb—it may itself be viewed as having the measure of a thumb. The individual soul also can be said to have the measure of a thumb only in so far as dwelling within the heart; for scripture directly states that its real size is that of the point of a goad, i.e. minute. And as men only are capable of devout meditation, and hence alone have a claim on scripture, the fact that the hearts of other living creatures also, such as donkeys, horses, snakes, &c., have the same size, cannot give rise to any objection.—The discussion of this matter will be completed later on[1].

25. Also beings above them (i.e. men), Bâdarâya*n*a thinks, on account of possibility.

In order to prove that the highest Brahman may be

[1] The 'pramitâdhikara*n*a' is resumed in Sûtra 41.

viewed as having the size of a thumb, it has been declared that the scriptural texts enjoining meditation on Brahman are the concern of men. This offers an opportunity for the discussion of the question whether also other classes of individual souls, such as devas, are qualified for knowledge of Brahman. The Pûrvapakshin denies this qualification in the case of gods and other beings, on the ground of absence of capability. For, he says, bodiless beings, such as gods, are incapable of the accomplishment of meditation on Brahman, which requires as its auxiliaries the seven means enumerated above (p. 17). This must not be objected to on the ground of the devas, and so on, having bodies; for there is no means of proof establishing such embodiedness. We have indeed proved above that the Vedânta-texts may intimate accomplished things, and hence are an authoritative means for the cognition of Brahman; but we do not meet with any Vedânta-text, the purport of which is to teach that the devas, and so on, possess bodies. Nor can this point be established through mantras and arthavâda texts; for these are merely supplementary to the injunctions of actions (sacrificial, and so on), and therefore have a different aim. And the injunctions themselves prove nothing with regard to the devas, except that the latter are that with a view to which those actions are performed. In the same way it also cannot be shown that the gods have any desires or wants (to fulfil or supply which they might enter on meditation of Brahman). For the two reasons above we therefore conclude that the devas, and so on, are not qualified for meditation on Brahman.—This view is contradicted by the Sûtra. Such meditation is possible in the case of higher beings also, Bâdarâya*n*a thinks; on account of the possibility of want and capacity on their part also. Want and wish exist in their case since they also are liable to suffering, springing from the assaults, hard to be endured, of the different kinds of pain, and since they also know that supreme enjoyment is to be found in the highest Brahman, which is untouched by the shadow even of imperfection, and is a mass of auspicious qualities in their highest perfection.

'Capability,' on the other hand, depends on the possession of a body and sense-organs of whatever degree of tenuity; and that the devas, from Brahmâ downward, possess a body and sense-organs, is declared in all the Upanishads, in the chapters treating of creation and the chapters enjoining meditation. In the *Kh*ândogya, e.g. it is related how the highest Being having resolved on creation, evolved the aggregate of non-sentient matter with its different kinds, and then produced the fourfold multitude of living creatures, each having a material body corresponding to its karman, and a suitable name of its own. Similarly, all the other scriptural accounts of creation declare that there are four classes of creatures—devas, men, animals, and non-moving beings, such as plants—and the difference of these classes depends on the individual Selfs being joined to various bodies capacitating them to experience the results of their works, each in that one of the fourteen worlds—beginning with the world of Brahmâ—which is the suitable place for retribution. For in themselves, apart from bodies, the individual Selfs are not distinguished as men, gods, and so on. In the same way the story of the devas and Asuras approaching Pra*g*âpati with fuel in their hands, staying with him as pupils for thirty-two years, &c. (*Kh*. Up. VIII, 7 ff.), clearly shows that the devas possess bodies and sense-organs. Analogously, mantras and arthavâdas, which are complementary to injunctions of works, contain unmistakeable references to the corporeal nature of the gods ('Indra holding in his hand the thunderbolt'; 'Indra lifted the thunderbolt,' &c.); and as the latter is not contradicted by any other means of proof it must be accepted on the authority stated. Nor can it be said that those mantras and arthavâdas are really meant to express something else (than those details mentioned above), in so far, namely, as they aim at proclaiming or glorifying the action with which they are connected; for those very details subserve the purpose of glorification, and so on, and without them glorification is not possible. For we praise or glorify a thing by declaring its qualities; if such qualities do not exist all glorification lapses. It cannot by any means be maintained that anything may be glorified by the proclamation of its qualities, even if such qualities do not really exist. Hence the arthavâdas which glorify a certain action, just thereby intimate the real existence of the qualities and details of the action. The mantras again, which are prescribed in connexion with the actions, serve the purpose of throwing light on the use to be derived from the performance of the actions, and this they accomplish by making statements as to the particular qualities, such as embodiedness and the like, which belong to the devas and other classes of beings. Otherwise Indra, and so on, would not be remembered at the time of performance; for the idea of a divinity presents itself to the mind only in connexion with the special attributes of that divinity. In the case of such qualities as are not established by other means of proof, the primary statement is made by the arthavâda or the mantra: the former thereby glorifies the action, and the latter proclaims it as possessing certain qualities or details; and both these ends are accomplished by making statements as to the gods, &c., possessing certain qualities, such as embodiedness and the like. In the case, again, of certain qualities being already established by other means of proof, the mantras and arthavâdas merely refer to them (as something already known), and in this way perform their function of glorification and elucidation. And where, thirdly, there is a contradiction between the other means of knowledge and what mantras and arthavâdas state (as when, e. g. a text of the latter kind says that 'the sacrificial post is the sun'), the intention of the text is metaphorically to denote, by means of those apparently unmeaning terms, certain other qualities which are not excluded by the other means of knowledge; and in this way the function of glorification and elucidation is again accomplished. Now what the injunction of a sacrificial action demands as its supplement, is a statement as to the power of the divinity to whom the sacrifice is offered; for the performance which scripture enjoins on men desirous of certain results, is itself of a merely transitory nature, and hence requires some agent capable of bringing about, at some future time, the result desired as, e.g. the heavenly world. 'Vâyu is the swiftest god; he (the sacrificer) approaches Vâyu with his own share; the god then leads him to prosperity' (Taitt. Sa*m*h. I, 2, 1); 'What he seeks by means of that offering, may he obtain that, may he prosper therein, may the gods favourably grant him that' (Taitt. Br. III, 5, 10, 5); these and similar arthavâdas and mantras intimate that the gods when propitiated by certain sacrificial works, give certain rewards and possess the power to do so; and they thus connect themselves with the general context of scripture as supplying an evidently required item of information. Moreover, the mere verb 'to sacrifice' (ya*g*), as denoting worship of the gods, intimates the presence of a deity which is to be propitiated by the action called sacrifice, and thus constitutes the main element of that action. A careful consideration of the whole context thus reveals that everything which is wanted for the due accomplishment of the action enjoined is to be learned from the text itself, and that hence we need not have recourse to such entities as the 'unseen principle' (apûrva), assumed to be denoted by, or to be imagined in connexion with, the passages enjoining certain actions. Hence the dharma*s*âstras, itihâsas, and purâ*n*as also, which are founded on the different brâhma*n*as, mantras and arthavâdas, clearly teach that Brahmâ and the other gods, as well as the Asuras and other superhuman beings, have bodies and sense-organs, constitutions of different kinds, different abodes, enjoyments, and functions.—Owing to their having bodies, the gods therefore are also qualified for meditation on Brahman.

26. If it be said that there results a contradiction to work; we deny this, on account of the observation of the assumption of several (bodies).

An objection here presents itself. If we admit the gods to have bodies, a difficulty arises at the sacrifices, as it is impossible that one and the same corporeal Indra—who is at the same time invited by many sacrificers 'come,

O Indra,' 'come, O Lord of the red horses,' &c.—should be present at all those places. And that the gods, Agni and so on, really do come to the sacrifices is proved by the following scriptural text: 'To whose sacrifice do the gods go, and to whose not? He who first receives the gods, sacrifices to them on the following day' (Taitt. Sa*m*h. I, 6, 7, 1). In refutation of this objection the Sûtra points out that there is seen, i. e. recorded, the assumption of several bodies at the same time, on the part of beings endowed with special powers, such as Saubhari.

27. If it be said (that a contradiction will result) with regard to words; we say no, since beings originate from them (as appears) from perception and inference.

Well then let us admit that there is no difficulty as far as sacrifices are concerned, for the reason stated in the preceding Sûtra. But another difficulty presents itself with regard to the words of which the Veda consists. For if Indra and the other gods are corporeal beings, it follows that they are made up of parts and hence non-permanent. This implies either that the Vedic words denoting them—not differing therein from common worldly words such as Devadatta—are totally devoid of meaning during all those periods which precede the origination of the beings called Indra and so on, or follow on their destruction; or else that the Veda itself is non-permanent, non-eternal.—This objection is not valid, the Sûtra points out, for the reason that those beings, viz. Indra and so on, again and again originate from the Vedic words. To explain. Vedic words, such as Indra and so on, do not, like the word Devadatta and the like, denote, on the basis of convention, one particular individual only: they rather denote by their own power particular species of beings, just as the word 'cow' denotes a particular species of animals. When therefore a special individual of the class called Indra has perished, the creator, apprehending from the Vedic word 'Indra' which is present to his mind the class characteristics of the beings denoted by that word, creates another Indra possessing those very same characteristics; just as the potter fashions a new jar, on the basis of the word 'jar' which is stirring in *his* mind.—But how is this known?—'Through perception and inference,' i. e. through Scripture and Sm*ri*ti. Scripture says, e. g. 'By means of the Veda Pra*g*âpati evolved names and forms, the being and the non-being'; and 'Saying "bhûh" (earth) he created the earth; saying "bhuva*h*" he created the air,' and so on; which passages teach that the creator at first bethinks himself of the characteristic make of a thing, in connexion with the word denoting it, and thereupon creates an individual thing characterised by that make. Sm*ri*ti makes similar statements; compare, e. g. 'In the beginning there was sent forth by the creator, divine speech—beginningless and endless—in the form of the Veda, and from it there originated all creatures'; and 'He, in the beginning, separately created from the words of the Veda the names and works and shapes of all things'; and 'The names and forms of beings, and all the multiplicity of works He in the beginning created from the Veda.' This proves that from the corporeality of the gods, and so on, it follows neither that the words of the Veda are unmeaning nor that the Veda itself is non-eternal.

28. And for this very reason eternity (of the Veda).

As words such as Indra and Vasish*th*a, which denote gods and *Ri*shis, denote (not individuals only, but) classes, and as the creation of those beings is preceded by their being suggested to the creative mind through those words; for this reason the eternity of the Veda admits of being reconciled with what scripture says about the mantras and kâ*nd*as (sections) of the sacred text having 'makers' and about *Ri*shis seeing the hymns; cp. such passages as 'He chooses the makers of mantras'; 'Reverence to the *Ri*shis who are the makers of mantras'; 'That is Agni; this is a hymn of Vi*s*vâmitra.' For by means of these very texts Pra*g*âpati presents to his own mind the characteristics and powers of the different *Ri*shis who make the different sections, hymns, and mantras, thereupon creates them endowed with those characteristics and powers, and appoints them to remember the very same sections, hymns, &c. The *Ri*shis being thus gifted by Pra*g*âpati with the requisite powers, undergo suitable preparatory austerities and finally *see* the mantras, and so on, proclaimed by the Vasish*th*as and other *Ri*shis of former ages of the world, perfect in all their sounds and accents, without having learned them from the recitation of a teacher. There is thus no conflict between the eternity of the Veda and the fact that the *Ri*shis are the *makers* of its sections, hymns, and so on. A further objection is raised. Let it be admitted that after each pralaya of the kind called 'contingent' (naimittika), Pra*g*âpati may proceed to create new Indras, and so on, in the way of remembering on the basis of the Veda the Indras, and so on, of preceding periods. In the case, on the other hand, of a pralaya of the kind called elemental (prâk*ri*tika), in which the creator, Pra*g*âpati himself, and words—which are the effects of the elemental ahaṅkâra—pass away, what possibility is there of Pra*g*âpati undertaking a new creation on the basis of Vedic words, and how can we speak of the permanency of a Veda which perishes? He who maintains the eternity of the Veda and the corporeality of gods, and so on, is thus really driven to the hypothesis of the course of mundane existence being without a beginning (i. e. not preceded by a pralaya).—Of this difficulty the next Sûtra disposes.

29. And on account of the equality of names and forms there is no contradiction, even in the renovation (of the world); as appears from *S*ruti and Sm*ri*ti.

On account of the sameness of names and forms, as stated before, there is no difficulty in the way of the origination of the world, even in the case of total pralayas. For what actually takes place is as follows. When the period of a great pralaya draws towards its close, the divine supreme Person, remembering the constitution of the world previous to the pralaya, and forming the volition 'May I become manifold,' separates into its constituent elements the whole mass of enjoying souls and objects of enjoyment which, during the pralaya state, had been merged in him so as to possess a separate existence (not actual but) potential only, and then emits the entire world just as it had been before, from the so-called Mahat down to the Brahman-egg, and Hira*n*yagarbha (Pra*g*âpati). Having thereupon manifested the Vedas in exactly the same order and arrangement they had had before, and having taught them to Hira*n*yagarbha, he entrusts to him the new creation of the different classes of beings, gods, and so on, just as it was before; and at the same time abides himself within the world so created as its inner Self and Ruler. This view of the process removes all difficulties. The superhuman origin and the eternity of the Veda really mean that intelligent agents having received in their minds an impression due to previous recitations of the Veda in a fixed order of words, chapters, and so on, remember and again recite it in that very same order of succession. This holds good both with regard to us men and to the highest Lord of all; there however is that difference between the two cases that the representations of the Veda which the supreme Person forms in his own mind are spontaneous, not dependent on an impression previously made.

To the question whence all this is known, the Sûtra replies 'from Scripture and Sm*ri*ti.' The scriptural passage is 'He who first creates Brahmâ and delivers the Vedas to him' (*S*vet. Up. VI, 18). And as to Sm*ri*ti we have the following statement in Manu, 'This universe existed in the shape of darkness, &c.—He desiring to produce beings of many kinds from his own body, first with a thought created the waters and placed his seed in them. That seed became a golden egg equal to the sun in brilliancy; in that he himself was born as Brahmâ, the progenitor of the whole world' (Manu I, 5; 8–9). To the same effect are the texts of the Paurâ*n*ikas, 'From the navel of the sleeping divinity there sprung up a lotus, and in that lotus there was born Brahmâ fully knowing all Vedas and Vedâṅgas. And then Brahmâ was told by him (the highest Divinity),

'Do thou create all beings, O Great-minded one'; and the following passage, 'From the highest Nârâya*n*a there was born the Four-faced one.'—And in the section which begins 'I will tell the original creation,' we read 'Because having created water (nâra) I abide within it, therefore my name shall be Nârâya*n*a. There I lie asleep in every Kalpa, and as I am sleeping there springs from my navel a lotus, and in that lotus there is born the Four-faced one, and I tell him "Do thou, Great-minded one, create all beings."'—Here terminates the adhikara*n*a of 'the deities.'

30. On account of the impossibility (of qualification for the madhuvidyâ, &c.) *G*aimini maintains the non-qualification (of gods, &c.).

So far it has been proved that also the gods, and so on, are qualified for the knowledge of Brahman. But a further point here presents itself for consideration, viz. whether the gods are qualified or not to undertake those meditations of which they themselves are the objects. The Sûtra states as a pûrvapaksha view held by *G*aimini, that they are not so qualified, for the reason that there are no other Âdityas, Vasus, and so on, who could be meditated on by the Âdityas and Vasus themselves; and that moreover for the Âdityas and Vasus the qualities and position of those classes of deities cannot be objects of desire, considering that they possess them already. The so-called Madhuvidyâ (*Kh*. Up. III) represents as objects of devout meditation certain parts of the sun which are being enjoyed by the different classes of divine beings, Vasus, Âdityas, and so on—the sun being there called 'madhu,' i.e. honey or nectar, on account of his being the abode of a certain nectar to be brought about by certain sacrificial works to be known from the *Ri*g-veda, and so on; and as the reward of such meditation the text names the attainment of the position of the Vasus, Âdityas, and so on.

31. And on account of (meditating on the part of the gods) being in the Light.

'Him the devas meditate upon as the light of lights, as

immortal time' (B*ri*. Up. IV, 4, 16). This text declares that the meditation of the gods has for its object the Light, i. e. the highest Brahman. Now this express declaration as to the gods being meditating devotees with regard to meditations on Brahman which are common to men and gods, implies a denial of the gods being qualified for meditations on other objects. The conclusion therefore is that the Vasus, and so on, are not qualified for meditations on the Vasus and other classes of deities.

32. But Bâdarâya*n*a (maintains) the existence (of qualification); for there is (possibility of such).

The Reverend Bâdarâya*n*a thinks that the Âdityas, Vasus, and so on, are also qualified for meditations on divinities. For it is in their case also possible that their attainment of Brahman should be viewed as preceded by their attainment of Vasu-hood or Âditya-hood, in so far, namely, as they meditate on Brahman as abiding within themselves. They may be Vasus and Âdityas in the present age of the world, but at the same time be desirous of holding the same position in future ages also. In the Madhuvidyâ we have to distinguish two sections, concerned respectively with Brahman in its causal and its effected state. The former section, extending from the beginning up to 'when from thence he has risen upwards,' enjoins meditation on Brahman in its condition as effect, i. e. as appearing in the form of creatures such as the Vasus, and so on; while the latter section enjoins meditation on the causal Brahman viewed as abiding within the sun as its inner Self. The purport of the whole vidyâ is that he who meditates on Brahman in this its twofold form will in a future age of the world enjoy Vasu-hood, and will finally attain Brahman in its causal aspect, i.e. the very highest Brahman. From the fact that the text, 'And indeed to him who thus knows the Brahma-upanishad, the sun does not rise and does not set; for him there is day once and for all,' calls the whole Madhuvidyâ a '*Brahma*'-upanishad, and that the reward declared is the attainment of Vasu-hood, and so on, leading up to the attainment of Brahman, we clearly are entitled to infer that the meditations which the text enjoins, viz. on the different parts of the sun viewed as objects of enjoyment for the Vasus, and so on, really are meant as meditations on Brahman as abiding in those different forms. Meditation on the Vasus and similar beings is thus seen to be possible for the Vasus themselves. And as Brahman really constitutes the only object of meditation, we also see the appropriateness of the text discussed above, 'On him the gods meditate as the light of lights.' The V*ri*ttikâra expresses the same opinion, 'For there is possibility with regard to the Madhu-vidyâ, and so on, Brahman only being the object of meditation everywhere.'—Here terminates the adhikara*n*a of 'honey.'

The Sûtras now enter on a discussion of the question whether the *S*ûdras also are qualified for the knowledge of Brahman.

The Pûrvapakshin maintains that they are so qualified; for qualification, he says, depends on want and capacity, and both these are possible in the case of *S*ûdras also. The *S*ûdra is not indeed qualified for any works depending on a knowledge of the sacred fires, for from such knowledge he is debarred; but he possesses qualification for meditation on Brahman, which after all is nothing but a certain mental energy. The only works prerequisite for meditation are those works which are incumbent on a man as a member of a caste or â*s*rama, and these consist, in the *S*ûdra's case, in obedience to the higher castes. And when we read 'therefore the *S*ûdra is not qualified for sacrifices,' the purport of this passage is only to make a confirmatory reference to something already settled by reason, viz. that the *S*ûdra is not qualified for the performance of sacrifices which cannot be accomplished by one not acquainted with the sacred fires (and not to deny the *S*ûdra's competence for devout meditation).—But how can meditation on Brahman be undertaken by a man who has not studied the Vedas, inclusive of the Vedânta, and hence knows nothing about the nature of Brahman and the proper modes of meditation?—Those also, we reply, who do not study Veda and Vedânta may acquire the requisite knowledge by hearing Itihâsas and Purâ*n*as; and there are texts which allow *S*ûdras to become acquainted with texts of that kind; cp. e.g. 'one is to make the four castes to hear texts, the Brâhma*n*a coming first.' Moreover, those Purâ*n*as and Itihâsas make mention of *S*ûdras, such as Vidura, who had a knowledge of Brahman. And the Upanishads themselves, viz. in the so-called Sa*m*varga-vidyâ, show that a *S*ûdra is qualified for the knowledge of Brahman; for there the teacher Raikva addresses *G*âna*s*ruti, who wishes to learn from him, as *S*ûdra, and thereupon instructs him in the knowledge of Brahman (*Kh*. Up. IV, 2, 3). All this proves that *S*ûdras also have a claim to the knowledge of Brahman.

This conclusion we deny, on the ground of the absence of capability. It is impossible that the capability of performing meditations on Brahman should belong to a person not knowing the nature of Brahman and the due modes of meditation, and not qualified by the knowledge of the requisite preliminaries of such meditation, viz. recitation of the Veda, sacrifices, and so on. Mere want or desire does not impart qualification to a person destitute of the required capability. And this absence of capability is due, in the *S*ûdra's case, to absence of legitimate study of the Veda. The injunctions of sacrificial works naturally connect themselves with the knowledge and the means of knowledge (i.e. religious ceremonies and the like) that belong to the three higher castes, for these castes actually possess the knowledge (required for the sacrifices), owing to their studying the Veda in agreement with the injunction which prescribes such study for the higher castes; the same injunctions do not, on the other hand, connect themselves with the knowledge and means of knowledge belonging to others (than members of the three higher castes). And the same naturally holds good with regard to the injunctions of meditation on Brahman. And as thus only such knowledge as is acquired by study prompted by the Vedic injunction of study supplies a means for meditation on Brahman, it follows that the *S*ûdra for whom that injunction is not meant is incapable of such meditation. Itihâsas and Purâ*n*as hold the position of being helpful means towards meditation in so far only as they confirm or support the Veda, not independently of the Veda. And that *S*ûdras are allowed to hear Itihâsas and Purâ*n*as is meant only for the end of destroying their sins, not to prepare them for meditation on Brahman. The case of Vidura and other *S*ûdras having been 'founded on Brahman,' explains itself as follows:—Owing to the effect of former actions, which had not yet worked themselves out, they were born in a low caste, while at the same time they possessed wisdom owing to the fact that the knowledge acquired by them in former births had not yet quite vanished.

(On these general grounds we object to *S*ûdras being viewed as qualified for meditation on Brahman.) The Sûtra now refutes that argument, which the Pûrvapakshin derives from the use of the word '*S*ûdra' in the Sa*m*varga-vidyâ.

33. (That) grief of him (arose), this is intimated by his (*G*âna*s*ruti's) resorting to him (Raikva) on hearing a disrespectful speech about himself.

From what the text says about *G*âna*s*ruti Pautrâya*n*a having been taunted by a flamingo for his want of knowledge of Brahman, and having thereupon resorted to Raikva, who possessed the knowledge of Brahman, it appears that sorrow (*suk*) had taken possession of him; and it is with a view to this that Raikva addresses him as *S*ûdra. For the word *S*ûdra, etymologically considered, means one who grieves or sorrows (*sok*ati). The appellation '*s*ûdra' therefore refers to his sorrow, not to his being a member of the fourth caste. This clearly appears from a consideration of the whole story. *G*âna*s*ruti Pautrâya*n*a was a very liberal and pious king. Being much pleased with his virtuous life, and wishing to rouse in him the desire of knowing Brahman, two noble-minded beings, assuming the shape of flamingoes, flew past him at night time, when one of them addressed the other, 'O Bhallâksha, the light of *G*âna*s*ruti has spread like the sky; do not go near that it may not burn thee.' To this praise of *G*ânas*r*uti the other flamingo replied, 'How can you speak of him, being what he is, as if he were Raikva "sayuktvân"?' i. e. 'how can you speak of *G*ânas*r*uti, being what he is, as if he were Raikva, who knows Brahman and is endowed with the most eminent qualities? Raikva, who knows Brahman, alone in this world is truly eminent. *G*ânas*r*uti may be very pious, but as he does not know Brahman what quality of his could produce splendour capable of burning me like the splendour of Raikva?' The former flamingo thereupon asks who that Raikva is, and its companion replies, 'He in whose work and knowledge there are comprised all the works done by good men and all the knowledge belonging to intelligent creatures, that is Raikva.' *G*ânas*r*uti, having heard this speech of the flamingo—which implied a reproach to himself as being destitute of the knowledge of Brahman, and a glorification of Raikva as possessing that knowledge—at once sends his door-keeper to look for Raikva; and when the door-keeper finds him and brings word, the king himself repairs to him with six hundred cows, a golden necklace, and a carriage yoked with mules, and asks him to teach him the deity on which he meditates, i. e. the highest deity. Raikva, who through the might of his Yoga-knowledge is acquainted with everything that passes in the three worlds, at once perceives that *G*ânas*r*uti is inwardly grieved at the slighting speech of the flamingo, which had been provoked by the king's want of knowledge of Brahman, and is now making an effort due to the wish of knowing Brahman; and thus recognises that the king is fit for the reception of that knowledge. Reflecting thereupon that a knowledge of Brahman may be firmly established in this pupil even without long attendance on the teacher if only he will be liberal to the teacher to the utmost of his capability, he addresses him: 'Do thou take away (apâhara) (these things), O *S*ûdra; keep (the chariot) with the cows for thyself.' What he means to say is, 'By so much only in the way of gifts bestowed on me, the knowledge of Brahman cannot be established in thee, who, through the desire for such knowledge, art plunged in grief'—the address 'O *S*ûdra' intimating that Raikva knows *G*ânas*r*uti to be plunged in grief, and on that account fit to receive instruction about Brahman. *G*ânas*r*uti thereupon approaches Raikva for a second time, bringing as much wealth as he possibly can, and moreover his own daughter. Raikva again intimates his view of the pupil's fitness for receiving instruction by addressing him a second time as '*S*ûdra,' and says, 'You have brought these, O *S*ûdra; by this mouth only you made me speak,' i.e. 'You now have brought presents to the utmost of your capability; by this means only you will induce me, without lengthy service on your part, to utter speech containing that instruction about Brahman which you desire.'—Having said this he begins to instruct him.—We thus see that the appellation '*s*ûdra' is meant to intimate the grief of *G*ânas*r*uti—which grief in its turn indicates the king's fitness for receiving instruction; and is not meant to declare that *G*ânas*r*uti belongs to the lowest caste.

34. And on account of (*G*ânas*r*uti's) kshattriya-hood being understood.

The first section of the vidyâ tells us that *G*ânas*r*uti bestowed much wealth and food; later on he is represented as sending his door-keeper on an errand; and in the end, as bestowing on Raikva many villages—which shows him to be a territorial lord. All these circumstances suggest *G*ânas*r*uti's being a Kshattriya, and hence not a member of the lowest caste.—The above Sûtra having declared that the kshattriya-hood of *G*ânas*r*uti is indicated in the introductory legend, the next Sûtra shows that the same circumstance is indicated in the concluding legend.

35. On account of the inferential sign further on, together with *K*aitraratha.

The kshattriya-hood of *G*ânas*r*uti is further to be accepted on account of the Kshattriya Abhipratârin *K*aitraratha, who is mentioned further on in this very same Sa*m*varga-vidyâ which Raikva imparts to *G*ânas*r*uti.—But why?—As follows. The section beginning 'Once a Brahma*k*ârin begged of *S*aunaka Kâpeya and Abhipratârin Kâkshaseni while being waited on at their meal,' and ending 'thus do we, O Brahma*k*ârin, meditate on that being,' shows Kâpeya, Abhipratârin, and the Brahma*k*ârin to be connected with the Sa*m*varga-vidyâ. Now Abhipratârin is a Kshattriya, the other two are Brâhma*n*as. This shows that there are connected with the vidyâ, Brâhma*n*as, and from among non-Brâhma*n*as, a Kshattriya only, but not a *S*ûdra. It therefore appears appropriate to infer that the person, other than the Brâhma*n*a Raikva, who is likewise connected with this vidyâ, viz. *G*ânа*s*ruti, is likewise a Kshattriya, not a *S*ûdra.—But how do we know that Abhipratârin is a *K*aitraratha and a Kshattriya? Neither of these circumstances is stated in the legend in the Sa*m*varga-vidyâ! To this question the Sûtra replies, 'on account of the inferential mark.' From the inferential mark that *S*aunaka Kâpeya and Abhipratârin Kâkshaseni are said to have been sitting together at a meal we understand that there is some connexion between Abhipratârin and the Kâpeyas. Now another scriptural passage runs as follows: 'The Kâpeyas made *K*aitraratha perform that sacrifice' (Tâ*nd*. Brâ. XX, 12, 5), and this shows that one connected with the Kâpeyas was a *K*aitraratha; and a further text shows that a *K*aitraratha is a Kshattriya, 'from him there was descended a *K*aitraratha who was a prince.' All this favours the inference that Abhipratârin was a *K*aitraratha and a Kshattriya.

So far the Sûtras have shown that there is no inferential mark to prove what is contradicted by reasoning, viz. the qualification of the *S*ûdras. The next Sûtra declares that the non-qualification of the *S*ûdra proved by reasoning is confirmed by Scripture and Sm*ri*ti.

36. On account of the reference to ceremonial purifications, and on account of the declaration of their absence.

In sections the purport of which is to give instruction about Brahman the ceremony of initiation is referred to, 'I will initiate you; he initiated him' (*Kh*. Up. IV, 4).

And at the same time the absence of such ceremonies in the case of *S*ûdras is stated: 'In the *S*ûdra there is not any sin, and he is not fit for any ceremony' (Manu X, 126); and 'The fourth caste is once born, and not fit for any ceremony' (Manu X, 4).

37. And on account of the procedure, on the ascertainment of the non-being of that.

That a *S*ûdra is not qualified for knowledge of Brahman appears from that fact also that as soon as Gautama has convinced himself that *G*âbâla, who wishes to become his pupil, is not a *S*ûdra, he proceeds to teach him the knowledge of Brahman.

38. And on account of the prohibition of hearing, studying, and performance of (Vedic) matter.

The *S*ûdra is specially forbidden to hear and study the Veda and to perform the things enjoined in it. 'For a *S*ûdra is like a cemetery, therefore the Veda must not be read in the vicinity of a *S*ûdra;' 'Therefore the *S*ûdra is like a beast, unfit for sacrifices.' And he who does not hear the Veda recited cannot learn it so as to understand and perform what the Veda enjoins. The prohibition of hearing thus implies the prohibition of understanding and whatever depends on it.

39. And on account of Sm*ri*ti.

Sm*ri*ti also declares this prohibition of hearing, and so on. 'The ears of him who hears the Veda are to be filled with molten lead and lac; if he pronounces it his tongue is to be slit; if he preserves it his body is to be cut through.' And 'He is not to teach him sacred duties or vows.'—It is thus a settled matter that the *S*ûdras are not qualified for meditations on Brahman.

We must here point out that the non-qualification of *S*ûdras for the cognition of Brahman can in no way be asserted by those who hold that a Brahman consisting of pure non-differenced intelligence constitutes the sole reality; that everything else is false; that all bondage is unreal;

that such bondage may be put an end to by the mere cognition of the true nature of Reality—such cognition resulting from the hearing of certain texts; and that the cessation of bondage thus effected constitutes final Release. For knowledge of the true nature of Reality, in the sense indicated, and the release resulting from it, may be secured by any one who learns from another person that Brahman alone is real and that everything else is falsely superimposed on Brahman. That the cognition of such truth can be arrived at only on the basis of certain Vedic texts, such as 'Thou art that,' is a restriction which does not admit of proof; for knowledge of the truth does not depend on man's choice, and at once springs up in the mind even of an unwilling man as soon as the conditions for such origination are present. Nor can it be proved in any way that bondage can be put an end to only through such knowledge of the truth as springs from Vedic texts; for error comes to an end through the knowledge of the true nature of things, whatever agency may give rise to such knowledge. True knowledge, of the kind described, will spring up in the mind of a man as soon as he hears the non-scriptural declaration, 'Brahman, consisting of non-differenced intelligence, is the sole Reality; everything else is false,' and this will suffice to free him from error. When a competent and trustworthy person asserts that what was mistaken for silver is merely a sparkling shell, the error of a *S*ûdra no less than of a Brâhma*n*a comes to an end; in the same way a *S*ûdra also will free himself from the great cosmic error as soon as the knowledge of the true nature of things has arisen in his mind through a statement resting on the traditional lore of men knowing the Veda. Nor must you object to this on the ground that men knowing the Veda do not instruct *S*ûdras, and so on, because the text, 'he is not to teach him sacred things,' forbids them to do so; for men who have once learned—from texts such as 'Thou art that'—that Brahman is their Self, and thus are standing on the very top of the Veda as it were, move no longer in the sphere of those to whom injunctions and prohibitions apply, and the prohibition quoted does not therefore touch them. Knowledge of Brahman may thus spring up in the mind of *S*ûdras and the like, owing to instruction received from one of those men who have passed beyond all prohibition. Nor must it be said that the instance of the shell and the silver is not analogous, in so far, namely, as the error with regard to silver in the shell comes to an end as soon as the true state of things is declared; while the great cosmic error that clouds the *S*ûdra's mind does not come to an end as soon as, from the teaching of another man, he learns the truth about Reality. For the case of the *S*ûdra does not herein differ from that of the Brâhma*n*a; the latter also does not at once free himself from the cosmic error. Nor again will it avail to plead that the sacred texts originate the demanded final cognition in the mind of the Brâhma*n*a as soon as meditation has dispelled the obstructive imagination of plurality; for in the same way, i.e. helped by meditation, the non-Vedic instruction given by another person produces the required cognition in the mind of the *S*ûdra. For meditation means nothing but a steady consideration of the sense which sentences declaratory of the unity of Brahman and the Self may convey, and the effect of such meditation is to destroy all impressions opposed to such unity; you yourself thus admit that the injunction of meditation aims at something visible (i.e. an effect that can be definitely assigned, whence it follows that the *S*ûdra also is qualified for it, while he would not be qualified for an activity having an 'ad*ri*sh*t*a,' i.e. supersensuous, transcendental effect). The recital of the text of the Veda also and the like (are not indispensable means for bringing about cognition of Brahman, but) merely subserve the origination of the *desire* of knowledge. The desire of knowledge may arise in a *S*ûdra also (viz. in some other way), and thereupon real knowledge may result from non-Vedic instruction, obstructive imaginations having previously been destroyed by meditation. And thus in his case also non-real bondage will come to an end.—The same conclusion may also be arrived at by a different road. The mere ordinary instruments of knowledge, viz. perception and inference assisted by reasoning, may suggest to the *S*ûdra the theory that there is an inward Reality constituted by non-differenced self-luminous intelligence, that this inward principle witnesses Nescience, and that owing to Nescience the entire apparent world, with its manifold distinctions of knowing subjects and objects of knowledge, is superimposed upon the inner Reality. He may thereupon, by uninterrupted meditation on this inner Reality, free himself from all imaginations opposed to it, arrive at the intuitive knowledge of the inner principle, and thus obtain final release. And this way being open to release, there is really no use to be discerned in the Vedânta-texts, suggesting as they clearly do the entirely false view that the real being (is not absolutely homogeneous intelligence, but) possesses infinite transcendent attributes, being endowed with manifold powers, connected with manifold creations, and so on. In this way the qualification of *S*ûdras for the knowledge of Brahman is perfectly clear. And as the knowledge of Brahman may be reached in this way not only by *S*ûdras but also by Brâhma*n*as and members of the other higher castes, the poor Upanishad is practically defunct.—To this the following objection will possibly be raised. Man being implicated in and confused by the beginningless course of mundane existence, requires to receive from somewhere a suggestion as to this empirical world being a mere error and the Reality being something quite different, and thus only there arises in him a desire to enter on an enquiry, proceeding by means of perception, and so on. Now that which gives the required suggestion is the Veda, and hence we cannot do without it.—But this objection is not valid. For in the minds of those who are awed by all the dangers and troubles of existence, the desire to enter on a philosophical investigation of Reality, proceeding by means of Perception and Inference, springs up quite apart from the Veda, owing to the observation that there are various sects of philosophers, Sâṅkhyas, and so on, who make it their business to carry on such investigations. And when such desire is once roused, Perception and Inference alone (in the way allowed by the *S*âṅkaras themselves) lead on to the theory that the only Reality is intelligence eternal, pure, self-luminous, non-dual, non-changing, and that everything else is fictitiously superimposed thereon. That this self-luminous Reality possesses no other attribute to be learned from scripture is admitted; for according to your opinion also scripture sublates everything that is not Brahman and merely superimposed on it. Nor should it be said that we must have recourse to the Upanishads for the purpose of establishing that the Real found in the way of perception and inference is at the same time of the nature of bliss; for the merely and absolutely Intelligent is seen of itself to be of that nature, since it is different from everything that is not of that nature.—There are, on the other hand, those who hold that the knowledge which the Vedânta-texts enjoin as the means of Release is of the nature of devout meditation; that such meditation has the effect of winning the love of the supreme Spirit and is to be learned from scripture only; that the injunctions of meditation refer to such knowledge only as springs from the legitimate study of the Veda on the part of a man duly purified by initiation and other ceremonies, and is assisted by the seven means (see above, p. 17); and that the supreme Person pleased by such meditation bestows on the devotee knowledge of his own true nature, dissolves thereby the Nescience springing from works, and thus releases him from bondage. And on this view the proof of the non-qualification of the *S*ûdra, as given in the preceding Sûtras, holds good.—Here terminates the adhikara*n*a of 'the exclusion of the *S*ûdras.'

Having thus completed the investigation of qualification which had suggested itself in connexion with the matter in hand, the Sûtras return to the being measured by a thumb, and state another reason for its being explained as Brahman—as already understood on the basis of its being declared the ruler of what is and what will be.

40. On account of the trembling.

In the part of the Ka*th*a-Upanishad which intervenes between the passage 'The Person of the size of a thumb stands in the middle of the Self' (II, 4, 12), and the passage 'The Person of the size of a thumb, the inner Self' (II, 6, 17), we meet with the text 'whatever there is, the whole world, when gone forth, trembles in its breath. A great terror, a raised thunderbolt; those who knew it became immortal. From fear of it fire burns, from fear the sun shines, from fear Indra and Vâyu, and Death as the fifth run away' (II, 6, 2; 3). This text declares that the whole world and Agni, Sûrya, and so on, abiding within that Person of the size of a thumb, who is here designated by the term 'breath,' and going forth from him, tremble from their great fear of him. 'What will happen to us if we transgress his commandments?'—thinking thus the whole world trembles on account of great fear, as if it were a raised thunderbolt. In this explanation we take the clause 'A great fear, a raised thunderbolt,' in the sense of '(the world trembles) from great fear,' &c., as it is clearly connected in meaning with the following clause: 'from fear the fire burns,' &c.—Now what is described here is the nature of the highest Brahman; for that such power belongs to Brahman only we know from other texts, viz.: 'By the command of that Imperishable, O Gârgî, sun and moon stand apart' (B*ri*. Up. III, 8, 9); and 'From fear of it the wind blows, from fear the sun rises; from fear of it Agni and Indra, yea Death runs as the fifth' (Taitt. Up. II, 8, 1).—The next Sûtra supplies a further reason.

41. On account of light being seen (declared in the text).

Between the two texts referring to the Person of the size of a thumb, there is a text declaring that to that Person there belongs light that obscures all other light, and is the cause and assistance of all other light; and such light is characteristic of Brahman only. 'The sun does not shine there, nor the moon and the stars, nor these lightnings, and much less this fire. After him, the shining one, everything shines; by his light all this is lighted' (Ka. Up. II, 5, 15). This very same *s*loka is read in the Âtharva*n*a (i. e.

Mu*nd*aka) with reference to Brahman. Everywhere, in fact, the texts attribute supreme luminousness to Brahman only. Compare: 'Having approached the highest light he manifests himself in his own shape' (*Kh.* Up. VIII, 12, 3); 'Him the gods meditate on as the light of lights, as immortal time' (B*ri.* Up. IV, 4, 16); 'Now that light which shines above this heaven' (*Kh.* Up. III, 13, 7).—It is thus a settled conclusion that the Person measured by a thumb is the highest Brahman.—Here terminates the adhikara*n*a of 'him who is measured' (by a thumb).

42. The ether, on account of the designation of something different, and so on.

We read in the *Kh*ândogya 'The ether is the evolver of forms and names. That within which these forms and names are (or "that which is within—or without—these forms and names") is Brahman, the Immortal, the Self' (VIII, 14). A doubt here arises whether the being here called ether be the released individual soul, or the highest Self.—The Pûrvapakshin adopts the former view. For, he says, the released soul is introduced as subject-matter in an immediately preceding clause, 'Shaking off all as a horse shakes his hair, and as the moon frees himself from the mouth of Râhu; having shaken off the body I obtain, satisfied, the uncreated world of Brahman.' Moreover, the clause 'That which is without forms and names' clearly designates the released soul freed from name and form. And 'the evolver of names and forms' is again that same soul characterised with a view to its previous condition; for the individual soul in its non-released state supported the shapes of gods, and so on, and their names. With a view, finally, to its present state in which it is free from name and form, the last clause declares 'that is Brahman, the Immortal.' The term 'ether' may very well be applied to the released soul which is characterised by the possession of non-limited splendour.—But, as the text under discussion is supplementary to the section dealing with the small ether within the heart (VIII, 1, 1 ff.), we understand that

that small ether is referred to here also; and it has been proved above that that small ether is Brahman!—Not so, we reply. The text under discussion is separated from the section treating of the small ether within the heart, by the teaching of Pra*g*âpati, and that teaching is concerned with the characteristics of the individual soul in its different conditions up to Release; and moreover the earlier part of the section under discussion speaks of the being which shakes off evil, and this undoubtedly is the released individual soul introduced in the teaching of Pra*g*âpati. All this shows that the ether in our passage denotes the released individual soul.

This view is set aside by the Sûtra. The ether in our passage is the highest Brahman, because the clause 'Ether is the evolver of forms and names' designates something other than the individual soul. The ether which evolves names and forms cannot be the individual soul either in the state of bondage or that of release. In the state of bondage the soul is under the influence of karman, itself participates in name and form, and hence cannot bring about names and forms. And in its released state it is expressly said not to take part in the world-business (Ve. Sû. IV, 4, 17), and therefore is all the less qualified to evolve names and forms. The Lord, on the other hand, who is the ruling principle in the construction of the Universe is expressly declared by scripture to be the evolver of names and forms; cp. 'Entering into them with this living Self, let me evolve names and forms' (*Kh*. Up. VI, 3, 2); 'Who is all-knowing, whose brooding consists of knowledge, from him is born this Brahman, name, form, and matter' (Mu. Up. I, 1, 9), &c. Hence the ether which brings about names and forms is something different from the soul for which name and form are brought about; it is in fact the highest Brahman. This the next clause of the text confirms, 'That which is within those forms and names'; the purport of which is: because that ether is within names and forms, not being touched by them but being something apart, therefore it is the evolver of them; this also following from his being free from evil and endowed with the power of realising his purposes. The 'and so on' in the Sûtra refers to the Brahma-hood, Self-hood, and immortality mentioned in the text ('That is the Brahman, the Immortal, the Self'). For Brahma-hood, i. e. greatness, and so on, in their unconditioned sense, belong to the highest Self only. It is thus clear that the ether is the highest Brahman.—Nor is the Pûrvapakshin right in maintaining that a clause immediately preceding ('shaking off all evil') introduces the individual soul as the general topic of the section. For what the part of the text immediately preceding the passage under discussion does introduce as general topic, is the highest Brahman, as shown by the clause 'I obtain the Brahma-world.' Brahman is, it is true, represented there as the object to be obtained by the released soul; but as the released soul cannot be the evolver of names and forms, &c., we must conclude that it is Brahman (and not the released soul), which constitutes the topic of the whole section. Moreover (to take a wider view of the context of our passage) the term 'ether' prompts us to recognise here the small ether (mentioned in the first section of the eighth book) as the general topic of the book; and as the teaching of Pra*g*âpati is meant to set forth (not the individual soul by itself but) the nature of the soul of the meditating devotee, it is proper to conclude that the text under discussion is meant finally to represent, as the object to be obtained, the small ether previously inculcated as object of meditation. In conclusion we remark that the term 'ether' is nowhere seen to denote the individual Self.—The ether that evolves names and forms, therefore, is the highest Brahman.

But, an objection is raised, there is no other Self different from the individual Self; for scripture teaches the unity of all Selfs and denies duality. Terms such as 'the highest Self,' 'the highest Brahman,' 'the highest Lord,' are merely designations of the individual soul in the state of Release. The Brahma-world to be attained, therefore, is nothing different from the attaining individual soul; and hence the ether also that evolves names and forms can be that soul only.—To this objection the next Sûtra replies.

43. On account of difference in deep sleep and departing.

We have to supply 'on account of designation' from the preceding Sûtra. Because the text designates the highest Self as something different from the individual Self in the state of deep sleep as well as at the time of departure, the highest Self is thus different. For the Vâgasaneyaka, after having introduced the individual Self in the passage 'Who is that Self?—He who consisting of knowledge is among the prânas,' &c. (Bri. Up. IV, 3, 7), describes how, in the state of deep sleep, being not conscious of anything it is held embraced by the all-knowing highest Self, 'embraced by the intelligent Self it knows nothing that is without, nothing that is within' (IV, 3, 21). So also with reference to the time of departure, i. e. dying 'Mounted by the intelligent Self it moves along groaning' (IV, 3, 35). Now it is impossible that the unconscious individual Self, either lying in deep sleep or departing from the body, should at the same time be embraced or mounted by itself, being all-knowing. Nor can the embracing and mounting Self be some other individual Self; for no such Self can be all-knowing.—The next Sûtra supplies a further reason.

44. And on account of such words as Lord.

That embracing highest Self is further on designated by terms such as Lord, and so on. 'He is the Lord of all, the master of all, the ruler of all. He does not become greater by good works, nor smaller by evil works. He is the lord of all, the king of beings, the protector of beings. He is a bank and a boundary so that these worlds may not be confounded. Brâhmanas seek to know him by the study of the Veda. He who knows him becomes a Muni. Wishing for that world only, mendicants leave their homes' (IV, 4, 22). 'This indeed is the great unborn Self, the strong, the giver of wealth,—undecaying, undying, immortal, fearless is Brahman' (IV, 4, 24; 25). Now all the qualities here declared, viz. being the lord of all, and so on, cannot possibly belong to the individual Self even in the state of Release; and we thus again arrive at the conclusion that the ether evolving forms and names is something different from the released individual soul. The declarations of general Unity which we meet with in the texts rest thereon, that all sentient and non-sentient beings are effects of Brahman, and hence have Brahman for their inner Self. That this is the meaning of texts such as 'All this is Brahman,' &c., we have explained before. And the texts denying plurality are to be understood in the same way.—Here terminates the adhikara*n*a of 'the designation of something different, and so on.'

## FOURTH PÂDA.

1. If it be said that some (mention) that which rests on Inference; we deny this because (the form) refers to what is contained in the simile of the body; and (this the text) shows.

So far the Sûtras have given instruction about a Brahman, the enquiry into which serves as a means to obtain what is the highest good of man, viz. final release; which is the cause of the origination, and so on, of the world; which differs in nature from all non-sentient things such as the Pradhâna, and from all intelligent beings whether in the state of bondage or of release; which is free from all shadow of imperfection; which is all knowing, all powerful, has the power of realising all its purposes, comprises within itself all blessed qualities, is the inner Self of all, and possesses unbounded power and might. But here a new special objection presents itself. In order to establish the theory maintained by Kapila, viz. of there being a Pradhâna and individual souls which do *not* have their Self in Brahman, it is pointed out by some that in certain branches of the Veda there are met with certain passages which appear to adumbrate the doctrine of the Pradhâna being the universal cause. The Sûtras now apply themselves to the refutation of this view, in order thereby to confirm the theory of Brahman being the only cause of all.

We read in the Ka*th*a-Upanishad, 'Beyond the senses there are the objects, beyond the objects there is the mind, beyond the mind there is the intellect, the great Self is beyond the intellect. Beyond the Great there is the Unevolved, beyond the Unevolved there is the Person. Beyond the Person there is nothing—this is the goal, the highest road' (Ka. Up. I, 3, 11). The question here arises whether by the 'Unevolved' be or be not meant the

Pradhâna, as established by Kapila's theory, of which Brahman is not the Self.—The Pûrvapakshin maintains the former alternative. For, he says, in the clause 'beyond the Great is the Unevolved, beyond the Unevolved is the Person,' we recognise the arrangement of entities as established by the Sâṅkhya-system, and hence must take the 'Unevolved' to be the Pradhâna. This is further confirmed by the additional clause 'beyond the Person there is nothing,' which (in agreement with Sâṅkhya principles) denies that there is any being beyond the soul, which itself is the twenty-fifth and last of the principles recognised by the Sâṅkhyas. This primâ facie view is expressed in the former part of the Sûtra, 'If it be said that in the *s*âkhâs of some that which rests on Inference, i.e. the Pradhâna, is stated as the universal cause.'

The latter part of the Sûtra refutes this view. The word 'Unevolved' does not denote a Pradhâna independent of Brahman; it rather denotes the body represented as a chariot in the simile of the body, i.e. in the passage instituting a comparison between the Self, body, intellect, and so on, on the one side, and the charioteer, chariot, &c. on the other side.—The details are as follows. The text at first—in the section beginning 'Know the Self to be the person driving,' &c., and ending 'he reaches the end of the journey, and that is the highest place of Vish*n*u' (I, 3, 3-9)—compares the devotee desirous of reaching the goal of his journey through the sa*m*sâra, i.e. the abode of Vish*n*u, to a man driving in a chariot; and his body, senses, and so on, to the chariot and parts of the chariot; the meaning of the whole comparison being that he only reaches the goal who has the chariot, &c. in his control. It thereupon proceeds to declare which of the different beings enumerated and compared to a chariot, and so on, occupy a superior position to the others in so far, namely, as they are that which requires to be controlled—'higher than the senses are the objects,' and so on. Higher than the senses—compared to the horses—are the objects—compared to roads,—because even a man who generally controls his senses finds it difficult to master them when they are in contact with their objects; higher than the objects is the mind—compared to the reins—because when the mind inclines towards the objects even the non-proximity of the latter does not make much difference; higher than the mind (manas) is the intellect (buddhi)—compared to the charioteer—because in the absence of decision (which is the characteristic quality of buddhi) the mind also has little power; higher than the intellect again is the (individual) Self, for that Self is the agent whom the intellect serves. And as all this is subject to the wishes of the Self, the text characterises it as the 'great Self.' Superior to that Self again is the body, compared to the chariot, for all activity whereby the individual Self strives to bring about what is of advantage to itself depends on the body. And higher finally than the body is the highest Person, the inner Ruler and Self of all, the term and goal of the journey of the individual soul; for the activities of all the beings enumerated depend on the wishes of that highest Self. As the universal inner Ruler that Self brings about the meditation of the Devotee also; for the Sûtra (II, 3, 41) expressly declares that the activity of the individual soul depends on the Supreme Person. Being the means for bringing about the meditation and the goal of meditation, that same Self is the highest object to be attained; hence the text says 'Higher than the Person there is nothing—that is the goal, the highest road.' Analogously scripture, in the antaryâmin-Brâhma*n*a, at first declares that the highest Self within witnesses and rules everything, and thereupon negatives the existence of any further ruling principle 'There is no other seer but he,' &c. Similarly, in the Bhagavad-gîtâ, 'The abode, the agent, the various senses, the different and manifold functions, and fifth the Divinity (i.e. the highest Person)' (XVIII, 14); and 'I dwell within the heart of all; memory and perception, as well as their loss, come from me' (XV, 15). And if, as in the explanation of the text under discussion, we speak of that highest Self being 'controlled,' we must understand thereby the soul's taking refuge with it; compare the passage Bha. Gî. XVIII, 61–62, 'The Lord dwells in the heart of all creatures, whirling them round as if mounted on a machine; to Him go for refuge.'

Now all the beings, senses, and so on, which had been mentioned in the simile, are recognised in the passage 'higher than the senses are the objects,' &c., being designated there by their proper names; but there is no mention made of the body which previously had been compared to the chariot; we therefore conclude that it is the body which is denoted by the term 'the Unevolved.' Hence there is no reason to see here a reference to the Pradhâna as established in the theory of Kapila. Nor do we recognise, in the text under discussion, the general system of Kapila. The text declares the objects, i.e. sounds and so on, to be superior to the senses; but in Kapila's system the objects are not viewed as the causes of the senses. For the same reason the statement that the manas is higher than the objects does not agree with Kapila's doctrine. Nor is this the case with regard to the clause 'higher than the buddhi is the great one, the Self'; for with Kapila the 'great one' (mahat) is the buddhi, and it would not do to say 'higher than the great one is the great one.' And finally the 'great one,' according to Kapila, cannot be called the 'Self.' The text under discussion thus refers only to those entities which had previously appeared in the simile. The text itself further on proves this, when saying 'That Self is hidden in all beings and does not shine forth, but it is seen by subtle seers through their sharp and subtle intellect. A wise man should keep down speech in the mind, he should keep that within knowledge (which is) within the Self; he should keep knowledge within the great Self, and that he should keep within the quiet Self.' For this passage, after having stated that the highest Self is difficult to see with the inner and outer organs of knowledge, describes the mode in which the sense-organs, and so on, are to be held in control. The wise man should restrain the sense-organs and the organs of activity within the mind; he should restrain that (i.e. the mind) within knowledge, i.e. within the intellect (buddhi), which abides within the Self; he should further restrain the intellect within the great Self, i.e. the active individual Self; and that Self finally he should restrain within the quiet Self, i.e. the highest Brahman, which is the inner ruler of all; i.e. he should reach, with his individual Self so qualified, the place of Vish*n*u, i.e. Brahman.—But how can the term 'the Unevolved' denote the evolved body?—To this question the next Sûtra furnishes a reply.

2. But the subtle (body), on account of its capability.

The elements in their fine state are what is called the 'Unevolved,' and this entering into a particular condition becomes the body. It is the 'Unevolved' in the particular condition of the body, which in the text under discussion is called the 'Unevolved.' 'On account of its capability,' i.e. because unevolved non-sentient matter, when assuming certain states and forms, is capable of entering on activities promoting the interest of man. But, an objection is raised, if the 'Unevolved' is taken to be matter in its subtle state, what objection is there to our accepting for the explanation of our text that which is established in the Sâṅkhya-system? for there also the 'Unevolved' means nothing else but matter in its subtle state.

To this the next Sûtra replies—

3. (Matter in its subtle state) subserves an end, on account of its dependence on him (viz. the Supreme Person).

Matter in its subtle state subserves ends, in so far only as it is dependent on the Supreme Person who is the cause of all. We by no means wish to deny unevolved matter and all its effects in themselves, but in so far only as they are maintained not to have their Self in the Supreme Person. For the fact is that they constitute his body and He thus constitutes their Self; and it is only through this their relation to him that the Pradhâna, and so on, are capable of accomplishing their several ends. Otherwise the different essential natures of them all could never exist,—nor persist, nor act. It is just on the ground of this dependence on the Lord not being acknowledged by the Sâṅkhyas that their system is disproved by us. In Scripture and Smriti alike, wherever the origination and destruction of the world are described, or the greatness of the Supreme Person is glorified, the Pradhâna and all its effects, no less than the individual souls, are declared to have their Self in that Supreme Person. Compare, e.g. the text which first says that the earth is merged in water, and further on 'the elements are merged in the Mahat, the Mahat in the Unevolved, the Unevolved in the Imperishable, the Imperishable in Darkness; Darkness becomes one with the highest divinity.' And 'He of whom the earth is the body,' &c. up to 'he of whom the Unevolved is the body; of whom the Imperishable is the body; of whom death is the body; he the inner Self of all beings, free from all evil, the divine one, the one God Nârâyana.' And 'Earth, water, fire, air, ether, mind, intellect, egoity—thus eightfold is my nature divided. Lower is this nature; other than this and higher know that nature of mine which has become the individual soul by which this world is supported. Remember that all beings spring from this; I am the origin and the dissolution of the whole Universe. Higher than I there is none else; all this is strung on me as pearls on a thread' (Bha. Gî. VII, 4-7). And 'the Evolved is Vishnu, and the Unevolved, he is the Person and time.—The nature (prakriti) declared by me, having the double form of the Evolved and the Unevolved, and the soul—both these are merged in the highest Self. That Self is the support of all, the Supreme Person who under the name of Vishnu is glorified in the Vedas and the Vedânta books.'

4. And on account of there being no statement of its being an object of knowledge.

If the text meant the Non-evolved as understood by the Sâṅkhyas it would refer to it as something to be known; for the Sâṅkhyas, who hold the theory of Release resulting from the discriminative knowledge of the Evolved, the

Non-evolved, and the soul, admit that all these are objects of knowledge. Now our text does not refer to the Unevolved as an object of knowledge, and it cannot therefore be the Pradhâna assumed by the Sâṅkhyas.

5. Should it be said that (the text) declares (it); we say, not so; for the intelligent Self (is meant), on account of subject-matter.

'He who has meditated on that which is without sound, without touch, without form, without decay, without taste, eternal, without smell, without beginning, without end, beyond the Great, unchangeable; is freed from the jaws of death' (Ka. Up. II, 3, 15), this scriptural text, closely following on the text under discussion, represents the 'Unevolved' as the object of knowledge!—Not so, we reply. What that *s*loka represents as the object of meditation is (not the Unevolved but) the intelligent Self, i. e. the Supreme Person. For it is the latter who forms the general subject-matter, as we infer from two preceding passages, viz. 'He who has knowledge for his charioteer, and who holds the reins of the mind, he reaches the end of his journey, the highest place of Vish*n*u'; and 'That Self is hidden in all beings and does not shine forth, but it is seen by subtle seers through their sharp and subtle intellect.' For this reason, also, the clause 'Higher than the person there is nothing' cannot be taken as meant to deny the existence of an entity beyond the 'purusha' in the Sâṅkhya sense. That the highest Self possesses the qualities of being without sound, &c., we moreover know from other scriptural texts, such as Mu. Up. I, 1, 6 'That which is not to be seen, not to be grasped,' &c. And the qualification 'beyond the Great, unchangeable' is meant to declare that the highest Self is beyond the individual Self which had been called 'the Great' in a previous passage 'beyond the intellect is the Great Self.'

6. And of three only there is this mention and question.

In the Upanishad under discussion there is mention

made of three things only as objects of knowledge—the three standing to one another in the relation of means, end to be realised by those means, and persons realising,—and questions are asked as to those three only. There is no mention of, nor question referring to, the Unevolved.—Na*k*iketas desirous of Release having been allowed by Death to choose three boons, chooses for his first boon that his father should be well disposed towards him—without which he could not hope for spiritual welfare. For his second boon he chooses the knowledge of the Nâ*k*iketa-fire, which is a means towards final Release. 'Thou knowest, O Death, the fire-sacrifice which leads to heaven; tell it to me, full of faith. Those who live in the heaven-world reach Immortality—this I ask as my second boon.' The term 'heaven-world' here denotes the highest aim of man, i. e. Release, as appears from the declaration that those who live there enjoy freedom from old age and death; from the fact that further on (I, 1, 26) works leading to perishable results are disparaged; and from what Yama says in reply to the second demand 'He who thrice performs this Nâ*k*iketa-rite overcomes birth and death.' As his third boon he, in the form of a question referring to final release, actually enquires about three things, viz. 'the nature of the end to be reached, i. e. Release; the nature of him who wishes to reach that end; and the nature of the means to reach it, i. e. of meditation assisted by certain works. Yama, having tested Na*k*iketas' fitness to receive the desired instruction, thereupon begins to teach him. 'The Ancient who is difficult to be seen, who has entered into the dark, who is hidden in the cave, who dwells in the abyss; having known him as God, by means of meditation on his Self, the wise one leaves joy and sorrow behind.' Here the clause 'having known the God,' points to the divine Being that is to be meditated upon; the clause 'by means of meditation on his Self' points to the attaining agent, i. e. the individual soul as an object of knowledge; and the clause 'having known him the wise ones leave joy and sorrow behind' points to the meditation through which Brahman is to be reached. Na*k*iketas, pleased with the general instruction received, questions again in order to receive clearer information on those three matters, 'What thou seest as different from dharma and different from adharma, as different from that, from that which is done and not done, as different from what is past or future, tell me that'; a question referring to three things, viz. an object to be effected, a means to effect it, and an effecting agent—each of which is to be different from anything else past, present, or future[1]. Yama thereupon at first instructs him as to the Pra*n*ava, 'That word which all the Vedas record, which all penances proclaim, desiring which men become religious students; that word I tell thee briefly—it is Om'—an instruction which implies praise of the Pra*n*ava, and in a general way sets forth that which the Pra*n*ava expresses, e. g. the nature of the object to be reached, the nature of the person reaching it, and the means for reaching it, such means here consisting in the word 'Om,' which denotes the object to be reached[2]. He then continues to glorify the Pra*n*ava (I, 2, 16–17), and thereupon gives special information in the first place about the nature of the attaining subject, i. e, the individual soul, 'The knowing Self is not born, it dies not,' &c. Next he teaches Na*k*iketas as to the true nature of the object to be attained, viz. the highest Brahman or Vish*n*u, in the section beginning 'The Self smaller than small,' and ending 'Who then knows where he is?' (I, 2, 20–25). Part of this section, viz. 'That Self cannot be gained by the Veda,' &c.,

[1] The commentary proposes different ways of finding those three objects of enquiry in the words of Na*k*iketas. According to the first explanation, 'that which is different from dharma' is a means differing from all ordinary means; 'adharma' 'not-dharma' is what is not a means, but the result to be reached: hence 'that which is different from adharma' is a result differing from all ordinary results. 'What is different from that' is an agent different from 'that'; i. e. an ordinary agent, and so on. (*S*ru. Prakâ*s*. p. 1226.)

[2] The syllable 'Om,' which denotes Brahman, is a means towards meditation (Brahman being meditated upon under this form), and thus indirectly a means towards reaching Brahman.

at the same time teaches that the meditation through which Brahman is attained is of the nature of devotion (bhakti). Next the *s*loka I, 3, 1 'There are the two drinking their reward' shows that, as the object of devout meditation and the devotee abide together, meditation is easily performed. Then the section beginning 'Know the Self to be him who drives in the chariot,' and ending 'the wise say the path is hard' (I, 3, 3–14), teaches the true mode of meditation, and how the devotee reaches the highest abode of Vish*n*u; and then there is a final reference to the object to be reached in I, 3, 15, 'That which is without sound, without touch,' &c. It thus appears that there are references and questions regarding those three matters only; and hence the 'Unevolved' cannot mean the Pradhâna of the Sâṅkhyas.

7. And as in the case of the 'Great.'

In the case of the passage 'Higher than the intellect is the Great Self,' we conclude from the co-ordination of 'the Great' with the Self that what the text means is not the 'Great' principle of the Sâṅkhyas; analogously we conclude that the 'Unevolved,' which is said to be higher than the Self, cannot be the Pradhâna of Kapila's system.

8. On account of there being no special characteristic; as in the case of the cup.

In the discussion of the following passages also we aim only at refuting the system of the Sâṅkhyas; not at disproving the existence and nature of Prak*ri*ti, the 'great' principle, the aha*m*kâra, and so on, viewed as dependent on Brahman. For that they exist in this latter relation is proved by Scripture as well as Sm*ri*ti.—A text of the followers of the Atharvan runs as follows: 'Her who produces all effects, the non-knowing one, the unborn one, wearing eight forms, the firm one—she is known (by the Lord) and ruled by him, she is spread out and incited and ruled by him, gives birth to the world for the benefit of the souls. A cow she is without beginning and end, a mother producing all beings; white, black, and red, milking all wishes for the Lord. Many babes unknown drink her, the impartial one;

but one God only, following his own will, drinks her submitting to him. By his own thought and work the mighty God strongly enjoys her, who is common to all, the milkgiver, who is pressed by the sacrifices. The Non-evolved when being counted by twenty-four is called the Evolved.' This passage evidently describes the nature of Prak*ri*ti, and so on, and the same Upanishad also teaches the Supreme Person who constitutes the Self of Prak*ri*ti, and so on. 'Him they call the twenty-sixth or also the twenty-seventh; as the Person devoid of all qualities of the Sâṅkhyas he is known by the followers of the Atharvan [1].'—Other followers of the Atharvan read in their text that there are sixteen originating principles (prak*ri*ti) and eight effected things (vikâra; Garbha Up. 3).—The *S*vetâ*s*vataras again set forth the nature of Prak*ri*ti, the soul and the Lord as follows. 'The Lord supports all this together, the Perishable and the Imperishable, the Evolved and the Unevolved; the other one is in bondage, since he is an enjoyer; but having known the God he is free from all fetters. There are two unborn ones, the one knowing and a Lord, the other without knowledge and lordly power; there is the one unborn female on whom the enjoyment of all enjoyers depends; and there is the infinite Self appearing in all shapes, but itself inactive. When a man finds out these three, that is Brahman. The Perishable is the Pradhâna, the Immortal and Imperishable is Hara; the one God rules the Perishable and the Self. From meditation on him, from union with him, from becoming one with him there is in the end cessation of all Mâyâ' (*S*vet. Up. I, 8–10). And 'The sacred verses, the offerings, the sacrifices, the vows, the past, the future, and all that the Vedas declare—from that the Ruler of Mâyâ creates all this; and in this the other one is bound up through Mâyâ. Know then Prak*ri*ti to be Mâyâ and the great Lord the ruler of Mâyâ; with his members this

[1] These quotations are from the *K*ulikâ-Upanishad (transl. by Deussen, Seventy Upanishads, p. 638 ff.) The translation as given above follows the readings adopted by Râmânuga and explained in the *S*ruta-Prakâ*s*ikâ.

whole world is filled' (*S*vet. Up. V, 9–10). And, further on, 'The master of Pradhâna and the soul, the lord of the gu*n*as, the cause of the bondage, existence, and release of worldly existence' (VI, 16). Thus likewise in Sm*ri*ti, 'Do thou know both Nature and the soul to be without beginning, and know all effects and qualities to have sprung from Nature. Nature is declared to be the cause of the activity of causes and effects, whilst the soul is the cause of there being enjoyment of pleasure and pain. For the soul abiding in Nature experiences the qualities derived from Nature, the reason being its connexion with the qualities, in its births in good and evil wombs' (Bha. Gî. XIII, 19–21). And 'Goodness, Passion, and Darkness—these are the qualities which, issuing from nature, bind in the body the embodied soul, the undecaying one' (XIV, 5). And 'All beings at the end of a kalpa return into my Nature, and again, at the beginning of a kalpa, do I send them forth. Presiding over my own nature again and again do I send forth this vast body of beings which has no freedom of its own, being subject to Nature.—With me as ruler Nature brings forth all moving and non-moving things, and for this reason the world does ever go round' (Bha. Gî. IX, 7, 8, 10). What we therefore refuse to accept are a Prak*ri*ti, and so on, of the kind assumed by Kapila, i. e. not having their Self in Brahman.—We now proceed to explain the Sûtra.

We read in the *S*vetâ*s*vatara-Upanishad 'There is one a*g*â, red, white, and black, producing manifold offspring of the same nature. One a*g*a loves her and lies by her; another leaves her after having enjoyed her.' A doubt arises here whether this mantra declares a mere Prak*ri*ti as assumed in Kapila's system, or a Prak*ri*ti having its Self in Brahman.

The Pûrvapakshin maintains the former alternative. For, he points out, the text refers to the non-originatedness of Prak*ri*ti, calling her a*g*â, i. e. unborn, and further says that she by herself independently produces manifold offspring resembling herself. This view is rejected by the Sûtra, on the ground that there is no intimation of a special circumstance determining the acceptance of the Prak*ri*ti as assumed by the Sâṅkhyas, i. e. independent of Brahman; for that she is a*g*â, i. e. not born, is not a sufficiently special characteristic. The case is analogous to that of the 'cup.' In the mantra 'There is a cup having its mouth below and its bottom above' (B*ri*. Up. II, 2, 3), the word *k*amasa conveys to us only the idea of some implement used in eating, but we are unable to see what special kind of *k*amasa is meant; for in the case of words the meaning of which is ascertained on the ground of their derivation (as '*k*amasa' from 'kam,' to eat or drink), the special sense of the word in any place cannot be ascertained without the help of considerations of general possibility, general subject-matter, and so on. Now in the case of the cup we are able to ascertain that the cup meant is the head, because there is a complementary passage 'What is called the cup with its mouth below and its bottom above is the head'; but if we look out for a similar help to determine the special meaning of a*g*â, we find nothing to convince us that the a*g*â, i. e. the 'unborn' principle, is the Prak*ri*ti of the Sâṅkhyas. Nor is there anything in the text to convey the idea of that a*g*â having the power of independent creation; for the clause 'giving birth to manifold offspring' declares only that she creates, not that she creates unaided. The mantra does not therefore tell us about an 'unborn' principle independent of Brahman.—There moreover is a special reason for understanding by the a*g*â something that depends on Brahman. This the following Sûtra states.

9. But she begins with light; for thus some read in their text.

The 'but' has assertory force. 'Light' in the Sûtra means Brahman, in accordance with the meaning of the term as known from texts such as 'On him the gods meditate, the light of lights' (B*ri*. Up. X, 4, 16); 'That light which shines beyond heaven' (*Kh*. Up. III, 13, 7). 'She begins with light' thus means 'she has Brahman for her cause.'—'For thus some read in their text,' i. e. because the members of one *S*âkhâ, viz. the Taittirîyas read in their text that this 'agâ' has Brahman for her cause. The Mahânârâyana-Upanishad (of the Taittirîyas) at first refers to Brahman abiding in the hollow of the heart as the object of meditation. 'Smaller than the small, greater than the great, the Self placed in the hollow of this creature'; next declares that all the worlds and Brahmâ and the other gods originated from that Self; and then says that there sprung from it also this agâ which is the cause of all 'The one agâ (goat), red, white and black, which gives birth to numerous offspring of the same shape, one aga (he-goat) loves and lies by her; another one forsakes her after having enjoyed her.' The subject-matter of the entire section evidently is to give instruction as to the whole aggregate of things other than Brahman originating from Brahman and thus having its Self in it; hence we conclude that also the agâ which gives birth to manifold creatures like her, and is enjoyed by the soul controlled by karman, while she is abandoned by the soul possessing true knowledge is, no less than vital airs, seas, mountains, &c., a creature of Brahman, and hence has its Self in Brahman. We then apply to the interpretation of the Svetâsvatara-text the meaning of the analogous Mahânârâyana-text, as determined by the complementary passages, and thus arrive at the conclusion that the agâ in the former text also is a being having its Self in Brahman.

That this is so, moreover, appears from the Svetâsvatara itself. For in the early part of that Upanishad, we have after the introductory question, 'Is Brahman the cause?' the passage 'The sages devoted to meditation and concentration have seen the person whose Self is the divinity, hidden in its own qualities' (I, 1, 3); which evidently refers to the agâ as being of the nature of a power of the highest Brahman. And as further on also (viz. in the passages 'From that the Mâyin creates all this, and in this the other is bound up through Mâyâ'; 'Know then Prakriti to be Mâyâ and the Great Lord the ruler of Mâyâ'; and 'he who rules every place of birth,' V, 9–11) the very same being is referred to, there remains not even a shadow of proof for the assertion that the mantra under discussion refers to an independent Prak*ri*ti as assumed by the Sâṅkhyas.

But a further objection is raised, if the Prak*ri*ti denoted by a*g*â begins with, i. e. is caused by Brahman, how can it be called a*g*â, i. e. the non-produced one; or, if it is non-produced, how can it be originated by Brahman? To this the next Sûtra replies.

10. And on account of the teaching of formation (i. e. creation) there is no contradiction; as in the case of the honey.

The 'and' expresses disposal of a doubt that had arisen. There is no contradiction between the Prak*ri*ti being a*g*â and originating from light. On account of instruction being given about the formation (kalpana), i. e. creation of the world. This interpretation of 'kalpana' is in agreement with the use of the verb k*li*p in the text, 'as formerly the creator made (akalpayat) sun and moon.'

In our text the *s*loka 'from that the Lord of Mâyâ creates all this' gives instruction about the creation of the world. From that, i. e. from matter in its subtle causal state when it is not yet divided, the Lord of all creates the entire Universe. From this statement about creation we understand that Prak*ri*ti exists in a twofold state according as it is either cause or effect. During a pralaya it unites itself with Brahman and abides in its subtle state, without any distinction of names and forms; it then is called the 'Unevolved,' and by other similar names. At the time of creation, on the other hand, there reveal themselves in Prak*ri*ti Goodness and the other gu*n*as, it divides itself according to names and forms, and then is called the 'Evolved,' and so on, and, transforming itself into fire, water, and earth, it appears as red, white, and black. In its causal condition it is a*g*â, i. e. unborn, in its effected condition it is 'caused by light, i. e. Brahman'; hence there is no contradiction. The case is analogous to that of the 'honey.' The sun in his causal state is one only, but in his effected state the Lord makes him into honey in so far namely as he then, for the purpose of enjoyment on the part of the Vasus and other gods, is the abode of nectar brought about by sacrificial works to be learned from the *Ri*k and the other Vedas; and further makes him to rise and to set. And between these two conditions there is no contradiction. This is declared in the Madhuvidyâ (*Kh*. Up. III), from 'The sun is indeed the honey of the Devas,' down to 'when from thence he has risen upwards he neither rises nor sets; being one he stands in the centre'—'one' here means 'of one nature.'—The conclusion therefore is that the *S*vetâ*s*vatara mantra under discussion refers to Prak*ri*ti as having her Self in Brahman, not to the Prak*ri*ti assumed by the Sâṅkhyas.

Others, however, are of opinion that the one a*g*â of which the mantra speaks has for its characteristics light, water, and earth. To them we address the following questions. Do you mean that by what the text speaks of as an a*g*â, consisting of fire, water, and earth, we have to understand those three elements only; or Brahman in the form of those three elements; or some power or principle which is the cause of the three elements? The first alternative is in conflict with the circumstance that, while fire, water, and earth are several things, the text explicitly refers to *one* a*g*â. Nor may it be urged that fire, water, and earth, although several, become one, by being made tripartite (*Kh*. Up. VI, 3, 3); for this making them tripartite, does not take away their being several; the text clearly showing that each several element becomes tripartite, 'Let me make each of these three divine beings tripartite.'—The second alternative again divides itself into two alternatives. Is the one a*g*â Brahman in so far as having passed over into fire, water, and earth; or Brahman in so far as abiding within itself and not passing over into effects? The former alternative is excluded by the consideration that it does not remove plurality (which cannot be reconciled with the *one* a*g*â). The second alternative is contradicted by the text calling that a*g*â red, white, and black; and moreover Brahman viewed as abiding within itself cannot be characterised by fire, water, and earth. On the third alternative it has to be assumed that the text denotes by the term '*ag*â' the three elements, and that on this basis there is imagined a causal condition of these elements; but better than this assumption it evidently is to accept the term '*ag*â' as directly denoting the causal state of those three elements as known from scripture.

Nor can we admit the contention that the term '*ag*â' is meant to teach that Prak*ri*ti should metaphorically be viewed as a she-goat; for such a view would be altogether purposeless. Where—in the passage 'Know the Self to be him who drives in the chariot'—the body, and so on, are compared to a chariot, and so on, the object is to set forth the means of attaining Brahman; where the sun is compared to honey, the object is to illustrate the enjoyment of the Vasus and other gods; but what similar object could possibly be attained by directing us to view Prak*ri*ti as a goat? Such a metaphorical view would in fact be not merely useless; it would be downright irrational. Prak*ri*ti is a non-intelligent principle, the causal substance of the entire material Universe, and constituting the means for the experience of pleasure and pain, and for the final release, of all intelligent souls which are connected with it from all eternity. Now it would be simply contrary to good sense, metaphorically to transfer to Prak*ri*ti such as described the nature of a she-goat—which is a sentient being that gives birth to very few creatures only, enters only occasionally into connexion with others, is of small use only, is not the cause of herself being abandoned by others, and is capable of abandoning those connected with her. Nor does it recommend itself to take the word *ag*â (understood to mean 'she-goat') in a sense different from that in which we understand the term '*ag*a' which occurs twice in the same mantra.—Let then all three terms be taken in the same metaphorical sense (*ag*a meaning he-goat).—It would be altogether senseless, we reply, to compare the soul which absolutely dissociates itself from Prak*ri*ti ('Another *ag*a leaves her after having enjoyed her') to a he-goat which is able to enter again into connexion with what he has abandoned, or with anything else.—Here terminates the adhikara*n*a of 'the cup.'

11. Not from the mention of the number even, on account of the diversity and of the excess.

The Vâ*g*asaneyins read in their text 'He in whom the five "five-people" and the ether rest, him alone I believe to be the Self; I, who know, believe him to be Brahman' (B*ri*. Up. IV, 4, 17). The doubt here arises whether this text be meant to set forth the categories as established in Kapila's doctrine, or not.—The Pûrvapakshin maintains the former view, on the ground that the word 'five-people,' qualified by the word 'five,' intimates the twenty-five categories of the Sâṅkhyas. The compound 'five-people' (pa*ñk*a*g*anâ*h*) denotes groups of five beings, just as the term pa*ñk*a-pûlya*h* denotes aggregates of five bundles of grass. And as we want to know how many such groups there are, the additional qualification 'five' intimates that there are five such groups; just as if it were said 'five five-bundles, i. e. five aggregates consisting of five bundles each.' We thus understand that the 'five five-people' are twenty-five things, and as the mantra in which the term is met with refers to final release, we recognise the twenty-five categories known from the Sâṅkhya-sm*ri*ti which are here referred to as objects to be known by persons desirous of release. For the followers of Kapila teach that 'there is the fundamental causal substance which is not an effect. There are seven things, viz. the Mahat, and so on, which are causal substances as well as effects. There are sixteen effects. The soul is neither a causal substance nor an effect' (Sâṅ. Kâ. 3). The mantra therefore is meant to intimate the categories known from the Sâṅkhya.—To this the Sûtra replies that from the mention of the number twenty-five supposed to be implied in the expression 'the five five-people,' it does not follow that the categories of the Sâṅkhyas are meant. 'On account of the diversity,' i. e. on account of the five-people further qualified by the number five being different from the categories of the Sâṅkhyas. For in the text 'in whom the five five-people and the ether rest,' the 'in whom' shows the five-people to have their abode, and hence their Self, in Brahman; and in the continuation of the text, 'him I believe the Self,' the 'him' connecting itself with the preceding 'in whom' is recognised to be Brahman. The five five-people must therefore be different from the categories of the Sâṅkhya-system. 'And on account of the excess.' Moreover there is, in the text under discussion, an excess over and above the Sâṅkhya categories, consisting in the Self denoted by the relative pronoun 'in whom,' and in the specially mentioned Ether. What the text designates therefore is the Supreme Person who is the Universal Lord in whom all things abide—such as he is described in the text quoted above, 'Therefore some call him the twenty-sixth, and others the twenty-seventh.' The 'even' in the Sûtra is meant to intimate that the 'five five-people' can in no way mean the twenty-five categories, since there is no pentad of groups consisting of five each. For in the case of the categories of the Sâṅkhyas there are no generic characteristics or the like which could determine the arrangement of those categories in fives. Nor must it be urged against this that there *is* a determining reason for such an arrangement in so far as the tattvas of the Sâṅkhyas form natural groups comprising firstly, the five organs of action; secondly, the five sense-organs; thirdly, the five gross elements; fourthly, the subtle parts of those elements; and fifthly, the five remaining tattvas; for as the text under discussion mentions the ether by itself, the possibility of a group consisting of the five gross elements is precluded. We cannot therefore take the compound 'five people' as denoting a group consisting of five constituent members, but, in agreement with Pâ*n*. II, 1, 50, as merely being a special name. There are certain beings the special name of which is 'five-people,' and of these beings the additional word 'pa*ñk*a' predicates that they are five in number. The expression is thus analogous to the term 'the seven seven-*ri*shis' (where the term 'seven-*ri*shis' is to be understood as the name of a certain class of *ri*shis only).—Who then are the beings called 'five-people?' —To this question the next Sûtra replies.

12. The breath, and so on, on the ground of the complementary passage.

We see from a complementary passage, viz. 'They who know the breath of breath, the eye of the eye, the ear of the ear, the food of food, the mind of mind,' that the 'five-people' are the breath, and eye, and so on, all of which have their abode in Brahman.

But, an objection is raised, while the mantra 'in whom the five five-people,' &c., is common to the Kâ*n*vas and the Mâdhyandinas, the complementary passage 'they who know the breath of breath,' &c., in the text of the former makes no mention of food, and hence we have no reason to say that the 'five-people' in their text are the breath, eye, and so on.

To this objection the next Sûtra replies.

13. By light, food not being (mentioned in the text) of some.

In the text of some, viz. the Kâ*n*vas, where food is not mentioned, the five-people are recognised to be the five senses, owing to the phrase 'of lights' which is met with in another complementary passage. In the mantra, 'him the gods worship as the light of lights,' which precedes the mantra about the 'five-people,' Brahman is spoken of as the light of lights, and this suggests the idea of certain lights the activity of which depends on Brahman. The mantra leaves it undetermined what these lights are; but from what follows about the 'five-people,' &c., we learn that what is meant are the senses which light up as it were their respective objects. In 'the breath of breath' the second 'breath' (in the genitive case) denotes the sense-organ of touch, as that organ is connected with air, and as the vital breath (which would otherwise suggest itself as the most obvious explanation of prâ*n*a) does not harmonise with the metaphorical term 'light.' 'Of the eye' refers to the organ of sight; 'of the ear' to the organ of hearing. 'Of food' comprises the senses of smell and taste together: it denotes the sense of smell on the ground that that sense is connected with earth, which may be 'food,' and the sense of taste in so far as 'anna' may be also explained as that by means of which eating goes on (adyate). 'Of mind' denotes mind, i. e. the so-called internal organ. Taste and smell thus being taken in combination, we have the required number of five, and we thus explain the 'five-people' as the sense-organs which throw light on their objects, together with the internal organ, i. e. mind. The meaning of the clause about the 'five-people' therefore is that the senses—called 'five-people'—and the elements, represented by the Ether, have their basis in Brahman; and as thus all beings are declared to abide in Brahman, the five 'five-people' can in no way be the twenty-five categories assumed by the Sâṅkhyas.—The general conclusion is that the Vedânta-texts, whether referring to numbers or not, nowhere set forth the categories established in Kapila's system.

14. And on account of (Brahman) as described being declared to be the cause with regard to Ether, and so on.

Here the philosopher who holds the Pradhâna to be the general cause comes forward with another objection. The Vedânta-texts, he says, do not teach that creation proceeds from one and the same agent only, and you therefore have no right to hold that Brahman is the sole cause of the world. In one place it is said that our world proceeded from 'Being,' 'Being only this was in the beginning' (*Kh.* Up. VI, 2, 1). In other places the world is said to have sprung from 'Non-being,' 'Non-being indeed this was in the beginning' (Taitt. Up. II, 7, 1); and 'Non-being only was this in the beginning; it became Being' (*Kh.* Up. III, 19, 1). As the Vedânta-texts are thus not consequent in their statements regarding the creator, we cannot conclude from them that Brahman is the sole cause of the world. On the other hand, those texts do enable us to conclude that the Pradhâna only is the universal cause. For the text 'Now all this was then undeveloped' (B*ri*. Up. I, 4, 7) teaches that the world was merged in the undeveloped Pradhâna, and the subsequent clause, 'That developed itself by form and name,' that from that Undeveloped there resulted the creation of the world. For the Undeveloped is that which is not distinguished by names and forms, and this is none other than the Pradhâna. And as this Pradhâna is at the same time eternal, as far as its essential nature is concerned, and the substrate of all change, there is nothing contradictory in the different accounts of creation calling it sometimes 'Being' and sometimes 'Non-being'; while, on the other hand, these terms cannot, without contradiction, both be applied to Brahman. The causality of the Undeveloped having thus been ascertained, such expressions as 'it *thought*, may I be many,' must be interpreted as meaning its being about to proceed to creation. The terms 'Self' and 'Brahman' also may be applied to the Pradhâna in so far as it is all-pervading (âtman from âpnoti), and preeminently great (b*ri*hat). We therefore conclude that the only cause of the world about which the Vedânta-texts give information is the Pradhâna.

This view is set aside by the Sûtra. The word *and* is used in the sense of *but*. It is possible to ascertain from the Vedânta-texts that the world springs from none other than the highest Brahman, which is all-knowing, lord of all, free from all shadow of imperfection, capable of absolutely realising its purposes, and so on; since scripture declares Brahman as described to be the cause of Ether, and so on. By 'Brahman as described' is meant 'Brahman distinguished by omniscience and other qualities, as described in the Sûtra "that from which the origination, and so on, of the world proceed," and in other places.' That Brahman only is declared by scripture to be the cause of Ether, and so on, i. e. the being which is declared to be the cause in passages such as 'From that Self sprang Ether' (Taitt. Up. II, 1); 'that sent forth fire' (*Kh*. Up. VI, 2, 3), is none other than Brahman possessing omniscience and similar qualities. For the former of these texts follows on the passage 'The True, intelligence, infinite is Brahman; he reaches all desires together with the intelligent Brahman,' which introduces Brahman as the general subject-matter—that

Brahman being then referred to by means of the connecting words 'from that.' In the same way the 'that' (in 'that sent forth fire') refers back to the omniscient Brahman introduced in the clause 'that thought, may I be many.' This view is confirmed by a consideration of all the accounts of creation, and we hence conclude that Brahman is the sole cause of the world.—But the text 'Non-being indeed this was in the beginning' calls the general cause 'something that is not'; how then can you say that we infer from the Vedânta-texts as the general cause of the world a Brahman that is all-knowing, absolutely realises its purposes, and so on?—To this question the next Sûtra replies.

15. From connexion.

The fact is that Brahman intelligent, consisting of bliss, &c., connects itself also with the passage 'Non-being was this in the beginning' (Taitt. Up. II, 7). For the section of the text which precedes that passage (viz. 'Different from this Self consisting of understanding is the Self consisting of Bliss;—he wished, may I be many;—he created all whatever there is. Having created he entered into it; having entered it he became sat and tyat') clearly refers to Brahman consisting of Bliss, which realises its purposes, creates all beings, and entering into them is the Self of all. When, therefore, after this we meet with the *s*loka ('Non-being this was in the beginning') introduced by the words 'On this there is also this *s*loka'—which shows that the *s*loka is meant to throw light on what precedes; and when further on we have the passage 'From fear of it the wind blows,' &c., which, referring to the same Brahman, predicates of it universal rulership, bliss of nature, and so on; we conclude with certainty that the *s*loka about 'Non-being' also refers to Brahman. As during a pralaya the distinction of names and forms does not exist, and Brahman also then does not exist in so far as connected with names and forms, the text applies to Brahman the term 'Non-being.' The text 'Non-being only this was in the beginning' explains itself in the same way.—Nor can we admit the contention that the text 'Now all this was then undeveloped' refers to the Pradhâna as the cause of the world; for the Undeveloped there spoken of is nothing else but Brahman in so far as its body is not yet evolved. For the text continues 'That same being entered thither to the very tips of the finger-nails;' 'When seeing, eye by name; when hearing, ear by name; when thinking, mind by name;' 'Let men meditate upon him as Self;' where the introductory words 'that same being' refer back to the Undeveloped—which thus is said to enter into all things and thereby to become their ruler. And it is known from another text also (*Kh.* Up. VI, 3, 2) that it is the all-creative highest Brahman which enters into its creation and evolves names and forms. The text 'Having entered within, the ruler of creatures, the Self of all' moreover shows that the creative principle enters into its creatures for the purpose of ruling them, and such entering again cannot be attributed to the non-sentient Pradhâna. The Undeveloped therefore is Brahman in that state where its body is not yet developed; and when the text continues 'it developed itself by names and forms' the meaning is that Brahman developed itself in so far as names and forms were distinguished in the world that constitutes Brahman's body. On this explanation of the texts relating to creation we further are enabled to take the thought, purpose, &c., attributed to the creative principle, in their primary literal sense. And, we finally remark, neither the term 'Brahman' nor the term 'Self' in any way suits the Pradhâna, which is neither absolutely great nor pervading in the sense of entering into things created with a view to ruling them. It thus remains a settled conclusion that Brahman is the sole cause of the world.—Here terminates the adhikara*n*a of '(Brahman's) causality.'

16. Because it denotes the world.

The Sâṅkhya comes forward with a further objection. Although the Vedânta-texts teach an intelligent principle to be the cause of the world, they do not present to us as objects of knowledge anything that could be the cause of the world, apart from the Pradhâna and the soul as established by the Sâṅkhya-system. For the Kaushîtakins declare in their text, in the dialogue of Bâlâki and A*g*âta*s*atru, that none but the enjoying (individual) soul is to be known as the cause of the world, 'Shall I tell you Brahman? He who is the maker of those persons and of whom this is the work (or "to whom this work belongs") he indeed is to be known' (Kau. Up. IV, 19). Bâlâki at the outset proposes Brahman as the object of instruction, and when he is found himself not to know Brahman, A*g*âta*s*atru instructs him about it, 'he indeed is to be known.' But from the relative clause 'to whom this work belongs,' which connects the being to be known with work, we infer that by Brahman we have here to understand the enjoying soul which is the ruler of Prak*ri*ti, not any other being. For no other being is connected with work; work, whether meritorious or the contrary, belongs to the individual soul only. Nor must you contest this conclusion on the ground that 'work' is here to be explained as meaning the object of activity, so that the sense of the clause would be 'he of whom this entire world, as presented by perception and the other means of knowledge, is the work.' For in that case the separate statements made in the two clauses, 'who is the maker of those persons' and 'of whom this is the work,' would be devoid of purport (the latter implying the former). Moreover, the generally accepted meaning of the word 'karman,' both in Vedic and worldly speech, is work in the sense of good and evil actions. And as the origination of the world is caused by actions of the various individual souls, the designation of 'maker of those persons' also suits only the individual soul. The meaning of the whole passage therefore is 'He who is the cause of the different persons that have their abode in the disc of the sun, and so on, and are instrumental towards the retributive experiences of the individual souls; and to whom there belongs karman, good and evil, to which there is due his becoming such a cause; *he* indeed is to be known, *his* essential nature is to be cognised in distinction from Prak*ri*ti.' And also in what follows, 'The two came to a person who was asleep. He pushed him with a stick,' &c., what is said about the sleeping man being pushed, roused, &c., all points only to the individual soul being the topic of instruction. Further on also the text treats of the individual soul only, 'As the master feeds with his people, nay as his people feed on the master, thus does this conscious Self feed with the other Selfs.' We must consider also the following passage—which contains the explanation given by A*g*âta*s*atru to Bâlâki, who had been unable to say where the soul goes at the time of deep sleep—'There are the arteries called Hitas. In these the person is; when sleeping he sees no dream, then he (*or* that, i.e. the aggregate of the sense-organs) becomes one with this prâ*n*a alone. Then speech goes to him with all names, &c., the mind with all thoughts. And when he awakes, then, as from a burning fire sparks proceed in all directions, thus from that Self the prâ*n*as proceed each towards its place, from the prâ*n*as the gods, from the gods the worlds.' The individual soul which passes through the states of dream, deep sleep and waking, and is that into which there are merged and from which there proceed speech and all the other organs, is here declared to be the abode of deep sleep 'then it (viz. the aggregate of the organs) becomes one in that prâ*n*a.' Prâ*n*a here means the individual soul in so far as supporting life; for the text continues 'when *that* one awakes' and neither the vital breath nor the Lord (both of whom might be proposed as explanations of prâ*n*a) can be said to be asleep and to wake. Or else 'asmin prâ*n*e' might be explained as 'in the vital breath (which abides) in the individual soul,' the meaning of the clause being 'all the organs, speech and so on, become one in the vital breath which itself abides in this soul.' The word 'prâ*n*a' would thus be taken in its primary literal sense; yet all the same the soul constitutes the topic of the section, the vital breath being a mere instrument of the soul. The Brahman mentioned at the outset therefore is none other than the individual soul, and there is nothing to prove a lord different from it. And as the attributes which the texts ascribe to the general cause, viz. thought and so on, are attributes of intelligent beings only, we arrive at the conclusion that what constitutes the cause of the world is the non-intelligent Pradhâna guided by the intelligent soul.

This primâ facie view the Sûtra disposes of, by saying 'because (the work) denotes the world.' It is not the insignificant individual soul—which is under the influence of its good and evil works, and by erroneously imputing to itself the attributes of Prak*ri*ti becomes the cause of the effects of the latter—that is the topic of our text; but rather the Supreme Person who is free from all shadow of imperfection such as Nescience and the like, who is a treasure of all possible auspicious qualities in their highest degree of perfection, who is the sole cause of this entire world. This is proved by the circumstance that the term 'work' connected with 'this' (in 'of whom this (is) the work') denotes the Universe which is an effect of the Supreme Person. For the word 'this' must, on account of its sense, the general topic of the section and so on, be taken in a non-limited meaning, and hence denotes the entire world, as presented by Perception and the other means of knowledge, with all its sentient and non-sentient beings. That the term 'work' does not here denote good and evil actions, appears from the following consideration of the context. Bâlâki at first offers to teach Brahman ('Shall I tell you Brahman?') and thereupon holds forth on various persons abiding in the sun, and so on, as being Brahman. A*g*âta*s*atru however refuses to accept this instruction as not setting forth Brahman, and finally, in order to enlighten Bâlâki, addresses him 'He, O Bâlâki, who is the maker of those persons,' &c. Now as the different personal souls abiding in the sun, &c., and connected with karman in the form of good and evil actions, are known already by Bâlâki, the term 'karman'—met with in the next clause—is clearly meant to throw light on some Person so far not known to Bâlâki, and therefore must be taken to mean not good and evil deeds or action in general, but rather the entire Universe in so far as being the outcome of activity. On this interpretation only the passage gives instruction about something not known before. Should it be said that this would be the case also if the subject to which the instruction refers were the true essential nature of the soul, indicated here by its connexion with karman, we reply that this would involve the (objectionable) assumption of so-called implication (lakshanâ), in so far namely as what the clause would directly intimate is (not the essential nature of the soul as free from karman but rather) the connexion of the soul with karman. Moreover if the intention of the passage were this, viz. to give instruction as to the soul, the latter being pointed at by means of the reference to karman, the intention would be fully accomplished by saying 'to whom karman belongs, he is to be known;' while in the text as it actually stands 'of whom this is the karman' the 'this' would be unmeaning. The meaning of the two separate clauses 'who is the maker of those persons' and 'of whom this is the work' is as follows. He who is the creator of those persons whom you called Brahman, and of whom those persons are the creatures; he of whom this entire world is the effect, and before whom all things sentient and non-sentient are equal in so far as being produced by him; he, the highest and universal cause, the Supreme Person, is the object to be known. The meaning implied here is—although the origination of the world has for its condition the deeds of individual souls, yet those souls do not independently originate the means for their own retributive experience, but experience only what the Lord has created to that end in agreement with their works. The individual soul, hence, cannot stand in creative relation to those persons.—What the text under discussion inculcates as the object of knowledge therefore is the highest Brahman which is known from all Vedânta-texts as the universal cause.

17. Should it be said that this is not so on account of the inferential marks of the individual soul and the chief vital air; we reply that this has been explained before.

With reference to the plea urged by the Pûrvapakshin

that, owing to inferential marks pointing to the individual soul, and the circumstance of mention being made of the chief vital air, we must decide that the section treats of the enjoying individual soul and not of the highest Self, the Sûtra remarks that this argumentation has already been disposed of, viz. in connexion with the Pratardana vidyâ. For there it was shown that when a text is ascertained, on the ground of a comprehensive survey of initial and concluding clauses, to refer to Brahman, all inferential marks which point to other topics must be interpreted so as to fall in with the principal topic. Now in our text Brahman is introduced at the outset 'Shall I tell you Brahman?' it is further mentioned in the middle of the section, for the clause 'of whom this is the work' does not refer to the soul in general but to the highest Person who is the cause of the whole world; and at the end again we hear of a reward which connects itself only with meditations on Brahman, viz. supreme sovereignty preceded by the conquest of all evil. 'Having overcome all evil he obtains pre-eminence among all beings, sovereignty and supremacy—yea, he who knows this.' The section thus being concerned with Brahman, the references to the individual soul and to the chief vital air must also be interpreted so as to fall in with Brahman. In the same way it was shown above that the references to the individual soul and the chief vital air which are met with in the Pratardana vidyâ really explain themselves in connexion with a threefold meditation on Brahman. As in the passage 'Then with this prâ*n*a alone he becomes one' the two words 'this' and 'prâ*n*a' may be taken as co-ordinated and it hence would be inappropriate to separate them (and to explain 'in the prâ*n*a which abides in this soul'), and as the word 'prâ*n*a' is ascertained to mean Brahman also, we must understand the mention of prâ*n*a to be made with a view to meditation on Brahman in so far as having the prâ*n*a for its body. But how can the references to the individual soul be put in connexion with Brahman?—This point is taken up by the next Sûtra.

18. But *G*aimini thinks that it has another purport,

on account of the question and answer; and thus some also.

The 'but' is meant to preclude the idea that the mention made of the individual soul enables us to understand the whole section as concerned with that soul.—The teacher *G*aimini is of opinion that the mention made of the individual soul has another meaning, i.e. aims at conveying the idea of what is different from the individual soul, i.e. the nature of the highest Brahman. 'On account of question and answer.' According to the story told in the Upanishad, A*g*âta*s*atru leads Bâlâki to where a sleeping man is resting, and convinces him that the soul is different from breath, by addressing the sleeping person, in whom breath only is awake, with names belonging to prâ*n*a [1] without the sleeper being awaked thereby, and after that rousing him by a push of his staff. Then, with a view to teaching Bâlâki the difference of Brahman from the individual soul, he asks him the following questions: 'Where, O Bâlâki, did this person here sleep? Where was he? Whence did he thus come back?' To these questions he thereupon himself replies, 'When sleeping he sees no dream, then he becomes one in that prâ*n*a alone.—From that Self the organs proceed each towards its place, from the organs the gods, from the gods the worlds.' Now this reply, no less than the questions, clearly refers to the highest Self as something different from the individual Self. For that entering into which the soul, in the state of deep sleep, attains its true nature and enjoys complete serenity, being free from the disturbing experiences of pleasure and pain that accompany the states of waking and of dream; and

---

[1] The names with which the king addresses the sleeper are *Great one, clad in white raiment, Soma, king*. The *S*ru. Pra. comments as follows: *Great one*; because according to *S*ruti Prâ*n*a is the oldest and best. *Clad in white raiment*; because *S*ruti says that water is the raiment of Prâ*n*a; and elsewhere, that what is white belongs to water. *Soma*; because scripture says 'of this prâ*n*a water is the body, light the form, viz. yonder moon.' *King*; for *S*ruti says 'Prâ*n*a indeed is the ruler.'

that from which it again returns to the fruition of pleasure and pain; that is nothing else but the highest Self. For, as other scriptural texts testify ('Then he becomes united with the True,' *Kh*. Up. VI, 8, 1; 'Embraced by the intelligent Self he knows nothing that is without, nothing that is within,' B*ri*. Up. IV, 3, 21), the abode of deep sleep is the intelligent Self which is different from the individual Self, i. e. the highest Self. We thus conclude that the reference, in question and answer, to the individual soul subserves the end of instruction being given about what is different from that soul, i. e. the highest Self. We hence also reject the Pûrvapakshin's contention that question and answer refer to the individual soul, that the veins called hita are the abode of deep sleep, and that the well-known clause as to the prâ*n*a must be taken to mean that the aggregate of the organs becomes one in the individual soul called prâ*n*a. For the veins are the abode, not of deep sleep, but of dream, and, as we have shown above, Brahman only is the abode of deep sleep; and the text declares that the individual soul, together with all its ministering organs, becomes one with, and again proceeds from, Brahman only—which the text designates as Prâ*n*a. —Moreover some, viz. the Vâ*g*asaneyins in this same colloquy of Bâlâki and A*g*âta*s*atru as recorded in their text, clearly distinguish from the vi*gñ*âna-maya, i. e. the individual soul in the state of deep sleep, the highest Self which then is the abode of the individual soul. 'Where was then the person, consisting of intelligence, and from whence did he thus come back?—When he was thus asleep, then the intelligent person, having through the intelligence of the senses absorbed within himself all intelligence, lies in the ether that is within the heart.' Now the word 'ether' is known to denote the highest Self; cf. the text 'there is within that the small ether' (*Kh*. Up. VIII, 1, 1). This shows us that the individual soul is mentioned in the Vâ*g*asaneyin passage to the end of setting forth what is different from it, viz. the prâ*gñ*a Self, i.e. the highest Brahman. The general conclusion therefore is that the Kaushîtaki-text under discussion proposes as the object of knowledge something that is different from the individual soul, viz. the highest Brahman which is the cause of the whole world, and that hence the Vedânta-texts nowhere intimate that general causality belongs either to the individual soul or to the Pradhâna under the soul's guidance. Here terminates the adhikara*n*a of 'denotation of the world.'

19. On account of the connected meaning of the sentences.

In spite of the conclusion arrived at there may remain a suspicion that here and there in the Upanishads texts are to be met with which aim at setting forth the soul as maintained in Kapila's system, and that hence there is no room for a being different from the individual soul and called Lord. This suspicion the Sûtra undertakes to remove, in connexion with the Maitreyî-brâhma*n*a, in the B*ri*hadâra*n*yaka. There we read 'Verily, a husband is dear, not for the love of the husband, but for the love of the Self a husband is dear, and so on. Everything is dear, not for the love of everything, but for the love of the Self everything is dear. The Self should be seen, should be heard, should be reflected on, should be meditated upon. When the Self has been seen, heard, reflected upon, meditated upon, then all this is known' (B*ri*. Up. IV, 5, 6).—Here the doubt arises whether the Self enjoined in this passage as the object of seeing, &c., be the soul as held by the Sâṅkhyas, or the Supreme Lord, all-knowing, capable of realising all his purposes, and so on. The Pûrvapakshin upholds the former alternative. For, he says, the beginning no less than the middle and the concluding part of the section conveys the idea of the individual soul only. In the beginning the individual soul only is meant, as appears from the connexion of the Self with husband, wife, children, wealth, cattle, and so on. This is confirmed by the middle part of the section where the Self is said to be connected with origination and destruction, 'a mass of knowledge, he having risen from these elements vanishes again into them. When he has departed there is no more consciousness.' And in the end we have 'whereby should he know the knower'; where we again recognise the knowing subject, i. e. the individual soul, not the Lord. We thus conclude that the whole text is meant to set forth the soul as held by the Sâṅkhyas.—But in the beginning there is a clause, viz. 'There is no hope of immortality by wealth,' which shows that the whole section is meant to instruct us as to the means of immortality; how then can it be meant to set forth the individual soul only?—You state the very reason proving that the text is concerned with the individual soul only! For according to the Sâṅkhya-system immortality is obtained through the cognition of the true nature of the soul viewed as free from all erroneous imputation to itself of the attributes of non-sentient matter; and the text therefore makes it its task to set forth, for the purpose of immortality, the essential nature of the soul free from all connexion with Prak*ri*ti, 'the *Self* should be heard,' and so on. And as the souls dissociated from Prak*ri*ti are all of a uniform nature, all souls are known through the knowledge of the soul free from Prak*ri*ti, and the text therefore rightly says that through the Self being known everything is known. And as the essential nature of the Self is of one and the same kind, viz. knowledge or intelligence, in all beings from gods down to plants, the text rightly asserts the unity of the Self 'that Self is all this'; and denies all otherness from the Self, on the ground of the characteristic attributes of gods and so on really being of the nature of the Not-self, 'he is abandoned by everything,' &c. The clause, 'For where there is duality as it were,' which denies plurality, intimates that the plurality introduced into the homogeneous Self by the different forms—such as of gods, and so on—assumed by Prak*ri*ti, is false. And there is also no objection to the teaching that 'the *Ri*g-veda and so on are breathed forth from that great being (i. e. Prak*ri*ti); for the origination of the world is caused by the soul in its quality as ruler of Prak*ri*ti.—It thus being ascertained that the whole Maitreyî-brâhma*n*a is concerned with the soul in the Sâṅkhya sense, we, according to the principle of the unity of purport of all Vedânta-texts, conclude that they all treat of the Sâṅkhya soul only, and that hence the cause of the world is to be found not in a so-called Lord but in Prak*ri*ti ruled and guided by the soul.

This primâ facie view is set aside by the Sûtra. The whole text refers to the Supreme Lord only; for on this supposition only a satisfactory connexion of the parts of the text can be made out. On being told by Yâ*gñ*avalkya that there is no hope of immortality through wealth, Maitreyî expresses her slight regard for wealth and all such things as do not help to immortality, and asks to be instructed as to the means of immortality only ('What should I do with that by which I do not become immortal? What my lord knows tell that clearly to me'). Now the Self which Yâ*gñ*avalkya, responding to her requests, points out to her as the proper object of knowledge, can be none other than the highest Self; for other scriptural texts clearly teach that the only means of reaching immortality is to know the Supreme Person—'Having known him thus man passes beyond death'; 'Knowing him thus he becomes immortal here, there is no other path to go' (*S*vet. Up. III, 8). The knowledge of the true nature of the individual soul which obtains immortality, and is a mere manifestation of the power of the Supreme Person, must be held to be useful towards the cognition of the Supreme Person who brings about Release, but is not in itself instrumental towards such Release; the being the knowledge of which the text declares to be the means of immortality is therefore the highest Self only. Again, the causal power with regard to the entire world which is expressed in the passage, 'from that great Being there were breathed forth the *Ri*g-veda,' &c., cannot possibly belong to the mere individual soul which in its state of bondage is under the influence of karman and in the state of release has nothing to do with the world; it can in fact belong to the Supreme Person only. Again, what the text says as to everything being known by the knowledge of one thing ('By the seeing indeed of the Self,' &c.) is possible only in the case of a Supreme Self which constitutes the Self of all. What the Pûrvapakshin said as to everything being known through the cognition of the one individual soul, since all individual souls are of the same type—this also cannot be upheld; for as long as there is a knowledge of the soul only and not also of the world of non-sentient things, there is no knowledge of everything. And when the text enumerates different things ('this Brahman class, this Kshatra class,' &c.), and then concludes 'all this is that Self'—where the 'this' denotes the entire Universe of animate and inanimate beings as known through Perception, Inference, and so on—universal unity such as declared here is possible only through a highest Self which is the Self of all. It is not, on the other hand, possible that what the word 'this' denotes, i. e. the whole world of intelligent and non-intelligent creatures, should be one with the personal soul as long as it remains what it is, whether connected with or disassociated from non-sentient matter. In the same spirit the passage, 'All things abandon him who views all things elsewhere than in the Self,' finds fault with him who views anything apart from the universal Self. The qualities also which in the earlier Maitreyî-brâhma*n*a (II, 4, 12) are predicated of the being under discussion, viz. greatness, endlessness, unlimitedness, cannot belong to any one else but the highest Self. That Self therefore is the topic of the Brâhma*n*a.

We further demur to our antagonist's maintaining that the entire Brâhma*n*a treats of the individual soul because that soul is at the outset represented as the object of enquiry, this being inferred from its connexion with husband, wife, wealth, &c. For if the clause 'for the love (literally, *for the desire*) of the Self' refers to the individual Self, we cannot help connecting (as, in fact, we must do in any case) that Self with the Self referred to in the subsequent clause, 'the Self indeed is to be seen,' &c.; the connexion having to be conceived in that way that the information given in the former clause somehow subserves the cognition of the Self enjoined in the latter clause. 'For the desire of the Self' would then mean 'for the attainment of the objects desired by the Self.' But if it is first said that husband, wife, &c., are dear because they fulfil the wishes of the individual Self, it could hardly be said further on that the nature of that Self must be enquired into; for what, in the circumstances of the case, naturally is to be enquired into and searched for are the dear objects but not the true nature of him to whom those objects are dear, apart from the objects themselves. It would certainly be somewhat senseless to declare that since husband, wife, &c., are dear because they fulfil the desires of the individual soul, therefore, setting aside those dear objects, we must enquire into the true nature of that soul apart from all the objects of its desire. On the contrary, it having been declared that husband, wife, &c., are dear not on account of husband, wife, &c., but on account of the Self, they should not be dropped, but included in the further investigation, just because they subserve the Self. And should our opponent (in order to avoid the difficulty of establishing a satisfactory connexion between the different clauses) maintain that the clause, 'but everything is dear for the love of the Self,' is not connected with the following clause, 'the Self is to be seen,' &c., we point out that this would break the whole connexion of the Brâhma*n*a. And if we allowed such a break, we should then be unable to point out what is the use of the earlier part of the Brâhma*n*a. We must therefore attempt to explain the connexion in such a way as to make it clear why all search for dear objects—husband, wife, children, wealth, &c.—should be abandoned and the Self only should be searched for. This explanation is as follows. After having stated that wealth, and so on, are no means to obtain immortality which consists in permanent absolute bliss, the text declares that the pleasant experiences which we derive from wealth, husband, wife, &c., and which are not of a permanent nature and always alloyed with a great deal of pain, are caused not by wealth, husband, wife, &c., themselves, but rather by the highest Self whose nature is absolute bliss. He therefore who being himself of the nature of perfect bliss causes other beings and things also to be the abodes of partial bliss, he—the highest Self—is to be constituted the object of knowledge. The clauses, 'not for the wish of the husband a husband is dear,' &c., therefore must be understood as follows—a husband, a wife, a son, &c., are not dear to us in consequence of a wish or purpose on their part, 'may I, for my own end or advantage be dear to him,' but they are dear to us for the wish of the Self, i.e. to the end that there may be accomplished the desire of the highest Self—which desire aims at the devotee obtaining what is dear to him. For the highest Self pleased with the works of his devotees imparts to different things such dearness, i.e. joy-giving quality as corresponds to those works, that 'dearness' being bound in each case to a definite place, time, nature and degree. This is in accordance with the scriptural text, 'For he alone bestows bliss' (Taitt. Up. II, 7). Things are not dear, or the contrary, to us by themselves, but only in so far as the highest Self makes them such. Compare the text, 'The same thing which erst gave us delight later on becomes the source of grief; and what was the cause of wrath afterwards tends to peace. Hence there is nothing that in itself is of the nature either of pleasure or of pain.'

But, another view of the meaning of the text is proposed, even if the Self in the clause 'for the desire of the Self' were accepted as denoting the individual Self, yet the clause 'the Self must be seen' would refer to the highest Self only. For in that case also the sense would be as follows—because the possession of husband, wife, and other so-called dear things is aimed at by a person to whom they are dear, not with a view of bringing about what is desired by them (viz. husband, wife, &c.), but rather to the end of bringing about what is desired by himself; therefore that being which is, to the individual soul, absolutely and unlimitedly dear, viz. the highest Self, must be constituted the sole object of cognition, not such objects as husband, wife, wealth, &c., the nature of which depends on various external circumstances and the possession of which gives rise either to limited pleasure alloyed with pain or to mere pain.—But against this we remark that as, in the section under discussion, the words designating the individual Self denote the highest Self also[1], the term 'Self' in both clauses, 'For the desire of the Self' and 'The Self is to be seen,' really refers to one and the same being (viz. the highest Self), and the interpretation thus agrees with the one given above.—In order to prove the tenet that words denoting the individual soul at the same time denote the highest Self, by means of arguments made use of by other teachers also, the Sûtrakâra sets forth the two following Sûtras.

20. (It is) a mark indicating that the promissory statement is proved; thus Âsmarathya thinks.

According to the teacher Âsmarathya the circumstance that terms denoting the individual soul are used to denote Brahman is a mark enabling us to infer that the promissory declaration according to which through the knowledge of one thing everything is known is well established. If the individual soul were not identical with Brahman in so far as it is the effect of Brahman, then the knowledge of the soul—being something distinct from Brahman—would not follow from the knowledge of the highest Self. There are the texts declaring the oneness of Brahman previous to creation, such as 'the Self only was this in the beginning' (Ait. Âr. II, 4, 1, 1), and on the other hand those texts which declare that the souls spring from and again are merged in Brahman; such as 'As from a blazing fire sparks being like unto fire fly forth a thousandfold, thus are various beings brought forth from the Imperishable, and return thither also' (Mu. Up. II, 1, 1). These two sets of texts together make us apprehend that the souls are one with Brahman in so far as they are its effects. On this ground a word denoting the individual soul denotes the highest Self as well.

[1] If it be insisted upon that the Self in 'for the desire of the Self' is the individual Self, we point out that terms denoting the individual Self at the same time denote the highest Self also. This tenet of his Râmânuga considers to be set forth and legitimately proved in Sûtra 23, while Sûtras 21 and 22 although advocating the right principle fail to assign valid arguments.

21. Because (the soul) when it will depart is such; thus Au*d*ulomi thinks.

It is wrong to maintain that the designation of Brahman by means of terms denoting the individual soul is intended to prove the truth of the declaration that through the knowledge of one thing everything is known, in so far namely as the soul is an effect of Brahman and hence one with it. For scriptural texts such as 'the knowing Self is not born, it dies not' (Ka. Up. I, 2, 18), declare the soul not to have originated, and it moreover is admitted that the world is each time created to the end of the souls undergoing experiences retributive of their former deeds; otherwise the inequalities of the different parts of the creation would be inexplicable. If moreover the soul were a mere effect of Brahman, its Release would consist in a mere return into the substance of Brahman,—analogous to the refunding into Brahman of the material elements, and that would mean that the injunction and performance of acts leading to such Release would be purportless. Release, understood in that sense, moreover would not be anything beneficial to man; for to be refunded into Brahman as an earthen vessel is refunded into its own causal substance, i. e. clay, means nothing else but complete annihilation. How, under these circumstances, certain texts can speak of the origination and reabsorption of the individual soul will be set forth later on.—According to the opinion of the teacher Au*d*ulomi, the highest Self's being denoted by terms directly denoting the individual soul is due to the soul's becoming Brahman when departing from the body. This is in agreement with texts such as the following, 'This serene being having risen from this body and approached the highest light appears in its true form' (*Kh.* Up. VIII, 3, 4); 'As the flowing rivers disappear in the sea, losing their name and form, thus a wise man freed from name and form goes to the divine Person who is higher than the high' (Mu. Up. III, 2, 8).

22. On account of (Brahman's) abiding (within the individual soul); thus Kâ*s*ak*ri*tsna (holds).

We must object likewise to the view set forth in the preceding Sûtra, viz. that Brahman is denoted by terms denoting the individual soul because that soul when departing becomes one with Brahman. For that view cannot stand the test of being submitted to definite alternatives.—Is the soul's not being such, i. e. not being Brahman, previously to its departure from the body, due to its own essential nature or to a limiting adjunct, and is it in the latter case real or unreal? In the first case the soul can never become one with Brahman, for if its separation from Brahman is due to its own essential nature, that separation can never vanish as long as the essential nature persists. And should it be said that its essential nature comes to an end together with its distinction from Brahman, we reply that in that case it perishes utterly and does not therefore become Brahman. The latter view, moreover, precludes itself as in no way beneficial to man, and so on.—If, in the next place, the difference of the soul from Brahman depends on the presence of real limiting adjuncts, the soul is Brahman even before its departure from the body, and we therefore cannot reasonably accept the distinction implied in saying that the soul becomes Brahman only when it departs. For on this view there exists nothing but Brahman and its limiting adjuncts, and as those adjuncts cannot introduce difference into Brahman which is without parts and hence incapable of difference, the difference resides altogether in the adjuncts, and hence the soul is Brahman even before its departure from the body.—If, on the other hand, the difference due to the adjuncts is not real, we ask—what is it then that becomes Brahman on the departure of the soul?—Brahman itself whose true nature had previously been obscured by Nescience, its limiting adjunct!—Not so, we reply. Of Brahman whose true nature consists in eternal, free, self-luminous intelligence, the true nature cannot possibly be hidden by Nescience. For by 'hiding' or 'obscuring' we understand the cessation of the light that belongs to the essential nature of a thing. Where, therefore, light itself and alone constitutes the essential nature of a thing, there can either be no obscuration at all, or if there is such it means complete annihilation of the thing. Hence Brahman's essential nature being manifest at all times, there exists no difference on account of which it could be said to *become* Brahman at the time of the soul's departure; and the distinction introduced in the last Sûtra ('when departing') thus has no meaning. The text on which Au*d*ulomi relies, 'Having risen from this body,' &c., does not declare that that which previously was not Brahman becomes such at the time of departure, but rather that the true nature of the soul which had previously existed already becomes manifest at the time of departure. This will be explained under IV, 4, 1.

The theories stated in the two preceding Sûtras thus having been found untenable, the teacher Kâ*s*ak*ri*tsna states his own view, to the effect that words denoting the *g*îva are applied to Brahman because Brahman abides as its Self within the individual soul which thus constitutes Brahman's body. This theory rests on a number of well-known texts, 'Entering into them with this living (individual) soul let me evolve names and forms' (*Kh.* Up. VI, 3, 2); 'He who dwelling within the Self, &c., whose body the Self is,' &c. (B*ri*. Up. III, 7, 22); 'He who moves within the Imperishable, of whom the Imperishable is the body,' &c.; 'Entered within, the ruler of beings, the Self of all.' That the term '*g*îva' denotes not only the *g*îva itself, but extends in its denotation up to the highest Self, we have explained before when discussing the text, 'Let me evolve names and forms.' On this view of the identity of the individual and the highest Self consisting in their being related to each other as body and soul, we can accept in their full and unmutilated meaning all scriptural texts whatever—whether they proclaim the perfection and omniscience of the highest Brahman, or teach how the individual soul steeped in ignorance and misery is to be saved through meditation on Brahman, or describe the origination and reabsorption of the world, or aim at showing how the world is identical with Brahman. For this reason the author of the Sûtras, rejecting other views, accepts the theory of Kâ*s*akr*i*tsna. Returning to the Maitreyî-brâhma*n*a we proceed to explain the general sense, from the passage previously discussed onwards. Being questioned by Maitreyî as to the means of immortality, Yâ*gñ*avalkya teaches her that this means is given in meditation on the highest Self ('The Self is to be seen,' &c.). He next indicates in a general way the nature of the object of meditation ('When the Self is seen,' &c.), and—availing himself of the similes of the drum, &c.—of the government over the organs, mind, and so on, which are instrumental towards meditation. He then explains in detail that the object of meditation, i. e. the highest Brahman, is the sole cause of the entire world; and the ruler of the aggregate of organs on which there depends all activity with regard to the objects of the senses ('As clouds of smoke proceed,' &c.; 'As the ocean is the home of all the waters'). He, next, in order to stimulate the effort which leads to immortality, shows how the highest Self abiding in the form of the individual Self, is of one uniform character, viz. that of limitless intelligence ('As a lump of salt,' &c.), and how that same Self characterised by homogeneous limitless intelligence connects itself in the Sa*m*sâra state with the products of the elements ('a mass of knowledge, it rises from those elements and again vanishes into them'). He then adds, 'When he has departed, there is no more knowledge'; meaning that in the state of Release, where the soul's unlimited essential intelligence is not contracted in any way, there is none of those specific cognitions by which the Self identifying itself with the body, the sense-organs, &c., views itself as a man or a god, and so on. Next—in the passage, 'For where there is duality as it were'—he, holding that the view of a plurality of things not having their Self in Brahman is due to ignorance, shows that for him who has freed himself from the shackles of ignorance and recognises this whole world as animated by Brahman, the view of plurality is dispelled by the recognition of the absence of any existence apart from Brahman. He then proceeds, 'He by whom he knows all this, by what means should he know Him?' This means—He, i.e. the highest Self, which abiding within the individual soul as its true Self bestows on it the power of knowledge so that the soul knows all this through the highest Self; by what means should the soul know Him? In other words, there is no such means of knowledge: the highest Self cannot be fully understood by the individual soul. 'That Self,' he continues, 'is to be expressed as—not so, not so!' That means—He, the highest Lord, different in nature from everything else, whether sentient or non-sentient, abides within all beings as their Self, and hence is not touched by the imperfections of what constitutes his body merely. He then concludes, 'Whereby should he know the Knower? Thus, O Maitreyî, thou hast been instructed. Thus far goes Immortality'; the purport of these words being—By what means, apart from the meditation described, should man know Him who is different in nature from all other beings, who is the sole cause of the entire world, who is the Knower of all, Him the Supreme Person? It is meditation on Him only which shows the road to Immortality. It thus appears that the Maitreyî-brâhma*n*a is concerned with the highest Brahman only; and this confirms the conclusion that Brahman only, and with it Prak*ri*ti as ruled by Brahman, is the cause of the world.—Here terminates the adhikara*n*a of 'the connexion of sentences.'

23. (Brahman is) the material cause on account of this not being in conflict with the promissory statements and the illustrative instances.

The claims raised by the atheistic Sâṅkhya having thus been disposed of, the theistic Sâṅkhya comes forward as an opponent. It must indeed be admitted, he says, that the Vedânta-texts teach the cause of the world to be an all-knowing Lord; for they attribute to that cause thought and similar characteristics. But at the same time we learn from those same texts that the material cause of the world is none other than the Pradhâna; with an all-knowing, unchanging superintending Lord they connect a Pradhâna, ruled by him, which is non-intelligent and undergoes changes, and the two together only they represent as the cause of the world. This view is conveyed by the following texts, 'who is without parts, without actions, tranquil, without fault, without taint' (*S*vet. Up. VI, 18); 'This great unborn Self, undecaying, undying' (B*ri*. Up. IV, 4, 25); 'He knows her who produces all effects, the non-knowing one, the unborn one, wearing eight forms, the firm one. Ruled by him she is spread out, and incited and guided by him gives birth to the world for the benefit of the souls. A cow she is without beginning and end, a mother producing all beings' (see above, p. 363). That the Lord creates this world in so far only as guiding Prak*ri*ti, the material cause, we learn from the following text, 'From that the Lord of Mâyâ creates all this. Know Mâyâ to be Prak*ri*ti and the Lord of Mâyâ the great Lord' (*S*vet. Up. IV, 9, 10). And similarly Sm*ri*ti, 'with me as supervisor Prak*ri*ti brings forth the Universe of the movable and the immovable' (Bha. Gî. IX, 10). Although, therefore, the Pradhâna is not expressly stated by Scripture to be the material cause, we must assume that there is such a Pradhâna and that, superintended by the Lord, it constitutes the material cause, because otherwise the texts declaring Brahman to be the cause of the world would not be fully intelligible. For ordinary experience shows us on all sides that the operative cause and the material cause are quite distinct: we invariably have on the one side clay, gold, and other material substances which form the material causes of pots, ornaments, and so on, and on the other hand, distinct from them, potters, goldsmiths, and so on, who act as operative causes. And we further observe that the production of effects invariably requires several instrumental agencies. The Vedânta-texts therefore cannot possess the strength to convince us, in open defiance of the two invariable rules, that the one Brahman is at the same time the material and the operative cause of the world; and hence we maintain that Brahman is only the operative but not the material cause, while the material cause is the Pradhâna guided by Brahman.

This primâ facie view the Sûtra combats. Prak*ri*ti, i.e. the material cause, not only the operative cause, is Brahman only; this view being in harmony with the promissory declaration and the illustrative instances. The promissory declaration is the one referring to the knowledge of all things through the knowledge of one, 'Did you ever ask for that instruction by which that which is not heard becomes heard?' &c. (*Kh.* Up. VI, 1, 3). And the illustrative instances are those which set forth the knowledge of the effect as resulting from the knowledge of the cause, 'As by one lump of clay there is made known all that is made of clay; as by one nugget of gold, &c.; as by one instrument for paring the nails,' &c. (*Kh.* Up. VI, 1, 4). If Brahman were merely the operative cause of the world, the knowledge of the entire world would not result from the knowledge of Brahman; not any more than we know the pot when we know the potter. And thus scriptural declaration and illustrative instances would be stultified. But if Brahman is the general material cause, then the knowledge of Brahman implies the knowledge of its effect, i.e. the world, in the same way as the knowledge of such special material causes as a lump of clay, a nugget of gold, an instrument for paring the nails, implies the knowledge of all things made of clay, gold or iron—such as pots, bracelets, diadems, hatchets, and so on. For an effect is not a substance different from its cause, but the cause itself which has passed into a different state. The initial declaration thus being confirmed by the instances of clay and its products, &c., which stand in the relation of cause and effect, we conclude that Brahman only is the material cause of the world. That Scripture teaches the operative and the material causes to be separate, is not true; it rather teaches the unity of the two. For in the text, 'Have you asked for that âde*s*a (above, and generally, understood to mean "instruction"), by which that which is not heard becomes heard?' the word 'âde*s*a' has to be taken to mean *ruler*, in agreement with the text, 'by the command—or rule—of that Imperishable sun and moon stand apart' (B*ri*. Up. III, 8, 9), so that the passage means, 'Have you asked for that

Ruler by whom, when heard and known, even that which is not heard and known, becomes heard and known?' This clearly shows the unity of the operative (ruling or supervising) cause and the material cause; taken in conjunction with the subsequent declaration of the unity of the cause previous to creation, 'Being only, this was in the beginning, one only,' and the denial of a further operative cause implied in the further qualification 'advitîyam,' i.e. 'without a second.'—But how then have we to understand texts such as the one quoted above (from the *K*ûlika-Upanishad) which declare Prak*ri*ti to be eternal and the material cause of the world?—Prak*ri*ti, we reply, in such passages denotes Brahman in its causal phase when names and forms are not yet distinguished. For a principle independent of Brahman does not exist, as we know from texts such as 'Everything abandons him who views anything as apart from the Self'; and 'But where for him the Self has become all, whereby should he see whom?' (B*ri*. Up. II, 4, 6; 15). Consider also the texts, 'All this is Brahman' (*Kh*. Up. III, 14, 1); and 'All this has its Self in that' (*Kh*. Up. VI, 8, 7); which declare that the world whether in its causal or its effected condition has Brahman for its Self. The relation of the world to Brahman has to be conceived in agreement with scriptural texts such as 'He who moves within the earth,' &c., up to 'He who moves within the Imperishable'; and 'He who dwells within the earth,' &c., up to 'He who dwells within the Self' (B*ri*. Up. III, 7, 3-23). The highest Brahman, having the whole aggregate of non-sentient and sentient beings for its body, ever is the Self of all. Sometimes, however, names and forms are not evolved, not distinguished in Brahman; at other times they are evolved, distinct. In the latter state Brahman is called an effect and manifold; in the former it is called one, without a second, the cause. This causal state of Brahman is meant where the text quoted above speaks of the cow without beginning and end, giving birth to effects, and so on.—But, the text, 'The great one is merged in the Unevolved, the Unevolved is merged in the Imperishable,' intimates that the Unevolved originates and again passes away; and similarly the Mahâbhârata says, 'from that there sprung the Non-evolved comprising the three gu*n*as; the Non-evolved is merged in the indivisible Person.'—These texts, we reply, present no real difficulty. For Brahman having non-sentient matter for its body, that state which consists of the three gu*n*as and is denoted by the term 'Unevolved' is something effected. And the text, 'When there was darkness, neither day nor night,' states that also in a total pralaya non-sentient matter having Brahman for its Self continues to exist in a highly subtle condition. This highly subtle matter stands to Brahman the cause of the world in the relation of a mode (prakâra), and it is Brahman viewed as having such a mode that the text from the *K*ûl. Upanishad refers to. For this reason also the text, 'the Imperishable is merged in darkness, darkness becomes one with the highest God,' declares not that darkness is completely merged and lost in the Divinity but only that it becomes one with it; what the text wants to intimate is that state of Brahman in which, having for its mode extremely subtle matter here called 'Darkness,' it abides without evolving names and forms. The mantra, 'There was darkness, hidden in darkness,' &c. (*Ri*. Sa*m*h. X, 129, 3), sets forth the same view; and so does Manu (I, 5), 'This universe existed in the shape of Darkness, unperceived, destitute of distinctive marks, unattainable by reasoning, unknowable, wholly immersed as it were in deep sleep.' And, as to the text, 'from that the Lord of Mâyâ creates everything,' we shall prove later on the unchangeableness of Brahman, and explain the scriptural texts asserting it.

As to the contention raised by the Pûrvapakshin that on the basis of invariable experience it must be held that one and the same principle cannot be both material and operative cause, and that effects cannot be brought about by one agency, and that hence the Vedânta-texts can no more establish the view of Brahman being the sole cause than the command 'sprinkle with fire' will convince us that fire may perform the office of water; we simply remark that the highest Brahman which totally differs in nature from all other beings, which is omnipotent and omniscient, can by itself accomplish everything. The invariable rule of experience holds good, on the other hand, with regard to clay and similar materials which are destitute of intelligence and hence incapable of guiding and supervising; and with regard to potters and similar agents who do not possess the power of transforming themselves into manifold products, and cannot directly realise their intentions.—The conclusion therefore remains that Brahman alone is the material as well as the operative cause of the Universe.

24. And on account of the statement of reflection.

Brahman must be held to be both causes for that reason also that texts such as 'He desired, may I be many, may I grow forth,' and 'It thought, may I be many, may I grow forth,' declare that the creative Brahman forms the purpose of its own Self multiplying itself. The text clearly teaches that creation on Brahman's part is preceded by the purpose 'May I, and no other than I, become manifold in the shape of various non-sentient and sentient beings.'

25. And on account of both being directly declared.

The conclusion arrived at above is based not only on scriptural declaration, illustrative instances and statements of reflection; but in addition Scripture directly states that Brahman alone is the material as well as operative cause of the world. 'What was the wood, what the tree from which they have shaped heaven and earth? You wise ones, search in your minds, whereon it stood, supporting the worlds.—Brahman was the wood, Brahman the tree from which they shaped heaven and earth; you wise ones, I tell you, it stood on Brahman, supporting the worlds.'—Here a question is asked, suggested by the ordinary worldly view, as to what was the material and instruments used by Brahman when creating; and the answer—based on the insight that there is nothing unreasonable in ascribing all possible powers to Brahman which differs from all other beings—declares that Brahman itself is the material and the instruments;—whereby the ordinary view is disposed of.—The next Sûtra supplies a further reason.

26. On account of (the Self) making itself.

Of Brahman which the text had introduced as intent on creation, 'He wished, may I be many' (Taitt. Up. II, 6), a subsequent text says, 'That itself made its Self' (II, 7), so that Brahman is represented as the object as well as the agent in the act of creation. It being the Self only which here is made many, we understand that the Self is material cause as well as operative one. The Self with names and forms non-evolved is agent (cause), the same Self with names and forms evolved is object (effect). There is thus nothing contrary to reason in one Self being object as well as agent.

A new doubt here presents itself.—'The True, knowledge, infinite is Brahman' (Taitt. Up. II, 1); 'Bliss is Brahman' (B*ri*. Up. III, 9, 28); 'Free from sin, free from old age, free from death and grief, free from hunger and thirst' (*Kh*. Up. VIII, 1, 5); 'Without parts, without action, tranquil, without fault, without taint' (*S*vet. Up. VI, 19); 'This great unborn Self, undecaying, undying' (B*ri*. Up. IV, 4, 25)—from all these texts it appears that Brahman is essentially free from even a shadow of all the imperfections which afflict all sentient and non-sentient beings, and has for its only characteristics absolutely supreme bliss and knowledge. How then is it possible that this Brahman should form the purpose of becoming, and actually become, manifold, by appearing in the form of a world comprising various sentient and non-sentient beings—all of which are the abodes of all kinds of imperfections and afflictions? To this question the next Sûtra replies.

27. Owing to modification.

This means—owing to the essential nature of modification (pari*n*âma). The modification taught in our system is not such as to introduce imperfections into the highest Brahman, on the contrary it confers on it limitless glory. For our teaching as to Brahman's modification is as follows.

Brahman—essentially antagonistic to all evil, of uniform goodness, differing in nature from all beings other than itself, all-knowing, endowed with the power of immediately realising all its purposes, in eternal possession of all it wishes for, supremely blessed—has for its body the entire universe, with all its sentient and non-sentient beings—the universe being for it a plaything as it were—and constitutes the Self of the Universe. Now, when this world which forms Brahman's body has been gradually reabsorbed into Brahman, each constituent element being refunded into its immediate cause, so that in the end there remains only the highly subtle, elementary matter which Scripture calls Darkness; and when this so-called Darkness itself, by assuming a form so extremely subtle that it hardly deserves to be called something separate from Brahman, of which it constitutes the body, has become one with Brahman; then Brahman invested with this ultra-subtle body forms the resolve 'May I again possess a world-body constituted by all sentient and non-sentient beings, distinguished by names and forms just as in the previous aeon,' and modifies (pari*n*âmayati) itself by gradually evolving the world-body in the inverse order in which reabsorption had taken place.

All Vedânta-texts teach such modification or change on Brahman's part. There is, e.g., the text in the B*ri*had-Âra*n*yaka which declares that the whole world constitutes the body of Brahman and that Brahman is its Self. That text teaches that earth, water, fire, sky, air, heaven, sun, the regions, moon and stars, ether, darkness, light, all beings, breath, speech, eye, ear, mind, skin, knowledge form the body of Brahman which abides within them as their Self and Ruler. Thus in the Kâ*n*va-text; the Mâdhyandina-text reads 'the Self' instead of 'knowledge'; and adds the worlds, sacrifices and vedas. The parallel passage in the Subâla-Upanishad adds to the beings enumerated as constituting Brahman's body in the B*ri*had-Âra*n*yaka, buddhi, aha*m*kâra, the mind (*k*itta), the Unevolved (avyakta), the Imperishable (akshara), and concludes 'He who moves within death, of whom death is the body, whom death does not know, he is the inner Self of all, free from all evil, divine, the one god Nârâya*n*a.' The term 'Death' here denotes matter in its extremely subtle form, which in other texts is called Darkness; as we infer from the order of enumeration in another passage in the same Upanishad, 'the Unevolved is merged in the Imperishable, the Imperishable in Darkness.' That this Darkness is called 'Death' is due to the fact that it obscures the understanding of all souls and thus is harmful to them. The full text in the Subâla-Up. declaring the successive absorption of all the beings forming Brahman's body is as follows, 'The earth is merged in water, water in fire, fire in air, air in the ether, the ether in the sense-organs, the sense-organs in the tanmâtras, the tanmâtras in the gross elements, the gross elements in the great principle, the great principle in the Unevolved, the Unevolved in the Imperishable; the Imperishable is merged in Darkness; Darkness becomes one with the highest Divinity.' That even in the state of non-separation (to which the texts refer as 'becoming one') non-sentient matter as well as sentient beings, together with the impressions of their former deeds, persists in an extremely subtle form, will be shown under II, 1, 35. We have thus a Brahman all-knowing, of the nature of supreme bliss and so on, one and without a second, having for its body all sentient and non-sentient beings abiding in an extremely subtle condition and having become 'one' with the Supreme Self in so far as they cannot be designated as something separate from him; and of this Brahman Scripture records that it forms the resolve of becoming many—in so far, namely, as investing itself with a body consisting of all sentient and non-sentient beings in their gross, manifest state which admits of distinctions of name and form—and thereupon modifies (pari*n*âma) itself into the form of the world. This is distinctly indicated in the Taittirîya-Upanishad, where Brahman is at first described as 'The True, knowledge, infinite,' as 'the Self of bliss which is different from the Self of Understanding,' as 'he who bestows bliss'; and where the text further on says, 'He desired, may I be many, may

I grow forth. He brooded over himself, and having thus brooded he sent forth all whatever there is. Having sent forth he entered it. Having entered it he became sat and tyat, defined and undefined, supported and non-supported, knowledge and non-knowledge, real and unreal.' The 'brooding' referred to in this text denotes knowing, viz. reflection on the shape and character of the previous world which Brahman is about to reproduce. Compare the text 'whose brooding consists of knowledge' (Mu. Up. I, 1, 9). The meaning therefore is that Brahman, having an inward intuition of the characteristics of the former world, creates the new world on the same pattern. That Brahman in all kalpas again and again creates the same world is generally known from *S*ruti and Sm*ri*ti. Cp. 'As the creator formerly made sun and moon, and sky and earth, and the atmosphere and the heavenly world,' and 'whatever various signs of the seasons are seen in succession, the same appear again and again in successive yugas and kalpas.'

The sense of the Taittirîya-text therefore is as follows. The highest Self, which in itself is of the nature of unlimited knowledge and bliss, has for its body all sentient and non-sentient beings—instruments of sport for him as it were—in so subtle a form that they may be called non-existing; and as they are his body he may be said to consist of them (tan-maya). Then desirous of providing himself with an infinity of playthings of all kinds he, by a series of steps beginning with Prak*ri*ti and the aggregate of souls and leading down to the elements in their gross state, so modifies himself as to have those elements for his body—when he is said to consist of them—and thus appears in the form of our world containing what the text denotes as sat and tyat, i.e. all intelligent and non-intelligent things, from gods down to plants and stones. When the text says that the Self having entered into it became sat and tyat, the meaning is that the highest Self, which in its causal state had been the universal Self, abides, in its effected state also, as the Self of the different substances undergoing changes and thus becomes this and that. While the highest Self thus undergoes a change—in the form of a world comprising the whole aggregate of sentient and non-sentient beings—all imperfection and suffering are limited to the sentient beings constituting part of its body, and all change is restricted to the non-sentient things which constitute another part. The highest Self is *effected* in that sense only that it is the ruling principle, and hence the Self, of matter and souls in their gross or evolved state; but just on account of being this, viz. their inner Ruler and Self, it is in no way touched by their imperfections and changes. Consisting of unlimited knowledge and bliss he for ever abides in his uniform nature, engaged in the sport of making this world go round. This is the purport of the clause 'it became the real and the unreal': although undergoing a change into the multiplicity of actual sentient and non-sentient things, Brahman at the same time was the Real, i. e. that which is free from all shadow of imperfection, consisting of nothing but pure knowledge and bliss. That all beings, sentient and non-sentient, and whether in their non-evolved or evolved states, are mere playthings of Brahman, and that the creation and reabsorption of the world are only his sport, this has been expressly declared by Dvaipâyana, Parâ*s*ara and other *Ri*shis, 'Know that all transitory beings, from the Unevolved down to individual things, are a mere play of Hari'; 'View his action like that of a playful child,' &c. The Sûtrakâra will distinctly enounce the same view in II, 1, 33. With a similar view the text 'from that the Lord of Mâyâ sends forth all this; and in that the other is bound by Mâyâ' (*S*vet. Up. IV, 9), refers to Prak*ri*ti and soul, which together constitute the body of Brahman, as things different from Brahman, although then, i. e. at the time of a pralaya, they are one with Brahman in so far as their extreme subtlety does not admit of their being conceived as separate; this it does to the end of suggesting that even when Brahman undergoes the change into the shape of this world, all changes exclusively belong to non-sentient matter which is a mode of Brahman, and all imperfections and sufferings to the individual souls which also are modes of Brahman. The text has to be viewed as agreeing in meaning with 'that Self made itself.' Of a similar purport is the account given in Manu, 'He being desirous to send forth from his body beings of many kinds, first with a thought created the waters and placed his seed in them' (I, 8).

It is in this way that room is found for those texts also which proclaim Brahman to be free from all imperfection and all change. It thus remains a settled conclusion that Brahman by itself constitutes the material as well as the operative cause of the world.

28. And because it is called the womb.

Brahman is the material as well as the operative cause of the world for that reason also that certain texts call it the womb, 'the maker, the Lord, the Person, Brahman, the womb' (Mu. Up. III, 1, 3); 'that which the wise regard as the womb of all beings' (I, 1, 6). And that 'womb' means as much as material cause, appears from the complementary passage 'As a spider sends forth and draws in its threads' (I, 1, 7).

29. Herewith all (texts) are explained, explained.

Hereby, i. e. by the whole array of arguments set forth in the four pâdas of the first adhyâya; all those particular passages of the Vedânta-texts which give instruction as to the cause of the world, are explained as meaning to set forth a Brahman all-wise, all-powerful, different in nature from all beings intelligent and non-intelligent. The repetition of the word 'explained' is meant to indicate the termination of the adhyâya.

## SECOND ADHYÂYA.

### FIRST PÂDA.

1. If it be said that there would result the fault of there being no room for (certain) Sm*ri*tis: (we reply) 'no,' because there would result the fault of want of room for other Sm*ri*tis.

The first adhyâya has established the truth that what the Vedânta-texts teach is a Supreme Brahman, which is something different as well from non-sentient matter known through the ordinary means of proof, viz. Perception and so on, as from the intelligent souls whether connected with or separated from matter; which is free from even a shadow of imperfection of any kind; which is an ocean as it were of auspicious qualities and so on; which is the sole cause of the entire Universe; which constitutes the inner Self of all things. The second adhyâya is now begun for the purpose of proving that the view thus set forth cannot be impugned by whatever arguments may possibly be brought forward. The Sûtrakâra at first turns against those who maintain that the Vedânta-texts do not establish the view indicated above, on the ground of that view being contradicted by the Sm*ri*ti of Kapila, i. e. the Sâṅkhya-system.

But how can it be maintained at all that Scripture does not set forth a certain view because thereby it would enter into conflict with Sm*ri*ti? For that Sm*ri*ti if contradicted by Scripture is to be held of no account, is already settled in the Pûrva Mîmâ*m*sâ ('But where there is contradiction Sm*ri*ti is not to be regarded,' I, 3, 3).—Where, we reply, a matter can be definitely settled on the basis of Scripture—as e.g. in the case of the Vedic injunction, 'he is to sing, after having touched the U*d*umbara branch' (which clearly contradicts the Sm*ri*ti injunction that the whole branch is to be covered up)—Sm*ri*ti indeed need not be regarded. But the topic with which the Vedânta-texts are concerned is hard to understand, and hence, when a conflict arises between those texts and a Sm*ri*ti propounded by some great *Ri*shi, the matter does not admit of immediate decisive settlement: it is not therefore unreasonable to undertake to prove by Sm*ri*ti that Scripture does not set forth a certain doctrine. That is to say—we possess a Sm*ri*ti composed with a view to teach men the nature and means of supreme happiness, by the great *Ri*shi Kapila to whom Scripture, Sm*ri*ti, Itihâsa and Purâ*n*a alike refer as a person worthy of all respect (compare e.g. 'the *Ri*shi Kapila,' *S*vet. Up. V, 2), and who moreover (unlike B*ri*haspati and other Sm*ri*ti-writers) fully acknowledges the validity of all the means of earthly happiness which are set forth in the karmakâ*nd*a of the Veda, such as the daily oblations to the sacred fires, the New and Full Moon offerings and the great Soma sacrifices. Now, as men having only an imperfect knowledge of the Veda, and moreover naturally slow-minded, can hardly ascertain the sense of the Vedânta-texts without the assistance of such a Sm*ri*ti, and as to be satisfied with that sense of the Vedânta which discloses itself on a mere superficial study of the text would imply the admission that the whole Sâṅkhya Sm*ri*ti, although composed by an able and trustworthy person, really is useless; we see ourselves driven to acknowledge that the doctrine of the Vedânta-texts cannot differ from the one established by the Sâṅkhyas. Nor must you object that to do so would force on us another unacceptable conclusion, viz. that those Sm*ri*tis, that of Manu e.g., which maintain Brahman to be the universal cause, are destitute of authority; for Manu and similar works inculcate practical religious duty and thus have at any rate the uncontested function of supporting the teaching of the karmakâ*nd*a of the Veda. The Sâṅkhya Sm*ri*ti, on the other hand, is entirely devoted to the setting forth of theoretical truth (not of practical duty), and if it is not accepted in that quality, it is of no use whatsoever.—On this ground the Sûtra sets forth the primâ facie view,

'If it be said that there results the fault of there being no room for certain Sm*ri*tis.'

The same Sûtra replies 'no; because there would result the fault of want of room for other Sm*ri*tis.' For other Sm*ri*tis, that of Manu e.g., teach that Brahman is the universal cause. Thus Manu says, 'This (world) existed in the shape of darkness, and so on. Then the divine Self existent, indiscernible but making discernible all this, the great elements and the rest, appeared with irresistible power, dispelling the darkness. He, desiring to produce beings of many kinds from his own body, first with a thought created the waters, and placed his seed in them' (Manu I, 5–8). And the Bhagavad-gîtâ, 'I am the origin and the dissolution of the whole Universe' (VII, 6). 'I am the origin of all; everything proceeds from me' (X, 8). Similarly, in the Mahâbhârata, to the question 'Whence was created this whole world with its movable and immovable beings?' the answer is given, 'Nârâya*n*a assumes the form of the world, he the infinite, eternal one'; and 'from him there originates the Unevolved consisting of the three gu*n*as'; and 'the Unevolved is merged in the non-acting Person.' And Parâ*s*ara says, 'From Vish*n*u there sprang the world and in him it abides; he makes this world persist and he rules it—he is the world.' Thus also Âpastamba, 'The living beings are the dwelling of him who lies in all caves, who is not killed, who is spotless'; and 'From him spring all bodies; he is the primary cause, he is eternal, permanent' (Dharmasû. I, 8, 22, 4; 23, 2).—If the question as to the meaning of the Vedânta-texts were to be settled by means of Kapila's Sm*ri*ti, we should have to accept the extremely undesirable conclusion that all the Sm*ri*tis quoted are of no authority. It is true that the Vedânta-texts are concerned with theoretical truth lying outside the sphere of Perception and the other means of knowledge, and that hence students possessing only a limited knowledge of the Veda require some help in order fully to make out the meaning of the Vedânta. But what must be avoided in this case is to give any opening for the conclusion that the very numerous

Sm*ri*tis which closely follow the doctrine of the Vedânta, are composed by the most competent and trustworthy persons and aim at supporting that doctrine, are irrelevant; and it is for this reason that Kapila's Sm*ri*ti which contains a doctrine opposed to Scripture must be disregarded. The support required is elucidation of the sense conveyed by Scripture, and this clearly cannot be effected by means of a Sm*ri*ti contradicting Scripture. Nor is it of any avail to plead, as the Pûrvapakshin does, that Manu and other Sm*ri*tis of the same kind fulfil in any case the function of elucidating the acts of religious duty enjoined in the karmakâ*nd*a. For if they enjoin acts of religious duty as means to win the favour of the Supreme Person but do not impress upon us the idea of that Supreme Person himself who is to be pleased by those acts, they are also not capable of impressing upon us the idea of those acts themselves. That it is the character of all religious acts to win the favour of the Supreme Spirit, Sm*ri*ti distinctly declares, 'Man attains to perfection by worshipping with his proper action Him from whom all Beings proceed; and by whom all this is stretched out' (Bha. Gî. XVIII, 46); 'Let a man meditate on Nârâya*n*a, the divine one, at all works, such as bathing and the like; he will then reach the world of Brahman and not return hither' (Daksha-sm*ri*ti); and 'Those men with whom, intent on their duties, thou art pleased, O Lord, they pass beyond all this Mâyâ and find Release for their souls' (Vi. Pu.). Nor can it be said that Manu and similar Sm*ri*tis have a function in so far as setting forth works (not aiming at final Release but) bringing about certain results included in transmigratory existence, whether here on earth or in a heavenly world; for the essential character of those works also is to please the highest Person. As is said in the Bhagavad-gîtâ (IX, 23, 24); 'Even they who devoted to other gods worship them with faith, worship me, against ordinance. For I am the enjoyer and the Lord of all sacrifices; but they know me not in truth and hence they fall,' and 'Thou art ever worshipped by me with sacrifices; thou alone, bearing the form of pit*ri*s and of gods, enjoyest all the offerings made to either.' Nor finally can we admit the contention that it is rational to interpret the Vedânta-texts in accordance with Kapila's Sm*ri*ti because Kapila, in the *S*vetâ*s*vatara text, is referred to as a competent person. For from this it would follow that, as B*ri*haspati is, in *S*ruti and Sm*ri*ti, mentioned as a pattern of consummate wisdom, Scripture should be interpreted in agreement with the openly materialistic and atheistic Sm*ri*ti composed by that authority.—But, it may here be said, the Vedânta-texts should after all be interpreted in agreement with Kapila's Sm*ri*ti, for the reason that Kapila had through the power of his concentrated meditation (yoga) arrived at an insight into truth.—To this objection the next Sûtra replies.

2. And on account of the non-perception (of truth on the part) of others.

The 'and' in the Sûtra has the force of 'but,' being meant to dispel the doubt raised. There are many other authors of Sm*ri*tis, such as Manu, who through the power of their meditation had attained insight into the highest truth, and of whom it is known from Scripture that the purport of their teaching was a salutary medicine to the whole world ('whatever Manu said that was medicine'). Now, as these *Ri*shis did not see truth in the way of Kapila, we conclude that Kapila's view, which contradicts Scripture, is founded on error, and cannot therefore be used to modify the sense of the Vedânta-texts.—Here finishes the adhikara*n*a treating of 'Sm*ri*ti.'

3. Hereby the Yoga is refuted.

By the above refutation of Kapila's Sm*ri*ti the Yoga-sm*ri*ti also is refuted.—But a question arises, What further doubt arises here with regard to the Yoga system, so as to render needful the formal extension to the Yoga of the arguments previously set forth against the Sâṅkhya?—It might appear, we reply, that the Vedânta should be supported by the Yoga-sm*ri*ti, firstly, because the latter admits the existence of a Lord; secondly, because the Vedânta-texts mention Yoga as a means to bring about final Release; and thirdly, because Hira*n*yagarbha, who proclaimed the Yoga-sm*ri*ti, is qualified for the promulgation of all Vedânta-texts.—But these arguments refute themselves as follows. In the first place the Yoga holds the Pradhâna, which is independent of Brahman, to be the general material cause, and hence the Lord acknowledged by it is a mere operative cause. In the second place the nature of meditation, in which Yoga consists, is determined by the nature of the object of meditation, and as of its two objects, viz. the soul and the Lord, the former does not have its Self in Brahman, and the latter is neither the cause of the world nor endowed with the other auspicious qualities (which belong to Brahman), the Yoga is not of Vedic character. And as to the third point, Hira*n*yagarbha himself is only an individual soul, and hence liable to be overpowered by the inferior gu*n*as, i. e. passion and darkness; and hence the Yoga-sm*ri*ti is founded on error, no less than the Purâ*n*as, promulgated by him, which are founded on ra*g*as and tamas. The Yoga cannot, therefore, be used for the support of the Vedânta.—Here finishes the adhikara*n*a of 'the refutation of the Yoga.'

4. Not, on account of the difference of character of that; and its being such (appears) from Scripture.

The same opponent who laid stress on the conflict between Scripture and Sm*ri*ti now again comes forward, relying this time (not on Sm*ri*ti but) on simple reasoning. Your doctrine, he says, as to the world being an effect of Brahman which you attempted to prove by a refutation of the Sâṅkhya Sm*ri*ti shows itself to be irrational for the following reason. Perception and the other means of knowledge show this world with all its sentient and non-sentient beings to be of a non-intelligent and impure nature, to possess none of the qualities of the Lord, and to have pain for its very essence; and such a world totally differs in nature from the Brahman, postulated by you, which is said to be all-knowing, of supreme lordly power, antagonistic to all evil, enjoying unbroken uniform blessedness. This difference in character of the world from Brahman is, moreover, not only known through Perception, and so on, but is seen to be directly stated in Scripture itself; compare 'Knowledge and non-knowledge' (Taitt. Up. II, 6, 1); 'Thus are these objects placed on the subjects, and the subjects on the prâ*n*a' (Kau. Up. III, 9); 'On the same tree man sits grieving, immersed, bewildered by his own impotence' (*S*vet. Up. IV, 7); 'The soul not being a Lord is bound because he has to enjoy' (*S*vet. Up. I, 8); and so on; all which texts refer to the effect, i.e. the world as being non-intelligent, of the essence of pain, and so on. The general rule is that an effect is non-different in character from its cause; as e.g. pots and bracelets are non-different in character from their material causes—clay and gold. The world cannot, therefore, be the effect of Brahman from which it differs in character, and we hence conclude that, in agreement with the Sâṅkhya Sm*ri*ti, the Pradhâna which resembles the actual world in character must be assumed to be the general cause. Scripture, although not dependent on anything else and concerned with supersensuous objects, must all the same come to terms with ratiocination (tarka); for all the different means of knowledge can in many cases help us to arrive at a decisive conclusion, only if they are supported by ratiocination. For by tarka we understand that kind of knowledge (intellectual activity) which in the case of any given matter, by means of an investigation either into the essential nature of that matter or into collateral (auxiliary) factors, determines what possesses proving power, and what are the special details of the matter under consideration: this kind of cognitional activity is also called ûha. All means of knowledge equally stand in need of tarka; Scripture however, the authoritative character of which specially depends on expectancy (âkâṅkshâ), proximity (sannidhi), and compatibility (yogyatâ), throughout requires to be assisted by tarka. In accordance with this Manu says, 'He who investigates by means of reasoning, he only knows religious duty, and none other.' It is with a view to such confirmation of the sense of Scripture by means of Reasoning that the texts declare that certain topics such as the Self must be 'reflected on' (mantavya).—Now here it might possibly be said that as Brahman is ascertained from Scripture to be the sole cause of the world, it must be admitted that intelligence exists in the world also, which is an effect of Brahman. In the same way as the consciousness of an intelligent being is not perceived when it is in the states of deep sleep, swoon, &c., so the intelligent nature of jars and the like also is not observed, although it really exists; and it is this very difference of manifestation and non-manifestation of intelligence on which the distinction of intelligent and non-intelligent beings depends.—But to this we reply that permanent non-perception of intelligence proves its non-existence. This consideration also refutes the hypothesis of things commonly called non-intelligent possessing the power, or potentiality, of consciousness. For if you maintain that a thing possesses the power of producing an effect while yet that effect is never and nowhere *seen* to be produced by it, you may as well proclaim at a meeting of sons of barren women that their mothers possess eminent procreative power! Moreover, to prove at first from the Vedânta-texts that Brahman is the material cause of the world, and from this that pots and the like possess potential consciousness, and therefrom the existence of non-manifested consciousness; and then, on the other hand, to start from the last principle as proved and to deduce therefrom that the Vedânta-texts prove Brahman to be the material cause of the world, is simply to argue in a circle; for that the relation of cause and effect should exist between things different in character is just what cannot be proved.—What sameness of character, again, of causal substance and effects, have you in mind when you maintain that from the absence of such sameness it follows that Brahman cannot be proved to be the material cause of the world? It cannot be complete sameness of all attributes, because in that case the relation of cause and effect (which after all requires *some* difference) could not be established. For we do not observe that in pots and jars which are fashioned out of a lump of clay there persists the quality of 'being a lump' which belongs to the causal substance. And should you say that it suffices that there should be equality in some or any attribute, we point out that such is actually the case with regard to Brahman and the world, both of which have the attribute of 'existence' and others. The true state of the case rather is as follows. There is equality of nature between an effect and a cause, in that sense that those essential characteristics by which the causal substance distinguishes itself from other things persist in its effects also: those characteristic features, e.g., which distinguish gold from clay and other materials, persist also in things made of gold—bracelets and the like. But applying this consideration to Brahman and the world we find that Brahman's essential nature is to be antagonistic to all evil, and to consist of knowledge, bliss and power, while the world's essential nature is to be the opposite of all this. Brahman cannot, therefore, be the material cause of the world.

But, it may be objected, we observe that even things of different essential characteristics stand to each other in the relation of cause and effect. From man, e.g., who is a sentient being, there spring nails, teeth, and hair, which are non-sentient things; the sentient scorpion springs from non-sentient dung; and non-sentient threads proceed from the sentient spider.—This objection, we reply, is not valid; for in the instances quoted the relation of cause and effect rests on the non-sentient elements only (i.e. it is only the non-sentient matter of the body which produces nails, &c.).

But, a further objection is raised, Scripture itself declares in many places that things generally held to be non-sentient really possess intelligence; compare 'to him the earth said'; 'the water desired'; 'the prâ*n*as quarrelling among themselves as to their relative pre-eminence went to Brahman.' And the writers of the Purâ*n*as also attribute consciousness to rivers, hills, the sea, and so on. Hence there is after all no essential difference in nature between sentient and so-called non-sentient beings.—To this objection the Pûrvapakshin replies in the next Sûtra.

5. But (there is) denotation of the superintending (deities), on account of distinction and entering.

The word 'but' is meant to set aside the objection started. In texts such as 'to him the earth said,' the terms 'earth' and so on, denote the divinities presiding over earth and the rest.—How is this known?—'Through distinction and connexion.' For earth and so on are denoted by the distinctive term 'divinities'; so e.g. 'Let me enter into those three divinities' (*Kh.* Up. VI, 3, 2), where fire, water, and earth are called divinities; and Kau. Up. II, 14, 'All divinities contending with each other as to pre-eminence,' and 'all these divinities having recognised pre-eminence in prâ*n*a.' The 'entering' of the Sûtra refers to Ait. Âr. II, 4, 2, 4, 'Agni having become speech entered into the mouth; Âditya having become sight entered into the eyes,' &c., where the text declares that Agni and other divine beings entered into the sense-organs as their superintendents.

We therefore adhere to our conclusion that the world, being non-intelligent and hence essentially different in nature from Brahman, cannot be the effect of Brahman; and that therefore, in agreement with Sm*ri*ti confirmed by reasoning, the Vedânta-texts must be held to teach that the Pradhâna is the universal material cause. This primâ facie view is met by the following Sûtra.

6. But it is seen.

The 'but' indicates the change of view (introduced in the present Sûtra). The assertion that Brahman cannot be the material cause of the world because the latter differs from it in essential nature, is unfounded; since it is a matter of observation that even things of different nature stand to each other in the relation of cause and effect. For it is observed that from honey and similar substances there originate worms and other little animals.—But it has been said above that in those cases there is sameness of nature, in so far as the relation of cause and effect holds good only between the non-intelligent elements in both!—This assertion was indeed made, but it does not suffice to prove that equality of character between cause and effect which you have in view. For, being apprehensive that from the demand of equality of character in some point or other only it would follow that, as all things have certain characteristics in common, anything might originate from anything, you have declared that the equality of character necessary for the relation of cause and effect is constituted by the persistence, in the effect, of those characteristic points which differentiate the cause from other things. But it is evident that this restrictive rule does not hold good in the case of the origination of worms and the like from honey and so on; and hence it is not unreasonable to assume that the world also, although differing in character from Brahman, may originate from the latter. For in the case of worms originating from honey, scorpions from dung, &c., we do *not* observe—what indeed we *do* observe in certain other cases, as of pots made of clay, ornaments made of gold—that the special characteristics distinguishing the causal substance from other things persist in the effects also.

7. If it be said that (the effect is) non-existing; we say no, there being a mere denial.

But, an objection is raised, if Brahman, the cause, differs in nature from the effect, viz. the world, this means that cause and effect are separate things and that hence the effect does not exist in the cause, i. e. Brahman; and this again implies that the world originates from what has no existence!—Not so, we reply. For what the preceding Sûtra has laid down is merely the denial of an absolute rule demanding that cause and effect should be of the same nature; it was not asserted that the effect is a thing altogether different and separate from the cause. We by no means abandon our tenet that Brahman the cause modifies itself so as to assume the form of a world differing from it in character. For such is the case with the honey and the worms also. There is difference of characteristics, but—as in the case of gold and golden bracelets—there is oneness of substance.—An objection is raised.

8. On account of such consequences in reabsorption (the Vedânta-texts would be) inappropriate.

The term 'reabsorption' here stands as an instance of all the states of Brahman, reabsorption, creation, and so on—among which it is the first as appears from the texts giving instruction about those several states 'Being only was this in the beginning'; 'The Self only was this in the beginning.' If we accept the doctrine of the oneness of substance of cause and effect, then, absorption, creation, &c. of the world all being in Brahman, the different states of the world would connect themselves with Brahman, and the latter would thus be affected by all the imperfections of its effect; in the same way as all the attributes of the bracelet are present in the gold also. And the undesirable consequence of this would be that contradictory attributes as predicated in different Vedânta-texts would have to be attributed to one and the same substance; cp. 'He who is all-knowing' (Mu. Up. I, 1, 9); 'Free from sin, free from old age and death' (*Kh*. Up. VIII, 1, 5); 'Of him there is known neither cause nor effect' (*S*vet. Up. VI, 8); 'Of these two one eats the sweet fruit' (*S*vet. Up. IV, 6); 'The Self that is not a Lord is bound because he has to enjoy' (*S*vet. Up. I, 8); 'On account of his impotence he laments, bewildered' (*S*vet. Up. IV, 7).—Nor can we accept the explanation that, as Brahman in its causal as well as its effected state has all sentient and non-sentient beings for its body; and as all imperfections inhere in that body only, they do not touch Brahman in either its causal or effected state. For it is not possible that the world and Brahman should stand to each other in the relation of effect and cause, and if it were possible, the imperfections due to connexion with a body would necessarily cling to Brahman. It is not, we say, possible that the intelligent and non-ntelligent beings together should constitute the body of Brahman. For a body is a particular aggregate of earth and the other elements, depending for its subsistence on vital breath with its five modifications, and serving as an abode to the sense-organs which mediate the experiences of pleasure and pain retributive of former works: such is in Vedic and worldly speech the sense connected with the term 'body.' But numerous Vedic texts—'Free from sin, from old age and death' (*Kh.* Up. VIII, 1); 'Without eating the other one looks on' (*S*vet. Up. IV, 6); 'Grasping without hands, hasting without feet, he sees without eyes, he hears without ears' (*S*vet. Up. III, 19); 'Without breath, without mind' (Mu. Up. II, 1, 2)—declare that the highest Self is free from karman and the enjoyment of its fruits, is not capable of enjoyment dependent on sense-organs, and has no life dependent on breath: whence it follows that he cannot have a body constituted by all the non-sentient and sentient beings. Nor can either non-sentient beings in their individual forms such as grass, trees, &c., or the aggregate of all the elements in their subtle state be viewed as the abode of sense-activity (without which they cannot constitute a body); nor are the elements in their subtle state combined into earth and the other gross elements (which again would be required for a body). And sentient beings which consist of mere intelligence are of course incapable of all this, and hence even less fit to constitute a body. Nor may it be said that to have a body merely means to be the abode of fruition, and that Brahman may possess a body in this latter sense; for there are abodes of fruition, such as palaces and the like, which are not considered to be bodies. Nor will it avail, narrowing the last definition, to say that that only is an abode of enjoyment directly abiding in which a being enjoys pain and pleasure; for if a soul enters a body other than its own, that body is indeed the abode in which it enjoys the pains and pleasures due to such entering, but is not admitted to be in the proper sense of the word the *body* of the soul thus entered. In the case of the Lord, on the other hand, who is in the enjoyment of self-established supreme bliss, it can in no way be maintained that he must be joined to a body, consisting of all sentient and non-sentient beings, for the purpose of enjoyment.—That view also according to which a 'body' means no more than a *means* of enjoyment is refuted hereby.

You will now possibly try another definition, viz. that the body of a being is constituted by that, the nature, subsistence and activity of which depend on the will of that being, and that hence a body may be ascribed to the Lord in so far as the essential nature, subsistence, and activity of all depend on him.—But this also is objectionable; since in the first place it is not a fact that the nature of a body depends on the will of the intelligent soul joined with it; since, further, an injured body does not obey in its movements the will of its possessor; and since the persistence of a dead body does not depend on the soul that tenanted it. Dancing puppets and the like, on the other hand, are things the nature, subsistence, and motions of which depend on the will of intelligent beings, but we do not on that account consider them to be the bodies of those beings. As, moreover, the nature of an eternal intelligent soul does not depend on the will of the Lord, it cannot be its body under the present definition.—Nor again can it be said that the body of a being is constituted by that which is exclusively ruled and supported by that being and stands towards it in an exclusive subservient relation (*s*esha); for this definition would include actions also. And finally it is a fact that several texts definitely declare that the Lord is without a body, 'Without hands and feet he grasps and hastens' &c.

As thus the relation of embodied being and body cannot subsist between Brahman and the world, and as if it did subsist, all the imperfections of the world would cling to Brahman; the Vedânta-texts are wrong in teaching that Brahman is the material cause of the world.

To this primâ facie view the next Sûtra replies.

9. Not so; as there are parallel instances.

The teaching of the Vedânta-texts is not inappropriate, since there are instances of good and bad qualities being separate in the case of one thing connected with two different states. The 'but' in the Sûtra indicates the impossibility of Brahman being connected with even a shadow of what is evil. The meaning is as follows. As Brahman has all sentient and non-sentient things for its body, and constitutes the Self of that body, there is nothing contrary to reason in Brahman being connected with two states, a causal and an effected one, the essential characteristics of which are expansion on the one hand and contraction on the other; for this expansion and contraction belong (not to Brahman itself, but) to the sentient and non-sentient beings. The imperfections adhering to the body do not affect Brahman, and the good qualities belonging to the Self do not extend to the body; in the same way as youth, childhood, and old age, which are attributes of embodied beings, such as gods or men, belong to the body only, not to the embodied Self; while knowledge, pleasure and so on belong to the conscious Self only, not to the body. On this understanding there is no objection to expressions such as 'he is born as a god or as a man' and 'the same person is a child, and then a youth, and then an old man.' That the character of a god or man belongs to the individual soul only in so far as it has a body, will be shown under III, 1, 1.

The assertion made by the Pûrvapakshin as to the impossibility of the world, comprising matter and souls and being either in its subtle or its gross condition, standing to Brahman in the relation of a body, we declare to be the vain outcome of altogether vicious reasoning springing from the idle fancies of persons who have never fully considered the meaning of the whole body of Vedânta-texts as supported by legitimate argumentation. For as a matter of fact all Vedânta-texts distinctly declare that the entire world, subtle or gross, material or spiritual, stands to the highest Self in the relation of a body. Compare e.g. the antaryâmin-brâhma*n*a, in the Kâ*n*va as well as the Mâdhyandina-text, where it is said first of non-sentient things ('he who dwells within the earth, whose body the earth is' &c.), and afterwards separately of the intelligent soul ('he who dwells in understanding,' according to the

Kâ*n*vas; 'he who dwells within the Self,' according to the Mâdhyandinas) that they constitute the body of the highest Self. Similarly the Subâla-Upanishad declares that matter and souls in all their states constitute the body of the highest Self ('He who dwells within the earth' &c.), and concludes by saying that that Self is the soul of all those beings ('He is the inner Self of all' &c.). Similarly Sm*ri*ti, 'The whole world is thy body'; 'Water is the body of Vish*n*u'; 'All this is the body of Hari'; 'All these things are his body'; 'He having reflected sent forth from his body'—where the 'body' means the elements in their subtle state. In ordinary language the word 'body' is not, like words such as *jar*, limited in its denotation to things of one definite make or character, but is observed to be applied directly (not only secondarily or metaphorically) to things of altogether different make and characteristics—such as worms, insects, moths, snakes, men, four-footed animals, and so on. We must therefore aim at giving a definition of the word that is in agreement with general use. The definitions given by the Pûrvapakshin—'a body is that which causes the enjoyment of the fruit of actions' &c.—do not fulfil this requirement; for they do not take in such things as earth and the like which the texts declare to be the body of the Lord. And further they do not take in those bodily forms which the Lord assumes according to his wish, nor the bodily forms released souls may assume, according to 'He is one' &c. (*Kh*. Up. VII, 26, 2); for none of those embodiments subserve the fruition of the results of actions. And further, the bodily forms which the Supreme Person assumes at wish are not special combinations of earth and the other elements; for Sm*ri*ti says, 'The body of that highest Self is not made from a combination of the elements.' It thus appears that it is also too narrow a definition to say that a body is a combination of the different elements. Again, to say that a body is that, the life of which depends on the vital breath with its five modifications is also too narrow, viz. in respect of plants; for although vital air is present in plants, it does not in them support the body by appearing in five special forms. Nor again does it answer to define a body as either the abode of the sense-organs or as the cause of pleasure and pain; for neither of these definitions takes in the bodies of stone or wood which were bestowed on Ahalyâ and other persons in accordance with their deeds. We are thus led to adopt the following definition—Any substance which a sentient soul is capable of completely controlling and supporting for its own purposes, and which stands to the soul in an entirely subordinate relation, is the body of that soul. In the case of bodies injured, paralysed, &c., control and so on are not actually perceived because the power of control, although existing, is obstructed; in the same way as, owing to some obstruction, the powers of fire, heat, and so on may not be actually perceived. A dead body again begins to decay at the very moment in which the soul departs from it, and is actually dissolved shortly after; it (thus strictly speaking is not a body at all but) is spoken of as a body because it is a part of the aggregate of matter which previously constituted a body. In this sense, then, all sentient and non-sentient beings together constitute the body of the Supreme Person, for they are completely controlled and supported by him for his own ends, and are absolutely subordinate to him. Texts which speak of the highest Self as 'bodiless among bodies' (e. g. Ka. Up. I, 2, 22), only mean to deny of the Self a body due to karman; for as we have seen, Scripture declares that the Universe *is* his body. This point will be fully established in subsequent adhikara*n*as also. The two preceding Sûtras (8 and 9) merely suggest the matter proved in the adhikara*n*a beginning with II, 1, 21.

10. And on account of the objections to his view.

The theory of Brahman being the universal cause has to be accepted not only because it is itself free from objections, but also because the pradhâna theory is open to objections, and hence must be abandoned. For on this latter theory the origination of the world cannot be accounted for. The Sâṅkhyas hold that owing to the soul's approximation to Prak*ri*ti the attributes of the latter are fictitiously superimposed upon the soul which in itself consists entirely of pure intelligence free from all change, and that thereon depends the origination of the empirical world. Now here we must raise the question as to the nature of that approximation or nearness of Prak*ri*ti which causes the superimposition on the changeless soul of the attributes of Prak*ri*ti. Does that nearness mean merely the existence of Prak*ri*ti or some change in Prak*ri*ti? or does it mean some change in the soul?—Not the latter; for the soul is assumed to be incapable of change.—Nor again a change in Prak*ri*ti; for changes in Prak*ri*ti are supposed, in the system, to be the effects of superimposition, and cannot therefore be its cause. And if, finally, the nearness of Prak*ri*ti means no more than its existence, it follows that even the released soul would be liable to that superimposition (for Prak*ri*ti exists always).—The Sâṅkhya is thus unable to give a rational account of the origination of the world. This same point will be treated of fully in connexion with the special refutation of the Sâṅkhya theory. (II, 2, 6.)

11. Also in consequence of the ill-foundedness of reasoning.

The theory, resting on Scripture, of Brahman being the universal cause must be accepted, and the theory of the Pradhâna must be abandoned, because all (mere) reasoning is ill-founded. This latter point is proved by the fact that the arguments set forth by Buddha, Ka*n*âda, Akshapâda, *G*ina, Kapila and Pata*ñg*ali respectively are all mutually contradictory.

12. Should it be said that inference is to be carried on in a different way; (we reply that) thus also it follows that (the objection raised) is not got rid of.

Let us then view the matter as follows. The arguments actually set forth by Buddha and others may have to be considered as invalid, but all the same we may arrive at the Pradhâna theory through other lines of reasoning by which the objections raised against the theory are refuted.—But, we reply, this also is of no avail. A theory which rests exclusively on arguments derived from human reason may, at some other time or place, be disestablished by arguments devised by people more skilful than you in reasoning; and thus there is no getting over the objection founded on the invalidity of all mere argumentation. The conclusion from all this is that, with regard to supersensuous matters, Scripture alone is authoritative, and that reasoning is to be applied only to the support of Scripture. In agreement herewith Manu says, 'He who supports the teaching of the *Ri*shis and the doctrine as to sacred duty with arguments not conflicting with the Veda, he alone truly knows sacred duty' (Manu XII, 106). The teaching of the Sâṅkhyas which conflicts with the Veda cannot therefore be used for the purpose of confirming and elucidating the meaning of the Veda.—Here finishes the section treating of 'difference of nature.'

13. Thereby also the remaining (theories) which are not comprised (within the Veda) are explained.

Not comprised means those theories which are not known to be comprised within (countenanced by) the Veda. The Sûtra means to say that by the demolition given above of the Sâṅkhya doctrine which is not comprised within the Veda the remaining theories which are in the same position, viz. the theories of Ka*n*âda, Akshapâda, *G*ina, and Buddha, must likewise be considered as demolished.

Here, however, a new objection may be raised, on the ground namely that, since all these theories agree in the view of atoms constituting the general cause, it cannot be said that their reasoning as to the causal substance is ill-founded.—They indeed, we reply, are agreed to that extent, but they are all of them equally founded on Reasoning only, and they are seen to disagree in many ways as to the nature of the atoms which by different schools are held to be either fundamentally void or nonvoid, having either a merely cognitional or an objective existence, being either momentary or permanent, either of a definite nature or the reverse, either real or unreal, &c. This disagreement proves all those theories to be ill-founded, and the objection is thus disposed of.—Here finishes the section of 'the remaining (theories) non-comprised (within the Veda).'

14. If it be said that from (Brahman) becoming an enjoyer, there follows non-distinction (of Brahman and the individual soul); we reply—it may be as in ordinary life.

The Sâṅkhya here comes forward with a new objection. You maintain, he says, that the highest Brahman has the character either of a cause or an effect according as it has for its body sentient and non-sentient beings in either their subtle or gross state; and that this explains the difference in nature between the individual soul and Brahman. But such difference is not possible, since Brahman, if embodied, at once becomes an enjoying subject (just like the individual soul). For if, possessing a body, the Lord necessarily experiences all pain and pleasure due to embodiedness, no less than the individual soul does.—But we have, under I, 2, 8, refuted the view of the Lord's being liable to experiences of pleasure and pain!—By no means! There you have shown only that the Lord's abiding within the heart of a creature so as to constitute the object of its devotion does not imply fruition on his part of pleasure and pain. Now, however, you maintain that the Lord is embodied just like an individual soul, and the unavoidable inference from this is that, like that soul, he undergoes pleasurable and painful experiences. For we observe that embodied souls, although not capable of participating in the changing states of the body such as childhood, old age, &c., yet experience pleasures and pains caused by the normal or abnormal condition of the matter constituting the body. In agreement with this Scripture says, 'As long as he possesses a body there is for him no escape from pleasure and pain; but when he is free of the body then neither pleasure nor pain touches him' (*Kh.* Up. VIII, 12, 1). As thus, the theory of an embodied Brahman constituting the universal cause does not allow of a distinction in nature between the Lord and the individual soul; and as, further, the theory of a mere Brahman (i.e. an absolutely homogeneous Brahman) leads to the conclusion that Brahman is the abode of all the imperfections attaching to the world, in the same way as a lump of clay or gold participates in the imperfections of the thing fashioned out of it; we maintain that the theory of the Pradhâna being the general cause is the more valid one.

To this objection the Sûtra replies in the words, 'it may be, as in ordinary life.' The desired distinction in nature between the Lord and the individual soul may exist all the same. That a soul experiences pleasures and pains caused by the various states of the body is not due to the fact of its being joined to a body, but to its karman in the form of good and evil deeds. The scriptural text also which you quote refers to that body only which is originated by karman; for other texts ('He is onefold, he is threefold'; 'If he desires the world of the Fathers'; 'He moves about there eating, playing, rejoicing'; *Kh.* Up. VII, 26, 2; VIII, 2, 1; 12, 3) show that the person who has freed himself from the bondage of karman and become manifest in his true nature is not touched by a shadow of evil while all the same he has a body. The highest Self, which is essentially free from all evil, thus has the entire world in its gross and its subtle form for its body; but being in no way connected with karman it is all the less connected with evil of any kind.—'As in ordinary life.' We observe in ordinary life that while those who either observe or transgress the ordinances of a ruler experience pleasure or pain according as the ruler shows them favour or restrains them, it does not follow from the mere fact of the ruler's having a body that he himself also experiences the pleasure and pain due to the observance or transgression of his commands. The author of the Drami*d*a-bhâshya gives expression to the same view, 'As in ordinary life a prince, although staying in a very unpleasant place infested with mosquitoes and full of discomforts of all kind is yet not touched by all these troubles, his body being constantly refreshed by fans and other means of comfort, rules the countries for which he cares and continues to enjoy all possible pleasures, such as fragrant odours and the like; so the Lord of creation, to whom his power serves as an ever-moving fan as it were, is not touched by the evils of that creation, but rules the world of Brahman and the other worlds for which he cares, and continues to enjoy all possible delights.' That the nature of Brahman should undergo changes like a lump of clay or gold we do not admit, since many texts declare Brahman to be free from all change and imperfection.—Others give a different explanation of this Sûtra. According to them it refutes the pûrvapaksha that on the view of Brahman being the general cause the distinction of enjoying subjects and objects of enjoyment cannot be accounted for—proving the possibility of such distinction by means of the analogous instance of the sea and its waves and flakes of foam. But this interpretation is inappropriate, since for those who hold that creation proceeds from Brahman connected with some power or Nescience or a limiting adjunct (upâdhi) no such primâ facie view can arise. For on their theory the enjoying subject is that which is conditioned by the power or Nescience or upâdhi inhering in the causal substance, and the power or Nescience or upâdhi is the object of enjoyment; and as the two are of different nature, they cannot pass over into each other. The view of Brahman itself undergoing an essential change (on which that primâ facie view might possibly be held to arise) is not admitted by those philosophers; for Sûtra II, i, 35 teaches that the individual souls and their deeds form a stream which has no beginning (so that the distinction of enjoying subjects and objects of enjoyment is eternal). But even if it be held that Brahman itself undergoes a change, the doubt as to the non-distinction of subjects and objects of enjoyment does not arise; for the distinction of the two groups will, on that view, be analogous to that of jars and platters which are modifications of the one substance clay, or to that of bracelets and crowns fashioned out of the one substance gold. And on the view of Brahman itself undergoing a change there arises a further difficulty, viz. in so far as Brahman (which is nothing but pure non-conditioned intelligence) is held to transform itself into (limited) enjoying souls and (non-sentient) objects of enjoyment.

15. The non-difference (of the world) from that (viz. Brahman) follows from what begins with the word ârambhana.

Under II, 1, 7 and other Sûtras the non-difference of the effect, i.e. the world from the cause, i.e. Brahman was assumed, and it was on this basis that the proof of Brahman being the cause of the world proceeded. The present Sûtra now raises a primâ facie objection against that very non-difference, and then proceeds to refute it.

On the point in question the school of Ka*n*âda argues as follows. It is in no way possible that the effect should be non-different from the cause. For cause and effect are the objects of different ideas: the ideas which have for their respective objects threads and a piece of cloth, or a lump of clay and a jar, are distinctly not of one and the same kind. The difference of words supplies a second argument; nobody applies to mere threads the word 'piece of cloth,' or vice versâ. A third argument rests on the difference of effects: water is not fetched from the well in a lump of clay, nor is a well built with jars. There, fourthly, is the difference of time; the cause is prior in time, the effect posterior. There is, fifthly, the difference of form: the cause has the shape of a lump, the effect (the jar) is shaped like a belly with a broad basis; clay in the latter condition only is meant when we say 'The jar has gone to pieces.' There, sixthly, is a numerical difference: the threads are many, the piece of cloth is one only. In the seventh place, there is the uselessness of the activity of the producing agent (which would result from cause and effect being identical); for if the effect were nothing but the cause, what could be effected by the activity of the agent?—Let us then say that, although the effect *exists* (at all times), the activity of the agent must be postulated as helpful towards the effect.—But in that case the activity of the agent would have to be assumed as taking place perpetually, and as hence everything would exist always, there would be no distinction between eternal and non-eternal things!—Let us then say that the effect, although always existing, is at first non-manifest and then is manifested through the activity of the agent; in this way that activity will not be purposeless, and there will be a distinction between eternal and non-eternal things!—This view also is untenable. For if that manifestation requires another manifestation (to account for it) we are driven into a *regressus in infinitum*. If, on the other hand, it is independent of another manifestation (and hence eternal), it follows that the effect also is eternally perceived. And if, as a third alternative, the manifestation is said to originate, we lapse into the asatkâryavâda (according to which the effect does not exist before its origination). Moreover, if the activity of the agent serves to manifest the effect, it follows that the activity devoted to a jar will manifest also waterpots and similar things. For things which admittedly possess manifesting power, such as lamps and the like, are not observed to be restricted to particular objects to be manifested by them: we do not see that a lamp lit for showing a jar does *not* at the same time manifest waterpots and other things. All this proves that the activity of the agent has a purpose in so far only as it is the cause of the origination of an effect which previously did *not* exist; and thus the theory of the previous existence of the effect cannot be upheld. Nor does the fact of definite causes having to be employed (in order to produce definite effects; clay e.g. to produce a jar) prove that that only which already exists can become an effect; for the facts explain themselves also on the hypothesis of the cause having definite potentialities (determining the definite effect which will result from the cause).

But, an objection is raised, he also who holds the theory of the previous non-existence of the effect, can really do nothing with the activity of the agent. For as, on his view, the effect has no existence before it is originated, the activity of the agent must be supposed to operate elsewhere than on the effect; and as this 'elsewhere' comprises without distinction all other things, it follows that the agent's activity with reference to threads may give rise to water-pots also (not only to cloth).—Not so, the Vai*s*eshika replies. Activity applied to a certain cause gives rise to those effects only the potentiality of which inheres in that cause.

Now, against all this, the following objection is raised. The effect is non-different from the cause. For in reality there is no such thing as an effect different from the cause, since all effects, and all empirical thought and speech about effects, are based on Nescience. Apart from the causal substance, clay, which is seen to be present in effected things such as jars, the so-called effect, i. e. the jar or pot, rests altogether on Nescience. All effected things whatever, such as jars, waterpots, &c., viewed as different from their causal substance, viz. clay, which is perceived to exist in these its effects, rest merely on empirical thought and speech, and are fundamentally false, unreal; while the causal substance, i.e. clay, alone is real. In the same way the entire world in so far as viewed apart from its cause, i. e. Brahman which is nothing but pure non-differenced Being, rests exclusively on the empirical assumption of Egoity and so on, and is false; while reality belongs to the causal Brahman which is mere Being. It follows that there is no such thing as an effect apart from its cause; the effect in fact is identical with the cause. Nor must you object to our theory on the ground that the corroborative instance of the silver erroneously imagined in the shell is inappropriate because the non-reality of such effected things as jars is by no means well proved while the non-reality of the shell-silver is so proved; for as a matter of fact it *is* determined by reasoning that it is the causal substance of jars, viz. clay, only that is real while the reality of everything apart from clay is disproved by reasoning. And if you ask whereupon that reasoning rests, we reply—on the fact that the clay only is continuous, permanent, while everything different from it is discontinuous, non-permanent. For just as in the case of the snake-rope we observe that the continuously existing rope only—which forms the substrate of the imagined snake—is real, while the snake or cleft in the ground, which is non-continuous, is unreal; so we conclude that it is the permanently enduring clay-material only which is real, while the non-continuous effects, such as jars and pots, are unreal. And, further, since what is real, i.e. the Self, does not perish, and what is altogether unreal, as e.g. the horn of a hare, is not perceived, we conclude that an effected thing, which on the one hand is perceived and on the other is liable to destruction, must be viewed as something to be defined neither as that which is nor as that which is not. And what is thus undefinable, is false, no less than the silver imagined in the shell, the anirva*k*anîyatva of which is proved by perception and sublation (see above, p. 102 ff.).—We further ask, 'Is a causal substance, such as clay, when producing its effect, in a non-modified state, or has it passed over into some special modified condition?' The former alternative cannot be allowed, because thence it would follow that the cause originates effects at all times; and the latter must equally be rejected, because the passing over of the cause into a special state would oblige us to postulate a previous passing over into a different state (to account for the latter passing over) and again a previous one, &c., so that a *regressus in infinitum* would result.—Let it then be said that the causal substance when giving rise to the effect is indeed unchanged, but connected with a special operative cause, time and place (this connexion accounting for the origination of the effect).—But this also we cannot allow; for such connexion would be with the causal substance either as unchanged or as having entered on a changed condition; and thus the difficulties stated above would arise again.—Nor may you say that the origination of jars, gold coins, and sour milk from clay, gold, and milk respectively is actually perceived; that this perception is not sublated with regard to time and place—while, on the other hand, the perception of silver in the shell is so sublated—and that hence all those who trust perception must necessarily admit that the effect *does* originate from the cause. For this argumentation does not stand the test of being set forth in definite alternatives. Does the mere gold, &c., by itself originate the svastika-ornament? or is it the gold coins (used for making ornaments) which originate? or is it the gold, as forming the substrate of the coins[1]? The mere gold, in the first place, cannot be originative as there exists no effect different from the gold (to which the originative activity could apply itself); and a thing cannot possibly display originative activity with regard to itself.—But, an objection is raised, the svastika-ornament is perceived as different from the gold!—It is not, we reply, different from the gold; for the gold is recognised in it, and no other thing but gold is perceived.—But the existence of another thing is proved by the fact of there being a different idea, a different word, and so on!—By no means, we reply. Other ideas, words, and so on, which have reference to an altogether undefined thing are founded on error, no less than the idea of, and the word denoting, shell-silver, and hence have no power of proving the existence of another thing. Nor, in the second place, is the *gold coin* originative of the svastika-ornament; for we do not perceive the coin in the svastika, as we do perceive the threads in the cloth. Nor, in the third place, is the effect originated by the gold in so far as being the substrate of the coin; for the gold in so far as forming the substrate of the coin is not perceived in the svastika. As it thus appears that all effects viewed apart from their causal

[1] In other words—is the golden ornament originated by the mere formless substance, gold; or by the form belonging to that special piece of gold (a coin, a bar, &c.), out of which the ornament is fashioned; or by the substance, gold, in so far as possessing that special form? The ru*k*aka of the text has to be taken in the sense of nishka.

substances are unreal, we arrive at the conclusion that the entire world, viewed apart from Brahman, is also something unreal; for it also is an effect.

In order to facilitate the understanding of the truth that everything apart from Brahman is false, we have so far reasoned on the assumption of things such as clay, gold, &c., being real, and have thereby proved the non-reality of all effects. In truth, however, all special causal substances are unreal quite as much as jars and golden ornaments are; for they are all of them equally effects of Brahman.

'In that all this has its Self; it is the True' (*Kh.* Up. VI, 8, 7); 'There is here no plurality; from death to death goes he who sees here plurality as it were' (B*ri.* Up. IV, 4, 19); 'For where there is duality as it were, there one sees another; but when for him the Self only has become all, whereby then should he see and whom should he see?' (B*ri.* Up. II, 4, 13); 'Indra goes manifold by means of his mâyâs' (B*ri.* Up. II, 5, 19);—these and other similar texts teach that whatever is different from Brahman is false. Nor must it be imagined that the truth intimated by Scripture can be in conflict with Perception; for in the way set forth above we prove that all effects are false, and moreover Perception really has for its object pure Being only (cp. above, p. 30). And if there is a conflict between the two, superior force belongs to Scripture, to which no imperfection can be attributed; which occupies a final position among the means of knowledge; and which, although dependent on Perception, and so on, for the apprehension of the form and meaning of words, yet is independent as far as proving power is concerned. Hence it follows that everything different from Brahman, the general cause, is unreal.

Nor must this conclusion be objected to on the ground that from the falsity of the world it follows that the individual souls also are non-real. For it is Brahman itself which constitutes the individual souls: Brahman alone takes upon itself the condition of individual soul in all living bodies; as we know from many texts: 'Having entered into them with this living Self' (*Kh.* Up. VI, 3);

'The one god hidden within all beings' (*S*vet. Up. VI, 11); 'The one god entered in many places'; 'That Self hidden in all beings does not shine forth' (Ka. Up. I, 3, 12); 'There is no other seer but he' (B*ri*. Up. III, 3, 23); and others.—But if you maintain that the one Brahman constitutes the soul in all living bodies, it follows that any particular pain or pleasure should affect the consciousness of all embodied beings, just as an agreeable sensation affecting the foot gives rise to a feeling of pleasure in the head; and that there would be no distinction of individual soul and Lord, released souls and souls in bondage, pupils and teachers, men wise and ignorant, and so on.

Now, in reply to this, some of those who hold the non-duality of Brahman give the following explanation. The many individual souls are the reflections of the one Brahman, and their states of pain, pleasure, and so on, remain distinct owing to the different limiting adjuncts (on which the existence of each individual soul as such depends), in the same way as the many reflected images of one and the same face in mirrors, crystals, sword-blades, &c., remain distinct owing to their limiting adjuncts (viz. mirrors, &c.); one image being small, another large, one being bright, another dim, and so on.—But you have said that scriptural texts such as 'Having entered with this living Self' show that the souls are not different from Brahman!—They are indeed not different in reality, but we maintain their distinction on the basis of an imagined difference.—To whom then does that imagination belong? Not to Brahman surely whose nature, consisting of pure intelligence, allows no room for imagination of any kind! Nor also to the individual souls; for this would imply a faulty mutual dependence, the existence of the soul depending on imagination and that imagination residing in the soul!—Not so, the advaita-vâdin replies. Nescience (wrong imagination) and the existence of the souls form an endless retrogressive chain; their relation is like that of the seed and the sprout. Moreover, mutual dependence and the like, which are held to constitute defects in the case of real things, are unable to disestablish Nescience, the very nature of which consists in being that which cannot rationally be established, and which hence may be compared to somebody's swallowing a whole palace and the like (as seen in a dream or under the influence of a magical illusion). In reality the individual souls are non-different from Brahman, and hence essentially free from all impurity; but as they are liable to impurity caused by their limiting adjuncts—in the same way as the face reflected in a mirror is liable to be dimmed by the dimness of the mirror—they may be the abodes of Nescience and hence may be viewed as the figments of wrong imagination. Like the dimness of the reflected face, the imperfection adhering to the soul is a mere error; for otherwise it would follow that the soul can never obtain release. And as this error of the souls has proceeded from all eternity, the question as to its cause is not to be raised.

This, we reply, is the view of teachers who have no insight into the true nature of aduality, and are prompted by the wish of capturing the admiration and applause of those who believe in the doctrine of duality. For if, as a first alternative, you should maintain that the abode of Nescience is constituted by the soul in its essential, not fictitiously imagined, form; this means that Brahman itself is the abode of Nescience. If, in the second place, you should say that the abode of Nescience is the soul, viewed as different from Brahman and fictitiously imagined in it, this would mean that the Non-intelligent (*gada*) is the abode of Nescience. For those who hold the view of Non-duality do not acknowledge a third aspect different from these two (i.e. from Brahman which is pure intelligence, and the Non-intelligent fictitiously superimposed on Brahman). And if, as a third alternative, it be maintained that the abode of Nescience is the soul in its essential nature, this nature being however qualified by the fictitiously imagined aspect; we must negative this also, since that which has an absolutely homogeneous nature cannot in any way be shown to be qualified, apart from Nescience. The soul is qualified in so far only as it is the abode of Nescience, and you therefore define nothing.—Moreover, the theory of Nescience abiding within the individual soul is resorted to for the purpose of establishing a basis for the distinction of bondage and release, but it really is quite unable to effect this. For if by Release be understood the destruction of Nescience, it follows that when one soul attains Release and Nescience is thus destroyed, the other souls also will be released.—But Nescience persists because other souls are not released!—Well then the one soul also is not released since Nescience is not destroyed!—But we assume a different Nescience for each soul; that soul whose Nescience is destroyed will be released, and that whose Nescience is not destroyed will remain in Bondage!—You now argue on the assumption of a special avidyâ for each soul. But what about the distinction of souls implied therein? Is that distinction essential to the nature of the soul, or is it the figment of Nescience? The former alternative is excluded, as it is admitted that the soul essentially is pure, non-differenced intelligence; and because on that alternative the assumption of avidyâ to account for the distinction of souls would be purposeless. On the latter alternative two subordinate alternatives arise—Does this avidyâ which gives rise to the fictitious distinction of souls belong to Brahman? or to the individual souls?—If you say 'to Brahman,' your view coincides with mine.—Well then, 'to the souls'!—But have you then quite forgotten that Nescience is assumed for the purpose of accounting for the distinction of souls?—Let us then view the matter as follows—those several avidyâs which are assumed for the purpose of establishing the distinction of souls bound and released, to those same avidyâs the distinction of souls is due.—But here you reason in a manifest circle: the avidyâs are established on the basis of the distinction of souls, and the distinction of souls is established when the avidyâs are established. Nor does the argument of the seed and sprout apply to the present question. For in the case of seeds and plants each several seed gives rise to a different plant; while in the case under discussion you adopt the impossible procedure of establishing the several avidyâs on the basis of the very souls which are assumed to be due to those avidyâs. And if you attempt to give to the argument a somewhat different turn, by maintaining that it is the avidyâs abiding in the earlier souls which fictitiously give rise to the later souls, we point out that this implies the souls being short-lived only, and moreover that each soul would have to take upon itself the consequences of deeds not its own and escape the consequences of its own deeds. The same reasoning disposes of the hypothesis that it is Brahman which effects the fictitious existence of the subsequent souls by means of the avidyâs abiding within the earlier souls. And if there is assumed a beginningless flow of avidyâs, it follows that there is also a beginningless flow of the condition of the souls dependent on those avidyâs, and that steady uniformity of the state of the souls which is supposed to hold good up to the moment of Release could thus not be established. Concerning your assertion that, as Nescience is something unreal and hence altogether unproved, it is not disestablished by such defects as mutual dependence which touch real things only; we remark that in that case Nescience would cling even to released souls and the highest Brahman itself.—But impure Nescience cannot cling to what has for its essence pure cognition!—Is Nescience then to be dealt with by rational arguments? If so, it will follow that, on account of the arguments set forth (mutual dependence, and so on), it likewise does not cling to the individual souls. We further put the following question—When the Nescience abiding in the individual soul passes away, owing to the rise of the knowledge of truth, does then the soul also perish or does it not perish? In the former case Release is nothing else but destruction of the essential nature of the soul; in the latter case the soul does not attain Release even on the destruction of Nescience, since it continues to exist as soul different from Brahman.—You have further maintained that the distinction of souls as pure and impure, &c., admits of being accounted for in the same way as the dimness or clearness, and so on, of the different images of a face as seen reflected in mirrors, crystals, sword-blades and the like. But here the following point requires consideration. On what occasion do the smallness, dimness and other imperfections due to the limiting adjuncts (i.e. the mirrors, &c.) pass away?—When the mirrors and other limiting adjuncts themselves pass away!—Does then, we ask, the reflected image which is the substrate of those imperfections persist or not? If you say that it persists, then by analogy the individual soul also must be assumed to persist, and from this it follows that it does not attain Release. And if the reflected image is held to perish together with its imperfections, by analogy the soul also will perish and then Release will be nothing but annihilation.—Consider the following point also. The destruction of a non-advantageous (apurushârtha) defect is of advantage to him who is conscious of that disadvantage. Is it then, we ask, in the given case Brahman—which corresponds to the thing reflected—that is conscious of the imperfections due to the limiting adjuncts? or is it the soul which corresponds to the reflected image? or is it something else? On the two former alternatives it appears that the comparison (between Brahman and the soul on the one hand, and the thing reflected and the reflection on the other—on which comparison your whole theory is founded) does not hold good; for neither the face nor the reflection of the face is conscious of the imperfections due to the adjuncts; for neither of the two is a being capable of consciousness. And, moreover, Brahman's being conscious of imperfections would imply its being the abode of Nescience. And the third alternative, again, is impossible, since there is no other knowing subject *but* Brahman and the soul.—It would, moreover, be necessary to define who is the imaginatively shaping agent (kalpaka) with regard to the soul as formed from Nescience. It cannot be Nescience itself, because Nescience is not an intelligent principle. Nor can it be the soul, because this would imply the defect of what has to be proved being presupposed for the purposes of the proof; and because the existence of the soul is that which *is formed* by Nescience, just as shell-silver is. And if, finally, you should say that Brahman is the fictitiously forming agent, we have again arrived at a Brahman that is the abode of Nescience.—If Brahman is not allowed to be the abode of Nescience, we further must ask whether Brahman sees (is conscious of) the individual souls or not. If not, it is not possible that Brahman should give rise to this manifold creation which, as Scripture declares, is preceded by 'seeing' on his part, and to the differentiation of names and forms. If, on the other hand, Brahman which is of an absolutely homogeneous nature *sees* the souls, it cannot do so without Nescience; and thus we are again led to the view of Nescience abiding in Brahman.

For similar reasons the theory of the distinction of Mâyâ and Nescience must also be abandoned. For even if Brahman possesses Mâyâ, i. e. illusive power, it cannot, without Nescience, be conscious of souls. And without being conscious of others the lord of Mâyâ is unable to delude them by his Mâyâ; and Mâyâ herself cannot bring about the consciousness of others on the part of its Lord, for it is a mere means to delude others, after they have (by other means) become objects of consciousness.—Perhaps you will say that the Mâyâ of Brahman causes him to be conscious of souls, and at the same time is the cause of those souls' delusion. But if Mâyâ causes Brahman—which is nothing but self-illuminated intelligence, absolutely homogeneous and free from all foreign elements—to become conscious of other beings, then Mâyâ is nothing but another name for Nescience.—Let it then be said that Nescience is the cause of the cognition of what is contrary to truth; such being the case, Mâyâ which presents all false things different from Brahman *as* false, and thus is not the cause of wrong cognition on the part of Brahman, is *not* avidyâ.—But this is inadmissible; for, when the oneness of the moon is known, that which causes the idea of the moon being double can be nothing else but avidyâ. Moreover, if Brahman recognises all beings apart from himself as false, he does not delude them; for surely none but a madman would aim at deluding beings known by him to be unreal!—

Let us then define avidyâ as the cause of a disadvantageous cognition of unreal things. Mâyâ then, as not being the cause of such a disadvantageous cognition on Brahman's part, cannot be of the nature of avidyâ!—But this also is inadmissible; for although the idea of the moon being double is not the cause of any pain, and hence not disadvantageous to man, it is all the same caused by avidyâ; and if, on the other hand, Mâyâ which aims at dispelling that idea (in so far as it presents the image and idea of one moon) did not present what is of disadvantage, it would not be something to be destroyed, and hence would be permanently connected with Brahman's nature.—Well, if it were so, what harm would there be?—The harm would be that such a view implies the theory of duality, and hence would be in conflict with the texts inculcating non-duality such as 'For where there is duality as it were, &c.; but when for him the Self only has become all, whereby then should he see, and whom should he see?'—But those texts set forth the Real; Mâyâ on the other hand is non-real, and hence the view of its permanency is not in real conflict with the texts!—Brahman, we reply, has for its essential nature unlimited bliss, and hence cannot be conscious of, or affected with, unreal Mâyâ, without avidyâ. Of what use, we further ask, should an eternal non-real Mâyâ be to Brahman?—Brahman by means of it deludes the individual souls!—But of what use should such delusion be to Brahman?—It affords to Brahman a kind of sport or play!—But of what use is play to a being whose nature is unlimited bliss?—Do we not then see in ordinary life also that persons in the enjoyment of full happiness and prosperity indulge all the same in play?—The cases are not parallel, we reply. For none but persons not in their right mind would take pleasure in an unreal play, carried on by means of implements unreal and known by them to be unreal, and in the consciousness, itself, unreal of such a play!—The arguments set forth previously also prove the impossibility of the fictitious existence of an individual soul considered as the abode of avidyâ, apart from Brahman considered as the abode of Mâyâ.

We thus arrive at the conclusion that those who hold the non-duality of Brahman must also admit that it is Brahman alone which is affected with beginningless avidyâ, and owing to this avidyâ is conscious of plurality within itself. Nor must it be urged against him who holds this view of avidyâ belonging to Brahman that he is unable to account for the distinction of bondage and release, for as there is only the one Brahman affected with Nescience and to be released by the cessation of that Nescience, the distinction of souls bound and released, &c., has no true existence: the empirical distinction of souls bound and released, of teachers and pupils, &c. is a merely fictitious one, and all such fiction can be explained by means of the avidyâ of one intelligent being. The case is analogous to that of a person dreaming: the teachers and pupils and all the other persons and things he may see in his dream are fictitiously shaped out of the avidyâ of the one dreaming subject. For the same reason there is no valid foundation for the assumption of many avidyâs. For those also who hold that avidyâ belongs to the individual souls do not maintain that the distinction of bondage and release, of one's own self and other persons, is real; and if it is unreal it can be accounted for by the avidyâ of one subject. This admits of being stated in various technical ways.—The distinctions of bondage and of one's own self and other persons are fictitiously shaped by one's own avidyâ; for they are unreal like the distinctions seen by a dreaming person.—Other bodies also have a Self through me only; for they are bodies like this my body.—Other bodies also are fictitiously shaped by my avidyâ; for they are bodies or effects, or non-intelligent or fictitious creations, as this my body is.—The whole class of intelligent subjects is nothing but *me*; for they are of intelligent nature; what is *not me* is seen to be of non-intelligent nature; as e. g. jars.—It thus follows that the distinctions of one's own self and other persons, of souls bound and released, of pupils and teachers, and so on, are fictitiously created by the avidyâ of one intelligent subject.

The fact is that the upholder of Duality himself is not

able to account for the distinction of souls bound and released. For as there is an infinity of past aeons, it follows that, even if one soul only should attain release in each aeon, all souls would by this time have attained release; the actual existence of non-released souls cannot thus be rationally accounted for.—But the souls are 'infinite'; this accounts for there being souls not yet released!—What, pray, do you understand by this 'infinity' of souls? Does it mean that they cannot be counted? This we cannot allow, for although a being of limited knowledge may not be able to count them, owing to their large number, the all-knowing Lord surely can count them; if he could not do so it would follow that he is not all-knowing.—But the souls are really numberless, and the Lord's not knowing a definite number which does not exist does not prove that he is not all-knowing!—Not so, we reply. Things which are definitely separate (bhinna) from each other cannot be without number. Souls have a number, because they are separate; just as mustard seeds, beans, earthen vessels, pieces of cloth, and so on. And from their being separate it moreover follows that souls, like earthen vessels, and so on, are non-intelligent, not of the nature of Self, and perishable; and it further follows therefrom that Brahman is not infinite. For by infinity we understand the absence of all limitation. Now on the theory which holds that there is a plurality of separate existences, Brahman which is considered to differ in character from other existences cannot be said to be free from substantial limitation; for substantial limitation means nothing else than the existence of other substances. And what is substantially limited cannot be said to be free from temporal and spatial limitation; for observation shows that it is just those things which differ in nature from other things and thus are substantially limited—such as earthen vessels, and so on—which are also limited in point of space and time. Hence all intelligent existences, including Brahman, being substantially limited, are also limited in point of space and time. But this conclusion leads to a conflict with those scriptural texts which declare Brahman to be free from all limitation whatsoever

('The True, knowledge, infinite is Brahman,' and similar texts), and moreover would imply that the souls as well as Brahman are liable to origination, decay, and so on; for limitation in time means nothing else but a being's passing through the stages of origination, decay, and so on.

The dvaita-view thus being found untenable on all sides, we adhere to our doctrine that this entire world, from Brahmâ down to a blade of grass, springs from the avidyâ attached to Brahman which in itself is absolutely unlimited; and that the distinctions of consciousness of pleasure and pain, and all similar distinctions, explain themselves from the fact of all of them being of the nature of avidyâ, just as the distinctions of which a dreaming person is conscious. The one Brahman, whose nature is eternal self-illuminedness, free from all heterogeneous elements, owing to the influence of avidyâ illusorily manifests itself (vivarttate) in the form of this world; and as thus in reality there exists nothing whatever different from Brahman, we hold that the world is 'non-different' from Brahman.

To this the Dvaitavâdin, i.e. the Vais*eshika, replies as follows. The doctrine that Brahman, which in itself is pure, non-differenced self-illuminedness, has its own true nature hidden by avidyâ and hence sees plurality within itself, is in conflict with all the valid means of right knowledge; for as Brahman is without parts, obscuration, i.e. cessation, of the light of Brahman, would mean complete destruction of Brahman; so that the hypothesis of obscuration is altogether excluded. This and other arguments have been already set forth; as also that the hypothesis of obscuration contradicts other views held by the Advaitin. Nor is there any proof for the assertion that effects apart from their causes are mere error, like shell-silver, the separate existence of the effect being refuted by Reasoning; for as a matter of fact there is no valid reasoning of the kind. The assertion that the cause only is real because it persists, while the non-continuous effects —such as jars and waterpots—are unreal, has also been refuted before, on the ground that the fact of a thing not existing at one place and one time does not sublate its real existence at another time and place. Nor is there any soundness in the argumentation that the effect is false because, owing to its being perceived and its being perishable, it cannot be defined either as real or unreal. For a thing's being perceived and its being perishable does not prove the thing's falseness, but only its non-permanency. To prove a thing's falseness it is required to show that it is sublated (i. e. that its non-existence is proved by valid means) with reference to that very place and time in connexion with which it is perceived; but that a thing is sublated with reference to a place and time *other* than those in connexion with which it is perceived, proves only that the thing does not exist in connexion with that place and time, but not that it is false. This view also may be put in technical form, viz. effects such as jars and the like are real because they are not sublated with regard to their definite place and time; just as the Self is.—Nor is there any truth in the assertion that the effect cannot originate from the cause either modified or unmodified; for the effect may originate from the cause if connected with certain favouring conditions of place, time, &c. Nor can you show any proof for the assertion that the cause, whether modified or non-modified, cannot enter into connexion with such favouring conditions; as a matter of fact the cause may very well, without being modified, enter into such connexion.—But from this it follows that the cause must have been previously connected with those conditions, since previously also it was equally unmodified!—Not so, we reply. The connexion with favouring conditions of time, place, &c., into which the cause enters, depends on some other cause, and not therefore on the fact of its not being modified. No fault then can be found with the view of the cause, when having entered into a special state depending on its connexion with time, place, &c., producing the effect. Nor can it be denied in any way that the cause possesses originative agency with regard to the effect; for such agency is actually observed, and cannot be proved to be irrational.—Further there is no proof for the assertion that originative agency cannot belong either to mere gold or to a (first) effect of gold such as coined gold, or to gold in so far as forming the substrate for coins and the like; for as a matter of fact mere gold (gold in general), if connected with the helpful factors mentioned above, may very well possess originative capacity. To say that we do not perceive any effect different from gold is futile; for as a matter of fact we perceive the svastika-ornament which is different from mere gold, and the existence of different terms and ideas moreover proves the existence of different things. Nor have we here to do with a mere error analogous to that of shell-silver. For a real effected thing, such as a golden ornament, is perceived during the whole period intervening between its origination and destruction, and such perception is not sublated with regard to that time and place. Nor is there any valid line of reasoning to sublate that perception. That at the same time when the previously non-perceived svastika-ornament is perceived the gold also is recognised, is due to the fact of the gold persisting as the substrate of the ornament, and hence such recognition of the causal substance does not disprove the reality of the effect.—And the attempts to prove the unreality of the world by means of scriptural texts we have already disposed of in a previous part of this work.

We further object to the assertion that it is one Self which bestows on all bodies the property of being connected with the Self; as from this it would follow that one person is conscious of all the pains and pleasures caused by all bodies. For, as seen in the case of Saubhari and others, it is owing to the oneness of the Self that one person is conscious of the pains and pleasures due to several bodies. Nor again must you allege that the non-consciousness (on the part of one Self of all pleasures and pains whatever) is due to the plurality of the Egos, which are the subjects of cognition, and not to the plurality of Selfs; for the Self is none other than the subject of cognition and the Ego. The organ of egoity (aha*m*kâra), on the other hand, which is the same as the internal organ (anta*h*kara*n*a), cannot be the knowing subject, for it is of a non-intelligent nature, and is a mere instrument like the body and the sense-organs. This also has been proved before.—Nor is there any proof for your assertion that all bodies must be held to spring from the avidyâ of one subject, because they are bodies, non-intelligent, effects, fictitious. For that all bodies are the fictitious creations of avidyâ is not true; since that which is not sublated by valid means of proof must be held to be real.—Nor again can you uphold the assertion that all intelligent subjects are non-different, i.e. one, because we observe that whatever is other than a subject of cognition is non-intelligent; for this also is disproved by the fact of the plurality of intelligent subjects as proved by the individual distribution, among them, of pleasures and pains.—You have further maintained 'Through me only all bodies are animated by a Self; they are the fictitious creations of *my* avidyâ; *I* alone constitute the whole aggregate of intelligent subjects,' and, on the basis of these averments, have attempted to prove the oneness of the Ego. But all this is nothing but the random talk of a person who has not mastered even the principles of his own theory; for according to your theory the Self is pure intelligence to which the whole distinction of 'I,' 'Thou,' &c., is altogether foreign. Moreover, if it be held that everything different from pure, non-differenced intelligence is false, it follows that all effort spent on learning the Veda with a view to Release is fruitless, for the Veda also is the effect of avidyâ, and the effort spent on it therefore is analogous to the effort of taking hold of the silver wrongly imagined in the shell. Or, to put it from a different point of view, all effort devoted to Release is purposeless, since it is the effect of knowledge depending on teachers of merely fictitious existence. Knowledge produced by texts such as 'Thou art that' does not put an end to bondage, because it is produced by texts which are the fictitious product of avidyâ; or because it is itself of the nature of avidyâ; or because it has for its abode knowing subjects, who are mere creatures of avidyâ; or because it is the product of a process of study which depends on teachers who are the mere creatures of avidyâ; it is thus no better than knowledge resting on texts teaching how bondage is to be put an end to, which one might have heard in a dream. Or, to put the matter again from a different point of view, Brahman constituted by pure non-differenced intelligence is false, since it is to be attained by knowledge, which is the effect of avidyâ; or since it is to be attained by knowledge abiding in knowing subjects who are mere figments of avidyâ; or because it is attained through knowledge which is the mere figment of avidyâ. For whatever is attained through knowledge of that kind is false; as e.g. the things seen in dreams or a town of the Gandharvas (Fata Morgana).

Nor does Brahman, constituted by pure non-differenced intelligence, shine forth by itself, so as not to need—for its cognition—other means of knowledge. And that that self-luminous knowledge which you declare to be borne witness to by itself, really consists in the knowledge of particular objects of knowledge—such knowledge abiding in particular cognising subjects—this also has been proved previously. And the different arguments which were set forth as proving Brahman's non-differenced nature, are sufficiently refuted by what we have said just now as to all such arguments themselves being the products of avidyâ.

Nor again is there any sense in the theory that the principle of non-differenced intelligence 'witnesses' avidyâ, and implicates itself in the error of the world. For 'witnessing' and error are observed to abide only in definite conscious subjects, not in consciousness in general. Nor can that principle of pure intelligence be proved to possess illumining power or light depending on itself only. For by light (enlightenment) we can understand nothing but definite well-established knowledge (siddhi) on the part of some knowing subject with regard to some particular object. It is on this basis only that you yourself prove the self-illuminedness of your universal principle; to an absolutely non-differenced intelligence not implying the distinction of subject and object such 'svayamprakâsatâ' could not possibly belong. With regard again to what you so loudly proclaim at your meetings, viz. that real effects are seen to spring even from unreal causes, we point out that although you allow to such effects, being non-sublated as it were, a kind of existence called 'empirical' (or 'conventional'—vyâvahârika), you yourself acknowledge that fundamentally they are nothing but products of avidyâ; you thus undermine your own position. We have, on the other hand, already disposed of this your view above, when proving that in all cases effects are originated by real causes only. Nor may you plead that what perception tells us in such cases is contradicted by Scripture; for as, according to you, Scripture itself is an effect, and hence of the essence of avidyâ, it is in no better case than the instances quoted.—You have further declared that, although Brahman is to be attained only through unreal knowledge, yet it is real since when once attained it is not sublated by any subsequent cognition. But this reasoning also is not valid; for when it has once been ascertained that some principle is attained through knowledge resting on a vicious basis, the fact that we are not aware of a subsequent sublation of that principle is irrelevant. That the principle 'the reality of things is a universal Void' is false, we conclude therefrom that the reasoning leading to that principle is ascertained to be ill-founded, although we are not aware of any subsequent truth sublating that principle. Moreover, for texts such as 'There is here no plurality whatsoever,' 'Knowledge, bliss is Brahman,' the absence of subsequent sublation is claimed on the ground that they negative the whole aggregate of things different from mere intelligence, and hence are later in order than all other texts (which had established that aggregate of things). But somebody may rise and say 'the Reality is a Void,' and thus negative the existence of the principle of mere Intelligence also; and the latter principle is thus sublated by the assertion as to the Void, which is later in order than the texts which it negatives. On the other hand the assertion as to the Void being the universal principle is not liable to subsequent sublation; for it is impossible for any negation to go beyond it. And as to resting on a vicious basis, there is in that respect no difference between Perception and the other means of knowledge, and the view of general unreality, founded on the Vedânta. The proper conclusion therefore is that all cognitions whatsoever abide in real subjects of cognition and are themselves real, consisting in mental certainty with regard to special objects. Some of these cognitions rest on defects which themselves are real; others spring from a combination of causes, real and free from all defect. Unless we admit all this we shall not be able to account in a satisfactory way for the distinction of things true and things false, and for all empirical thought. For empirical thought, whether true or of the nature of error, presupposes inward light (illumination) in the form of certainty with regard to a particular object, and belonging to a real knowing subject; mere non-differenced Being, on the other hand (not particularised in the form of a knowing subject), cannot be the cause of states of consciousness, whether referring to real or unreal things, and cannot therefore form the basis of empirical thought.

Against our opponent's argument that pure Being must be held the real substrate of all erroneous superimposition (adhyâsa), for the reason that no error can exist without a substrate, we remark that an error may take place even when its substrate is unreal, in the same way as an error may exist even when the defect (giving rise to the error), the abode of the defect, the subject of cognition and the cognition itself are unreal. The argument thus loses its force. Possibly he will now argue that as an error is never seen to exist where the substrate is unreal, the reality of pure Being (as furnishing the required basis for error) must necessarily be admitted. But, we point out, it also is a fact that errors are never observed where the defect, the abode of the defect, the knowing subject and the act of knowledge are unreal; and if we pay regard to observation, we must therefore admit the reality of all these factors as well. There is really no difference between the two cases, unless our opponent chooses to be obstinate.

You further asserted that, on the theory of many really different Selfs, it would follow from the infinity of the past aeons that all souls must have been released before this, none being left in the state of bondage; and that hence the actually observed distinction of souls bound and released remains unexplained. But this argumentation is refuted by the fact of the souls also being infinite. You indeed maintained that, if the souls are really separate, they must necessarily have a definite number like beans, mustard-seeds, earthen vessels, and so on; but these instances are beside the point, as earthen vessels, and so on, are also infinite in number.—But do we not actually see that all these things have definite numbers, 'Here are ten jars; a thousand beans,' &c.?—True, but those numbers do not belong to the essential nature of jars, and so on, but only to jars in so far as connected with time, place, and other limiting adjuncts. And that souls also have definite numbers in this sense, we readily admit. And from this it does not follow that all souls should be released; for essentially the souls are infinite (in number).—Nor are you entitled to maintain that the real separation of individual souls would imply that, as earthen vessels and the like, they are non-intelligent, not of the nature of Self, and perishable. For the circumstance of individuals of one species being distinct from each other, does in no way imply that they possess the characteristics of things belonging to another species: the individual separation of jars does not imply their having the characteristics of pieces of cloth.—You further maintain that from the hypothesis of a real plurality of souls it follows that Brahman is substantially limited, and in consequence of this limited with regard to time and space also, and that hence its infinity is disproved. But this also is a mistaken conclusion. Things substantially limited may be limited more or less with regard to time and place: there is no invariable rule on this point, and the measure of their connexion with space and time has hence to be determined in dependence on other means of knowledge. Now Brahman's connexion with *all* space and *all* time results from such other means of proof, and hence there is no contradiction (between this non-limitation with regard to space and time, and its limitation in point of substance—

which is due to the existence of other souls).—But mere substantial limitation, as meaning the absence of non-limitation of any kind, by itself proves that Brahman is not infinite!—Well, then you yourself are in no better case; for you admit that Brahman is something different from avidyâ. From this admission it follows that Brahman also is something 'different,' and thus all the disadvantages connected with the view of difference cling to your theory as well. If on the other hand it should not be allowed that Brahman differs in nature from avidyâ, then Brahman's nature itself is constituted by avidyâ, and the text defining Brahman as 'the True, knowledge, infinite' is contrary to sense.—If the reality of 'difference' is not admitted, then there is no longer any distinction between the proofs and the mutual objections set forth by the advocates of different theories, and we are landed in general confusion. The proof of infinity, we further remark, rests altogether on the absence of limitation of space and time, not on absence of substantial limitation; absence of such limitation is something very much akin to the 'horn of a hare' and is perceived nowhere. On the view of difference, on the other hand, the whole world, as constituting Brahman's body, is its mode, and Brahman is thus limited neither through itself nor through other things.—We thus arrive at the conclusion that, as effects are real in so far as different from their cause, the effect of Brahman, i.e. the entire world, is different from Brahman.

Against this view the Sûtra now declares itself as follows.—The non-difference of the world from Brahman, the highest cause, follows from 'what begins with the word ârambhana'—which proves such non-difference; 'what begins with the word ârambhana' means those clauses at the head of which that word is met with, viz. 'vâ*k*ârambhana*m* vikâro nâmadheya*m* m*ri*ttikety eva satyam'; 'Being only this was in the beginning, one only, without a second'; 'it thought, may I be many, may I grow forth; it sent forth fire'; 'having entered with this living Self'; 'In the True, my son, all these creatures have their root, in the True they dwell, in the True they rest'; 'In that all that exists has its Self; it is the True, it is the Self; and thou art it, O *S*vetaketu' (*Kh.* Up. VI, 1-8)—it is these clauses and others of similar purport which are met with in other chapters, that the Sûtra refers to. For these texts prove the non-difference from Brahman of the world consisting of non-sentient and sentient beings. This is as follows. The teacher, bearing in his mind the idea of Brahman constituting the sole cause of the entire world and of the non-difference of the effect from the cause, asks the pupil, 'Have you ever asked for that instruction by which the non-heard is heard, the non-perceived is perceived, the not known is known'; wherein there is implied the promise that, through the knowledge of Brahman the general cause, its effect, i.e. the whole Universe, will be known? The pupil, not knowing that Brahman is the sole cause of the Universe, raises a doubt as to the possibility of one thing being known through another, 'How then, Sir, is that instruction?' and the teacher thereupon, in order to convey the notion of Brahman being the sole universal cause, quotes an instance showing that the non-difference of the effect from the cause is proved by ordinary experience, 'As by one clod of clay there is known everything that is made of clay'; the meaning being 'as jars, pots, and the like, which are fashioned out of one piece of clay, are known through the cognition of that clay, since their substance is not different from it.' In order to meet the objection that according to Ka*n*âda's doctrine the effect constitutes a substance different from the cause, the teacher next proceeds to prove the non-difference of the effect from the cause by reference to ordinary experience, 'vâ*k*ârambhana*m* vikâro nâmadheya*m* m*ri*ttikety eva satyam.' Ârambhanam must here be explained as that which is taken or touched (â-rabh = â-labh; and 'âlambha*h* spar*s*a-hi*m*sayo*h*'); compare Pâ*n*ini III, 3, 113, as to the form and meaning of the word. 'Vâ*k*â,' 'on account of speech,' we take to mean 'on account of activity preceded by speech'; for activities such as the fetching of water in a pitcher are preceded by speech, 'Fetch water in the pitcher,' and so on. For the bringing about of such activity, the material clay (which had been mentioned just before) touches (enters into contact with) an effect (vikâra), i. e. a particular make or configuration, distinguished by having a broad bottom and resembling the shape of a belly, and a special name (nâmadheya), viz. *pitcher*, and so on, which is applied to that effect; or, to put it differently, to the end that certain activities may be accomplished, the substance clay receives a new configuration and a new name[1]. Hence jars and other things of clay are clay (m*ri*ttikâ), i. e. are of the substance of clay, only; this *only* is true (satyam), i. e. known through authoritative means of proof; *only* (eva), because the effects are not known as different substances. One and the same substance therefore, such as clay or gold, gives occasion for different ideas and words only as it assumes different configurations; just as we observe that one and the same Devadatta becomes the object of different ideas and terms, and gives rise to different effects, according to the different stages of life—youth, old age, &c.—which he has reached.—The fact of our saying 'the jar has perished' while yet the clay persists, was referred to by the Pûrvapakshin as proving that the effect is something different from the cause; but this view is disproved by the view held by us that origination, destruction, and so on, are merely different states of one and the same causal substance. According as one and the same substance is in this or that state, there belong to it different terms and different activities, and these different states may rightly be viewed as depending on the activity

[1] The meaning of the four words constituting the clause therefore would be, 'On account of speech (i. e. for the sake of the accomplishment of certain activities such as the bringing of water, which are preceded by speech), there is touched (by the previously mentioned substance clay) an effect and a name; i. e. for the sake of, &c., clay modifies itself into an effect having a special name.' The Commentary remarks that 'ârambhanam' cannot be taken in the sense of upâdâna; since, on the theory of the unreality of effects, the effect is originated not by speech but by thought (imagination) only; and on the pari*n*âma doctrine the effect is likewise not originated by speech but by Brahman.

of an agent. The objections again which are connected with the theory of 'manifestation' are refuted by our not acknowledging such a thing at all as 'manifestation.' Nor does the admission of origination render the doctrine of the reality of the effect irrational; for it is only the Real that originates.—But it is a contradiction to maintain that that which previously exists is originated!—This, we reply, is the objection of a person who knows nothing about the true nature of origination and destruction. A substance enters into different states in succession; what passes away is the substance in its previous states, what originates is the substance in its subsequent states. As thus the substance in all its states has being, there is nothing irrational in the satkârya theory.—But the admission of the origination of a non-existing state lands us in the asatkârya theory!—If he, we retort, who holds the asatkârya theory is of opinion that the origination of the effect does not itself originate, he is similarly landed in the satkârya theory; and if he holds that the origination itself originates, he is led into a *regressus in infinitum*. According to us, on the other hand, who hold that states are incapable of being apprehended and of acting apart from that of which they are states, origination, destruction, and so on, belong only to a substance which is in a certain state; and on this theory no difficulty remains. And in the same way as the state of being a jar results from the clay abandoning the condition of being either two halves of a jar or a lump of clay, plurality results from a substance giving up the state of oneness, and oneness from the giving up of plurality; hence this point also gives rise to no difficulty.

We now consider the whole *Kh*ândogya-text in connexion. 'Sad eva somye*dam agra âsîd ekam evâdvitîyam.' This means—That which is Being, i.e. this world which now, owing to the distinction of names and forms, bears a manifold shape, was in the beginning one only, owing to the absence of the distinction of names and forms. And as, owing to the 'Sat' being endowed with all powers, a further ruling principle is out of the question, the world was also 'without a second.' This proves the non-difference of the world from Brahman. In the same way the next clause also, 'It thought, may I be many, may I grow forth,' which describes the creation of the world as proceeding from a resolve of the Self to differentiate itself into a world consisting of manifold beings movable and immovable, viz. Fire, and so on, enables us to determine that the effect, i. e. the world, is non-different from the highest cause, i. e. the highest Brahman.

And as now a further doubt may arise as to how the highest Brahman with all its perfections can be designated as one with the world, and how the world can be designated as one, without a second, not dependent on another guiding principle; and how this thought, i.e. the resolution, on the part of the Supreme cause, of differentiating itself into a manifold world, and the creation corresponding to that resolution are possible; the text continues, 'That deity thought—Let me now enter those three beings with this living Self (*g*îva âtman) and distinguish names and forms'—which means, 'Let me make the aggregate of non-sentient things (for this is meant by the "three beings") to possess various names and forms, by entering into them by means of the *g*îva which is of the nature of my Self.' The possession of names and forms must thus be understood to be effected by the *g*îva entering into matter as its Self. There is another scriptural text also which makes it clear that the highest Brahman enters, so as to be their Self, into the world together with the *g*îvas. 'Having sent forth that he entered into it. Having entered into it he became sat and tyat (i.e. sentient and non-sentient beings).' And that the entire aggregate of sentient and non-sentient beings, gross or subtle, in their effected or their causal state, constitutes the body of the highest Brahman, and that on the other hand the highest Brahman constitutes their Self—this is proved by the antaryâmin-brâhma*n*a and similar texts. This disposes of the doubt raised above. Since Brahman abides, as their Self, in all non-sentient matter together with the *g*îvas, Brahman is denoted by the term 'world' in so far only as it (i.e.

Brahman) has non-sentient and sentient beings for its body, and hence utterances such as 'This which is Being only was in the beginning one only' are unobjectionable in every way. All change and all imperfection belongs only to the beings constituting Brahman's body, and Brahman itself is thus proved to be free from all imperfection, a treasure as it were of all imaginable holy qualites. This point will be further elucidated under II, 1, 22.—The *Kh*ândogya-text then further teaches that all sentient and non-sentient beings have their Self in Brahman 'in that all this has its Self'; and further inculcates this truth in 'Thou art that.'

Texts met with in other sections also teach this same non-difference of the general cause and its effect: 'All this indeed is Brahman' (*Kh.* Up. III, 14, 1); 'When the Self has been seen, heard, perceived, and known, then all this is known' (B*ri*. Up. IV, 5, 6); 'That Self is all this' (B*ri*. Up. II, 4, 6); 'Brahman indeed is all this' (Mai. Up. IV, 6); 'The Self only is all this' (*Kh.* Up. VII, 25, 2). Other texts, too, negative difference: 'Everything abandons him who looks for anything elsewhere than in the Self' (B*ri*. Up. II, 4, 6); 'There is not any plurality here' (B*ri*. Up. IV, 4, 19); 'From death to death goes he who sees here any plurality' (B*ri*. Up. IV, 4, 19). And in the same spirit the passage 'For where there is duality as it were, one sees the other; but when for him the Self has become all, whereby then should he see and whom?' (B*ri*. Up. II, 4, 13)—in setting forth that the view of duality belongs to him who does not know and the view of non-duality to him who knows—intimates that non-difference only is real.

It is in this way that we prove, by means of the texts beginning with ârambha*n*a, that the world is non-different from the universal cause, i.e. the highest Brahman. Brahman only, having the aggregate of sentient and non-sentient beings for its body and hence for its modes (prakâra), is denoted by all words whatsoever. The body of this Brahman is sometimes constituted by sentient and non-sentient beings in their subtle state, when—just owing to that subtle state—they are incapable of being (conceived and) designated as apart from Brahman whose body they form: Brahman is then in its so-called causal condition. At other times the body of Brahman is constituted by all sentient and non-sentient beings in their gross, manifest state, owing to which they admit of being thought and spoken of as having distinct names and forms: Brahman then is in its 'effected' state. The effect, i. e. the world, is thus seen to be non-different from the cause, i. e. the highest Brahman. And that in the effected as well as the causal state of Brahman's body as constituted by sentient and non-sentient beings, and of Brahman embodied therein, perfections and imperfections are distributed according to the difference of essential nature between Brahman and its body, as proved by hundreds of scriptural texts, we have shown above.

Those on the other hand who establish the non-difference of cause and effect, on the basis of the theory of the effect's non-reality, are unable to prove what they wish to prove; for the True and the False cannot possibly be one. If these two were one, it would follow either that Brahman is false or that the world is real.—Those again who (like Bhâskara) hold the effect also to be real—the difference of the soul and Brahman being due to limiting conditions, while their non-difference is essential; and the difference as well as the non-difference of Brahman and matter being essential—enter into conflict with all those texts which declare that the soul and Brahman are distinct in so far as the soul is under the power of karman while Brahman is free from all evil, &c., and all those texts which teach that non-sentient matter undergoes changes while Brahman does not. For as, according to them, nothing exists but Brahman and the limiting adjuncts, Brahman—as being indivisible—must be undivided while entering into connexion with the upâdhis, and hence itself undergoes a change into inferior forms. And if they say that it is only the power (*s*akti), not Brahman itself, which undergoes a change; this also is of no avail since Brahman and its power are non-different.

Others again (Yâdavaprakâ*s*a) hold that the general

cause, i.e. Brahman, is pure Being in which all distinctions and changes such as being an enjoying subject, and so on, have vanished, while however it is endowed with all possible potentialities. During a pralaya this causal substance abides self-luminous, with all the distinctions of consciousness of pleasure and pain gone to rest, comparable to the soul of a man held by dreamless sleep, different however in nature from mere non-sentient matter. During the period of a creation, on the other hand, just as the substance called clay assumes the forms of jars, platters, and so on, or as the water of the sea turns itself into foam, waves, bubbles, and so on, the universal causal substance abides in the form of a triad of constituent parts, viz. enjoying subjects, objects of enjoyment, and a ruler. The attributes of being a ruler, or an object of enjoyment, or an enjoying subject, and the perfections and imperfections depending on those attributes, are therefore distributed in the same way as the attributes of being a jar or pitcher or platter; and the different effects of these attributes are distributed among different parts of the substance, clay. The objects of enjoyment, subjects of enjoyment, and the ruler are one, on the other hand, in so far as 'that which is' constitutes their substance; just as jars, platters and pitchers are one in so far as their substance is constituted by clay. It is thus one substance only, viz. 'that which is,' that appears in different conditions, and it is in this sense that the world is non-different from Brahman.—But this theory is really in conflict with all Scripture, Sm*ri*ti, Itihâsa, Purâ*n*a and Reasoning. For Scripture, Sm*ri*ti, Itihâsa and Purâ*n*a alike teach that there is one supreme cause, viz. Brahman—a being that is the Lord of all Lords, all-knowing, all-powerful, instantaneously realising all its purposes, free of all blemish, not limited either by place or time, enjoying supreme unsurpassable bliss. Nor can it be held that above the Lord there is 'pure Being' of which the Lord is a part only. For 'This which is "being" only was in the beginning one only, without a second; it thought, may I be many, may I grow forth' (*Kh*. Up. VI, 2, 3); 'Verily, in the beginning this was Brahman, one only. Being one it was not strong enough. It created the most excellent Kshattra, viz. those Kshattras among the Devas—Indra, Varu*n*a, Soma, Rudra, Par*g*anya, Yama, M*ri*tyu, Î*s*âna' (B*ri*. Up. I, 4, 11); 'In the beginning all this was Self, one only; there was nothing whatsoever else blinking. He thought, shall I send forth worlds' (Ait. Âr. II, 4, 1, 1, 2); 'There was in truth Nârâya*n*a only, not Brahmâ, not Î*s*âna, nor heaven and earth, nor the nakshatras, nor the waters, nor Agni, nor Soma, nor Sûrya. Being alone he felt no delight. Of him merged in meditation' &c. (Mahânâ. Up. I, 1)—these and other texts prove that the highest cause is the Lord of all Lords, Nârâya*n*a. For as the terms 'Being,' 'Brahman,' 'Self,' which are met with in sections treating of the same topic, are in one of those parallel sections particularised by the term 'Nârâya*n*a,' it follows that they all mean Nârâya*n*a. That the Lord only is the universal cause is shown by the following text also, 'He the highest great lord of lords, the highest deity of deities—he is the cause, the lord of the lords of the organs, and there is of him neither parent nor lord' (*S*vet. Up. VI, 7, 9). Similarly the Manu Sm*ri*ti, 'Then the divine Self-existent (Brahmâ)—desirous to produce from his own body beings of many kind—first with a thought created the waters and placed his seed in them' (Ma. I, 6–8). Itihâsas and Purâ*n*as also declare the Supreme Person only to be the universal cause, 'Nârâya*n*a, of whom the world is the body, of infinite nature, eternal, when desirous to create sent forth from a thousandth part of himself the souls in two divisions.' 'From Vish*n*u the world originated and in him it abides.'

Nor is it possible to hold that the Lord is pure 'Being' only, for such 'Being' is admitted to be an element of the Lord; and moreover all 'Being' has difference. Nor can it be maintained that the Lord's connexion with all his auspicious qualities—knowledge, bliss, and so on—is occasional (adventitious) merely; it rather is essential and hence eternal. Nor may you avail yourself of certain texts—viz. 'His high power (*s*akti) is revealed as manifold, as essential, and (so) his knowledge, strength and action'

(*S*vet. Up. VI, 8); 'He who is all-knowing, all-cognising' (Mu. Up. I, 1, 9), and others—to the end of proving that what is essential is only the Lord's connexion with the *potentialities* (*s*akti) of knowledge, bliss, and so on. For in the *S*vetâ*s*vatara-text the word 'essential' independently qualifies 'knowledge, strength, and action' no less than '*s*akti'; and your explanation would necessitate so-called implication (laksha*n*â). Nor again can it be said that in words such as sarva*gñ*a (all-knowing), the formative suffix expresses potentiality only, as it admittedly does in other words such as pâ*k*aka (cook); for grammar does not teach that all these (k*ri*t) affixes in general express potentiality or capability only. It rather teaches (cp. Pâ*n*ini III, 2, 54) that a few k*ri*t-affixes only have this limited meaning; and in the case of pâ*k*aka and similar words we must assume capability to be denoted, because there is no other explanation open to us.—If, moreover, the Lord were held to be only a part of the Sat it would follow that the Sat, as the whole, would be superior to the Lord just as the ocean is superior to a wave, and this would be in conflict with ever so many scriptural texts which make statements about the Lord, cp. e.g. 'Him the highest great lord of lords'; 'There is none seen like to him or superior' (*S*vet. Up. VI, 7, 8). If, moreover, mere Being is held to be the Self of all and the general whole, and the Lord only a particular part of it, this would imply the stultification of all those texts which declare the Lord to be the general Self and the whole of which all beings are parts; for jars and platters certainly cannot be held to be parts of, and to have their being in, pitchers (which themselves are only special things made of clay). Against this you perhaps will plead that as Being in general is fully present in all its parts, and hence also in that part which is the Lord, all other things may be viewed as having their Self in, and being parts of, him.—But from your principles we might with equal right draw the inference that as Being in general is fully present in the jar, the Lord is a part of the jar and has his Self in that! From enunciations such as 'the jar is,' 'the cloth is,' it appears that Being is an attribute of things, and cannot therefore be a substance and a cause. By the 'being' of a thing we understand the attribute of its being suitable for some definite practical effect; while its 'non-being' means its suitability for an effect of an opposite nature.—Should it on the other hand be held that substances only have being, the (unacceptable) consequence would be that actions, and so on, are non-existent. And if (to avoid this consequence) it were said that the being of actions, and so on, depends on their connexion with substances, it would be difficult to show (what yet should be shown) that 'being' is everywhere of one and the same nature. Moreover, if everything were non-different in so far as 'being,' there would be a universal consciousness of the nature of everything, and from this there would follow a general confusion of all good and evil (i. e. every one would have conscious experience of everything) This point we have explained before. For all these reasons non-difference can only have the meaning set forth by us.—Here the following doubt may arise. In the case of childhood, youth, and so on, we observe that different ideas and different terms are applied to different states of one and the same being; in the case of clay, wood, gold, &c., on the other hand, we observe that different ideas and terms are applied to different things. On what ground then do you determine that in the case of causes and effects, such as e.g. clay and jars, it is mere difference of state on which the difference of ideas and terms is based?—To this question the next Sûtra gives a reply.

16. And because (the cause) is perceived in the existence of the effect.

This means—because gold which is the cause is perceived in the existence of its effects, such as earrings and the like; i.e. on account of the recognition of gold which expresses itself in the judgment 'this earring is gold.' We do not on the other hand perceive the presence of clay, and so on, in gold, and so on. The case of the cause and the effect is thus analagous to that of the child and the youth: the word 'effect' denotes nothing else but the causal substance which has passed over into a different condition. He also who holds the effect to be a new thing acknowledges that the effect is connected with a different state, and as this different state suffices to account for the difference of ideas and words, we are not entitled to assume a new substance which is not perceived. Nor must it be said that the recognition of the gold in the earring is due to generic nature (the two *things* being different, but having the same generic nature); for we perceive no new substance which could be the abode of the generic character. What we actually perceive is one and the same substance possessing the generic characteristics of gold, first in the causal state and then in the effected state. Nor again can it be said that even on the supposition of difference of substance, recognition of the cause in the effect results from the continuity of the so-called intimate cause (samavâyi-kâra*n*a). For where there is difference of substances we do not observe that mere continuity of the abode gives rise to the recognition (of one substance) in the other substance residing in that abode.—But in the case of certain effects, as e.g. scorpions and other vermin which originate from dung, that recognition of the causal substance, i.e. dung (to which you refer as proving the identity of cause and effect), is not observed to take place!—You misstate the case, we reply; here also we *do* recognise in the effect that substance which is the primal cause, viz. earth.—But in smoke, which is the effect of fire, we do not recognise fire!—True! but this does not disprove our case. Fire is only the operative cause of smoke; for smoke originates from damp fuel joined with fire. That smoke is the effect of damp fuel is proved thereby, as well as that both have smell (which shows them to be alike of the substance of earth).—As thus the identity of the substance is perceived in the effect also, we are entitled to conclude that the difference of ideas and terms rests on difference of state only. The effect, therefore, is non-different from the cause.—This is so for the following reason also.

17. And on account of the existence of that which is posterior.

On account of the existence of the posterior, i.e. the effect existing in the cause—for this reason also the effect is non-different from the cause. For in ordinary language as well as in the Veda the effect is spoken of in terms of the cause; as when we say, 'all these things—jars, platters, &c.—were clay only this morning'; or when the Veda says, 'Being only was this in the beginning.'

18. If it be said 'not, on account of the designation of the (effect as the) non-existent; we reply, not so, on account (of such designation being due to) another attribute, (as appears) from the complementary passage, from Reasoning, and from another Vedic text.

The assertion that ordinary speech as well as the Veda acknowledges the existence of the effect in the cause cannot be upheld 'on account of the designation of (the effect as) the non-existent.' For the Veda says, 'Non-being only was this in the beginning' (*Kh.* Up. III, 19, 1); 'Non-being indeed was this in the beginning' (Taitt. Up. II, 6, 1); 'In the beginning truly this was not anything whatever.' And in ordinary language we say 'In the morning all this—jars, platters, and so on,—was not.'—This objection the Sûtra proceeds to refute. 'Not so, on account of such designation being due to another attribute.' The designation of the effected substance as the non-existent is due to the effect having at an earlier time a different quality, i.e. a different constitution; not to its being, as you think, absolutely non-existing. The quality different from the quality of existence is non-existence; that is to say, of the world designated as *this*, the quality of existence is constituted by name and form, while the quality of non-existence consists in the subtle state opposed to name and form.—But how is this known?—'From the complementary passage, from Reasoning, and from another text.' The complementary passage is the one following on the last text quoted above, viz. 'that Non-existent formed the resolve "may I be."' The resolve referred to in this complementary text serving as an inferential sign to determine that the Non-existence spoken of is other than absolute Non-existence, we, on the basis of the observation that all the three texts quoted treat of the same matter, conclude that in the other two texts also the Non-existent has to be understood in the same sense. 'From Reasoning.' Reasoning shows Being and Non-being to be attributes of things. The possession, on the part of clay, of a certain shape, a broad base, a belly-shaped body, and so on, is the cause of our thinking and saying 'the jar exists,' while the connexion, on the part of the clay, with a condition opposed to that of a jar is the cause of our thinking and saying 'the jar does not exist.' A condition of the latter kind is e. g. the clay's existing in the form of two separate halves of a jar, and it is just this and similar conditions of the clay which account for our saying that the jar does not exist. We do not perceive any non-existence of the jar different from the kind of non-existence described; and as the latter sufficiently accounts for all current ideas and expressions as to non-existence, there is no occasion to assume an additional kind of non-existence.—And also 'from another text.' The text meant is that often quoted, 'Being only was this in the beginning.' For there the view of the absolute non-being of the effect is objected to, 'But how could it be thus?' &c., and then the decision is given that from the beginning the world was 'being.' This matter is clearly set forth in the text 'This was then undistinguished; it became distinguished by name and form' (B*ri*. Up. I, 4, 7).

The next two Sûtras confirm the doctrine of the non-difference of the effect from the cause by two illustrative instances.

19. And like a piece of cloth.

As threads when joined in a peculiar cross-arrangement are called a piece of cloth, thus acquiring a new name, a new form, and new functions, so it is with Brahman also.

20. And as the different vital airs.

As the one air, according as it undergoes in the body

different modifications, acquires a new name, new characteristics, and new functions, being then called prâ*n*a, apâna, and so on; thus the one Brahman becomes the world, with its manifold moving and non-moving beings.—The non-difference of the world from Brahman, the highest cause, is thus fully established.

Here terminates the 'ârambha*n*a' adhikara*n*a.

21. From the designation of the 'other' (as non-different from Brahman) there result (Brahman's) not creating what is beneficial, and other imperfections.

'Thou art that'; 'this Self is Brahman'—these and similar texts which declare the non-difference of the world from Brahman, teach, as has been said before, at the same time the non-difference from Brahman of the individual soul also. But an objection here presents itself. If these texts really imply that the 'other one,' i. e. the soul, is Brahman, there will follow certain imperfections on Brahman's part, viz. that Brahman, endowed as it is with omniscience, the power of realising its purposes, and so on, does not create a world of a nature beneficial to itself, but rather creates a world non-beneficial to itself; and the like. This world no doubt is a storehouse of numberless pains, either originating in living beings themselves or due to the action of other natural beings, or caused by supernatural agencies. No rational independent person endeavours to produce what is clearly non-beneficial to himself. And as you hold the view of the non-difference of the world from Brahman, you yourself set aside all those texts which declare Brahman to be different from the soul; for were there such difference, the doctrine of general non-difference could not be established. Should it be maintained that the texts declaring difference refer to difference due to limiting adjuncts, while the texts declaring non-difference mean essential non-difference, we must ask the following question—does the non-conditioned Brahman know, or does it not know, the soul which is essentially non-different from it? If it does not know it, Brahman's omniscience has to be abandoned. If, on the other hand, it knows it, then

Brahman is conscious of the pains of the soul—which is non-different from Brahman—as its own pains; and from this there necessarily follows an imperfection, viz. that Brahman does not create what is beneficial and does create what is non-beneficial to itself. If, again, it be said that the difference of the soul and Brahman is due to Nescience on the part of both, and that the texts declaring difference refer to difference of this kind, the assumption of Nescience belonging to the soul leads us to the very alternatives just stated and to their respective results. Should the a*gñ*âna, on the other hand, belong to Brahman, we point out that Brahman, whose essential nature is self-illuminedness, cannot possibly be conscious of a*gñ*âna and the creation of the world effected by it. And if it be said that the light of Brahman is obscured by a*gñ*âna, we point to all the difficulties, previously set forth, which follow from this hypothesis—to obscure light means to make it cease, and to make cease the light of Brahman, of whom light is the essential nature, means no less than to destroy Brahman itself. The view of Brahman being the cause of the world thus shows itself to be untenable.—This primâ facie view the next Sûtra refutes.

22. But (Brahman is) additional, on account of the declaration of difference.

The word 'but' sets aside the primâ facie view. To the individual soul capable of connexion with the various kinds of pain there is additional, i.e. from it there is different, Brahman.—On what ground?—'Owing to the declaration of difference.' For Brahman is spoken of as different from the soul in the following texts:—'He who dwells in the Self and within the Self, whom the Self does not know, of whom the Self is the body, who rules the Self within, he is thy Self, the ruler within, the immortal' (B*ri*. Up. III, 7, 22); 'Knowing as separate the Self and the Mover, blessed by him he gains Immortality' (*S*vet. Up. I, 6); 'He is the cause, the Lord of the lords of the organs' (i.e. the individual souls) (*S*vet. Up. VI, 9); 'One of them eats the sweet fruit; without eating the other looks on' (*S*vet. Up.

IV, 6); 'There are two, the one knowing, the other not knowing, both unborn, the one a ruler, the other not a ruler' (*S*vet. Up. I, 9); 'Embraced by the prâ*g*ña Self' (B*ri*. Up. IV, 3, 21); 'Mounted by the prâ*g*ña Self' (B*ri*. Up. IV, 3, 35); 'From that the ruler of mâyâ sends forth all this, in that the other is bound up through mâyâ (*S*vet. Up. IV, 9); 'the Master of the Pradhâna and the souls, the lord of the gu*n*as' (*S*vet. Up. VI, 16); 'the eternal among eternals, the intelligent among the intelligent, who, one, fulfils the desires of many' (*S*vet. Up. VI, 13); 'who moves within the Unevolved, of whom the Unevolved is the body, whom the Unevolved does not know; who moves within the Imperishable, of whom the Imperishable is the body, whom the Imperishable does not know; who moves within Death, of whom Death is the body, whom Death does not know; he is the inner Self of all beings, free from evil, the divine one, the one God, Nârâya*n*a'; and other similar texts.

23. And as in the analogous case of stones and the like, there is impossibility of that.

In the same way as it is impossible that the different non-sentient things such as stones, iron, wood, herbs, &c., which are of an extremely low constitution and subject to constant change, should be one in nature with Brahman, which is faultless, changeless, fundamentally antagonistic to all that is evil, &c. &c.; so it is also impossible that the individual soul, which is liable to endless suffering, and a mere wretched glowworm as it were, should be one with Brahman who, as we know from the texts, comprises within himself the treasure of all auspicious qualities, &c. &c. Those texts, which exhibit Brahman and the soul in co-ordination, must be understood as conveying the doctrine, founded on passages such as 'of whom the Self is the body,' that as the *g*îva constitutes Brahman's body and Brahman abides within the *g*îva as its Self, Brahman has the *g*îva for its mode; and with this doctrine the co-ordination referred to is not only not in conflict but even confirms it—as we have shown repeatedly, e.g. under Sû. I, 4, 22. Brahman in all its states has the souls and matter for its body; when the souls and matter are in their subtle state Brahman is in its causal condition; when, on the other hand, Brahman has for its body souls and matter in their gross state, it is 'effected' and then called world. In this way the co-ordination above referred to fully explains itself. The world is non-different from Brahman in so far as it is its effect. There is no confusion of the different characteristic qualities; for liability to change belongs to non-sentient matter, liability to pain to sentient souls, and the possession of all excellent qualities to Brahman: hence the doctrine is not in conflict with any scriptural text. That even in the state of non-separation—described in texts such as, 'Being only this was in the beginning'—the souls joined to non-sentient matter persist in a subtle condition and thus constitute Brahman's body must necessarily be admitted; for that the souls at that time also persist in a subtle form is shown under Sûtras II, 1, 34; 35. Non-division, at that time, is possible in so far as there is no distinction of names and forms. It follows from all this that Brahman's causality is not contrary to reason.

Those, on the other hand, who explain the difference, referred to in Sûtra 22, as the difference between the *g*îva in its state of bondage and the *g*îva in so far as free from avidyâ, i. e. the unconditioned Brahman, implicate themselves in contradictions. For the *g*îva, in so far as free from avidyâ, is neither all-knowing, nor the Lord of all, nor the cause of all, nor the Self of all, nor the ruler of all—it in fact possesses none of those characteristics on which the scriptural texts found the difference of the released soul; for according to the view in question all those attributes are the mere figment of Nescience. Nor again can the Sûtra under discussion be said to refer to the distinction, from the individual soul, of a Lord fictitiously created by avidyâ—a distinction analogous to that which a man in the state of avidyâ makes between the shell and the silver; for it is the task of the Vedânta to convey a knowledge of that true Brahman which is introduced as the object of enquiry in the first Sûtra ('Now then the enquiry into Brahman') and which is the cause of the origination and so on of the world, and what they at this point are engaged in is to refute the objections raised against the doctrine of that Brahman on the basis of Smriti and Reasoning.—The two Sûtras II, 1, 8; 9 really form a complementary statement to what is proved in the present adhikarana; for their purport is to show also that things of different nature can stand to each other in the relation of cause and effect. And the Sûtra II, 1, 7 has reference to what is contained in the previous adhikarana.

Here terminates the adhikarana of 'designation of the other.'

24. Should it be said that (it is) not, on account of the observation of employment; we say, not so; for as in the case of milk.

We have so far determined that it is in no way unreasonable to hold that the highest Brahman, which is all-knowing, capable of realising its purposes, &c., has all beings, sentient and non-sentient, for its body, and hence constitutes the Self of all and differs in nature from everything else. We now proceed to show that it is not unreasonable to hold that, possessing all those attributes, it is able to effect by its mere will and wish the creation of this entire manifold Universe.—But, it may here be said, it is certainly a matter of observation that agents of limited power are obliged to employ a number of instrumental agencies in order to effect their purposes; but how should it follow therefrom that the view of the all-powerful Brahman producing the world without such instrumental agencies is in any way irrational?—As, we reply, it is observed in ordinary life that even such agents as possess the capability of producing certain effects stand in need of certain instruments, some slow-witted person may possibly imagine that Brahman, being destitute of all such instruments, is incapable of creating the world. It is this doubt which we have to dispel. It is seen that potters, weavers, &c., who produce jars, cloth, and the like, are incapable of actually producing unless they make use of certain implements, although they may fully possess the specially required skill. Men destitute of such skill are not capable of production, even with the help of implements; those having the capacity produce by means of the instruments only. This leads to the conclusion that Brahman also, although possessing all imaginable powers, is not capable of creating the world without employing the required instrumental agencies. But before creation there existed nothing that could have assisted him, as we know from texts such as 'Being only this was in the beginning'; 'there was Nârâya*n*a alone.' Brahman's creative agency thus cannot be rendered plausible; and hence the primâ facie view set forth in the earlier part of the Sûtra, 'Should it be said that (it is) not; on account of the observation of employment (of instruments).'

This view is set aside by the latter part of the Sûtra, 'not so; for as in the case of milk.' It is by no means a fact that every agent capable of producing a certain effect stands in need of instruments. Milk, e.g. and water, which have the power of producing certain effects, viz. sour milk and ice respectively, produce these effects unaided. Analogously Brahman also, which possesses the capacity of producing everything, may actually do so without using instrumental aids. The 'for' in the Sûtra is meant to point out the fact that the proving instances are generally known, and thus to indicate the silliness of the objection. Whey and similar ingredients are indeed sometimes mixed with milk, but not to the end of making the milk turn sour, but merely in order to accelerate the process and give to the sour milk a certain flavour.

25. And as in the case of the gods and so on, in (their) world.

As the gods and similar exalted beings create, each in his own world, whatever they require by their mere volition, so the Supreme Person creates by his mere volition the entire world. That the gods about whose powers we know from the Veda only (not through perception) are here quoted as supplying a proving instance, is done in order to facilitate the comprehension of the creative power of Brahman, which is also known through the Veda.—Here terminates the adhikara*n*a of 'the observation of employment.'

26. Or the consequence of the entire (Brahman entering into the effect), and stultification of (Brahman's) being devoid of parts.

'Being only was this in the beginning'; 'This indeed was in the beginning not anything'; 'The Self alone indeed was this in the beginning'—these and other texts state that in the beginning Brahman was one only, i. e. without parts—that means: Brahman, in its causal state, was without parts because then all distinction of matter and souls had disappeared. This one, non-divided, Brahman thereupon having formed the resolution of being many divided itself into the aggregate of material things—ether, air, and so on—and the aggregate of souls from Brahmâ down to blades of grass. This being so, it must be held that the entire highest Brahman entered into the effected state; that its intelligent part divided itself into the individual souls, and its non-intelligent part into ether, air, and so on. This however stultifies all those often-quoted texts which declare Brahman in its causal state to be devoid of parts. For although the cause is constituted by Brahman in so far as having for its body matter and souls in their subtle state, and the effect by Brahman invested with matter and souls in their gross state; the difficulty stated above cannot be avoided, since also that element in Brahman which is embodied is held to enter into the effect. If, on the other hand, Brahman is without parts, it cannot become many, and it is not possible that there should persist a part not entering into the effected state. On the ground of these unacceptable results we conclude that Brahman cannot be the cause.—This objection the next Sûtra disposes of.

27. But on account of Scripture; (Brahman's possession of various powers) being founded upon the word.

The 'but' sets aside the difficulty raised. There is no

inappropriateness; 'on account of Scripture.' Scripture declares on the one hand that Brahman is not made up of parts, and on the other that from it a multiform creation proceeds. And in matters vouched for by Scripture we must conform our ideas to what Scripture actually says.—But then Scripture might be capable of conveying to us ideas of things altogether self-contradictory; like as if somebody were to tell us 'Water with fire'!—The Sûtra therefore adds 'on account of its being founded on the word.' As the possession, on Brahman's part, of various powers (enabling it to emit the world) rests exclusively on the authority of the word of the Veda and thus differs altogether from other matters (which fall within the sphere of the other means of knowledge also), the admission of such powers is not contrary to reason. Brahman cannot be either proved or disproved by means of generalisations from experience.

28. And thus in the Self; for (there are) manifold (powers).

If attributes belonging to one thing were on that account to be ascribed to other things also, it would follow that attributes observed in non-sentient things, such as jars and the like, belong also to the intelligent eternal Self, which is of an altogether different kind. But that such attributes do not extend to the Self is due to the variety of the essential nature of things. This the Sûtra expresses in 'for (there are) manifold (powers).' We perceive that fire, water, and so on, which are of different kind, possess different powers, viz. heat, and so on: there is therefore nothing unreasonable in the view that the highest Brahman which differs in kind from all things observed in ordinary life should possess innumerous powers not perceived in ordinary things. Thus Parâsara also—in reply to a question founded on ordinary observation—viz. 'How can creative energy be attributed to Brahman, devoid of qualities, pure, &c.?'—declares 'Numberless powers, lying beyond the sphere of all ordinary thought, belong to Brahman, and qualify it for creation, and so on; just as heat belongs to fire.' Similarly, Scripture says, 'what was that wood, what was that tree from which they built heaven and earth?' &c. (*Ri.* Sa*m*h. X, 81); and 'Brahman was that wood, Brahman was that tree,' and so on.—Objections founded on ordinary generalisations have no force against Brahman which differs in nature from all other things.

29. And on account of the defects of his view also.

On his view, i.e. on the view of him who holds the theory of the Pradhâna or something similar, the imperfections observed in ordinary things would attach themselves to the Pradhâna also, since it does not differ in nature from those things. The legitimate conclusion therefore is that Brahman only which differs in nature from all other things can be held to be the general cause.

The Pradhâna, moreover, is without parts; how then is it possible that it should give rise to a manifold world, comprising the 'great principle,' and so on?—But there *are* parts of the Pradhâna, viz. Goodness, Passion, and Darkness!—This we reply necessitates the following distinction. Does the aggregate of Goodness, Passion, and Darkness constitute the Pradhâna? or is the Pradhâna the effect of those three? The latter alternative is in conflict with your own doctrine according to which the Pradhâna is cause only. It moreover contradicts the number of tattvas (viz. 24) admitted by you; and as those three gu*n*as also have no parts one does not see how they can produce an effect. On the former alternative, the gu*n*as not being composed of parts must be held to aggregate or join themselves without any reference to difference of space, and from such conjunction the production of gross effects cannot result.—The same objection applies to the doctrine of atoms being the general cause. For atoms, being without parts and spatial distinction of parts, can join only without any reference to such spatial distinction, and hence do not possess the power of originating effects.

30. And (the divinity is) endowed with all powers, because that is seen.

The highest divinity which is different in nature from all other things is endowed with all powers; for scriptural texts show it to be such, 'His high power is revealed as manifold, as essential, and so his knowledge, force, and action' (*S*vet. Up. VI, 8). In the same way another text first declares the highest divinity to differ in nature from everything else, 'Free from sin, from old age, from death and grief, from hunger and thirst,' and then goes on to represent it as endowed with all powers, 'realising all its wishes, realising all its intentions,' &c. (*Kh*. Up. VIII, 1, 5). Compare also 'He, consisting of mind, having prâ*n*a for his body, whose form is light, who realises his wishes,' &c. (*Kh*. Up. III, 14, 2).

31. Not, on account of the absence of organs; this has been explained (before).

Although the one Brahman is different from all other beings and endowed with all powers, we yet infer from the text 'Of him there is known no effect and no instrument,' that as it is destitute of instruments it cannot produce any effect.—To this objection an answer has already been given in II, 1, 27; 28, 'on account of its being founded on the word,' and 'for there are manifold (powers).' That for which the sacred word is the only means of knowledge, and which is different from all other things, is capable of producing those effects also of the instrumental means of which it is destitute. It is in this spirit that Scripture says 'He sees without eyes, he hears without ears, without hands and feet he hastens and grasps' (*S*vet. Up. III, 19).—Here terminates the adhikara*n*a of 'the consequence of the entire (Brahman).'

32. (Brahman is) not (the cause); on account of (the world) having the nature of what depends on a motive.

Although the Lord, who before creation is alone, is endowed with all kinds of powers since he differs in nature from all other beings, and hence is by himself capable of creating the world; we all the same cannot ascribe to him actual causality with regard to the world; for this manifold world displays the nature of a thing depending on a motive, and the Lord has no motive to urge him to creation. In the case of all those who enter on some activity after having formed an idea of the effect to be accomplished, there exists a motive in the form of something beneficial either to themselves or to others. Now Brahman, to whose essential nature it belongs that all his wishes are eternally fulfilled, does not attain through the creation of the world any object not attained before. Nor again is the second alternative possible. For a being, all whose wishes are fulfilled, could concern itself about others only with a view to benefitting them. No merciful divinity would create a world so full, as ours is, of evils of all kind—birth, old age, death, hell, and so on;—if it created at all, pity would move it to create a world altogether happy. Brahman thus having no possible motive cannot be the cause of the world. —This primâ facie view is disposed of in the next Sûtra.

33. But (it is) mere sport, as in ordinary life.

The motive which prompts Brahman—all whose wishes are fulfilled and who is perfect in himself—to the creation of a world comprising all kinds of sentient and non-sentient beings dependent on his volition, is nothing else but sport, play. We see in ordinary life how some great king, ruling this earth with its seven dvîpas, and possessing perfect strength, valour, and so on, has a game at balls, or the like, from no other motive than to amuse himself; hence there is no objection to the view that sport only is the motive prompting Brahman to the creation, sustentation, and destruction of this world which is easily fashioned by his mere will.

34. Not inequality and cruelty, on account of there being regard; for so (Scripture) declares.

It must indeed be admitted that the Lord, who differs in nature from all other beings, intelligent and non-intelligent, and hence possesses powers unfathomable by thought, is capable of creating this manifold world, although before creation he is one only and without parts. But the assumption of his having actually created the world would lay him open to the charge of partiality, in so far as the world contains beings of high, middle, and low station—gods, men, animals, immovable beings; and to that of cruelty, in so far as he would be instrumental in making his creatures experience pain of the most dreadful kind.—The reply to this is 'not so, on account of there being regard'; i.e. 'on account of the inequality of creation depending on the deeds of the intelligent beings, gods, and so on, about to be created.' *S*ruti and Sm*ri*ti alike declare that the connexion of the individual souls with bodies of different kinds—divine, human, animal, and so on—depends on the karman of those souls; compare 'He who performs good works becomes good, he who performs bad works becomes bad. He becomes pure by pure deeds, bad by bad deeds' (B*ri*. Up. IV, 4, 5). In the same way the reverend Parâ*s*ara declares that what causes the difference in nature and status between gods, men, and so on, is the power of the former deeds of the souls about to enter into a new creation—'He (the Lord) is the operative cause only in the creation of new beings; the material cause is constituted by the potentialities of the beings to be created. The being to be embodied requires nothing but an operative cause; it is its own potentiality which leads its being into that condition of being (which it is to occupy in the new creation).' Potentiality here means karman.

35. If it be said 'not so, on account of non-distinction of deeds'; we say, 'not so, on account of beginninglessness'; this is reasonable, and it is also observed.

But before creation the individual souls do not exist; since Scripture teaches non-distinction 'Being only this was in the beginning.' And as then the souls do not exist, no karman can exist, and it cannot therefore be said that the inequality of creation depends on karman.—Of this objection the Sûtra disposes by saying 'on account of beginninglessness,' i. e. although the individual souls and their deeds form an eternal stream, without a beginning, yet non-distinction of them 'is reasonable' (i. e. may reasonably be asserted) in so far as, previous to creation, the substance of the souls abides in a very subtle condition, destitute of names and forms, and thus incapable of being designated as something apart from Brahman, although in reality then also they constitute Brahman's body only. If it were not admitted (that the distinctions in the new creation are due to karman), it would moreover follow that souls are requited for what they have not done, and not requited for what they have done. The fact of the souls being without a beginning is observed, viz., to be stated in Scripture, 'The intelligent one is not born and dies not' (Ka. Up. I, 2, 18); so also the fact of the flow of creation going on from all eternity, 'As the creator formed sun and moon formerly.' Moreover, the text, 'Now all this was then undeveloped. It became developed by form and name' (B*ri*. Up. I, 4, 7), states merely that the names and forms of the souls were developed, and this shows that the souls themselves existed from the beginning. Sm*ri*ti also says, 'Dost thou know both Prak*ri*ti and the soul to be without beginning?' (Bha. Gî. XIII, 19.)—As Brahman thus differs in nature from everything else, possesses all powers, has no other motive than sport, and arranges the diversity of the creation in accordance with the different karman of the individual souls, Brahman alone can be the universal cause.

36. And because all the attributes are proved (to be present in Brahman).

As all those attributes required to constitute causality which have been or will be shown to be absent in the Pradhâna, the atoms, and so on, can be shown to be present in Brahman, it remains a settled conclusion that Brahman only is the cause of the world. Here terminates the adhikara*n*a of 'that which has the nature of depending on a motive.'

## SECOND PÂDA.

1. Not that which is inferred, on account of the impossibility of construction, and on account of activity.

The Sûtras have so far set forth the doctrine that the highest Brahman is the cause of the origination and so on of the world, and have refuted the objections raised by others. They now, in order to safeguard their own position, proceed to demolish the positions held by those very adversaries. For otherwise it might happen that some slow-witted persons, unaware of those other views resting on mere fallacious arguments, would imagine them possibly to be authoritative, and hence might be somewhat shaken in their belief in the Vedic doctrine. Another pâda therefore is begun to the express end of refuting the theories of others. The beginning is made with the theory of Kapila, because that theory has several features, such as the view of the existence of the effect in the cause, which are approved of by the followers of the Veda, and hence is more likely, than others, to give rise to the erroneous view of its being the true doctrine. The Sûtras I, 1, 5 and ff. have proved only that the Vedic texts do not set forth the Sâṅkhya view, while the task of the present pâda is to demolish that view itself: the Sûtras cannot therefore be charged with needless reiteration.

The outline of the Sâṅkhya doctrine is as follows. 'There is the fundamental Prak*ri*ti, which is not an effect; there are the seven effects of Prak*ri*ti, viz. the Mahat and so on, and the sixteen effects of those effects; and there is the soul, which is neither Prak*ri*ti nor effect'—such is the comprehensive statement of the principles. The entity called 'fundamental Prak*ri*ti' is constituted by the three substances called Sattva, Ra*g*as, and Tamas, (when) in a state of complete equipoise, none of the three being either in defect or in excess; the essential nature of those three consists respectively in pleasure, pain, and dullness; they have for their respective effects lightness and illumination, excitement and mobility, heaviness and obstruction; they are absolutely non-perceivable by means of the senses, and to be defined and distinguished through their effects only. Prak*ri*ti, consisting in the equipoise of Sattva, Ra*g*as, and Tamas, is one, itself non-sentient but subserving the enjoyment and final release of the many sentient beings, eternal, all-pervading, ever active, not the effect of anything, but the one general cause. There are seven Principles which are the effects of Prak*ri*ti and the causal substances of everything else; these seven are the Mahat, the ahaṅkâra, the subtle matter (tanmâtra) of sound, the subtle matter of touch, the subtle matter of colour, the subtle matter of taste, and the subtle matter of smell. The ahaṅkâra is threefold, being either modified (vaikârika), or active (tai*g*asa), or the originator of the elements (bhûtâdi).

The vaikârika is of sattva-nature and the originator of the sense-organs; the bhûtâdi is of tamas-nature, and the cause of those subtle matters (tanmâtra) which in their turn are the cause of the gross elements; the tai*g*asa is of the nature of ra*g*as, and assists the other two. The five gross elements are the ether and so on; the five intellectual senses are hearing and so on; the five organs of action are speech and so on. With the addition of the internal organ (manas) these are the sixteen entities which are mere effects.—The soul, not being capable of any change, is not either the causal matter or the effect of anything. For the same reason it is without attributes, consisting of mere intelligence, eternal, non-active, all-pervading, and different in each body. Being incapable of change and non-active, it can neither be an agent nor an enjoyer; but although this is so, men in their confusion of mind, due to the closeness to each other of Prak*ri*ti and the soul, erroneously attribute to Prak*ri*ti the intelligence of the soul, and to the soul the activity of Prak*ri*ti—just as the redness of the rose superimposes itself on the crystal near it,—and thus consider the soul to be an 'I' and an enjoyer. Fruition thus results from ignorance, and release from knowledge of the truth. This their theory the Sâṅkhyas prove by means of perception, inference, and authoritative tradition. Now with regard to those matters which are proved by perception, we Vedântins have no very special reason for dissenting from the Sâṅkhyas; and what they say about their authoritative tradition, claiming to be founded on the knowledge of all-knowing persons such as Kapila, has been pretty well disproved by us in the first adhyâya. If, now, we further manage to refute the inference which leads them to assume the Pradhâna as the cause of the world, we shall have disestablished their whole theory. We therefore proceed to give this refutation.

On this point the Sâṅkhyas reason as follows. It must necessarily be admitted that the entire world has one cause only; for if effects were assumed to originate from several causes we should never arrive at an ultimate cause. Assume that parts such as e.g. threads produce a whole (i.e. in the case of threads, a piece of cloth) in the way of their being joined together by means of their six sides, which are parts of the threads. You must then further assume that the threads themselves are in the same way produced by their parts, having a similar constitution. And these parts again by their parts, until you reach the atoms; these also must be assumed to produce their immediate effects by being joined together with their six sides, for otherwise solid extension (prathiman) could not be brought about. And then the atoms also as being wholes, consisting of parts[1], must be viewed as produced by their parts, and these again by their parts and so on, so that we never arrive at an ultimate cause. In order therefore to establish such an ultimate cause we must have recourse to the hypothesis of the general cause being constituted by one substance, which possesses the power of transforming itself in various different ways, without at the

[1] As follows from their having six sides.

same time forfeiting its own essential nature, and which forms the general substrate for an infinity of different effects, from the Mahat downwards. This one general cause is the Pradhâna constituted by the equipoise of the three gu*n*as. The reasons for the assumption of this Pradhâna are as follows :—'On account of the limitedness of particular things; of connexion (anvaya); of activity proceeding from special power; and of the difference and non-difference of cause and effect—the Non-evolved (Pradhâna) is the general cause of this many-natured Universe' (vai*s*varûpya) (Sâṅkhya Kâ. I, 15; 16).—The term 'vai*s*varûpya' denotes that which possesses all forms, i. e. the entire world with its variously constituted parts—bodies, worlds, and so on. This world, which on account of its variegated constitution must be held to be an effect, has for its cause the Unevolved (avyakta = Prak*ri*ti), which is of the same nature as the world. Why so? Because it is an effect; for we perceive that every effect is different from its special cause—which has the same nature as the effect—and at the same time is non-different. Such effected things as e. g. a jar and a gold ornament are different from their causes, i. e. clay and gold, which have the same nature as the effects, and at the same time non-different. Hence the manifold-natured world originates from the Pradhâna which has the same nature, and is again merged in it: the world thus has the Pradhâna alone for its cause. This Pradhâna is constituted by the equipoise of the three gu*n*as, and thus is a cause possessing a nature equal to that of its effect, i. e. the world; for the world is of the nature of pleasure, pain, and dullness, which consist of sattva, ra*g*as, and tamas respectively. The case is analogous to that of a jar consisting of clay; of that also the cause is none other than the substance clay. For in every case observation shows that only such causal substances as are of the same nature as the effects possess that power which is called the origination of the effect. That the general cause can be found only in the unevolved Pradhâna, which consists of the three gu*n*as in a state of equipoise and is unlimited with regard to space as well as time, follows from the limitedness of the particular things, viz. the Mahat, the ahankâra, and so on. These latter things are limited like jars and so on, and hence incapable of originating the entire world. Hence it follows that this world, consisting of the three gu*n*as, has for its only cause the Pradhâna, which is constituted by those three gu*n*as in a state of equipoise.

Against this argumentation the Sûtra says, 'Not that which is inferred, on account of the impossibility of construction, and on account of activity.'—'Inference' means 'that which is inferred,' i. e. the Pradhâna. The Pradhâna postulated by you is not capable of constructing this manifold-natured world, because while itself being non-intelligent it is not guided by an intelligent being understanding its nature. Whatever is of this latter kind is incapable of producing effects; as e. g. wood and the like by themselves are not capable of constructing a palace or a carriage. As it is matter of observation that non-intelligent wood, not guided by an intelligent agent understanding its nature, cannot produce effects; and as it is observed that if guided by such an agent matter does enter on action so as to produce effects; the Pradhâna, which is not ruled by an intelligent agent, cannot be the general cause. The 'and' in the Sûtra is meant to add as a further argument that 'presence' (anvaya) has no proving force. For whiteness present in cows and so on is not invariably accompanied by the quality of being the cause of the class characteristics of cows. Nor must it be said that qualities such as whiteness, although present in the effect, may not indeed be causes, but that substances such as gold and the like which are present in certain effects are invariably accompanied by the quality of being causes, and that hence also the substances called sattva, ra*g*as, and tamas, which are found present in all effects, are proved to be the causes of all those effects. For sattva and so on are attributes of substances, but not themselves substances. Sattva and so on are the causes of the lightness, light, &c., belonging to substances such as earth and the like, and hence distinctive attributes of the essential nature of those substances, but they are not observed to be present in any effects in a substantial form, as clay, gold, and other substances are. It is for this reason that they are known as 'gu*n*as.' You have further said that the world's having one cause only must be postulated in order that an ultimate cause may be reached. But as the sattva, ra*g*as, and tamas are not one but three, you yourself do not assume one cause, and hence do not manage to arrive at an ultimate cause. For your Pradhâna consists in the equipoise of the three gu*n*as; there are thus several causes, and you have no more an ultimate cause than others. Nor can you say that this end is accomplished through the three gu*n*as being unlimited. For if the three gu*n*as are all alike unlimited, and therefore omnipresent, there is nowhere a plus or minus of any of them, and as thus no inequality can result, effects cannot originate. In order to explain the origination of results it is therefore necessary to assume limitation of the gu*n*as.

Nor is our view confirmed by those cases only in which it is clearly perceived that matter produces effects only when guided by an intelligent principle; other cases also (where the fact is not perceived with equal clearness) are in favour of our view. This the next Sûtra declares.

2. If it be said—like milk or water; there also (intelligence guides).

What has been said—the Sâṅkhya rejoins—as to the impossibility of the Pradhâna not guided by an intelligent principle constructing this variously constituted world, is unfounded; for the Pradhâna may be supposed to act in the same way as milk and water do. Milk, when turning into sour milk, is capable of going by itself through a series of changes: it does not therefore depend on anything else. In the same way we observe that the homogeneous water discharged from the clouds spontaneously proceeds to transform itself into the various saps and juices of different plants, such as palm trees, mango trees, wood-apple trees, lime trees, tamarind trees, and so on. In the same way the Pradhâna, of whose essential nature it is to change, may, without being guided by another agent, abide in the interval between two creations in a state of homogeneousness, and then when the time for creation comes modify itself into many various effects due to the loss of equilibrium on the part of the gu*n*as. As has been said '(the Pradhâna acts), owing to modification, as water according to the difference of the abodes of the several gu*n*as' (Sâṅkhya Kâ. I, 16). In this way the Unevolved acts independently of anything else.

To this reasoning the Sûtra replies 'there also.' Also, in the instances of milk and water, activity is not possible in the absence of an intelligent principle, for these very cases have already been referred to as proving our position. The Sûtra II, 1, 24 (where the change of milk into sour milk is instanced) meant to prove only that a being destitute of other visible instruments of action is able to produce its own special effect, but not to disprove the view of all agency presupposing an intelligent principle. That even in water and so on an intelligent principle is present is proved by scriptural texts, 'he who dwells in water' and so on.

3. And because from the independence (of the Pradhâna) there would follow the non-existence of what is different (from creation, i.e. of the pralaya condition).

That the Pradhâna which is not guided by an intelligent principle is not the universal cause is proved also by the fact that, if we ascribe to it a power for change independent of the guidance of a Lord capable of realising all his purposes, it would follow that the pralaya state, which is different from the state of creation, would not exist; while on the other hand the guidance of the Pradhâna by a Lord explains the alternating states of creation and pralaya as the effects of his purposes. Nor can the Sâṅkhya retort that our view gives rise to similar difficulties in so far, namely, as the Lord, all whose wishes are eternally accomplished, who is free from all imperfection, &c. &c., cannot be the originator of either creation or pralaya, and as the creation of an unequal world would lay him open to the charge of mercilessness. For, as explained before, even a being perfect and complete may enter on activity for the sake of sport; and as the reason for a particular creation on the part of an all-knowing Lord may be his recognition of Prak*ri*ti having reached a certain special state, it is the deeds of the individual souls which bring about the inequalities in the new creation.—But if this is so, all difference of states is caused exclusively by the good and evil deeds of the individual souls; and what position remains then for a ruling Lord? Prak*ri*ti, impressed by the good and evil deeds of the souls, will by herself modify herself on such lines as correspond to the deserts of the individual souls; in the same way as we observe that food and drink, if either vitiated by poison or reinforced by medicinal herbs and juices, enter into new states which render them the causes of either pleasure or pain. Hence all the differences between states of creation and pralaya, as also the inequalities among created beings such as gods, men, and so on, and finally the souls reaching the condition of Release, may be credited to the Pradhâna, possessing as it does the capability of modifying itself into all possible forms!—You do not, we reply, appear to know anything about the nature of good and evil works; for this is a matter to be learned from the *S*âstra. The *S*âstra is constituted by the aggregate of words called Veda, which is handed on by an endless unbroken succession of pupils learning from qualified teachers, and raised above all suspicion of imperfections such as spring from mistake and the like. It is the Veda which gives information as to good and evil deeds, the essence of which consists in their pleasing or displeasing the Supreme Person, and as to their results, viz. pleasure and pain, which depend on the grace or wrath of the Lord. In agreement herewith the Drami*d*â*k*ârya says, 'From the wish of giving rise to fruits they seek to please the Self with works; he being pleased is able to bestow fruits, this is the purport of the *S*âstra.' Thus *S*ruti also says, 'Sacrifices and pious works which are performed in many forms, all that he bears (i.e. he takes to himself); he the navel of the Universe' (Mahânâr. Up. I, 6). And in the same spirit the Lord himself declares, 'From whom there proceed all beings, by whom all this is pervaded—worshipping him with the proper works man attains to perfection' (Bha. Gî. XVIII, 46); and 'These evil and malign haters, lowest of men, I hurl perpetually into transmigrations and into demoniac wombs' (Bha. Gî. XVI, 19). The divine Supreme Person, all whose wishes are eternally fulfilled, who is all-knowing and the ruler of all, whose every purpose is immediately realised, having engaged in sport befitting his might and greatness and having settled that work is of a twofold nature, such and such works being good and such and such being evil, and having bestowed on all individual souls bodies and sense-organs capacitating them for entering on such work and the power of ruling those bodies and organs; and having himself entered into those souls as their inner Self abides within them, controlling them as an animating and cheering principle. The souls, on their side, endowed with all the powers imparted to them by the Lord and with bodies and organs bestowed by him, and forming abodes in which he dwells, apply themselves on their own part, and in accordance with their own wishes, to works either good or evil. The Lord, then, recognising him who performs good actions as one who obeys his commands, blesses him with piety, riches, worldly pleasures, and final release; while him who transgresses his commands he causes to experience the opposites of all these. There is thus no room whatever for objections founded on deficiency, on the Lord's part, of independence in his dealings with men, and the like. Nor can he be arraigned with being pitiless or merciless. For by pity we understand the inability, on somebody's part, to bear the pain of others, coupled with a disregard of his own advantage. When pity has the effect of bringing about the transgression of law on the part of the pitying person, it is in no way to his credit; it rather implies the charge of unmanliness (weakness), and it is creditable to control and subdue it. For otherwise it would follow that to subdue and chastise one's enemies is something to be blamed. What the Lord himself aims at is ever to increase happiness to the highest degree, and to this end it is instrumental that he should reprove and reject the infinite and intolerable mass of sins which accumulates in the course of beginning and endless aeons, and thus check the tendency on the part of individual beings to transgress his laws. For thus he says: 'To them ever devoted, worshipping me in love, I give that means of wisdom by which they attain to me. In mercy only to them, dwelling in their hearts, do I destroy the darkness born of ignorance with the brilliant light of knowledge' (Bha. Gî. X, 10, 11).—It thus remains a settled conclusion that the Pradhâna, which is not guided by an intelligent principle, cannot be the general cause.—Here a further objection is raised. Although Prak*ri*ti, as not being ruled by an intelligent principle, is not capable of that kind of activity which springs from effort, she may yet be capable of that kind of activity which consists in mere transformation. For we observe parallel cases; the grass and water e.g. which are consumed by a cow change on their own account into milk. In the same way, then, Prak*ri*ti may on her own account transform herself into the world.—To this the next Sûtra replies.

4. Nor like grass and so on; because (milk) does not exist elsewhere.

This argumentation does not hold good; for as grass and the like do not transform themselves without the guidance of an intelligent principle, your proving instance is not established.—But why is it not established?—'Because it does not exist elsewhere.' If grass, water and so on changed into milk even when consumed by a bull or when not consumed at all, then indeed it might be held that they change without the guidance of an intelligent principle. But nothing of the kind takes place, and hence we conclude that it is the intelligent principle only which turns the grass eaten by the cow into milk.—This point has been set forth above under Sûtra 3; the present Sûtra is meant to emphasise and particularise it.

5. And if you say—as the man and the stone; thus also.

Here the following view might be urged. Although the soul consists of mere intelligence and is inactive, while the Pradhâna is destitute of all power of thought; yet the non-sentient Pradhâna may begin to act owing to the mere nearness of the soul. For we observe parallel instances. A man blind but capable of motion may act in some way, owing to the nearness to him of some lame man who has no power of motion but possesses good eyesight and assists the blind man with his intelligence. And through the nearness of the magnetic stone iron moves. In the same way the creation of the world may result from the connexion of Prak*ri*ti and the soul. As has been said, 'In order that the soul may know the Pradhâna and become isolated, the connexion of the two takes place like that of the lame and the blind; and thence creation springs' (Sâṅkhya Kâ. 21). This means—to the end that the soul may experience the Pradhâna, and for the sake of the soul's emancipation, the Pradhâna enters on action at the beginning of creation, owing to the nearness of the soul.

To this the Sûtra replies 'thus also.' This means—the inability of the Pradhâna to act remains the same, in spite of these instances. The lame man is indeed incapable of walking, but he possesses various other powers—he can see the road and give instructions regarding it; and the blind man, being an intelligent being, understands those instructions and directs his steps accordingly. The magnet again possesses the attribute of moving towards the iron and so on. The soul on the other hand, which is absolutely inactive, is incapable of all such changes. As, moreover, the mere nearness of the soul to the Pradhâna is something eternal, it would follow that the creation also is eternal. If, on the other hand, the soul is held to be eternally free, then there can be no bondage and no release.

6. And on account of the impossibility of the relation of principal (and subordinate) matter.

You Sâṅkhyas maintain that the origination of the world results from a certain relation between principal and subordinate entities which depends on the relative inferiority and superiority of the gu*n*as—'according to the difference of the abodes of the several gu*n*as' (Sâṅkhya Kâ. I, 16).

But, as in the pralaya state the three gu*n*as are in a state of equipoise, none of them being superior or inferior to the others, that relation of superiority and subordination cannot then exist, and hence the world cannot originate. Should it, on the other hand, be maintained that even in the pralaya state there is a certain inequality, it would follow therefrom that creation is eternal.

7. And if another inference be made (the result remains unchanged), on account of (the Pradhâna) being destitute of the power of a knowing subject.

Even if the Pradhâna were inferred by some reasoning different from the arguments so far refuted by us, our objections would remain in force because, anyhow, the Pradhâna is devoid of the power of a cognising subject. The Pradhâna thus cannot be established by any mode of inference.

8. And even if it be admitted; on account of the absence of a purpose.

Even if it were admitted that the Pradhâna is established by Inference, the Sâṅkhya theory could not be accepted for the reason that the Pradhâna is without a purpose. For, according to the view expressed in the passage, 'In order that the soul may know the Pradhâna and become isolated' (Sâṅkhya Kâ. I, 21), the purpose of the Pradhâna is fruition and final release on the part of the soul; but both these are impossible. For, as the soul consists of pure intelligence, is inactive, changeless, and spotless, and hence eternally emancipated, it is capable neither of fruition which consists in consciousness of Prak*ri*ti, nor of Release which consists in separation from Prak*ri*ti. If, on the other hand, it be held that the soul constituted as described is, owing to the mere nearness of Prak*ri*ti, capable of fruition, i.e. of being conscious of pleasure and pain, which are special modifications of Prak*ri*ti, it follows that, as Prak*ri*ti is ever near, the soul will never accomplish emancipation.

9. And (it is) objectionable on account of the contradictions.

The Sâṅkhya-system, moreover, labours from many internal contradictions.—The Sâṅkhyas hold that while Prak*ri*ti is for the sake of another and the object of knowledge and fruition, the soul is independent, an enjoying and knowing agent, and conscious of Prak*ri*ti; that the soul reaches isolation through the instrumentality of Prak*ri*ti only, and that as its nature is pure, permanent, unchanging consciousness, absence of all activity and isolation belong to that nature; that for this reason the accomplishing of the means of bondage and release and of release belong to Prak*ri*ti only; and that, owing to Prak*ri*ti's proximity to the unchanging non-active soul, Prak*ri*ti, by a process of mutual superimposition (adhyâsa), works towards the creation of a world and subserves the purposes of the soul's fruition and emancipation.—'Since the aggregate of things is for the sake of another; since there is an opposite of the three gu*n*as and the rest; since there is superintendence; since there is an experiencing subject; and since there is activity for the sake of isolation; the soul exists' (Sâṅkhya Kâ. 17); 'And from that contrast the soul is proved to be a witness, isolated, neutral, cognising, and inactive' (18).—And after having stated that the activity of the Pradhâna is for the purpose of the release of the Self, the text says, 'therefore no (soul) is either bound or released, nor does it migrate; it is Prak*ri*ti, which, abiding in various beings, is bound and released and migrates' (62). And 'From this connexion therewith (i.e. with the soul) the non-intelligent appears as intelligent; and although all agency belongs to the gu*n*as, the indifferent (soul) becomes an agent. In order that the soul may know the Pradhâna and become isolated, the connexion of the two takes place like that of the lame and the blind; and thence creation springs' (20, 21).—Now to that which is eternally unchanging, non-active and isolated, the attributes of being a witness and an enjoying and cognising agent can in no way belong. Nor also can such a being be subject to error resting on superimposition; for error and superimposition both are of the nature of change. And, on the other hand, they also cannot belong to Prak*ri*ti, since they are attributes of intelligent beings. For by superimposition we understand the attribution, on the part of an intelligent being, of the qualities of one thing to another thing; and this is the doing of an intelligent being, and moreover a change. Nor is it possible that superimposition and the like should take place in the soul only if it is in approximation to Prak*ri*ti. —They may take place just on account of the non-changing nature of the soul!—Then, we reply, they would take place permanently. And that mere proximity has no effective power we have already shown under II, 1, 4. And if it is maintained that it is Prak*ri*ti only that migrates, is bound and released, how then can she be said to benefit the soul, which is eternally released? That she does so the Sâṅkhyas distinctly assert, 'By manifold means Prak*ri*ti, helpful and endowed with the gu*n*as, without any benefit to herself, accomplishes the purpose of the soul, which is thankless and not composed of the gu*n*as' (Sâṅkhya Kâ. 60).—The Sâṅkhyas further teach that Prak*ri*ti, on being seen by any soul in her true nature, at once retires from that soul —'As a dancer having exhibited herself on the stage withdraws from the soul, so Prak*ri*ti withdraws from the soul when she has manifested herself to it' (59); 'My opinion is that there exists nothing more sensitive than Prak*ri*ti, who knowing "I have been seen" does not again show itself to the soul' (61). But this doctrine also is inappropriate. For, as the soul is eternally released and above all change, it never sees Prak*ri*ti, nor does it attribute to itself her qualities; and Prak*ri*ti herself does not see herself since she is of non-intelligent nature; nor can she wrongly impute to herself the soul's seeing of itself as her own seeing of herself, for she herself is non-intelligent and the soul is incapable of that change which consists in seeing or knowing.—Let it then be said that the 'seeing' means nothing more than the proximity of Prak*ri*ti to the soul!—But this also does not help you; for, as said above, from that there would follow eternal seeing, since the two are in eternal proximity. Moreover, the ever unchanging soul is not capable of an approximation which does not form an element of its unchanging nature.—Moreover, if you define the seeing as mere proximity and declare this to be the cause of Release, we point out that it equally is the cause of bondage—so that bondage and release would both be permanent.—Let it then be said that what causes bondage is wrong seeing—while intuition of the true nature of things is the cause of Release!—But as both these kinds of seeing are nothing but proximity, it would follow that both take place permanently. And if, on the other hand, the proximity of Soul and Prak*ri*ti were held not to be permanent, then the cause of such proximity would have to be assigned, and again the cause of that, and so on *ad infinitum*.—Let us then, to escape from these difficulties, define proximity as nothing more than the true nature of soul and Prak*ri*ti! —As the true nature is permanent, we reply, it would follow therefrom that bondage and release would be alike permanent.—On account of all these contradictory views the system of the Sâṅkhyas is untenable.

We finally remark that the arguments here set forth by us at the same time prove the untenableness of the view of those who teach that there is an eternally unchanging Brahman whose nature is pure, non-differenced intelligence, and which by being conscious of Nescience experiences unreal bondage and release. For those philosophers can show no more than the Sâṅkhyas do how their Brahman can be conscious of Nescience, can be subject to adhyâsa, and so on. There is, however, the following difference between the two theories. The Sâṅkhyas, in order to account for the definite individual distribution of birth, death, and so on, assume a plurality of souls. The Vedântins, on the other hand, do not allow even so much, and their doctrine is thus all the more irrational. The assertion that there is a difference (in favour of the Vedântins) between the two doctrines, in so far as the Vedântins hold Prak*ri*ti to be something unreal, while the Sâṅkhyas consider it to be real, is unfounded; for pure, homogeneous intelligence, eternally non-changing, cannot possibly be conscious of anything different from itself, whether it be unreal or real. And if that thing is held to be unreal, there arise further difficulties, owing to its having to be viewed as the object of knowledge, of refutation, and so on.

Here terminates the adhikara*n*a of 'the impossibility of construction.'

10. Or in the same way as the big and long from the short and the atomic.

We have shown that the theory of the Pradhâna being the universal cause is untenable, since it rests on fallacious arguments, and suffers from inner contradictions. We shall now prove that the view of atoms constituting the universal cause is untenable likewise. 'Or in the same way as the big and long from the short and the atomic.'—'Is untenable' must be supplied from the preceding Sûtra; 'or' has to be taken in the sense of 'and.' The sense of the Sûtra is—in the same way as the big and long, i.e. as the theory of ternary compounds originating from the short and the atomic, i.e. from binary compounds and simple atoms is untenable, so everything else which they (the Vai*s*eshikas) maintain is untenable; or, in other words—as the theory of the world originating from atoms through binary compounds is untenable, so everything else is likewise untenable.—Things consisting of parts, as e.g. a piece of cloth, are produced by their parts, e.g. threads, being joined by means of the six sides which are parts of those parts. Analogously the atoms also must be held to originate binary compounds in the way of combining by means of their six sides; for if the atoms possessed no distinction of parts (and hence filled no space), a group of even a thousand atoms would not differ in extension from a single atom, and the different kinds of extension—minuteness, shortness, bigness, length, &c.—would never emerge. If, on the other hand, it is admitted that the atoms also have distinct sides, they have parts and are made up of those parts, and those parts again are made up of their parts, and so on *in infinitum*.—But, the Vai*s*eshika may object, the difference between a mustard seed and a mountain is due to the paucity of the constituent parts on the one hand, and their multitude on the other. If, now, it be held that the atom itself contains an infinity of parts, the mustard seed and the mountain alike will contain an infinity of parts, and thus their inequality cannot be accounted for. We must therefore assume that there is a limit of subdivision (i.e. that there are real atoms which do not themselves consist of parts).—Not so, we reply. If the atoms did not possess distinct parts, there could originate no extension greater than the extension of one atom (as already shown), and thus neither mustard seed nor mountain would ever be brought about.—But what, then, are we to do to get out of this dilemma?—You have only to accept the Vedic doctrine of the origination of the world!

Others explain the above Sûtra as meant to refute an objection against the doctrine of Brahman being the general cause. But this does not suit the arrangement of the Sûtras, and would imply a meaningless iteration. The objections raised by some against the doctrine of Brahman have been disposed of in the preceding pâda, and the present pâda is devoted to the refutation of other theories. And that the world admits of being viewed as springing from an intelligent principle such as Brahman was shown at length under II, 1, 4. The sense of the Sûtra, therefore, is none other than what we stated above.—But what are those other untenable views to which the Sûtra refers?—To this question the next Sûtra replies.

11. On both assumptions also there is no motion, and thence non-being (of the origination of the world).

The atomic theory teaches that the world is produced by the successive formation of compounds, binary, ternary, and so on, due to the aggregation of atoms—such aggregation resulting from the motion of the atoms. The primary motion of the atoms—which are the cause of the origination of the entire world—is assumed to be brought about by the unseen principle (ad*r*ish*t*a), 'The upward flickering of fire, the sideway motion of air, the primary motion on the part of atoms and of the manas are caused by the unseen principle.'—Is then, we ask, this primary motion of the atoms caused by an ad*ri*sh*t*a residing in them, or by an ad*ri*sh*t*a residing in the souls? Neither alternative is possible. For the unseen principle which is originated by the good and evil deeds of the individual souls cannot possibly reside in the atoms; and if it could, the consequence would be that the atoms would constantly produce the world. Nor again can the ad*ri*sh*t*a residing in the souls be the cause of motion originating in the atoms.—Let it then be assumed that motion originates in the atoms, owing to their being in contact with the souls in which the ad*ri*sh*t*a abides!—If this were so, we reply, it would follow that the world would be permanently created, for the ad*ri*sh*t*a of the souls forms an eternal stream.—But the ad*ri*sh*t*a requires to be matured in order to produce results. The ad*ri*sh*t*as of some souls come to maturity in the same state of existence in which the deeds were performed; others become mature in a subsequent state of existence only; and others again do not become mature before a new Kalpa has begun. It is owing to this dependence on the maturation of the ad*ri*sh*t*as that the origination of the world does not take place at all times. —But this reasoning also we cannot admit. For there is nothing whatever to establish the conclusion that all the different ad*ri*sh*t*as which spring from the manifold actions performed at different times, without any previous agreement, by the infinite multitude of individual Selfs should reach a state of uniform maturation at one and the same moment of time (so as to give rise to a new creation). Nor does this view of yours account for the fact of the entire world being destroyed at the same time, and remaining in a state of non-maturation for the period of a dviparârdha.—Nor can you say that the motion of the atoms is due to their conjunction with (souls whose) ad*ri*sh*t*a possesses certain specific qualities imparted to them by the will of the Lord; for by mere inference the existence of a Lord cannot be proved, as we have shown under I, 1.

The origin of the world cannot, therefore, be due to any action on the part of the atoms.

12. And because owing to the acknowledgment of samavâya, there results a *regressus in infinitum* from equality.

The Vai*s*eshika doctrine is further untenable on account of the acknowledgment of samavâya.—Why so?—Because the samavâya also, like part, quality, and generic characteristics, requires something else to establish it, and that something else again requires some further thing to establish it—from which there arises an infinite regress. To explain. The Vai*s*eshikas assume the so-called samavâya relation, defining it as 'that connexion which is the cause of the idea "this is here," in the case of things permanently and inseparably connected, and standing to each other in the relation of abode and thing abiding in the abode.' Now, if such a samavâya relation is assumed in order to account for the fact that things observed to be inseparably connected—as, e.g., class characteristics are inseparably connected with the individuals to which they belong—are such, i.e. inseparably connected, a reason has also to be searched for why the samavâya, which is of the same nature as those things (in so far, namely, as it is also inseparably connected with the things connected by it), is such; and for that reason, again, a further reason has to be postulated, and so on, *in infinitum*. Nor can it be said that inseparable connexion must be assumed to constitute the essential nature of samavâya (so that no further reason need be demanded for its inseparable connexion); for on this reasoning you would have to assume the same essential nature for class characteristics, qualities, and so on (which would render the assumption of a samavâya needless for them also). Nor is it a legitimate proceeding to postulate an unseen entity such as the samavâya is, and then to assume for it such and such an essential nature.—These objections apply to the samavâya whether it be viewed as eternal or non-eternal. The next Sûtra urges a further objection against it if viewed as eternal.

13. And because (the world also) would thus be eternal.

The samavâya is a relation, and if that relation is eternal that to which the relation belongs must also be eternal, so that we would arrive at the unacceptable conclusion that the world is eternal.

14. And on account of (the atoms) having colour and so on, the reverse (takes place); as it is observed.

From the view that the atoms of four kinds—viz. of earth or water or fire or air—possess colour, taste, smell, and touch, it would follow that the atoms are non-eternal, gross, and made up of parts—and this is the reverse of what the Vai*s*eshikas actually teach as to their atoms, viz. that they are eternal, subtle, and not made up of parts. For things possessing colour, e.g. jars, are non-eternal, because it is observed that they are produced from other causes of the same, i.e. non-eternal nature, and so on. To a non-perceived thing which is assumed in accordance with what is actually perceived, we may not ascribe any attributes that would be convenient to us; and it is in accordance with actual experience that you Vai*s*eshikas assume the atoms to possess colour and other qualities. Hence your theory is untenable.—Let it then, in order to avoid this difficulty, be assumed that the atoms do not possess colour and other sensible qualities. To this alternative the next Sûtra refers.

15. And as there are objections in both cases.

A difficulty arises not only on the view of the atoms having colour and other sensible qualities, but also on the view of their being destitute of those qualities. For as the qualities of effected things depend on the qualities of their causes, earth, water, and so on, would in that case be destitute of qualities. And if to avoid this difficulty, it be held that the atoms do possess qualities, we are again met by the difficulty stated in the preceding Sûtra. Objections thus arising in both cases, the theory of the atoms is untenable.

16. And as it is not accepted, it is altogether disregarded.

Kapila's doctrine, although to be rejected on account of its being in conflict with Scripture and sound reasoning, yet recommends itself to the adherents of the Veda on some accounts—as e.g. its view of the existence of the effect in the cause. Ka*n*âda's theory, on the other hand, of which no part can be accepted and which is totally destitute of proof, cannot but be absolutely disregarded by all those who aim at the highest end of man.—Here terminates the adhikara*n*a of 'the big and long.'

17. Even on the aggregate with its two causes, there is non-establishment of that.

We so far have refuted the Vai*s*eshikas, who hold the doctrine of atoms constituting the general cause. Now the followers of Buddha also teach that the world originates from atoms, and the Sûtras therefore proceed to declare that on their view also the origination, course, and so on, of the world cannot rationally be accounted for. These Bauddhas belong to four different classes. Some of them hold that all outward things, which are either elements (bhûta) or elemental (bhautika), and all inward things which are either mind (*k*itta) or mental (*k*aitta),—all these things consisting of aggregates of the atoms of earth, water, fire and air—are proved by means of Perception as well as Inference. Others hold that all external things, earth, and so on, are only to be inferred from ideas (vi*gñ*âna). Others again teach that the only reality are ideas to which no outward things correspond; the (so-called) outward things are like the things seen in dreams. The three schools mentioned agree in holding that the things admitted by them have a momentary existence only, and do not allow that, in addition to the things mentioned, viz. elements and elemental things, mind and mental things, there are certain further independent entities such as ether, Self, and so on.—Others finally assert a universal void, i.e. the non-reality of everything.

The Sûtras at first dispose of the theory of those who acknowledge the real existence of external things. Their opinion is as follows. The atoms of earth which possess the qualities of colour, taste, touch and smell; the atoms of water which possess the qualities of colour, taste and touch; the atoms of fire which possess the qualities of colour and touch; and the atoms of air which possess the quality of touch only, combine so as to constitute earth, water, fire and air; and out of the latter there originate the aggregates called bodies, sense-organs, and objects of sense-organs. And that flow of ideas, which assumes the form of the imagination of an apprehending agent abiding within the body, is what constitutes the so-called Self. On the agencies enumerated there rests the entire empiric world.—On this view the Sûtra remarks, 'Even on the aggregate with its two causes, there is non-establishment of that.' That aggregate which consists of earth and the other elements and of which the atoms are the cause; and that further aggregate which consists of bodies, sense-organs and objects, and of which the elements are the cause—on neither of these two aggregates with their twofold causes can there be proved establishment of that, i. e. can the origination of that aggregate which we call the world be rationally established. If the atoms as well as earth and the other elements are held to have a momentary existence only, when, we ask, do the atoms which perish within a moment, and the elements, move towards combination, and when do they combine? and when do they become the objects of states of consciousness? and when do they become the abodes of the activities of appropriation, avoidance and so on (on the part of agents)? and what is the cognising Self? and with what objects does it enter into contact through the sense-organs? and which cognising Self cognises which objects, and at what time? and which Self proceeds to appropriate which objects, and at what time? For the sentient subject has perished, and the object of sensation has perished; and the cognising subject has perished, and the object cognised has perished. And how can one subject cognise what has been apprehended through the senses of another? and how is one subject to take to itself what another subject has cognised? And should it be said that each stream of cognitions is one (whereby a kind of unity of the cognising subject is claimed to be established), yet this affords no sufficient basis for the ordinary notions and activities of life, since the stream really is nothing different from the constituent parts of the stream (all of which are momentary and hence discrete).—That in reality the Ego constitutes the Self and is the knowing subject, we have proved previously.

18. If it be said that (this) is to be explained through successive causality; we say 'no,' on account of their not being the causes of aggregation.

'If it be said that through the successive causality of Nescience and so on, the formation of aggregates and other matters may be satisfactorily accounted for.' To explain. Although all the entities (acknowledged by the Bauddhas) have a merely momentary existence, yet all that is accounted for by avidyâ. Avidyâ means that conception, contrary to reality, by which permanency, and so on, are ascribed to what is momentary, and so on. Through avidyâ there are originated desire, aversion, &c., which are comprised under the general term 'impression' (sa*m*skâra); and from those there springs cognition (vi*gñ*âna) which consists in the 'kindling' of mind; from that mind (*k*itta) and what is of the nature of mind (*k*aitta) and the substances possessing colour, and so on, viz. earth, water, &c. From that again the six sense-organs, called 'the six abodes'; from that the body, called 'touch' (spar*s*a); from that sensation (vedanâ), and so on. And from that again avidyâ, and the whole series as described; so that there is an endlessly revolving cycle, in which avidyâ, and so on, are in turn the causes of the links succeeding them. Now all this is not possible without those aggregates of the elements and elemental things which are called earth, and so on; and thereby the rationality of the formation of those aggregates is proved.

To this the second half of the Sûtra replies 'Not so, on

account of (their) not being the causes of aggregation.' This cannot rationally be assumed, because avidyâ, and so on, cannot be operative causes with regard to the aggregation of earth and the other elements and elemental things. For avidyâ, which consists in the view of permanency and so on, belonging to what is non-permanent, and desire, aversion and the rest, which are originated by avidyâ, cannot constitute the causes of (other) momentary things entering into aggregation; not any more than the mistaken idea of shell-silver is the cause of the aggregation of things such as shells. Moreover, on the Bauddha doctrine, he who views a momentary thing as permanent himself perishes at the same moment; who then is the subject in whom the so-called sa*m*skâras, i. e. desire, aversion, and so on, originate? Those who do not acknowledge one permanent substance constituting the abode of the sa*m*skâras have no right to assume the continuance of the sa*m*skâras.

19. And on account of the cessation of the preceding one on the origination of the subsequent one.

For the following reason also the origination of the world cannot be accounted for on the view of the momentariness of all existence. At the time when the subsequent momentary existence originates, the preceding momentary existence has passed away, and it cannot therefore stand in a causal relation towards the subsequent one. For if non-existence had causal power, anything might originate at any time at any place.—Let it then be said that what constitutes a cause is nothing else but existence in a previous moment.—But, if this were so, the previous momentary existence of a jar, let us say, would be the cause of all things whatever that would be met with in this threefold world in the subsequent moment—cows, buffaloes, horses, chairs, stones, &c.!—Let us then say that a thing existing in a previous moment is the cause only of those things, existing in the subsequent moment, which belong to the same species.—But from this again it would follow that one jar existing in the previous moment would be the cause of all jars, to be met with in any place, existing in the following moment!—Perhaps you mean to say that one thing is the cause of one subsequent thing only. But how then are we to know which thing is the cause of which one subsequent thing?—Well then I say that the momentarily existing jar which exists in a certain place is the cause of that one subsequent momentary jar only which exists at the very same place!—Very good, then you hold that a place is something permanent! (while yet your doctrine is that there is nothing permanent).—Moreover as, on your theory, the thing which has entered into contact with the eye or some other sense-organ does no longer exist at the time when the idea originates, nothing can ever be the object of a cognition.

20. There not being (a cause), there results contradiction of the admitted principle; otherwise simultaneousness.

If it be said that the effect may originate even when a cause does not exist, then—as we have pointed out before—anything might originate anywhere and at any time. And not only would the origination of the effect thus remain unexplained, but an admitted principle would also be contradicted. For you hold the principle that there are four causes bringing about the origination of a cognition, viz. the adhipati-cause, the sahakâri-cause, the âlambhana-cause, and the samanantara-cause. The term adhipati denotes the sense-organs.—And if, in order to avoid opposition to an acknowledged principle, it be assumed that the origination of a further momentary jar takes place at the time when the previous momentary jar still exists, then it would follow that the two momentary jars, the causal one and the effected one, would be perceived together; but as a matter of fact they are not so perceived. And, further, the doctrine of general momentariness would thus be given up. And should it be said that (this is not so, but that) momentariness remains, it would follow that the connexion of the sense-organ with the object and the cognition are simultaneous.

21. There is non-establishment of pratisaṅkhyâ

and apratisaṅkhyâ destruction, on account of non-interruption.

So far the hypothesis of origination from that which is not has been refuted. The present Sûtra now goes on to declare that also the absolute (niranvaya) destruction of that which is cannot rationally be demonstrated. Those who maintain the momentariness of all things teach that there are two kinds of destruction, one of a gross kind, which consists in the termination of a series of similar momentary existences, and is capable of being perceived as immediately resulting from agencies such as the blow of a hammer (breaking a jar, e.g.); and the other of a subtle kind, not capable of being perceived, and taking place in a series of similar momentary existences at every moment. The former is called pratisaṅkhyâ-destruction; the latter apratisaṅkhyâ-destruction.—Both these kinds of destruction are not possible.—Why?—On account of the non-interruption, i.e. on account of the impossibility of the complete destruction of that which is. The impossibility of such destruction was proved by us under II, 1, 14, where we showed that origination and destruction mean only the assumption of new states on the part of one and the same permanent substance, and therefrom proved the non-difference of the effect from the cause.—Here it may possibly be objected that as we see that a light when extinguished passes away absolutely, such absolute destruction may be inferred in other cases also. But against this we point out that in the case of a vessel of clay being smashed we perceive that the material, i.e. clay, continues to exist, and that therefrom destruction is ascertained to be nothing else but the passing over of a real substance into another state. The proper assumption, therefore, is that the extinguished light also has passed over into a different state, and that in that state it is no longer perceptible may be explained by that state being an extremely subtle one.

22. And on account of the objections presenting themselves in either case.

It has been shown that neither origination from nothing, as held by the advocates of general momentariness, is possible; nor the passing away into nothing on the part of the thing originated. The acknowledgment of either of these views gives rise to difficulties. If the effect originates from nothing, it is itself of the nature of nothing; for it is observed that effects share the nature of what they originate from. Pitchers and ornaments, e. g. which are produced from clay and gold respectively, possess the nature of their causal substances. But you hold yourself that the world is not seen to be of the nature of nothingness; and certainly it is not observed to be so.—Again, if that which is underwent absolute destruction, it would follow that after one moment the entire world would pass away into nothingness; and subsequently the world again originating from nothingness, it would follow that, as shown above, it would itself be of the nature of nothingness (i. e. there would no longer be a *real* world).—There being thus difficulties on both views, origination and destruction cannot take place as described by you.

23. And in the case of space also, on account of there being no difference.

In order to prove the permanency of external and internal things, we have disproved the view that the two forms of destruction called pratisaṅkhyâ and apratisaṅkhyâ mean reduction of an existing thing to nothing. This gives us an opportunity to disprove the view of Ether (space) being likewise a mere irrational non-entity, as the Bauddhas hold it to be. Ether cannot be held to be a mere irrational non-entity, because, like those things which are admitted to be positive existences, i. e. earth, and so on, it is proved by consciousness not invalidated by any means of proof. For the formation of immediate judgments such as 'here a hawk flies, and there a vulture,' implies our being conscious of ether as marking the different places of the flight of the different birds. Nor is it possible to hold that Space is nothing else but the non-existence (abhâva) of earth, and so on; for this view collapses as soon as set forth in definite alternatives. For whether we define Space as the antecedent and subsequent non-existence of earth, and so on, or as their mutual non-existence, or as their absolute non-existence—on none of these alternatives we attain the proper idea of Space. If, in the first place, we define it as the antecedent and subsequent non-existence of earth, and so on, it will follow that, as the idea of Space can thus not be connected with earth and other things existing at the present moment, the whole world is without Space.

If, in the second place, we define it as the mutual non-existence of earth, and so on, it will follow that, as such mutual non-existence inheres in the things only which stand towards each other in the relation of mutual non-existence, there is no perception of Space in the intervals between those things (while as a matter of fact there is). And, in the third place, absolute non-existence of earth, and so on, cannot of course be admitted. And as non-existence (abhâva) is clearly conceived as a special state of something actually existing, Space even if admitted to be of the nature of abhâva, would not on that account be a futile non-entity (something 'tu*kkh*a' or 'nirupâkhya').

24. And on account of recognition.

We return to the proof of the, previously mooted, permanence of things. The 'anusm*ri*ti' of the Sûtra means cognition of what was previously perceived, i. e. recognition. It is a fact that all things which were perceived in the past may be recognised, such recognition expressing itself in the form 'this is just that (I knew before).' Nor must you say that this is a mere erroneous assumption of oneness due to the fact of the thing now perceived being similar to the thing perceived before, as in the case of the flame (where a succession of flames continually produced anew is mistaken for one continuous flame); for you do not admit that there is one permanent knowing subject that could have that erroneous idea. What one person has perceived, another cannot judge to be the same as, or similar to, what he is perceiving himself. If therefore you hold that there is an erroneous idea of oneness due to the perception of similarity residing in different things perceived at different times, you necessarily must acknowledge oneness on the part of the cognising subject. In the case of the flame there is a valid means of knowledge to prove that there really is a succession of similar flames, but in the case of the jar, we are not aware of such a means, and we therefore have no right to assume that recognition is due to the similarity of many successive jars.—Perhaps you will here argue as follows. The momentariness of jars and the like is proved by Perception as well as Inference. Perception in the first place presents as its object the present thing which is different from non-present things, in the same way as it presents the blue thing as different from the yellow; it is in this way that we know the difference of the present thing from the past and the future. Inference again proceeds as follows—jars and the like are momentary because they produce effects and have existence (sattva); what is non-momentary, such as the horn of a hare, does not produce effects and does not possess existence. We therefore conclude from the existence of the last momentary jar that the preceding jar-existences also are perishable, just because they are momentary existences like the existence of the last jar.—But both this perception and this inference have already been disproved by what was said above about the impossibility of momentary existences standing to one another in the relation of cause and effect. Moreover, that difference of the present object from the non-present object which is intimated by Perception does not prove the present object to be a different *thing* (from the past object of Perception), but merely its being connected with the present time. This does not prove it to be a different thing, for the same thing can be connected with different times. The two reasons again which were said to prove the momentariness of jars are invalid because they may be made to prove just the contrary of what they are alleged to prove. For we may argue as follows—From existence and from their having effects it follows that jars, and so on, are permanent; for whatever is non-permanent, is non-existent, and does not produce effects, as e.g. the horn of a hare. The capacity of producing effects can in fact be used only to prove non-momentariness on the part of jars, and so on; for as things perishing within a moment are not capable of acting, they are not capable of producing effects. Further, as it is seen in the case of the last momentary existence that its destruction is due to a visible cause (viz. the blow of a hammer or the like), the proper conclusion is that also the other momentary jars (preceding the last one) require visible causes for their destruction; and (as no such causes are seen, it follows that) the jar is permanent and continuous up to the time when a destructive cause, such as the blow of a hammer, supervenes. Nor can it be said that hammers and the like are not the causes of destruction, but only the causes of the origination of a new series of momentary existences dissimilar to the former ones—in the case of the jar, e.g. of a series of momentary fragments of a jar; for we have proved before that the destruction of jars, and so on, means nothing but their passing over into a different condition, e.g. that of fragments. And even if destruction were held to be something different from the origination of fragments, it would yet be reasonable to infer, on the ground of immediate succession in time, that the cause of the destruction is the blow of the hammer.

Hence it is impossible to deny in any way the permanency of things as proved by the fact of recognition. He who maintains that recognition which has for its object the oneness of a thing connected with successive points of time has for its objects different things, might as well say that several cognitions of, let us say, blue colour have for their object something different from blue colour. Moreover, for him who maintains the momentariness of the cognising subject and of the objects of cognition, it would be difficult indeed to admit the fact of Inference which presupposes the ascertainment and remembrance of general propositions. He would in fact not be able to set forth the reason required to prove his assertion that things are momentary; for the speaker perishes in the very moment when he states the proposition to be proved, and another person is unable to complete what has been begun by another and about which he himself does not know anything.

25. Not from non-entity, this not being observed.

So far we have set forth the arguments refuting the views of the Vaibhâshikas as well as the Sautrântikas—both which schools maintain the reality of external things.—Now the Sautrântika comes forward and opposes one of the arguments set forth by us above, viz. that, on the view of general momentariness, nothing can ever become an object of cognition, since the thing which enters into connexion with the sense-organ is no longer in existence when the cognition originates.—It is not, he says, the persistence of the thing up to the time of cognition which is the cause of its becoming an object of cognition. To be an object of cognition means nothing more than to be the cause of the origination of cognition. Nor does this definition imply that the sense-organs also are the objects of cognition. For a cause of cognition is held to be an object of cognition only in so far as it imparts to the cognition its own form (and this the sense-organs do not). Now even a thing that has perished may have imparted its form to the cognition, and on the basis of that form, blue colour, and so on, the thing itself is inferred. Nor can it be said (as the Yogâkâras do) that the form of subsequent cognitions is due to the action of previous cognitions (and not to the external thing); for on this hypothesis it could not be explained how in the midst of a series of cognitions of blue colour there all at once arises the cognition of yellow colour. The manifold character of cognitions must therefore be held to be due to the manifold character of real things.—To this we reply 'not from non-entity; this not being observed.' The special forms of cognition, such as blue colour, and so on, cannot be the forms of things that have perished, and therefore are not in Being, since this is not observed. For it is not observed that when a substrate of attributes has perished, its attributes pass over into another thing. (Nor can it be said that the thing that perished leaves in cognition a reflection of itself, for) reflections also are only of persisting things, not of mere attributes. We therefore conclude that the manifoldness of cognitions can result from the manifoldness of things only on the condition of the thing persisting at the time of cognition.—The Sûtras now set forth a further objection which applies to both schools.

26. And thus there would be accomplishment on the part of non-active people also.

Thus, i.e. on the theory of universal momentariness, origination from the non-existent, causeless cognition, and so on, it would follow that persons also not making any efforts may accomplish all their ends. It is a fact that the attainment of things desired and the warding off of things not desired is effected through effort, and so on. But if all existences momentarily perish, a previously existing thing, or special attributes of it, such as after-effects (through which Svarga and the like are effected) or knowledge (through which Release is effected) do not persist, and hence nothing whatever can be accomplished by effort. And as thus all effects would be accomplished without a cause, even perfectly inert men would accomplish all the ends to be reached in this and in the next life, including final release.—Here terminates the adhikara*n*a of 'the aggregates.'

27. Not non-existence, on account of consciousness.

Here now come forward the Yogâ*k*âras, who hold that cognitions (ideas) only are real. There is no reasonable ground, they say, for the view that the manifoldness of ideas is due to the manifoldness of things, since ideas themselves—no less than the things assumed by others—have their distinct forms, and hence are manifold. And this manifold nature of ideas is sufficiently explained by so-called vâsanâ. Vâsanâ means a flow of ideas (states of consciousness—pratyaya) of different character. We observe, e.g., that a cognition which has the form of a jar (i.e. the idea of a jar) gives rise to the cognition of the two halves of a jar, and is itself preceded and produced by the cognition of a jar, and this again by a similar cognition, and so on; this is what we call a stream or flow of ideas.—But how, then, is it that internal cognitions have the forms of external things, mustard-grains, mountains, and so on?—Even if real things are admitted, the Yogâ*k*âra replies, their becoming objects of thought and speech depends altogether on the light of knowledge, for otherwise it would follow that there is no difference between the objects known by oneself and those known by others. And that cognitions thus shining forth to consciousness have forms (distinctive characteristics) must needs be admitted; for if they were without form they could not shine forth. Now we are conscious only of one such form, viz. that of the cognition; that this form at the same time appears to us as something external (i.e. as the form of an outward thing) is due to error. From the general law that we are conscious of ideas and things together only, it follows that the thing is not something different from the idea.

As, moreover, the fact of one idea specially representing one particular thing only, whether it be a jar or a piece of cloth or anything else, requires for its explanation an equality in character of the idea and the thing, those also who hold the existence of external things must needs assume that the idea has a form similar to that of the thing; and as this suffices for rendering possible practical thought and intercourse, there is nothing authorising us to assume the existence of things in addition to the ideas. Hence cognitions only constitute reality; external things do not exist.

To this the Sûtra replies, 'Not non-existence, on account of consciousness.' The non-existence of things, apart from ideas, cannot be maintained, because we are conscious of cognitions as what renders the knowing subject capable of thought and intercourse with regard to particular *things*. For the consciousness of all men taking part in worldly life expresses itself in forms such as 'I know the jar.' Knowledge of this kind, as everybody's consciousness will testify, presents itself directly as belonging to a knowing subject and referring to an object; those therefore who attempt to prove, on the basis of this very knowledge, that Reality is constituted by mere knowledge, are fit subjects for general derision. This point has already been set forth in detail in our refutation of those crypto-Bauddhas who take shelter under a pretended Vedic theory.—To maintain, as the Yogâkâras do, that the general rule of idea and thing presenting themselves together proves the non-difference of the thing from the idea, implies a self-contradiction; for 'going together' can only be where there are different things. To hold that it is a general rule that of the idea—the essential nature of which is to make the thing to which it refers capable of entering into common thought and intercourse—we are always conscious together with the thing, and then to prove therefrom that the thing is not different from the idea, is a laughable proceeding indeed. And as, according to you, cognitions perish absolutely, and do not possess any permanently persisting aspect, it is rather difficult to prove that such cognitions form a series in which each member colours or affects the next one (vâsanâ); for how is the earlier cognition, which has absolutely perished, to affect the later one, which has not yet arisen? We conclude therefore that the manifoldness of cognitions is due solely to the manifoldness of things. We are directly conscious of cognitions (ideas) as rendering the things to which they refer capable of being dealt with by ordinary thought and speech, and the specific character of each cognition thus depends on the relation which connects it with a particular thing. This relation is of the nature of conjunction (sa*m*yoga), since knowledge (cognition) also is a substance. Just as light (prabhâ), although a substance, stands to the lamp in the relation of an attribute (gu*n*a), so knowledge stands in the relation of an attribute to the Self, but, viewed in itself, it is a substance.—From all this it follows that external things are not non-existent.

The next Sûtra refutes the opinion of those who attempt to prove the baselessness of the cognitions of the waking state by comparing them to the cognitions of a dreaming person.

28. And on account of difference of nature (they are) not like dreams.

Owing to the different nature of dream-cognitions, it cannot be said that, like them, the cognitions of the waking state also have no things to correspond to them. For dream-cognitions are originated by organs impaired by certain defects, such as drowsiness, and are moreover sublated by the cognitions of the waking state; while the cognitions of the waking state are of a contrary nature. There is thus no equality between the two sets.—Moreover, if all cognitions are empty of real content, you are unable to prove what you wish to prove since your inferential cognition also is devoid of true content. If, on the other hand, it be held to have a real content, then it follows that no cognition is devoid of such content; for all of them are alike cognitions, just like the inferential cognition.

29. The existence (is) not, on account of the absence of perception.

The existence of mere cognitions devoid of corresponding things is not possible, because such are nowhere perceived. For we nowhere perceive cognitions not inherent in a cognising subject and not referring to objects. That even dream-cognitions are not devoid of real matter we have explained in the discussion of the different khyâtis (above, p. 118).—Here terminates the adhikara*n*a of '*perception*.'

30. And on account of its being unproved in every way.

Here now come forward the Mâdhyamikas who teach that there is nothing but a universal Void. This theory of a universal Nothing is the real purport of Sugata's doctrine; the theories of the momentariness of all existence, &c., which imply the acknowledgment of the reality of things, were set forth by him merely as suiting the limited intellectual capacities of his pupils.—Neither cognitions nor external objects have real existence; the Void (the '*Nothing*') only constitutes Reality, and final Release means passing over into Non-being.

This is the real view of Buddha, and its truth is proved by the following considerations. As the Nothing is not to be proved by any argument, it is self-proved. For a cause has to be assigned for that only which *is*. But what *is* does not originate either from that which is or that which is not. We never observe that which is to originate from Being; for things such as jars, and so on, do not originate as long as the lump of clay, &c., is non-destroyed. Nor can Being originate from Non-being; for if the jar were supposed to originate from Non-being, i. e. that non-being which results from the destruction of the lump of clay, it would itself be of the nature of Non-being. Similarly it can be shown that nothing can originate either from itself or from anything else. For the former hypothesis would imply the vicious procedure of the explanation presupposing the thing to be explained; and moreover no motive can be assigned for a thing originating from itself. And on the hypothesis of things originating from other things, it would follow that anything might originate from anything, for all things alike are *other* things. And as thus there is no origination there is also no destruction. Hence the *Nothing* constitutes Reality: origination, destruction, Being, Non-being, and so on, are mere illusions (bhrânti). Nor must it be said that as even an illusion cannot take place without a substrate we must assume something real to serve as a substrate; for in the same way as an illusion may arise even when the defect, the abode of the defect, and the knowing subject are unreal, it also may arise even when the substrate of the illusion is unreal. Hence the *Nothing* is the only reality.—To this the Sûtra replies, 'And on account of its being in every way unproved'—the theory of general Nothingness which you hold cannot stand. Do you hold that everything is being or non-being, or anything else? On none of these views the Nothingness maintained by you can be established. For the terms *being* and *non-being* and the ideas expressed by them are generally understood to refer to particular states of actually *existing* things only. If therefore you declare 'everything is nothing,' your declaration is equivalent to the declaration, 'everything is being,' for your statement also can only mean that everything that *exists* is capable of abiding in a certain condition (which you call 'Nothing'). The absolute Nothingness you have in mind cannot thus be established in any way. Moreover, he who tries to establish the tenet of universal Nothingness can attempt this in so far only as, through some means of knowledge, he has come to know Nothingness, and he must therefore acknowledge the truth of that means. For if it were not true it would follow that everything is real. The view of general Nothingness is thus altogether incapable of proof.—Here terminates the adhikara*n*a of 'unprovedness in every way.'

31. Not so, on account of the impossibility in one.

The Bauddhas have been refuted. As now the *G*ainas also hold the view of the world originating from atoms and similar views, their theory is reviewed next.—The *G*ainas hold that the world comprises souls (*g*îva), and non-souls (a*g*îva), and that there is no Lord. The world further comprises six substances (dravya), viz. souls (*g*îva), merit (dharma), demerit (adharma), bodies (pudgala), time (kâla), and space (âkâ*s*a). The souls are of three different kinds—bound (in the state of bondage), perfected by Yoga (Yogasiddha), and released (mukta). 'Merit' is that particular world-pervading substance which is the cause of the motion of all things moving; 'demerit' is that all-pervading substance which is the cause of stationariness, 'Body' is that substance which possesses colour, smell, taste, and touch. It is of two kinds, atomic or compounded of atoms; to the latter kind belong wind, fire, water, earth, the bodies of living creatures, and so on. 'Time' is a particular atomic substance which is the cause of the current distinction of past, present, and future. 'Space' is one, and of infinite extent. From among these substances those which are not atomic are comprehended under the term 'the five astikâyas (existing bodies)'—the astikâya of souls, the astikâya of merit, the astikâya of demerit, the astikâya of matter, the astikâya of space. This term 'astikâya' is applied to substances occupying several parts of space.—They also use another division of categories which subserves the purpose of Release; distinguishing souls, non-souls, influx (âsrava), bondage, nir*g*ara, sa*m*vara, and Release. *Release* comprises the means of Release also, viz. perfect knowledge, good conduct, and so on. The soul is that which has knowledge, seeing, pleasure, strength (vîrya) for its qualities. Non-soul is the aggregate of the things enjoyed by the souls. 'Influx' is whatever is instrumental towards the souls having the fruition of objects, viz. the sense-organs, and so on.—Bondage is of eight different kinds, comprising the four ghâtikarman, and the four aghâtikarman. The former term denotes whatever obstructs the essential qualities of the soul, viz. knowledge, intuition, strength, pleasure; the latter whatever causes pleasure, pain, and indifference, which are due to the persistence of the wrong imagination that makes the soul identify itself with its body.—'Decay' means the austerities (tapas), known from the teaching of the Arhat, which are the means of Release.—Sa*m*vara is such deep meditation (Samâdhi) as stops the action of the sense-organs.—Release, finally, is the manifestation of the Self in its essential nature, free from all afflictions such as passion, and so on.—The atoms which are the causes of earth and the other compounds, are not, as the Vai*s*eshikas and others hold, of four different kinds, but have all the same nature; the distinctive qualities of earth, and so on, are due to a modification (pari*n*âma) of the atoms. The *G*ainas further hold that the whole complex of things is of an ambiguous nature in so far as being existent and non-existent, permanent and non-permanent, separate and non-separate. To prove this they apply their so-called sapta-bhaṅgî-nyâya ('the system of the seven paralogisms')—'May be, it is'; 'May be, it is not'; 'May be, it is and is not'; 'May be, it is not predicable'; 'May be, it is and is not predicable'; 'May be, it is not, and is not predicable'; 'May be, it is and is not, and is not predicable.' With the help of this they prove that all things—which they declare to consist of substance (dravya), and paryâya—to be existing, one and permanent in so far as they are substances, and the opposite in so far as they are paryâyas. By paryâya they understand the particular states of substances, and as those are of the nature of Being as well as Non-being, they manage to prove existence, non-existence, and so on.—With regard to this the Sûtra remarks that no such proof is possible, 'Not so, on account of the impossibility in one'; i. e. because contradictory attributes such as existence and non-existence cannot at the same time belong to one thing, not any more than light and darkness. As a substance and particular states qualifying it—and (by the *G*ainas), called paryâya—are different things (padârtha), one substance cannot be connected with opposite attributes. It is thus not possible that a substance qualified by one particular state, such as existence, should at the same time be qualified by the opposite state, i. e. non-existence. The non-permanency, further, of a substance consists in its being the abode of those particular states which are called origination and destruction; how then should permanency, which is of an opposite nature, reside in the substance at the same time? Difference (bhinnatva) again consists in things being the abodes of contradictory attributes; non-difference, which is the opposite of this, cannot hence possibly reside in the same things which are the abode of difference; not any more than the generic character of a horse and that of a buffalo can belong to one animal. We have explained this matter at length, when—under Sûtra I, 1—refuting the bhedâbheda-theory. Time we are conscious of only as an attribute of substances (not as an independent substance), and the question as to its being and non-being, and so on, does not therefore call for a separate discussion. To speak of time as being and non-being in no way differs from generic characteristics (*g*âti), and so on, being spoken of in the same way; for—as we have explained before—of *g*âti and the like we are conscious only as attributes of substances.—But (the *G*aina may here be supposed to ask the Vedântin), how can you maintain that Brahman, although one only, yet at the same time is the Self of all?—Because, we reply, the whole aggregate of sentient and non-sentient beings constitutes the body of the Supreme Person, omniscient, omnipotent, and so on. And that the body and the person embodied and their respective attributes are of totally different nature (so that Brahman is not touched by the defects of his body), we have explained likewise.—Moreover, as your six substances, soul, and so on, are not one substance and one paryâya, their being one substance, and so on, cannot be used to prove their being one and also not one, and so on.—And if it should be said that those six substances are such (viz. one and several, and so on), each owing to its own paryâya and its own nature, we remark that then you cannot avoid contradicting your own theory of everything being of an ambiguous nature. Things which stand to each other in the relation of mutual non-existence cannot after all be identical.—Hence the theory of the *G*ainas is not reasonable. Moreover it is liable to the same objections which we have above set forth as applying to all theories of atoms constituting the universal cause, without the guidance of a Lord.

33. And likewise non-entireness of the Self.

On your view there would likewise follow non-entireness of the Self. For your opinion is that souls abide in numberless places, each soul having the same size as the body which it animates. When, therefore, the soul previously abiding in the body of an elephant or the like has to enter into a body of smaller size, e.g. that of an ant, it would follow that as the soul then occupies less space, it would not remain entire, but would become incomplete.—Let us then avoid this difficulty by assuming that the soul passes over into a different state—which process is called paryâya,—which it may manage because it is capable of contraction and dilatation.—To this the next Sûtra replies.

34. Nor also is there non-contradiction from paryâya; on account of change, and so on.

Nor is the difficulty to be evaded by the assumption of the soul assuming a different condition through contraction or dilatation. For this would imply that the soul is subject to change, and all the imperfections springing from it, viz. non-permanence, and so on, and hence would not be superior to non-sentient things such as jars and the like.

35. And on account of the endurance of the final (size), and the (resulting) permanency of both; there is no difference.

The final size of the soul, i. e. the size it has in the state of Release, is enduring since the soul does not subsequently pass into another body; and both, i. e. the soul in the state of Release and the size of that soul, are permanent (nitya). From this it follows that that ultimate size is the true essential size of the soul and also belongs to it previously to Release. Hence there is no difference of sizes, and the soul cannot therefore have the size of its temporary bodies. The Ârhata theory is therefore untenable.—Here terminates the adhikara*n*a of 'the impossibility in one.'

36. (The system) of the Lord (must be disregarded), on account of inappropriateness.

So far it has been shown that the doctrines of Kapila, Ka*n*âda, Sugata, and the Arhat must be disregarded by men desirous of final beatitude; for those doctrines are all alike untenable and foreign to the Veda. The Sûtras now declare that, for the same reasons, the doctrine of Pa*s*upati also has to be disregarded. The adherents of this view belong to four different classes—Kâpâlas, Kâlâmukhas, Pâ*s*upatas, and *S*aivas. All of them hold fanciful theories of Reality which are in conflict with the Veda, and invent various means for attaining happiness in this life and the next. They maintain the general material cause and the operative cause to be distinct, and the latter cause to be constituted by Pa*s*upati. They further hold the wearing of the six so-called 'mudrâ' badges and the like to be means to accomplish the highest end of man.

Thus the Kâpâlas say, 'He who knows the true nature of the six mudrâs, who understands the highest mudrâ, meditating on himself as in the position called bhagâsana, reaches Nirvâ*n*a. The necklace, the golden ornament, the earring, the head-jewel, ashes, and the sacred thread are called the six mudrâs. He whose body is marked with these is not born here again.'—Similarly the Kâlâmukhas teach that the means for obtaining all desired results in this world as well as the next are constituted by certain practices—such as using a skull as a drinking vessel, smearing oneself with the ashes of a dead body, eating the flesh of such a body, carrying a heavy stick, setting up a liquor-jar and using it as a platform for making offerings to the gods, and the like. 'A bracelet made of Rudrâksha-seeds on the arm, matted hair on the head, a skull, smearing oneself with ashes, &c.'—all this is well known from the sacred writings of the *S*aivas. They also hold that by some special ceremonial performance men of different castes may become Brâhma*n*as and reach the highest â*s*rama: 'by merely entering on the initiatory ceremony (dîkshâ) a man becomes a Brâhma*n*a at once; by undertaking the kâpâla rite a man becomes at once an ascetic.'

With regard to these views the Sûtra says 'of pati, on account of inappropriateness.' A 'not' has here to be supplied from Sûtra 32. The system of Pa*s*upati has to be disregarded because it is inappropriate, i.e. because the different views and practices referred to are opposed to one another and in conflict with the Veda. The different practices enumerated above, the wearing of the six mudrâs and so on, are opposed to each other; and moreover the theoretical assumptions of those people, their forms of devotion and their practices, are in conflict with the Veda. For the Veda declares that Nârâya*n*a who is the highest Brahman is alone the operative and the substantial cause of the world, 'Nârâya*n*a is the highest Brahman, Nârâya*n*a is the highest Reality, Nârâya*n*a is the highest light, Nârâya*n*a is the highest Self'; 'That thought, may I be many, may I grow forth' (*Kh*. Up. VI, 2, 3); 'He desired, may I be many, may I grow forth' (Taitt. Up. II, 6, 1), and so on. In the same way the texts declare meditation on the Supreme Person, who is the highest Brahman, to be the only meditation which effects final release; cp. 'I know that great Person of sunlike lustre beyond the darkness. A man who knows him passes over death; there is no other path to go' (*S*vet. Up. III, 8). And in the same way all texts agree in declaring that the works subserving the knowledge of Brahman are only those sacrificial and other works which the Veda enjoins on men in the different castes and stages of life: 'Him Brâhma*n*as seek to know by the study of the Veda, by sacrifice, by gifts, by penance, by fasting. Wishing for that world only, mendicants wander forth from their homes' (B*ri*. Up. XI, 4, 22). In some texts enjoining devout meditation, and so on, we indeed meet with terms such as Pra*g*âpati, *S*iva, Indra, Âkâ*s*a, Prâ*n*a, &c., but that these all refer to the supreme Reality established by the texts concerning Nârâya*n*a—the aim of which texts it is to set forth the highest Reality in its purity—, we have already proved under I, 1, 30. In the same way we have proved under Sû. I, 1, 2 that in texts treating of the creation of the world, such as 'Being only this was in the beginning,' and the like, the words *Being*, *Brahman*, and so on, denote nobody else but Nârâya*n*a, who is set forth as the universal creator in the account of creation given in the text, 'Alone indeed there was Nârâya*n*a, not Brahmâ, not I*s*âna—he being alone did not rejoice' (Mahopanishad I).—As the Pa*s*upati theory thus teaches principles, meditations and acts conflicting with the Veda, it must be disregarded.

37. And on account of the impossibility of rulership.

Those who stand outside the Veda arrive through inference at the conclusion that the Lord is a mere operative cause. This being so, they must prove the Lord's being the ruler (of the material cause) on the basis of observation. But it is impossible to prove that the Lord is the ruler of the Pradhâna in the same way as the potter e.g. is the ruler of the clay. For the Lord is without a body, while the power of ruling material causes is observed only in the case of embodied beings such as potters. Nor may you have recourse to the hypothesis of the Lord being embodied; for—as we have shown under I, 1, 3—there arise difficulties whether that body, which as body must consist of parts, be viewed as eternal or as non-eternal.

38. If you say, as in the case of the organs; we deny this, on account of enjoyment and so on.

It may possibly be said that, in the same way as the enjoying (individual) soul, although in itself without a body, is seen to rule the sense-organs, the body, and so on, the great Lord also, although without a body, may rule the Pradhâna. But this analogy cannot be allowed 'on account of enjoyment,' and so on. The body's being ruled by the soul is due to the unseen principle in the form of good and evil works, and has for its end the requital of those works. Your analogy would thus imply that the Lord also is under the influence of an unseen principle, and is requited for his good and evil works.—The Lord cannot therefore be a ruler.

39. Finiteness or absence of omniscience.

'Or' here has the sense of 'and.' If the Lord is under the influence of the ad*ri*sh*t*a, it follows that, like the individual soul, he is subject to creation, dissolution, and so on, and that he is not omniscient. The Pa*s*upati theory cannot therefore be accepted.—It is true that the Sûtra, 'but in case of conflict (with Scripture) it is not to be regarded' (Pû. Mî. Sû. I, 3, 3), has already established the non-acceptability of all views contrary to the Veda; the present adhikara*n*a, however, raises this question again in order specially to declare that the Pa*s*upati theory *is* contrary to the Veda. Although the Pâ*s*upata and the *S*aiva systems exhibit some features which are not altogether contrary to the Veda, yet they are unacceptable because they rest on an assumption contrary to the Veda, viz. of the difference of the general, instrumental and material causes, and imply an erroneous interchange of higher and lower entities.—Here terminates the adhikara*n*a of 'Pa*s*upati.'

40. On account of the impossibility of origination.

The Sûtras now proceed to refute a further doubt, viz.

that the Pa*ñk*arâtra tantra—which sets forth the means of attaining supreme beatitude, as declared by the Lord (Bhagavat)—may also be destitute of authority, in so far, namely, as belonging to the same class as the tantras of Kapila and others. The above Sûtra raises the doubt.

The theory of the Bhâgavatas is that from Vâsudeva, who is the highest Brahman and the highest cause, there originates the individual soul called Saṅkarsha*n*a; from Saṅkarsha*n*a the internal organ called Pradyumna; and from Pradyumna the principle of egoity called Aniruddha. Now this theory implies the origination of the individual soul, and this is contrary to Scripture. For scriptural texts declare the soul to be without a beginning—cp. 'the intelligent one is not born and does not die' (Ka. Up. II, 18), and other texts.

41. And there is not (origination) of the instrument from the agent.

'The internal organ called Pradyumna originates from Saṅkarsha*n*a,' i.e. the internal organ originates from the individual soul which is the agent. But this is inadmissible, since the text 'from him there is produced breath, mind, and all sense-organs' (Mu. Up. II, 1, 3) declares that the mind also springs from none else but the highest Brahman. As the Bhâgavata doctrine thus teaches things opposed to Scripture, its authoritativeness cannot be admitted.—Against these objections the next Sûtra declares itself.

42. Or, if they are of the nature of that which is knowledge and so on, there is no contradiction to that (i.e. the Bhâgavata doctrine).

The 'or' sets aside the view previously maintained. By 'that which is knowledge and so on'[1] we have to understand the highest Brahman. If Saṅkarsha*n*a, Pradyumna, and Aniruddha are of the nature of the highest Brahman, then truly there can be no objection to a body of doctrine

[1] Or 'by that which is knowledge and cause.'

which sets forth this relation. The criticism that the Bhâgavatas teach an inadmissible origination of the individual soul, is made by people who do not understand that system. What it teaches is that the highest Brahman, there called Vâsudeva, from kindness to those devoted to it, voluntarily abides in a fourfold form, so as to render itself accessible to its devotees. Thus it is said in the Paushkara-sa*m*hitâ, 'That which enjoins that Brâhma*n*as have to worship, under its proper names, the fourfold nature of the Self; that is the authoritative doctrine.' That this worship of that which is of a fourfold nature means worship of the highest Brahman, called Vâsudeva, is declared in the Sâtvata-sa*m*hitâ, 'This is the supreme *s*âstra, the great Brahmopanishad, which imparts true discrimination to Brâhma*n*as worshipping the real Brahman under the name of Vâsudeva.' That highest Brahman, called Vâsudeva, having for its body the complete aggregate of the six qualities, divides itself in so far as it is either the 'Subtle' (sûkshma), or 'division' (vyûha), or 'manifestation' (vibhava), and is attained in its fulness by the devotees who, according to their qualifications, do worship to it by means of works guided by knowledge. 'From the worship of the vibhava-aspect one attains to the vyûha, and from the worship of the vyûha one attains to the "Subtile" called Vâsudeva, i.e. the highest Brahman'—such is their doctrine. By the 'vibhava' we have to understand the aggregate of beings, such as Râma, K*r*ish*n*a, &c., in whom the highest Being becomes manifest; by the 'vyûha' the fourfold arrangement or division of the highest Reality, as Vâsudeva, Sankarsha*n*a, Pradyumna, and Aniruddha; by the 'Subtle' the highest Brahman itself, in so far as it has for its body the mere aggregate of the six qualities—as which it is called 'Vâsudeva.' Compare on this point the Paushkara, 'That body of doctrine through which, by means of works based on knowledge, one fully attains to the imperishable highest Brahman, called Vâsudeva,' and so on. Sankarsha*n*a, Pradyumna, and Aniruddha are thus mere bodily forms which the highest Brahman voluntarily assumes. Scripture already declares, 'Not born he is born in many ways,' and it is this birth—consisting in the voluntary assumption of bodily form, due to tenderness towards its devotees—which the Bhâgavata system teaches; hence there lies no valid objection to the authoritativeness of that system. And as Sankarsha*n*a, Pradyumna, and Aniruddha are the beings ruling over the individual souls, internal organs and organs of egoity, there can be no objection to their being themselves denoted by those latter terms, viz. individual soul, and so on. The case is analogous to that of Brahman being designated, in some texts, by terms such as ether, breath, and the like.

43. And on account of contradiction.

The origination of the *g*îva is, moreover, distinctly controverted in the books of the Bhâgavatas also. Thus in the Parama-sa*m*hitâ 'The nature of Prak*ri*ti consists therein that she is non-sentient, for the sake of another, eternal, ever-changing, comprising within herself the three gu*n*as, and constituting the sphere of action and experience for all agents. With her the soul (purusha) is connected in the way of inseparable association; that soul is known to be truly without beginning and without end.' And as all Sa*m*hitâs make similar statements as to the eternity of the soul, the Pa*ñk*arâtra doctrine manifestly controverts the view of the essential nature of the *g*îva being something that originates. How it is possible that in the Veda as well as in common life the soul is spoken of as being born, dying, &c., will be explained under Sû. II, 3, 17. The conclusion, therefore, is that the Bhâgavata system also denies the origination of the soul, and that hence the objections raised on this ground against its authoritativeness are without any force. Another objection is raised by some. *S*â*nd*ilya, they argue, is said to have promulgated the Pa*ñk*arâtra doctrine because he did not find a sure basis for the highest welfare of man in the Veda and its auxiliary disciplines, and this implies that the Pa*ñk*arâtra is opposed to the Veda.—This objection, we reply, springs from nothing else but the mere unreasoning faith of men who do not possess the faintest knowledge of the teachings of the Veda, and have never considered the hosts of arguments which confirm that teaching. When the Veda says, 'Morning after morning those speak untruth who make the Agnihotra offering before sunrise,' it is understood that the censure there passed on the offering before sunrise is really meant to glorify the offering after sunrise. We meet with a similar case in the 'bhûma-vidyâ' (*Kh.* Up. VII, 2). There at the beginning Nârada says, 'I know the *Ri*g-veda, the Ya*g*ur-veda, the Sâma-veda, the Âtharva*n*a as the fourth, the Itihâsa-purâ*n*a as the fifth,' and so on, enumerating all the various branches of knowledge, and finally summing up 'with all this I know the mantras only, I do not know the Self.' Now this declaration of the knowledge of the Self not being attainable through any branch of knowledge except the knowledge of the Bhûman evidently has no other purpose but to glorify this latter knowledge, which is about to be expounded. Or else Nârada's words refer to the fact that from the Veda and its auxiliary disciplines he had not obtained the knowledge of the highest Reality. Analogous to this is the case of *S*â*nd*ilya's alleged objection to the Veda. That the Bhâgavata doctrine is meant to facilitate the understanding of the sense of the Veda which by itself is difficult of comprehension, is declared in the Parama-sa*m*hitâ, 'I have read the Vedas at length, together with all the various auxiliary branches of knowledge. But in all these I cannot see a clear indication, raised above all doubt, of the way to blessedness, whereby I might reach perfection'; and 'The wise Lord Hari, animated by kindness for those devoted to him, extracted the essential meaning of all the Vedânta-texts and condensed it in an easy form.' The incontrovertible fact then is as follows. The Lord who is known from the Vedânta-texts, i.e. Vâsudeva, called there the highest Brahman—who is antagonistic to all evil, whose nature is of uniform excellence, who is an ocean, as it were, of unlimited exalted qualities, such as infinite intelligence, bliss, and so on, all whose purposes come true—perceiving that those devoted to him, according as they are differently placed in the four castes and the four stages of life, are intent on the different ends of life, viz. religious observances, wealth, pleasure, and final release; and recognising that the Vedas—which teach the truth about his own nature, his glorious manifestations, the means of rendering him propitious and the fruits of such endeavour—are difficult to fathom by all beings other than himself, whether gods or men, since those Vedas are divided into *Ri*k, Ya*g*us, Sâman, and Atharvan; and being animated by infinite pity, tenderness, and magnanimity; with a view to enable his devotees to grasp the true meaning of the Vedas, himself composed the Pa*ñk*arâtra-*s*âstra. The author of the Sûtras (Vyâsa)—who first composed the Sûtras, the purport of which it is to set forth the arguments establishing the Vedânta doctrine, and then the Bhârata-sa*m*hitâ (i.e. the Mahâbhârata) in a hundred thousand *s*lokas in order to support thereby the teaching of the Veda—himself says in the chapter called Mokshadharma, which treats of knowledge, 'If a householder, or a Brahma*k*ârin, or a hermit, or a mendicant wishes to achieve success, what deity should he worship?' and so on; explains then at great length the Pa*ñk*arâtra system, and then says, 'From the lengthy Bhârata story, comprising one hundred thousand *s*lokas, this body of doctrine has been extracted, with the churning-staff of mind, as butter is churned from curds—as butter from milk, as the Brâhma*n*a from men, as the Âra*n*yaka from the Vedas, as Am*ri*ta from medicinal herbs.—This great Upanishad, consistent with the four Vedas, in harmony with Sâṅkhya and Yoga, was called by him by the name of Pa*ñk*arâtra. This is excellent, this is Brahman, this is supremely beneficial. Fully agreeing with the *Ri*k, the Ya*g*us, the Sâman, and the Atharvâṅgiras, this doctrine will be truly authoritative.' The terms Sâṅkhya and Yoga here denote the concentrated application of knowledge and of works. As has been said, 'By the application of knowledge on the part of the Sâṅkhya, and of works on the part of the Yogins.' And in the Bhîshmaparvan we read, 'By Brâhma*n*as, Kshattriyas, Vai*s*yas and *S*ûdras, Mâdhava is to be honoured, served and worshipped—he who was proclaimed by Saṅkarsha*n*a in agreement with the Sâtvata law.'—How then could these utterances of Bâdarâya*n*a, the foremost among all those who understand the teaching of the Veda, be reconciled with the view that in the Sûtras he maintains the non-authoritativeness of the Sâtvata doctrine, the purport of which is to teach the worship of, and meditation on, Vâsudeva, who is none other than the highest Brahman known from the Vedânta-texts?

But other passages in the Mahâbhârata, such as 'There is the Sâṅkhya, the Yoga, the Pa*ñk*arâtra, the Vedas, and the Pâ*s*upata doctrine; do all these rest on one and the same basis, or on different ones?' and so on, declare that the Sâṅkhya and other doctrines also are worthy of regard, while yet in the *S*ârîraka Sûtras those very same doctrines are formally refuted. Why, therefore, should not the same hold good in the case of the Bhâgavata doctrine?—Not so, we reply. In the Mahâbhârata also Bâdarâya*n*a applies to the Sâṅkhya and other doctrines the same style of reasoning as in the Sûtras. The question, asked in the passage quoted, means 'Do the Sâṅkhya, the Yoga, the Pâ*s*upata, and the Pa*ñk*arâtra set forth one and the same reality, or different ones? If the former, what is that reality? If the latter, they convey contradictory doctrines, and, as reality is not something which may be optionally assumed to be either such or such, one of those doctrines only can be acknowledged as authoritative, and the question then arises which is to be so acknowledged?'—The answer to the question is given in the passage beginning, 'Know, O royal Sage, all those different views. The promulgator of the Sâṅkhya is Kapila,' &c. Here the human origin of the Sâṅkhya, Yoga, and Pâ*s*upata is established on the ground of their having been produced by Kapila, Hira*n*yagarbha, and Pa*s*upati. Next the clause 'Aparântatamas is said to be the teacher of the Vedas' intimates the non-human character of the Vedas; and finally the clause 'Of the whole Pa*ñk*arâtra, Nârâya*n*a himself is the promulgator' declares that Nârâya*n*a himself revealed the Pa*ñk*arâtra doctrine. The connected purport of these different clauses is as follows. As the systems of human origin set forth doctrines mutually contradictory, and, moreover, teach what is in conflict with the matter known from the Veda—which, on account of its non-human character, is raised above all suspicion of error and other imperfections—they cannot be accepted as authoritative with regard to anything not depending on human action and choice. Now the matter to be known from the Veda is Nârâyana, who is none other than the highest Brahman. It hence follows that the entities set forth in those different systems—the pradhâna, the soul (purusha), Pasupati, and so on—have to be viewed as real only in so far as Nârâyana, i.e. the highest Brahman, as known from the Vedânta-texts, constitutes their Self. This the text directly declares in the passage, 'In all those doctrines it is seen, in accordance with tradition and reasoning, that the lord Nârâyana is the only basis.' This means—'To him who considers the entities set forth in those systems with the help of argumentation, it is evident that Nârâyana alone is the basis of all those entities.' In other words, as the entities set forth in those systems are not Brahman, any one who remembers the teaching of texts such as 'all this indeed is Brahman,' 'Nârâyana is all,' which declare Brahman to be the Self of all, comes to the conclusion that Nârâyana alone is the basis of those entities. As thus it is settled that the highest Brahman, as known from the Vedânta-texts, or Nârâyana, himself is the promulgator of the entire Pañkarâtra, and that this system teaches the nature of Nârâyana and the proper way of worshipping him, none can disestablish the view that in the Pañkarâtra all the other doctrines are comprised. For this reason the Mahâbhârata says, 'Thus the Sâṅkhya-yoga and the Veda and the Âranyaka, being members of one another, are called the Pañkarâtra,' i.e. the Sâṅkhya, the Yoga, the Vedas, and the Âranyakas, which are members of one another because they are one in so far as aiming at setting forth one Truth, together are called the Pañkarâtra.—The Sâṅkhya explains the twenty-five principles, the Yoga teaches certain practices and means of mental concentration, and the Âranyakas teach that all the subordinate principles have their true Self in Brahman, that the mental concentration enjoined in the Yoga is a mode of meditation on Brahman, and that the rites and works which are set forth in the Veda are means to win the favour of Brahman —thus giving instruction as to Brahman's nature. Now all these elements, in their inward connexion, are clearly set forth in the Pa*ñk*arâtra by the highest Brahman, i.e. Nârâya*n*a, himself. The *S*ârîraka *S*âstra (i.e. the Vedânta) does not disprove the principles assumed by the Sâṅkhyas, but merely the view of their not having Brahman for their Self; and similarly in its criticism on the Yoga and Pâ*s*upata systems, it merely refutes the view of the Lord being a mere instrumental cause, the erroneous assumptions as to the relative position of higher and lower entities, and certain practices not warranted by the Veda; but it does not reject the Yoga itself, nor again the lord Pa*s*upati. Hence Sm*ri*ti says, 'The Sâṅkhya, the Yoga, the Pa*ñk*arâtra, the Vedas, and the Pâ*s*upata doctrine—all these having their proof in the Self may not be destroyed by arguments.' The essential points in all these doctrines are to be adopted, not to be rejected absolutely as the teaching of *G*ina or Sugata is to be rejected. For, as said in the Sm*ri*ti text quoted above, 'in all those doctrines it is seen, according to tradition and reasoning, that the lord Nârâya*n*a is the only basis.'—Here terminates the adhikara*n*a of 'the impossibility of origination.'

## THIRD PÂDA.

1. Not Ether; on account of the absence of scriptural statement.

We have demonstrated that the Sâṅkhya-system and other systems standing outside the Veda are untenable since they rest on fallacious reasoning and are self-contradictory. In order to prove that our own view is altogether free from all objections of this kind, we shall now explain in detail the mode in which this world, with all its sentient and non-sentient beings, is produced by Brahman, whom we hold to be the general creator.

The first doubt here presenting itself is whether Ether be something produced or not.—The Pûrvapakshin maintains that it is not produced, since there is no scriptural statement to that effect. A scriptural statement may be expected with regard to what is possible; but what is impossible—as e. g. the origination of a sky-flower or of Ether—cannot possibly be taught by Scripture. For the origination of Ether, which is not made up of parts and is all pervasive, cannot be imagined in any way. For this very reason, i. e. the impossibility of the thing, the *Kh*ândogya, in its account of creation, mentions the origination of fire, water, &c. only (but not of Ether)—'It thought, may I be many, may I grow forth,' 'It sent forth fire,' and so on. When therefore the Taittirîya, the Âtharva*n*a, and other texts tell us that Ether did originate—'From that Self sprang Ether' (Taitt. Up. II, 1); 'From him is born breath, mind, and all organs of sense, Ether, air, light, water,' &c. (Mu. Up. II, 1, 4)—such statements are contrary to sense, and hence refute themselves.—To this the Sûtra replies.

2. But there is.

But there is origination of Ether. For Scripture, which is concerned with matters transcending sense perception, is able to establish the truth even of the origination of Ether, although this be not proved by other means of knowledge.

And in a matter known from Scripture a contradictory inference, such as that Ether cannot originate because it is without parts, is not of sufficient force. That the non-originatedness of the Self also does not rest on its being without parts will be shown further on.—Here the Pûrvapakshin raises an objection.

3. It has a secondary sense, on account of impossibility and of the text.

It is reasonable to assume that in passages such as 'From that Self there sprang Ether,' the origination of Ether is not to be taken in its literal sense; for according to the *Kh*ândogya-text 'it sent forth fire.' Brahman engaged in creation first produces fire, and fire thus having the first place, the text cannot possibly mean to say that Ether also was produced. Moreover, there is another text, viz. 'Vâyu and antariksha (i.e. Ether), this is the Immortal,' according to which Ether is immortal, i.e. non-produced. —But how can one and the same word, viz. it 'sprang' (i.e. originated), be taken in a metaphorical sense with reference to Ether, and in its literal sense with reference to fire, and so on?—To this the next Sûtra replies.

4. There may be (a double sense) of the one (word), as in the case of the word 'Brahman.'

Since in the clause 'from that Self there sprang Brahman,' the word 'sprang' cannot be taken in its literal sense, it may be used there in a secondary sense; while the same word as connected with the subsequent clauses 'from Vâyu Agni,' &c., may have its primary sense. This would be analogous to the use of the word Brahman in Mu. Up. I, 1. There in the clause 'From him is born that Brahman, name, form, and matter' (9), the word *Brahman* is used in a secondary sense, i.e. denotes the Pradhâna; while in the same chapter, in the clause 'Brahman swells by means of brooding' (8), the same word denotes Brahman in its primary sense. It is true indeed that in this latter case the word 'Brahman' occurs twice; while in the Taitt. text the word 'sambhûta' occurs once only, and has to be carried over from the first clause into the subsequent ones; but this makes no difference, for, in the case of such carrying over of a word, no less than in the case of actual repetition, the general denotation of the word is repeated.—The next Sûtra refutes this objection.

5. The non-abandonment of the promissory statement (results) from non-difference.

It is not appropriate to assume, from deference to the *Kh*ândogya-text, a secondary meaning for those other texts also which declare Ether to have originated. For the *Kh*ândogya itself virtually admits the origination of Ether; in so far, namely, as the clause 'that by which the non-heard is heard,' &c., declares that through the knowledge of Brahman everything is known. This declaration is not abandoned, i. e. is adhered to, only if the Ether also is an effect of Brahman and thus non-different from it.

6. (As follows also) from (other) texts.

That Ether is an originated thing follows from other clauses also in the *Kh*ândogya: 'Being only this was in the beginning, one without a second' affirms the oneness of everything before creation, and 'In that all this has its Self' implies that everything is an effect of, and hence non-different from, Brahman.—Nor does the statement as to the creation of fire, 'it sent forth fire,' exclude the creation of Ether. For the first place which there is assigned to fire rests only thereon that no mention is made of the creation of Ether, and this has no force to negative the creation of Ether as positively stated in other texts.

7. But the division (origination) extends over all effects; as in ordinary life.

The 'but' has the sense of 'and.' As the clause 'In that all this has its Self' and similar ones directly state that Ether also is a creation of Brahman, the division, i. e. the origination of Ether from Brahman, is implicitly declared thereby. As in ordinary life. When in ordinary life somebody has said 'all these men are the sons of

Devadatta,' it is known that any particulars which may afterwards be given about the descent of some of them are meant to apply to all.—In accordance with this our conclusion we interpret the text 'Air and Ether, this is the Immortal,' as asserting only that air and Ether continue to exist for a long time, as the Devas do.

8. Hereby air is explained.

The same argumentation explains the origination of air also. That a special Sûtra is devoted to the origination of air—instead of disposing in one Sûtra of Ether and air—is for the sake of Sûtra 10, which states that 'hence (i. e. from air) there originated fire.'

9. But there is non-origination of that which is (only); on account of impossibility.

The 'but' has an affirmative sense. There is non-origination of that which is, i. e. of Brahman only; of whatever is different from Brahman non-origination cannot possibly be established. This means—the origination of Ether and air has been proved only in order to illustrate a general truth. Only that which *is*, i. e. Brahman, which is the general cause, cannot originate. Whatever is other than Brahman, i. e. the entire world comprising the Unevolved, the great principle (mahat), ahankâra, the tanmâtras, the sense-organs, the Ether, the air, and so on, cannot possibly be shown to be non-originated, since its being an effect is proved by the text declaring that everything is known through one thing, and in other ways.—Here terminates the adhikara*n*a of 'the Ether.'

10. Fire (is produced) thence, for thus Scripture declares.

It has been stated that everything different from Brahman is the effect of Brahman. The doubt now arises whether the more remote effects of Brahman originate, each of them, only from that substance which is their immediately antecedent cause or from Brahman in the form of that substance.—The decision is that they originate from those substances only; for the text 'from air fire' directly states the origination of fire from air.

11. Water (from fire).

Water also originates 'thence,' i. e. from fire; for so the texts declare 'From fire water' (Taitt. Up. II, 1, 1); 'that sent forth water' (*Kh.* Up. VI, 2, 3).

12. Earth (from water).

Earth originates from water; for so the texts declare 'From water earth' (Taitt. Up. II, 1, 1). 'It (water) sent forth food' (*Kh.* Up. VI, 2, 3). But how can the word 'food' denote earth?—To this the next Sûtra replies.

13. Earth on account of the subject-matter, the colour, and other texts.

That the word 'food' denotes the earth is to be inferred from the fact that the section in which the word occurs has for its subject-matter the creation of the elements; as everything eatable is a product of the earth, the term denoting the effect is there applied to denote the cause. In the same chapter, where the colour of the elements is mentioned ('The red colour of a flame is the colour of fire, the white one that of water, the black one that of food'), the collocation of words clearly shows that 'food' means something of the same kind as fire and water, viz. the elements of earth. And there are other texts also which treat of the same topic and declare the origination of earth from water, cp. Taitt. Up. II, 1, 'from fire sprang water, from water earth.' All this proves that the term 'food' denotes earth, and that hence earth originates from water.

Fire and the other substances, the origination of which has been detailed, are mentioned merely as instances, and it must be understood that also other entities, such as the 'Mahat,' and so on, originate only from the immediately preceding cause, in agreement with scriptural statements. And texts such as 'From him is born breath, mind, and all organs of sense, ether, air, light, water, and the earth, the support of all' (Mu. Up. II, 1, 3); 'From him is born that

Brahman, name, form, and food' (Mu. Up. I, 1, 9); 'From that Self there sprang ether' (Taitt. Up. II, 1, 1); 'It (i.e. that which is) sent forth fire' (*Kh.* Up. VI, 2, 3)—(which seems to teach the direct origination from Brahman of the different elements, and so on)—may be interpreted on the understanding of Brahman being their mediate cause also.—This primâ facie view the next Sûtra disposes of.

14. But he; from the inferential mark supplied by their reflection.

The 'but' indicates the setting aside of the primâ facie view raised. Of all effected things, the *Mahat*, and so on, the highest Person himself, in so far as embodied in the immediately preceding substance, is the direct cause.—How is this known?—'From the inferential mark supplied by the reflection of them.' By 'reflection' the Sûtra means the resolve expressed in the recurring phrase, 'May I be many'; 'That fire thought, may I be many'; 'That water thought, may I be many' (*Kh.* Up. VI, 2, 3; 4). As these texts declare that there was thought—in the form of a resolve of self-multiplication—which thought can belong to a Self only, we conclude that also the Mahat, the ahaṅkâra, the Ether, and so on, accomplish the sending forth of their respective effects only after similar thought, and such thought can belong only to the highest Brahman embodied in the Mahat, ahaṅkâra, and so on. That the highest Brahman is embodied in all beings and constitutes their Self, is directly stated in the antaryâmin-brâhma*n*a, 'He who abiding in the earth; abiding in water; abiding in fire,' &c. &c. (B*ri*. Up. III, 7, 3 ff.); and likewise in the Subâla-Up., 'Whose body is the earth,' &c. &c., up to 'Whose body is the Unevolved.'—The Pûrvapakshin had maintained that the creation, from Brahman, of breath, and so on, which is declared in texts such as 'From him are born breath, mind,' &c., may be understood as a mediate creation. This point is taken up by the next Sûtra.

15. But the order of succession (which is stated) in reverse order (of the true one) is possible, (only

if the origination of all effects is) thence (i.e. from Brahman).

The 'but' has an asseverative sense. The direct origination from Brahman of all effects—which in passages such as the one quoted by the Pûrvapakshin is stated in a form the reverse of the (true) order of origination according to which the Unevolved, the Mahat, the ahankâra, Ether, and so on, succeed each other—is possible only on the supposition of the origination of each effect being really from Brahman itself in the form of a special causal substance. To understand the causality of Brahman as a merely mediate one would be to contradict all those statements of immediate origination. Texts such as the one quoted thus confirm the conclusion that everything originates from Brahman directly.

16. If it be said that knowledge and mind (which are mentioned) between (breath and the elements) (are stated) in order of succession, owing to an inferential mark of this; we say, not so, on account of non-difference.

'Knowledge' in the Sûtra denotes the means of knowledge, i. e. the sense-organs.—An objection is raised against the conclusion arrived at under the preceding Sûtra. We cannot, the opponent says, admit the conclusion that the passage from the Mu*nd*aka Up. 'from him is born breath, mind,' &c., declares the immediate origination from Brahman of all things, and that hence the passage confirms the view, first suggested by the inferential mark of 'thought' (see above, Sû. 14), that everything springs from Brahman direct. For the purport of the text is to state a certain order of succession, and we hence conclude that all the beings mentioned were successively created. In the second half of the text we recognise the series of ether, air, fire, &c., which is known to us from other texts, and from the fact of their being exhibited in one and the same text we conclude that knowledge and mind—which are mentioned between breath on the one side and the elements on the other—must be viewed as created in that order. The text therefore in no way confirms the direct origination of everything from Brahman. To this the Sûtra replies, 'Not so, on account of non-difference.' The first words of the text 'from him is born' connect themselves equally with breath, and knowledge, and mind, and the series of elements beginning with ether; and the meaning of the whole therefore is to declare that all the entities spring directly from Brahman, not to teach the order of succession in which they are produced. It moreover cannot have the purport of teaching a certain order of succession, because the order stated contradicts the order established by other scriptural passages; such as the one beginning 'the earth is merged in water,' and ending 'darkness becomes one.' We hence hold to the conclusion that all effects originate from Brahman only, in so far as embodied in the Unevolved, and so on, and that the terms 'fire' and so on denote Brahman, which is the Self of all those substances.—But to interpret all these words as denoting Brahman is to set aside their special denotative power as established by etymology!—To this objection the next Sûtra replies.

17. But that which abides in the things movable and immovable, i.e. the terms denoting those things, are non-secondary (i.e. of primary denotative power, viz. with regard to Brahman); since (their denotative power) is effected by the being of that (i.e. Brahman).

The 'but' sets aside the objection raised. (The primâ facie view here is as follows.) As Brahman, which has all things for its modes, is not the object of Perception and the other means of knowledge which give rise to the apprehension of the things only which are Brahman's modes, and as hence, previously to the study of the Vedânta-texts, the idea of that to which the modes belong (i. e. of Brahman) does not arise, and as the knowledge of all words finally denoting Brahman depends on the existence of the idea of that to which the modes belong (i. e. Brahman); all the individual words are used in worldly language only separately to denote special things. In other words, as the terms 'fire' and so on have denotative power with regard to particular things only, their denotative power with regard to Brahman is secondary, indirect only.—Of this view the Sûtra disposes by saying 'that which abides in the moving and the non-moving,' &c. The meaning is—the terms which abide in, i. e. are connected with, the different moving and non-moving things, and hence denote those things, possess with regard to Brahman a denotative power which is not 'bhâkta,' i.e. secondary or figurative, but primary and direct. 'Why so?' Because the denotative power of all words is dependent on the being of Brahman. For this we know from the scriptural passage which tells how names and forms were evolved by Brahman.—Here terminates the adhikara*n*a of 'fire.'

18. Not the Self, on account of scriptural statement, and on account of the eternity (which results) from them.

The Sûtras so far have stated that this entire world, from Ether downwards, originates from the highest Brahman. It now becomes a matter for discussion whether the individual soul also originates in the same way or not.—It does so originate, the Pûrvapakshin maintains. For on this assumption only the scriptural statement as to the cognition of all things through the cognition of one thing holds good, and moreover Scripture declares that before creation everything was one. Moreover, there are texts directly stating that the soul also was produced in the same way as Ether and other created things.

'Pra*g*âpati sent forth all creatures'; 'All these creatures have their root in the True, they abide in the True, they rest on the True' (*Kh.* Up. VI, 8, 6); 'From whence these beings are produced' (Taitt. Up. III, 1, 1). As these passages declare the origination of the world inclusive of sentient beings, we conclude that the souls also originate. Nor must this be objected to on the ground that from the fact that Brahman is eternal, and the other fact that texts such as 'That art thou' teach the soul to be of the nature of Brahman, it follows that the soul also is eternal. For if we reasoned in this style we should have to admit also that the Ether and the other elements are eternal, since texts such as 'in that all this has its Self' and 'all this indeed is Brahman' intimate them also to be of the nature of Brahman. Hence the individual soul also originates no less than Ether and the rest.—To this the Sûtra replies, 'Not the Self, on account of scriptural statement.' The Self is not produced, since certain texts directly deny its origination; cp. 'the intelligent one is not born nor does he die' (Ka. Up. I, 2, 18); 'There are two unborn ones, one intelligent and strong, the other non-intelligent and weak' (*S*vet. Up. I, 9). And the eternity of the soul is learned from the same texts, cp. 'There is one eternal thinker,' &c. (Ka. Up. II, 5, 13); 'Unborn, eternal, everlasting is that ancient one; he is not killed though the body is killed' (Ka. Up. I, 2, 18).—For these reasons the soul is not produced.

But how then about the declaration that through the cognition of one thing everything is known?—There is no difficulty here, since the soul also is an effect, and since effect and cause are non-different.—But this implies that the soul is an originated thing just like Ether and so on!—Not so, we reply. By a thing being an effect we mean its being due to a substance passing over into some other state; and from this point of view the soul also is an effect. There is, however, the difference, that the 'other condition' which is represented by the soul is of a different kind from that which constitutes non-sentient things, such as Ether and so on. The 'otherness' on which the soul depends consists in the contraction and expansion of intelligence; while the change on which the origination of Ether and so on depends is a change of essential nature. And change of the latter kind is what we deny of the soul. We have shown that there are three entities of distinct nature, viz. objects of fruition, enjoying subjects, and a Ruler; that origination and so on which are characteristic of the objects do not belong to the subjects, and that the latter are eternal; that the characteristic qualities of the objects and likewise those of the subjects—viz. liability to pain and suffering—do not belong to the Ruler; that the latter is eternal, free from all imperfections, omniscient, immediately realising all his purposes, the Lord of the lords of the organs, the highest Lord of all; and that sentient and non-sentient beings in all their states constitute the body of the Lord while he constitutes their Self. While Brahman thus has for its modes (prakâra) the sentient and non-sentient beings in which it ever is embodied, during certain periods those beings abide in so subtle a condition as to be incapable of receiving designations different from that of Brahman itself; Brahman then is said to be in its causal state. When, on the other hand, its body is constituted by all those beings in their gross state, when they have separate, distinct names and forms, Brahman is said to be in its effected condition. When, now, Brahman passes over from the causal state into the effected state, the aggregate of non-sentient things which in the causal state were destitute of name and form undergoes an essential change of nature—implying the possession of distinct names and so on—so as to become fit to constitute objects of fruition for sentient beings; the change, on the other hand, which the sentient beings (the souls) undergo on that occasion is nothing more than a certain expansion of intelligence (or consciousness), capacitating them to experience the different rewards or punishments for their previous deeds. The ruling element of the world, i. e. the Lord, finally, who has the sentient and non-sentient beings for his modes, undergoes a change in so far as he is, at alternating periods, embodied in all those beings in their alternating states. The two modes, and he to whom the modes belong, thus undergo a common change in so far as in the case of all of them the causal condition passes over into a different condition.

It is with reference to this change undergone by one substance in passing over into a different state that the *Kh*ândogya says that through the knowledge of one thing everything is known, and illustrates this by the case of the lump of clay (knowing which we know all things made of clay). Texts such as 'Pra*g*âpati sent forth the creatures,' which declare the origination of the soul, really mean only to state that the souls are by turns associated with or dissociated from bodies—the effect of which is that their intelligence is either contracted or expanded. Texts again which deny the origination of the soul and affirm its permanency ('He is not born and does not die,' &c.) mean to say that the soul does not, like the non-sentient element of creation, undergo changes of essential nature. And finally there are texts the purport of which it is to declare the absence of change of essential nature as well as of alternate expansion and contraction of intelligence—cp. 'That is the great unborn Self, undecaying, undying, immortal, Brahman' (B*ri*. Up. IV, 4, 25); 'the eternal thinker,' &c. (Ka. Up. II, 5, 13); such texts have for their subject the highest Lord.—All this also explains how Brahman, which is at all times differentiated by the sentient and non-sentient beings that constitute its body, can be said to be one only previous to creation; the statement is possible because at that time the differentiation of names and forms did not exist. That that which makes the difference between plurality and unity is the presence or absence of differentiation through names and forms, is distinctly declared in the text, 'Now all this was undifferentiated. It became differentiated by form and name' (B*ri*. Up. I, 4, 7).—Those also who hold that the individual soul is due to Nescience; and those who hold it to be due to a real limiting adjunct (upâdhi); and those who hold that Brahman, whose essential nature is mere Being, assumes by itself the threefold form of enjoying subjects, objects of enjoyment, and supreme Ruler; can all of them explain the unity which Scripture predicates of Brahman in the pralaya state, only on the basis of the absence of differentiation by names and forms; for according to them also (there is no absolute unity at any time, but) either the potentiality of Nescience, or the potentiality of the limiting adjunct, or the potentialities of enjoying subjects, objects of enjoyment, and supreme Ruler persist in the pralaya condition also. And, moreover, it is proved by the two Sûtras, II, 1, 33; 35, that the distinction of the several individual souls and the stream of their works are eternal.

There is, however, the following difference between those several views. The first-mentioned view implies that Brahman itself is under the illusive influence of beginningless Avidyâ. According to the second view, the effect of the real and beginningless limiting adjunct is that Brahman itself is in the state of bondage; for there is no other entity but Brahman and the adjunct. According to the third view, Brahman itself assumes different forms, and itself experiences the various unpleasant consequences of deeds. Nor would it avail to say that that part of Brahman which is the Ruler is not an experiencing subject; for as Brahman is all-knowing it recognises the enjoying subject as non-different from itself, and thus is itself an enjoying subject.—According to our view, on the other hand, Brahman, which has for its body all sentient and non-sentient beings, whether in their subtle or their gross state, is always—in its effected as well as in its causal condition—free from all shadow of imperfection, and a limitless ocean as it were of all exalted qualities. All imperfections, and suffering, and all change belong not to Brahman, but only to the sentient and non-sentient beings which are its modes. This view removes all difficulties.—Here terminates the adhikara*n*a of 'the Self.'

19. For this very reason (the individual soul is) a knower.

It has been shown that, different therein from Ether and the rest, the soul is not produced. This leads to the consideration of the soul's essential nature. Is that essential nature constituted by mere intelligence as Sugata and Kapila hold; or is the soul as Ka*n*âda thinks, essentially non-intelligent, comparable to a stone, while intelligence is merely an adventitious quality of it; or is it essentially a knowing subject?—The soul is mere intelligence, the Pûrvapakshin maintains; for the reason that Scripture declares it to be so. For in the antaryâmin-brâhma*n*a the clause which in the Mâdhyandina-text runs as follows, 'he who abides in the Self,' is in the text of the Kâ*n*vas represented by the clause 'he who abides in knowledge.'

Similarly the text 'knowledge performs the sacrifice and all sacred acts' (Taitt. Up. II, 5, 1) shows that it is knowledge only which is the true nature of the active Self. And Sm*ri*ti texts convey the same view, as e.g. 'it in reality is of the nature of absolutely spotless intelligence.' A second Pûrvapakshin denies the truth of this view. If, he says, we assume that the Self's essential nature consists either in mere knowledge or in its being a knowing subject, it follows that as the Self is omnipresent there must be consciousness at all places and at all times. On that doctrine we, further, could not account for the use of the instruments of cognition (i.e. the sense-organs, &c.); nor for the fact that in the states of deep sleep, swoon and so on, the Self although present is not observed to be conscious, while on the other hand consciousness is seen to arise as soon as the conditions of the waking state are realised. We therefore conclude that neither intelligence or consciousness, nor being a knowing agent, constitutes the essence of the soul, but that consciousness is a mere adventitious or occasional attribute. And the omnipresence of the Self must needs be admitted since its effects are perceived everywhere. Nor is there any valid reason for holding that the Self moves to any place; for as it is assumed to be present everywhere the actual accomplishment of effects (at certain places only) may be attributed to the moving of the body only.—Scripture also directly declares that in the state of deep sleep there is no consciousness, 'I do not indeed at the present moment know myself, so as to be able to say "that am I," nor do I know those beings.' Similarly Scripture declares the absence of consciousness in the state of final release, 'when he has departed there is no consciousness' (B*ri*. Up. II, 4, 12); where the Self is spoken of as having knowledge for its essential nature, the meaning only is that knowledge constitutes its specific quality, and the expression is therefore not to be urged in its literal sense.

Against all this the Sûtra declares 'for this very reason a knower.' This Self is essentially a knower, a knowing subject; not either mere knowledge or of non-sentient nature.—Why?—'For this very reason,' i.e. on account of Scripture itself. 'For this reason' refers back to the 'on account of Scripture' in the preceding Sûtra. For in the *Kh*ândogya, where the condition of the released and the non-released soul is described, the text says 'He who knows, let me smell this, he is the Self—with the mind seeing those pleasures he rejoices—the devas who are in the world of Brahman—whose desires are true, whose purposes are true—not remembering the body into which he was born' (*Kh.* Up. VIII, 12, 4-5; 1, 5; 12, 3). And elsewhere 'The seer does not see death' (*Kh.* Up. VII, 26, 2). Similarly we read in the Vâ*g*asaneyaka, in reply to the question 'Who is that Self?'—'He who is within the heart, surrounded by the Prâ*n*as, the person of light, consisting of knowledge' (B*ri*. Up. IV, 3, 7); 'By what should one know the knower?' (B*ri*. Up. IV, 5, 15); 'That person knows.' And 'for he is the knower, the hearer, the smeller, the taster, the perceiver, the thinker, the agent—he the person whose Self is knowledge'; and 'thus these sixteen parts of that seer' (Pra. Up. IV, 9; VI, 5). To the objection that if being a cognising subject constituted the essential nature of the Self it would follow that as the Self is omnipresent, there would be consciousness always and everywhere, the next Sûtra replies.

20. On account of (its) passing out, moving and returning.

The Self is not omnipresent, but on the contrary, of atomic size (a*n*u).—How is this known?—Since Scripture says that it passes out, goes and returns. Its passing out is described in the following passage 'by that light this Self departs, either through the eye, or through the skull, or through other parts of the body' (B*ri*. Up. IV, 4, 2). Its going in the following text 'all those who pass away out of this world go to the moon,' and its returning in the text 'from that world he comes again into this world, for action.' All this going, and so on, cannot be reconciled with the soul being present everywhere.

21. And on account of the latter two (being effected) through the Self.

The 'and' has affirming power. The 'passing out' might somehow be reconciled with a non-moving Self (such as the omnipresent Self would be) if it were taken in the sense of the Self separating from the body; but for the going and returning no analogous explanation is possible. They, therefore, must be taken as effected by the Self itself (which, then, cannot be omnipresent and non-moving).

22. If it be said that (the soul) is not atomic, on account of scriptural statement of (what is) not that; we say no, on account of the other one being the topic.

The passage 'He who is within the heart, surrounded by the Prâ*n*as, the person consisting of knowledge' (B*ri*. Up. IV, 3, 7) introduces as the topic of discussion the personal Self, and further on in the same chapter we read 'the unborn Self, the great one' (IV, 4, 22). The personal Self, being expressly called *great*, cannot, therefore, be atomic!—Not so, we reply. 'Since the other one is the topic.' In the second text quoted that Self which is other than the personal Self—i.e. the highest Self (prâg*ñ*a) constitutes the topic. In the beginning of the chapter, indeed, the individual Self is introduced, but later on, between the two texts quoted, the instruction begins to concern itself with the highest Self, 'he by whom there is known the Self of intelligence' (pratibuddha âtmâ; IV, 4, 13). It is this latter Self which, in 22, is called *great*, not the individual Self.

23. And on account of the very word, and of measure.

Scripture directly applies the word 'a*n*u' to the individual Self, 'By thought is to be known that atomic Self into which Breath has entered fivefold' (Mu. Up. III, 1, 9). —By the term 'unmâna' in the Sûtra we have to understand measurement by selection of comparative instances.

Scripture declares the minuteness of the individual Self by reference to things which are like atoms in size, 'The individual soul is to be known as part of the hundredth part of the point of a hair divided a hundred times, and yet it is to be infinite' (*S*vet. Up. V, 9); 'that lower one is seen of the measure of the point of a goad' (V, 8). For these reasons also the individual Self must be viewed as atomic.—But this conflicts with the fact that sensation extends over the whole body!—This objection the next Sûtra refutes by means of an analogous instance.

24. There is no contradiction, as in the case of sandal-ointment.

As a drop of sandal-ointment, although applied to one spot of the body only, yet produces a refreshing sensation extending over the whole body; thus the Self also, although dwelling in one part of the body only, is conscious of sensations taking place in any part of the body.

25. Should it be said (that this is not so) on account of specialisation of abode; we say no, on account of the acknowledgment (of a place of the Self), viz. in the heart.

There is a difference. The drop of ointment can produce its effect as at any rate it is in contact with a definite part of the body. But we know of no such part in the case of the soul!—Not so, we reply. Scripture informs us that the Self abides in a definite part of the body, viz. the heart. 'For that Self is in the heart, there are a hundred and one veins.' And in reply to the question 'What is that Self?' the text has 'He who is within the heart, surrounded by the Prâ*n*as, the Person of light, consisting of knowledge' (B*ri*. Up. IV, 3, 7).—The parallel case of the sandal-ointment is referred to in order to point out that the Self abides in some particular part of the body; while the ointment is not bound to any special place.—In the next Sûtra the Sûtrakâra proceeds to state how, according to his own view, the Self, although abiding in one spot only, gives rise to effects extending over the whole body.

26. Or on account of its quality as light.

The 'or' is meant to set aside the view previously stated. The Self extends through the whole body by means of its quality, viz. knowledge or consciousness. 'As light.' As the light of things abiding in one place—such as gems, the sun, and so on—is seen to extend to many places, so the consciousness of the Self dwelling in the heart pervades the entire body. That the knowledge of the knowing subject may extend beyond its substrate, as the light of a luminous body does, we have already explained under the first Sûtra.—But it has been said that the Self is *mere* knowledge; how then can knowledge be said to be a quality—which is something different from the essential nature of a thing?—This the next Sûtra explains.

27. There is distinction as in the case of smell; and thus Scripture declares.

Just as smell, which is perceived as a quality of earth, is distinct from earth; thus knowledge of which we are conscious as the quality of a knowing subject—which relation expresses itself in judgments such as 'I know'—is different from the knowing subject. Scriptural texts also prove this relation, as e.g. 'This Person knows.'

28. On account of the separate statement.

Scripture even states quite directly that knowledge is something distinct from the knowing subject, viz. in the passage 'For there is not known any intermission of the knowing of the knower' (B*ri*. Up. IV, 3, 30).—It has been said that in passages such as 'he who abiding in knowledge' (B*ri*. Up. III, 7, 22); 'Knowledge performs the sacrifice' (Taitt. Up. II, 5, 1); 'having knowledge for its nature, absolutely free from stain,' Scripture speaks of the Self as being mere knowledge (not a knower). This point the next Sûtra elucidates.

29. But (the Self) is designated as that because it has that quality (viz. knowledge) for its essential quality; as in the case of the intelligent (prâ*gñ*a) Self.

The 'but' discards the objection. Because that quality, viz. the quality of knowledge, is the essential quality, therefore the Self is, in the passages quoted, designated as knowledge. For knowledge constitutes the essential quality of the Self. Similarly, the intelligent highest Self is occasionally called 'Bliss,' because bliss is its essential quality. Compare 'If that bliss existed not in the ether' (Taitt. Up. II, 7, 1); 'He perceived that bliss is Brahman' (Taitt. Up. III, 6, 1). That bliss is the essential attribute of Brahman is proved by texts such as 'That is one bliss of Brahman'; 'He who knows the bliss of Brahman is afraid of nothing' (Taitt. Up. II, 4, 1).—Or else the analogous case to which the Sûtra refers may be that of the intelligent Brahman being designated by the term 'knowledge,' in texts such as 'Truth, knowledge, the Infinite is Brahman' (Taitt. Up. II, 1). That knowledge is the essential quality of Brahman is known from passages such as 'together with the intelligent Brahman' (Taitt. Up. II, 1, 1); 'He who is all-knowing' (Mu. Up. I, 1, 9).

30. And there is no objection, since (the quality of knowledge) exists wherever the Self is; this being observed.

Since knowledge is an attribute which is met with wherever a Self is, there is no objection to the Self being designated by that attribute. Similarly we observe that special kinds of cows, as e.g. hornless ones, are designated by the term 'cow,' since the quality of possessing the generic character of cows is met with everywhere in connexion with the essential character of such animals with mutilated horns; since in fact that quality contributes to define their essential character. The 'and' of the Sûtra is meant to suggest a further argument, viz. that to apply to the Self the term 'knowledge' is suitable for that reason also that like knowledge the Self is self-illuminated. The objection that knowledge or consciousness cannot be an attribute inseparably connected with the essential nature of the Self as there is no consciousness in deep sleep and similar states is taken up in the next Sûtra.

31. Since there may be manifestation of that which exists; as in the case of virile power and so on.

The 'but' is meant to set the raised objection aside. The case may be that while consciousness is present also in deep sleep, and so on, it is manifested in the waking state only; whence there would be no objection to viewing consciousness as an essential attribute of the Self. 'As in the case of virile power and the like.' Special substances such as the virile element are indeed present in the male child already, but then are not manifest, while later on they manifest themselves with advancing youth; but all the same the possession of those substances is essential to the male being, not merely adventitious. For to be made up of seven elementary substances (viz. blood, humour, flesh, fat, marrow, bone, and semen) is an essential property of the body. That even in deep sleep and similar states the 'I' shines forth we have explained above. Consciousness is always there, but only in the waking state and in dreams it is observed to relate itself to objects. And that to be a subject of cognition, and so on, are essential attributes of the Self, we have also proved before. The conclusion, therefore, is that to be a knowing subject is the essential character of the Self. And that Self is of atomic size. The text 'when he has departed there is no consciousness' (sa*m*g*ñ*â; B*ri*. Up. II, 4, 12) does not declare that the released Self has no consciousness; but only that in the case of that Self there is absent that knowledge (experience) of birth, death, and so on, which in the Sa*m*sâra state is caused by the connexion of the Self with the elements—as described in the preceding passage, 'that great being having risen from out these elements again perishes after them.' For the text as to the absence of sa*m*g*ñ*â after death must be interpreted in harmony with other texts describing the condition of the released soul, such as 'the seeing one does not see death nor illness nor pain; the seeing one sees everything and obtains everything everywhere' (*Kh*. Up. VII, 25, 2); 'not remembering that body into which he was born—seeing these pleasures with the mind he rejoices' (VIII, 12, 3; 5).

The Sûtras now proceed to refute the doctrine of the Self being (not a knower) but mere knowledge, and being omnipresent.

32. There would result permanent consciousness or non-consciousness, or else limitative restriction to either.

On the other view, i. e. on the view of the Self being omnipresent and mere knowledge, it would follow either that consciousness and also non-consciousness would permanently take place together everywhere; or else that there would be definite permanent restriction to either of the two, i. e. either permanent consciousness or permanent non-consciousness.—If the omnipresent Self, consisting of mere knowledge only, were the cause of all that actual consciousness and non-consciousness on the part of Selfs which takes place in the world, it might be conceived either as the cause of both—i. e. consciousness and non-consciousness—and this would mean that there is everywhere and at all times simultaneous consciousness and non-consciousness. If, on the other hand, it were the cause of consciousness only, there would never and nowhere be unconsciousness of anything; and if it were the cause of non-consciousness only, there would never and nowhere be consciousness of anything. On our view, on the other hand, the actually perceived distribution of consciousness and non-consciousness explains itself, since we hold the Self to abide within bodies only, so that naturally consciousness takes place there only, not anywhere else.—The view, finally (held by the Vaiseshikas), of the consciousness of the Self depending on its organs (mind, senses, &c.; while the omnipresent Self is, apart from those organs, non-sentient, *gad*a), results in the same difficulties as the view criticised above; for as all the Selfs are omnipresent they are in permanent conjunction with all organs; and moreover it would follow that the ad*r*ish*t*as (due to the actions of the different bodies) could not thus be held apart (but would cling to all Selfs, each of which is in contact with all bodies).

Here terminates the adhikara*n*a of 'the *knower*.'

33. (The soul is) an agent, on account of Scripture (thus) having a purport.

It has been shown that the individual Self is a knowing subject and atomic. Now the question arises whether that Self is an agent or, being itself non-active, erroneously ascribes to itself the activity of the non-sentient gu*n*as. The primâ facie answer is that the individual Self is not an agent, since the sacred texts concerned with the Self declare that the Self does not act, while the gu*n*as do act. Thus, e. g. in the Ka*th*avallî, where the text at first denies of the individual Self all the attributes of Prak*ri*ti, such as being born, ageing and dying ('he is not born, he does not die'), and then also denies that the Self is the agent in acts such as killing and the like, 'If the slayer thinks that he slays, if the slain thinks that he is slain, they both do not understand; for this one does not slay, nor is that one slain' (I, 2, 19). This means—if one thinks the Self to be the slayer one does not know the Self. And the Lord himself teaches that non-agency is the essential nature of the individual soul, and that it is mere delusion on the Self's part to ascribe to itself agency. 'By the attributes (gu*n*a) of Prak*ri*ti, actions are wrought all round.' He who is deluded by self-conceit thinks 'I am the agent'; 'when the seer beholds no other agent than the gu*n*as'; 'Prak*ri*ti is said to be the cause of all agency of causes and effects, whilst the soul is the cause of all enjoyment of pleasure and pain' (Bha. Gî. III, 27; XIV, 19; XIII, 20).—The soul, therefore, is an enjoyer only, while all agency belongs to Prak*ri*ti.—To this the Sûtra replies, 'an agent, on account of Scripture thus having a meaning.' The Self only is an agent, not the gu*n*as, because thus only Scripture has a meaning. For the scriptural injunctions, such as 'he who desires the heavenly world is to sacrifice,' 'He who desires Release is to meditate on Brahman,' and similar ones, enjoin action on him only who will enjoy the fruit of the action—whether the heavenly world, or Release, or anything else. If a non-sentient thing were the agent, the injunction would not be addressed to another being (viz. to an intelligent being—to which it actually is addressed). The term '*s*âstra' (scriptural injunction) moreover comes from *s*âs, to command, and commanding means impelling to action. But scriptural injunctions impel to action through giving rise to a certain conception (in the mind of the being addressed), and the non-sentient Pradhâna cannot be made to conceive anything. Scripture therefore has a sense only, if we admit that none but the intelligent enjoyer of the fruit of the action is at the same time the agent. Thus the Pûrva Mîmâ*m*sâ declares 'the fruit of the injunction belongs to the agent' (III, 7, 18). The Pûrvapakshin had contended that the text 'if the slayer thinks, &c.,' proves the Self not to be the agent in the action of slaying; but what the text really means is only that the Self as being eternal cannot be killed. The text, from Sm*ri*ti, which was alleged as proving that the gu*n*as only possess active power, refers to the fact that in all activities lying within the sphere of the sa*m*sâra, the activity of the Self is due not to its own nature but to its contact with the different gu*n*as. The activity of the gu*n*as, therefore, must be viewed not as permanent, but occasional only. In the same sense Sm*ri*ti says 'the reason is the connexion of the soul with the gu*n*as, in its births, in good and evil wombs' (Bha. Gî. XIII, 21). Similarly it is said there (XVIII, 16) that 'he who through an untrained understanding looks upon the isolated Self as an agent, that man of perverted mind does not see'; the meaning being that, since it appears from a previous passage that the activity of the Self depends on five factors (as enumerated in *s*l. 16), he who views the isolated Self to be an agent has no true insight.

34. On account of taking and the declaration as to its moving about.

The text beginning 'And as a great king,' &c., declares that 'the Self taking the prâ*n*as moves about in its own body, according to its pleasure' (B*ri*. Up. II, 1, 18), i. e. it teaches that the Self is active in taking to itself the prâ*n*as and moving about in the body.

35. And on account of the designation (of the Self as the agent) in actions. If not so, there would be change of grammatical expression.

Because in the text 'Knowledge performs the sacrifice, it performs all works' (Taitt. Up. II, 5) the Self is designated as the agent in all worldly and Vedic works, for this reason also the Self must be held to be an agent. And should it be said that the word 'knowledge' in that text denotes not the Self, but the internal organ or buddhi, we point out that in that case there would be a change of grammatical expression, that is to say, as the buddhi is the instrument of action, the text would exhibit the instrumental case instead of the nominative case 'by knowledge, and so on' (vi*gñ*ânena instead of vi*gñ*ânam).

36. (There would be) absence of definite rule, as in the case of consciousness.

The Sûtra points out a difficulty which arises on the view of the Self not being an agent. Sûtra 32 has declared that if the Self were all-pervading it would follow that there would be no definite determination with regard to consciousness. Similarly, if the Self were not an agent but all activity belonged to Prak*ri*ti, it would follow that as Prak*ri*ti is a common possession of all souls, all actions would result in enjoyment (experience) on the part of all souls, or else on the part of none; for as each Self is held to be omnipresent, they are all of them in equal proximity to all parts of the Pradhâna. For the same reason it could not be maintained that the distribution of results between the different souls depends on the different internal organs which are joined to the souls; for if the souls are omnipresent, no soul will be exclusively connected with any particular internal organ.

37. On account of the inversion of power.

If the internal organ were the agent, then—since it is

impossible that a being other than the agent should be the enjoyer of the fruit of the action—the power of enjoyment also would belong to the internal organ, and would consequently have to be denied of the Self. But if this were so, there would be no longer any proof for the existence of the Self; for they expressly teach that 'the person (i.e. the soul) exists, on account of the fact of enjoyment.'

38. And on account of the absence of samâdhi.

If the internal organ were the agent, it would be such even in that final state of meditation, called samâdhi, which is the instrument of Release. But that state consists therein that the meditating being realises its difference from Prak*ri*ti, and this is a conception which Prak*ri*ti itself (of which the internal organ is only a modification) cannot form.—The Self alone, therefore, is the agent.—But this would imply that the activity of the Self is never at rest!—Of this difficulty the next Sûtra disposes.

39. And as the carpenter, in both ways.

The Self, although always provided with the instruments of action, such as the organ of speech, and so on, acts when it wishes to do so, and does not act when it does not wish to do so. Just as a carpenter, although having his axe and other implements ready at hand, works or does not work just as he pleases.—If the internal organ, on the contrary, were essentially active, it would constantly be acting, since as a non-intelligent being it could not be influenced by particular reasons for action, such as the desire for enjoyment.

Here terminates the adhikara*n*a of 'the agent.'

40. But from the highest, this being declared by Scripture.

Is the activity of the individual soul independent (free), or does it depend on the highest Self?—It is free; for if it were dependent on the highest Self, the whole body of scriptural injunctions and prohibitions would be unmeaning. For commandments can be addressed to such agents only as are capable of entering on action or refraining from action, according to their own thought and will.

This primâ facie view is set aside by the Sûtra. The activity of the individual soul proceeds from the highest Self as its cause. For Scripture teaches this. 'Entered within, the ruler of creatures, the Self of all'; 'who dwelling in the Self is different from the Self, whom the Self does not know, whose body the Self is, who rules the Self from within, he is thy Self, the inward ruler, the immortal one.' Sm*ri*ti teaches the same, 'I dwell within the heart of all; memory and knowledge as well as their loss come from me' (Bha. Gî. XV, 15); 'The Lord, O Ar*g*una, dwells in the heart of all creatures, whirling, by his mysterious power, all creatures as if mounted on a machine' (Bha. Gî. XVIII, 61).—But this view implies the meaninglessness of all scriptural injunctions and prohibitions!—To this the next Sûtra replies.

41. But with a view to the efforts made (the Lord makes the soul act) on account of the (thus resulting) non-meaninglessness of injunctions and prohibitions and the rest.

The inwardly ruling highest Self promotes action in so far as it regards in the case of any action the volitional effort made by the individual soul, and then aids that effort by granting its favour or permission (anumati); action is not possible without permission on the part of the highest Self. In this way (i.e. since the action primarily depends on the volitional effort of the soul) injunctions and prohibitions are not devoid of meaning. The 'and the rest' of the Sûtra is meant to suggest the grace and punishments awarded by the Lord.—The case is analogous to that of property of which two men are joint owners. If one of these wishes to transfer that property to a third person he cannot do so without the permission of his partner, but that that permission is given is after all his own doing, and hence the fruit of the action (reward or anything) properly belongs to him only.—That, in the case of evil actions, allowance of the action on the part of one able to stop it does not necessarily prove hardheartedness, we have shown above when explaining the Sâṅkhya doctrine. —But there is a scriptural text.—'He (the Lord) makes him whom he wishes to lead up from these worlds do a good deed, and the same makes him whom he wishes to lead down from these worlds do a bad deed' (Kau. Up. III, 8)—which means that the Lord himself causes men to do good and evil actions, and this does not agree with the partial independence claimed above for the soul.—The text quoted, we reply, does not apply to all agents, but means that the Lord, wishing to do a favour to those who are resolved on acting so as fully to please the highest Person, engenders in their minds a tendency towards highly virtuous actions, such as are means to attain to him; while on the other hand, in order to punish those who are resolved on lines of action altogether displeasing to him, he engenders in their minds a delight in such actions as have a downward tendency and are obstacles in the way of the attainment of the Lord. Thus the Lord himself says, 'I am the origin of all, everything proceeds from me; knowing this the wise worship me with love. To them ever devoted, worshipping me in love, I give that means of wisdom by which they attain to me. In mercy only to them, dwelling in their hearts, do I destroy the darkness born of ignorance, with the brilliant light of knowledge' (Bha. Gî. X, 8; 10–11). And further on the Lord—after having described 'demoniac' people, in the passus beginning 'they declare the world to be without a Truth, without a resting-place, without a Ruler,' and ending 'malignantly hating me who abides in their own bodies and those of others'—declares, 'These evil and malign haters, most degraded of men, I hurl perpetually into transmigrations and into demoniac wombs' (XVI, 8–19).

Here terminates the adhikaraṇa of 'that which depends on the Highest.'

42. (The soul is) a part, on account of the declarations of difference and otherwise; some also record

(that Brahman is of) the nature of slaves, fishermen, and so on.

The Sûtras have declared that the individual soul is an agent, and as such dependent on the highest Person. The following question now arises—Is the individual soul absolutely different from Brahman? or is it nothing else than Brahman itself in so far as under the influence of error? or is it Brahman in so far as determined by a limiting adjunct (upâdhi)? or is it a part (a*ms*a) of Brahman?—The doubt on this point is due to the disagreement of the scriptural texts.—But this whole matter has already been decided under Sû. II, 1, 22.—True. But as a difficulty presents itself on the ground of the conflicting nature of the texts—some asserting the difference and some the unity of the individual soul and Brahman—the matter is here more specially decided by its being proved that the soul is a part of Brahman. As long as this decision remains unsettled, the conclusions arrived at under the two Sûtras referred to, viz. that the soul is non-different from Brahman and that Brahman is 'additional' to the soul, are without a proper basis.

Let it then first be said that the soul is absolutely different from Brahman, since texts such as 'There are two, the one knowing, the other not knowing, both unborn, the one strong, the other weak' (*S*vet. Up. I, 9) declare their difference. Texts which maintain the non-difference of a being which is knowing and another which is not knowing, if taken literally, convey a contradiction—as if one were to say, 'Water the ground with fire'!—and must therefore be understood in some secondary metaphorical sense. To hold that the individual soul is a part of Brahman does not explain matters; for by a 'part' we understand that which constitutes part of the extension of something. If, then, the soul occupied part of the extension of Brahman, all its imperfections would belong to Brahman. Nor can the soul be a part of Brahman if we take 'part' to mean a *piece* (kha*nd*a); for Brahman does not admit of being divided into pieces, and moreover, the difficulties connected with the former interpretation would present themselves here also. That something absolutely different from something else should yet be a part of the latter cannot in fact be proved.

Or else let it be said that the soul is Brahman affected by error (bhrama). For this is the teaching of texts such as 'Thou art that'; 'this Self is Brahman.' Those texts, on the other hand, which declare the difference of the two merely restate what is already established by perception and the other means of knowledge, and therefore are shown, by those texts the purport of which it is to teach non-duality not established by other means, to lie—like perception and the other means of knowledge themselves—within the sphere of Nescience.

Or let it be assumed, in the third place, that the individual soul is Brahman as determined by a beginningless limiting adjunct (upâdhi). For it is on this ground that Scripture teaches the Self to be Brahman. And that upâdhi must not be said to be a mere erroneous imagination, for on that view the distinction of bondage, release, and so on, would be impossible.

Against all these views the Sûtra declares that the soul is a part of Brahman; since there are declarations of difference and also 'otherwise,' i.e. declarations of unity. To the former class belong all those texts which dwell on the distinction of the creator and the creature, the ruler and the ruled, the all-knowing and the ignorant, the independent and the dependent, the pure and the impure, that which is endowed with holy qualities and that which possesses qualities of an opposite kind, the lord and the dependent. To the latter class belong such texts as 'Thou art that' and 'this Self is Brahman.' Some persons even record that Brahman is of the nature of slaves, fishermen, and so on. The Âtharva*n*ikas, that is to say, have the following text, 'Brahman are the slaves, Brahman are these fishers,' and so on; and as Brahman there is said to comprise within itself all individual souls, the passage teaches general non-difference of the Self. In order, then, that texts of both these classes may be taken in their primary, literal sense, we must admit that the individual soul is a part of Brahman. Nor is it a fact that the declarations of difference refer to matters settled by other means of knowledge, such as perception and so on, and on that account are mere reiterations of something established otherwise (in consequence of which they would have no original proving force of their own, and would be sublated by the texts declaring non-duality). For the fact that the soul is created by Brahman, is ruled by it, constitutes its body, is subordinate to it, abides in it, is preserved by it, is absorbed by it, stands to it in the relation of a meditating devotee, and through its grace attains the different ends of man, viz. religious duty, wealth, pleasure and final release—all this and what is effected thereby, viz. the distinction of the soul and Brahman, does not fall within the cognisance of perception and the other means of proof, and hence is not established by something else. It is therefore not true that the texts declaring the creation of the world, and so on, are mere reiterations of differences established by other means of authoritative knowledge, and hence have for their purport to teach things that are false.—[Nor will it do to say that the texts declaring duality teach what indeed is not established by other means of knowledge but is erroneous.] 'Brahman conceives the thought of differentiating itself, forms the resolution of becoming many, and accordingly creates the ether and the other elements, enters into them as individual soul, evolves all the different forms and names, takes upon himself all the pleasures and pains which spring from experiencing the infinite multitude of objects thus constituted, abides within and inwardly rules all beings, recognises itself in its *g*îva-condition to be one with the universal causal Brahman, and finally accomplishes its release from the sa*m*sâra and the body of sacred doctrine by which this release is effected'—all this the Veda indeed declares, but its real purport is that all this is only true of a Brahman under the influence of an illusion, and therefore is unreal!—while at the same time Brahman is defined as that the essential nature of which is absolutely pure intelligence! Truly, if such were the purport of the Veda, what more would the Veda be than the idle talk of a person out of his mind!

Nor finally is there any good in the theory of the soul being Brahman in so far as determined by a limiting adjunct. For this view also is in conflict with the texts which distinguish Brahman as the ruling and the soul as the ruled principle, and so on. One and the same Devadatta does not become double as it were—a ruler on the one hand and a ruled subject on the other—because he is determined by the house in which he is, or by something else.

In order to be able to account for the twofold designations of the soul, we must therefore admit that the soul is a *part* of Brahman.

43. And on account of the mantra.

'One part (quarter) of it are all beings, three feet (quarters) of it are the Immortal in heaven' (*Kh.* Up. III, 12, 6)—on account of this mantra also the soul must be held to be a part of Brahman. For the word 'foot' denotes a part. As the individual souls are many the mantra uses the plural form 'all beings.' In the Sûtra (42) the word 'part' is in the singular, with a view to denote the whole class. For the same reason in II, 3, 18 also the word 'âtman' is in the singular. For that the individual Selfs are different from the Lord, and are many and eternal, is declared by texts such as 'He who, eternal and intelligent, fulfils the desires of many who likewise are eternal and intelligent' (Ka. Up. II, 5, 13). Since thus the plurality of the eternal individual Selfs rests on good authority, those who have an insight into the true nature of Selfs will discern without difficulty different characteristics distinguishing the individual Selfs, although all Selfs are alike in so far as having intelligence for their essential nature. Moreover the Sûtra II, 3, 48 directly states the plurality of the individual Selfs.

44. Moreover it is so stated in Sm*ri*ti.

Sm*ri*ti moreover declares the individual soul to be a part of the highest Person, 'An eternal part of myself becomes the individual soul (*g*îva) in the world of life' (Bha. Gî. XV, 7).—For this reason also the soul must be held to be a part of Brahman.

But if the soul is a part of Brahman, all the imperfections of the soul are Brahman's also!—To this objection the next Sûtra replies.

45. But as in the case of light and so on. Not so is the highest.

The 'but' discards the objection.—'Like light and so on.' The individual soul is a part of the highest Self; as the light issuing from a luminous thing such as fire or the sun is a part of that body; or as the generic characteristics of a cow or horse, and the white or black colour of things so coloured, are attributes and hence parts of the things in which those attributes inhere; or as the body is a part of an embodied being. For by a part we understand that which constitutes one place (de*s*a) of some thing, and hence a distinguishing attribute (vi*s*esha*n*a) is a part of the thing distinguished by that attribute. Hence those analysing a thing of that kind discriminate between the *distinguishing* element or part of it, and the *distinguished* element or part. Now although the distinguishing attribute and the thing distinguished thereby stand to each other in the relation of part and whole, yet we observe them to differ in essential character. Hence there is no contradiction between the individual and the highest Self—the former of which is a vi*s*esha*n*a of the latter—standing to each other in the relation of part and whole, and their being at the same time of essentially different nature. This the Sûtra declares 'not so is the highest,' i.e. the highest Self is not of the same nature as the individual soul. For as the luminous body is of a nature different from that of its light, thus the highest Self differs from the individual soul which is a part of it. It is this difference of character—due to the individual soul being the distinguishing element and the highest Self being the substance distinguished thereby—to which all those texts refer which declare difference. Those texts, on the other hand, which declare non-difference are based on the circumstance that attributes which are incapable of separate existence are ultimately bound to the substance which they distinguish, and hence are fundamentally valid. That in declarations such as 'Thou art that' and 'this Self is Brahman,' the words *thou* and *Self*, no less than the words *that* and *Brahman*, denote Brahman in so far as having the individual souls for its body, and that thus the two sets of words denote fundamentally one and the same thing, has been explained previously.

46. And Sm*ri*ti texts declare this.

That the world and Brahman stand to each other in the relation of part and whole, the former being like the light and the latter like the luminous body, or the former being like the power and the latter like that in which the power inheres, or the former being like the body and the latter like the soul; this Parâ*s*ara also and other Sm*ri*ti writers declare, 'As the light of a fire which abides in one place only spreads all around, thus this whole world is the power (*s*akti) of the highest Brahman.' The 'and' in the Sûtra implies that scriptural texts also ('of whom the Self is the body' and others) declare that the individual Self is a part of Brahman in so far as it is its body.

But if all individual souls are equal in so far as being alike parts of Brahman, alike actuated by Brahman, and alike knowing subjects, what is the reason that, as Scripture teaches, some of them are allowed to read the Veda and act according to its injunctions, while others are excluded therefrom; and again that some are to see, feel, and so on, while others are excluded from these privileges?—This question is answered by the next Sûtra.

47. Permission and exclusion (result) from connexion with a body; as in the case of light and so on.

Although all souls are essentially of the same nature in so far as they are parts of Brahman, knowing subjects and so on, the permissions and exclusions referred to are possible for the reason that each individual soul is joined to some particular body, pure or impure, whether of a Brâhma*n*a or Kshattriya or Vai*s*ya or *S*ûdra, and so on. 'As in the case of fire and so on.' All fire is of the same kind, and yet one willingly fetches fire from the house of a Brâhma*n*a, while one shuns fire from a place where dead bodies are burnt. And from a Brâhma*n*a one accepts food without any objection, while one refuses food from a low person.

48. And on account of non-connectedness there is no confusion.

Although the souls, as being parts of Brahman and so on, are of essentially the same character, they are actually separate, for each of them is of atomic size and resides in a separate body. For this reason there is no confusion or mixing up of the individual spheres of enjoyment and experience. The Sûtrakâra introduces this reference to an advantage of his own view of things, in order to intimate that the views of the soul being Brahman deluded or else Brahman affected by a limiting adjunct are on their part incapable of explaining how it is that the experiences of the individual Self and the highest Self, and of the several individual Selfs, are not mixed up.

But may not, on the view of the soul being Brahman deluded, the distinction of the several spheres of experience be explained by means of the difference of the limiting adjuncts presented by Nescience?—This the next Sûtra negatives.

49. And it is a mere apparent argument.

The argumentation by which it is sought to prove that that being whose nature is constituted by absolutely uniform light, i. e. intelligence, is differentiated by limiting adjuncts which presuppose an obscuration of that essential nature, is a mere apparent (fallacious) one. For, as we have shown before, obscuration of the light of that which is nothing but light means destruction of that light.—If we accept as the reading of the Sûtra 'âbhâsâ*h*' (in plural) the meaning is that the various reasons set forth by the adherents of that doctrine are all of them fallacious. The 'and' of the Sûtra is meant to point out that that doctrine, moreover, is in conflict with texts such as 'thinking himself to be different from the Mover' (*S*vet. Up. I, 6); 'there are two unborn ones, one a ruler, the other not a ruler' (I, 9); 'of those two one eats the sweet fruit' (V, 6); and others. For even if difference is due to upâdhis which are the figment of Nescience, there is no escaping the conclusion that the spheres of experience must be mixed up, since the theory admits that the thing itself with which all the limiting adjuncts connect themselves is one only.

But this cannot be urged against the theory of the individual soul being Brahman in so far as determined by real limiting adjuncts; for on that view we may explain the difference of spheres of experience as due to the beginningless ad*ri*sh*t*as which are the cause of the difference of the limiting adjuncts!—To this the next Sûtra replies.

50. On account of the non-determination of the ad*ri*sh*t*as.

As the ad*ri*sh*t*as also which are the causes of the series of upâdhis have for their substrate Brahman itself, there is no reason for their definite allotment (to definite individual souls), and hence again there is no definite separation of the spheres of experience. For the limiting adjuncts as well as the ad*ri*sh*t*as cannot by their connexion with Brahman split up Brahman itself which is essentially one.

51. And it is thus also in the case of purposes and so on.

For the same reason there can be no definite restriction in the case of purposes and so on which are the causes of the different ad*ri*sh*t*as. (For they also cannot introduce plurality into Brahman that is fundamentally one.)

52. Should it be said (that that is possible) owing to the difference of place; we deny this, on account of (all upâdhis) being within (all places).

Although Brahman is one only and not to be split by the several limiting adjuncts with which it is connected, yet the separation of the spheres of enjoyment is not impossible since the places of Brahman which are connected with the upâdhis are distinct.—This the Sûtra negatives on the ground that, as the upâdhis move here and there and hence all places enter into connexion with all upâdhis, the mixing up of spheres of enjoyment cannot be avoided. And even if the upâdhis were connected with different places, the pain connected with some particular place would affect the whole of Brahman which is one only.—The two Sûtras II, 3, 32 and 37 have stated an objection against those who, without taking their stand on the Veda, held the view of an all-pervading soul. The Sûtras II, 3, 50 and ff., on the other hand, combat the view of those who, while basing their doctrine on the Veda, teach the absolute unity of the Self.—Here terminates the adhikara*n*a of 'the part.'

## FOURTH PÂDA.

1. Thus the prâ*n*as.

After having taught that Ether and all the other elements are effects, and hence have originated, the Sûtras had shown that the individual soul, although likewise an effect, does not originate in the sense of undergoing a change of essential nature; and had in connexion therewith clearly set forth wherein the essential nature of the soul consists. They now proceed to elucidate the question as to the origination of the instruments of the individual soul, viz. the organs and the vital breath.

The point here to be decided is whether the organs are effects as the individual soul is an effect, or as ether and the other elements are. As the soul is, thus the prâ*n*as are, the Pûrvapakshin maintains. That means—as the soul is not produced, thus the organs also are not produced. For the latter point no less than the former is directly stated in Scripture; the wording of the Sûtra 'thus the prâ*n*as' being meant to extend to the case of the prâ*n*as also, the authority of Scripture to which recourse was had in the case of the soul.—But what is the scriptural text you mean?

'Non-being, truly this was in the beginning. Here they say, what was that? Those *Ri*shis indeed were that Non-being, thus they say. And who were those *Ri*shis? The prâ*n*as indeed were those *Ri*shis.' This is the passage which declares that before the origination of the world the *Ri*shis existed. As 'prâ*n*â*h*' is in the plural, we conclude that what is meant is the organs and the vital air. Nor can this text be interpreted to mean only that the prâ*n*as exist for a very long time (but are not uncreated); as we may interpret the texts declaring Vâyu and the atmosphere (antariksha) to be immortal: 'Vâyu and the atmosphere are immortal'; 'Vâyu is the deity that never sets' (B*ri*. Up. II, 3, 3; I, 5, 22). For the clause 'Non-being indeed was this in the beginning' declares that the prâ*n*as existed even at the time when the entire world was in the pralaya state. Those texts, then, which speak of an origination of the prâ*n*as must be explained somehow, just as we did with the texts referring to the origination of the individual soul.

To this the Siddhântin replies, 'the prâ*n*as also originate in the same way as ether, and so on.'—Why?—Because we have scriptural texts directly stating that before creation everything was one, 'Being only this was in the beginning,' 'The Self only was this in the beginning.' And moreover, the text 'from that there is produced the prâ*n*a and the mind and all organs' (Mu. Up. II, 3, 1) declares that the organs originated; they therefore cannot have existed before creation. Nor is it permissible to ascribe a different meaning to the texts which declare the origination of the sense-organs—as we may do in the case of the texts declaring the origination of the soul. For we have no texts directly denying the origination of the sense-organs, or affirming their eternity, while we *have* such texts in the case of the individual soul. In the text quoted by the Pûrvapakshin, 'Non-being indeed was this in the beginning,' &c., the word prâ*n*a can denote the highest Self only; for from texts such as 'All these beings indeed enter into breath alone, and from breath they arise' (*Kh*. Up. I, 11, 5), the word prâ*n*a is known to be one of the designations of the highest Self. And as to the clause 'the prâ*n*as indeed are those *Ri*shis,' we remark that the term *Ri*shi may properly be applied to the all-seeing highest Self, but not to the non-intelligent organs.

But how then is the plural form 'the *Ri*shis are the prâ*n*as' to be accounted for? This the next Sûtra explains.

2. (The scriptural statement of the plural) is secondary, on account of impossibility; and since (the highest Self) is declared before that.

The plural form exhibited by the text must be taken (not in its literal, but) in a secondary figurative sense, since there is no room there for a plurality of things. For Scripture declares that previous to creation the highest Self only exists.

3. On account of speech having for its antecedent that.

For the following reason also the word 'prâ*n*a,' in the text quoted, can denote Brahman only. Speech, i. e. the names which have for their object all things apart from Brahman, presupposes the existence of the entire universe of things—ether, and so on—which is the object of speech. But, as according to the text 'this was then non-differentiated; it was thereupon differentiated by names and forms,' then (i. e. before the differentiation of individual things), no things having name and form existed, there existed also no effects of speech and the other organs of action and sensation, and hence it cannot be inferred that those organs themselves existed.—Here terminates the adhikara*n*a of 'the origination of the prâ*n*as.'

4. (They are seven) on account of the going of the seven and of specification.

The question here arises whether those organs are seven only, or eleven—the doubt on this point being due to the conflicting nature of scriptural texts.—The Pûrvapakshin maintains the former alternative.—On what grounds?—'On account of going, and of specification.' For the text refers to the 'going,' i. e. to the moving about in the different worlds, together with the soul when being born or dying, of seven prâ*n*as only, 'seven are these worlds in which the prâ*n*as move which rest in the cave, being placed there as seven and seven' (Mu. Up. II, 1, 8)—where the repetition 'seven and seven' intimates the plurality of souls to which the prâ*n*as are attached. Moreover those moving prâ*n*as are distinctly specified in the following text, 'when the five instruments of knowledge stand still, together with the mind (manas), and when the buddhi does not move, that they call the highest "going"' (gati—Ka. Up. II, 6, 10). The 'highest going' here means the moving towards Release, all movement within the body having come to an end. As thus the text declares that at the time of birth and death seven prâ*n*as only accompany the soul, and as, with regard to the condition of final concentration, those prâ*n*as are distinctly specified as forms of knowledge (*gñ*ânâni), we conclude that the prâ*n*as are the seven following instruments of the soul—the organs of hearing, feeling, seeing, tasting and smelling, the buddhi and the manas. In various other passages indeed, which refer to the prâ*n*as, higher numbers are mentioned, viz. up to fourteen, speech, the hands, the feet, the anus, the organ of generation, the ahaṅkâra and the *k*itta being added to those mentioned above; cp. e.g. 'there are eight grahas' (B*ri*. Up. III, 2, 1); 'Seven are the prâ*n*as of the head, two the lower ones' (Taitt. Sa*m*h. V, 3, 2, 5). But as the text says nothing about those additional organs accompanying the soul, we assume that they are called prâ*n*as in a metaphorical sense only, since they all, more or less, assist the soul.—This view the next Sûtra sets aside.

5. But the hands and so on also; (since they assist the soul) abiding (in the body). Hence (it is) not so.

The organs are not seven only, but eleven, since the hands and the rest also contribute towards the experience and fruition of that which abides in the body, i.e. the soul, and have their separate offices, such as seizing, and so on. Hence it is not so, i.e. it must not be thought that the hands and the rest are not organs. Buddhi, ahaṅkâra and *k*itta, on the other hand, are (not independent organs but) mere designations of the manas, according as the latter is engaged in the functions of deciding (adhyavasâya), or misconception (abhimâna), or thinking (*k*intâ). The organs therefore are eleven. From this it follows that in the passage 'Ten are these prâ*n*as in man, and Âtman is the eleventh' (B*ri*. Up. II, 4, 11), the word Âtman denotes the manas. The number *eleven* is confirmed by scriptural and Sm*ri*ti passages, cp. 'the ten organs and the one' (Bha. Gî. XIII, 5); 'ten are the vaikârika beings, the manas is the eleventh,' and others. Where more organs are mentioned, the different functions of the manas are meant; and references to smaller numbers are connected with special effects of the organs, such as accompanying the soul, and the like.—Here terminates the adhikara*n*a of 'the going of the seven.'

6. And (they are) minute.

As the text 'these are all alike, all infinite' (B*ri*. Up. I, 5, 13), declares speech, mind, and breath to be infinite, we conclude that the prâ*n*as are all-pervading.—To this the Sûtra replies, that they are minute; for the text 'when the vital breath passes out of the body, all the prâ*n*as pass out after it' (B*ri*. Up. V, 4, 2), proves those prâ*n*as to be of limited size, and as when passing out they are not perceived by bystanders, they must be of minute size.—The text which speaks of them as infinite is a text enjoining meditation ('he who meditates on them as infinite'), and infinity there means only that abundance of activities which is an attribute of the prâ*n*a to be meditated on.

7. And the best.

By 'the best' we have to understand the chief vital air (mukhya prâ*n*a), which, in the colloquy of the prâ*n*as, is determined to be the best because it is the cause of the preservation of the body. This chief vital air the Pûrvapakshin maintains to be something non-created, since Scripture (*Ri*. Sa*m*h. V, 129, 2), 'By its own law the One was breathing without wind,' shows that an effect of it, viz. the act of breathing, existed even previously to creation, at the time of a great pralaya; and because texts declaring it to have been created—such as 'from him is born breath' (Mu. Up. II, 1, 3)—may be interpreted in the same way as the texts declaring that the soul is something created (see p. 540 ff.).—To this the reply is that, since this view contradicts scriptural statements as to the oneness of all, previous to creation; and since the Mu*nd*aka-text declares the prâ*n*a to have been created in the same way as earth and the other elements; and since there are no texts plainly denying its createdness, the chief vital air also must be held to have been created. The words 'the One was breathing without wind' by no means refer to the vital breath of living creatures, but intimate the existence of the highest Brahman, alone by itself; as indeed appears from the qualification 'without wind.'—That the vital breath, although really disposed of in the preceding Sûtras, is specially mentioned in the present Sûtra, is with a view to the question next raised for consideration.—Here terminates the adhikara*n*a of 'the minuteness of the prâ*n*as.'

8. Neither air nor function, on account of its being stated separately.

Is this main vital breath nothing else but air, the second of the elements? Or is it a certain motion of the air? Or is it air that has assumed some special condition?—The first alternative may be adopted, on account of the text 'prâ*n*a is air.'—Or, since mere air is not called breath, while this term is generally applied to that motion of air which consists in inhalation and exhalation, we may hold that breath is a motion of air.—Of both these views the Sûtra disposes by declaring 'not so, on account of separate statement.' For in the passage 'From him there is produced breath, mind, and all sense-organs, ether and air,' &c., breath and air are mentioned as two separate things. For the same reason breath also cannot be a mere motion or function of air; for the text does not mention any functions of fire and the other elements, side by side with these elements, as separate things (and this shows that breath also cannot, in that text, be interpreted to denote a function of air). The text 'prâ*n*a is air,' on the other hand, intimates (not that breath is identical with air, but) that breath is air having assumed a special form, not a thing altogether different from it, like fire. In ordinary language, moreover, the word *breath* does not mean a mere motion but a substance to which motion belongs; we say, 'the breath moves to and fro in inhalation and exhalation.'

Is breath, which we thus know to be a modification of air, to be considered as a kind of elementary substance, like fire, earth, and so on? Not so, the next Sûtra replies.

9. But like the eye and the rest, on account of being taught with them, and for other reasons.

Breath is not an element, but like sight and the rest, a special instrument of the soul. This appears from the fact that the texts mention it together with the recognised organs of the soul, the eye, and so on; so e.g. in the colloquy of the prâ*n*as. And such common mention is suitable in the case of such things only as belong to one class.—The 'and for other reasons' of the Sûtra refers to the circumstance of the principal breath being specially mentioned among the organs comprised under the term 'prâ*n*a'; cp. 'that principal breath' (*Kh.* Up. I, 2, 7); 'that central breath' (B*ri.* Up. I, 5, 21).—But if the chief breath is, like the eye and the other organs, an instrument of the soul, there must be some special form of activity through which it assists the soul, as the eye e. g. assists the soul by seeing. But no such activity is perceived, and the breath cannot therefore be put in the same category as the organs of sensation and action!—To this objection the next Sûtra replies.

10. And there is no objection on account of its not having an activity (kara*n*a); for (Scripture) thus declares.

The kara*n*a of the Sûtra means kriyâ, action. The objection raised on the ground that the principal breath does not exercise any form of activity helpful to the soul, is without force, since as a matter of fact Scripture declares that there is such an activity, in so far as the vital breath supports the body with all its organs. For the text (*Kh.* Up. V, 1, 7 ff.) relates how on the successive departure of speech, and so on, the body and the other organs maintained their strength, while on the departure of the vital breath the body and all the organs at once became weak and powerless.—The conclusion therefore is that the breath, in its fivefold form of prâ*n*a, apâna, and so on, subserves the purposes of the individual soul, and thus occupies the position of an instrument, no less than the eye and the other organs.

But as those five forms of breath, viz. prâ*n*a, udâna, &c., have different names and functions they must be separate principles (and hence there is not *one* principal breath)! To this the next Sûtra replies.

11. It is designated as having five functions like mind.

As desire, and so on, are not principles different from mind, although they are different functions and produce different effects—according to the text, 'Desire, purpose, doubt, faith, want of faith, firmness, absence of firmness, shame, reflection, fear—all this is mind' (B*ri*. Up. I, 5, 3); so, on the ground of the text, 'prâ*n*a, apâna, vyâna, udâna, samâna—all this is prâ*n*a' (ibid.), apâna and the rest must be held to be different functions of prâ*n*a only, not independent principles.—Here terminates the adhikara*n*a of what is 'a modification of air.'

12. And (it is) minute.

This prâ*n*a also is minute, since as before (i.e. as in the case of the organs) the text declares it to pass out of the body, to move, and so on, 'him when he passes out the prâ*n*a follows after' (B*ri*. Up. V, 4, 2). A further doubt arises, in the case of prâ*n*a, owing to the fact that in other texts it is spoken of as of large extent, 'It is equal to these three worlds, equal to this Universe' (B*ri*. Up. I, 3, 22); 'On prâ*n*a everything is founded'; 'For all this is shut up in prâ*n*a.' But as the texts declaring the passing out, and so on, of the prâ*n*a, prove it to be of limited size, the all-embracingness ascribed to prâ*n*a in those other texts must be interpreted to mean only that the life of all living and breathing creatures depends on breath.—Here terminates the adhikara*n*a of 'the minuteness of the best.'

13. But the rule (over the prâ*n*as) on the part of Fire and the rest, together with him to whom the prâ*n*as belong (i.e. the soul), is owing to the thinking of that (viz. the highest Self); on account of scriptural statement.

It has been shown that the prâ*n*as, together with the main prâ*n*a, originate from Brahman, and have a limited size. That the prâ*n*as are guided by Agni and other divine beings has also been explained on a previous occasion, viz. under Sû. II, 1, 5. And it is known from ordinary experience that the organs are ruled by the individual soul, which uses them as means of experience and fruition. And this is also established by scriptural texts, such as 'Having taken these prâ*n*as he (i.e. the soul) moves about in his own body, according to his pleasure' (B*ri*. Up. II, 1, 18). The question now arises whether the rule of the soul and of the presiding divine beings over the prâ*n*as depends on them (i.e. the soul and the divinities) only, or on some other being.—On them only, since they depend on no one else!—Not so, the Sûtra declares. The rule which light, and so on, i.e. Agni and the other divinities, together with him to whom the prâ*n*as belong, i.e. the soul, exercise over the prâ*n*as, proceeds from the thinking of that, i.e. from the will of the highest Self.—How is this known?—'From scriptural statement.' For Scripture teaches that the organs, together with their guiding divinities and the individual soul, depend in all their doings on the thought of the highest Person. 'He, who abiding within Fire, rules Fire from within.—He, who abiding within air—within the Self—within the eye, and so on' (B*ri*. Up. III, 7); 'From fear of it the wind blows, from fear of it the sun rises, from fear of it Agni and Indra, yea Death runs as the fifth' (Taitt. Up. II, 8, 1); 'By the command of that Imperishable one, sun and moon stand, held apart' (B*ri*. Up. III, 8, 9).

14. And on account of the eternity of this.

As the quality, inhering in all things, of being ruled by the highest Self, is eternal and definitely fixed by being connected with his essential nature, it is an unavoidable conclusion that the rule of the soul and of the divinities over the organs depends on the will of the highest Self. The text, 'Having sent forth this he entered into it, having entered into it he became sat and tyat' (Taitt. Up. II, 6), shows that the entering on the part of the highest Person into all things, so as to be their ruler, is connected with his essential nature. Similarly Smriti says, 'Pervading this entire Universe by a portion of mine I do abide' (Bha. Gî. X, 42).—Here terminates the adhikarana of 'the rule of Fire and the rest.'

15. They, with the exception of the best, are organs, on account of being so designated.

Are all principles called prânas to be considered as 'organs' (indriyâni), or is the 'best,' i. e. the chief prâna, to be excepted?—All of them, without exception, are organs; for they all are called prânas equally, and they all are instruments of the soul.—Not so, the Sûtra replies. The 'best' one is to be excepted, since only the prânas other than the best are designated as *organs*. Texts such as 'the organs are ten and one' (Bha. Gî. XIII, 5) apply the term 'organ' only to the senses of sight and the rest, and the internal organ.

16. On account of scriptural statement of difference, and on account of difference of characteristics.

Texts such as 'from him is born prâna, and the internal organ, and all organs' (Mu. Up. II, 1, 3) mention the vital breath separately from the organs, and this shows that the breath is not one of the organs. The passage indeed mentions the internal organ (manas) also as something separate; but in other passages the manas is formally included in the organs, 'the (five) organs with mind as the sixth' (Bha. Gî. XV, 7). That the vital breath differs in nature from the organ of sight and the rest, is a matter of observation. For in the state of deep sleep the function of breath is seen to continue, while those of the eye, and so on, are not perceived. The work of the organs, inclusive of the manas, is to act as instruments of cognition and action, while the work of breath is to maintain the body and the organs. It is for the reason that the subsistence of the organs depends on breath, that the organs themselves are called prânas. Thus Scripture says, 'they all became the form of that (breath), and therefore they are called after him prânas' (*Bri*. Up. I, 5, 21). 'They became its form' means—they became its body, their activity depended on it.—Here terminates the adhikara*n*a of 'the *organs*.'

17. But the making of names and forms (belongs) to him who renders tripartite, on account of scriptural teaching.

The Sûtras have shown that the creation of the elements and organs in their collective aspect (samash*t*i) and the activity of the individual souls proceed from the highest Self; and they have also further confirmed the view that the rule which the souls exercise over their organs depends on the highest Self. A question now arises with regard to the creation of the world in its discrete aspect (vyash*t*i), which consists in the differentiation of names and forms (i.e. of individual beings). Is this latter creation the work of Hira*n*yagarbha only, who represents the collective aggregate of all individual souls; or, fundamentally, the work of the highest Brahman having Hira*n*yagarbha for its body—just as the creation of water e.g. is the work of the highest Brahman having fire for its body?—The Pûrvapakshin maintains the former alternative. For, he says, the text 'Having entered with this living-soul-self (anena *g*îvenâtmanâ), let me differentiate names and forms' (*Kh*. Up. VI, 3, 2), declares the *g*îva-soul to be the agent in differentiation. For the resolve of the highest deity is expressed, not in the form 'let me differentiate names and forms by myself' (svena rûpe*n*a), but 'by this soul-self,' i.e. by a part of the highest Self, in the form of the individual soul.—But on this interpretation the first person in 'vyâkaravâ*n*i' (let me enter), and the grammatical form of 'having entered,' which indicates the agent, could not be taken in their literal, but only in an implied, sense—as is the case in a sentence such as 'Having entered the hostile army by means of a spy, I will estimate its strength' (where the real agent is not the king, who is the speaker, but the spy).—The cases are not analogous, the Pûrvapakshin replies. For the king and the spy are fundamentally separate, and hence the king is agent by implication only. But in the case under discussion the soul is a part, and hence contributes to constitute the essential nature of, the highest Self; hence that highest Self itself enters and differentiates in the form of the soul. Nor can it be said that the instrumental case ('with this soul-self') has the implied meaning of association ('together with this soul-self'); for if a case can be taken in its primary sense, it is not proper to understand it in a sense which has to be expressed by means of a preposition. But the third case, *g*îvena, cannot here be understood even in its primary sense, i.e. that of the instrument of the action; for if Brahman is the agent in the acts of entering and differentiating, the soul is not that which is most suitable to accomplish the end of action (while yet grammar defines the *instrumental* case—kara*n*a —on this basis). Nor can it be said that the activity of the soul comes to an end with the entering, while the differentiation of names and forms is Brahman's work, for the past participle (pravi*s*ya) indicates (according to the rules of grammar) that the two actions—of entering and differentiating—belong to the same agent. And although the soul as being a part of the highest Self shares in its nature, yet in order to distinguish it from the highest Self, the text by means of the clause 'with *that* living Self' refers to it as something outward (not of the nature of the Self). The agent in the action of differentiation of names and forms therefore is Hira*n*yagarbha. Sm*ri*ti texts also ascribe to him this activity; cp. 'he in the beginning made, from the words of the Veda, the names and forms of beings, of the gods and the rest, and of actions.'

Against this view the Sûtra declares itself. The differentiation of names and forms belongs to him who renders tripartite, i. e. the highest Brahman; since it is assigned by Scripture to the latter only. For the text 'That divinity thought, let me, having entered these three beings with this living-soul-self, differentiate names and forms—let me make each of these three tripartite,' shows that all the activities mentioned have one and the same agent. But the rendering tripartite cannot belong to Brahmâ (Hira*n*yagarbha), who abides within the Brahma-egg, for that egg itself is produced from fire, water, and earth, only after these elements have been rendered tripartite; and Sm*ri*ti says that Brahmâ himself originated in that egg, 'in that egg there originated Brahmâ, the grandfather of all the worlds.' As thus the action of rendering tripartite can belong to the highest Brahman only, the differentiation of names and forms, which belongs to the same agent, also is Brahman's only.—But how then does the clause 'with that living-soul-self' fit in?—The co-ordination 'with that soul, with the Self,' shows that the term 'soul' here denotes the highest Brahman as having the soul for its body; just as in the clauses 'that fire thought'; 'it sent forth water'; 'water thought,' and so on, what is meant each time is Brahman having fire, water, and so on, for its body. The work of differentiating names and forms thus belongs to the highest Brahman which has for its body Hira*n*yagarbha, who represents the soul in its aggregate form. On this view the first person (in 'let me differentiate') and the agency (conveyed by the form of 'pravi*s*ya') may, without any difficulty, be taken in their primary literal senses; and the common agency, implied in the connexion of pravi*s*ya and vyâkaravâ*n*i, is accounted for. The view here set forth as to the relation of Brahman and Hira*n*yagarbha also explains how the accounts of Hira*n*yagarbha's (Brahmâ's) creative activity can say that *he* differentiated names and forms.

The whole passus beginning 'that divinity thought,' therefore has the following meaning—'Having entered into those three beings, viz. Fire, Water, and Earth, with my Self which is qualified by the collective soul (as constituting its body), let me differentiate names and forms, i.e. let me produce gods and all the other kinds of individual beings, and give them names; and to that end, since fire, water, and earth have not yet mutually combined, and hence are incapable of giving rise to particular things, let me make each of them tripartite, and thus fit them for creation.'—The settled conclusion then is, that the differentiation of names and forms is the work of the highest Brahman only.

But, an objection is raised, the fact that the differentiation of names and forms must be due to the same agent as the rendering tripartite, does not after all prove that the former is due to the highest Self. For the rendering tripartite may itself belong to the individual soul. For the text relates how, after the creation of the cosmic egg, a process of tripartition was going on among the individual living beings created by Brahmâ. 'Learn from me, my friend, how those three beings having reached man become tripartite, each of them. The earth when eaten is disposed of in three ways; its grossest portion becomes feces, its middle portion flesh, its subtlest portion mind,' and so on. Similarly, in the preceding section, it is described how the process of tripartition goes on in the case of fire, sun, moon, and lightning, which all belong to the world created by Brahmâ, 'the red colour of burning fire is the colour of fire,' &c. And the text moreover states the original tripartition to have taken place after the differentiation of names and forms: 'That divinity having entered into these three beings differentiated names and forms. Each of these (beings) it rendered tripartite.'—To this objection the next Sûtra replies.

18. Flesh is of earthy nature; in the case of the two others also according to the text.

The view that the description of tripartition, given in the passage 'each of these he made tripartite,' refers to a time subsequent to the creation of the mundane egg and to the gods created by Brahmâ, cannot be upheld. For from it there would follow that, as in the passage 'earth when eaten is disposed of in three ways,' &c., flesh is declared to be more subtle than feces, and mind yet subtler, it would have to be assumed—in agreement with the nature of the causal substance—that flesh is made of water and manas of fire[1]. And similarly we should have to assume that urine

[1] I.e. if the tripartition of earth (i.e. solid food) when eaten, which is described in VI, 5, 1, were the same tripartition which is described in VI, 3, 3–4, we should have to conclude that the former tripartition consists, like the latter, in an admixture to earth of water and fire.

—which is the grossest part of water drunk (cp. VI, 5, 2)—is of the nature of earth, and breath, which is its subtlest part, of the nature of fire. But this is not admissible; for as the text explicitly states that earth when eaten is disposed of in three ways, flesh and mind also must be assumed to be of an earthy nature. In the same way we must frame our view concerning 'the two others,' i. e. water and fire, 'according to the text.' That means—the three parts into which water divides itself when drunk, must be taken to be all of them modifications of water, and the three parts of fire when consumed must be held to be all of them modifications of fire. Thus feces, flesh and mind are alike transformations of earth; urine, blood and breath transformations of water; bones, marrow and speech transformations of fire.

This moreover agrees with the subsequent statement (VI, 5, 4), 'For, truly, mind consists of earth, breath of water, speech of fire.' The process of tripartition referred to in VI, 3, 4, is not therefore the same as the one described in the section that tells us what becomes of food when eaten, water when drunk, &c. Were this (erroneous) assumption made, and were it thence concluded that mind, breath and speech—as being the subtlest created things—are made of fire, this would flatly contradict the complementary text quoted above ('mind consists of earth,' &c.). When the text describes how earth, water and fire, when eaten, are transformed in a threefold way, it refers to elements which had already been rendered tripartite; the process of tripartition must therefore have taken place before the creation of the cosmic egg. Without such tripartition the elements would be incapable of giving rise to any effects; such capability they acquire only by being mutually conjoined, and that is just the process of tripartition. In agreement herewith Sm*ri*ti says, 'Separate from each other, without connexion, those elements with their various powers were incapable of producing creatures. But having combined completely, entered into mutual conjunction, abiding one within the other, the principles—from the highest Mahat down to individual things—produced the mundane egg.'—When the text therefore says (VI, 3, 3) 'The divinity having entered into those three beings with that soul-self differentiated names and forms; he made each of these tripartite,' the order in which the text mentions the activities of differentiation and tripartition is refuted by the order demanded by the sense[1].—The text then proceeds to exemplify the process of tripartition, by means of burning fire, the sun and lightning, which indeed are things contained within the mundane egg (while yet the tripartition of elements took place before the egg, with all its contents, was created); but this is done for the information of *S*vetaketu, who himself is a being within the mundane egg, and has to be taught with reference to things he knows.

But, a final objection is raised, as on this view of the matter the elements—earth, water and fire—which are eaten and drunk, are already tripartite, each of them containing portions of all, and thus are of a threefold nature, how can they be designated each of them by a simple term—*earth*, *water*, *fire*?—To this the next Sûtra replies.

19. But on account of their distinctive nature there is that designation, that designation.

Each element indeed is of a threefold nature, owing to the primary tripartition; but as in each mixed element one definite element prevails—so that each element has a distinctive character of its own—a definite designation is given to each.—The repetition (of 'that designation') in the Sûtra indicates the completion of the adhyâya.—Here terminates the adhikara*n*a of 'the fashioning of names and forms.'

---

[1] That means—in reality the tripartition of the elements came first, and after that the creation of individual beings.

# THIRD ADHYÂYA.

## FIRST PÂDA.

1. In obtaining another of that, it goes enveloped, (as appears) from question and explanation.

That the Vedânta-texts establish as the proper object of meditation, on the part of all men desirous of Release, the highest Brahman, which is the only cause of the entire world, which is not touched by even a shadow of imperfection, which is an ocean, as it were, of supremely exalted qualities, and which totally differs in nature from all other beings—this is the point proved in the two previous adhyâyas; there being given at the same time arguments to disprove the objections raised against the Vedânta doctrine on the basis of Sm*ri*ti and reasoning, to refute the views held by other schools, to show that the different Vedânta-texts do not contradict each other, and to prove that the Self is the object of activities (enjoined in injunctions of meditation, and so on). In short, those two adhyâyas have set forth the essential nature of Brahman. The subsequent part of the work now makes it its task to enquire into the mode of attaining to Brahman, together with the means of attainment. The third adhyâya is concerned with an enquiry into meditation—which is the means of attaining to Brahman; and as the motive for entering on such meditation is supplied by the absence of all desire for what is other than the thing to be obtained, and by the desire for that thing, the points first to be enquired into are the imperfections of the individual soul—moving about in the different worlds, whether waking or dreaming or merged in dreamless sleep, or in the state of swoon; and those blessed characteristics by which Brahman is raised above all these imperfections. These are the topics of the first and second pâdas of the adhyâya.

The first question to be considered is whether the soul,

when moving from one body into another, is enveloped by those subtle rudiments of the elements from which the new body is produced, or not. The Pûrvapakshin maintains the latter alternative; for, he says, wherever the soul goes it can easily provide itself there with those rudiments. Other reasons supporting this primâ facie view will be mentioned and refuted further on.—The Sûtra states the view finally accepted, 'In obtaining another "of that" it goes enveloped.' The 'of that' refers back to the form, i.e. body, mentioned in II, 4, 17. The soul when moving towards another embodiment goes enveloped by the rudiments of the elements. This is known 'from question and explanation,' i.e. answer. Question and answer are recorded in the 'Knowledge of the five fires' (*Kh.* Up. V, 3–10), where Pravâha*n*a, after having addressed to *S*vetaketu several other questions, finally asks 'Do you know why in the fifth libation water is called man?' In answer to this last question the text then explains how the Devas, i.e. the prâ*n*as attached to the soul, offer into the heavenly world, imagined as a sacrificial fire, the oblation called *s*raddhâ; how this *s*raddhâ changes itself into a body consisting of am*ri*ta, which body is called moon; how the same prâ*n*as offer this body of am*ri*ta in Par*g*anya, imagined as a fire, whereupon the body so offered becomes rain; how the same prâ*n*as throw that rain on to the earth, also imagined as a sacrificial fire, whereupon it becomes food; how this food is then offered into man, also compared to fire, where it becomes seed; and how, finally, this seed is offered into woman, also compared to a fire, and there becomes an embryo. The text then goes on, 'Thus in the fifth oblation water becomes purushava*k*as,' i.e. to be designated by the term *man*. And this means that the water which, in a subtle form, was throughout present in the previous oblations also, now, in that fifth oblation, assumes the form of a man.—From this question and answer it thus appears that the soul moves towards a new embodiment, together with the subtle rudiments from which the new body springs.—But the words, 'water becomes purushava*k*as,' only intimate that water assumes the form of a man, whence we conclude that water only invests the soul during its wanderings; how then can it be held that the soul moves invested by the rudiments of all elements?—To this question the next Sûtra replies.

2. But on account of (water) consisting of the three elements; on account of predominance.

Water alone could not produce a new body; for the text *Kh*. Up. VI, 3, 4, 'Each of these he made tripartite,' shows that all the elements were made tripartite to the end of producing bodies. That the text under discussion mentions water only, is due to the predominance of water; and that among the elements giving rise to a new body water predominates, we infer from the fact that blood and the other humours are the predominating element in the body.

3. And on account of the going of the prâ*n*as.

That the soul goes embedded in the subtle rudiments of the elements follows therefrom also that when passing out of the old body it is said to be followed by the prâ*n*as, 'when he thus passes out, the chief prâ*n*a follows after him,' &c. (B*ri*. Up. V, 4, 2). Compare also Sm*ri*ti: 'It draws to itself the organs of sense, with the mind for the sixth. When the Ruler (soul) obtains a new body, and passes out of another, he takes with him those organs and then moves on, as the wind takes the odours from their abodes (the flowers)' (Bha. Gî. XV, 8). But the prâ*n*as cannot move without a substrate, and hence we must admit that the rudiments of the elements—which are their substrate—are also moving.

4. If it be said (that it is not so) on account of scriptural statement as to going to Agni and the rest; we say no, on account of the secondary nature (of the statement).

But the text, 'when the speech of the dead person enters into fire,' &c. (B*ri*. Up. III, 2, 13), declares that when a person dies his organs go into fire, and so on; they cannot therefore accompany the soul. Hence the text which asserts the latter point must be explained in some other way!—Not so, the Sûtra replies. The text stating that the organs go to fire, and so on, cannot be taken in its literal sense; for it continues, 'the hairs of the body enter into herbs, the hair of the head into trees' (which manifestly is not true, in its literal sense). The going of speech, the eye, and so on, must therefore be understood to mean that the different organs approach the divinities (Agni and the rest) who preside over them.

5. Should it be said, on account of absence of mention in the first (reply); we say no, for just that (is meant), on the ground of fitness.

An objection is raised to the conclusion arrived at under III, 1, 1; on the ground that in the first oblation, described in *Kh.* Up. V, 4, 2, as being made into the heavenly world, water is not mentioned at all as the thing offered. The text says, 'on that altar the gods offer *s*raddhâ'; and by *s*raddhâ (belief) everybody understands a certain activity of mind. Water therefore is not the thing offered.—Not so, we reply. It is nothing else but water, which there is called *s*raddhâ. For thus only question and answer have a sense. For the question is, 'Do you know why in the fifth libation water is called man?' and at the outset of the reply *s*raddhâ is mentioned as constituting the oblation made into the heavenly world viewed as a fire. If here the word *s*raddhâ did not denote water, question and answer would refer to different topics, and there would be no connexion. The form in which the final statement is introduced (iti tu pa*ñk*amyâm, &c., 'but thus in the fifth oblation,' &c.), moreover, also intimates that *s*raddhâ means water. The word 'iti,' *thus*, here intimates that the answer is meant to dispose of the question, 'Do you know *how*?' &c. *S*raddhâ becomes moon, rain, food, seed, embryo in succession, and *thus* the water comes to be called man. Moreover, the word *s*raddhâ is actually used in the Veda in the sense of 'water'; 'he carries water, *s*raddhâ indeed is water' (Taitt. Sa*m*h. I, 6, 8, 1). And what the text says as to king Soma (the moon) originating from *s*raddhâ when offered, also shows that *s*raddhâ must mean water.

6. 'On account of this not being stated by Scripture'; not so, on account of those who perform sacrifices and so on being understood.

But, a further objection is raised, in the whole section under discussion no mention at all is made of the soul; the section cannot therefore prove that the soul moves, enveloped by water. The text speaks only of different forms of water—*s*raddhâ and the rest.—This, the Sûtra points out, is not so, on account of those who perform sacrifices being understood. For further on in the same chapter it is said, that those who, while destitute of the knowledge of Brahman, practise sacrifices, useful works and alms, reach the heavenly world and become there of the essence of the moon (somarâ*g*âna*h*); whence, on the results of their good works being exhausted, they return again and enter on a new embryonic state (*Kh*. Up. V, 10). Now in the preceding section (V, 9) it is said that they offer *s*raddhâ in the heavenly world, and that from that oblation there arises the king Soma—an account which clearly refers to the same process as the one described in V, 10. We herefrom infer that what is meant in V, 9 is that that being which was distinguished by a body of *s*raddhâ, becomes a being distinguished by a body of the nature of the moon. The word *body* denotes that the nature of which it is to be the attribute of a soul, and thus extends in its connotation up to the soul. The meaning of the section therefore is that it is the soul which moves enveloped by water and the other rudimentary elements.—But the phrase 'him the gods eat' (V, 10, 4) shows that the king Soma cannot be the soul, for that cannot be eaten!—To this the next Sûtra replies.

7. Or it is metaphorical, on account of their not knowing the Self. For thus Scripture declares.

He who performs sacrifices, and so on, and thus does not know the Self, is here below and in yonder world a mere means of enjoyment for the devas. He serves them here, by propitiating them with sacrifices, and so on; and when the gods, pleased with his service, have taken him up into yonder world, he there is a common means of enjoyment for them (since they are gratified by the presence of a faithful servant). That those not knowing the Self serve and benefit the gods, Scripture explicitly declares, 'He is like a beast for the devas' (B*ri*. Up. I, 4, 10). Sm*ri*ti also declares, that while those who know the Self attain to Brahman, those who do not know it are means of enjoyment for the devas, 'To the gods go the worshippers of the gods, and they that are devoted to me go to me' (Bha. Gî. VII, 23). When Scripture speaks of the soul being eaten by the gods, it therefore only means that the soul is to them a source of enjoyment. That eating the soul means no more than satisfaction with it, may also be inferred from the following scriptural passage, 'The gods in truth do not eat nor do they drink; by the mere sight of that am*ri*ta they are satisfied.'—It thus remains a settled conclusion that the soul moves enveloped by the subtle rudiments of the elements.—Here terminates the adhikara*n*a of 'the obtaining of another body.'

8. On the passing away of the works, with a remainder, according to Scripture and Sm*ri*ti; as it went and not so.

The text declares that those who only perform sacrifices and useful works ascend by the road of the fathers, and again return to the earth when they have fully enjoyed the fruit of their works, 'having dwelt there yâvat sa*m*pâtam, they return by the same way' (*Kh*. Up. V, 10, 5). The question here arises whether the descending soul carries a certain remainder (anu*s*aya) of its works or not.—It does not, since it has enjoyed the fruit of all its works. For by 'anu*s*aya' we have to understand that part of the karman which remains over and above the part retributively enjoyed; but when the fruit of the entire karman has been enjoyed, there is no such remainder. And that this is so we learn from the phrase 'yâvat sa*m*pâtam ushitvâ,' which means 'having dwelt there as long as the karman lasts' (sampatanty anena svargalokam iti sampâta*h*). Analogously another text says, 'Having obtained the end of whatever deed he does on earth, he again returns from that world to this world to action' (B*ri*. Up. V, 4, 6).—Against this primâ facie view the Sûtra declares 'with a remainder he descends, on account of what is seen, i. e. scriptural text, and Sm*ri*ti.' The scriptural text is the one 'Those whose conduct has been good' (V, 10, 7), which means that among the souls that have returned, those whose karman is good obtain a good birth as Brâhma*n*as or the like, while those whose karman is bad are born again as low creatures—dogs, pigs, *K*â*nd*âlas, and the like. This shows that the souls which have descended are still connected with good or evil karman. Sm*ri*ti also declares this: 'Men of the several castes and orders, who always stand firm in the works prescribed for them, enjoy after death the rewards of their works, and by virtue of a remnant (of their works) they are born again in excellent countries, castes and families, endowed with beauty, long life, learning in the Vedas, wealth, good conduct, happiness and wisdom. Those who act in a contrary manner perish' (Gautama Dha. Sû. XI, 29); 'Afterwards when a man returns to this world he obtains, by virtue of a remainder of works, birth in a good family, beauty of form, beauty of complexion, strength, aptitude for learning, wisdom, wealth, and capacity for fulfilling his duties. Therefore, rolling like a wheel (from the one to the other), in both worlds he dwells in happiness' (Âpast. Dha. Sû. II, 1, 2, 3). The clause 'as long as his works last' (yâvat-sa*m*pâtam) refers to that part of his works only which was performed with a view to reward (as promised for those works by the Veda); and the same holds true with regard to the passage 'whatever work man does here on earth' (B*ri*. Up. V, 4, 6). Nor is it possible that works, the fruit of which has not yet been enjoyed, and those the result of which has not been wiped out by expiatory ceremonies, should be destroyed by the enjoyment of the fruits of other works. Hence those who have gone to that world return with a remnant of their works, 'as they went and not so'—i. e. in the same way as they ascended and also in a different way. For the ascent takes place by the following stages—smoke, night, the dark half of the moon, the six months of the sun's southern progress, the world of the fathers, ether, moon. The descent, on the other hand, goes from the place of the moon, through ether, wind, smoke, mist, cloud. The two journeys are alike in so far as they pass through ether, but different in so far as the descent touches wind, and so on, and does not touch the world of the fathers, and other stages of the ascent.

9. 'On account of conduct'; not so, since (*k*ara*n*a) connotes works; thus Kârsh*n*â*g*ini thinks.

In the phrases 'those whose works were good' (rama*n*îya-*k*ara*n*â*h*), and 'those whose works were bad' (kapûyâ-*k*ara*n*â*h*), the word *k*ara*n*a does not denote good and evil works (i. e. not such works as the Veda on the one hand enjoins as leading to certain rewards, and on the other prohibits, threatening punishment), for, in Vedic as well as ordinary language, the term *k*ara*n*a is generally used in the sense of â*k*âra, i. e. general conduct. In ordinary speech such words as â*k*âra, *s*îla, v*ri*tta are considered synonymous, and in the Veda we read 'whatever works (karmâ*n*i) are blameless, those should be regarded, not others. Whatever our good conduct (su-*k*aritâni) was, that should be observed by thee, nothing else' (Taitt. Up. I, 11, 2)—where 'works' and 'conduct' are distinguished. Difference in quality of birth therefore depends on conduct, not on the remainder of works performed with a view to certain results.—This primâ facie view the Sûtra sets aside, 'not so, because the scriptural term *k*ara*n*a connotes works; thus the teacher Kârsh*n*â*g*ini thinks.' For mere conduct does not lead to experiences of pleasure and pain; pleasure and pain are the results of *works* in the limited sense.

10. 'There is purposelessness'; not so, on account of the dependence on that.

But if conduct has no result, it follows that good conduct, as enjoined in the Sm*ri*tis, is useless!—Not so, we reply; for holy works enjoined by the Veda depend on conduct, in so far as a man of good conduct only is entitled to perform those works. This appears from passages such as the following: 'A man who is not pure is unfit for all religious work,' and 'Him who is devoid of good conduct the Vedas do not purify.' Kârsh*n*â*g*ini's view thus is, that the *k*ara*n*a of the text implies karman.

11. But only good and evil works, thus Bâdari thinks.

As the verb â-*k*ar takes karman for its object (pu*n*ya*m* karmâ*k*arati, &c.), and as the separate denotation (i.e. the use of apparently equivalent words, viz. â*k*ar and karman) can be accounted for on the ground that one of them refers to works established by manifest texts, and the other to texts inferred from actually existing rules of good conduct; and as, when the primary meaning is possible, no secondary meaning must be adopted; nothing else but good and evil works (in the Vedic sense) are denoted by the word *k*ara*n*a: such is the opinion of the teacher Bâdari. This opinion of Bâdari, the author of the Sûtra states as representing his own. On the other hand, he adopts the view of Kârsh*n*â*g*ini in so far as he considers such items of virtuous *conduct* as the Sandhyâ—which are enjoined by scriptural texts, the existence of which is inferred on the basis of conduct as enjoined by Sm*ri*ti—to have the result of qualifying the agent for the performance of other works.—The conclusion therefore is that the souls descend, carrying a remnant of their works.—Here terminates the adhikara*n*a of 'the passing of works.'

12. Of those also who do not perform sacrifices (the ascent) is declared by Scripture.

It has been said that those who perform only sacrifices, and so on, go to the moon and thence return with a remainder of their works. The question now arises whether those also who do not perform sacrifices go to the moon. The phrase 'who do not perform sacrifices' denotes evil-doers of two kinds, viz. those who do not do what is enjoined, and those who do what is forbidden.—These also go to the moon, the Pûrvapakshin maintains; for the text contains a statement to that effect, 'All who depart from this world go to the moon' (Ka. Up. I, 2)—where it is said that all go, without any distinction. So that those who perform good works and those who perform evil works, equally go to the moon.—This the next Sûtra negatives.

13. But of the others having enjoyed in Sa*m*yamana, there is ascent and descent; as such a course is declared.

Of the others, i. e. those who do not perform sacrifices, and so on, there is ascent to the moon and descent from there, only after they have in the kingdom of Yama suffered the punishments due to their actions. For the text declares that evil-doers fall under the power of Yama, and have to go to him, 'He who thinks, this is the world there is no other, falls again and again under my sway' (Ka. Up. I, 2, 6); 'the son of Vivasvat, the gathering place of men' (*Ri*k Sa*m*h. X, 14, 1); 'King Yama,' and other texts.

14. Smr*i*ti texts also declare this.

That all beings are under the sway of Yama, Parâ*s*ara also and other Smr*i*ti writers declare, 'And all these pass under the sway of Yama.'

15. Moreover there are seven.

The Smr*i*tis moreover declare that there are seven hells, called Raurava, and so on, to which evil-doers have to go.—But how do they, if moving about in those seven places, reach the palace of Yama?

16. On account of his activity there also, there is no contradiction.

As their going to those seven places also is due to the command of Yama, there is no contradiction.—Thus those also who do not perform sacrifices, and so on, after having gone to the world of Yama, and there undergone punishments according to the nature of their works, later on ascend to the moon and again descend from there.—Of this conclusion the next Sûtra disposes.

17. But, of knowledge and work—as these are the leading topics.

The 'but' sets aside the view developed so far. It cannot be admitted that those also who do not perform sacrifices, and so on, reach the moon; because the path of the gods and the path of the fathers are meant for the enjoyment of the fruits 'of knowledge and work.' That is to say—as those who do not perform sacrifices cannot ascend by the path of the gods, since they are destitute of knowledge; so they also cannot go by the path of the fathers, since they are destitute of meritorious works. And that these two paths are dependent respectively on knowledge and works, we know from the fact that these two are the leading topics. For knowledge forms the leading topic with regard to the path of the gods, 'Those who know this, and those who in the forest follow faith and austerities, go to light,' &c.; and works have the same position with regard to the path of the fathers, 'they who living in a village perform sacrifices, &c. go to the smoke,' &c. The text, 'all those who depart from this world go to the moon,' must therefore be interpreted to mean 'all those who perform sacrifices go to the moon.'—But if evil-doers do not go to the moon, the fifth oblation cannot take place, and no new body can be produced. For the text says, 'In the fifth oblation water is called man,' and, as we have shown, that fifth oblation presupposes the soul's going to the moon. In order, therefore, to understand how in their case also a new embodiment is possible, it must needs be admitted that they also ascend to the moon.—To this the next Sûtra replies.

18. Not in the case of the third (place), as it is thus perceived.

The third 'place' does not, for the origination of a new body, depend on the fifth oblation. The term, 'the third place,' denotes mere evil-doers. That these do not, for the origination of a new body, depend on the fifth oblation, is seen from Scripture. For, in answer to the question 'Do you know why that world never becomes full?' the text says, 'On neither of these two ways are those small creatures continually returning, of whom it may be said, Live and die. This is the third place. Therefore that world never becomes full.' As this passage states that in consequence of 'the third place' (i. e. the creatures forming a third class) not ascending to and descending from the heavenly world that world never becomes full, it follows that that third place does not, for the origination of bodies, depend on the fifth oblation. The clause, 'in the fifth oblation,' moreover, merely states that the connexion of water with the fifth fire is the cause of the water 'being called man' (i. e. becoming an embryo), but does not deny the origination of embryos in other ways; for the text contains no word asserting such a limitation.

19. It moreover is recorded, in the world.

Sm*ri*ti, moreover, states that the bodies of some specially meritorious persons, such as Draupadî, Dh*rish*t*a*dyumna and others, were formed independently of the fifth oblation' (i. e. sexual union).

20. And on account of its being seen.

And it is seen in Scripture also, that the bodies of some beings originate independently of the fifth oblation: 'Of all beings there are indeed three origins only, that which springs from an egg, that which springs from a living being, that which springs from a germ' (*Kh*. Up. VI, 3, 1). It is observed that from among these beings those springing from a germ and those springing from heat originate without that fifth oblation.—But the text quoted does not refer to the creatures springing from heat; for it says that there are three origins only!—To this the next Sûtra replies.

21. The third term includes that which springs from heat.

Creatures sprung from heat are included in the third term—viz. that which springs from a germ—which is exhibited in the text quoted. The settled conclusion therefore is that the evil-doers do not go to the moon.—Here terminates the adhikara*n*a of 'those who do not perform sacrifices.'

22. There is entering into similarity of being with those, there being a reason.

The text describes the manner in which those who perform sacrifices, and so on, descend from the moon as follows: 'They return again that way as they came, to the ether, from the ether to the air. Then having become air they become smoke, having become smoke they become mist,' &c. The doubt here arises whether the soul when reaching ether, and so on, becomes ether in the same sense as here on earth it becomes a man or other being, or merely becomes similar to ether, and so on.—The former view is the true one; for as the soul in the *s*raddhâ state becomes the moon, so it must likewise be held to *become* ether, and so on, there being no reason for a difference in the two cases.—This primâ facie view the Sûtra sets aside. The descending soul enters into similarity of being with ether, and so on; since there is a reason for this. When the soul becomes a man or becomes the moon, there is a reason for that, since it thereby becomes capacitated for the enjoyment of pain and pleasure. But there is no similar reason for the soul becoming ether, and so on, and hence the statement that the soul becomes ether, and so on, can only mean that, owing to contact with them, it becomes similar to them.—Here terminates the adhikara*n*a of 'entering into similarity of being.'

23. Not very long; on account of special statement.

Does the soul in its descent through ether, and so on, stay at each stage for a not very long time, or is there nothing to define that time?—It stays at each stage for an indefinite time, there being nothing to define the time.—

Not so, the Sûtra decides. For there is a special statement, i.e. the text says that when the soul has become rice or grain or the like, the passing out of that stage is beset with difficulties. From this we infer that as there is no such statement concerning the earlier stages, the soul stays at each of them for a short time only.—Here terminates the adhikara*n*a of 'the not very long time.'

24. Into (plants) animated by other souls, because the statement is as in the previous cases.

The text declares that the descending souls are born as rice, corn, &c., 'they are born here as rice, corn, herbs, trees,' &c. The question here is whether the souls cling to plants animated by other souls which have those plants for their bodies; or whether the descending souls themselves are born with those plants for their bodies.—The latter view is the right one; for the text says, 'they are born as rice, grain,' and so on, and this expression is of the same kind as when we say 'he is born as a man, as a deva,' and so on. The text therefore means that the souls are embodied in the different plants.—This view the Sûtra rejects. The souls merely cling to those plants which constitute the bodies of other souls; 'since the statement is as in the previous cases,' i.e. because the text only says that the souls become plants as it had previously been said that they become ether, and so on. Where the text means to say that the soul enters on the condition of an enjoying soul (i.e. of a soul assuming a new body for the purpose of retributive enjoyment), it refers to the deeds which lead to such enjoyment; so e.g. in the passage, 'Those whose works have been good obtain a good birth,' &c. But in the text under discussion there is no such reference to karman. For those works—viz. sacrifices and the like—which were undertaken with a view to reward, such as enjoyment of the heavenly world, are, in the case of the descending souls, completely wiped out by the enjoyment of the heavenly world (which precedes the descent of the souls); and those works on the other hand, the action of which has not yet begun, lead to the embodiments mentioned further on ('Those whose works are good'). And in the interval between those two conditions no new karman originates. When, therefore, the text says that the souls are born as plants, the statement cannot be taken in its literal sense.

25. It is unholy. Not so, on the ground of Scripture.

The conclusion arrived at above cannot be accepted, since there is a reason why the descending soul should enter on the condition of an enjoying soul. Such works as sacrifices, the fruit of which is the enjoyment of the heavenly world, are mixed with evil, for they imply injury to living beings as in the case of the goat offered to Agnîshomau. And such injury is evil as it is forbidden by texts such as 'let him not harm any creature.' Nor can it be said that the injunctions of sacrificing animals constitute exceptions to the general rule of not harming any creature.—For the two injunctions refer to different things. The injunction to kill the goat for Agnîshomau intimates that the killing of the animal subserves the accomplishment of the sacrifice, while the injunction not to 'harm' teaches that such harming has disastrous consequences. Should it be said that the prohibition of harming does not refer to such actions as the sacrifice of the goat which proceed on the basis of scriptural injunction, but only to such actions as spring from natural passion or desire (râga); we remark that in the case of sacrifices also the action is equally prompted by natural desire. Injunctions such as 'He who desires the heavenly world is to sacrifice,' teach that sacrifices are to be undertaken by persons desirous of certain pleasant results, and such persons having thus learned by what means the result is to be accomplished proceed to action from the natural desire of the result. This applies to the killing of the goat also which is offered to Agnîshomau; man learns from Scripture that such actions help to accomplish the sacrifice which effects the result, and then performs those actions from natural desire. The case in no way differs from that of harm done in ordinary life—where the agent always is prompted by natural desire, having somehow arrived at the conclusion that his action will accomplish something aimed at by himself. The same holds good with regard to works of permanent obligation. Men learn from Scripture that through the performance of the special duties of their caste they attain happiness of the highest kind, and then apply themselves to their duties from a natural desire of such happiness, and therefore such works also are mixed with evil. Hence the souls of those who have performed sacrifices, and so on, which contain an element of evil, at first experience in the heavenly world that result which is to be enjoyed there, and then embodying themselves in non-moving things such as plants, experience the fruit of that part of their actions which is of a harmful nature. That embodiment in non-moving beings is the result of evil deeds Sm*ri*ti declares: 'Owing to those defects of work which are due to the body, a man becomes a non-moving being.' From all this it follows that the souls embody themselves in plants to the end of enjoying the fruits of their works.—To this the Sûtra replies—it is not so, on account of scriptural statement. For Scripture declares that the killing of sacrificial animals makes them to go up to the heavenly world, and therefore is not of the nature of harm. This is declared in the text, 'The animal killed at the sacrifice having assumed a divine body goes to the heavenly world'; 'with a golden body it ascends to the heavenly world.' An action which is the means of supreme exaltation is not of the nature of harm, even if it involves some little pain; it rather is of beneficial nature.—With this the mantra also agrees: 'Thou dost not die, thou goest to the gods on easy paths; where virtuous men go, not evil-doers, there the divine Savit*ri* may lead thee.' An act which has a healing tendency, although it may cause a transitory pain, men of insight declare to be preservative and beneficial.

26. After that conjunction with him who performs the act of generation.

The declaration that the descending souls *become* rice plants, and so on, cannot be taken literally for that reason also, that the text afterwards declares them to *become* those who perform the act of generation: 'Whoever the being may be that eats the food and begets offspring, that being he (i.e. the soul that has descended) becomes.' Now the meaning of this latter text can only be that the soul enters into conjunction with the creature which eats the grain; and hence we have to interpret the previous text, as to the soul's becoming a plant, in the same way.

27. From the yoni the body.

Only after having reached a yoni the soul, affected with a remnant of its works, obtains a new body, and only in a body there can be the enjoyment of pleasure and pain. When, therefore, previous to that the soul is said to reach ether, wind, and so on, this can only mean that it enters into conjunction with them.—Here terminates the adhikara*n*a of 'that animated by another soul.'

## SECOND PÂDA.

1. In the intermediate sphere the creation (is effected by the soul); for (Scripture) says (so).

So far it has been shown that the soul in the waking state suffers affliction since, in accordance with its deeds, it goes, returns, is born, and so on. Next an enquiry is instituted into its condition in the state of dream. With reference to the state of dreaming Scripture says, 'There are no chariots in that state, no horses, no roads; then he creates chariots, horses and roads. There are no blessings, no happiness, no joys; then he himself creates blessings, happiness, joys, and so on. For he is the creator' (B*ri*. Up. IV, 3, 10). A doubt here arises whether this creation of chariots and the rest is accomplished by the individual soul, or by the Lord.—'The creation in the intermediate state' is due to the individual soul only. 'The intermediate state' means the sphere of dreams, in agreement with the passage 'There is a third intermediate state, the place of dreams' (B*ri*. Up. IV, 3, 1). And that creation is effected by the soul only; for what is referred to in the passages 'he creates,' 'For he is the maker,' is none other but the dreaming soul.

2. And some (state the soul to be) the shaper; and sons, and so on.

And the followers of one *s*âkhâ state in their text that the dreaming soul is the shaper of its desires: 'He, the person who is awake in those who sleep, shaping one desired thing (kâma) after the other.' The term 'kâma' there denotes not mère desires, but such things as sons and the like which are objects of desire. For sons and so on are introduced as 'kâmas' in previous passages: 'Ask for all kâmas according to thy wish'; 'Choose sons and grandsons living a hundred years' (Ka. Up. I, 1, 25; 23). The individual soul thus creates chariots, and so on, in its dreams. That the soul has the power of realising all its wishes is known from the declaration of Pra*g*âpati. It is therefore able to create, even in the absence of special instruments.—This view is set aside by the next Sûtra.

3. But it is mere Mâyâ; on account of the true nature (of the soul) not being fully manifested.

The things appearing in dreams—chariots, lotus tanks, and so on—are absolute Mâyâ, i. e. things created by the Supreme Person. For the term 'Mâyâ' denotes wonderful things, as appears from passages such as 'She was born in the race of *G*anaka, appearing like the wonderful power of the divine being in bodily shape' (devamâyâ). The sense of the passage 'there are no chariots,' &c. then is—there are no chariots and horses to be perceived by any other person but the dreaming one; and then 'he creates chariots,' &c.—i. e. the Supreme Person creates things to be perceived by the dreamer and persisting for a certain time only. Those things therefore are of a wonderful nature (but not illusions). And the creation of such wonderful things is possible for the Supreme Person who can immediately realise all his wishes; but not for the individual soul. The latter also, indeed, fundamentally possesses that power; but as in the Sa*m*sâra state the true nature of the soul is not fully manifested, it is then incapable of accomplishing such wonderful creations. The text 'the person shaping one desired thing after the other' declares the Supreme Person to be the creator, for the clauses immediately preceding and following that text (viz. 'He who is awake in those who sleep'; and 'that is the Bright, that is Brahman, that alone is called the Immortal; all worlds are contained in it and no one goes beyond'—Ka. Up. II, 5, 8) mention attributes distinctively characteristic of the Supreme Person. And the B*ri*. Up. text, 'For he is the maker,' must therefore, in agreement with the Ka*th*a-text, also be understood as declaring that it is the Supreme Person only that creates the things seen in a dream.—But if it is the true nature of the soul to be free from all imperfections, and so on, why then does this not manifest itself?—To this the next Sûtra replies.

4. But owing to the wish of the highest it is hidden; for from that are its bondage and the opposite state.

The *but* sets the objection aside. Owing to the wish of the highest, i. e. the Supreme Person, the essential nature of the individual soul is hidden. The Supreme Person hides the true, essentially blessed, nature of the soul which is in a state of sin owing to the endless chain of karman. For this reason we find it stated in Scripture that the bondage and release of the soul result from the wish of the Supreme Person only 'when he finds freedom from fear and rest in that invisible, incorporeal, undefined, unsupported; then he has gone to fearlessness'; 'for he alone causes blessedness'; 'from fear of it the wind blows' (Taitt. Up. II, 7, 8).

5. Or that (results) also from connexion with the body.

The obscuration of the soul's true nature results either from the soul's connexion with the body or from its connexion with the power of matter in a subtle state. As long as the creation lasts, the soul is obscured by its connexion with matter in the form of a body; at the time of a pralaya, on the other hand, by its connexion with matter of so exceedingly subtle a kind as not to admit of differentiation by means of name and form. As thus its true nature is not manifest, the soul is unable to create, in dreams, chariots, lotus tanks, and so on, by its mere wish. And what the texts say about a being that is awake in those who sleep and is the abode of all worlds ('in that all the worlds abide, and no one goes beyond it'—Ka. Up. II, 4, 9) can apply to the Supreme Person only. The things seen by an individual soul in its dreams therefore are specially created by the Supreme Person, and are meant by him to be a retribution—whether reward or punishment—for deeds of minor importance; they therefore last for the time of the dream only, and are perceived by that one soul only.

6. And it is suggestive, according to Scripture; this the experts also declare.

The things seen in dreams are not created by the wish of the individual soul for this reason also, that according to Scripture dreams are prophetic of future good or ill fortune. 'When a man engaged in some work undertaken for some special wish sees a woman in his dream, he may infer success from his dream vision.' Those also who understand the science of dreams teach that dreams foreshadow good and evil fortune. But that which depends on one's own wish can have no prophetic quality; and as ill fortune is not desired the dreamer would create for himself only such visions as would indicate good fortune. Hence the creation which takes place in dreams can be the Lord's work only.—Here terminates the adhikara*n*a of 'the intermediate state.'

7. The absence of that takes place in the nâ*d*îs and in the Self, according to scriptural statement.

Next the state of deep dreamless sleep is enquired into. Scripture says, 'When a man is asleep, reposing and at perfect rest, so that he sees no dream, then he lies asleep in those nâ*d*îs' (*Kh.* Up. VIII, 6, 3); 'When he is in profound sleep and is conscious of nothing, there are seventy-two thousand veins called hita which from the heart spread through the pericardium. Through them he moves forth and rests in the pericardium' (B*ri*. Up. II, 1, 19). 'When a man sleeps here, he becomes united with the True' (*Kh.* Up. VI, 8, 1). These texts declare the veins, the pericardium, and Brahman to be the place of deep sleep; and hence there is a doubt whether each of them in turns, or all of them together, are that place.—There is an option between them, since they are not in mutual dependence, and since the sleeping soul cannot at the same time be in several places!—To this the Sûtra replies—the absence of dreams, i.e. deep sleep takes place in the veins, in the pericardium, and in the highest Self together; since these three are declared by Scripture. When different alternatives may be combined, on the ground of there being different effects in each case, it is improper to assume an option which implies sublation of some of the alternatives. And in the present case such combination is possible, the veins and the pericardium holding the position of a mansion, as it were, and a couch within the mansion, while Brahman is the pillow, as it were. Thus Brahman alone is the immediate resting-place of the sleeping soul.

8. Hence the awaking from that.

Since Brahman alone directly is the place of deep sleep, Scripture is able to declare that the souls awake from that, i. e. Brahman; compare 'Having come back from the True they do not know that they come from the True' (*Kh.* Up. VI, 10, 2), and other texts.—Here terminates the adhikara*n*a of 'the absence of that.'

9. But the same, on account of work, remembrance, text, and injunction.

Does the same person who had gone to sleep rise again at the time of waking, or a different one?—Since the soul in deep sleep frees itself from all limiting adjuncts, unites itself with Brahman, and thus being in no way different from the released soul, is no longer in any way connected with its previous body, organs, and so on; the person rising from sleep is a different one.—This view the Sûtra sets aside, saying 'but the same.' For there remains the work, i. e. the good and evil deeds previously done by the sleeper, for which the same person has to undergo retribution before the knowledge of truth arises. There is next remembrance—'I, the waking person, am the same as I who was asleep.' Scripture also declares this: 'Whatever these creatures are here, whether a lion, or tiger, or wolf, &c., that they become again' (*Kh.* Up. VI, 10, 2). And, lastly, the injunctions which enjoin certain acts for the sake of final Release would be purportless if the person merged in deep sleep attained Release. Nor can it be said that the sleeping soul is free from all limiting adjuncts and manifests itself in its true nature (so as not to be different from the released soul). For with regard to the sleeping person the text says, 'In truth he thus does not know himself that he is I, nor does he know anything that exists. He is gone to utter annihilation. I see no good in this' (*Kh.* Up. VIII, 11, 1); while, on the other hand, the texts, 'Having approached the highest light he manifests himself in his true nature; he moves about there laughing, playing, delighting himself'; 'He becomes a Self-ruler; he moves about in all the worlds according to his wish'; 'The seeing one sees everything, and attains everything everywhere' (*Kh.* Up. VIII, 12, 3; VII, 25, 2; 26, 2), declare that the released soul is all-knowing, and so on. What is true about the sleeping person is that he is still comprised within the Sa*m*sâra, but for the time having put off all instruments of knowledge and action and become incapable of knowledge and enjoyment repairs to the place of utter rest, i. e. the highest Self, and having there refreshed himself, again rises to new enjoyment of action.—Here terminates the adhikara*n*a of 'work, remembrance, text, and injunction.'

10. In the swooning person there is half-combination; this being the remaining (hypothesis).

With regard to a person lying in a swoon or stunned, the question arises whether that state of swoon is one of the other states, viz. deep sleep and so on, or whether it is a special condition of its own.—The former alternative must be accepted. For the term 'swoon' may be explained as denoting either deep sleep or some other acknowledged state, and there is no authority for assuming an altogether different new state.—This view the Sûtra sets aside. The condition of a swooning person consists in reaching half, viz. of what leads to death; for this is the only hypothesis remaining. A swoon cannot be either dreaming or being awake; for in a swoon there is no consciousness. And as it is different in character as well as in the occasions giving rise to it from deep sleep and death, it cannot be either of those two states; for there are special circumstances occasioning a swoon, such as a blow on the head. The only possible alternative then is to view a swoon as a state in which there is made a half-way approach to death. For while death consists in the complete cessation of the soul's connexion with the body or organs of any kind, a swoon consists in the soul's remaining connected with the subtle body and organs only.—Here terminates the adhikara*n*a of 'the swooning person.'

11. Not on account of place even (is there any imperfection) of the Highest; for everywhere (it is described) as having twofold characteristics.

The different states of the individual soul have been discussed, to the end that an insight into their imperfections may give rise to indifference towards all worldly enjoyments. Next now, in order to give rise to the desire of attaining to Brahman, the Sûtras proceed to expound how Brahman's nature is raised above all imperfections and constituted by mere blessed qualities. The following point requires to be considered first. Do those imperfections which cling to the individual soul in consequence of its different states—viz. the waking state, dreams, deep sleep, swoon, departure from the body—affect also the highest Brahman which as its inner Ruler abides within the soul in those different states, or not?—They do affect it, since Brahman abides within the bodies which are in those different states.—But Sûtras such as I, 2, 8 have already declared that the highest Brahman, because not subject to the influence of karman, is free from all imperfections; how then can imperfections cling to it for the reason that it is connected with this or that place?—In the following way. As was shown under III, 2, 6, works give rise to imperfection and suffering in so far as they cause the connexion of the soul with a body. The efficient cause therein is the imperfection inherent in the connexion with a body; for otherwise the works themselves would directly give rise to pain, and what then would be the use of the connexion with a body? Hence, even in the case of a being not subject to karman, its connexion with various unholy bodies will cause imperfection and suffering. And even when such a being voluntarily enters into such bodies in order to rule them, connexion with imperfections is unavoidable ; no less than to be immersed in blood and purulent matter, even if done voluntarily, will make a man unclean. Although therefore Brahman is the sole cause of the world and a treasure-house of all blessed qualities, yet it is affected by the imperfections springing therefrom that, as declared by Scripture, it abides within matter, bodies, and their parts, and thus is connected with them (cp. 'he who abides within earth, within the soul, within the eye, within the seed,' &c., B*ri*. Up. III, 7, 3).

Of this primâ facie view the Sûtra disposes by saying—'Not even from place, such as earth, soul, &c., is there possible for the highest Self a shadow even of imperfection ; since everywhere in Scripture as well as Sm*ri*ti Brahman is described as having characteristics of a double kind ; viz. on the one hand freedom from all imperfections, and on the other possession of all blessed qualities. For Scripture says that the Supreme Person is free from evil, free from old age, free from death, free from grief, free from hunger and thirst ; that all his wishes realise themselves, that all its purposes realise themselves' (*Kh*. Up. VIII, 1, 5). And Sm*ri*ti says, 'He comprises within himself all blessed qualities, by a particle of his power the whole mass of beings is supported. In him there are combined energy, strength, might, wisdom, valour, and all other noble qualities. He is the Highest of the high, no pain or other imperfections affect him, the Lord of all, high or low. From all evil he is free, he whose name is Vish*n*u, the highest abode.' These and other passages teach that Brahman possesses the double characteristics stated above.

12. Should it be said 'on account of difference'; not so, because with reference to each the text says what is not that.

But, an objection is raised, we observe, that the individual soul also, although in reality possessing the same twofold attributes, viz. freedom from all evil and so on, as we learn from the teaching of Pra*g*âpati (*Kh*. Up. VIII, 7), yet is affected with imperfections owing to the fact that it is connected with bodies, divine, human, and so on, and thus undergoes a variety of conditions. Analogously we cannot avoid the conclusion that the inner Ruler also, although in reality possessing those same twofold attributes, is also affected by imperfection, because through its connexion with those different bodies it likewise undergoes a variety of conditions.—This objection the Sûtra sets aside in the words, 'not so, because with reference to each the text says what is not that,' i. e. what is contrary. For where the text says that the inner Ruler dwells within the earth, within the soul, within the eye, and so on, it concludes each clause by saying, 'that is thy Self, the inner Ruler, the immortal one,' i. e. declares the inner Ruler to be immortal, and thus denies of him any imperfections due to his connexion with the bodies which he voluntarily enters in order to rule them. The true (perfect) nature of the individual soul, on the other hand, is obscured as long as it is connected with a body, as we have explained under III, 2, 5.—But, as the Pûrvapakshin has pointed out, even if the highest Self voluntarily enters into bodies, it cannot escape connexion with the imperfections which depend on the essential nature of those bodies.—Not so, we reply. The fact is, that not even non-sentient things are, essentially or intrinsically, bad; but in accordance with the nature of the works of those beings which are under the rule of karman, one thing, owing to the will of the Supreme Person, causes pain to one man at one time and pleasure at another time, and causes pleasure or pain to one person and the opposite to another person. If the effects of things depended on their own nature only, everything would at all times be productive for all persons, either of pleasure only or of pain only. But this is not observed to be the case. In agreement herewith Smriti says, 'Because one and the same thing causes pain and pleasure and envy and wrath, the nature of a thing cannot lie in itself. As the same thing which erst gave rise to love causes pain later on, and that which once caused anger now causes satisfaction, nothing is in itself of the nature either of pleasure or of pain.' To the soul therefore which is subject to karman the connexion with different things is the source of imperfection and suffering, in agreement with the nature of its works; while to the highest Brahman, which is subject to itself only, the same connexion is the source of playful sport, consisting therein that he in various ways guides and rules those things.

13. Some also (teach) thus.

Moreover, the followers of one *s*âkhâ explicitly teach that the connexion with one and the same body is for the individual soul a source of disadvantage, while for the highest Brahman it is nothing of the kind, but constitutes an accession of glory in so far as it manifests him as a Lord and Ruler, 'Two birds, inseparable friends, cling to the same tree. One of them eats the sweet fruit, the other looks on without eating' (Mu. Up. III, 1, 1).—But the text, 'Having entered by means of that *g*îva-self I will differentiate names and forms,' teaches that the differentiation of names and forms depends on the entering into the elements of the *g*îva-soul whose Self is Brahman, and this implies that Brahman also, as the Self of the individual soul, possesses definite shapes, divine, human, and so on, and is to be denominated by the corresponding names. Brahman thus falls within the sphere of beings to which injunctions and prohibitions are addressed—such as 'a Brâhma*n*a is to sacrifice'—and hence necessarily is under the power of karman.—To this the next Sûtra replies.

14. For (Brahman is) without form merely, since it is the principal agent with regard to that.

Brahman, although by entering into bodies, human, divine, and so on, it becomes connected with various forms, yet is in itself altogether devoid of form, and therefore does not share that subjection to karman which in the case of the soul is due to its embodiedness.—Why?—Because as it is that which brings about names and forms it stands to them in the relation of a superior (pradhâna). For the text, 'The Ether (Brahman) indeed is the accomplisher of names and forms; that which is without these two is Brahman,' teaches that Brahman, although entering into all beings, is not touched by name and form, but is that which brings about name and form.—But, an objection is raised, if Brahman is the inner ruler of beings in so far as he has them for its body, how can it be said that it is altogether destitute of form?—There is a difference, we reply. The individual soul is connected with the shape of the body in which it dwells because it participates in the pleasures and pains to which the body gives rise; but as Brahman does not share those pleasures and pains, it has no shape or form. And the scriptural injunctions and prohibitions apply to those only who are under the power of karman. The highest Brahman therefore is like a being without form, and hence, although abiding within all things, free from all imperfection and endowed with all blessed qualities.

But, an objection is raised, texts such as 'the True, knowledge, infinite is Brahman' suggest a Brahman whose nature is constituted exclusively by non-differentiated light; while at the same time a Brahman endowed with qualities—such as omniscience, being the cause of the world, being the inner Self of all, having the power of immediately realising its wishes and purposes—is expressly negatived by texts such as 'not so, not so' (*Bri.* Up. II, 3, 6), and therefore must be held to be false. How then can it be maintained that Brahman possesses the 'twofold characteristics' mentioned under Sûtra 11?—To this the next Sûtra replies.

15. And in the same way as (a Brahman) consisting of light; (the texts thus) not being devoid of meaning.

In order that texts such as 'the True, knowledge, infinite is Brahman' may not be devoid of meaning, we have to admit that light (intelligence) constitutes the essential nature of Brahman. But analogously we have also to admit that Brahman possesses the 'twofold characteristics'; for otherwise the texts declaring it to be free from all imperfections, all-knowing, the cause of the world, and so on, would in their turn be devoid of meaning.

16. And (the text) says so much only.

Moreover the text 'the True, knowledge, infinite is Brahman' only teaches that Brahman has light for its essential nature, and does not negative those other attributes of Brahman—omniscience, being the cause of the world, &c.—which are intimated by other texts. What is the object of the negation in 'not so, not so' will be shown further on.

17. (This Scripture) also shows, and it is also stated in Sm*ri*ti.

That Brahman is a treasure as it were of all blessed qualities and free from all imperfections, the whole body of Vedânta-texts clearly declares: 'That highest great lord of lords, that highest deity of deities'; 'He is the cause, the lord of the lords of the organs, and there is of him neither parent nor lord'; 'There is no effect and no cause known of him, no one is seen like unto him or higher. His high power is revealed as manifold, as essential action of knowledge and strength' (*S*vet. Up. VI, 7-9); 'He who is all-knowing, whose brooding consists of knowledge' (Mu. I, 1, 9); 'From fear of him the wind blows, from fear of him the sun moves'; 'That is one bliss of Brahman' (Taitt. Up. II, 8); 'That from which all speech with the mind turns away, not having reached it, knowing the bliss of that Brahman man fears nothing' (Taitt. Up. II, 9); 'He who is without parts, without action, tranquil, without fault, without taint' (*S*vet. Up. VI, 19).—And Sm*ri*ti: 'He who knows me to be unborn and without a beginning, the Supreme Lord of the worlds'; 'Pervading this entire universe, by one part of mine I do abide'; 'With me as supervisor Prak*ri*ti brings forth the universe of the movable and the immovable, and for this reason the world does ever move round'; 'But another is the Supreme Person, who is called the Supreme Spirit, who pervading the three worlds supports them—the eternal Lord' (Bha.

Gî. X, 3; 42; IX, 10; XV, 17); 'The all-working, all-powerful one, rich in knowledge and strength, who becomes neither less nor more, who is self-dependent, without beginning, master of all; who knows neither weariness nor exhaustion, nor fear, wrath and desire; the blameless one, raised above all, without support, imperishable.'—As thus Brahman in whatever place it may abide has the 'twofold characteristics,' the imperfections dependent on those places do not touch it.

18. For this very reason comparisons, such as reflected images of the sun and the like.

Because Brahman, although abiding in manifold places, ever possesses the twofold characteristics, and hence does not share the imperfections due to those places, scriptural texts illustrate its purity in the midst of inferior surroundings by comparing it to the sun reflected in water, mirrors, and the like. Compare e.g. 'As the one ether is rendered manifold by jars and the like, or as the one sun becomes manifold in several sheets of water; thus the one Self is rendered manifold by abiding in many places. For the Self of all beings, although one, abides in each separate being and is thus seen as one and many at the same time, as the moon reflected in water.'

19. But because it is not apprehended like water, there is no equality.

The 'but' indicates an objection.—The highest Self is not apprehended in earth and other places in the same way as the sun or a face is apprehended in water or a mirror. For the sun and a face are erroneously apprehended as abiding in water or a mirror; they do not really abide there. When, on the other hand, Scripture tells us that the highest Self dwells in the earth, in water, in the soul, &c., we apprehend it as really dwelling in all those places. That the imperfections caused by water and mirrors do not attach themselves to the sun or a face is due to the fact that the sun and the face do not really abide in the water and the mirror. Hence there is no real parallelism between the thing compared (the highest Self) and the thing to which it is compared (the reflected image).

20. The participation (on Brahman's part) in increase and decrease, due to its abiding within (is denied); on account of the appropriateness of both (comparisons), and because thus it is seen.

The comparison of the highest Self to the reflected sun and the rest is meant only to deny of the Self that it participates in the imperfections—such as increase, decrease, and the like—which attach to the earth and the other beings within which the Self abides.—How do we know this?—From the circumstance that on this supposition both comparisons are appropriate. In the scriptural text quoted above Brahman is compared to ether, which although one becomes manifold through the things—jars and so on—within it; and to the sun, which is multiplied by the sheets of water in which he is reflected. Now the employment of these comparisons—with ether which really does abide within the jars and so on, and with the sun which in reality does not abide in the water—is appropriate only if they are meant to convey the idea that the highest Self does not participate in the imperfections inherent in earth and so on. Just as ether, although connecting itself separately with jars, pots, and so on, which undergo increase and decrease, is not itself touched by these imperfections; and just as the sun, although seen in sheets of water of unequal extent, is not touched by their increase and decrease; thus the highest Self, although abiding within variously-shaped beings, whether non-sentient like earth or sentient, remains untouched by their various imperfections—increase, decrease, and so on—, remains one although abiding in all of them, and ever keeps the treasure of its blessed qualities unsullied by an atom even of impurity.—The comparison of Brahman with the reflected sun holds good on the following account. As the sun is not touched by the imperfections belonging to the water, since he does not really abide in the water and hence there is no reason for his sharing those imperfections, thus the highest Self, which really abides within earth and the rest, is not affected by their imperfections; for as the nature of the highest Self is essentially antagonistic to all imperfection, there is no reason for its participating in the imperfection of others.—'And as this is seen.' This means—Since we observe in ordinary life also that comparisons are instituted between two things for the reason that although they do not possess all attributes in common, they yet have some attribute in common. We say, e.g. 'this man is like a lion.'—The conclusion from all this is that the highest Self, which is essentially free from all imperfections and a treasure as it were of all blessed qualities, in no way suffers from dwelling within the earth and the rest.

An objection is raised. In the B*ri*had-âra*n*yaka, in the chapter beginning 'There are two forms of Brahman, the material and the immaterial,' the whole material world, gross and subtle, is at first referred to as constituting the form of Brahman, and next a special form of Brahman is mentioned: 'And what is the form of that Person? Like a saffron-coloured raiment,' &c. But thereupon the text proceeds, 'Now follows the teaching—not so, not so; for there is not anything else higher than this "not so."' This passage, referring to all the previously mentioned forms of Brahman by means of the word 'so,' negatives them; intimating thereby that Brahman is nothing else than pure Being, and that all distinctions are mere imaginations due to Brahman not knowing its own essential nature. How then can Brahman possess the twofold characteristics?—To this the next Sûtra replies.

21. For the text denies the previously declared so-muchness; and declares more than that.

It is impossible to understand the text 'not so, not so' as negativing those distinctions of Brahman which had been stated previously. If the text meant that, it would be mere idle talk. For none but a person not in his right mind would first teach that all the things mentioned in the earlier part of the section are distinctive attributes of Brahman—as which they are not known by any other means of proof—and thereupon deliberately negative his own teaching. Although among the things mentioned there are some which, in themselves, are known through other means of proof, yet they are not thus known to be modes of Brahman, and others again are known neither in themselves nor as modes of Brahman. The text therefore cannot merely refer to them as things otherwise known, but gives fundamental instruction about them. Hence the later passage cannot be meant as a sheer negation, but must be taken as denying the previously described 'so-muchness' of Brahman ; i.e. the passage denies that limited nature of Brahman which would result from Brahman being viewed as distinguished by the previously stated attributes only. The word *so* refers to that limited nature, and the phrase *not so* therefore means that Brahman is not distinguished by the previously stated modes *only*. This interpretation is further confirmed by the fact that after that negative phrase further qualities of Brahman are declared by the text : 'For there is not anything higher than this *not so*. Then comes the name, the *True of the True* ; for the prâ*n*as are the True, and he is the True of them.' That means : Than that Brahman which is expressed by the phrase 'not so' there is no other thing higher, i.e. there is nothing more exalted than Brahman either in essential nature or in qualities. And of that Brahman the name is the 'True of the True.' This name is explained in the next clause, 'for the prâ*n*as,' &c. The term prâ*n*as here denotes the individual souls, so called because the prâ*n*as accompany them. They are the 'True' because they do not, like the elements, undergo changes implying an alteration of their essential nature. And the highest Self is the 'True of the True' because while the souls undergo, in accordance with their karman, contractions and expansions of intelligence, the highest Self which is free from all sin knows of no such alternations. He is therefore more eminently *true* than they are. As thus the complementary passage declares Brahman to be connected with certain qualities, the clause 'not so, not so' (to which that passage is complementary) cannot deny that Brahman possesses distinctive attributes, but only that Brahman's nature is confined to the attributes previously stated.—Brahman therefore possesses the twofold characteristics. That the clause 'not so' negatives Brahman's being fully described by the attributes previously mentioned, was above proved on the ground that since Brahman is not the object of any other means of proof, those previous statements cannot refer to what is already proved, and that the final clause cannot therefore be meant to deny what the previous clauses expressly teach. The next Sûtra now confirms this circumstance of Brahman not lying within the sphere of the other means of proof.

22. That (is) unmanifested; for (this Scripture) declares.

Brahman is not manifested by other means of proof; for Scripture says, 'His form is not to be seen, no one beholds him with the eye' (Ka. Up. II, 6, 9); 'He is not apprehended by the eye nor by speech' (Mu. Up. III, 1, 8).

23. Also in perfect conciliation, according to Scripture and Sm*ri*ti.

Moreover, it is only in the state of perfect conciliation or endearment, i.e. in meditation bearing the character of devotion, that an intuition of Brahman takes place, not in any other state. This Scripture and Sm*ri*ti alike teach. 'That Self cannot be gained by the Veda, nor by understanding, nor by much learning. He whom the Self chooses by him the Self can be gained. The Self chooses him as his own' (Ka. Up. I, 2, 23); 'When a man's nature has become purified by the serene light of knowledge, then he sees him, meditating on him as without parts' (Mu. Up. III, 1, 9). Sm*ri*ti: 'Neither by the Vedas, nor austerities, nor gifts, nor by sacrifice, but only by exclusive devotion, may I in this form be known and beheld in truth and also entered into' (Bha. Gî. XI, 53, 54). The scriptural text beginning 'Two are the forms of Brahman,' which declares the nature of Brahman for the purposes of devout meditation, cannot therefore refer to Brahman's being characterised by two forms, a material and an immaterial, as something already known; for apart from Scripture nothing is known about Brahman.

24. And there is non-difference (of the intention of Brahman's distinguishing attributes), as in the case of light; and the light (is) intuited as constituting Brahman's essential nature by repetition of the practice (of meditation).

That the clause 'not so' negatives not Brahman's possessing two forms, a material and an immaterial one, but only Brahman's nature being restricted to those determinations, follows therefrom also that in the vision of Vâmadeva and others who had attained to intuition into Brahman's nature, the fact of Brahman having all material and immaterial beings for its attributes is apprehended in non-difference, i. e. in the same way as the fact of light (i. e. knowledge) and bliss constituting Brahman's essential nature. Compare the text 'Seeing this the *Ri*shi Vâmadeva understood, I am Manu and the sun' (B*ri*. Up. I, 4, 10). And that light and bliss constitute Brahman's nature was perceived by Vâmadeva and the rest through repeated performance of the practice of devout meditation. In the same way then, i. e. by repeated meditation, they also became aware that Brahman has all material and immaterial things for its distinguishing modes.—The next Sûtra sums up the proof of Brahman's possessing twofold characteristics.

25. Hence (Brahman is distinguished) by what is infinite; for thus the characteristics (hold good).

By the arguments stated it is proved that Brahman is distinguished by the infinite multitude of blessed qualities. And this being so, it follows that Brahman possesses the twofold characteristics.—Here terminates the adhikara*n*a of 'that which has twofold characteristics.'

26. But on account of twofold designation, as the snake and its coils.

It has been shown in the preceding adhikara*n*a that

the entire non-sentient universe is the outward form of Brahman. For the purpose of proving Brahman's freedom from all imperfection, an enquiry is now begun into the particular mode in which the world may be conceived to constitute the form of Brahman. Is the relation of the two like that of the snake and its coils; or like that of light and the luminous body, both of which fall under the same genus; or like that of the individual soul and Brahman, the soul being a distinguishing attribute and for that reason a part (a*ms*a) of Brahman?—On the assumption of this last alternative, which is about to be established here, it has been already shown under two preceding Sûtras (I, 4, 23; II, 1, 14), that from Brahman, as distinguished by sentient and non-sentient beings in their subtle form, there originates Brahman as distinguished by all those beings in their gross form.

Which then of the alternatives stated above is the true one?—The material world is related to Brahman as the coils to the snake, 'on account of twofold designation.' For some texts declare the identity of the two: 'Brahman only is all this'; 'The Self only is all this.' Other texts again refer to the difference of the two: 'Having entered into these three deities with this *g*îva-self, let me differentiate names and forms.' We therefore consider all non-sentient things to be special forms or arrangements of Brahman, as the coils are of a coiled-up snake or a coiled-up rope.

27. Or else like light and its abode, both being fire.

The *or* sets aside the other two alternatives. If Brahman itself only appeared in the form of non-sentient things—as the snake itself only constitutes the coils—both sets of texts, those which declare difference as well as those which declare the unchangeableness of Brahman, would be contrary to sense. We therefore, adopting the second alternative, hold that the case under discussion is analogous to that of light and that in which it abides, i. e. the luminous body. The two are different, but at the same time they are identical in so far as they both are fire (te*g*as). In the same way the non-sentient world constitutes the form of Brahman.

28. Or else in the manner stated above.

The *but* sets aside the two preceding alternatives. One substance may indeed connect itself with several states, but the former of the two alternatives implies that Brahman itself constitutes the essential nature of non-sentient matter, and thus there is no escape from the objections already stated under Sûtra 27. Let then the second alternative be adopted according to which Brahma-hood (brahmatva) constitutes a genus inhering in Brahman as well as in non-sentient matter, just as fire constitutes the common genus for light and luminous bodies. But on this view Brahman becomes a mere abstract generic character inhering in the Lord (î*s*vara), sentient souls and non-sentient matter, just as the generic character of horses (a*s*vatva) inheres in concrete individual horses; and this contradicts all the teaching of *S*ruti and Sm*ri*ti (according to which Brahman is the highest concrete entity). We therefore hold that non-sentient matter stands to Brahman in the same relation as the one previously proved for the individual soul in Sûtra II, 3, 43; 46; viz. that it is an attribute incapable of being realised apart from Brahman and hence is a part (a*ms*a) of the latter. The texts referring to the two as non-different may thus be taken in their primary sense; for the part is only a limited place of that of which it is a part. And the texts referring to the two as different may also be taken in their primary sense; for the distinguishing attribute and that to which the attribute belongs are essentially different. Thus Brahman's freedom from all imperfection is preserved.—Lustre is an attribute not to be realised apart from the gem, and therefore is a part of the gem; the same relation also holds good between generic character and individuals having that character, between qualities and things having qualities, between bodies and souls. In the same way souls as well as non-sentient matter stand to Brahman in the relation of parts.

29. And on account of denial.

Texts such as 'This is that great unborn Self, undecaying, undying' (B*ri*. Up. IV, 4, 25), 'By the old age of the body that does not age' (*Kh*. Up. VIII, 1, 5), deny of Brahman the properties of non-sentient matter. From this it follows that the relation of the two can only be that of distinguishing attribute and thing distinguished, and hence of part and whole. Brahman distinguished by sentient and non-sentient beings in their subtle state is the cause; distinguished by the same beings in their gross state is the effect: the effect thus is non-different from the cause, and by the knowledge of the causal Brahman the effect is likewise known. All these tenets are in full mutual agreement. Brahman's freedom from defects also is preserved; and this and Brahman's being the abode of all blessed qualities prove that Brahman possesses the 'twofold characteristics.'—Here terminates the adhikara*n*a of 'the coils of the snake.'

30. (There is something) higher than that; on account of the designations of bridge, measure, connexion, and difference.

The Sûtras now proceed to refute an erroneous view based on some fallacious arguments, viz. that there is a being higher even than the highest Brahman, the supreme cause, material as well as operative, of the entire world—a refutation which will confirm the view of Brahman being free from all imperfections and a treasure as it were of countless transcendentally exalted qualities.—There is some entity higher than the Brahman described so far as being the cause of the world and possessing the twofold characteristics. For the text 'That Self is a bank (or bridge), a boundary' (*Kh*. Up. VIII, 4, 1) designates the Self as a bank or bridge (setu). And the term 'setu' means in ordinary language that which enables one to reach the other bank of a river; and from this we conclude that in the Vedic text also there must be meant something to be reached. The text further says that that bridge is to be crossed:

'He who has crossed that bridge, if blind,' &c.; this also indicates that there must be something to be reached by crossing. Other texts, again, speak of the highest Brahman as something measured, i.e. limited. 'Brahman has four feet (quarters), sixteen parts.' Such declarations of Brahman being something limited suggest the existence of something unlimited to be reached by that bridge. Further there are texts which declare a connexion of the bridge as that which is a means towards reaching, and a thing connected with the bridge as that to be reached: 'the highest bridge of the Immortal' (*S*vet. Up. VI, 19); 'he is the bridge of the Immortal' (Mu. Up. II, 2, 5). For this reason also there is something higher than the Highest.—And other texts again expressly state that being beyond the Highest to be something different: 'he goes to the divine Person who is higher than the Highest' (Mu. Up. III, 2, 8); 'by this Person this whole universe is filled; what is higher than that is without form and without suffering' (*S*vet. Up. III, 9–10). All this combined shows that there is something higher than the highest Brahman.—The next Sûtra disposes of this view.

31. But on account of resemblance.

The 'but' sets aside the pûrvapaksha. There is no truth in the assertion that from the designation of the Highest as a bridge (or bank) it follows that there is something beyond the Highest. For Brahman in that text is not called a bank with regard to something to be reached thereby; since the additional clause 'for the non-confounding of these worlds' declares that it is compared to a bridge or bank in so far as it binds to itself (*setu* being derived from *si*, to bind) the whole aggregate of sentient and non-sentient things without any confusion. And in the clause 'having passed beyond that bridge' the *passing beyond* means *reaching*; as we say, 'he passes beyond the Vedânta,' meaning 'he has fully mastered it.'

32. It subserves the purpose of thought; as in the case of the feet.

Where the texts speak of Brahman as having four quarters, and sixteen parts, or say that 'one quarter of him are all these beings' (*Kh.* Up. III, 12, 6), they do so for the purpose of thought, i. e. meditation, only. For as texts such as 'the Truth, knowledge, infinite is Brahman' teach Brahman, the cause of the world, to be unlimited, it cannot in itself be subject to measure. The texts referring to measure therefore aim at meditation only, in the same way as texts such as 'Speech is one foot (quarter) of him, breath another, the eye another, the mind another' (*Kh.* Up. III, 18, 2).—But how can something that in itself is beyond all measure, for the purpose of meditation, be spoken of as measured? To this the next Sûtra replies.

33. Owing to difference of place, as in the case of light, and so on.

Owing to the difference of limiting adjuncts constituted by special places, such as speech, and so on, Brahman in so far as connected with these adjuncts may be viewed as having measure; just as light and the like although spread everywhere may be viewed as limited, owing to its connexion with different places—windows, jars, and so on.

34. And on account of possibility.

Nor is there any truth in the assertion that, because texts such as 'he is the bridge of the Immortal' intimate a distinction between that which causes to reach and the object reached, there must be something to be reached different from that which causes to reach; for the highest Self may be viewed as being itself a means towards itself being reached; cp. 'The Self cannot be reached by the Veda, and so on; he whom the Self chooses by him the Self can be gained' (*Kh.* Up. I, 2, 23).

35. Thus, from the denial of anything else.

Nor can we allow the assertion that there is something higher than the highest because certain texts ('the Person which is higher than the highest'; 'beyond the Imperishable there is the highest,' &c.) refer to such a difference.

For the same texts expressly deny that there is anything else higher than the highest—'than whom there is nothing else higher, than whom there is nothing smaller or larger' (*S*vet. Up. III, 9). So also other texts: 'For there is nothing else higher than this "not so"' (i. e. than this Brahman designated by the phrase 'not so'; B*ri*. Up. II, 3, 6); 'Of him none is the Lord, his name is great glory' (Mahânâr. Up. I, 10).

But what then is the entity referred to in the text 'tato yad uttarataram'? (*S*vet. Up. III, 10)?—The passage immediately preceding (8), 'I know that great person, &c.; a man who knows him passes over death,' had declared that the knowledge of Brahman is the only way to immortality; and the clause (9), 'Higher than whom there is nothing else,' had confirmed this by declaring that Brahman is the Highest and that there is no other thing higher. In agreement herewith we must explain stanza 10 as giving a reason for what had been said, 'Because that which is the highest (uttarataram), viz. the Supreme Person is without form and without suffering, therefore (tata*h*) those who know him become immortal,' &c. On any other explanation stanza 10 would not be in harmony with stanza 8 where the subject is introduced, and with what is declared in stanza 9.—Analogously in the text 'He goes to the divine Person who is higher than the highest' (Mu. Up. III, 2, 8) 'the highest' means the aggregate soul (samash*t*i-purusha), which in a previous passage had been said to be 'higher than the high Imperishable' (II, 1, 2); and the 'higher' refers to the Supreme Person, with all his transcendent qualities, who is superior to the aggregate soul.

36. The omnipresence (possessed) by that, (understood) from the declaration of extent.

That omnipresence which is possessed 'by that,' i. e. by Brahman, and which is known 'from declarations of extent,' and so on, i. e. from texts which declare Brahman to be all-pervading, is also known from texts such as 'higher than that there is nothing.' Declarations of extent are e. g. the following: 'By this Person this whole Universe is filled'

(*S*vet. Up. III. 9); 'whatever is seen or heard in this world, is pervaded inside and outside by Nârâya*n*a' (Mahânâr. Up.); 'The eternal, pervading, omnipresent, which the Wise consider as the source of all beings' (Mu. Up. I, 1, 6). The 'and the rest' in the Sûtra comprises passages such as 'Brahman indeed is all this,' 'The Self indeed is all this,' and the like. The conclusion is that the highest Brahman is absolutely supreme.—Here terminates the adhikara*n*a of 'the Highest.'

37. From thence the reward; on account of possibility.

It has been shown, for the purpose of giving rise to a desire for devout meditation, that the soul in all its states is imperfect, while the Supreme Person to be reached by it is free from imperfections, the owner of blessed qualities and higher than everything else. Being about to investigate the nature of meditation, the Sûtrakâra now declares that the meditating devotee receives the reward of meditation, i.e. Release, which consists in attaining to the highest Person, from that highest Person only; and that analogously the rewards for all works prescribed by the Veda—whether to be enjoyed in this or the next world—come from the highest Person only. The Sûtra therefore says generally, 'from thence the reward.'—'Why so?'—'Because that only is possible.'

For it is he only—the all-knowing, all-powerful, supremely generous one—who being pleased by sacrifices, gifts, offerings, and the like, as well as by pious meditation, is in a position to bestow the different forms of enjoyment in this and the heavenly world, and Release which consists in attaining to a nature like his own. For action which is non-intelligent and transitory is incapable of bringing about a result connected with a future time.

38. And on account of scriptural declaration.

That he bestows all rewards—whether in the form of enjoyment or Release—Scripture also declares 'This indeed is the great, the unborn Self, the eater of food, the giver of wealth' (Bri. Up. IV, 4, 24); and 'For he alone causes delight' (Taitt. Up. II, 7).—Next a primâ facie view is stated.

39. For the same reasons *G*aimini (thinks it to be) religious action.

For the same reasons, viz. possibility and scriptural declaration, the teacher *G*aimini thinks that religious works, viz. sacrifices, gifts, offerings, and meditation, of themselves bring about their rewards. For we observe that in ordinary life actions such as ploughing and the like, and charitable gifts and so on, bring about their own reward, directly or indirectly. And although Vedic works do not bring about their rewards immediately, they may do so mediately, viz. by means of the so-called *apûrva*. This follows also from the form of the Vedic injunctions, such as 'He who is desirous of the heavenly world is to sacrifice.' As such injunctions enjoin sacrifices as the means of bringing about the object desired to be realised, viz. the heavenly world and the like, there is no other way left than to assume that the result (which is seen not to spring directly from the sacrifice) is accomplished by the mediation of the apûrva.

40. But the former, Bâdarâya*n*a (thinks), on account of the designation (of deities) as the cause.

The reverend Bâdarâya*n*a maintains the previously declared awarding of rewards by the Supreme Person since the scriptural texts referring to the different sacrifices declare that the deities only, Agni, Vâyu, and so on, who are propitiated by the sacrifices—which are nothing else but means to propitiate deities—are the cause of the rewards attached to the sacrifices. Compare texts such as 'Let him who is desirous of prosperity offer a white animal to Vâyu. For Vâyu is the swiftest god. The man thus approaches Vâyu with his proper share, and Vâyu leads him to prosperity.' And the whole instruction which the texts give, as to the means by which men desirous of certain results are to effect those results, is required on account of the injunctions only, and hence it cannot be doubted that it has reference to the injunctions. The apparatus of means to bring about the results thus being learnt from the text only, no person acquainted with the force of the means of proof will assent to that apparatus, as stated by the text, being set aside and an apûrva about which the text says nothing being fancifully assumed. And that the imperative verbal forms of the injunctions denote as the thing to be effected by the effort of the sacrificer, only that which on the basis of the usage of language and grammatical science is recognised as the meaning of the root-element of such words as 'ya*g*eta,' viz. the sacrifice (yâga), which consists in the propitiation of a divine being, and not some additional supersensuous thing such as the apûrva, we have already proved above (p. 153 ff.). Texts such as 'Vâyu is the swiftest god' teach that Vâyu and other deities are the bestowers of rewards. And that it is fundamentally the highest Self—as constituting the inner Self of Vâyu and other deities—which is pleased by offerings, and bestows rewards for them is declared by texts such as 'Offerings and pious works, all this he bears who is the nave of the Universe. He is Agni and Vâyu, he is Sun and Moon' (Mahânâr. Up. I, 6, 7). Similarly in the antaryâmin-brâhma*n*a, 'He who dwells in Vâyu, of whom Vâyu is the body'; 'He who dwells in Agni,' &c. Sm*ri*ti expresses itself similarly, 'Whatsoever devotee wishes to worship with faith whatsoever divine form, of him do I make that faith unshakable. Endued with such faith he endeavours to propitiate him and obtains from him his desires—those indeed being ordained by me' (Bha. Gî. VII, 21–22); 'For I am the enjoyer and the Lord of all sacrifices' (IX, 24)—where Lord means him who bestows the reward for the sacrifices. 'To the gods go the worshippers of the gods, and those devoted to me go to me' (VII, 23).—In ordinary life men, by agriculture and the like, acquire wealth in various forms, and by means of this propitiate their king, either directly or through his officials and servants; and the king thereupon is seen to reward them in a manner corresponding to the measure of their services and presents. The Vedânta-texts, on the other hand, give instruction on a subject which transcends the sphere of all the other means of knowledge, viz. the highest Person who is free from all shadow even of imperfection, and a treasure-house as it were of all exalted qualities in their highest state of perfection ; on sacrifices, gifts, oblations, which are helpful towards the propitiation of that Person ; on praise, worship, and meditation, which directly propitiate him ; and on the rewards which he, thus propitiated, bestows, viz. temporal happiness and final Release.—Here terminates the adhikara*n*a of 'reward.'

## THIRD PÂDA.

1. What is understood from all the Vedânta-texts (is one), on account of the non-difference of injunction and the rest.

The Sûtras have stated whatever has to be stated to the end of rousing the desire of meditation—concluding with the fact that Brahman bestows rewards. Next the question is introduced whether the vidyâs (i. e. the different forms of meditation on Brahman which the Vedânta-texts enjoin) are different or non-different, on the decision of which question it will depend whether the qualities attributed to Brahman in those vidyâs are to be comprised in one act of meditation or not.—The first subordinate question arising here is whether one and the same meditation—as e.g. the vidyâ of Vai*s*vânara—which is met with in the text of several *s*âkhâs, constitutes one vidyâ or several.—The vidyâs are separate, the Pûrvapakshin maintains; for the fact that the same matter is, without difference, imparted for a second time, and moreover stands under a different heading—both which circumstances necessarily attend the text's being met with in different *s*âkhâs—proves the difference of the two meditations. It is for this reason only that a restrictive injunction, such as the one conveyed in the text, 'Let a man tell this science of Brahman to those only who have performed the rite of carrying fire on their head' (Mu. Up. III, 2, 10)—which restricts the imparting of knowledge to the Âtharva*n*ikas, to whom that rite is peculiar—has any sense; for if the vidyâs were one, then the rite mentioned, which is a part of the vidyâ, would be valid for the members of other *s*âkhâs also, and then the restriction enjoined by the text would have no meaning.—This view is set aside by the Sûtra, 'What is understood from all the Vedânta-texts' is one and the same meditation, 'because there is non-difference of injunction and the rest.' By injunction is meant the injunction of special activities denoted by different verbal roots—such as upâsîta 'he should meditate,' vidyât 'he should know.' The 'and the rest' of the Sûtra is meant to comprise as additional reasons the circumstances mentioned in the Pûrva Mîmâ*m*sâ-sûtras (II, 4, 9). Owing to all these circumstances, non-difference of injunction and the rest, the same vidyâ is recognised in other *s*âkhâs also. In the *Kh*ândogya (V, 12, 2) as well as in the Vâ*g*asaneyaka we meet with one and the same injunction (viz. 'He should meditate on Vai*s*vânara'). The form (character, rûpa) of the meditations also is the same, for the form of a cognition solely depends on its object; and the object is in both cases the same, viz. Vai*s*vânara. The name of the two vidyâs also is the same, viz. the knowledge of Vai*s*vânara. And both vidyâs are declared to have the same result, viz. attaining to Brahman. All these reasons establish the identity of vidyâs even in different *s*âkhâs.—The next Sûtra refers to the reasons set forth for his view by the Pûrvapakshin and refutes them.

2. If it be said (that the vidyâs are not one) on account of difference, we deny this, since even in one (vidyâ there may be repetition).

If it be said that there is no oneness of vidyâ, because the fact of the same matter being stated again without difference, and being met with in a different chapter, proves the object of injunction to be different; we reply that even in one and the same vidyâ some matter may be repeated without any change, and under a new heading (in a different chapter); if, namely, there is difference of cognising subjects. Where the cognising person is one only, repetition of the same matter under a new heading can only be explained as meaning difference of object enjoined, and hence separation of the two vidyâs. But where the cognising persons are different (and this of course is eminently so in the case of different *s*âkhâs), the double statement of one and the same matter explains itself as subserving the cognition of those different persons, and hence does not imply difference of matter enjoined.—The next Sûtra refutes the argument founded on a rite enjoined in the Mu*nd*aka.

3. For (the *s*irovrata) concerns the mode of the study of the Veda; also on account of (that rite) being a heading in the samâ*k*âra; and the restriction is like that of the libations.

What the text says as to a restriction connected with the 'vow of the head,' does not intimate a difference of vidyâs. For that vow does not form part of the vidyâ. The restriction refers only to a peculiarity of the *study* of the Veda on the part of the Âtharva*n*ikas, being meant to establish that they should possess that special qualification which the rite produces; but it does not affect the vidyâ itself. This is proved by the subsequent clause, 'a man who has not performed that rite may not *read* the text,' which directly connects the rite with the studying of the text. And it is further proved by the fact that in the book of the Âtharva*n*ikas, called 'samâ*k*âra,' that rite is referred to as a rite connected with the Veda (not with the special vidyâ set forth in the Mu*nd*aka), viz. in the passage, 'this is explained already by the Veda-observance' (which extends the details of the *s*irovrata, there called veda-vrata, to other observances). By the *knowledge of Brahman* (referred to in the Mu*nd*aka-text 'let a man tell this science of Brahman to those only,' &c.), we have therefore to understand knowledge of the Veda in general. And that restriction is 'like that of the libations'—i. e. it is analogous to the restriction under which the sava-libations, beginning with the Saptasûrya-libation, and terminating with the *S*ataudana-libation, are offered in the one fire which is used by the followers of the Atharvan, and not in the ordinary three fires.

4. Scripture also declares this.

Scripture also shows that (identical) meditation is what all the Vedânta-texts intimate. The *Kh*ândogya (VIII, 1, 1 ff.) declares that that which is within the small space in the heart is to be enquired into, and then in reply to the question what the thing to be enquired into is, says that it is the highest Self possessing the eight attributes, freedom from all evil and the rest, which is to be meditated upon within the heart. And then the Taittirîya-text, referring to this declaration in the *Kh*ândogya, says, 'Therein is a small space, free from all grief; what is within that is to be meditated upon' (Mahânâr. Up. X, 23), and thus likewise enjoins meditation on the highest Self possessing the eight qualities. And this is possible only if, owing to unity of vidyâ, the qualities mentioned in the first text are included also in the meditation enjoined in the second text.—Having thus established the unity of meditations, the Sûtras proceed to state the practical effect of such unity.

5. (Meditation) thus being equal, there is combination (of gu*n*as); on account of non-difference of purport in the case of what subserves injunction.

The meditation in all Vedânta-texts thus being the same, the qualities mentioned in one text are to be combined with those mentioned in another; 'on account of non-difference of purport in the case of what subserves injunction.' We find that in connexion with certain injunctions of meditation—such as the meditation on Vai*s*vânara, or the small ether within the heart—the text of some individual Vedânta-book mentions certain secondary matters (qualities, gu*n*a) which subserve that meditation; and as these gu*n*as are connected with the meditation they are to be comprised in it, so that they may accomplish their aim, i. e. of subserving the meditation. For the same reason therefore we have to enclose in the meditation gu*n*as mentioned in other Vedânta-texts; for being also connected with the meditation they subserve it in the same way.—Here terminates the adhikara*n*a of 'what is intimated by all Vedânta-texts.

6. If it be said that there is difference on account of the text; we say no; on account of non-difference.

So far it has been shown that the non-difference of injunction, and so on, establishes the unity of meditations, and that owing to the latter the special features of meditation enjoined in different texts have to be combined. Next, an enquiry is entered upon whether in the case of certain particular meditations there actually exists, or not, that non-difference of injunction which is the cause of meditations being recognised as identical. A meditation on the Udgîtha is enjoined in the text of the *Kh*andogas, as well as in that of the Vâ*g*asaneyins (*Kh.* Up. I, 2; B*ri.* Up. I, 3); and the question arises whether the two are to be viewed as one meditation or not. The Pûrvapakshin maintains the former alternative. For, he says, there is no difference of injunction, and so on, since both texts enjoin as the object of meditation the Udgîtha viewed under the form of Prâ*n*a; since there is the same reward promised in both places, viz. mastering of one's enemies; since the form of meditation is the same, the Udgîtha being in both cases viewed under the form of Prâ*n*a; since the injunction is the same, being conveyed in both cases by the same verbal root (vid, to know); and since both meditations have the same technical name, viz. udgîtha-vidyâ. The Sûtra states this view in the form of the refutation of an objection raised by the advocate of the final view. We do not admit, the objector says, the unity maintained by you, since the texts clearly show a difference of form. The text of the Vâ*g*asaneyins represents as the object of meditation that which is the agent in the act of singing out the Udgîtha; while the text of the *Kh*andogas enjoins meditation on what is the object of the action of singing out (i. e. the Udgîtha itself). This discrepancy establishes difference in the character of the meditation, and as this implies difference of the object enjoined, the mere non-difference of injunction, and so on, is of no force, and hence the two meditations are separate ones.—This objection the Pûrvapakshin impugns, 'on account of non-difference.' For both texts, at the outset, declare that the Udgîtha is the means to bring about the conquest of enemies ('Let us overcome the Asuras at the sacrifices by means of the Udgîtha' (B*ri.* Up.); 'The gods took the Udgîtha, thinking they would with that overcome the Asuras'—*Kh.* Up.). In order therefore not to stultify this common beginning, we must assume that in the clause 'For them that breath sang out' (B*ri*. Up.), the Udgîtha, which really is the object of the action of singing, is spoken of as the agent. Otherwise the term udgîtha in the introductory passage ('by means of the Udgîtha') would have to be taken as by implication denoting the agent (while directly it indicates the instrument).—Hence there is oneness of the two vidyâs.—Of this view the next Sûtra disposes.

7. Or not, on account of difference of subject-matter; as in the case of the attribute of being higher than the high, and so on.

There is no unity of the two vidyâs, since the subject-matter of the two differs. For the tale in the *Kh*ândogya-text, which begins 'when the Devas and the Asuras struggled together,' connects itself with the pra*n*ava (the syllable Om) which is introduced as the object of meditation in *Kh*ând. I, 1, 1, 'Let a man meditate on the syllable Om as the Udgîtha'; and the clause forming part of the tale, 'they meditated on that chief breath as Udgîtha,' therefore refers to a meditation on the pra*n*ava which is a part only of the Udgîtha. In the text of the Vâ*g*asaneyins, on the other hand, there is nothing to correspond to the introductory passage which in the *Kh*ândogya-text determines the subject-matter, and the text clearly states that the meditation refers to the whole Udgîtha (not only the pra*n*ava). And this difference of leading subject-matter implies difference of matter enjoined, and this again difference of the character of meditation, and hence there is no unity of vidyâs. Thus the object of meditation for the *Kh*andogas is the pra*n*ava viewed under the form of Prâ*n*a; while for the Vâ*g*asaneyins it is the Udgât*ri* (who sings the Udgîtha), imaginatively identified with Prâ*n*a. Nor does there arise, on this latter account, a contradiction between the later and the earlier part of the story of the Vâ*g*asaneyins. For as a meditation on the Udgât*ri* necessarily extends to the Udgîtha, which is the object of the activity of singing, the latter also helps to bring about the result, viz. the mastering of enemies.—There is thus no unity of vidyâ, although there may be non-difference of injunction, and so on.—'As in the case of the attribute of being higher than the high,' &c. In one and the same *s*âkhâ there are two meditations, in each of which the highest Self is enjoined to be viewed under the form of the pra*n*ava (*Kh.* Up. I, 6; I, 9), and in so far the two vidyâs are alike. But while the former text enjoins that the pra*n*ava has to be viewed under the form of a golden man, in the latter he has to be viewed as possessing the attributes of being higher than the high, and owing to this difference of attributes the two meditations must be held separate (*a fortiori*, then, those meditations are separate which have different objects of meditation).

8. If that be declared on account of name; (we object, since) that is also (where the objects of injunction differ).

If the oneness of the vidyâs be maintained on the ground that both have the same name, viz. udgîtha-vidyâ, we point out that oneness is found also where the objects enjoined are different. The term agnihotra is applied equally to the permanent agnihotra and to that agnihotra which forms part of the sacrifice called 'Ku*nd*apâyinâm ayanam'; and the term udgîtha is applied equally to the many different meditations described in the first prapâ*th*aka of the *Kh*ândogya.

9. And (this is) appropriate, on account of the extension.

Since the pra*n*ava, which is a part of the udgîtha, is introduced as the subject of meditation in the first prapâ*th*aka of the *Kh*ândogya, and extends over the later vidyâs also, it is appropriate to assume that also in the clause 'the gods took the udgîtha'—which stands in the middle—the term udgîtha denotes the pra*n*ava. Expressions such as 'the cloth is burned' show that frequently the whole denotes the part.—The conclusion from all this is that in the *Kh*ândogya the object of meditation is constituted by the pra*n*ava—there termed udgîtha—viewed under the form of prâ*n*a; while in the Vâ*g*asaneyaka the term udgîtha denotes the whole udgîtha, and the object of meditation is he who produces the udgîtha, i.e. the udgât*ri*, viewed under the form of prâ*n*a. And this proves that the two vidyâs are separate.—Here terminates the adhikara*n*a of 'difference.'

10. On account of non-difference of everything, those elsewhere.

The *Kh*ândogya and the Vâ*g*asaneyaka alike record a meditation on Prâ*n*a; the object of meditation being Prâ*n*a as possessing the qualities of being the oldest and the best, and also as possessing certain other qualities such as being the richest, and so on (*Kh*. Up. V, 1; B*ri*. Up. VI, 1). In the text of the Kaushîtakins, on the other hand, there is a meditation on Prâ*n*a which mentions the former qualities ('being the best' and 'being the oldest'), but not the latter ('being the richest,' and so on). This, the Pûrvapakshin maintains, constitutes a difference between the objects of meditation, and hence between the meditations themselves.—This view the Sûtra sets aside 'on account of non-difference of everything, those elsewhere.' There is no difference of meditation. Those qualities, viz. being the richest, and so on, are to be meditated upon in the other place also, viz. in the meditation on Prâ*n*a of the Kaushîtakins; 'since there is non-difference of everything,' i.e. since the text of the Kaushîtakins also exhibits the very same method, in all its details, for proving what it is undertaken to prove, viz. that Prâ*n*a is the oldest and best. And for that proof it is required that Prâ*n*a should be viewed as possessing also the quality of being the richest, and so on, and these qualities therefore have to be comprised in the meditation of the Kaushîtakins also. Hence there is no difference of meditation.—Here terminates the adhikara*n*a of 'non-difference of everything.'

In the same way as the meditation on Prâ*n*a as the

oldest and best cannot be accomplished without Prâ*n*a being also meditated upon as the richest, and so on, and as hence these latter qualities have to be comprised in the meditation on Prâ*n*a of the Kaushîtakins, although they are not expressly mentioned there; thus those qualities of Brahman also, without which the meditation on Brahman cannot be accomplished, must be included in all meditations on Brahman—this is the point to be proved next.

11. Bliss and other qualities, as belonging to the subject of the qualities.

The point to be decided here is whether, or not, the essential qualities of Brahman are to be included in all meditations on the highest Brahman.—Since there is no valid reason for including in a meditation those qualities which are not expressly mentioned in the section containing that meditation, only those qualities which are thus expressly mentioned should be included!—This primâ facie view is negatived by the Sûtra. The clause, 'on account of non-difference,' has to be carried on from the preceding Sûtra. As the 'subject of the qualities,' i. e. Brahman is the same in all meditations, the qualities which do not exist apart from their subject, viz. bliss, and so on, are to be comprised in all meditations.—But for the same reason then such qualities as 'having joy for its head' (Taitt. Up. II, 5) would also have to be included in all meditations on Brahman!—This the next Sûtra negatives.

12. Such qualities as having joy for its head, and so on, are not established, for if there were difference (of members) there would be increase and decrease.

The declaration that the essential qualities of Brahman are established for all meditations, does not imply that such attributes as 'having joy for its head' are equally established. For the latter are not qualities of Brahman, since they are mere elements in a figurative representation of Brahman under the form of an animal body. Otherwise, i. e. if Brahman really possessed different members, such as head, wings, and so on, it would be liable to increase and decrease, and this would be in conflict with texts such as 'the True, knowledge, infinite is Brahman.'—But if this reasoning holds good, then all the infinite qualities belonging to Brahman such as lordly power, generosity, compassion, and so on—all of which are incapable of existing apart from the subject to which they belong—would have to be comprehended in all those meditations on Brahman where they are not expressly mentioned; and this could not possibly be done, as those qualities are infinite in number.—This difficulty the next Sûtra removes.

13. But the others, on account of equality with the thing.

Those other qualities which are 'equal to the thing,' i. e. which are attributes determining the essential character of the thing, and therefore necessarily entering into the idea of the thing, must be included in all meditations, no less than the thing itself. To this class belong qualities such as true being, knowledge, bliss, purity, infinity, and so on. For of Brahman—which by texts such as 'that from which all these beings,' &c. had been suggested as the cause of the world—the essential definition is given in texts such as 'the True, knowledge, infinite is Brahman'; 'bliss is Brahman,' and others; and hence, in order that a true notion may be formed of Brahman as the object of meditation, such qualities as true being, bliss, and so on, have to be included in all meditations on Brahman. Such additional qualities, on the other hand, as e. g. compassion, which indeed cannot exist apart from the subject to which they belong, but are not necessary elements of the idea of Brahman, are to be included in those meditations only where they are specially mentioned.

But, an objection is raised, if 'having joy for its head' and the like are not qualities of Brahman, but merely serve the purpose of a figurative representation of Brahman, for what purpose then is this representation introduced? For if something is represented as something else, there must be some motive for doing so. Where, e. g. the sacred text compares the meditating devotee to a charioteer, its body and organs to a chariot, and so on, it does so for the purpose of assisting the subjection to the Self of the means of meditation, i. e. the body, the senses, and so on. But in the present case no such purpose is to be discerned, and hence it must needs be admitted that having joy for its head, and so on, are real qualities of Brahman.—The next Sûtra disposes of this difficulty.

14. For meditation, owing to the absence of purpose.

As no other purpose can be assigned, the text must be supposed to represent Brahman as having joy for its head, and so on, for the purpose of meditation. In order to accomplish the meditation on Brahman which is enjoined in the text 'he who knows (i.e. meditates on) Brahman reaches the Highest,' the text represents the Brahman consisting of bliss as made up of joy, satisfaction, &c., and compares these to the head, the wings, and so on. The Self of bliss, which is the inmost of all the Selfs mentioned in the text, is by this means represented to the mind in a definite shape; just as in the preceding sections the Self of food, the Self of breath, and the rest had similarly been represented in definite shapes, consisting of head, wings, and so on. As thus the qualities of having joy for its head, &c. are merely secondary marks of the Self of bliss, they are not necessarily included in each meditation that involves the idea of that Self.

15. And on account of the term 'Self.'

That this is so further follows from the fact that in the clause 'different from this is the inner Self consisting of bliss' the term 'Self' is used. For as the Self cannot really possess a head, wings, and tail, its having joy for its head, and so on, can only be meant in a metaphorical sense, for the sake of easier comprehension.—But, in the preceding sections, the term *Self* had been applied to what is *not* of the nature of Self—the text speaking of the Self of breath, the Self of mind, and so on; how then are we able to determine that in the phrase 'the Self of bliss' the term

Self denotes a true *Self*?—To this the next Sûtra replies.

16. There is reference to the Self, as in other places; on account of the subsequent passage.

In the clause, 'different from that is the Self of bliss,' the term Self can refer to the highest Self only; 'as in other cases,' i.e. as in other passages—'the Self only was this in the beginning; it thought, let me send forth the worlds,' and similar ones—the term 'Self' denotes the highest Self only.—But whereby is this proved?—'By the subsequent passage', i.e. by the passage, 'he desired, may I be many, may I grow forth,' which refers to the Self of bliss.

17. If it be said 'on account of connexion'; it may be so, on account of ascertainment.

But as in the preceding sections the term Self is seen to be connected with what is not of the nature of the Self, such as the Self of breath, and so on, it is not possible to draw a valid conclusion from the subsequent passage!—It *is* possible, the Sûtra replies, 'on account of ascertainment.' For the previous clause, 'from that Self there originated the Ether,' settles in the mind the idea of the highest Self, and that idea then is transferred in succession to the (so-called) Self of breath, the Self of mind, and so on, until it finally finds rest in the Self of bliss, beyond which there is no other Self; while at the same time the subsequent clause 'he desired' confirms the idea of the highest Self. The term *Self* thus connects itself from the beginning with things which are not true Selfs, because the highest Self is as it were viewed in them.—Here terminates the adhikara*n*a of 'bliss and the rest.'

18. The new (thing is enjoined); on account of the statement of what has to be done.

The Sûtra discusses an additional question connected with the meditation on breath. Both texts—the *K*h*â*ndogya as well as the Vâ*g*asaneyaka—declare that water constitutes a dress for prâ*n*a, and refer to the rinsing of the mouth with water. The doubt here arises whether what the texts mean to enjoin is the rinsing of the mouth, or a meditation on prâ*n*a as having water for its dress.—The Pûrvapakshin maintains the former view; for, he says, the Vâ*g*asaneyaka uses the injunctive form 'he is to rinse,' while there is no injunctive form referring to the meditation; and what the text says in praise of the breath thus not being allowed to remain naked may be taken as a mere glorification of the act of rinsing. And as ordinary rinsing of the mouth, subsequent to eating, is already established by Sm*ri*ti and custom, we must conclude that the text means to enjoin rinsing of the mouth of a different kind, viz. as auxiliary to the meditation on prâ*n*a.—To this the Sûtra replies that what the text enjoins is the 'new' thing, i. e. the previously non-established meditation on water as forming the dress of prâ*n*a. 'On account of the statement of what has to be done,' i. e. on account of the statement of what is not established—for only on the latter condition Scripture has a meaning. The beginning as well as the end of the Vâ*g*asaneyaka-text clearly refers to a meditation on the water used for rinsing as forming a dress for prâ*n*a; and as rinsing is already established by Sm*ri*ti and custom, we naturally infer that what the text enjoins is a meditation on breath as having the water used in rinsing for its dress. This also explains why the *Kh*ândogya-text does not mention the rinsing at all, but merely the clothing of breath with water.—Here terminates the adhikara*n*a of 'the statement of what has to be done.'

19. And (the qualities) thus being equal, on account of non-difference.

In the book of the Vâ*g*asaneyaka, called Agnirahasya, we meet with a meditation on Brahman called *S*â*nd*ilya-vidyâ; and there is also a *S*â*nd*ilya-vidyâ in the B*ri*hadâra*n*yaka. The Pûrvapakshin holds that these two meditations are different since the latter text mentions qualities—such as Brahman being the lord of all—which are not mentioned in the former; the objects of meditation thus being different, the meditations themselves are different.

—This the Sûtra negatives. The object of meditation is 'equal,' for both texts state the same qualities, such as 'consisting of mind,' and so on; and the additional qualities stated in the B*ri*had-âra*n*yaka, such as the rulership of Brahman, 'do not differ' from those equally stated by both texts, such as Brahman realising all its purposes, and so on. Thus the objects of meditation do not differ in character.—Here terminates the adhikara*n*a of 'what is equal.'

20. On account of connexion, thus elsewhere also.

In the B*ri*had-âra*n*yaka (V, 5) it is said that Brahman is to be meditated upon as abiding within the orb of the sun and within the right eye; and then the text mentions two secret names of Brahman—*aham* and *ahar*. Here the Pûrvapakshin holds that both these names are to be comprehended in each of the two meditations 'On account of connexion,' i. e. on account of the object of meditation, i. e. Brahman being one only, although connected with different abodes, it is 'thus elsewhere also,' i. e. the same conclusion which had been arrived at in the case of the *S*â*nd*ilya-vidyâs, has to be accepted with regard to Brahman abiding in the sun and in the eye. The meditation is one only, and hence the two secret names apply to Brahman in both its abodes.—This view the next Sûtra negatives.

21. Or not so, on account of difference.

This is not so, for as Brahman is to be meditated upon in two different abodes, the meditations are separate. In both the *S*â*nd*ilya-vidyâs, on the other hand, Brahman is to be meditated upon as abiding within the heart.

22. The text also declares this.

That the qualities of that which abides within the sun and that which abides in the eye are not to be combined, the text itself moreover shows by specially stating that the characteristics of the one are those of the other. For such a special transfer of qualities is needed only where the qualities are not of themselves established, i. e. where the two things are naturally different.—Here terminates the adhikara*n*a of 'connexion.'

23. And for the same reason the holding together and the pervading the sky.

In the Taittirîyaka and in the khilas of the Râ*n*âyanîyas we have the following passage: 'Gathered together are the powers among which Brahman is the oldest; Brahman as the oldest in the beginning stretched out the sky. Brahman was born as the first of all beings; who may rival that Brahman?' which declares that Brahman gathered together all the most ancient powers, that it pervades the sky, and so on. And as these attributes are not stated in connexion with any special meditation, we must infer that they are to be included in all meditations whatever on Brahman.—This primâ facie view is controverted by the Sûtra. The holding together of all powers, &c., although not mentioned in connexion with any special meditation, is not to be included in all meditations whatever, but to be connected with particular meditations 'on the same ground,' i. e. according to difference of place. *Where* those qualities have to be included must be decided on the ground of feasibility. The attribute of pervading the whole heaven cannot be included in a meditation on Brahman as abiding within a small place such as the heart, and hence the other attributes also which are stated together with the attribute mentioned cannot be included in those meditations. And when we find that in meditations on Brahman as abiding within a small place it is said that Brahman is greater than the earth, or that the ether within the heart is as great as the universal ether, these attributes cannot be taken in their literal sense and hence included in those meditations, but must be viewed as merely meant to glorify the object proposed for meditation.—Herewith terminates the adhikara*n*a of 'holding together.'

24. And although (they both be) meditations on man; on account of others not being recorded.

In the Taittirîyaka as well as the *Kh*ândogya we meet with a meditation on man (purusha-vidyâ), in which parts of the sacrifice are fancifully identified with the parts of the human body.—Here the Pûrvapakshin maintains that these two meditations are identical; for, he says, both meditations have the same name (purusha-vidyâ), and the same character as stated above; and as the Taittirîyaka mentions no fruit of the meditation, the fruit declared in the *Kh*ândogya holds good for the Taittirîyaka also, and thus there is no difference of fruit.—This view the Sûtra negatives. Although both meditations are meditations on man, yet they are separate 'on account of the others not being recorded,' i. e. on account of the qualities recorded in one *s*âkhâ not being recorded in the other. For the Taittirîyaka mentions the three libations, while the *Kh*ândogya does not, and so on. The character of the two meditations thus differs. And there is a difference of result also. For an examination of the context in the Taittirîyaka shows that the purusha-vidyâ is merely a subordinate part of a meditation on Brahman, the fruit of which the text declares to be that the devotee reaches the greatness of Brahman; while the *Kh*ândogya meditation is an independent one, and has for its reward the attainment of long life. The two meditations are thus separate, and hence the details of one must not be included in the other.—Here terminates the adhikara*n*a of 'the meditation on man.'

25. On account of the difference of sense of piercing and so on.

The text of the Âtharva*n*ikas exhibits at the beginning of their Upanishad some mantras, 'Pierce the *s*ukra, pierce the heart.' The followers of the Sâma-veda read at the beginning of their rahasya-brâhma*n*a 'O God Savit*ri*, promote the sacrifice.' The Kâ*th*akas and the Taittirîyakas have 'May Mitra be propitious to us, may Varu*n*a be propitious.' The *S*â*t*yâyanins have 'Thou art a white horse, a tawny and a black one!' The Kaushîtakins have a Brâhma*n*a referring to the Mahâvrata-ceremony, 'Indra having slain V*ri*tra became great.' The Kaushîtakins also have a Mahâvrata-brâhma*n*a, 'Pra*g*âpati is the year; his Self is that Mahâvrata.' The Vâ*g*asaneyins have a Brâhma*n*a referring to the Pravargya, 'The gods sat down for a sattra-celebration.' With reference to all this a doubt arises whether these mantras and the sacrificial works referred to in the Brâhma*n*a texts form parts of the meditations enjoined in the Upanishads or not.—The Pûrvapakshin affirms this, on the ground that as the mantras and works are mentioned in the immediate neighbourhood of the meditations the idea of their forming parts of the latter naturally presents itself. Such mantras as 'pierce the heart' and works such as the pravargya may indeed—on the basis of direct statement (*s*ruti), inferential mark (liṅga), and syntactical connexion (vâkya), which are stronger than mere proximity—be understood to be connected with certain actions; but, on the other hand, mantras such as 'May Varu*n*a be propitious' have no application elsewhere, and are suitable introductions to meditations. We therefore take them to be parts of the meditations, and hence hold that those mantras are to be included in all meditations.—This view the Sûtra sets aside 'on account of the difference of sense of piercing, and so on.' The inferential marks contained in texts such as 'pierce the *s*ukra, pierce the heart'; 'I shall speak the right, I shall speak the true,' show that the mantras have an application in connexion with certain magical practices, or else the study of the Veda, and the like, and do not therefore form part of meditations. That is to say—in the same way as the mantra 'pierce the heart' enables us to infer that also the mantra 'pierce the *s*ukra' belongs to some magical rite, so we infer from the special meaning of mantras such as 'I shall speak the right,' &c., that also mantras such as 'May Mitra be propitious' are connected with the study of the Veda, and do not therefore form part of meditations. That mantras of this kind and Brâhma*n*a passages relative to the Pravargya and the like are placed at the beginning of Upanishads is owing to their having, like the latter, to be studied in the forest.—Herewith terminates the adhikara*n*a of 'piercing and the like.'

26. But in the case of the getting rid of (it has to be combined with the obtaining), as it is supple-

mentary to statements of obtaining; as in the case of the kusas, the metres, the praise, and the singing. This has been explained.

The *Kh*andogas read in their text 'Shaking off all evil as a horse shakes his hair, and shaking off the body as the moon frees herself from the mouth of Râhu, I obtain the world of Brahman' (*Kh.* Up. VIII, 13). The Âtharva*n*ikas have 'He who knows, shaking off good and evil, free from passion, reaches the highest oneness.' The *S*â*t*yâyanins have 'His sons obtain his inheritance, his friends the good, his enemies the evil he has done.' The Kaushîtakins 'He shakes off his good and his evil deeds. His beloved relatives obtain the good, his unbeloved relatives the evil he has done.' Two of these texts mention only the shaking off, on the part of him who knows, of his good and evil works; one mentions only the obtainment of these works, on the part of friends and enemies; and one mentions both these occurrences.—Now both the occurrences, although mentioned in several meditations, must be considered elements of all meditations: for whoever, on the basis of a knowledge of Brahman, reaches Brahman, necessarily leaves behind all his good and evil works, and those works unless thus left behind cannot be obtained by others. Meditation on those two matters therefore enters as an element into all meditations. The doubtful point, however, is whether there is option between the meditation on the abandonment of works, and that on the obtainment of works by others, and that on both these events; or whether in each case all these meditations are to be combined.—There is option, the Pûrvapakshin holds; for the reason that the texts make different declarations on this point. For, if the meditations had to be combined, there would be in each case meditation on both the matters mentioned; and as such double meditation is established by the Kaushîtakin text, it would follow that the statements of the other texts are without meaning. Thus the only motive for the declarations made in different places can be to allow option. Nor must this conclusion be controverted on the ground that declarations of the same matter, made in different places, are made with reference to the difference of students severally reading the several texts; for this holds good in those cases only where identical statements are made in different texts; while in the case under discussion two *s*âkhâs mention the abandonment of works, and one their passing over to other persons. Nor can you account for the difference of statement on the ground of difference of vidyâs; for you yourself maintain that the meditations in question form part of all meditations.—This view the Sûtra impugns, 'but where the getting rid of is mentioned,' &c. Where a text mentions either the abandonment only of works or only their being obtained by others, both these matters must necessarily be combined, since the statement as to the works being obtained forms a supplement to the statement of their being abandoned. For the former statement declares the place to which the good and evil works, got rid of by him who knows Brahman, are transferred.—This supplementary relation of two statements the Sûtra illustrates by some parallel cases. A clause in the text of the *S*â*t*yâyanins, 'the ku*s*as are the children of the udumbara tree,' forms a defining supplement to a more general statement in the text of the Kaushîtakins, 'the ku*s*as are the children of the tree.' The clause, 'the metres of the gods are prior,' defines the order of the metres which in other texts mentioning 'the metres of the gods and Asuras' had been left undefined, and therefore forms a supplement to those texts. Analogous is the relation of the clause, 'he assists the stotra of the sho*d*a*s*in when the sun has half risen,' to the less definite statement 'he assists with gold the stotra of the sho*d*a*s*in;' and the relation of the clause, 'the adhvaryu is not to sing,' to the general injunction 'all the priests join in the singing.' Unless we admit that one statement, which defines some other more general statement, may stand to the latter in a supplementary relation, we are driven to assume an optional proceeding, and this is objectionable as long as there is any other way open; according to a principle laid down in the Pûrva Mîmâ*m*sâ (X, 8, 15). As the clauses referring to the abandonment of the works, and those referring to their being taken up by others, thus form one connected whole, there is no such thing as mere abandonment and mere taking up, and hence there can be no option between the two. That the text of the Kaushîtakins mentions both thus explains itself, on the ground that the several declarations of what is really only one and the same matter are directed to different hearers.—Here terminates the adhikara*n*a of 'getting rid of.'

27. At departing; there being nothing to be reached. For thus others (also declare).

The further question arises whether the putting off of all good and evil deeds takes place only at the time when the soul leaves the body, or also after it has departed and is on its journey to the world of Brahman. The Pûrvapakshin holds the latter view, for, he says, the texts declare both. The Kaushîtakins say that the soul shakes off its good and evil deeds when it crosses the river Vira*g*â in the world of Brahman; while the Tâ*nd*ins say 'Shaking off all evil, and shaking off the body,' &c., which shows that the deeds are shaken off at the time when the soul leaves the body. And when the *S*â*t*yâyanaka says that 'his sons obtain his inheritance, his friends his good deeds,' and so on, this also intimates that the deeds are shaken off at the time when the soul leaves the body. We therefore must conclude that a part of the deeds is left behind at the moment of death, and the remainder on the journey to the world of Brahman.—This view the Sûtra controverts. All the good and evil deeds of the dying man are left behind, without remainder, at the time when the soul parts from the body. For after the soul of him who knows has departed from the body, 'there is nothing to be reached,' i. e. there are no further pleasures and pains to be enjoyed as the result of good and evil deeds, different from the obtaining of Brahman, which is the fruit of knowledge. Thus others also declare that, subsequently to the soul's departure from the body, there is no enjoyment of any pain or pleasure different from the obtaining of Brahman. 'But when he is free of the body, then neither pleasure nor pain touches him'; 'Thus does that serene being, rising from this body, appear in its own form as soon as it has approached the highest light' (*Kh*. Up. VIII, 12, 1; 3); 'For him there is delay only so long as he is not freed (from the body); then he will be perfect' (VI, 14, 2).

28. As it is desired; on account of there being no contradiction of either.

The time when good and evil deeds are left behind thus having been determined on the basis of the reason of the thing, the several words of the passages must be construed as it is desired, i. e. so as not to contradict either, i.e. either the declaration of scripture or the reason of the thing. Thus in the text of the Kaushîtakins the later clause, 'he shakes off his good and evil deeds,' must be taken as coming before the earlier passage 'having entered on that path of the gods.'—Here the Pûrvapakshin raises a new objection.

29. There is meaning of the soul's going (only) on the twofold hypothesis; for otherwise there is contradiction.

It is only on the hypothesis of a part of the good and evil works being left behind at the time of the soul's departure from the body, and another part later on, and the effacement of works thus taking place in a double way, that a sense can be found in the scriptural declaration of the soul proceeding on the path of the gods. For otherwise there would be a contradiction. For if all the works perished at the time of the soul's departure from the body, the subtle body also would perish, and if this were so, no going on the part of the mere Self would be possible. It is not therefore possible that at the time of the soul's departure from the body all works should perish without a remainder.—To this the next Sûtra replies.

30. (That assumption) is justified; on account of the perception of things which are marks of that; as in ordinary experience.

The assumption of all the works perishing at the time of 'departure' involves no contradiction; since we perceive, in the sacred texts, matters which are marks of connexion with a body even on the part of the soul which has divested itself of all its works and become manifest in its true nature. Compare 'Having approached the highest light he manifests himself in his true form'; 'He moves about there laughing, playing, and rejoicing'; 'He becomes a self-ruler, he moves about in all worlds according to his will'; 'He becomes one, he becomes three,' &c. (*Kh.* Up. VIII, 12, 3; VII, 25, 2; 26, 2). All these texts refer to the soul's connexion with a body. The soul therefore, joined to the subtle body, may proceed on the path of the gods, even after all its works have passed away. But how can the subtle body persist, when the works which originate it have passed away? Through the power of knowledge, we reply. Knowledge does not indeed by itself originate the subtle body, but it possesses the power of making that body persist, even after the gross body—which is the instrument for the experience of all ordinary pains and pleasures—and all works have passed away, so as thereby to make the soul capable of moving on the path of the gods, and thus to obtain Brahman which is the fruit of knowledge. 'As in ordinary life.' As in ordinary life, a tank, which may have been made with a view to the irrigation of rice-fields and the like, is maintained and used for the purpose of drawing drinking-water, and so on, even after the intentions which originally led to its being made have passed away.—Here an objection is raised. It may be admitted, that at the time when a man possessing true knowledge dies, all his works pass away without a remainder, and that the subtle body only remains, enabling him to move towards Brahman; but it cannot be held that the soul in that state does not experience pain and pleasure; for we know from sacred tradition that Vasish*th*a, Avântaratamas, and others, who had reached intuition of the highest truth, entered after death on other embodiments, and experienced pain and pleasure due to the birth of sons, various calamities, and so on.—To this the next Sûtra replies.

31. Of those who have a certain office there is subsistence (of their works) as long as the office lasts.

We do not maintain that all those who have reached true knowledge divest themselves at the time of death of all their good and evil works; we limit our view to those who immediately after death attain to moving on the path, the first stage of which is light. Persons like Vasish*th*a, on the other hand, who are entrusted with certain offices, do not immediately after death attain to moving on the path beginning with light, since the duties undertaken by them are not completely accomplished. In the case of beings of this kind, who owing to particular deeds have been appointed to particular offices, the effect of the works which gave rise to the office does not pass away before those offices are completely accomplished; for the effect of a work is exhausted only through the complete enjoyment of its result. In the case of those persons, therefore, the effects of the works which gave rise to their office continue to exist as long as the office itself, and hence they do not after death enter on the path beginning with light.—Here terminates the adhikara*n*a of 'passing away.'

32. There is no restriction (since) all (have to go on that path). (Thus) there is non-contradiction of sacred text and Sm*ri*ti.

The question here is whether Brahman is to be reached on the path of the gods by those only who take their stand on those meditations which, like the Upako*s*ala-vidyâ, describe that path, or by all who practise any of the meditations on Brahman. The Pûrvapakshin holds the former view, since there is no proof to show that in other vidyâs the going on that path is not mentioned, and since those other vidyâs—such as the texts 'and those who in the forest meditate on faith and austerities,' and 'those who in the forest worship faith, the True' (*Kh*. Up. V, 10, 1; B*ri*. Up. VI, 2, 15)—suggest to the mind the idea of the knowledge of Brahman. This the Sûtra negatives.

There is no restriction to that limited class of devotees, since all who carry on meditations have to go on that path. For on this latter assumption only text and inference, i. e. scripture and authoritative tradition, are not contradicted. As to scripture, the *Kh*ândogya and the Vâ*g*asaneyaka alike, in the Pa*ñk*âgni-vidyâ, declare that all those who practise meditation go on that path. In the Vâ*g*asaneyaka the words 'who know this' refer to those who practise the meditation on the five fires, while the following words 'those who in the forest meditate on faith and the True' refer to those who meditate on Brahman; and the text then goes on to say that all those devotees go to Brahman, on the path of the gods. Texts such as 'the True, knowledge, infinite is Brahman,' and 'the True must be enquired into,' prove that the term 'the True' denotes Brahman; and as in the *Kh*ândogya the term 'tapas' occurs in the corresponding place, we conclude that both these terms, viz. *the True* and tapas, denote nothing else but Brahman. Meditation on Brahman, preceded by faith, is mentioned elsewhere also; in the text which begins 'The True must be enquired into' we read further on 'Faith must be enquired into' (*Kh*. Up. VII, 18, 16; 19). Sm*ri*ti also declares that all those who know Brahman proceed on the path of the gods, 'Fire, the light, the day, the bright fortnight, the six months of the sun's northern progress—proceeding by that road those who know Brahman go to Brahman' (Bha. Gî. VIII, 24). And there are many other *S*ruti and Sm*ri*ti passages of this kind. The conclusion therefore is that the Upako*s*alavidyâ and similar texts merely refer to that going of the soul which is common to all vidyâs.—Here terminates the adhikara*n*a of 'non-restriction.'

33. But the conceptions of the Imperishable are to be comprised (in all meditations). There being equality (of the Brahman to be meditated on) and (those conceptions) existing (in Brahman); as in the case of what belongs to the upasad. This has been explained.

We read in the B*ri*had-âra*n*yaka (III, 8, 9), 'O Gârgî, the Brâhma*n*as call that the Akshara. It is neither coarse nor fine,' and so on. And in the Âtharva*n*a (Mu. Up. I, 1, 5) we have 'The higher knowledge is that by which the Akshara is apprehended. That which cannot be seen nor seized,' &c. The doubt here arises whether all the qualities there predicated of Brahman—called akshara, i.e. the Imperishable—and constituting something contrary in nature to the apparent world, are to be included in all meditations on Brahman, or only those where the text specially mentions them. The Pûrvapakshin advocates the latter view; for, he says, there is no authority for holding that the qualities which characterise one meditation are characteristic of other meditations also; and such negative attributes as are mentioned in those two texts do not—as positive qualities such as bliss do—contribute to the apprehension of the true nature of Brahman. What those two texts do is merely to deny of Brahman, previously apprehended as having bliss, and so on, for its essential qualities, certain qualities belonging to the empirical world, such as grossness, and so on; for all negation must refer to an established basis.—This view the Sûtra refutes. The ideas of absence of grossness, and so on, which are connected with Brahman viewed as the Akshara, are to be included in all meditations on Brahman. For the imperishable (akshara) Brahman is the same in all meditations, and qualities such as non-grossness enter into the conception of its essential nature. The apprehension of a thing means the apprehension of its specific character. But mere bliss, and so on, does not suggest the specific character of Brahman, since those qualities belong also to the individual soul. What is specifically characteristic of Brahman is bliss, and so on, in so far as fundamentally opposed to all evil and imperfection. The individual soul, on the other hand, although fundamentally free from evil, yet is capable of connexion with evil. Now being fundamentally opposed to evil implies having a character the opposite of grossness and all similar qualities which belong to the empirical world, material and mental. He therefore who thinks of

Brahman must think of it as having for its essential nature bliss, knowledge, and so on, in so far as distinguished by absence of grossness and the like, and those qualities, being no less essential than bliss, and so on, must therefore be included in all meditations on Brahman.—The Sûtra gives an instance illustrating the principle that qualities (secondary matters) follow the principal matter to which they belong. As the mantra 'Agnir vai hotra*m* vetu,' although given in the Sâma-veda, yet has to be recited in the Ya*g*ur-veda style, with a subdued voice, because it stands in a subordinate relation to the upasad-offerings prescribed for the four-days' sacrifice called *G*âmadagnya; those offerings are the principal matter to which the subordinate matter—the mantra—has to conform. This point is explained in the first section, i. e. in the Pûrva Mîmâ*m*sâ-sûtras III, 3, 9.—But this being admitted, it would follow that as Brahman is the principal matter in all meditations on Brahman, and secondary matters have to follow the principal matter, also such qualities as 'doing all works, enjoying all odours and the like,' which are mentioned in connexion with special meditations only, would indiscriminately have to be included in all meditations.—With reference to this the next Sûtra says.

34. So much; on account of reflection.

Only so much, i. e. only those qualities which have to be included in all meditations on Brahman, without which the essential special nature of Brahman cannot be conceived, i. e. bliss, knowledge, and so on, characterised by absence of grossness and the like. Other qualities, such as doing all works and the like, although indeed following their substrate, are explicitly to be meditated on in special meditations only.—Here terminates the adhikara*n*a of 'the idea of the Imperishable.'

35. Should it be said that (the former reply refers) to that Self to which the aggregate of material things belongs (since) otherwise the difference (of the two replies) could not be accounted for; we say—no; as in the case of instruction.

In the B*ri*had-âra*n*yaka (III, 4; 5) the same question is asked twice in succession ('Tell me the Brahman which is visible, not invisible, the Self who is within all'), while Yâ*gñ*avalkya gives a different answer to each ('He who breathes in the upbreathing,' &c.; 'He who overcomes hunger and thirst,' &c.). The question here is whether the two meditations, suggested by these sections, are different or not. They are different, since the difference of reply effects a distinction between the two vidyâs. The former reply declares him who is the maker of breathing forth, and so on, to be the inner Self of all; the latter describes him as free from hunger, thirst, and so on. It thence appears that the former passage refers to the inner (individual) Self which is different from body, sense-organs, internal organ, and vital breath; while the latter refers to that which again differs from the inner Self, viz. the highest Self, free from hunger, thirst, and so on. As the individual soul is inside the aggregate of material things, it may be spoken of as being that inner Self of all. Although this kind of inwardness is indeed only a relative one, we nevertheless must accept it in this place; for if, desirous of taking this 'being the inner Self of all' in its literal sense, we assumed the highest Self to be meant, the difference of the two replies could not be accounted for. The former reply evidently refers to the individual soul, since the highest Self cannot be conceived as breathing forth, and so on; and the latter reply, which declares the Self to be raised above hunger, &c., evidently refers to the highest Self. This is expressed in the earlier part of the Sûtra: 'The former reply refers to the Self to which there belongs the aggregate of material things, i.e. the individual soul as being the inner Self of all; otherwise we could not account for the difference of the two replies.'—The last words of the Sûtra negative this—'not so,' i.e. there is no difference of vidyâs, since both assertions and replies refer to the highest Self. The question says in both places, 'the Brahman which is visible, not invisible, the Self who is within all,' and this clearly refers to the highest Self only. We indeed observe that in some places the term *Brahman* is, in a derived sense, applied to the individual soul also; but the text under discussion, for distinction's sake, adds the qualification 'the Brahman which is manifest' (sâkshât). The quality of 'aparokshatva' (i. e. being that which does not transcend the senses but lies openly revealed) also, which implies being connected with all space and all time, suits Brahman only, which from texts such as 'the True, knowledge, infinite is Brahman' is known to be infinite. In the same way the attribute of being the inner Self of all can belong to the highest Self only, which texts such as 'He who dwelling within the earth,' &c., declare to be the inner ruler of the universe. The replies to the two questions likewise can refer to Brahman only. The unconditional causal agency with regard to breath, declared in the clause 'he who breathes in the upbreathing,' &c., can belong to the highest Self only, not to the individual soul, since the latter possesses no such causal power when in the state of deep sleep. Ushasta thereupon, being not fully enlightened, since causality with regard to breathing may in a sense be attributed to the individual soul also, again asks a question, in reply to which Yâ*gñ*avalkya clearly indicates Brahman, 'Thou mayest not see the seer of sight,' &c., i.e. thou must not think that my previous speech has named as the causal agent of breathing the individual soul, which is the causal agent with regard to those activities which depend on the sense-organs, viz. seeing, hearing, thinking, and knowing; for in the state of deep sleep, swoon, and so on, the soul possesses no such power. And moreover another text also—'Who could breathe if that bliss existed not in the ether?' (Taitt. Up. II, 7)—declares that the highest Self only is the cause of the breathing of all living beings. In the same way the answer to the second question can refer to the highest Self only, which alone can be said to be raised above hunger, thirst, and so on. For this reason also both replies wind up with the same phrase, 'Everything else is of evil.' The iteration of question and reply serves the purpose of showing that the same highest Brahman which is the cause of all breathing is beyond all hunger, thirst, and so on.—The

Sûtra subjoins a parallel instance. 'As in the case of instruction.' As in the vidyâ of that which truly is (*Kh.* Up. VI, 1 ff.), question and reply are iterated several times, in order to set forth the various greatness and glory of Brahman.—Thus the two sections under discussion are of the same nature, in so far as setting forth that the one Brahman which is the inner Self of all is the cause of all life and raised beyond all imperfections; and hence they constitute one meditation only.—To this a new objection is raised. The two sections may indeed both refer to the highest Brahman; nevertheless there is a difference of meditation, as according to the one Brahman is to be meditated upon as the cause of all life, and according to the other as raised above all defects; this difference of character distinguishes the two meditations. And further there is a difference of interrogators; the first question being asked by Ushasta, the second by Kahola.

36. There is interchange (of ideas), for the texts distinguish; as in other cases.

There is no difference of vidyâ because both questions and answers have one subject-matter, and because the one word that possesses enjoining power proves the connexion of the two sections. Both questions have for their topic Brahman viewed as the inner Self of all; and in the second question the word 'eva' ('just,' 'very') in 'Tell me just that Brahman,' &c., proves that the question of Kahola has for its subject the Brahman, to the qualities of which the question of Ushasta had referred. Both answers again refer to the one Brahman, viewed as the Self of all. The idea of the injunction of the entire meditation again is suggested in the second section only, 'Therefore a Brâhma*n*a, after he has done with learning, is to wish to stand by real strength.' The object of meditation being thus ascertained to be one, there must be effected a mutual interchange of the ideas of Ushasta and Kahola, i. e. Ushasta's conception of Brahman being the cause of all life must be entertained by the interrogating Kahola also; and vice versâ the conception of Kahola as to Brahman being beyond hunger, thirst, and so on, must be entertained by Ushasta also. This interchange being made, the difference of Brahman, the inner Self of all, from the individual soul is determined by both sections. For this is the very object of Yâ*gñ*avalkya's replies: in order to intimate that the inner Self of all is different from the individual soul, they distinguish that Self as the cause of all life and as raised above hunger, thirst, and so on. Hence Brahman's being the inner Self of all is the only quality that is the subject of meditation; that it is the cause of life and so on are only means to prove its being such, and are not therefore to be meditated on independently.—But if this is so, to what end must there be made an interchange, on the part of the two interrogators, of their respective ideas?—Brahman having, on the ground of being the cause of all life, been ascertained by Ushasta as the inner Self of all, and different from the individual soul, Kahola renews the question, thinking that the inner Self of all must be viewed as different from the soul, on the ground of some special attribute which cannot possibly belong to the soul; and Yâ*gñ*avalkya divining his thought thereon declares that the inner Self possesses an attribute which cannot possibly belong to the soul, viz. being in essential opposition to all imperfection. The interchange of ideas therefore has to be made for the purpose of establishing the idea of the individual nature of the object of meditation.—'As elsewhere,' i. e. as in the case of the knowledge of that which truly is, the repeated questions and replies only serve to define one and the same Brahman, not to convey the idea of the object of meditation having to be meditated on under new aspects.—But a new objection is raised—As there is, in the Sad-vidyâ also, a difference between the several questions and answers, how is that vidyâ known to be one?—To this question the next Sûtra replies.

37. For one and the same (highest divinity), called the 'truly being,' and so on (is the subject of that meditation).

For the highest divinity, called there *that which is*—

which was introduced in the clause 'that divinity thought,' &c.—is intimated by all the following sections of that chapter. This is proved by the fact that the attributes—'*that which truly is*,' and so on—which were mentioned in the first section and confirmed in the subsequent ones, are finally summed up in the statement, 'in that all this has its Self, that is the True, that is the Self.'

Some interpreters construe the last two Sûtras as constituting two adhikara*n*as. The former Sûtra, they say, teaches that the text, 'I am thou, thou art I,' enjoins a meditation on the soul and the highest Self as interchangeable. But as on the basis of texts such as 'All this is indeed Brahman,' 'all this has its Self in Brahman,' 'Thou art that,' the text quoted is as a matter of course understood to mean that there is one universal Self, the teaching which it is by those interpreters assumed to convey would be nothing new; and their interpretation therefore must be rejected. The point as to the oneness of the individual and the highest Self will moreover be discussed under IV, 1, 3. Moreover, there is no foundation for a special meditation on Brahman as the individual soul and the individual soul as Brahman, apart from the meditation on the Self of all being one.—The second Sûtra, they say, declares the oneness of the meditation on the True enjoined in the text, 'whosoever knows this great wonderful first-born as the True Brahman' (B*ri*. Up. V, 4), and of the meditation enjoined in the subsequent passage (V, 5, 2), 'Now what is true, that is the Âditya, the person that dwells in yonder orb, and the person in the right eye.' But this also is untenable. For the difference of abode mentioned in the latter passage (viz. the abode in the sun and in the eye) establishes difference of vidyâ, as already shown under Sû. III, 3, 21. Nor is it possible to assume that the two meditations comprised in the latter text which have a character of their own in so far as they view the True as embodied in syllables, and so on, and which are declared to be connected with a special result ('he who knows this destroys evil and leaves it'), should be identical with the one earlier meditation which has an independent character of its own and a result of its own ('he conquers these worlds'). Nor can it be said that the declaration of a fruit in 'he destroys evil and leaves it' refers merely to the fruit (not of the entire meditation but) of a subordinate part of the meditation; for there is nothing to prove this. The proof certainly cannot be said to lie in the fact of the vidyâs being one; for this would imply reasoning in a circle, viz. as follows—it being settled that the vidyâs are one, it follows that the fruit of the former meditation only is the main one, while the fruits of the two later meditations are subordinate ones; and—it being settled that those two later fruits are subordinate ones, it follows that, as thus there is no difference depending on connexion with fruits, the two later meditations are one with the preceding one.—All this proves that the two Sûtras can be interpreted only in the way maintained by us.—Here terminates the adhikara*n*a of 'being within.'

38. Wishes and the rest, here and there; (as is known from the abode, and so on).

We read in the *Kh*ândogya (VIII, 1, 1), 'There is that city of Brahman, and in it the palace, the small lotus, and in it that small ether,' &c.; and in the Vâ*g*asaneyaka, 'He is that great unborn Self who consists of knowledge,' and so on. A doubt here arises whether the two texts constitute one meditation or not.—The two meditations are separate, the Pûrvapakshin maintains; for they have different characters. The *Kh*ândogya represents as the object of meditation the ether as distinguished by eight different attributes, viz. freedom from all evil and the rest; while, according to the Vâ*g*asaneyaka, the being to be meditated on is he who dwells within that ether, and is distinguished by attributes such as lordship, and so on.—To this we reply that the meditations are not distinct, since there is no difference of character. For desires and so on constitute that character 'here and there,' i.e. in both texts nothing else but Brahman distinguished by attributes, such as having true wishes, and so on, forms the subject of meditation. This is known 'from the abode and so on,' i.e. the meditation is recognised as the same because in both texts Brahman is referred to as abiding in the heart, being a bridge, and so on. Lordship and the rest, which are stated in the Vâ*g*asaneyaka, are special aspects of the quality of being capable to realise all one's purposes, which is one of the eight qualities declared in the *Kh*ândogya, and as such prove that all the attributes going together with that quality in the *Kh*ândogya are valid for the Vâ*g*asaneyaka also. The character of the two vidyâs therefore does not differ. The connexion with a reward also does not differ, for it consists in both cases in attaining to Brahman; cp. *Kh.* Up. VIII, 12, 3 'Having approached the highest light he is manifested in his own form,' and B*ri*. Up. V, 4, 24 'He becomes indeed the fearless Brahman.' That, in the *Kh*ândogya-text, the term *ether* denotes the highest Brahman, has already been determined under I, 3, 14. As in the Vâ*g*asaneyaka, on the other hand, he who abides in the ether is recognised as the highest Self, we infer that by the ether in which he abides must be understood the ether within the heart, which in the text 'within there is a little hollow space (sushira)' (Mahânâr. Up. XI, 9) is called sushira. The two meditations are therefore one. Here an objection is raised. It cannot be maintained that the attributes mentioned in the *Kh*ândogya have to be combined with those stated in the Vâ*g*asaneyaka (lordship, rulership, &c.), since even the latter are not truly valid for the meditation. For the immediately preceding passage, 'By the mind it is to be perceived that there is here no plurality: from death to death goes he who sees here any plurality; as one only is to be seen that eternal being, not to be proved by any means of proof,' as well as the subsequent text, 'that Self is to be described by No, no,' shows that the Brahman to be meditated upon is to be viewed as devoid of attributes; and from this we infer that the attributes of lordship and so on, no less than the qualities of grossness and the like, have to be denied of Brahman. From this again we infer that in the *Kh*ândogya also the attributes of satyakâmatva and so on are not meant to be declared as Brahman's true qualities. All such qualities—

as not being real qualities of Brahman—have therefore to be omitted in meditations aiming at final release.—This objection the next Sûtra disposes of.

39. On account of emphasis there is non-omission.

Attributes, such as having the power of immediately realising one's purposes, and so on, which are not by other means known to constitute attributes of Brahman, and are in the two texts under discussion, as well as in other texts, emphatically declared to be attributes of Brahman, as constituting the object of meditations undertaken with a view to final release, cannot be omitted from those meditations, but must be comprised within them. In the *Kh*ândogya the passage, 'Those who depart from hence, after having cognised the Self and those self-realising desires, move about at will in all those worlds,' enjoins the knowledge of Brahman as distinguished by the power of realising its desires and similar qualities, while the text, 'Those who depart from here not having cognised the Self, &c., do *not* move about at will,' &c., finds fault with the absence of such knowledge, and in this way emphasises the importance of the possession of it. In the same way the repeated declarations as to Brahman's ruling power ('the lord of all, the king of all beings,' &c.) show that stress is to be laid upon the quality indicated. It truly cannot be held that Scripture, which in tender regard to man's welfare is superior to a thousand of parents, should, deceitfully, give emphatic instruction as to certain qualities—not known through any other means of knowledge—which fundamentally would be unreal and hence utterly to be disregarded, and thus throw men desirous of release, who as it is are utterly confused by the revolutions of the wheel of Sa*m*sâra, into even deeper confusion and distress. That the text, 'there is not any diversity here; as one only is to be seen that eternal being,' teaches a unitary view of the world in so far as everything is an effect of Brahman and thus has Brahman for its Self, and negatives the view of plurality—established antecedently to Vedic teaching—as excluding Brahman's being the universal Self, we have explained before. In the clause 'not so, not so' the *so* refers back to the world as established by other means of proof, and the clause thus declares that Brahman who is the Self of all is different in nature from the world. This is confirmed by the subsequent passage, 'He is incomprehensible, for he is not comprehended, he is undecaying,' &c.; which means—as he is different in nature from what is comprehended by the other means of proof he is not grasped by those means; as he is different from what suffers decay he does not decay, and so on. And analogously, in the *Kh*ândogya, the text 'by the old age of the body he does not age' &c. first establishes Brahman's being different in nature from everything else, and then declares it to be satyakâma, and so on.—But, an objection is raised, the text, 'Those who depart from hence, having cognised the Self and those true desires, move about at will in all worlds. Thus he who desires the world of the fathers,' &c., really declares that the knowledge of Brahman as possessing the power of immediately realising its wishes has for its fruit something lying within the sphere of transmigratory existence, and from this we infer that for him who is desirous of release and of reaching Brahman the object of meditation is not to be found in Brahman in so far as possessing qualities. The fruit of the highest knowledge is rather indicated in the passage, 'Having approached the highest light it manifests itself in its own form'; and hence the power of realising its wishes and the rest are not to be included in the meditation of him who wishes to attain to Brahman.—To this objection the next Sûtra replies.

40. In the case of him who has approached (Brahman); just on that account, this being declared by the text.

When the soul, released from all bonds and manifesting itself in its true nature, has approached, i.e. attained to Brahman; then just on that account, i.e. on account of such approach, the text declares it to possess the power of moving about at will in all worlds. 'Having approached the highest light he manifests himself in his true form.

He is the highest Person. He moves about there laughing, playing,' &c. This point will be proved in greater detail in the fourth adhyâya. Meanwhile the conclusion is that such qualities as satyakâmatva have to be included in the meditation of him also who is desirous of release; for the possession of those qualities forms part of the experience of the released soul itself.—Here terminates the adhikara*n*a of 'wishes and the rest.'

41. There is non-restriction of determination, because this is seen; for there is a separate fruit, viz. non-obstruction.

There are certain meditations connected with elements of sacrificial actions; as e.g. 'Let a man meditate on the syllable Om as udgîtha.' These meditations are subordinate elements of the sacrificial acts with which they connect themselves through the udgîtha and so on, in the same way as the quality of being made of par*n*a wood connects itself with the sacrifice through the ladle (made of par*n*a wood), and are to be undertaken on that very account. Moreover the statement referring to these meditations, viz. 'whatever he does with knowledge, with faith, with the Upanishad, that becomes more vigorous,' does not allow the assumption of a special fruit for these meditations (apart from the fruit of the sacrificial performance); while in the case of the ladle being made of par*n*a wood the text mentions a special fruit ('he whose ladle is made of par*n*a wood does not hear an evil sound'). The meditations in question are therefore necessarily to be connected with the particular sacrificial performances to which they belong.—This view the Sûtra refutes, 'There is non-restriction with regard to the determinations.' By 'determination' we have here to understand the definite settling of the mind in a certain direction, in other words, meditation. The meditations on the udgîtha and so on are not definitely connected with the sacrificial performances; 'since that is seen,' i.e. since the texts themselves declare that there is no such necessary connexion; cp. the text, 'therefore both perform the sacrificial work, he who thus knows it

(i. e. who possesses the knowledge implied in the meditations on the sacrifice), as well as he who does not know'—which declares that he also who does not know the meditations may perform the work. Were these meditations auxiliary elements of the works, there could be no such absence of necessary connexion (as declared in this text). It thus being determined that they are not auxiliary elements, a special result must be assigned to the injunction of meditation, and this we find in the greater strength which is imparted to the sacrifice by the meditation, and which is a result different from the result of the sacrifice itself. The *greater strength* of the performance consists herein, that its result is not impeded, as it might be impeded, by the result of some other performance of greater force. This result, viz. absence of obstruction, is something apart from the general result of the action, such as the reaching of the heavenly world, and so on. This the Sûtra means when saying, 'for separate is non-obstruction.' As thus those meditations also which refer to auxiliary members of sacrifices have their own results, they may or may not be combined with the sacrifices, according to wish. Their case is like that of the godohana vessel which, with the view of obtaining a certain special result, may be used instead of the *k*amasa.—Here terminates the adhikara*n*a of 'non-restriction of determination.'

42. Just as in the case of the offerings. This has been explained.

In the daharavidyâ (*Kh*. Up. VIII, 1 ff.) the text, 'those who depart having known here the Self, and those true desires,' declares at first a meditation on the small ether, i. e. the highest Self, and separately therefrom a meditation on its qualities, viz. true desires, and so on. The doubt here arises whether, in the meditation on those qualities, the meditation on the highest Self—as that to which the qualities belong—is to be repeated or not.—It is not to be repeated, the Pûrvapakshin maintains; for the highest Self is just that which is constituted by the qualities—freedom from all evil, and so on—and as that Self so constituted can be comprised in one meditation, there is no need of repeating the meditation on account of the qualities. —This view the Sûtra sets aside. The meditation has to be repeated. The highest Self indeed is that being to which alone freedom from evil and the other qualities belong, and it forms the object of the first meditation; yet there is a difference between it as viewed in its essential being and as viewed as possessing those qualities; and moreover, the clause 'free from evil, from old age,' &c. enjoins a meditation on the Self as possessing those qualities. It is therefore first to be meditated on in its essential nature, and then there takes place a repetition of the meditation on it in order to bring in those special qualities. The case is analogous to that of 'the offerings.' There is a text 'He is to offer a puro*d*â*s*a on eleven potsherds to Indra the ruler, to Indra the supreme ruler, to Indra the self-ruler.' This injunction refers to one and the same Indra, possessing the qualities of rulership and so on; but as, through connexion with those several qualities, the aspects of Indra differ, the oblation of the puro*d*â*s*a has to be repeated. This is declared in the Sâṅkarsha*n*a, 'The divinities are different on account of separation.'—Here terminates the adhikara*n*a of 'offerings.'

43. On account of the plurality of indicatory marks; for that (proof) is stronger. This also is declared (in the Pûrva Mîmâ*m*sâ).

The Taittirîyaka contains another daharavidyâ, 'The thousand-headed god, the all-eyed one,' &c. (Mahânâr. Up. XI). Here the doubt arises whether this vidyâ, as being one with the previously introduced vidyâ, states qualities to be included in the meditation enjoined in that vidyâ, or qualities to be included in the meditations on the highest Self as enjoined in all the Vedânta-texts.—The former is the case, the Pûrvapakshin holds, on account of the leading subject-matter. For in the preceding section (X) the meditation on the small ether is introduced as the subject-matter. 'There is the small lotus placed in the middle of the town (of the body), free from all evil, the abode of the Highest; within that there is a small space, free from sorrow—what is within that should be meditated upon' (Mahânâr. Up. X, 23). Now, as the lotus of the heart is mentioned only in section X, the 'Nârâya*n*a-section' ('the heart resembling the bud of a lotus, with its point turned downwards,' XI, 6), we conclude that that section also is concerned with the object of meditation to which the daharavidyâ refers.—Against this view the Sûtra declares itself, 'on account of the majority of indicatory marks'; i.e. there are in the text several marks proving that that section is meant to declare characteristics of that which constitutes the object of meditation in all meditations on the highest being. For that being which in those meditations is denoted as the Imperishable, *S*iva, *S*ambhu, the highest Brahman, the highest light, the highest entity, the highest Self, and so on, is here referred to by the same names, and then declared to be Nârâya*n*a. There are thus several indications to prove that Nârâya*n*a is none other than that which is the object of meditation in all meditations on the Highest, viz. Brahman, which has bliss and the rest for its qualities. By 'liṅga' (inferential mark) we here understand clauses (vâkya) which contain a specific indication; for such clauses have, according to the Pûrva Mîmâ*m*sâ, greater proving power than leading subject-matter (prakara*n*a). The argumentation that the clause 'the heart resembling the bud of a lotus flower,' &c., proves that section to stand in a dependent relation to the daharavidyâ, is without force; for it being proved by a stronger argument that the section refers to that which is the object of meditation in all meditations, the clause mentioned may also be taken as declaring that in the daharavidyâ also the object of meditation is Nârâya*n*a. Nor must it be thought that the accusatives with which the section begins (sahasra*s*îrsham, &c.) are to be connected with the 'meditating' enjoined in the previous section; for the 'meditating' is there enjoined by a gerundive form ('tasmin yad antas tad upâsitavyam'), and with this the subsequent accusatives cannot be construed. Moreover, the subsequent clause ('all this is Nârâya*n*a,' &c., where the nominative case is used) shows that those accusatives are to be taken in the sense of nominatives.—Here terminates the adhikara*n*a of 'the plurality of indicatory marks.'

44. There is option with regard to what precedes (i. e. the altar made of bricks) on account of subject-matter, and hence there is action; as in the case of the mânasa cup.

In the Vâ*g*asaneyaka, in the Agnirahasya chapter, there are references to certain altars built of mind, 'built of mind, built of speech,' &c. The doubt here arises whether those structures of mind, and so on, which metaphorically are called fire-altars, should be considered as being of the nature of action, on account of their connexion with a performance which itself is of the nature of action; or merely of the nature of meditation, as being connected with an activity of the nature of meditation. The Sûtra maintains the former view. Since those things 'built of mind, and so on,' are, through being *built* (or *piled up*), constituted as fire-altars, they demand a performance with which to connect themselves; and as in immediate proximity to them no performance is enjoined, and as the general subject-matter of the section is the fire-altar built of bricks—introduced by means of the clause 'Non-being this was in the beginning'—which is invariably connected with a performance of the nature of outward action, viz. a certain sacrificial performance—we conclude that the altars built of mind, &c., which the text mentions in connexion with the same subject-matter, are themselves of the nature of action, and as such can be used as alternatives for the altar built of bricks[1]. An analogous case is presented by the so-called *mental* cup. On the tenth, so-called avivâkya, day of the Soma sacrifice extending over twelve days,

[1] So that for the actual outward construction of a brick altar there may optionally be substituted the merely mental construction of an imaginary altar.

there takes place the mental offering of a Soma cup, all the rites connected with which are rehearsed in imagination only; the offering of that cup is thus really of the nature of thought only, but as it forms an auxiliary element in an actual outward sacrificial performance it itself assumes the character of an action.

45. And on account of the transfer.

That the altar built of thought is an optional substitute for the altar built of bricks, and of the nature of an action, appears therefrom also that the clause 'of these each one is as great as that previous one,' explicitly transfers to the altars of mind, and so on, the powers of the previous altar made of bricks. All those altars thus having equal effects there is choice between them. The altars of mind, and so on, therefore are auxiliary members of the sacrificial performance which they help to accomplish, and hence themselves of the nature of action.—Against this view the next Sûtra declares itself.

46. But it is a meditation only, on account of assertion and what is seen.

The altars built of mind, and so on, are not of the nature of action, but of meditation only, i.e. they belong to a performance which is of the nature of meditation only. For this is what the text asserts, viz. in the clauses 'they are built of knowledge only,' and 'by knowledge they are built for him who thus knows.' As the energies of mind, speech, sight, and so on, cannot be piled up like bricks, it is indeed a matter of course that the so-called altars constructed of mind, and so on, can be mental constructions only; but the text in addition specially confirms this by declaring that those altars are elements in an activity of purely intellectual character, and hence themselves mere creatures of the intellect. Moreover there is seen in the text a performance consisting of thought only to which those fires stand in a subsidiary relation, 'by the mind they were established on hearths, by the mind they were built up, by the mind the Soma cups were drawn thereat;

by the mind they chanted, and by the mind they recited; whatever rite is performed at the sacrifice, whatever sacrificial rite there is, that, as consisting of mind, was performed by the mind only, on those (fire-altars) composed of mind, built up of mind.' From this declaration, that whatever sacrificial rite is actually performed in the case of fire-altars built of bricks is performed mentally only in the case of altars built of mind, it follows that the entire performance is a mental one only, i. e. an act of meditation. —But, an objection is raised, as the entire passus regarding the altars of mind does not contain any word of injunctive power, and as the text states no special result (from which it appears to follow that the passus does not enjoin a new independent performance), we must, on the strength of the fact that the leading subject-matter is an actual sacrificial performance as suggested by the altars built of brick, give up the idea that the altars built of mind, &c., are mental only because connected with a performance of merely mental nature.—This objection the next Sûtra refutes.

47. And on account of the greater strength of direct statement, and so on, there is no refutation.

The weaker means of proof, constituted by so-called leading subject-matter, cannot refute what is established by three stronger means of proof—direct statement, inferential mark, and syntactical connexion—viz. that there is an independent purely mental performance, and that the altars made of mind are parts of the latter. The direct statement is contained in the following passage, 'Those fire-altars indeed are built of knowledge,'—which is further explained in the subsequent passage, 'by knowledge alone these altars are built for him who knows this'—the sense of which is: the structures of mind, and so on, are built in connexion with a performance which consists of knowledge (i. e meditation).—The inferential mark is contained in the passage, 'For him all beings at all times build them, even while he is asleep.' And the syntactical connexion (vâkya) consists in the connexion of the two words eva*m*-

vide (for him who knows this), and *k*invanti (they build) —the sense being: for him who accomplishes the performance consisting of knowledge all beings at all times build those altars. The proving power of the passage above referred to as containing an indicatory mark (liṅga) lies therein that a construction mentally performed at all times by all beings cannot possibly connect itself with a sacrificial performance through the brick-altar, which is constructed by certain definite agents and on certain definite occasions only, and must therefore be an element in a mental performance, i. e. a meditation.—The next Sûtra disposes of the objection that the text cannot possibly mean to enjoin a new mental performance, apart from the actual performance, because it contains no word of injunctive force and does not mention a special result.

48. On account of connexions and the rest, as in the case of the separateness of other cognitions. And this is seen (elsewhere also); as declared (in the Pûrva Mîmâ*m*sâ).

That the text enjoins a meditative performance different from the actual performance of which the brick-altar is a constituent element, follows from the reasons proving separation, viz. *the connexions*, i.e. the things connected with the sacrifice, such as the Soma cups, the hymns, the recitations, and so on. What is meant is that the special mention of the cups, and so on, made in the passage 'by the mind the Soma cups were drawn thereat,' proves the difference of the performance.—The 'and the rest' of the Sûtra comprises the previously stated arguments, viz. direct statement, and so on. 'As other meditations,' i.e. the case is analogous to that of other meditations such as the meditation on the small ether within the heart, which are likewise proved by textual statement, and so on, to be different and separate from actual outward sacrificial performances.—The existence of a separate meditative act having thus been ascertained, the requisite injunction has to be construed on the basis of the text as it stands.

Such construction of injunctions on the basis of texts of arthavâda character is seen in other places also; the matter is discussed in Pû. Mî. Sûtras III, 5, 21.—The result of the meditative performance follows from the passage 'of these (altars made of mind, and so on) each is as great as that former one (i.e. the altar built of bricks)'—for this implies that the same result which the brick-altar accomplishes through the sacrifice of which it forms an element is also attained through the altars made of mind, and so on, through the meditations of which they form parts.—The next Sûtra disposes of the argumentation that, as this formal transfer of the result of the brick-altar to the altars built of mind, and so on, shows the latter to possess the same virtues as the former, we are bound to conclude that they also form constituent elements of an actual (not merely meditative) performance.

49. Not so, on account of this being observed on account of similarity also; as in the case of Death; for (the person in yonder orb) does not occupy the worlds (of Death).

From a transfer or assimilation of this kind it does not necessarily follow that things of different operation are equal, and that hence those altars of mind, and so on, must connect themselves with an actual outward performance. For it is observed that such assimilation rests sometimes on a special point of resemblance only; so in the text, 'The person in yonder orb is Death indeed,'—where the feature of resemblance is the destroying power of the two; for the person within yonder orb does certainly not occupy the same worlds, i.e. the same place as Death. Analogously, in the case under discussion, the fact that the altars made of mind are treated as, in a certain respect, equivalent to the altar built of bricks, does not authorise us to connect those altars with the sacrificial performance to which the altar of bricks belongs. When the text says that the altar made of mind is as great as the altar of bricks, this only means that the same result which is attained through the brick-altar in connexion with its own sacrificial performance is also attained through the altar of mind in connexion with the meditational performance into which it enters.

50. And by a subsequent (Brâhma*n*a) also the 'being of such a kind' of the word (is proved). But the connexion is on account of plurality.

The subsequent Brâhma*n*a (*S*at. Br. X, 5, 4) also proves that the text treating of the altars made of mind, and so on, enjoins a meditation only. For that Brâhma*n*a (which begins 'This brick-built fire-altar is this world; the waters are its enclosing-stones,' &c.) declares further on 'whosoever knows this thus comes to be that whole Agni who is the space-filler,' and from this it appears that what is enjoined there is a meditation with a special result of its own. And further on (X, 6) there is another meditation enjoined, viz. one on Vai*s*vânara. All this shows that the Agnirahasya book (*S*at. Br. X) is not solely concerned with the injunction of outward sacrificial acts.—But what then is the reason that such matters as the mental (meditative) construction of fire-altars which ought to be included in the B*ri*had-âra*n*yaka are included in the Agnirahasya?—'That connexion is on account of plurality,' i. e. the altars made of mind, and so on, are, in the sacred text, dealt with in proximity to the real altar made of bricks, because so many details of the latter are mentally to be accomplished in the meditation.—Here terminates the adhikara*n*a of 'option with the previous one.'

51. Some, on account of the existence of a Self within a body.

In all meditations on the highest Self the nature of the meditating subject has to be ascertained no less than the nature of the object of meditation and of the mode of meditation. The question then arises whether the meditating Self is to be viewed as the knowing, doing, and enjoying Self, subject to transmigration; or as that Self which Pragâpati describes (*Kh*. Up. VIII, 1), viz. a Self free from all sin and imperfection.—Some hold the former view, on the ground that the meditating Self is within a body. For as long as the Self dwells within a body, it *is* a knower, doer, enjoyer, and so on, and it can bring about the result of its meditation only as viewed under that aspect. A person who, desirous of the heavenly world or a similar result, enters on some sacrificial action may, after he has reached that result, possess characteristics different from those of a knowing, doing, and enjoying subject, but those characteristics cannot be attributed to him as long as he is in the state of having to bring about the means of accomplishing those ends; in the latter state he must be viewed as an ordinary agent, and there it would be of no use to view him as something different. And the same holds equally good with regard to a person engaged in meditation.—But, an objection is raised, the text 'as the thought of a man is in this world, so he will be when he has departed this life' (*Kh.* Up. III, 14, 1) *does* declare a difference (between the agent engaged in sacrificial action, and the meditating subject), and from this it follows that the meditating Self is to be conceived as having a nature free from all evil, and so on.—Not so, the Pûrvapakshin replies; for the clause, 'howsoever they meditate on him,' proves that that text refers to the equality of the object meditated upon (not of the meditating subject).—To this the next Sûtra replies.

52. But this is not so, (but rather) difference; since it is of the being of that; as in the case of intuition.

It is not true that the meditating subject must be conceived as having the ordinary characteristics of knowing, acting, &c.; it rather possesses those characteristic properties—freedom from evil, and so on—which distinguish the state of Release from the Sa*m*sâra state. At the time of meditation the Self of the devotee is of exactly the same nature as the released Self. 'For it is of the being of that,' i.e. it attains the nature of that—as proved by the texts, 'as the thought of a man is in this world, so he will be when he has departed,' and 'howsoever he meditate on him, such he becomes himself.' Nor can it be maintained that these texts refer only to meditation on the highest Self (without declaring anything as to the personal Self of the devotee); for the personal Self constitutes the body of Brahman which is the object of meditation, and hence itself falls under the category of object of meditation. The character of such meditation, therefore, is that it is a meditation on the highest Self as having for its body the individual Self, distinguished by freedom from evil and the other qualities mentioned in the teaching of Pra*g*âpati. And hence the individual Self is, in such meditation, to be conceived (not as the ordinary Self, but) under that form which it has to attain (i.e. the pure form which belongs to it in the state of Release). 'As in the case of intuition'—i.e. as in the case of intuition of Brahman. As the intuition of Brahman has for its object the essential nature of Brahman, so the intuition of the individual soul also has for its object its permanent essential nature. In the case of sacrificial works the conception of the true nature of the Self forms an auxiliary factor. An injunction such as 'Let him who is desirous of the heavenly world sacrifice,' enjoins the performance of the sacrifice to the end of a certain result being reached; while the conception of the Self as possessing characteristics such as being a knowing subject, and so on—which are separate from the body—has the function of proving its qualification for works meant to effect results which will come about at some future time. So much only (i.e. the mere cognition of the Self as something different from the body) is required for works (as distinguished from meditations).—Here terminates the adhikara*n*a of 'being in the body.'

53. But those (meditations) which are connected with members (of sacrifices) are not (restricted) to (particular) *s*âkhâs, but rather (belong) to all *s*âkhâs.

There are certain meditations connected with certain constituent elements of sacrifices—as e.g. 'Let a man meditate on the syllable Om (as) the Udgîtha' (*Kh.* Up. I, 1, 1); 'Let a man meditate on the fivefold Sâman as the five worlds' (*Kh.* Up. II, 2, 1), &c. The question here arises whether those meditations are restricted to the members of those *s*âkhâs in whose texts they are mentioned; or to be connected with the Udgîtha, and so on, in all *s*âkhâs. There is here a legitimate ground for doubt, in so far as, although the general agreement of all Vedânta-texts is established, the Udgîtha, and so on, are different in each Veda since the accents differ in the different Vedas.—The Pûrvapakshin declares that those meditations are limited each to its particular *s*âkhâ; for, he says, the injunction 'Let him meditate on the Udgîtha' does indeed, verbally, refer to the Udgîtha in general; but as what stands nearest to this injunction is the special Udgîtha of the *s*âkhâ, in whose text this injunction occurs, and which shares the peculiarities of accent characteristic of that *s*âkhâ, we decide that the meditation is enjoined on members of that *s*âkhâ only.—The Sûtra sets this opinion aside. The injunction of meditations of this type is valid for all *s*âkhâs, since the text expressly connects them with the Udgîtha in general. They therefore hold good wherever there is an Udgîtha. The individual Udgîthas of the several *s*âkhâs are indeed distinguished by different accentuation; but the general statement, 'Let him meditate on the Udgîtha,' suggests to the mind not any particular Udgîtha, but *the* Udgîtha in general, and hence there is no reason to restrict the meditation to a particular *s*âkhâ. From the principle moreover that all *s*âkhâs teach the same doctrine, it follows that the sacrifice enjoined in the different *s*âkhâs is one only; and hence there is no reason to hold that the Udgîtha suggested by the injunction of the meditation is a particular one. For the Udgîtha is only an element in the sacrifice, and the sacrifice is one and the same. The meditations are not therefore limited to particular *s*âkhâs.

54. Or there is no contradiction as in the case of mantras and the rest.

The 'or' here has the sense of 'and.' The 'and the rest' comprises generic characteristics, qualities, number, similarity, order of succession, substances, and actions. As there is nothing contrary to reason in mantras and the rest, although mentioned in the text of one *s*âkhâ only, finding, on the basis of such means of proof as direct statement, and so on, their application in all *s*âkhâs, since the sacrifice to which they belong is one and the same in all *s*âkhâs; so there is likewise no contradiction in the meditations under discussion being undertaken by members of all *s*âkhâs.—Here terminates the adhikara*n*a of 'what is connected with constituent elements of the sacrifice.'

55. There is pre-eminence of plenitude, as in the case of the sacrifice; for thus Scripture shows.

The sacred text (*Kh*. Up. V, 12 ff.) enjoins a meditation on Vai*s*vânara, the object of which is the highest Self, as having for its body the entire threefold world, and for its limbs the heavenly world, the sun, the wind, and so on. The doubt here arises whether separate meditations have to be performed on the highest Being in its separate aspects, or in its aggregate as well as in its distributed aspect, or in its aggregate aspect only.—In its separate aspects, the Pûrvapakshin maintains; since at the outset a meditation of that kind is declared. For on the *Ri*shis in succession telling A*s*vapati the objects of their meditation, viz. the sky, the sun, and so on, A*s*vapati explains to them that these meditations refer to the head, eye, and so on, of the highest Being, and mentions for each of these meditations a special fruit. And the concluding explanation 'he who worships Vai*s*vânara as a span long, &c.,' is merely meant to gather up into one, as it were, the preceding meditations on the parts of Vai*s*vânara.—Another Pûrvapakshin holds that this very concluding passage enjoins a further meditation on Vai*s*vânara in his collective aspect, in addition to the previously enjoined meditations on his limbs; for that passage states a separate result, 'he eats food in all worlds,' &c. Nor does this destroy the unity of the whole section. The case is analogous to that of the meditation on 'plenitude' (bhûman; *Kh.* Up. VII, 23). There, in the beginning, separate meditations are enjoined on name, and so on, with special results of their own; and after that a meditation is enjoined on bhûman, with a result of its own, 'He becomes a Self-ruler,' &c. The entire section really refers to the meditation on bhûman; but all the same there are admitted subordinate meditations on name, and so on, and a special result for each.—These views are set aside by the Sûtra, 'There is pre-eminence of plenitude,' i. e. there is reason to assume that Vai*s*vânara in his fulness, i. e. in his collective aspect, is meant; since we apprehend unity of the entire section. From the beginning of the section it is manifest that what the *Ri*shis desire to know is the Vai*s*vânara Self; it is that Self which A*s*vapati expounds to them as having the Universe for his body, and in agreement therewith the last clause of his teaching intimates that the intuition of Brahman (which is none other than the Vai*s*vânara Self)—which is there characterised as the food of all worlds, all beings, all Selfs—is the fruit of the meditation on Vai*s*vânara. This summing up proves the whole section to deal with the same subject. And on the basis of this knowledge we determine that what the text says as to meditations on the separate members of the Vai*s*vânara Self and their special results is merely of the nature of explanatory comment (anuvâda) on parts of the meditation on the collective Self.—This decision is arrived at as in the case of the sacrifice. For to the injunction of certain sacrifices—such as 'Let a man, on the birth of a son, offer a cake on twelve potsherds to Vai*s*vânara'—the text similarly adds remarks on parts of the oblation, 'there is an oblation on eight potsherds,' and so on.—The meditation therefore has to be performed on the entire Vai*s*vânara Self only, not on its parts. This, moreover, Scripture itself intimates, in so far, namely, as declaring the evil consequences of meditation on parts of the Self only, 'your head would have fallen off if you had not come to me'; 'you would have become blind,' and so on. This also shows that the reference to the text enjoining meditations on name, &c., proves nothing as to our passage. For there the text says nothing as to disadvantages connected with those special meditations; it only says that the meditation on plenitude (bhûman) has a more excellent result. The section, therefore, although really concerned with enjoining the meditation on the bhûman, at the same time means to declare that the special meditations also are fruitful; otherwise the meditation on the bhûman could not be recommended, for the reason that it has a more excellent result than the preceding meditations.—The conclusion, therefore, is that the text enjoins a meditation on the collective Vaisvânara Self only.—Here terminates the adhikara*n*a of 'the pre-eminence of plenitude.'

56. (The meditations are) separate, on account of the difference of words, and so on.

The instances coming under this head of discussion are all those meditations on Brahman which have for their only result final Release, which consists in attaining to Brahman—such as the meditation on that which is, the meditation on the bhûman, the meditation on the small space within the heart, the Upako*s*ala meditation, the *Sând*ilya meditation, the meditation on Vai*s*vânara, the meditation on the Self of bliss, the meditation on the Imperishable, and others—whether they be recorded in one *s*âkhâ only or in several *s*âkhâs. To a different category belong those meditations which have a special object such as Prâ*n*a, and a special result.—The doubt here arises whether the meditations of the former class are all to be considered as identical, or as separate.—The Pûrvapakshin holds that they are all one; for, he says, they all have one and the same object of meditation, viz. Brahman. For the nature of all cognition depends on the object cognised; and the nature of the meditations thus being one, the meditations themselves are one.—This view the Sûtra controverts.

The meditations are different, on account of the difference of terms and the rest. The 'and the rest' comprises repetition (abhyâsa), number (sa*m*khyâ), quality (gu*n*a), subject-matter (prakriyâ), and name (nâmadheya; cp. Pû. Mî. Sû. II, 2, 1 ff.). We meet in those meditations with difference of connexion, expressing itself in difference of words, and so on; which causes difference on the part of the meditations enjoined. The terms enjoining meditation, 'he knows,' 'he is to meditate' (veda; upâsîta), and so on, do indeed all of them denote a certain continuity of cognition, and all these cognitions have for their object Brahman only, but all the same those cognitions differ in so far as they have for their object Brahman, as variously qualified by special characteristics mentioned in the meditation; in one meditation he is spoken of as the sole cause of the world, in another as free from all evil, and so on. We therefore arrive at the decision that clauses which describe special forms of meditation having for their result the attainment to Brahman, and are complete in themselves, convey the idea of separate independent meditations, and thus effect separation of the vidyâs. This entire question was indeed already decided in the Pûrva Mîmâ*m*sâ-sûtras (II, 2, 1), but it is here argued again to the end of dispelling the mistaken notion that the Vedânta-texts aim at knowledge only, and not at the injunction of activities such as meditation. The meditations, therefore, are separate ones.—Here terminates the adhikara*n*a of 'difference of words and the rest.'

57. Option, on account of the non-difference of result.

It has been proved that the meditation on that which truly is, the meditation on the small ether within the heart, and so on—all of which have for their result the attainment to Brahman—are separate meditations. The question now arises whether all these meditations should be combined by each meditating devotee, on account of such combination being useful to him; or whether, in the absence of any use of such combination, they should be undertaken optionally.—They may be combined, the Pûrvapakshin holds; since it is observed that different scriptural matters are combined even when having one and the same result. The Agnihotra, the Darsapûrnamâsa oblation, and other sacrifices, all of them have one and the same result, viz. the possession of the heavenly world; nevertheless, one and the same agent performs them all, with a view to the greater fulness of the heavenly bliss aimed at. So the different meditations on Brahman also may be cumulated with a view to greater fulness of intuition of Brahman.—This view the Sûtra rejects. Option only between the several meditations is possible, on account of the non-difference of result. For to all meditations on Brahman alike Scripture assigns one and the same result, viz. intuitive knowledge of Brahman, which is of the nature of supreme, unsurpassable bliss. 'He who knows Brahman attains the Highest' (Taitt. Up. II, 1, 1), &c. The intuitive knowledge of Brahman constitutes supreme, unsurpassable bliss; and if such intuition may be reached through one meditation, of what use could other meditations be? The heavenly world is something limited in respect of place, time, and essential nature, and hence a person desirous of attaining to it may cumulate works in order to take possession of it to a greater extent, and so on. But an analogous proceeding cannot be resorted to with regard to Brahman, which is unlimited in every sense. All meditations on Brahman tend to dispel Nescience, which stands in the way of the intuition of Brahman, and thus equally have for their result the attaining to Brahman; and hence there is option between them. In the case, on the other hand, of those meditations which aim at other results than Brahman, there may either be choice between the several meditations, or they may be cumulated—as one may also do in the case of sacrifices aiming at the attainment of the heavenly world;—for as those results are not of an infinite nature one may aim at realising them in a higher degree. This the next Sûtra declares.

58. But meditations aiming at objects of desire

may, according to one's liking, be cumulated or not; on account of the absence of the former reason.

The last clause means—on account of their results not being of an infinite nature.—Here terminates the adhikara*n*a of 'option.'

59. They belong to the constituent members, as the bases.

A doubt arises whether meditations such as the one enjoined in the text, 'Let him meditate on the syllable Om as the Udgîtha,' which are connected with constituent elements of the sacrifice such as the Udgîtha, contribute towards the accomplishment of the sacrifice, and hence must be performed at the sacrifice as part of it; or whether they, like the godohana vessel, benefit the agent apart from the sacrifice, and therefore may be undertaken according to desire.—But has it not been already decided under III, 3, 42 that those meditations are generally beneficial to man, and not therefore restricted to the sacrifices?—True; it is just for the purpose of further confirming that conclusion that objections are now raised against it on the ground of some inferential marks (liṅga) and reasoning. For there it was maintained on the strength of the text 'therefore he does both' that those meditations have results independent of the sacrifice. But there are several reasons favouring the view that those meditations must be connected with the sacrifices as subordinate members, just as the Udgîtha and the rest to which the meditations refer.

Their case is by no means analogous to that of the godohana vessel, for, while in the case of the latter, the text expressly declares the existence of a special result, 'For him who is desirous of cattle he is to bring water in a godohana,' the texts enjoining those meditations do not state special results for them. For clauses such as 'he is to meditate on the Udgîtha' intimate only that the Udgîtha is connected with the meditation; while their connexion with certain results is known from other clauses, such as 'whatever he does with knowledge, with faith, with the

Upanishad, that is more vigorous' (according to which the result of such meditations is only to strengthen the result of the sacrifices). And when a meditation of this kind has, on the ground of its connexion with the Udgîtha or the like—which themselves are invariably connected with sacrifices—been cognised to form an element of a sacrifice, some other passage which may declare a fruit for that meditation can only be taken as an arthavâda; just as the passage which declares that he whose sacrificial ladle is made of par*n*a wood does not hear an evil sound. In the same way, therefore, as the Udgîtha and so on, which are the bases of those meditations, are to be employed only as constituent parts of the sacrifices, so the meditations also connected with those constituent parts are themselves to be employed as constituent parts of the sacrifices only.

60. And on account of injunction.

The above conclusion is further confirmed by the fact of injunction, i. e. thereby that clauses such as 'he is to meditate on the Udgîtha' enjoin the meditation as standing to the Udgîtha in the relation of a subordinate member. Injunctions of this kind differ from injunctions such as 'he is to bring water in the godohana vessel for him who desires cattle'; for the latter state a special qualification on the part of him who performs the action, while the former do not, and hence cannot claim independence.

61. On account of rectification.

The text 'from the seat of the Hot*ri* he sets right the wrong Udgîtha' shows that the meditation is necessarily required for the purpose of correcting whatever mistake may be made in the Udgîtha. This also proves that the meditation is an integral part of the sacrificial performance.

62. And on account of the declaration of a quality being common (to all the Vedas).

The text 'By means of that syllable the threefold knowledge proceeds. With *Om* the Adhvaryu gives orders, with *Om* the Hot*ri* recites, with *Om* the Udgât*ri* sings,' which declares the pra*n*ava—which is a 'quality' of the meditation, in so far as it is its basis—to be common to the three Vedas, further shows that the meditation has to be employed in connexion with the sacrifice. For the meditation is connected with the Udgîtha, and the Udgîtha is an integral part of all sacrificial performances whatever.

Of the primâ facie view thus far set forth the next Sûtra disposes.

63. Rather not, as the text does not declare their going together.

It is not true that the meditations on the Udgîtha and the rest are bound to the sacrifices in the same way as the Udgîtha, and so on, themselves are; for Scripture does not declare that they go together with, i. e. are subordinate constituents of the Udgîtha, and so on. The clause 'Let him meditate on the Udgîtha' does not indeed itself state another qualification on the part of the agent (i. e. does not state that the agent in entering on the meditation is prompted by a motive other than the one prompting the sacrifice); but the subsequent clause, 'whatever he does with knowledge, with faith, with the Upanishad, that becomes more vigorous,' intimates that knowledge is the means to render the sacrificial work more efficacious, and from this it follows that the meditation is enjoined as a means towards effecting a result other than the result of the sacrifice. And hence the meditation cannot be viewed as a subordinate member of the Udgîtha, which itself is a subordinate member of the sacrifice. It rather has the Udgîtha for its basis only. He only indeed who is qualified for the sacrifice is qualified for the meditation, since the latter aims at greater efficaciousness of the sacrifice; but this does not imply that the meditation necessarily goes with the sacrifice. By the greater vigour of the sacrifice is meant its non-obstruction by some other sacrificial work of greater strength, its producing its effect without any delay.—The case of a statement such as 'he whose ladle is of par*n*a wood hears no evil sound' is different. There the text does not declare that the quality of consisting of parna wood is the direct means of bringing about the result of no evil sound being heard; hence there is no valid reason why that quality should not be subordinate to the ladle, which itself is subordinate to the sacrifice; and as it is not legitimate to assume for the mere subordinate constituents of a sacrifice special fruits (other than the general fruit of the sacrifice), the declaration as to no evil sound being heard is to be viewed as a mere arthavâda (i.e. a mere additional statement meant further to glorify the result of the sacrifice—of which the ladle made of parna wood is a subordinate instrument).

64. And because (Scripture) shows it.

A scriptural text, moreover, shows that the meditation is necessary for, and restricted to, the sacrificial performance. For the text 'A Brahman priest who knows this saves the sacrifice, the sacrificer, and all the officiating priests'—which declares that all priests are saved through the knowledge of the Brahman—has sense only on the understanding that that knowledge is not restricted to the Udgâtri, and so on (i. e. not to those priests who are engaged in carrying out the details of the sacrifices which are the 'bases' of the meditations).—The conclusion, therefore, is that those meditations are not restricted to the sacrifices, subordinate members of which serve as their 'bases.'—This terminates the adhikarana of 'like the bases.'

## FOURTH PÂDA.

1. The benefit to man results from thence, on account of scriptural statement; thus Bâdarâya*n*a thinks.

We have concluded the investigation into the oneness or diverseness of meditations—the result of which is to indicate in which cases the special points mentioned in several meditations have to be combined, and in which not. A further point now to be investigated is whether that advantage to the meditating devotee, which is held to accrue to him from the meditation, results from the meditation directly, or from works of which the meditations are subordinate members.—The Reverend Bâdarâya*n*a holds the former view. The benefit to man results from thence, i. e. from the meditation, because Scripture declares this to be so. 'He who knows Brahman reaches the Highest' (Taitt. Up. II, 1, 1); 'I know that great Person of sun-like lustre beyond the darkness. A man who knows him truly passes over death; there is no other path to go' (*S*vet. Up. III, 8); 'As the flowing rivers disappear in the sea, losing their name and their form, thus a man who possesses knowledge, freed from name and form, goes to the divine Person who is greater than the great' (Mu. Up. III, 2, 8).—Against this view the Pûrvapakshin raises an objection.

2. On account of (the Self) standing in a complementary relation, they are arthavâdas, as in other cases; thus *G*aimini opines.

What has been said as to Scripture intimating that a beneficial result is realised through the meditations by themselves is untenable. For texts such as 'he who knows Brahman reaches the Highest' do not teach that the highest aim of man is attained through knowledge; their purport rather is to inculcate knowledge of Truth on the part of a Self which is the agent in works prescribed. Knowledge, therefore, stands in a complementary relation to sacrificial works, in so far as it imparts to the acting Self a certain mystic purification; and the texts which declare special results of knowledge, therefore, must be taken as mere arthavâdas. 'As in the case of other things; so *G*aimini thinks,' i.e. as *G*aimini holds that in the case of substances, qualities, and so on, the scriptural declaration of results is of the nature of arthavâda.—But it has been shown before that the Vedânta-texts represent as the object to be attained, by those desirous of Release, on the basis of the knowledge imparted by them, something different from the individual Self engaged in action; cp. on this point Sû. I, 1, 15; I, 3, 5; I, 2, 3; I, 3, 18. And Sû. II, 1, 22 and others have refuted the view that Brahman is to be considered as non-different from the personal soul, because in texts such as 'thou art that' it is exhibited in co-ordination with the latter. And other Sûtras have proved that Brahman must, on the basis of numerous scriptural texts, be recognised as the inner Self of all things material and immaterial. How then can it be said that the Vedânta-texts merely mean to give instruction as to the true nature of the active individual soul, and that hence all meditation is merely subservient to sacrificial works?—On the strength of numerous inferential marks, the Pûrvapakshin replies, which prove that in the Vedânta-texts all meditation is really viewed as subordinate to knowledge, and of the declarations of co-ordination of Brahman and the individual soul (which must be taken to imply that the two are essentially of the same nature), we cannot help forming the conclusion that the real purport of the Vedânta-texts is to tell us of the true nature of the individual soul in so far as different from its body.—But, again it is objected, the agent is connected no less with ordinary worldly works than with works enjoined by the Veda, and hence is not invariably connected with sacrifices (i.e. works of the latter type); it cannot, therefore, be maintained that meditations on the part of the agent necessarily connect themselves with sacrifices in so far as they effect a purification of the sacrificer's mind!—There is a difference, the Pûrvapakshin rejoins. Worldly works can proceed also if the agent is non-different from the body; while an agent is qualified for sacred works only in so far as he is different from the body, and of an eternal non-changing nature. Meditations, therefore, properly connect themselves with sacrifices, in so far as they teach that the agent really is of that latter nature. We thus adhere to the conclusion that meditations are constituents of sacrificial actions, and hence are of no advantage by themselves.—But what then are those inferential marks which, as you say, fully prove that the Vedânta-texts aim at setting forth the nature of the individual soul?—To this the next Sûtra replies.

3. On account of (such) conduct being seen.

It is seen, viz. in Scripture, that those who knew Brahman busied themselves chiefly with sacrifices.—A*s*vapati Kaikeya had a deep knowledge of the Self; but when three *Ri*shis had come to him to receive instruction regarding the Self, he told them 'I am about to perform a sacrifice, Sirs' (*Kh.* Up. V, 11). Similarly we learn from Sm*ri*ti that *G*anaka and other princes deeply versed in the knowledge of Brahman applied themselves to sacrificial works, 'By works only *G*anaka and others attained to perfection'; 'He also, well founded in knowledge, offered many sacrifices.' And this fact—that those who know Brahman apply themselves to works chiefly—shows that knowledge (or meditation) has no independent value, but serves to set forth the true nature of the active Self, and thus is subordinate to work.—An even more direct proof is set forth in the next Sûtra.

4. On account of direct scriptural statement.

Scripture itself directly declares knowledge to be subordinate to works, 'whatever he does with knowledge, with faith, with the Upanishad, that is more vigorous.' Nor can it be said that this text refers, on the ground of leading subject-matter (prakara*n*a), to the Udgîtha only; for direct scriptural statement (*s*ruti) is stronger than subject-matter, and the words 'whatever he does with knowledge' clearly refer to knowledge in general.

5. On account of the taking hold together.

The text 'then both knowledge and work take hold of him' (B*ri*. Up. IV, 4, 2) shows that knowledge and work go together, and this going together is possible only if, in the manner stated, knowledge is subordinate to work.

6. On account of injunction for such a one.

That knowledge is subordinate to works follows therefrom also that works are enjoined on him only who possesses knowledge. For texts such as 'He who has learnt the Veda from a family of teachers,' &c. (*Kh*. Up. VIII, 15), enjoin works on him only who has mastered the sacred texts so as fully to understand their meaning—for this is the sense of the term 'learning' (adhyayana). Hence the knowledge of Brahman also is enjoined with a view to works only: it has no independent result of its own.

7. On account of definite rule.

Another argument for our conclusion is that the text 'Doing works here let a man desire to live a hundred years,' &c. (Î*s*. Up. II), expressly enjoins lifelong works on him who knows the Self. The general conclusion, therefore, is that knowledge (meditation) is merely auxiliary to works. Of this view the next Sûtra finally disposes.

8. But on account of the teaching of the different one, Bâdarâya*n*a's (view is valid); as this is seen.

Knowledge by itself benefits man; since Scripture teaches that the object of knowledge is the highest Brahman which, as it is of an absolutely faultless and perfect nature, is other than the active individual soul.

Bâdarâya*n*a, therefore, holds that knowledge has an independent fruit of its own. Let the inferential marks (referred to by the Pûrvapakshin) be; the direct teaching of the texts certainly refers to a being different from the

Self that acts; for we clearly see that their object is the highest creative Brahman with all its perfections and exalted qualities, which cannot possibly be attributed to the individual Self whether in the state of Release or of bondage: 'Free from evil, free from old age,' &c. &c. In all those texts there is not the slightest trace of any reference to the wretched individual soul, as insignificant and weak as a tiny glow-worm, implicated in Nescience and all the other evils of finite existence. And the fruit of that knowledge of the highest Person the texts expressly declare, in many places, to be immortality—which consists in attaining to Him. The view of knowledge by itself benefitting man therefore is well founded.—The Sûtras proceed to dispose of the so-called inferential marks.

9. But the declarations are equal.

The argument that knowledge must be held subordinate to work because we learn from Scripture that those who know Brahman perform sacrificial works, will not hold good; since, on the other hand, we also see that men knowing Brahman abandoned all work; cp. texts such as 'The *Ri*shis descended from Kavasha said: For what purpose should we study the Veda? for what purpose should we sacrifice?' As it thus appears that those who know Brahman give up works, knowledge cannot be a mere auxiliary to works.—But how can it be accounted for that those who know Brahman both do and do not perform works?—Works may be performed in so far as sacrifices and the like, if performed by one not having any special wish, stand in subordinate relation to the knowledge of Brahman; hence there is no objection to texts enjoining works. And as, on the other hand, sacrifices and such-like works when aiming at results of their own are opposed to the knowledge of Brahman which has Release for its only result, there is all the less objection to texts which suggest the non-performance of works. If, on the other hand, knowledge were subordinate to works, works could on no account be dispensed with.—Against the assertion that

Scripture directly declares knowledge to be subordinate to works the next Sûtra declares itself.

10. (It is) non-comprehensive.

The scriptural declaration does not refer to all meditations, but only to the meditation on the Udgîtha. In the clause 'what he does with knowledge,' the 'what' is in itself indefinite, and therefore must be defined as connecting itself with the Udgîtha mentioned in the previous clause, 'Let him meditate on the Udgîtha.' The sentence cannot be construed to mean 'whatever he does is to be done with knowledge,' but means 'that which he does with knowledge becomes more vigorous,' and *that which is* done with knowledge is the Udgîtha. The next Sûtra refutes the argument set forth in Sûtra 5.

11. There is distribution, as in the case of the hundred.

As knowledge and work have different results, the text 'of him knowledge and work lay hold' must be understood in a distributive sense, i. e. as meaning that knowledge lays hold of him to the end of bringing about its own particular result, and that so likewise does work. 'As in the case of a hundred,' i. e. as it is understood that, when a man selling a field and a gem is said to receive two hundred gold pieces, one hundred are given for the field and one hundred for the gem.

12. Of him who has merely read the Veda.

Nor is there any force in the argument that knowledge is only auxiliary to work because works are enjoined on him who possesses knowledge. For the text which refers to the man 'who has read the Veda' enjoins works on him who has merely *read* the texts, and *reading* there means nothing more than the apprehension of the aggregate of syllables called Veda, without any insight into their meaning. A man who has thus mastered the words of the Veda apprehends therefrom that it makes statements as to works having certain results, and then on his own account applies himself to the enquiry into the meaning of those declarations; he who is desirous of work applies himself to the knowledge of works; he who is desirous of Release applies himself to the knowledge of Brahman. And even if the injunction of *reading* were understood as prompting to the understanding of the text also, all the same, knowledge would not be a subsidiary to works. For *knowledge*, in the sense of the Upanishads, is something different from mere cognition of sense. In the same way as the performance of such works as the *G*yotish*t*oma sacrifice is something different from the cognition of the true nature of those works; so that vidyâ, which effects the highest purpose of man, i. e. devout meditation (dhyâna, upâsanâ), is something different from the mere cognition of the true nature of Brahman. Knowledge of that kind has not the most remote connexion even with works.

13. Not so, on account of non-specification.

Nor is it true that the text 'Doing works here,' &c., is meant to divert him who knows the Self from knowledge and restrict him to works. For there is no special reason to hold that that text refers to works as independent means of a desirable result: it may as well be understood to refer to works merely subordinate to knowledge. As he who knows the Self has to practise meditation as long as he lives, he may also have to practise, for the same period, works that are helpful to meditation. Having thus refuted the objection on the ground of the reason of the matter, the Sûtrakâra proceeds to give his own interpretation of the text.

14. Or the permission is for the purpose of glorification.

The *or* has assertive force. The introductory words of the Upanishad, 'Hidden in the Lord is all this,' show knowledge to be the subject-matter; hence the permission of works can aim only at the glorification of knowledge. The sense of the text therefore is—owing to the power of knowledge a man although constantly performing works is not stained by them.

15. Some also, by proceeding according to their liking.

In some *s*âkhâs, moreover, we read that he who possesses the knowledge of Brahman may, according to his liking, give up the state of a householder, 'What shall we do with offspring, we who have this Self and this world?' (B*ri*. Up. V, 4, 22.) This text also proves knowledge not to be subsidiary to works; for if it were so subsidiary, it would not be possible for him who knows Brahman to give up householdership (with all the works obligatory on that state) according to his liking.

16. And destruction.

There is moreover a Vedânta-text which declares the knowledge of Brahman to destroy work—good and evil—which is the root of all the afflictions of transmigratory existence: 'The knot of the heart is broken, all doubts are solved, all his works perish when He has been beheld who is high and low' (Mu. Up. II, 2, 8). This also contradicts the view of knowledge being subordinate to works.

17. And of him who is chaste; for in Scripture (this is declared).

The knowledge of Brahman belongs to those who have to observe chastity, and men living in that state have not to perform the Agnihotra, the Dar*s*apûr*n*amâsa, and similar works. For this reason also knowledge cannot be subsidiary to works.—But, it may be objected, there is no such condition of life; for texts such as 'he is to perform the Agnihotra as long as he lives,' declare men to be obliged to perform sacrifices and the like up to the end of their lives, and Sm*ri*ti texts contradicting Scripture have no authority.—To meet this the Sûtra adds 'for in Scripture.' The three stages of life are recognised in Scripture only; cp. texts such as 'Those who in the forest practise penance and faith' (*Kh*. Up. V, 10, 1); 'Wishing for that world only mendicants wander forth from their homes' (B*ri*. Up. IV, 4, 22). The text as to the lifelong obligatoriness of the Agnihotra is valid for those only who do not retire from worldly life.

18. A reference (only) *G*aimini (holds them to be), on account of absence of injunction; for (Scripture) forbids.

The argument for the three stages of life, founded on their mention in Vedic texts, has no force, since all those references are only of the nature of anuvâda. For none of those texts contain injunctive forms. The text 'There are three branches of sacred observance,' &c. (*Kh*. Up. II, 23, 1), is meant to glorify the previous meditation on Brahman under the form of the pra*n*ava, as appears from the concluding clause 'he who is firmly grounded in Brahman obtains immortality'; it therefore cannot mean to enjoin the three conditions of life as valid states. In the same way the text 'And those who in the forest practise penance and faith' refers to the statements previously made as to the path of the gods, and cannot therefore be meant to make an original declaration as to another condition of life. Scripture moreover expressly forbids that other condition, 'a murderer of men is he who removes the fire,' &c. There are therefore no conditions of life in which men are bound to observe chastity. This is the opinion of the teacher *G*aimini.

19. It is to be accomplished, Bâdarâya*n*a holds, on account of scriptural statement of equality.

Bâdarâya*n*a is of opinion that, in the same way as the condition of householdership, those other conditions of life also are obligatory; since in the section beginning 'there are three branches of sacred duty' all the three conditions of life are equally referred to, with a view to glorifying him who is firmly grounded in Brahman. The reference there made to the condition of the householder necessarily presupposes that condition to be already established and obligatory, and the same reasoning then holds good with regard to the other conditions mentioned. Nor must it be said that the special duties mentioned at the beginning of the section—sacrifice, study, charity, austerity, Brahma*k*arya—all of them belong to the state of the householder (in which case the text would contain no reference to the other conditions of life); for on that supposition the definite reference to a threefold division of duties, 'Sacrifice, &c. are the first, austerity the second, Brahma*k*arya the third,' would be unmeaning. The proper explanation is to take the words 'sacrifice, study, and charity' as descriptive of the condition of the householder; the word 'austerity' as descriptive of the duties of the Vaikhânasa and the wandering mendicant, who both practise mortification; and the word 'Brahma*k*arya' as referring to the duties of the Brahma*k*ârin. The term 'Brahmasa*m*stha' finally, in the concluding clause, refers to all the three conditions of life, as men belonging to all those conditions may be founded on Brahman. Those, the text means to say, who are destitute of this foundation on Brahman and only perform the special duties of their condition of life, obtain the worlds of the blessed; while he only who at the same time founds himself on Brahman attains to immortality.—In the text 'and those who in the forest,' &c. the mention made of the forest shows that the statement as to the path of the gods has for its presupposition the fact that that stage of life which is especially connected with the forest is one generally recognised.—So far it has been shown that the other stages of life are no less obligatory than that of the householder, whether we take the text under discussion as containing merely a reference to those stages (as established by independent means of proof) or as directly enjoining them. The next Sûtra is meant to show that the latter view is after all the right one.

20. Or an injunction, as in the case of the carrying.

As the second part of the text 'Let him approach carrying the firewood below the ladle; for above he carries it for the gods' (which refers to a certain form of the Agnihotra), although having the form of an anuvâda, yet must be interpreted as an injunction, since the carrying of firewood above is not established by any other injunction; so the text under discussion also must be taken as an injunction of the different stages of life (which are not formally enjoined elsewhere). No account being taken of the text of the *G*âbâlas, 'Having completed his studentship he is to become a householder,' &c., it is thus a settled conclusion that the texts discussed, although primarily concerned with other topics, must at the same time be viewed as proving the validity of the several conditions of life. From this it follows that the text enjoining the performance of the Agnihotra up to the end of life, and similar texts, are not universally binding, but concern those only who do not retire from worldly life.—The final conclusion therefore is that as the knowledge of Brahman is enjoined on those who lead a life of austerity (which does not require the performance of sacrifices and the like), it is not subordinate to works, but is in itself beneficial to man.—Here terminates the adhikara*n*a of 'benefit to man.'

21. If it be said that they are mere glorification, on account of their reference; not so, on account of the newness.

The following point is next enquired into. Are texts such as 'That Udgîtha is the best of all essences, the highest, holding the supreme place, the eighth' (*Kh.* Up. I, 1, 3) meant to glorify the Udgîtha as a constituent element of the sacrifice, or to enjoin a meditation on the Udgîtha as the best of all essences, and so on? The Pûrvapakshin holds the former view, on the ground that the text declares the Udgîtha to be the best of all essences in so far as being a constituent element of the sacrifice. The case is analogous to that of texts such as 'the ladle is this earth, the âhavanîya is the heavenly world,' which are merely meant to glorify the ladle and the rest as constituent members of the sacrifice.—This view the latter part of the Sûtra sets aside 'on account of newness.'

Texts, as the one referring to the Udgîtha, cannot be mere glorifications; for the fact of the Udgîtha being the best of essences is not established by any other means of proof, and the text under discussion cannot therefore be understood as a mere anuvâda, meant for glorification. Nor is there, in proximity, any injunction of the Udgîtha on account of connexion with which the clause declaring the Udgîtha to be the best of all essences could naturally be taken as an anuvâda (glorifying the thing previously enjoined in the injunctive text); while there is such an injunction in connexion with the (anuvâda) text 'The ladle is this earth,' and so on. We thus cannot but arrive at the conclusion that the text is meant to enjoin a meditation on the Udgîtha as being the best of all essences, and so on—the fruit of such meditation being an increase of vigour and efficacy on the part of the sacrifice.

22. And on account of the words denoting becoming.

That the texts under discussion have an injunctive purport also follows from the fact that they contain verbal forms denoting becoming or origination—'he is to meditate' and the like; for all such forms have injunctive force. All these texts therefore are meant to enjoin special forms of meditation.—Here terminates the adhikara*n*a of 'mere glorification.'

23. Should it be said that (the stories told in the Upanishads) are for the purpose of the Pâriplava; not so, since (certain stories) are specified.

We meet in the Vedânta-texts with certain stories such as 'Pratardana the son of Divodâsa came to the beloved abode of Indra,' &c., and similar ones. The question here arises whether the stories are merely meant to be recited at the A*s*vamedha sacrifice or to convey knowledge of a special kind.—The Pûrvapakshin maintains that as the text 'they tell the stories' declares the special connexion of those stories with the so-called pâriplava performance, they cannot be assumed to be mainly concerned with knowledge.—This view the Sûtra negatives, on the ground that not all stories of that kind are specially connected with the pâriplava. The texts rather single out special stories only as suitable for that performance; on the general injunction quoted above there follows an injunction defining *which* stories are to be told, 'King Manu, the son of Vivasvat,' &c. The stories told in the Vedânta-texts do not therefore form parts of the pâriplava performance, but are connected with injunctions of meditations.

24. This follows also from the textual connexion (of those stories with injunctions).

That those stories subserve injunctions of meditation is proved thereby also that they are exhibited in textual connexion with injunctions such as 'the Self is to be seen,' and so on. Their position therefore is analogous to that of other stories told in the texts, which somehow subserve injunctions of works, and are not merely meant for purposes of recitation.—Here terminates the adhikara*n*a of 'the pâriplava.'

25. For this very reason there is no need of the lighting of the fire and so on.

The Sûtras return, from their digression into the discussion of two special points, to the question as to those whose condition of life involves chastity. The above Sûtra declares that as persons of that class are referred to by Scripture as specially concerned with meditation ('He who is founded on Brahman reaches immortality;' 'those who in the forest,' &c.), their meditation does not presuppose a knowledge of the kindling of fire and so on, i. e. a knowledge of the Agnihotra, the Dar*s*apûr*n*amâsa, and all those other sacrifices which require the preliminary establishment of the sacred fires, but a knowledge of those works only which are enjoined for their special condition of life.—Here terminates the adhikara*n*a of 'the kindling of the fire.'

26. And there is need of all (works), on account

of the scriptural statement of sacrifices and the rest; as in the case of the horse.

If knowledge (meditation), without any reference to sacrifices and the like, is able to bring about immortality, it must be capable of accomplishing this in the case of householders also; and the mention made of sacrifices and the rest in texts such as 'Brâhma*n*as seek to know him by the study of the Veda, by sacrifice, by gifts' (B*ri*. Up. IV, 4, 22), does not prove sacrifices and so on to be auxiliary to knowledge, since the stress there lies (not on the sacrifices and so on, but) on the desire of knowledge.—Of this view the Sûtra disposes. In the case of householders, for whom the Agnihotra and so on are obligatory, knowledge presupposes all those works, since scriptural texts such as the one quoted directly state that sacrifices and the like are auxiliary to knowledge. 'They seek to know by means of sacrifices' can be said only if sacrifices are understood to be a means through which knowledge is brought about; just as one can say 'he desires to slay with a sword,' because the sword is admitted to be an instrument wherewith one can kill. What we have to understand by knowledge in this connexion has been repeatedly explained, viz. a mental energy different in character from the mere cognition of the sense of texts, and more specifically denoted by such terms as dhyâna or upâsana, i.e. meditation; which is of the nature of remembrance (i.e. representative thought), but in intuitive clearness is not inferior to the clearest presentative thought (pratyaksha); which by constant daily practice becomes ever more perfect, and being duly continued up to death secures final Release. Such meditation is originated in the mind through the grace of the Supreme Person, who is pleased and conciliated by the different kinds of acts of sacrifice and worship duly performed by the Devotee day after day. This is what the text 'they seek to know through the sacrifice' really means. The conclusion therefore is that in the case of householders knowledge has for its pre-requisite all sacrifices and other works of permanent and occasional obligation. 'As a horse.' As the horse, which is a means of locomotion for man, requires attendants, grooming, &c., so knowledge, although itself the means of Release, demands the co-operation of the different works. Thus the Lord himself says, 'The work of sacrifice, giving, and austerities is not to be relinquished, but is indeed to be performed; for sacrifices, gifts, and austerities are purifying to the thoughtful.' 'He from whom all beings proceed and by whom all this is pervaded—worshipping Him with the proper works man attains to perfection' (Bha. Gî. XVIII, 5; 46).—Here terminates the adhikara*n*a of 'the need of all.'

27. But all the same he must be possessed of calmness, subjection of the senses, &c., since those are enjoined as auxiliaries to that, and must necessarily be accomplished.

The question is whether the householder also must practise calmness and so on, or not. The Pûrvapakshin says he must not, since the performance of works implies the activity of the outer and inner organs of action, and since calmness and so on are of an exactly opposite nature.—This view the Sûtra sets aside. The householder also, although engaged in outward activity, must, in so far as he possesses knowledge, practise calmness of mind and the rest also; for these qualities or states are by Scripture enjoined as auxiliaries to knowledge, 'Therefore he who knows this, having become calm, subdued, satisfied, patient, and collected, should see the Self in Self' (B*ri*. Up. IV, 4, 23). As calmness of mind and the rest are seen, in so far as implying composure and concentration of mind, to promote the origination of knowledge, they also must necessarily be aimed at and practised. Nor can it be said that between works on the one side and calmness and so on on the other, there is an absolute antagonism; for the two have different spheres of application. Activity of the organs of action is the proper thing in the case of works enjoined; quiescence in the case of works not enjoined and such as have no definite purpose. Nor also can it be objected that in the case of works implying the activity of organs, calmness of mind and so on are impossible, the mind then being necessarily engrossed by the impressions of the present work and its surroundings; for works enjoined by Scripture have the power of pleasing the Supreme Person, and hence, through his grace, to cause the destruction of all mental impressions obstructive of calmness and concentration of mind. Hence calmness of mind and the rest are to be aimed at and practised by householders also.—Here terminates the adhikara*n*a of 'calmness' and so on.

28. And there is permission of all food in the case of danger of life; on account of this being seen.

In the meditation on prâ*n*a, according to the Vâ*g*a-saneyins and the *Kh*andogas, there is a statement as to all food being allowed to him who knows the prâ*n*a, 'By him there is nothing eaten that is not food' (B*ri*. Up. VI, 1, 14; and so on). A doubt here arises whether this permission of all food is valid for him who possesses the knowledge of prâ*n*a, in all circumstances, or only in the case of life being in danger.—The Pûrvapakshin holds the former view, on account of no special conditions being stated in the text.—This the Sûtra sets aside 'in the case of danger to life'; for the reason that, as the text shows, the eating of food of all kinds is permitted even for those who know Brahman itself—the knowledge of which of course is higher than that of prâ*n*a—only when their life is in danger. The text alluded to is the one telling how Ushasta *K*âkrâya*n*a, who was well versed in the knowledge of Brahman, once, when in great distress, ate unlawful food. We therefore conclude that what the text says as to all food being lawful for him who knows prâ*n*a, can refer only to occasions when food of any kind must be eaten in order to preserve life.

29. And on account of non-sublation.

The conclusion above arrived at is confirmed by the consideration that thus only those texts are not stultified which enjoin, for those who know Brahman, purity in matters of food with a view to the origination of knowledge of Brahman. Cp. 'when the food is pure the mind becomes pure' (*Kh*. Up. VII, 26, 2).

30. This is said in Sm*ri*ti also.

That for those as well who know Brahman, as for others, the eating of food of any kind is lawful only in case of extreme need, Sm*ri*ti also declares, 'He who being in danger of his life eats food from anywhere is stained by sin no more than the lotus leaf by water.'

31. And hence also a scriptural passage as to non-proceeding according to liking.

The above conclusion is further confirmed by a scriptural passage prohibiting licence of conduct on the part of any one. The text meant is a passage in the Sa*m*hitâ of the Ka*th*as, 'Therefore a Brâhma*n*a does not drink spirituous liquor, thinking "may I not be stained by sin."'—Here terminates the adhikara*n*a of 'the allowance of all food.'

32. The works of the â*s*ramas also, on account of their being enjoined.

It has been said that sacrifices and other works are auxiliary to the knowledge of Brahman. The doubt now arises whether those works are to be performed by him also who merely wishes to fulfil the duties of his â*s*rama, without aiming at final Release, or not. They are not, the Pûrvapakshin holds, for that things auxiliary to knowledge should stand in subordinate relation to a certain state of life would imply the contradiction of permanent and non-permanent obligation.—Of this view the Sûtra disposes, 'The works of the â*s*ramas also.' The works belonging to each â*s*rama have to be performed by those also who do not aim at more than to live according to the â*s*rama; for they are specifically enjoined by texts such as 'as long as life lasts he is to offer the Agnihotra'; this implies a permanent obligation dependent on life. And that the same works are also to be performed as being auxiliary to knowledge appears from the texts enjoining them in that aspect, 'Him they seek to know by the study of the Veda' (Bri. Up. IV, 4, 22); this the next Sûtra declares.

33. And on account of co-operativeness.

These works are to be performed also on account of their being co-operative towards knowledge in so far, namely, as they give rise to the desire of knowledge; and their thus being enjoined for a double purpose does not imply contradiction any more than the double injunctions of the Agnihotra, which one text connects with the life of the sacrificer and another text with his desire to reach the heavenly world.—Nor does this imply a difference of works —this the next Sûtra declares.

34. In any case they are the same, on account of twofold inferential signs.

There is no radical difference of works; but in any case, i. e. whether they be viewed as duties incumbent on the âsrama or as auxiliary to knowledge, sacrifices and other works are one and the same. For Scripture, in enjoining them in both these aspects, makes use of the same terms, so that we recognise the same acts, and there is no means of proof to establish difference of works.

35. And Scripture also declares (knowledge) not to be overpowered.

Texts such as 'By works of sacred duty he drives away evil' declare that sacrifices and similar works have the effect of knowledge 'not being overpowered,' i. e. of the origination of knowledge not being obstructed by evil works. Sacrifices and similar works being performed day after day have the effect of purifying the mind, and owing to this, knowledge arises in the mind with ever increasing brightness. This proves that the works are the same in either case.—Here terminates the adhikarana of 'the being enjoined' (of sacrifices, and so on).

36. Also in the case of those outside, as this is seen.

It has been declared that the members of the four â*s*ramas have a claim to the knowledge of Brahman, and that the duties connected with each â*s*rama promote knowledge. A doubt now arises whether those men also who, on account of poverty and so on, stand outside the â*s*ramas are qualified for the knowledge of Brahman, or not.—They are not, the Pûrvapakshin holds, since such knowledge is to be attained in a way dependent on the special duties of each â*s*rama; while those who do not belong to an â*s*rama are not concerned with â*s*rama duties.—This view the Sûtra rejects. Those also who do not stand within any â*s*rama are qualified for knowledge, 'because that is seen,' i. e. because the texts declare that men such as Raikva, Bhîshma, Sa*m*varta and others who did not belong to â*s*ramas were well grounded in the knowledge of Brahman. It can by no means be maintained that it is â*s*rama duties only that promote knowledge; for the text 'by gifts, by penance, by fasting, and so on' (B*ri*. Up. IV, 4, 22) distinctly declares that charity also and other practices, which are not confined to the â*s*ramas, are helpful towards knowledge. In the same way as in the case of those bound to chastity—who, as the texts show, may possess the knowledge of Brahman—knowledge is promoted by practices other than the Agnihotra and the like, so—it is concluded—in the case of those also who do not belong to any â*s*rama knowledge may be promoted by certain practices not exclusively connected with any â*s*rama, such as prayer, fasting, charity, propitiation of the divinity, and so on.

37. Sm*ri*ti also states this.

Sm*ri*ti also declares that men not belonging to an â*s*rama grow in knowledge through prayer and the like. 'Through prayer also a Brâhma*n*a may become perfect. May he perform other works or not, one who befriends all creatures is called a Brâhma*n*a' (Manu Sm*ri*. II, 17).

38. And there is the promotion (of knowledge) through special acts (of duty).

The above conclusion is founded not only on Reasoning and Sm*ri*ti; but Scripture even directly states that knowledge is benefited by practices not exclusively prescribed for the â*s*ramas, 'By penance, abstinence, faith, and knowledge he is to seek the Self' (Pr. Up. I, 10).

39. But better than that is the other also on account of an inferential mark.

Better than to be outside the â*s*ramas is the condition of standing within an â*s*rama. The latter state may be due to misfortune; but he who can should be within an â*s*rama, which state is the more holy and beneficial one. This follows from inference only, i.e. Sm*ri*ti; for Sm*ri*ti says, 'A Brâhma*n*a is to remain outside the â*s*ramas not even for one day.' For one who has passed beyond the stage of Brahma*k*arya, or whose wife has died, the impossibility to procure a wife constitutes the misfortune (which prevents him from belonging to an â*s*rama).—Here terminates the adhikara*n*a of 'widowers.'

40. But of him who has become that there is no becoming not that, according to *G*aimini also, on account of (Scripture) restraining from the absence of the forms of that.

The doubt here arises whether those also who have fallen from the state of life of a Naish*th*ika, Vaikhânasa or Pârivrâ*g*aka are qualified for the knowledge of Brahman or not.—They are so, since in their case, no less than in that of widowers and the like, the growth of knowledge may be assisted by charity and other practices not confined to â*s*ramas.—This primâ facie view the Sûtra sets aside. 'He who has become that,' i.e. he who has entered on the condition of a Naish*th*ika or the like 'cannot become not that,' i.e. may not live in a non-â*s*rama condition; since scriptural texts restrain men who once have entered the Naish*th*ika, &c., state 'from the absence of the forms of that,' i.e. from the discontinuance of the special duties of their â*s*rama. Compare texts such as 'He is to go into the forest, and is not to return from thence'; 'Having renounced the world he is not to return.' And hence persons who have lapsed from their â*s*rama are not qualified for meditation on Brahman. This view of his the Sûtrakâra strengthens by a reference to the opinion of *G*aimini.—But cannot a Naish*th*ika who, through some sin, has lapsed from his duties and position, make up for his transgression by some expiatory act and thus again become fit for meditation on Brahman?—To this point the next Sûtra refers.

41. Nor the (expiatory performance) described in the chapter treating of qualification; that being impossible on account of the Sm*ri*ti referring to such lapse.

Those expiatory performances which are described in the chapter treating of qualification (Pû. Mî. Sû. VI) are not possible in the case of him who has lapsed from the condition of a Naish*th*ika; since such expiations do not apply to him, as is shown by a Sm*ri*ti text referring to such lapse, viz. 'He who having once entered on the duties of a Naish*th*ika lapses from them, for such a slayer of the Self I do not see any expiatory work by which he might become clean.' The expiatory ceremony referred to in the Pûrva Mîmâ*m*sâ therefore applies to the case of other Brahma*k*ârins only.

42. A minor one, thus some; (and hence they hold) the existence (of expiation), as in the case of eating. This has been explained.

Some teachers are of opinion that even on the part of Naish*th*ikas and the rest the lapse from chastity constitutes only a minor offence which can be atoned for by expiatory observances; in the same way as in the case of the eating of forbidden food the same prâya*sk*itta may be used by the ordinary Brahma*k*ârin and by Naish*th*ikas and the rest. This has been stated by the Sm*ri*ti writer, 'For the others also (i. e. the Naish*th*ikas and so on) the same (rules and practices as those for the Upakurvâna) hold good, in so far as not opposed to their âsrama.'

43. But in either case (such men) stand outside; on account of Smriti and custom.

Whether the point under discussion constitutes a minor or a major offence, in any case those who have lapsed stand outside the category of those qualified for the knowledge of Brahman. For Smriti, i. e. the text quoted above, 'I see no expiatory performance by which he, a slayer of Brahman as he is, could become pure again,' declares that expiations are powerless to restore purity. And custom confirms the same conclusion; for good men shun those Naishthikas who have lapsed, even after they have performed prâyaskittas, and do not impart to them the knowledge of Brahman. The conclusion, therefore, is that such men are not qualified for knowing Brahman.—Here terminates the adhikarana of 'him who has become that.'

44. By the Lord (of the sacrifice), since Scripture declares a fruit—thus Âtreya thinks.

A doubt arises whether the meditations on such constituent elements of the sacrifice as the Udgîtha, and so on, are to be performed by the sacrificer (for whose benefit the sacrifice is offered), or by the officiating priests. Âtreya advocates the former view; on the ground of Scripture showing that in the case of such meditations as the one on the small ether within the heart, fruit and meditation belong to the same person, and that in the case of such meditations as the one on the Udgîtha the fruit belongs to the sacrificer (whence we conclude that the meditation also is his). Nor can it be said that the sacrificer is not competent for such meditation, for the reason that like the godohana vessel it is connected with an element of the sacrifice (which latter the priests only can perform). For the godohana vessel serves to bring water, and this of course none else can do but the Adhvaryu; while a meditation on the Udgîtha as being the essence of all essences can very well be performed by the Sacrificer—true though it be that the Udgîtha itself can be performed by the Udgât*ri* priest only.—Against this view the next Sûtra declares itself.

45. (They are) the priest's work, Au*d*ulomi thinks; since for that he is engaged.

The teacher Au*d*ulomi is of opinion that the meditation on the Udgîtha and the like is the work of the priest, since it is he who is engaged for the purpose of performing that which gives rise to the fruit, i. e. of the entire sacrifice with all its subordinate parts. Injunctions referring to the performance of the sacrifices such as 'he chooses the priests; he gives to the priests their fee' indicate that the entire sacrificial performance is the work of the priests, and that hence all activities comprised within it—mental as well as bodily—belong to the priests. Capability or non-capability does not constitute the criterion in this case. For although the meditations in question aim directly at the benefit of man (not at the greater perfection of the sacrifice), yet since they fall within the sphere of qualification of those who are qualified for the sacrifice, and since the sacrifice with all its subordinate elements has to be performed by the priests, and since the text 'whatever he does with knowledge that becomes more vigorous' declares knowledge to belong to the same agent as the works which are benefited by such knowledge, we conclude that those meditations also are the exclusive duty of the priests. In the case of the meditations on the small ether, &c., on the other hand, the text says nothing as to their having to be performed by priests, and we therefore assume in accordance with the general principle that 'the fruit belongs to the performer,' that the agent there is the person to whom Scripture assigns the fruit.—Here terminates the adhikara*n*a of 'the lord (of the sacrifice).'

46. There is injunction of other auxiliary means for him who is such, as in the case of injunction and so on; (the term *mauna* denoting) according to an alternative meaning a third something.

'Therefore let a Brâhma*n*a after he has done with learning wish to stand by a childlike state; and after having done with the childlike state and learning (he is) a Muni' (B*ri*. Up. III, 5). A doubt arises whether this text enjoins Muni-hood in the same way as it enjoins learning and the childlike state, or merely refers to it as something already established.—The Pûrvapakshin holds the latter view on the ground that as 'Muni-hood' and 'learning' both connote knowledge, the word 'Muni' merely refers back to the knowledge already enjoined in the phrase 'after he has done with learning.' For the text presents no word of injunctive force with regard to Muni-hood.—This view the Sûtra controverts. 'For him who is such,' i.e. for those who possess knowledge, 'there is an injunction of a different co-operative factor' 'in the same way as injunctions and the rest.' By the *injunctions* in the last clause we have to understand the special duties of the different â*s*ramas, i.e. sacrifices and the like, and also such qualifications as quietness of mind and the like; and by the 'and the rest' is meant the learning of and pondering on the sacred texts. Stated at length, the meaning of the Sûtra then is as follows—in the same way as texts such as 'him Brâhma*n*as seek to know through the reciting of the Veda, through sacrifices and charity, and so on,' and 'Quiet, subdued,' &c. (B*ri*. Up. IV, 4, 23) enjoin sacrifices and so on, and quietness of mind and the like, as helpful towards knowledge; and as texts such as 'the Self is to be heard, to be pondered upon' (B*ri*. Up. II, 4, 5) mention hearing and pondering as helpful towards knowledge; thus the text under discussion enjoins learning, a childlike state of mind, and Muni-hood as three further different auxiliaries of knowledge.—'Muni-hood' does *not* denote the same thing as 'learning'—this the Sûtra intimates by the clause 'alternatively a third,' i.e. as the word muni is observed alternatively to denote persons such as Vyâsa distinguished by their power of profound reflection (manana), the abstract term munihood denotes a third thing different from *learning* and the 'childlike state.' Hence, although the phrase 'then a Muni' does not contain a word of directly injunctive power, we must all the same understand it in an injunctive sense, viz. 'then let him be or become a Muni'; for Muni-hood is not something previously established. Such munihood is also something different from mere *reflection* (manana); it is the reiterated representation before the mind of the object of meditation, the idea of that object thus becoming more and more vivid. The meaning of the entire text therefore is as follows. A Brâhma*n*a is at first fully to master knowledge, i. e. he is to attain, by means of hearing and pondering, to the knowledge of Brahman in all its fulness and perfection. This is to be effected through the growth of purity of mind and heart, due to the grace of the Lord; for this Sm*ri*ti declares, 'Neither by the Vedas nor by austerities, and so on, can I be so seen—; but by devotion exclusive I may be known' (Bha. Gî. XI, 53-54); and Scripture also says, 'Who has the highest devotion for God' (*S*vet. Up. VI, 23), and 'That Self cannot be gained by the study of the Veda,' &c. 'He whom the Self chooses by him the Self is to be attained' (Ka. Up. I, 2, 23). After that 'he is to stand by a childlike state'; what this means will be explained further on. And after that he is to be a Muni, i. e. he is to fix his thoughts so exclusively and persistently on Brahman as to attain to the mode of knowledge called meditation. Having by the employment of these three means reached true knowledge he—the text goes on to say—having done with amauna and mauna is a Brâhma*n*a. Amauna, i. e. non-mauna, denotes all the auxiliaries of knowledge different from mauna: employing these and mauna as well he reaches the highest goal of knowledge. And, the text further says, there is no other means but those stated whereby to become such, i. e. a true Brâhma*n*a. The entire text thus evidently means to enjoin on any one standing within any â*s*rama learning, a childlike state, and mauna as auxiliary means of knowledge, in addition to sacrifices and the other special duties of the â*s*ramas.—But, an objection is raised, if knowledge, aided by pâ*nd*itya and so on, and thus being auxiliary to the action of the special duties of the â*s*ramas, is thus declared to be the means of attaining to Brahman; how then are we to understand the *Kh*ândogya's declaring that a man, in order to attain to Brahman, is throughout his life to carry on the duties of a householder [1]?—To this the next Sûtra replies.

47. But on account of the existence (of knowledge) in all, there is winding up with the householder.

As knowledge belongs to the members of all â*s*ramas it belongs to the householder also, and for this reason the Upanishad winds up with the latter. This winding up therefore is meant to illustrate the duties (not of the householder only, but) of the members of all â*s*ramas. Analogously in the text under discussion (B*ri*. Up. III, 5) the clause 'A Brâhma*n*a having risen above the desire for sons, the desire for wealth, and the desire for worlds, wanders about as a mendicant,' intimates duties belonging exclusively to the condition of the wandering beggar, and then the subsequent clause 'therefore let a Brâhma*n*a having done with learning,' &c., enjoins pâ*nd*itya, bâlya, and mauna (not as incumbent on the pârivrâ*g*aka only, but) as illustrating the duties of all â*s*ramas.—This the next Sûtra explicitly declares.

48. On account of the others also being taught, in the same way as the condition of the Muni.

The injunction, on him who has passed beyond all desire, of mauna preceded by pârivrâ*g*ya (wandering about as a mendicant), is meant to illustrate the duties of all â*s*ramas. For the duties of the other â*s*ramas are taught by Scripture no less than those of the Muni (and the householder). Similarly it was shown above that in the text 'There are three branches of sacred duty—he who is founded on Brahman goes to immortality,' the term 'founded on Brahman' applies equally to members of all â*s*ramas.—It therefore remains a settled conclusion that

[1] *Kh*. Up. VIII, 13.

the text under discussion enjoins pâ*nd*itya, bâlya, and mauna as being auxiliaries to knowledge in the same way as the other duties of the â*s*ramas, such as sacrifices and the rest.—Here terminates the adhikara*n*a of 'the injunction of other auxiliaries.'

49. Not manifesting itself; on account of the connexion.

In the text discussed above we meet with the word 'bâlya,' which may mean either 'being a child' or 'being and doing like a child.' The former meaning is excluded, as that particular age which is called childhood cannot be assumed at will. With regard to the latter meaning, however, a doubt arises, viz. whether the text means to say that he who aims at perfect knowledge is to assume all the ways of a child, as e.g. its wilful behaviour, or only its freedom from pride and the like.—The former, the Pûrvapakshin maintains. For the text gives no specification, and texts enjoining restraints of different kinds (on the man desirous of knowledge) are sublated by this specific text which enjoins him to be in all points like a child.—This view the Sûtra disposes of. 'Not manifesting itself.' That aspect of a child's nature which consists in the child not manifesting its nature (viz. in pride, arrogance, and so on), the man aiming at true knowledge is to make his own. 'On account of connexion,' i.e. because thus only the 'bâlya' of the text gives a possible sense. The other characteristic features of 'childhood' the texts declare to be opposed to knowledge, 'He who has not turned away from wicked conduct, who is not tranquil and attentive, or whose mind is not at peace, he can never attain the Self by knowledge' (Ka. Up. I, 2, 24); 'When food is pure, the whole nature becomes pure' (*Kh.* Up. VII, 26, 2), and so on.—Here terminates the adhikara*n*a of 'non-manifestation.'

50. What belongs to this world, there being no obstruction at hand; as this is seen.

Knowledge, as enjoined by Scripture, is twofold, having

for its fruit either exaltation within the sphere of the Sa*m*sâra, or final Release. With regard to the former the question arises whether it springs up only immediately subsequent to the good works which are the means to bring it about; or, indefinitely, either subsequent to such works or at some later time.—The Pûrvapakshin holds the former view. A man reaches knowledge through his good deeds only, as the Lord himself declares, 'Four kinds of men doing good works worship me,' &c. (Bha. Gî. VII, 16); and when those works have been accomplished there is no reason why the result, i. e. knowledge, should be delayed.—This view the Sûtra disposes of. 'What is comprised in this world,' i. e. meditation, the result of which is worldly exaltation, springs up immediately after the works to which it is due, in case of there being no other works of greater strength obstructing the rise of knowledge; but if there is an obstruction of the latter kind, knowledge springs up later on only. 'For this is seen,' i. e. Scripture acknowledges the effects of such obstruction; for a statement such as 'what he does with knowledge, with faith, with the Upanishad that is more vigorous,' means that works joined with the knowledge of the Udgîtha, and so on, produce their results without obstruction (which implies that the action of other works is liable to be obstructed).—Here terminates the adhikara*n*a of 'what belongs to this world.'

51. In the same way there is non-determination with regard to what has Release for its result; that condition being ascertained, that condition being ascertained.

So likewise in the case of the origination, through works of very great merit, of such knowledge as has for its result final Release, the time is not definitely fixed; for here also there is ascertained the same condition, viz. the termination of the obstruction presented by other works. A further doubt might in this case be raised on the ground that such works as give rise to knowledge leading to final Release are stronger than all other works, and therefore not liable to obstruction. But this doubt is disposed of by the reflection that even in the case of a man knowing Brahman there may exist previous evil deeds of overpowering strength.—The repetition of the last words of the Sûtra indicates the completion of the adhyâya.—Here terminates the adhikara*n*a of 'what has Release for its result.'

# FOURTH ADHYÂYA.

## FIRST PÂDA.

1. Repetition, on account of the text teaching (what has to be done more than once).

The third adhyâya was concerned with the consideration of meditation, together with its means. The Sûtras now enter on a consideration of the results of meditation, after a further preliminary clearing up of the nature of meditation. The question here arises whether the act of knowledge of Brahman inculcated in Vedânta-texts, such as 'He who knows Brahman reaches the Highest,' 'Having known him thus he passes beyond death,' 'He knows Brahman, he becomes Brahman,' is, in the view of Scripture, to be performed once only, or to be repeated more than once.—Once suffices, the Pûrvapakshin maintains; for as the text enjoins nothing more than knowing there is no authority for a repetition of the act. Nor can it be said that the act of knowing, analogous to the act of beating the rice-grains until they are freed from the husks, is a visible means towards effecting the intuition of Brahman, and hence must, like the beating, be repeated until the effect is accomplished; for knowing is not a visible means towards anything. Such acts as the *G*yotish*t*oma sacrifice and the knowledge inculcated in the Vedânta-texts are alike of the nature of conciliation of the Supreme Person; through whom thus conciliated man obtains all that is beneficial to him, viz. religious duty, wealth, pleasure, and final Release. This has been shown under III, 2, 38. The meaning of Scripture therefore is accomplished by performing the act of knowledge once only, as the *G*yotish*t*oma is performed once.—This view the Sûtra sets aside. The meaning of Scripture is fulfilled only by repeated acts of knowledge 'on account of teaching,' i. e. because the teaching of Scripture is conveyed by means of the term 'knowing' (vedana), which is synonymous with meditating (dhyâna, upâsana). That these terms are so synonymous appears from the fact that the verbs vid, upâs, dhyâi are in one and the same text used with reference to one and the same object of knowledge. A text begins, e. g. 'Let him meditate (upâsîta) on mind as Brahman,' and concludes 'he who knows (veda) this shines, warms,' &c. (*Kh.* Up. III, 18). In the same way the knowledge of Raikva is at first referred to by means of vid, 'He who knows (veda) what he knows is thus spoken of by me,' and further on by means of upâs, 'teach me the deity on which you meditate' (*Kh.* Up. IV, 1, 2). Similarly texts which have the same meaning as the text 'He who knows Brahman reaches the Highest'—viz. 'the Self should be seen, be heard, be reflected on, be meditated upon (nididhyâsitavya)'—'Then he sees him meditating (dhyâyamâna) on him as without parts' (Mu. Up. III, 1, 8), and others—use the verb dhyâi to express the meaning of vid. Now dhyâi means to think of something not in the way of mere representation (sm*ri*ti), but in the way of *continued* representation. And upâs has the same meaning; for we see it used in the sense of thinking with uninterrupted concentration of the mind on one object. We therefore conclude that as the verb 'vid' is used interchangeably with dhyâi and upâs, the mental activity referred to in texts such as 'he knows Brahman' and the like is an often-repeated continuous representation.

2. And on account of an inferential mark.

Inferential mark here means Sm*ri*ti. Sm*ri*ti also declares that that knowledge which effects Release is of the nature of continued representation. Meditation therefore has to be repeated.—Here terminates the adhikara*n*a of 'repetition.'

3. But as the Self; this (the ancient Devotees) acknowledge (since the texts) make (them) apprehend (in that way).

The following point is now taken into consideration. Is Brahman to be meditated upon as something different from the meditating Devotee, or as the Self of the latter?—The Pûrvapakshin holds the former view. For, he says, the individual soul *is* something different from Brahman; as has been proved under II, 1, 22; III, 4, 8; I, 1, 15. And Brahman must be meditated upon as it truly is; for if it is meditated upon under an unreal aspect, the attaining to Brahman also will not be real, according to the principle expressed in the text, 'According as a man's thought is in this world, so will he be when he has departed this life' (*Kh.* Up. III, 14, 1). This view the Sûtra sets aside. Brahman is rather to be meditated upon as being the Self of the meditating Devotee. As the meditating individual soul is the Self of its own body, so the highest Brahman is the Self of the individual soul—this is the proper form of meditation.—Why?—Because the great Devotees of olden times acknowledged this to be the true nature of meditation; compare the text 'Then I am indeed thou, holy divinity, and thou art me.'—But how can the Devotees claim that Brahman which is a different being is their 'Ego'?—Because the texts enable them to apprehend this relation as one free from contradiction. 'He who dwelling within the Self is different from the Self, whom the Self does not know, of whom the Self is the body, who rules the Self from within; he is thy Self, the inner ruler, the immortal one' (B*ri*. Up. III, 7, 3); 'In the True all these beings have their root, they dwell in the True, they rest in the True;—in that all that exists has its Self' (*Kh.* Up. VI, 8); 'All this indeed is Brahman' (*Kh.* Up. III, 14, 1)—all these texts teach that all sentient and non-sentient beings spring from Brahman, are merged in him, breathe through him, are ruled by him, constitute his body; so that he is the Self of all of them. In the same way therefore as, on the basis of the fact that the individual soul occupies with regard to the body the position of a Self, we form such judgments of co-ordination as 'I am a god—I am a man'; the fact of the individual Self being of the nature of Self justifies us in viewing our own Ego as belonging to the highest Self. On the presupposition of all ideas being finally based on Brahman and hence all words also finally denoting Brahman, the texts therefore make such statements of mutual implication as 'I am thou, O holy divinity, and thou art me.' On this view of the relation of individual soul and highest Self there is no real contradiction between two, apparently contradictory, sets of texts, viz. those on the one hand which negative the view of the soul being different from the highest Self, 'Now if a man meditates upon another divinity, thinking "the divinity is one and I another," he does not know'; 'He is incomplete, let him meditate upon Him as the Self'; 'Everything abandons him who views anything apart from the Self' (B*ri*. Up. I, 4, 10; 7—II, 4, 6); and on the other hand those texts which set forth the view of the soul and the highest Self being different entities, 'Thinking of the (individual) Self and the Mover as different' (*S*vet. Up. I, 6). For our view implies a denial of difference in so far as the individual 'I' is of the nature of the Self; and it implies an acknowledgment of difference in so far as it allows the highest Self to differ from the individual soul in the same way as the latter differs from its body. The clause 'he is incomplete' (in one of the texts quoted above) refers to the fact that Brahman which is different from the soul constitutes the Self of the soul, while the soul constitutes the body of Brahman.—It thus remains a settled conclusion that Brahman is to be meditated upon as constituting the Self of the meditating Devotee.—Here terminates the adhikara*n*a of 'meditation under the aspect of Self.'

4. Not in the symbol; for (the symbol) is not that one (i. e. the Self of the Devotee).

'Let a man meditate on mind as Brahman' (*Kh*. Up. III, 18, 1); 'He who meditates on name as Brahman' (*Kh*. Up. VII, 15)—with regard to these and similar meditations on outward symbols (pratîka) of Brahman there arises a doubt, viz. whether in them the symbols are to be thought of as of the nature of Self or not. The Pûrvapakshin holds the former view. For, he says, in form those injunctions do not differ from other injunctions of meditation on Brahman, and Brahman, as we have seen, constitutes the Self of the meditating Devotee.—This view the Sûtra sets aside. A pratîka cannot be meditated on as being of the nature of Self; for the pratîka is not the Self of the meditating Devotee. What, in those meditations, is to be meditated upon is the pratîka only, not Brahman: the latter enters into the meditation only as qualifying its aspect. For by a meditation on a pratîka we understand a meditation in which something that is not Brahman is viewed under the aspect of Brahman, and as the pratîka—the object of meditation—is not the Self of the Devotee it cannot be viewed under that form.—But an objection is raised here also, it is Brahman which is the real object of meditation; for where Brahman *may* be viewed as the object of meditation, it is inappropriate to assume as objects non-sentient things of small power such as the mind, and so on. The object of meditation therefore is Brahman viewed under the aspect of mind, and so on.—This objection the next Sûtra disposes of.

5. The view of Brahman, on account of superiority.

The view of Brahman may appropriately be superimposed on mind and the like; but not the view of mind, and so on, on Brahman. For Brahman is something superior to mind, and so on; while the latter are inferior to Brahman. To view a superior person, a prince e.g., as a servant would be lowering; while, on the other hand, to view a servant as a prince is exalting.—Here terminates the adhikara*n*a of 'symbols.'

6. And the ideas of Âditya and the rest on the member; on account of this being rational.

'He who shines up there let a man meditate on him as the Udgîtha' (*Kh*. Up. I, 3, 1).—With regard to this and similar meditations connected with subordinate parts of sacrificial performances there arises the doubt whether the idea of Âditya and so on has to be superimposed on the subordinate part of the sacrifice, such as the Udgîtha, or vice versâ (i. e. whether Âditya should be meditated upon under the aspect of the Udgîtha, or vice versâ).—The Pûrvapakshin holds the former view. For the general principle is that the lower being should be viewed under the aspect of the higher, and the Udgîtha and so on, which are parts of the sacrifices through which certain results are effected, are superior to the divinities who do not accomplish any result.—Of this view the Sûtra disposes. The ideas of Âditya and so on are to be superimposed on the 'members,' i. e. the Udgîtha and so on, which are constituent members of the sacrifices; because of the gods only superiority can be established. For it is only through the propitiation of the gods that sacrifices are capable of bringing about their results. The Udgîtha and the rest therefore are to be viewed under the aspect of Âditya and so on.—Here terminates the adhikara*n*a of 'the ideas of Âditya and so on.'

7. Sitting; on account of possibility.

It has been shown that that special form of cognitional activity which the Vedânta-texts set forth as the means of accomplishing final Release and which is called meditation (dhyâna; upâsana) has to be frequently repeated, and is of the nature of continued representation. A question now arises as to the way in which it has to be carried on.—There being no special restrictive rule, the Pûrvapakshin holds that the Devotee may carry it on either sitting or lying down or standing or walking.—This view the Sûtra sets aside. Meditation is to be carried on by the Devotee in a sitting posture, since in that posture only the needful concentration of mind can be reached. Standing and walking demand effort, and lying down is conducive to sleep. The proper posture is sitting on some support, so that no effort may be required for holding the body up.

8. And on account of meditation.

Since, as intimated by the text, 'the Self is to be meditated upon,' the mental activity in question is of the nature of meditation, it requires as its necessary condition concentration of mind. For by meditation is understood thought directed upon one object and not disturbed by the ideas of other things.

9. And with reference to immobility.

And it is with reference to their immobility that the earth and other inanimate things—the air, the sky, the waters, the mountains—may be spoken of as thinking, 'the earth thinks (dhyâyati) as it were,' and so on. Movelessness hence is characteristic of the intensely meditating person also, and such movelessness is to be realised in the sitting posture only.

10. And Sm*ri*ti texts say the same.

Sm*ri*ti texts also declare that he only who sits can meditate, 'Having placed his steady seat upon a pure spot, there seated upon that seat, concentrating his mind he should practise Yoga' (Bha. Gî. VI, 11–12).

11. Where concentration of mind (is possible), there; on account of there being no difference.

As the texts do not say anything as to special places and times, the only requisite of such places and times is that they should favour concentration of mind. This agrees with the declaration 'Let a man apply himself to meditation in a level and clean place, &c., favourable to the mind' (*S*vet. Up. II, 10).—Here terminates the adhikara*n*a of 'the sitting one.'

12. Up to death; for there also it is seen.

The question now arises whether the meditation described which is the means of final Release is to be accomplished within one day, or to be continued day after day, until death.—The view that it is accomplished within one day, as this will satisfy the scriptural injunction, is disposed of by the Sûtra. Meditation is to be continued until death. For Scripture declares that meditation has to take place 'there,' i. e. in the whole period from the first effort after meditation up to death, 'Acting thus as long as life lasts he reaches the world of Brahman.'—Here terminates the adhikara*n*a of 'up to death.'

13. On the attainment of this, there result the non-clinging and the destruction of later and earlier sins; this being declared.

Having, so far, elucidated the nature of meditation, the Sûtras now begin to consider the result of meditation. Scripture declares that on the knowledge of Brahman being attained a man's later and earlier sins do not cling to him but pass away. 'As water does not cling to a lotus leaf, so no evil deed clings to him who knows this' (*Kh.* Up. IV, 14, 3); 'Having known that he is not sullied by any evil deed' (B*ri*. Up. IV, 4, 23); 'As the fibres of the Ishîkâ reed when thrown into the fire are burnt, thus all his sins are burnt' (*Kh.* Up. V, 24, 3); 'All his works perish when He has been beheld who is high and low' (Mu. Up. II, 2, 8).—The doubt here arises whether this non-clinging and destruction of all sins is possible as the result of mere meditation, or not.—It is not possible, the Pûrvapakshin maintains; for Scripture declares, 'no work the fruits of which have not been completely enjoyed perishes even in millions of aeons.' What the texts, quoted above, say as to the non-clinging and destruction of works occurs in sections complementary to passages inculcating knowledge as the means of final Release, and may therefore be understood as somehow meant to eulogize knowledge. Nor can it be said that knowledge is enjoined as an expiation of sins, so that the destruction of sins could be conceived as resulting from such expiation; for knowledge—as we see from texts such as 'He who knows Brahman reaches the Highest,' 'He knows Brahman and he becomes Brahman'—is enjoined as a means to reach Brahman. The texts as to the non-clinging and destruction of sins therefore can only be viewed as arthavâda passages supplementary to the texts enjoining knowledge of Brahman.—This view the Sûtra sets aside. When a man reaches knowledge, the non-clinging and destruction of all sins may be effected through the power of knowledge. For Scripture declares the power of knowledge to be such that 'to him who knows this, no evil deed clings,' and so on. Nor is this in conflict with the text stating that no work not fully enjoyed perishes; for this latter text aims at confirming the power of works to produce their results; while the texts under discussion have for their aim to declare that knowledge when once sprung up possesses the power of destroying the capability of previously committed sins to produce their own evil results and the power of obstructing that capability on the part of future evil actions. The two sets of texts thus refer to different matters, and hence are not mutually contradictory. There is in fact no more contradiction between them than there is between the power of fire to produce heat and the power of water to subdue such heat. By knowledge effecting the non-clinging of sin we have to understand its obstructing the origination of the power, on the part of sin, to cause that disastrous disposition on the part of man which consists in unfitness for religious works; for sins committed tend to render man unfit for religious works and inclined to commit further sinful actions of the same kind. By knowledge effecting the destruction of sin, on the other hand, we understand its destroying that power of sin after it has once originated. That power consists, fundamentally, in displeasure on the part of the Lord. Knowledge of the Lord, which, owing to the supreme dearness of its object is itself supremely dear, possesses the characteristic power of propitiating the Lord—the object of knowledge—and thus destroys the displeasure of the Lord due to the previous commission of sins on the part of the knowing Devotee; and at the same time obstructs the origination of further displeasure on the Lord's part, which otherwise would be caused by sins committed subsequently to the origination of such knowledge. What Scripture says about sin not clinging to him who knows can however be understood only with regard to such sins as spring from thoughtlessness; for texts such as 'he who has not turned away from evil conduct' (Ka. Up. I, 2, 24) teach that meditation, becoming more perfect day after day, cannot be accomplished without the Devotee having previously broken himself off from all evil conduct.—Here terminates the adhikara*n*a of 'the reaching of that.'

14. Of the other also there is thus non-clinging; but at death.

It has been said that, owing to knowledge, earlier and subsequent sins do not cling and are destroyed. The same holds good also with regard to the other, i.e. to good works—they also, owing to knowledge, do not cling and are destroyed; for there is the same antagonism between knowledge and the fruit of those works, and Scripture moreover expressly declares this. Thus we read, 'Day and night do not pass that bank—neither good nor evil deeds. All sins turn back from it' (*Kh.* Up. VIII, 4, 1); 'He shakes off his good and evil deeds' (Kau. Up. I, 4). In the former of these texts good works are expressly designated as 'sin' because their fruits also are something not desirable for him who aims at Release; there is some reason for doing this because after all good works are enjoined by Scripture and their fruits are desired by men, and they hence might be thought not to be opposed to knowledge.—But even to him who possesses the knowledge of Brahman, the fruits of good deeds—such as seasonable rain, good crops, &c.—are desirable because they enable him to perform his meditations in due form; how then can it be said that knowledge is antagonistic to them and destroys them?—Of this point the Sûtra disposes by means of the clause 'but on death.' Good works which produce results favourable to knowledge and meditation perish only on the death of the body (not during the lifetime of the Devotee).—Here terminates the adhikara*n*a of 'the other.'

15. But only those former works the effects of which have not yet begun; on account of that being the term.

A new doubt arises here, viz. whether all previous good and evil works are destroyed by the origination of knowledge, or only those the effects of which have not yet begun to operate.—All works alike, the Pûrvapakshin says; for the texts—as e.g. 'all sins are burned'—declare the fruits of knowledge to be the same in all cases; and the fact of the body continuing to exist subsequently to the rise of knowledge may be accounted for by the force of an impulse once imparted, just as in the case of the revolution of a potter's wheel.—This view the Sûtra sets aside. Only those previous works perish the effects of which have not yet begun to operate; for the text 'For him there is delay as long as he is not delivered from the body' (*Kh.* Up. VI, 14, 2) expressly states when the delay of the body's death will come to an end (the body meanwhile continuing to exist through the influence of the anârabdhakârya works). There is no proof for the existence of an impetus accounting for the continuance of the body's life, other than the Lord's pleasure or displeasure caused by good or evil deeds.—Here terminates the adhikara*n*a of 'the works the operation of which has not yet begun.'

16. But the Agnihotra and the rest, (because they tend) to that effect only; this being seen.

It might here be said that special works incumbent on the several â*s*ramas, as e.g. the Agnihotra, need not be undertaken by those who are not desirous of their results, since these works also fall under the category of good works the result of which does not 'cling.'—This view the Sûtra sets aside. Such works as the Agnihotra must be performed, since there is no possibility of their results *not* clinging; for him who knows, those works have knowledge for their exclusive effect. This we learn from Scripture itself: 'Him Brâhma*n*as seek to know by the study of the Veda, by sacrifices, gifts, austerities, and fasting.' This passage shows that works such as the Agnihotra give rise to knowledge, and as knowledge in order to grow and become more perfect has to be practised day after day until death, the special duties of the â*s*rama also, which assist the rise of knowledge, have daily to be performed. Otherwise, those duties being omitted, the mind would lose its clearness and knowledge would not arise.—But if good works such as the Agnihotra only serve the purpose of giving rise to knowledge, and if good works previous to the rise of knowledge perish, according to the texts 'Having dwelt there till their works are consumed' (*Kh.* Up. V, 10, 5) and 'having obtained the end of his deeds' (B*ri*. Up. IV, 4, 6), to what then applies the text 'His sons enter upon his inheritance, his friends upon his good works'?—This point is taken up by the next Sûtra.

17. According to some (a class of good works) other than these, of both kinds.

The text quoted above from one *s*âkhâ ('His friends enter upon his good deeds') refers to good works other than the Agnihotra and the rest, the only object of which is to give rise to knowledge, viz. to all those manifold good works, previous or subsequent to the attaining to knowledge, the results of which are obstructed by other works of greater strength. Those texts also which declare works not to cling or to be destroyed through knowledge refer to this same class of works.—The next Sûtra recalls the fact, already previously established, that the results of works actually performed may somehow be obstructed.

18. For (there is the text) 'whatever he does with knowledge.'

The declaration made in the text 'whatever he does with knowledge that is more vigorous,' viz. that the knowledge of the Udgîtha has for its result non-obstruction of the result of the sacrifice, implies that the result of works actually performed *may* be obstructed. We thus arrive at the conclusion that the text of the *S*â*t*yâyanins, 'his friends enter upon his good works,' refers to those good works of the man possessing knowledge the results of which were somehow obstructed (and hence did not act themselves out during his lifetime, so that on his death they may be transferred to others).—Here terminates the adhikara*n*a of 'the Agnihotra and the rest.'

19. But having destroyed by fruition the other two sets he becomes one with Brahman.

There now arises the doubt whether the good and evil

works other than those the non-clinging and destruction of which have been declared, that is to say those works the results of which have begun to act, come to an end together with that bodily existence in which knowledge of Brahman originates, or with the last body due to the action of the works last mentioned, or with another body due to the action of the anârabdhakârya.—The second of these alternatives is the one to be accepted, for there is a text declaring that works come to an end with the deliverance of the Self from the current bodily existence: 'For him there is delay so long as he is not delivered (from the body), then he will become one with Brahman' (*Kh.* Up. VI, 14, 2).—This view the Sûtra sets aside. Having destroyed the other good and evil works the results of which had begun to operate by retributive experience he, subsequently to the termination of such retributive enjoyment, becomes one with Brahman. If those good and evil works are such that their fruits may be fully enjoyed within the term of one bodily existence, they come to an end together with the current bodily existence; if they require several bodily existences for the full experience of their results, they come to an end after several existences only. This being so, the deliverance spoken of in the text quoted by the Pûrvapakshin means deliverance from those works when completely destroyed by retributive enjoyment, not deliverance from bodily existence about which the text says nothing. All those works, on the other hand, good and evil, which were performed before the rise of knowledge and the results of which have not yet begun to operate—works which have gradually accumulated in the course of infinite time so as to constitute an infinite quantity—are at once destroyed by the might of the rising knowledge of Brahman. And works performed subsequently to the rise of such knowledge do not 'cling.' And, as Scripture teaches, the friends of the man possessing true knowledge take over, on his death, his good works, and his enemies his evil deeds. Thus there remains no contradiction.—Here terminates the adhikara*n*a of 'the destruction of the others.'

## SECOND PÂDA.

1. Speech with mind, on account of this being seen and of scriptural statement.

The Sûtras now begin an enquiry into the mode of the going to Brahman of him who knows. At first the soul's departure from the body is considered. On this point we have the text, 'When a man departs from hence his speech is combined (sampadyate) with his mind, his mind with his breath, his breath with fire, fire with the highest deity' (*Kh.* Up. VI, 6, 1). The doubt here arises whether the speech's being combined with the mind, referred to in the text, means that the function of speech only is merged in mind, or the organ of speech itself.—The Pûrvapakshin holds the former view; for, he says, as mind is not the causal substance of speech, the latter cannot be merged in it; while the scriptural statement is not altogether irrational in so far as the functions of speech and other organs are controlled by the mind, and therefore may be conceived as being withdrawn into it.—This view the Sûtra sets aside. Speech itself becomes combined with mind; since that is seen. For the activity of mind is observed to go on even when the organ of speech has ceased to act.—But is this not sufficiently accounted for by the assumption of the mere function of speech being merged in mind?—To this the Sûtra replies 'and on account of the scriptural word.' The text says distinctly that speech itself, not merely the function of speech, becomes one with the mind. And when the function of speech comes to an end, there is no other means of knowledge to assure us that the function only has come to an end and that the organ itself continues to have an independent existence. The objection that speech cannot become one with mind because the latter is not the causal substance of speech, we meet by pointing out that the purport of the text is not that speech is merged in mind, but only that it is combined or connected with it.

2. And for the same reason all follow after.

Because speech's becoming one with mind means only conjunction with the latter, not merging within it; there is also no objection to what Scripture says as to all other organs that follow speech being united with mind.—Here terminates the adhikara*n*a of 'speech.'

3. That mind in breath, owing to the subsequent clause.

That mind, i. e. mind united with all the organs unites itself with breath; not merely the function of mind. This appears from the clause following upon the text quoted above, 'mind (unites itself) with breath.' Here, however, a further doubt suggests itself. The text 'Mind is made of earth' declares earth to be the causal substance of mind, and the text 'that (viz. water) sent forth earth' declares water to be the causal substance of earth; while the further text 'breath is made of water' shows water to be the causal substance of breath. Considering therefore that in the text 'mind becomes united with breath' the term *breath* is naturally understood to denote the causal substance of breath, i. e. water, the appropriate sense to be given to the statement that mind is united with water is that mind is completely refunded into its own causal substance—so that the 'being united' would throughout be understood 'as being completely merged.'—The reply to this, however, is, that the clauses 'Mind is made of food, breath is made of water,' only mean that mind and breath are nourished and sustained by food and water, not that food and water are the causal substances of mind and breath. The latter indeed is impossible; for mind consists of aha*m*kâra, and as breath is a modification of ether and other elements, the word *breath* may suggest water.—Here terminates the adhikara*n*a of 'mind.'

4. That (is united) with the ruler, on account of the going to it, and so on.

As from the statements that speech becomes united with mind and mind with breath it follows that speech and mind are united with mind and breath only; so we conclude from the subsequent clause 'breath with fire' that breath becomes united with fire only.—Against this primâ facie view the Sûtra declares 'that breath becomes united with the ruler of the organs, i. e. the individual soul, on account of the going to it, and so on.' That breath goes to the individual soul, the following text declares, 'At the time of death all the prâ*n*as go to the Self of a man about to expire' (B*ri*. Up. IV, 3, 38). Similarly Scripture mentions the departure of prâ*n*a together with the soul, 'after him thus departing the prâ*n*a departs'; and again its staying together with the soul, 'What is that by whose departure I shall depart, and by whose staying I shall stay?' (Pr. Up. VI, 3). We therefore conclude that the text 'breath with fire' means that breath joined with the individual soul becomes united with fire. Analogously we may say in ordinary life that the Yamunâ is flowing towards the sea, while in reality it is the Yamunâ joined with the Gaṅgâ which flows on.—Here terminates the adhikara*n*a of 'the ruler.'

5. With the elements, this being stated by Scripture.

There arises the further question whether breath joined with the soul unites itself with fire only or with all the elements combined. — With fire, so much only being declared by Scripture!—This view the Sûtra sets aside. Breath and soul unite themselves with all the elements; for Scripture declares the soul, when moving out, to consist of all the elements—'Consisting of earth, consisting of water, consisting of fire.'—But this latter text explains itself also on the assumption of breath and soul uniting themselves in succession with fire and the rest, one at a time!—This the next Sûtra negatives.

6. Not with one; for both declare this.

Not with one; because each element by itself is incapable of producing an effect. Such incapability is declared by Scripture and tradition alike. The text 'Having entered these beings with this *g*îva soul let me reveal names and forms—let me make each of these three tripartite' (*Kh*. Up.

VI, 3) teaches that the elements were rendered tripartite in order to be capable of evolving names and forms; and of similar import is the following Smriti text, 'Possessing various powers these (elements), being separate from one another, were unable to produce creatures without combining. But having entered into mutual conjunction they, from the Mahat down to individual beings, produce the Brahma egg.' From this it follows that in the clause 'breath is united with fire' the word *fire* denotes fire mixed with the other elements. Breath and soul therefore are united with the aggregate of the elements.—Here terminates the adhikarana of 'the elements.'

7. And it is common up to the beginning of the way; and the immortality (is that which is obtained), without having burned.

Is this departure of the soul common to him who knows and him who does not know?—It belongs to him only who does not know, the Pûrvapakshin holds. For Scripture declares that for him who knows there is no departure, and that hence he becomes immortal then and there (irrespective of any departure of the soul to another place), 'when all desires which once dwelt in his heart are undone, then the mortal becomes immortal, then he obtains Brahman' (Bri. Up. IV, 4, 7). This view the Sûtra sets aside. For him also who knows there is the same way of passing out up to the beginning of the path, i. e. previously to the soul's entering the veins. For another text expressly declares that the soul of him also who knows passes out by way of a particular vein: 'there are a hundred and one veins of the heart; one of them penetrates the crown of the head; moving upwards by that a man reaches immortality, the others serve for departing in different directions' (*Kh.* Up. VIII, 6, 5). Scripture thus declaring that the soul of him who knows passes out by way of a particular vein, it must of course be admitted that it *does* pass out; and as up to the soul's entering the vein no difference is mentioned, we must assume that up to that moment the departure of him who knows does not differ from that of him who does not know. A difference however is stated with regard to the stage of the soul's entering the vein, viz. B*ri*. Up. IV, 4, 2, 'By that light the Self departs, either through the eye, or through the skull, or through other parts of the body.' As this text must be interpreted in agreement with the text relative to the hundred and one veins, the departure by way of the head must be understood to belong to him who knows, while the other modes of departing belong to other persons. The last clause of the Sûtra 'and the immortality, without having burned' replies to what the Pûrvapakshin said as to the soul of him who knows being declared by Scripture to attain to immortality then and there. The immortality referred to in the text 'when all desires of his heart are undone' denotes that non-clinging and destruction of earlier and later sins which comes to him who knows, together with the rise of knowledge, without the connexion of the soul with the body, and the sense-organs being burned, i. e. dissolved at the time.—'He reaches Brahman' in the same text means that in the act of devout meditation the devotee has an intuitive knowledge of Brahman.

8. Since, up to the union with that (i. e. Brahman) the texts describe the Sa*m*sâra state.

The immortality referred to must necessarily be understood as not implying dissolution of the soul's connexion with the body, since up to the soul's attaining to Brahman the texts describe the Sa*m*sâra state. That attaining to Brahman takes place, as will be shown further on, after the soul—moving on the path the first stage of which is light—has reached a certain place. Up to that the texts denote the Sa*m*sâra state of which the connexion with a body is characteristic. 'For him there is delay so long as he is not delivered (from the body); then he will be united' (*Kh*. Up. VI, 14, 2); 'Shaking off all evil as a horse shakes his hairs, and as the moon frees herself from the mouth of Râhu; having shaken off the body I obtain self, made and satisfied, the uncreated world of Brahman' (VIII, 13).

9. And the subtle (body persists), on account of

a means of knowledge, it being thus observed (in Scripture).

The bondage of him who knows is not, at that stage, dissolved, for this reason also that the subtle body continues to persist.—How is this known?—Through a means of knowledge, viz. because it is thus seen in Scripture. For Scripture states that he who knows, when on the path of the gods, enters into a colloquy with the moon and others, 'he is to reply,' &c. (Kau. Up. I, 3 ff.). This implies the existence of a body, and thence it follows that, at that stage, the subtle body persists. The state of bondage therefore is not yet dissolved.

10. Hence not in the way of destruction of bondage.

It thus appears that the text 'when all desires which once entered his heart are undone, then does the mortal become immortal, then he obtains Brahman' (B*ri*. Up. IV, 4, 7), does not mean such immortality as would imply complete destruction of the state of bondage.

11. And to that very (subtle body) (there belongs) the warmth, this only being reasonable.

It is observed that when a man is about to die there is some warmth left in some part or parts of the gross body. Now this warmth cannot really belong to the gross body, for it is not observed in other parts of that body (while yet there is no reason why it should be limited to some part); but it may reasonably be attributed to the subtle body which may abide in some part of the gross body (and into which the warmth of the entire gross body has withdrawn itself). We therefore conclude that this partial perception of warmth is due to the departing subtle body. This confirms the view laid down in Sûtra 7.—The next Sûtra disposes of a further doubt raised as to the departure of the soul of him who knows.

12. If it be said that on account of the denial (it is not so); we deny this. From the embodied soul; for (that one is) clear, according to some.

The contention that the soul of him who knows departs from the body in the same way as other souls do cannot be upheld, since Scripture expressly negatives such departure. For B*ri*. Up. IV, 4, at first describes the mode of departure on the part of him who does not possess true knowledge ('He taking to himself those elements of light descends into the heart' up to 'after him thus departing the Prâ*n*a departs'); then refers to his assuming another body ('he makes to himself another, newer and more beautiful shape'); then concludes the account of him who does not possess true knowledge ('having attained the end of these works whatever he does here, he again returns from that world to this world of action. So much for the man who desires'); and thereupon proceeds explicitly to deny the departure from the body of him who possesses true knowledge, 'But he who does not desire, who is without desire, free from desire, who has obtained his desire, who desires the Self only, of him (tasya) the prâ*n*as do not pass forth,—being Brahman only he goes into Brahman.' Similarly a previous section also, viz. the one containing the questions put by Ârtabhâga, directly negatives the view of the soul of him who knows passing out of the body. There the clause 'he again conquers death' introduces him who knows as the subject-matter, and after that the text continues: 'Yâ*gñ*avalkya, he said, when that person dies, do the prâ*n*as pass out of him (asmât) or not?—No, said Yâ*gñ*avalkya, they are gathered up in him (atraiva), he swells, inflated the dead lies' (B*ri*. Up. III, 2, 10–11). From these texts it follows that he who knows attains to immortality *here* (without his soul passing out of the body and moving to another place).—This view the Sûtra rejects. 'Not so; from the embodied soul.' What those texts deny is the moving away of the prâ*n*as from the embodied individual soul, not from the body. 'Of him (tasya) the prâ*n*as do not pass forth'—here the 'of him' refers to the subject under discussion, i. e. the embodied soul which is introduced by the clause 'he who does not desire,' not to the body which the text had not previously mentioned. The sixth case (tasya) here denotes the embodied soul as that which is connected with the prâ*n*as ('the prâ*n*as belonging to that, i. e. the soul, do not pass out'), not as that from which the passing out takes its start.—But why should the 'tasya' not denote the body as the point of starting ('the prâ*n*as do not pass forth from that (tasya), viz. the body')?—Because, we reply, the soul which is actually mentioned in its relation of connexion with the prâ*n*as (as indicated by tasya) suggests itself to the mind more immediately than the body which is not mentioned at all; if therefore the question arises as to the starting-point of the passing forth of the prâ*n*as the soul is (on the basis of the text) apprehended as that starting-point also (i. e. the clause 'the prâ*n*as of him do not pass forth' implies at the same time 'the prâ*n*as do not pass forth from him, i. e. from the soul'). Moreover, as the prâ*n*as are well known to be connected with the soul and as hence it would serve no purpose to state that connexion, we conclude that the sixth case which expresses connexion in general is here meant to denote the starting-point in particular. And no dispute on this point is really possible; since 'according to some' it is 'clear' that what the text means to express is the embodied soul as the starting-point of the prâ*n*as. The *some* are the Mâdhyandinas, who in their text of the B*ri*had-âra*n*yaka read 'na tasmât prâ*n*â utkrâmanti'—'the prâ*n*as do not pass forth *from him*' (the 'tasya' thus being the reading of the Kâ*n*va *S*âkhâ only).—But, an objection is raised, there is no motive for explicitly negativing the passing away of the prâ*n*as from the soul; for there is no reason to assume that there should be such a passing away (and the general rule is that a denial is made of that only for which there is a presumption).—Not so, we reply. The *Kh*ândogya-text 'For him there is delay only as long as he is not delivered (from the body); then he will be united' declares that the soul becomes united with Brahman at the time of its separation from the body, and this suggests the idea of the soul of him who knows separating itself at that very time (i. e. the time of death) from the prâ*n*as also. But this would mean that the soul cannot reach union with Brahman by means of proceeding on the path of the gods, and for this reason the B*ri*had-âra*n*yaka ('of him the prâ*n*as do not pass forth') explicitly declares that the prâ*n*as do not depart from the soul of him who knows, before that soul proceeding on the path of the gods attains to union with Brahman.

The same line of refutation would have to be applied to the arguments founded by our opponent on the question of Ârtabhâga, if that question be viewed as referring to him who possesses true knowledge. The fact however is that that passage refers to him who does *not* possess that knowledge; for none of the questions and answers of which the section consists favours the presumption of the knowledge of Brahman being under discussion. The matters touched upon in those questions and answers are the nature of the senses and sense objects viewed as graha and atigraha; water being the food of fire; the non-separation of the prâ*n*as from the soul at the time of death; the continuance of the fame—there called *name*—of the dead man; and the attainment, on the part of the soul of the departed, to conditions of existence corresponding to his good or evil deeds. The passage immediately preceding the one referring to the non-departure of the prâ*n*as merely means that death is conquered in so far as it is a fire and fire is the food of water; this has nothing to do with the owner of true knowledge. The statement that the prâ*n*as of the ordinary man who does not possess true knowledge do not depart means that at the time of death the prâ*n*as do not, like the gross body, abandon the *g*îva, but cling to it like the subtle body and accompany it.

13. Sm*ri*ti also declares this.

Sm*ri*ti also declares that the soul of him who knows departs by means of an artery of the head. 'Of those, one is situated above which pierces the disc of the sun and passes beyond the world of Brahman; by way of that the soul reaches the highest goal' (Yâ*gñ*. Sm*ri*. III, 167).—Here terminates the adhikara*n*a of 'up to the beginning of the road.'

14. With the Highest; for thus it says.

It has been shown that at the time of departure from the body the soul together with the organs and prâ*n*as unites itself with the subtle elements, fire and the rest; and the notion that the soul of him who knows forms an exception has been disposed of. The further question now arises whether those subtle elements move on towards producing their appropriate effects, in accordance with the works or the nature of meditation (of some other soul with which those elements join themselves), or unite themselves with the highest Self.—The Pûrvapakshin holds that, as in the case of union with the highest Self, they could not give rise to their peculiar effects, i. e. the experience of pleasure and pain, they move towards some place where they can give rise to their appropriate effects.—Of this view the Sûtra disposes. They unite themselves with the highest Self; for Scripture declares 'warmth in the highest Being' (*Kh.* Up. VI, 8, 6). And the doings of those elements must be viewed in such a way as to agree with Scripture. As in the states of deep sleep and a pralaya, there is, owing to union with the highest Self, a cessation of all experience of pain and pleasure; so it is in the case under question also.—Here terminates the adhikara*n*a of 'union with the Highest.'

15. Non-division, according to statement.

Is this union with the highest Self to be understood as ordinary 'merging,' i. e. a return on the part of the effected thing into the condition of the cause (as when the jar is reduced to the condition of a lump of clay), or as absolute non-division from the highest Self, such as is meant in the clauses preceding the text last quoted, 'Speech is merged in mind'? &c.—The former view is to be adopted; for as the highest Self is the causal substance of all, union with it means the return on the part of individual beings into the condition of that causal substance.—This view the Sûtra rejects. Union here means non-division, i. e. connexion of such kind that those subtle elements are altogether incapable of being thought and spoken of as separate from Brahman. This the text itself declares, since the clause 'warmth in the highest Being' is connected with and governed by the preceding clause 'Speech is merged in mind.' This preceding clause intimates a special kind of connexion, viz. absolute non-separation, and there is nothing to prove that the dependent clause means to express something different; nor is there any reason why at the time of the soul's departure those elements should enter into the causal condition; nor is there anything said about their again proceeding from the causal substance in a new creation.—Here terminates the adhikara*n*a of 'non-separation.'

16. A lighting up of the point of the abode of that; having the door illuminated by that (the soul), owing to the power of its knowledge and the application of remembrance of the way which is an element of that (viz. of knowledge), being assisted by him who abides within the heart, (passes out) by way of the hundred and first artery.

So far it has been shown that, up to the beginning of the journey, the souls of them as well who possess true knowledge as of those who do not, pass out of the body in the same way. Now a difference is stated in the case of those who have true knowledge. We have on this point the following text: 'There are a hundred and one arteries of the heart; one of them penetrates the crown of the head; moving upwards by that a man reaches immortality; the others serve for departing in different directions' (*Kh.* Up. VIII, 6, 5). The doubt here arises whether he who knows departs by this hundred and first artery in the top of the head, while those who do not know depart by way of the other arteries; or whether there is no definite rule on this point.—There is no definite rule, the Pûrvapakshin holds. For as the arteries are many and exceedingly minute, they are difficult to distinguish, and the soul therefore is not able to follow any particular one. The text therefore (is not meant to make an original authoritative statement as to different arteries being followed by different souls, but) merely refers in an informal way to what is already settled (viz. by the reason of the thing), i.e. the casual departure of any soul by any artery.—This view the Sûtra rejects 'By way of the hundred and first.' The soul of him who possesses true knowledge departs only by way of the hundred and first artery in the crown of the head. Nor is that soul unable to distinguish that particular artery. For, through the power of his supremely clear knowledge which has the effect of pleasing the Supreme Person, and through the application of remembrance of the way—which remembrance is a part of that knowledge—the soul of him who knows wins the favour of the Supreme Person who abides within the heart, and is assisted by him. Owing to this the abode of that, i.e. the heart which is the abode of the soul, is illuminated, lit up at its tip, and thus, through the grace of the Supreme Soul, the individual soul has the door (of egress from the body) lit up and is able to recognise that artery. There is thus no objection to the view that the soul of him who knows passes out by way of that particular artery only.—Here terminates the adhikara*n*a of 'the abode of that.'

17. Following the rays.

Scripture teaches that the soul of him who knows, after having passed forth from the heart by way of the hundred and first artery, follows the rays of the sun and thus reaches the disc of the sun: 'when he departs from this body he goes upwards by these rays only' (eva) (*Kh.* Up. VIII, 6, 5). The idea here suggests itself that the going of the soul cannot be exclusively bound to those rays, since when a man dies during the night it *cannot* follow the rays of the sun. Hence the text quoted above can refer only to a part of the actual cases.—This view the Sûtra rejects. The soul moves upwards, following the rays only; the text expressly asserting this by means of the 'eva'—which would be out of place were there any alternative. Nor is there any strength in the argument that the soul of him who dies at night cannot follow the rays as there are none. For in summer the experience of heat at night-time shows that there are present rays then also; while in winter, as generally in bad weather, that heat is overpowered by cold and hence is not perceived (although actually present). Scripture moreover states that the arteries and rays are at all times mutually connected: 'As a very long highway goes to two villages, so the rays of the sun go to both worlds, to this one and to the other. They stretch themselves forth from the sun and enter into these arteries; they stretch themselves forth from these arteries and enter into yonder sun' (*Kh.* Up. VIII, 6, 2).—As thus there are rays at night also, the souls of those who know reach Brahman by way of the rays only.—Here terminates the adhikara*n*a of 'the following up the rays.'

18. Should it be said, not in the night; we say, no; because the connexion persists as long as the body does. Scripture also declares this.

It is now enquired into whether the soul of him who, while having true knowledge, dies at night reaches Brahman or not. Although, as solar rays exist at night, the soul may move on at night also following those rays; yet, since dying at night is spoken of in the Sûtras as highly objectionable, we conclude that he who dies at night cannot accomplish the highest end of man, viz. attainment to Brahman. The Sûtras eulogize death occurring in day-time and object to death at night-time: 'Day-time, the bright half of the month and the northern progress of the sun are excellent for those about to die; the contrary times are unfavourable.' According to this, their different nature, dying in day-time may be assumed to lead to a superior state of existence, and dying at night to an inferior state. He who dies at night cannot therefore ascend to Brahman.—This view the Sûtra refutes: 'Because, in the case of him who knows, the connexion with works exists as long as the body does.' This is to say—since those works which have not yet begun to produce their results and which are the cause of future inferior states of existence are destroyed by the contact with knowledge, while at the same time later works do not 'cling' (also owing to the presence of true knowledge), and those works which have begun to act come to an end with the existence of the last body; there is no reason why he who knows should remain in bondage, and hence he reaches Brahman even if dying at night-time. Scripture also declares this, 'for him there is delay only as long as he is not freed from the body, then he will be united.' The text which praises the advantages of night-time, the light half of the month, &c., therefore must be understood as referring to those who do not possess true knowledge.—Here terminates the adhikara*n*a of 'night.'

19. For the same reason also during the southern progress of the sun.

The reasoning stated above also proves that the owner of true knowledge who may happen to die during the southern progress of the sun reaches Brahman. A further doubt, however, arises here. The text 'He who dies during the sun's southern progress reaches the greatness of the Fathers and union with the moon' (Mahânâr. Up. 25) declares that he who dies during the southern progress reaches the moon; and the other text 'when this ceases they return again the same way' (B*ri*. Up. VI, 2, 16) states that he returns again to the earth. We further know that Bhîshma and others, although fully possessing the knowledge of Brahman, put off their death until the beginning of the northern progress. All this seems to prove that he who dies during the southern progress does not reach Brahman.—This doubt we dispose of as follows. Those only who do not possess true knowledge return from the moon; while he who has such knowledge does not return even after he has gone to the moon. For a complementary clause in the Mahânârâya*n*a Up., 'from there he reaches the greatness of Brahman,' shows that the abode in the moon forms for him, who having died during the southern progress wishes to reach Brahman, a mere stage of rest. And even if there were no such complementary passage, it would follow from the previously stated absence of any reason for bondage that the going of the wise man's soul to the moon in no way precludes his reaching Brahman. Bhîshma and others who through the power of Yoga were able to choose the time of their death put it off until the beginning of the northern progress in order to proclaim before the world the excellence of that season and thus to promote pious faith and practice.—But we also meet with an authoritative statement made with reference to wise men about to die, as to difference of time of death being the cause of a man either returning or not returning to this world, 'I will declare at which time the Yogins departing return not, and also the time at which they return. The fire, the light, the day, the bright fortnight, the six months of the sun's northern progress—the knowers of Brahman departing there go to Brahman. The smoke, the night, the dark fortnight, the six months of the southern progress—the Yogin departing there having reached the light of the moon returns again. These are held to be the perpetual paths of the world—the white and the black; by the one man goes not to return, by the other he returns again' (Bha. Gî. VIII, 23-26).—To this point the next Sûtra refers.

20. And those two (paths) are, with a view to the Yogins, mentioned as to be remembered.

The text quoted does not state an injunction for those about to die, of a special time of death; but there are rather mentioned in it those two matters belonging to Sm*ri*ti and therefore to be remembered, viz. the two paths —the path of the Gods and the path of the Fathers— with a view to those who know and practise Yoga; the text intimating that Yogins should daily think of those paths which are included in Yoga meditation. In agreement herewith the text concludes, 'Knowing these two paths no Yogin is ever deluded. Hence in all times, O Ar*g*una, be engaged in Yoga' (Bha. Gî. VIII, 27). Through the terms 'the fire, the light,' 'the smoke, the night,' &c. the path of the Gods and the path of the Fathers are recognised. Where, in the beginning, the text refers to 'the time when,' the word 'time' must be understood to denote the divine beings ruling time, since Fire and the rest cannot be time. What the Bha. Gî. aims at therefore is to enjoin on men possessing true knowledge the remembrance of that path of the Gods originally enjoined in the text, 'they go to light' (*Kh.* Up. IV, 15, 10); not to determine the proper time of dying for those about to die.—Here terminates the adhikara*n*a of 'the southern progress.'

## THIRD PÂDA.

1. On the path beginning with light, that being known.

The Sûtras now go on to determine the road which the soul of the wise man follows, after having—assisted by the Person within the heart—passed out of the body by way of one particular artery. Now of that road various accounts are given in Scripture. There is a detailed account in the *Kh*ândogya (IV, 15), 'now whether people perform obsequies for him or not,' &c. Another account is given in the eighth book of the same Upanishad, 'then he moves upwards by those very rays' (VIII, 6, 5).

The Kaushîtakins again give a different account: 'He having reached the path of the Gods comes to the world of Agni,' &c. (Kau. Up. I, 3). Different again in the B*ri*had-âra*n*yaka: 'Those who thus know this and those who in the forest meditate on faith and the True,' &c. (B*ri*. Up. VI, 2, 15). The same Upanishad, in another place (V, 10), gives a different account: 'When the person goes away from this world he comes to the wind,' &c.—A doubt here arises whether all these texts mean to give instruction as to one and the same road—the first stage of which is light—having to be followed by the soul of the wise man; or whether they describe different roads on any of which the soul may proceed.—The Pûrvapakshin holds the latter view; for he says the roads described differ in nature and are independent one of the other.—This view the Sûtra disposes of. All texts mean one and the same road only, viz. the one beginning with light, and the souls proceed on that road only. For that road is known, i. e. is recognised in all the various descriptions, although it is, in different texts, described with more or less fulness. We therefore have to proceed here as in the case of the details (gu*n*a) which are mentioned in different meditations referring to one and the same object, i. e. we have to combine the details mentioned in different places into one whole. The two *Kh*ândogya-texts—the one in the Upakos*a*lavidyâ and the one in the Vidyâ of the five fires—describe exactly the same road. And in the Vidyâ of the five fires as given in the B*ri*had-âra*n*yaka the same road, beginning with light, is also described, although there are differences in minor points; we therefore recognise the road described in the *Kh*ândogya. And in the other texts also we everywhere recognise the divinities of certain stages of the road, Agni, Âditya, and so on.—Here terminates the adhikara*n*a of 'that which begins with light.'

2. From the year to Vâyu; on account of non-specification and specification.

In their description of the path beginning with light the *Kh*andogas mention the year between the months and the sun, 'from the months to the year, from the year to the sun' (*Kh.* Up. V, 10, 1); while the Vâ*g*asaneyins mention, in that very place, the world of the Gods, 'from the months to the world of the Gods, from the world of the Gods to the sun' (B*ri.* Up. VI, 2, 15). Now, as the two paths are identical, we have to supplement each by the additional item given in the other (and the question then arises whether the order of the stages be 1. months, 2. year, 3. world of the Gods, 4. sun; or 1. months, 2. world of the Gods, 3. year, 4. sun). The year and the world of the Gods are equally entitled to the place after the months in so far as textual declaration goes; for both texts say '*from* the months.' But we observe that the advance is throughout from the shorter periods of time to the longer ones ('from the day to the bright fortnight, from the bright fortnight to the six months of the northern progress'), and as therefore the year naturally presents itself to the mind immediately after the six months, we decide that the order is—months, year, world of the Gods, sun.—In another place (B*ri.* Up. V, 10) the Vâ*g*asaneyins mention the wind as the stage preceding the sun ('the wind makes room for him—he mounts upwards; he comes to the sun'). The Kaushîtakins, on the other hand, place the world of the wind subsequent to light, referred to by them as the world of Agni ('Having entered on the path of the Gods he comes to the world of Agni, to the world of the wind,' &c., Kau. Up. I, 3). Now in this latter text the fact of the world of the wind following upon light is to be inferred only from the succession of the clauses ('to the world of Agni'—'to the world of the wind'), while the 'upwards' in the text of the Vâ*g*asaneyins is a direct statement of succession given by the text itself; and as this latter order of succession has greater force than the former, we have to place, in the series of stages, the world of Vâyu directly before the world of the sun. But above we have determined that the same place (after the year and before the sun) has to be assigned to the world of the Gods also; and hence a doubt arises whether the world of the Gods and Vâyu are two different things—the soul of the wise man passing by them in optional succession—or one and the same thing—the soul coming, after the year, to Vâyu who is the world of the Gods.—They are different things, the Pûrvapakshin says; for they are generally known to be so. And there are definite indications in the text that the world of the Gods as well as Vâyu is to be placed immediately before the sun—this being indicated for Vâyu by the 'upwards' referred to above, and for the world of the Gods by the ablative case (devalokât) in the *Kh*ând. text, 'from the world of the Gods he goes to the sun'—and as thus there is no difference between the two, we conclude that the soul passes by them in either order it may choose.—This view the Sûtra negatives: 'From the year to Vâyu.' The soul, having departed from the year, comes to Vâyu. This is proved 'by non-specification and specification.' For the term 'the world of the Gods' is a term of general meaning, and hence can denote Vâyu in so far as being the world of the Gods; while on the other hand the term Vâyu specifically denotes that divine being only. The Kaushîtakins speak of 'the world of Vâyu'; but this only means 'Vâyu who at the same time is a world.' That Vâyu may be viewed as the world of the Gods is confirmed by another scriptural passage, viz.

'he who blows (Vâyu) is the houses of the Gods.'—Here terminates the adhikara*n*a of 'Vâyu.'

3. Beyond lightning there is Varu*n*a, on account of connexion.

According to the text of the Kaushîtakins the soul goes on to the world of Vâyu, to the world of Varu*n*a, to the world of Indra, to the world of Pra*g*âpati, to the world of Brahman. The doubt here arises whether Varu*n*a and the divinities of the following stages are to be inserted in the series after Vâyu, in agreement with the order of enumeration in the text of the Kaushîtakins; or at the end of the whole series as stated in the *Kh*ândogya Up. (IV, 15, 5), Varu*n*a thus coming after lightning.—The decision is in favour of the latter view because Varu*n*a, the god of waters, is naturally connected with lightning which dwells within the clouds.—This terminates the adhikara*n*a of 'Varu*n*a.'

4. Conductors, this being indicated.

The decision here is that light, Vâyu, and the rest mentioned in the texts as connected with the soul's progress on the path of the Gods are to be interpreted not as mere marks indicating the road, nor as places of enjoyment for the soul, but as divinities appointed by the Supreme Person to conduct the soul along the stages of the road; for this is indicated by what the *Kh*ândogya says with regard to the last stage, viz. lightning, 'There is a person not human, he leads them to Brahman.' What here is said as to that person not human, viz. that he leads the soul, is to be extended to the other beings also, light and the rest.—But if that not-human person leads the souls from lightning to Brahman, what then about Varu*n*a, Indra, and Pra*g*âpati, who, as was decided above, are in charge of stages beyond lightning? Do they also lead the soul along their stages?

5. From thence by him only who belongs to lightning, the text stating that.

The only leader from lightning up to Brahman is the not-human person connected with lightning; for the text states this directly. Varu*n*a, Indra, and Pra*g*âpati take part in the work in so far only as they may assist the person connected with lightning.—Here terminates the adhikara*n*a of 'the conductors.'

6. (Him who meditates on) the effected Brahman, (thus opines) Bâdari; because for him going is possible.

The following question now presents itself for consideration. Does the troop of conducting divinities, Agni and the rest, lead on those who meditate on the effected Brahman, i.e. Hira*n*yagarbha; or those only who meditate on the highest Brahman; or those who meditate on the highest Brahman and those who meditate on the individual Self as having Brahman for its Self?—The teacher Bâdari is of opinion that the divinities lead on those only who meditate on the effected Brahman. For he only who meditates on Hira*n*yagarbha can move; while a person meditating on the highest Brahman which is absolutely complete, all-knowing, present everywhere, the Self of all, cannot possibly be conceived as moving to some other place in order to reach Brahman; for him Brahman rather is something already reached. For him the effect of true knowledge is only to put an end to that Nescience which has for its object Brahman, which, in reality, is eternally reached. He, on the other hand, who meditates on Hira*n*yagarbha may be conceived as moving in order to reach his object, which is something abiding within a special limited place. It is he therefore who is conducted on by Agni and the other escorting deities.

7. And on account of (Brahman) being specified.

The text 'a person not human leads them to the worlds of Brahman' (B*ri*. Up. VI, 2, 15) by using the word 'world,' and moreover in the plural, determines the specification that the not-human person leads those only who meditate on Hira*n*yagarbha, who dwells within some particular world.

Moreover, the text 'I enter the hall of Pra*g*âpati, the house' (*Kh*. Up. VIII, 14) shows that he who goes on the path beginning with light aims at approaching Hira*n*yagarbha. But if this is so, there is a want of appropriate denotation in the clause, 'There is a person not human, he leads them to Brahman'; if Hira*n*yagarbha is meant, the text should say 'He leads them to Brahmâ (Brahmâ*n*am).'

8. But on account of nearness there is that designation.

Hira*n*yagarbha is the first created being (as declared by the text 'he who creates Brahmâ'); he thus stands near to Brahman, and therefore may be designated by the same term (viz. Brahman). This explanation is necessitated by the reasons set forth in the preceding Sûtras (which show that the real highest Brahman cannot be meant).—But, if the soul advancing on the path of the Gods reaches Hira*n*yagarbha only, texts such as 'This is the path of the Gods, the path of Brahman; those who proceed on that path do not return to the life of man' (*Kh*. Up. IV, 15, 6), and 'moving upwards by that a man reaches immortality' (VIII, 6, 6), are wrong in asserting that that soul attains to immortality and does not return; for the holy books teach that Hira*n*yagarbha, as a created being, passes away at the end of a dviparârdha-period; and the text 'Up to the world of Brahman the worlds return again' (Bha. Gî. VIII, 16) shows that those who have gone to Hira*n*yagarbha necessarily return also.

9. On the passing away of the effected (world of Brahmâ), together with its ruler, (the souls go) to what is higher than that; on account of scriptural declaration.

On the passing away of the effected world of Brahmâ, together with its ruler Hira*n*yagarbha, who then recognises his qualification for higher knowledge, the soul also which had gone to Hira*n*yagarbha attains to true knowledge and thus reaches Brahman, which is higher than that, i.e. higher than the effected world of Brahmâ. This is known from the texts declaring that he who proceeds on the path of light reaches immortality and does not return; and is further confirmed by the text, 'They all, reaching the highest immortality, become free in the world of Brahman (Brahmâ) at the time of the great end' (Mu. Up. III, 2, 6).

10. And on account of Sm*ri*ti.

This follows from Sm*ri*ti also, which declares 'when the pralaya has come and the end of the Highest, they all together with Brahman enter the highest place.'—For all these reasons Bâdari holds that the troop of the conducting deities, beginning with Light, leads the souls of those only who meditate on the effected Brahman, i.e. Hira*n*ya-garbha.

11. The Highest, *G*aimini thinks; on account of primariness of meaning.

The teacher *G*aimini is of opinion that those deities lead on the souls of those only who meditate on the highest Brahman. For in the text 'a person not human leads them to Brahman' the word *Brahman* is naturally taken in its primary sense (i.e. the highest Brahman); the secondary sense (i.e. the effected Brahman) can be admitted only if there are other valid reasons to refer the passage to the effected Brahman. And the alleged impossibility of the soul's going is no such valid reason; for although Brahman no doubt is present everywhere, Scripture declares that the soul of the wise frees itself from Nescience only on having gone to some particular place. That the origination of true knowledge depends on certain conditions of caste, â*s*rama, religious duty, purity of conduct, time, place, and so on, follows from certain scriptural texts, as e.g. 'Brâhma*n*as desire to know him through the study of the Veda' (B*ri*. Up. IV, 4, 22); in the same way it follows from the text declaring the soul's going to Brahman that the final realisation of that highest knowledge which implies the cessation of all Nescience depends on the soul's going to some particular place. The arguments founded on texts alleged to declare that the soul of the wise does not pass out of the body at all we have refuted above. The argument that the specification implied in the text which mentions *Brahman-worlds* clearly points to the effected Brahman, i.e. Hira*n*yagarbha, is equally invalid. For the compound 'the Brahman-world' is to be explained as 'the world which is Brahman'; just as according to the Pûrva Mîmâ*m*sâ the compound 'Nishâda-sthapati' denotes a sthapati who is a Nishâda (not a sthapati of the Nishâdas). A thing even which is known as one only may be designated by a plural form, as in a mantra one girdle is spoken of as 'the fetters of Aditi.' And as to the case under discussion, we know on the authority of Scripture, Sm*ri*ti, Itihâsa, and Purâ*n*a, that the wonderful worlds springing from the mere will of a perfect and omnipresent being cannot be but infinite.

12. And because Scripture declares it.

And Scripture moreover directly declares that the soul which has departed by way of the artery in the upper part of the head and passed along the path of the Gods reaches the highest Brahman: 'This serene being having risen from the body, having reached the highest light manifests itself in its own shape' (*Kh.* Up. VIII, 12, 3).—Against the contention that the text 'I enter the hall of Pra*g*âpati, the house' shows that he who proceeds on the path beginning with light aims at the effected Brahman, the next Sûtra argues.

13. And there is no aiming at the effected (Brahman).

The aim of the soul is not at Hira*n*yagarbha, but at the highest Brahman itself. For the complementary sentence 'I am the glorious among Brâhma*n*as' shows that what the soul aims at is the condition of the universal Self, which has for its antecedent the putting off of all Nescience. For this appears from the preceding text, 'As a horse shakes his hairs and as the moon frees herself from the mouth of Râhu; having shaken off the body may I obtain—the uncreated Brahman-world' declares that the Brahman-world, which is the thing to be reached, is something non-created, and explicitly states that reaching that world implies freedom from all bondage whatsoever.—It is for these reasons that *G*aimini holds that the deities speeding the soul on its way lead on him only who has the highest Brahman for the object of his meditation.

Now the Reverend Bâdarâya*n*a declares his own view, which constitutes the final conclusion in this matter.

14. Those not depending on symbols he leads, thus Bâdarâya*n*a thinks; there being a defect in both cases; and he whose thought is that.

Bâdarâya*n*a is of opinion that the deities lead those not depending on symbols, i.e. all meditating devotees other than those depending on symbols. That is to say, the view that those are led who meditate on the effected Brahman cannot be upheld; nor is there an exclusive rule that those only should be led on who meditate on the highest Brahman. The truth is that those are led who meditate on the highest Brahman, and also those who meditate on the Self (soul) as different from matter (Prak*ri*ti) and having Brahman for its true Self. Souls of both these kinds are led on to Brahman. Those on the other hand whose object of meditation is such things as name and so on, which fall within what is a mere effect of Brahman—such things being viewed either under the aspect of Brahman, just as some valiant man may be viewed under the aspect of a lion (which view expresses itself in the judgment 'Devadatta is a lion'); or by themselves (without reference to Brahman)—all those are not led on to Brahman. Why so? 'Because there is a defect in both cases,' i.e. in both the views rejected by Bâdarâya*n*a. The view that those are led who meditate on the effected Brahman is in conflict with texts such as 'having risen from this body and reached the highest light' (*Kh*. Up. VIII, 12, 3)—for the nature of the fruit depends on the nature of the meditation; and the view that those only are led to the highest Brahman who meditate on the highest Brahman, would stultify texts such as the one which expressly declares Agni and the rest of the deities to lead on those who possess the knowledge of the five fires ('Those who know this, viz. the Vidyâ of the five fires, and those who in the forest meditate on faith and austerity go to light—there is a person not human, he leads them to Brahman,' *Kh.* Up. V, 10). Both these views thus being defective, we adhere to the conclusion that the deities lead on to Brahman the two classes of souls mentioned above.—This the Sûtra further declares in the words 'he whose thought is that' (tatkratu*h*), the sense of which is that he whose thought is that reaches that, i.e. that the nature of what is reached depends on the nature of the meditation. This argument is founded on the text, 'According to what his thought is (yathâ-kratu*h*) in this world, so will he be when he has departed this life' (*Kh.* Up. III, 14), which implies the principle that what a soul after death attains is according to its thought and meditation in this life; and moreover we have direct scriptural statements to the effect that those who possess the knowledge of the five fires proceed on the path of the Gods, and that those who proceed on that path reach Brahman and do not return. Analogous reasoning proves that meditation on the soul as free from matter and having Brahman for its true Self also leads to the highest Brahman. In the case of those, on the other hand, who rely on the symbols (in which they meditatively contemplate Brahman), beginning with name and terminating with prâ*n*a ('He who meditates on name as Brahman,' *Kh.* Up. VII, 1 ff.), the meditation is not proved by texts of the two kinds previously mentioned to lead to Brahman; it rather is contaminated by an element not of the nature of intelligence, and hence—according to the principle that the result of a meditation is the same in nature as the meditation itself—the soul of the inferior devotee practising such meditation does not proceed by the path of light and does not reach Brahman.—That this distinction is declared by Scripture itself, the next Sûtra shows.

15. And Scripture declares the difference.

The text, 'He who meditates on name as Brahman, for him there is movement as he wishes as far as name extends,' &c. (*Kh.* Up. VII, 1 ff.), declares that those who meditate on the series of symbols beginning with name and ending with prâ*n*a attain to a result of limited nature and not depending on any particular path. Those therefore who meditate on the Intelligent either as mixed with the Non-intelligent or by itself, viewing it either under the aspect of Brahman or as separated from Brahman, are not led on by the conducting deities. On the other hand, it remains a settled conclusion that the deities speed on their way those who meditate on the highest Brahman and on the soul as separated from Prak*ri*ti and having Brahman for its true Self.—Here terminates the adhikara*n*a of 'the effected.'

## FOURTH PÂDA.

1. (On the soul's) having approached (the highest light) there is manifestation; (as we infer) from the word 'own.'

The Sûtras now proceed to consider the *kind* of superior existence (aisvarya) which the released souls enjoy.—The text says, 'Thus does that serene being, having risen from the body and having approached the highest light, manifest itself in its own form' (*Kh.* Up. VIII, 12, 3). Does this passage mean that the soul having approached the highest light assumes a new body, to be brought about then, as e.g. the body of a deva; or that it only manifests its own natural character?—The text must be understood in the former sense, the Pûrvapakshin holds. For otherwise the scriptural texts referring to Release would declare what is of no advantage to man. We do not observe that its own nature is of any advantage to the soul. In the state of dreamless sleep the body and the sense-organs cease to act, and you may say the pure soul then abides by itself, but in what way does this benefit man? Nor can it be said that mere cessation of pain constitutes the well-being of the soul which has approached the highest light, and that in this sense manifestation of its own nature may be called Release; for Scripture clearly teaches that the released soul enjoys an infinity of positive bliss, 'One hundred times the bliss of Pragâpati is one bliss of Brahman and of a sage free from desires'; 'for having tasted a flavour he experiences bliss' (Taitt. Up. II, 7). Nor can it be said that the true nature of the soul is consciousness of the nature of unlimited bliss which, in the Samsâra condition, is hidden by Nescience and manifests itself only when the soul reaches Brahman. For, as explained previously, intelligence which is of the nature of light cannot be hidden; hiding in that case would be neither more nor less than destruction. Nor can that which is mere light be of the nature of bliss; for bliss is pleasure, and to be of the nature of pleasure is to be such as to agree with the Self. But, if the Self is mere light, where is the being by which light is to be apprehended as agreeable to its own nature? (i. e. where is the knowing subject conscious of bliss?) He, therefore, who holds the Self to be mere light, can in no way prove that it is of the nature of bliss. If, moreover, that which the soul effects on approaching the highest light is merely to attain to its own true nature, we point out that that nature is something eternally accomplished, and that hence the declaration that 'it manifests (accomplishes) itself in its own nature' would be purportless. We hence conclude that on approaching the highest light the soul connects itself with a new form only then brought about. On this view the term 'accomplishes itself' is taken in its direct sense, and the expression 'in its own shape' also is suitable in so far as the soul accomplishes itself in a nature specially belonging to it and characterised by absolute bliss.—This view the Sûtra rejects. That special condition into which the soul passes on having, on the path of the Gods, approached the highest light is a manifestation of its own true nature, not an origination of a new character. For this is proved by the specification implied in the term 'own,' in the phrase 'in its own nature.' If the soul assumed a new body, this specification would be without meaning; for, even without that, it would be clear that the new body belongs to the soul.—Against the assertion that the soul's own true nature is something eternally accomplished, and that hence a declaration of that nature 'accomplishing itself' would be unmeaning, the next Sûtra declares itself.

2. The released one; on account of the promise.

What the text says about the soul accomplishing itself in its own form refers to the released soul which, freed from its connexion with works and what depends thereon, i. e. the body and the rest, abides in its true essential nature. —That essential nature no doubt is something eternally accomplished, but as in the Sa*m*sâra state it is obscured by Nescience in the form of Karman; the text refers to the cessation of such obscuration as 'accomplishment.'—How is this known?—'From the promise,' i. e. from the fact that the text promises to set forth such cessation. For Pragâpati when saying again and again, 'I will explain that further to you,' does so with a view to throw light on the individual soul—first introduced in the clause 'that Self which is free from sin, &c.' (VIII, 7, 1)—in so far as freed from all connexion with the three empirical conditions of waking, dreaming and dreamless sleep, and released from the body which is due to Karman and the cause of joy and sorrow. When, therefore, he concludes 'that serene being, i. e. the soul, having risen from this body and having approached the highest light accomplishes itself in its true form,' we understand that such 'accomplishment' means the final release, i. e. the cessation of all bondage, which is gained by the soul, previously connected with Karman, as soon as it approaches the highest light.—The Pûrvapakshin had said that as in the state of deep sleep the manifestation of the true nature of the soul is seen in no way to benefit man, Scripture, if declaring that Release consists in a manifestation of the true nature of the soul, would clearly teach something likewise not beneficial to man; and that hence the 'accomplishment in its own form' must mean the soul's entering on such a new condition of existence as would be a cause of pleasure, viz. the condition of a deva or the like. To this the next Sûtra replies.

3. The Self, on account of subject-matter.

The subject-matter of the whole section shows that by the Self manifesting itself in its own form there is meant the Self as possessing the attributes of freedom from all evil and sin and so on. For the teaching of Pragâpati begins as follows: 'the Self which is free from sin, free from old age, from death and grief, from hunger and thirst, whose desires and thoughts spontaneously realise themselves.' And that this Self which forms the subject-matter of the entire section is the individual Self we have shown under I, 3, 19. The manifestation of the true nature of the soul when reaching the highest light therefore means the manifestation of that Self which has freedom from sin and so on for its essential attributes—that nature being in the Samsâra state obscured through Nescience. When therefore at the moment of Release those essential qualities assert themselves, the case is one of manifestation of what already exists, not one of origination. Thus the reverend Saunaka says, 'As the lustre of the gem is not created by the act of polishing, so the essential intelligence of the Self is not created by the putting off of imperfections. As the well is not the cause of the production of rain water, but only serves to manifest water which already exists—for whence should that originate which is not?—thus knowledge and the other attributes of the Self are only manifested through the putting off of evil qualities; they are not produced, for they are eternal.' Intelligence, therefore, bliss, and the other essential qualities of the soul which were obscured and contracted by Karman, expand and thus manifest themselves when the bondage due to Karman passes away and the soul approaches the highest light. On this view of 'manifestation' there remains no difficulty.—Here terminates the adhikarana of 'on approaching manifestation.'

4. In non-division; because that is seen.

Is the soul, when it has reached the highest light and freed itself from all bondage, conscious of itself as separate from the highest Self or as non-separate in so far as being a mere 'mode' (prakâra) of that Self?—The former view is the right one. For Scriptural and Smriti texts alike declare that the released soul stands to the highest Self in the relation of fellowship, equality, equality of attributes, and all this implies consciousness of separation. Compare 'He attains all desires together with the all-knowing Brahman' (Taitt. Up. II, 1, 1); 'When the seer sees the shining maker, the Lord, the Person who has his source in Brahman; then, possessing perfect knowledge, and shaking off good and evil, free from all passions he reaches the highest equality' (Mu. Up. III, 1, 3); 'Taking their stand upon this knowledge they, attaining to an equality of attributes with me, are neither born at the time of a creation nor are they agitated when a pralaya takes place' (Bha. Gî. XIV, 2).—Against this view the Sûtra declares itself 'in non-division.' The released soul is conscious of itself as non-divided from the highest Brahman. 'For this is seen,' i. e. for the soul having reached Brahman and freed itself from the investment of Nescience sees itself in its true nature. And this *true nature* consists herein that the souls have for their inner Self the highest Self while they constitute the body of that Self and hence are *modes* (prakâra) of it. This is proved by all those texts which exhibit the soul and Brahman in co-ordination—'Thou art that,' 'this Self is Brahman'; 'In that all this has its Self'; 'All this in truth is Brahman'; and by other texts, such as 'He who dwells within the Self, whom the Self does not know, of whom the Self is the body,' &c.; and 'He who abides within, the ruler of creatures, he is thy Self'; as explained by us under Sûtra I, 4, 22. The consciousness of the released soul therefore expresses itself in the following form: 'I am Brahman, without any division.' Where the texts speak of the soul's becoming equal to, or having equal attributes with, Brahman, the meaning is that the nature of the individual soul—which is a mere mode of Brahman—is equal to that of Brahman, i. e. that on putting off its body it becomes equal to Brahman in purity. The text declaring that the soul 'attains all its desires together with Brahman' intimates that the soul, together with Brahman of which it is a mode, is conscious of the attributes of Brahman. The different texts are thus in no conflict. Nor, on this view of the soul being non-divided from Brahman in so far as being its mode, is there any difficulty on account of what is said about the soul under Sû. IV, 4, 8; or on account of the doctrines conveyed in II, 1, 22; III, 4, 8.—Here terminates the adhikara*n*a of 'non-division, on account of its being seen.'

5. In (a nature like) that of Brahman, thus *G*aimini thinks; on account of suggestion and the rest.

Owing to the fact that different texts give different accounts, the question now arises of what character that essential nature of the Self is in which it manifests itself on reaching Brahman. Is that nature constituted by freedom from evil and sin and the rest (i. e. the attributes enumerated *Kh.* Up. VIII, 7, 1); or by mere intelligence (vi*gñ*âna); or by both, there being no opposition between intelligence and those other attributes?—The teacher *G*aimini holds that the soul manifests itself in its Brahman character, i. e. in a character constituted by freedom from sin, and so on. These latter attributes are, in the text of the 'small lotus,' mentioned as belonging to Brahman (*Kh.* Up. VIII, 1, 5), and may hence be referred to as the 'Brahman' character. And that this Brahman character is the character of the released soul also follows from 'suggestion and the rest.' For freedom from all evil and the rest are, in the teaching of Pra*g*âpati, referred to as attributes of the soul (VIII, 7, 1). The 'and the rest' of the Sûtra refers to the activities of the released soul—laughing, playing, rejoicing, and so on (mentioned in VIII, 12, 3)—which depend on the power belonging to the soul in that state to realise all its ideas and wishes. It is for these reasons that *G*aimini holds that mere intelligence does not constitute the true nature of the released soul.

6. In the sole nature of intelligence; as that is its Self. Thus Au*d*ulomi thinks.

Intelligence (consciousness; *k*aitanya) alone is the true nature of the soul, and hence it is in that character only that the released soul manifests itself; this is the view of the teacher Au*d*ulomi. That intelligence only constitutes the true being of the soul, we learn from the express statement 'As a lump of salt has neither inside nor outside, but is altogether a mass of taste; so this Self has neither inside nor outside, but is altogether a mass of knowledge' (B*ri*. Up. IV, 5, 13). When, therefore, the text attributes to the soul freedom from evil and the rest, it does not mean to predicate of it further positive qualities, but only to exclude all the qualities depending on avidyâ—change, pleasure, pain, and so on.—For these reasons Au*d*ulomi holds that the released soul manifests itself as mere intelligence.—Next the teacher Bâdarâya*n*a determines the question by propounding his own view.

7. Thus also, on account of existence of the former qualities (as proved) by suggestion, Bâdarâya*n*a holds absence of contradiction.

The teacher Bâdarâya*n*a is of opinion that even thus, i. e. although the text declares the soul to have mere intelligence for its essential nature, all the same the previously stated attributes, viz. freedom from all sin, and so on, are not to be excluded. For the authority of a definite statement in the Upanishads proves them to exist ('That Self which is free from sin,' &c.) ; and of authorities of equal strength one cannot refute the other. Nor must you say that the case is one of essential contradiction, and that hence we necessarily must conclude that freedom from sin, and so on (do not belong to the true nature of the soul, but) are the mere figments of Nescience (from which the released soul is free). For as there is equal authority for both sides, why should the contrary view not be held? (viz. that the soul is essentially free from sin, &c., and that the *k*aitanya is non-essential.) For the principle is that where two statements rest on equal authority, that only which suffers from an intrinsic impossibility is to be interpreted in a different way (i. e. different from what it means on the face of it), so as not to conflict with the other. But while admitting this we deny that the text which describes the Self as a mass of mere knowledge implies that the nature of the Self comprises nothing whatever but knowledge. —But what then *is* the purport of that text?—The meaning is clear, we reply; the text teaches that the entire Self, different from all that is non-sentient, is self-illumined, i. e. not even a small part of it depends for its illumination on something else. The fact, vouched for in this text, of the soul in its entirety being a mere mass of knowledge in no way conflicts with the fact, vouched for by other texts, of its possessing qualities such as freedom from sin and so on, which inhere in it as the subject of those qualities; not any more than the fact of the lump of salt being taste through and through—which fact is known through the sense of taste—conflicts with the fact of its possessing such other qualities as colour, hardness, and so on, which are known through the eye and the other sense-organs. The meaning of the entire text is as follows—just as the lump of salt has throughout one and the same taste, while other sapid things such as mangoes and other fruit have different tastes in their different parts, rind and so on; so the soul is throughout of the nature of knowledge or self-illuminedness.—Here terminates the adhikara*n*a of 'that which is like Brahman.'

8. By the mere will; Scripture stating that.

Concerning the released soul Scripture states, 'He moves about there, laughing, playing, rejoicing, be it with women, or chariots, or relatives' (*Kh.* Up. VIII, 12, 3). The doubt here arises whether the soul's meeting with relatives and the rest presupposes an effort on its part or follows on its mere will—as things spring from the mere will of the highest Person.—An effort is required; for we observe in ordinary life that even such persons as kings and the like who are capable of realising all their wishes do not accomplish the effects desired without some effort.—Against this view the Sûtra says 'by the mere will.' For, in a previous passage, Scripture expressly says, 'He who desires the world of the Fathers, by his mere will the Fathers rise to receive him,' &c. (VIII, 2, 1). And there is no other text declaring the need of effort which would oblige us to define and limit the meaning of the text last quoted.

9. And for this very reason without another ruler.

Since the released soul realises all its wishes, it does not stand under another ruler. For to be under a ruler means to be subject to injunction and prohibition, and to be such is opposed to being free in the realisation of all one's wishes. Hence Scripture says, 'he is a Self-ruler' (*Kh.* Up. VII, 25).—Here terminates the adhikara*n*a of 'wishes.'

10. The absence, Bâdari holds; for thus Scripture says.

A doubt arises whether the Released has a body and sense-organs, or not; or whether he has them or not just as he pleases. The teacher Bâdari holds that body and sense-organs are absent; since the text declares this. The text—'as long as he is embodied there is no freedom from pleasure and pain; but when he is free from the body then neither pleasure nor pain touches him' (*Kh.* Up. VIII, 12, 1)—declares that pleasure and pain are necessarily connected with embodiedness; and the text—'having risen from this body and reached the highest light he manifests himself in his own shape' (VIII, 12, 3)—declares that the Released one is without a body.

11. The presence, *G*aimini holds; because the text declares manifoldness.

The teacher *G*aimini holds that the Released one has a body and senses; because the text declares manifoldness—'He is onefold, he is threefold, he is fivefold, he is sevenfold' (*Kh.* Up. VII, 26, 2). The Self which is one and indivisible cannot be manifold, and the various forms of manifoldness of which the text speaks therefore must depend on the body. The text which speaks of the absence of a body refers to the absence of that body only which is due to Karman; for this latter body only is the cause of pleasure and pain. Next the Reverend Bâdarâya*n*a decides this point by the declaration of his own view.

12. For this reason Bâdarâya*n*a (holds him to be) of both kinds; as in the case of the twelve days' sacrifice.

'For this reason,' i.e. for the reason that the text refers to the wish of the Released, the Reverend Bâdarâya*n*a is of opinion that the Released may, at his liking, be with or without a body. This satisfies both kinds of texts. The case is analogous to that of the twelve days' sacrifice which, on the basis of twofold texts—'Those desirous of prosperity are to celebrate the dvâdasâha,' and 'The priest is to offer the dvâdasâha for him who desires offspring'—belongs, according to difference of wish, either to the sattra or the ahîna class of sacrifices.—The next Sûtra declares that the body and the sense-organs of the Released are not necessarily created by the Released himself.

13. In the absence of a body, as in the state of dream; that being possible.

As in the absence of a body and other instruments of enjoyment created by himself, the Released may undergo experiences of pleasure by means of instruments created by the highest Person, the Released, although capable of realising all his wishes, may not himself be creative. As in the state of dream the individual soul has experiences depending on chariots and other implements created by the Lord ('He creates chariots, horses,' &c., B*ri*. Up. IV, 3, 10); thus the released soul also may have experience of different worlds created by the Lord engaged in playful sport.

14. When there is a body, as in the waking state.

When, on the other hand, the released soul possesses a body created by its own will, then it enjoys its various delights in the same way as a waking man does.—In the same way as the highest Person creates out of himself, for his own delight, the world of the Fathers and so on; so he sometimes creates such worlds for the enjoyment of the released souls. But sometimes, again, the souls using their own creative will-power themselves create their own worlds, which however are included within the sphere of sport of the highest Person (so that the souls in enjoying them do not pass beyond the intuition of Brahman).

But it has been taught that the soul is of atomic size; how then can it connect itself with many bodies?—To this question the next Sûtra replies.

15. The entering is as in the case of a lamp; for thus Scripture declares.

Just as a lamp, although abiding in one place only, enters through the light proceeding from it into connexion with many places; so the soul also, although limited to one place, may through its light-like consciousness enter into several bodies. It may do this as well as in this life the soul, although abiding in one spot of the body only, viz. the heart, pervades the whole body by means of its consciousness and thus makes it its own. There is however the following difference between the two cases. The non-released soul has its intellectual power contracted by the influence of Karman, and hence is incapable of that expansive pervasion without which it cannot identify itself with other bodies. The released soul, on the other hand, whose intellectual power is non-contracted is capable of extending as far as it likes, and thus to make many bodies its own. For Scripture declares, 'That living soul is to be known as part of the hundredth part of the point of a hair divided a hundred times, and yet it is capable of infinity' (*S*vet. Up. V, 9). The non-released soul is ruled by Karman, the released one only by its will—this is the difference.—But, a new difficulty is raised, Scripture declares that when the soul reaches Brahman all its inner and outer knowledge is stopped: 'Embraced by the highest Self the soul knows nothing that is without, nothing that is within' (B*ri*. Up. IV, 3, 21). How then can it be said to know all things?—To this the next Sûtra replies.

16. It refers either to dreamless sleep or to union (sampatti); for this is manifested.

Texts as the one last quoted do not refer to the released soul, but either to deep sleep or to 'union' (sampatti), i. e. the time of dying; the latter in accordance with the text 'then his speech is united (sampadyate) with his mind,—heat with the highest divinity' (*Kh*. Up. VI, 15, 1). In both those states the soul attains to the highest Self and is unconscious. That in the states of deep sleep and dying the soul is unconscious and that the released soul is all-knowing, Scripture reveals. The text 'In truth he thus does not know himself that he is I, nor does he know anything that exists. He is gone to utter annihilation. I see no good in this' (*Kh.* Up. VIII, 11, 1) declares that the soul is unconscious in the state of deep sleep; and a subsequent text in the same section declares the released soul to be all-knowing, 'He seeing these pleasures with the divine eye, i.e. the mind, rejoices' (VIII, 12, 5). The same is clearly stated in the text, 'He who sees this sees everything, and obtains everything everywhere' (VII, 26, 2). That at death there is unconsciousness appears from the text, 'having risen from these elements he vanishes again in them. When he has departed there is no more knowledge' (B*ri*. Up. IV, 5, 13). From all this it follows that the text as to the soul being held in embrace by the prâ*gñ*a Self refers either to deep sleep or death.—Here terminates the adhikara*n*a of 'non-being.'

17. With the exception of world-energy; on account of leading subject-matter and of non-proximity.

The doubt here presents itself whether the power of the released soul is a universal power such as belongs to the Supreme Person, extending to the creation, sustentation, and so on, of the worlds; or is limited to the intuition of the Supreme Person.—The Pûrvapakshin maintains the former view. For he says Scripture declares that the soul reaches equality with the Supreme Person: 'Free from stain he reaches the highest equality' (Mu. Up. III, 1, 3); and moreover Scripture ascribes to the released soul the power of realising all its thoughts. And these two conditions are not fulfilled unless the soul possess the special powers of the Lord with regard to the government, &c., of the world.—To this the Sûtra replies, 'with the exception of world-energy.' The released soul, freed from all that hides its true nature, possesses the power of intuitively beholding the pure Brahman, but does not possess the power of ruling and guiding the different forms of motion and rest belonging to animate and inanimate nature.—How is this known?—'From subject-matter.' For it is with special reference to the highest Brahman only that the text mentions ruling and controlling power over the entire world. 'That from whence these beings are born, that through which they live when born, that into which they enter at death, endeavour to know that; that is Brahman' (Taitt. Up. III, 1, 1). If such universal ruling and controlling power belonged to the released soul as well, it would not be used—as the text actually uses it—for defining Brahman; for all definition rests on special individual attributes. Analogously many other texts speak of universal ruling and controlling power with exclusive reference to the Supreme Person—'Being only this was in the beginning, &c.—it thought, may I be many' (*Kh.* Up. VI, 2); 'In the beginning this was Brahman, one only—it created the most excellent Kshattra,' &c. (B*ri.* Up. I, 4, 11); 'In the beginning all this was Self, one only—it thought, let me send forth these worlds' (Ait. Âr. II, 4, 1, 1); 'There was Nârâya*n*a alone, not Brahmâ, and so on.' 'He who dwelling within the earth,' &c. (B*ri.* Up. III, 7, 3).—This also follows 'from non-proximity'; for in all those places which speak of world-controlling power the context in no way suggests the idea of the released soul, and hence there is no reason to ascribe such power to the latter.

18. If it be said that this is not so, on account of direct teaching; we reply not so, on account of the texts declaring that which abides within the spheres of those entrusted with special functions.

But, an objection is raised, certain texts directly declare that the released soul also possesses 'world-energy.' Compare 'He becomes a self-ruler; he moves in all worlds according to his wishes' (*Kh.* Up. VII, 25, 2); 'He moves through these worlds, enjoying any food he wishes, and assuming any shape he wishes' (Taitt. Up. III, 10, 5). We cannot therefore accept the restriction laid down in the last Sûtra.—Not so, the latter half of the present Sûtra declares, 'on account of the texts declaring that which abides in the spheres of those entrusted with special functions.' The meaning of the texts quoted is that the released soul participates in the enjoyments connected with the spheres of Hira*n*yagarbha and other beings which are entrusted with special functions. The soul whose knowledge is no longer obstructed by Karman freely enjoys all the different worlds in which the power of Brahman manifests itself and thus is fully satisfied.—But if the released soul, no less than the soul implicated in the Sa*m*sâra, experiences enjoyments belonging to the sphere of change, it follows that the sum of its enjoyments is finite and limited, and that hence the released soul is no better off than the soul in the state of bondage!—Of this doubt the next Sûtra disposes.

19. That which is not within change; for thus Scripture declares the abiding (of the soul).

That which is not within change, i. e. the highest Brahman which is free from all change and of an absolutely perfect and blessed nature—this, together with the manifestations of its glory, is what forms the object of consciousness for the released soul. The worlds which are subject to change thus form objects for that soul's experience, in so far as they form part of Brahman's manifestation. For Scripture declares that the released soul thus abides within, i. e. is conscious of the changeless highest Brahman, 'when he finds freedom from fear and an abode in that which is invisible, incorporeal, undefined, unsupported, then he obtains the fearless' (Taitt. Up. II, 7). And that the world is contained within Brahman as its manifestation is declared in the text, 'In that all the worlds abide, and no one goes beyond' (Ka. Up. II, 5, 8). The meaning of the text stating that the Released freely move in all worlds, and similar texts, therefore is only that the released soul while conscious of Brahman with its manifestations experiences also the enjoyments, lying within the sphere of change, which abide in the world of Hira*n*yagarbha and similar beings; not that it possesses the world-energies—creative, ruling, and so on—which are the distinctive attribute of the highest Lord.

20. And thus Perception and Inference show.

That the energies connected with the rule of the entire world are exclusive attributes of the highest Person, Scripture and Smriti alike declare. Compare scriptural texts such as 'From fear of him the wind blows,' &c. (Taitt. Up. II, 8, 1); 'By the command of that Imperishable one sun and moon stand, held apart' (B*ri*. Up. III, 9); 'He is the lord of all, the king of all beings, the protector of all beings' (B*ri*. Up. IV, 4, 22). And Sm*ri*ti texts such as 'With me as Supervisor, Prak*ri*ti brings forth the Universe of the movable and the immovable, and for this reason the world ever moves round'; 'Pervading this entire Universe by a portion of mine I do abide' (Bha. Gî. IX, 10; X, 42). Scripture and Sm*ri*ti likewise declare that of the bliss which is enjoyed by the released soul the highest Person alone is the cause—'For he alone causes blessedness' (Taitt. Up. II, 7); 'He who serves me with unswerving devotion, surpasses these qualities and is fitted for becoming one with Brahman. For I am the abode of Brahman, of infinite immortality, of everlasting virtue, and of absolute bliss' (Bha. Gî. XIV, 26–27). The exalted qualities of the soul—freedom from evil and sin and so on—which manifest themselves in the state of Release no doubt belong to the soul's essential nature; but that the soul is of such a nature fundamentally depends on the Supreme Person, and on him also depends the permanency of those qualities; they are permanent in so far as the Lord himself on whom they depend is permanent. It is in the same way that all the things which constitute the means of enjoyment and sport on the part of the Lord are permanent in so far as the Lord himself is permanent. It thus appears that the equality to the Lord which the released soul may claim does not extend to the world-ruling energies.

21. And on account of the indication of the equality of enjoyment only.

The previous conclusion is confirmed by the further fact that the text directly teaches the released soul to be equal to Brahman in so far only as enjoying direct insight into the true nature of Brahman. 'He reaches all objects of desire, together with the all-knowing Brahman' (Taitt. Up. II, 1, 1).—The conclusion thus is that we have to shape our ideas as to the powers of the released soul in accordance with what the texts say as to the Lord only possessing the power of ruling and controlling the entire world, and that hence the latter power cannot be attributed to the soul.—But if the powers of the released soul altogether depend on the Lord, it may happen that He, being independent in all his doings, may will the released soul to return into the Sa*m*sâra.—Of this doubt the next Sûtra disposes.

22. Non-return, according to Scripture; non-return, according to Scripture.

We know from Scripture that there is a Supreme Person whose nature is absolute bliss and goodness; who is fundamentally antagonistic to all evil; who is the cause of the origination, sustentation, and dissolution of the world; who differs in nature from all other beings, who is all-knowing, who by his mere thought and will accomplishes all his purposes; who is an ocean of kindness as it were for all who depend on him; who is all-merciful; who is immeasurably raised above all possibility of any one being equal or superior to him; whose name is the *highest Brahman*. And with equal certainty we know from Scripture that this Supreme Lord, when pleased by the faithful worship of his Devotees—which worship consists in daily repeated meditation on Him, assisted by the performance of all the practices prescribed for each caste and â*s*rama—frees them from the influence of Nescience which consists of karman accumulated in the infinite progress of time and hence hard to overcome; allows them to attain to that supreme bliss which consists in the direct intuition of His own true nature: and after that does *not* turn them back into the miseries of Sa*m*sâra. The text distinctly teaching this is 'He who behaves thus all his life through reaches the world of Brahman and does not return' (*Kh.* Up. VIII, 15). And the Lord himself declares 'Having obtained me great-souled men do not come into rebirth, the fleeting abode of misery; for they have reached the highest perfection. Up to the world of Brahmâ the worlds return again, O Arguna; but having attained to me, O son of Kunti, there is no rebirth' (Bha. Gî. VIII, 15-16). As, moreover, the released soul has freed itself from the bondage of karman, has its powers of knowledge fully developed, and has all its being in the supremely blissful intuition of the highest Brahman, it evidently cannot desire anything else nor enter on any other form of activity, and the idea of its returning into the Samsâra therefore is altogether excluded. Nor indeed need we fear that the Supreme Lord when once having taken to himself the Devotee whom he greatly loves will turn him back into the Samsâra. For He himself has said, 'To the wise man I am very dear, and dear he is to me. Noble indeed are all these, but the wise man I regard as my very Self. For he, with soul devoted, seeks me only as his highest goal. At the end of many births the wise man goes to me, thinking all is Vâsudeva. Such great-souled men are rarely met with' (Bha. Gî. VII, 17-19).—The repetition of the words of the Sûtra indicates the conclusion of this body of doctrine. Thus everything is settled to satisfaction.—Here terminates the adhikarana of 'with the exception of the world-energies.'

Here terminates the fourth pâda of the fourth adhyâya of the commentary on the Sârîraka Mîmâmsâ, composed by the reverend teacher Râmânuga. This completes the fourth adhyâya, and the whole work; and the entire body of doctrine is thus brought to a conclusion.

---

# INDEX OF QUOTATIONS.

# INDEX OF SANSKRIT WORDS.

# INDEX OF NAMES AND SUBJECTS.

## TRANSLITERATION OF ORIENTAL ALPHABETS ADOPTED FOR THE TRANSLATIONS OF THE SACRED BOOKS OF THE EAST.

| CONSONANTS. | MISSIONARY ALPHABET. I Class. | II Class. | III Class. | Sanskrit. | Zend. | Pehlevi. | Persian. | Arabic. | Hebrew. | Chinese. |
|---|---|---|---|---|---|---|---|---|---|---|
| **Gutturales.** | | | | | | | | | | |
| 1 Tenuis | k | ... | .... | क | 𐬐 | [Pehlevi character] | ک | ك | כּ | k |
| 2 „ aspirata | kh | ... | .... | ख | 𐬑 | [Pehlevi character] | ... | ... | כ | kh |
| 3 Media | g | ... | .... | ग | 𐬔 | [Pehlevi character] | گ | ... | גּ | ... |
| 4 „ aspirata | gh | ... | .... | घ | 𐬖 | [Pehlevi character] | ... | ... | ג | ... |
| 5 Gutturo-labialis | q | ... | .... | ... | .... | ... | ق | ق | ק | ... |
| 6 Nasalis | ṅ (ng) | ... | .... | ङ | 𐬧 (ng)<br>𐬣 (N) | ... | ... | ... | ... | ... |
| 7 Spiritus asper | h | ... | .... | ह | 𐬵 (𐬓 *hv*) | [Pehlevi character] | ه | ه | ה | h, hs |
| 8 „ lenis | ’ | ... | .... | ... | .... | ... | ا | ا | א | ... |
| 9 „ asper faucalis | ‘h | ... | .... | ... | .... | ... | ح | ح | ח | ... |
| 10 „ lenis faucalis | ’h | ... | .... | ... | .... | ... | ع | ع | ע | ... |
| 11 „ asper fricatus | ... | ‘*h* | .... | ... | .... | ... | خ | خ | ח | ... |
| 12 „ lenis fricatus | ... | ’*h* | .... | ... | .... | ... | ... | ... | ... | ... |
| **Gutturales modificatae (palatales, &c.)** | | | | | | | | | | |
| 13 Tenuis | ... | *k* | .... | च | 𐬗 | [Pehlevi character] | چ | ... | ... | *k* |
| 14 „ aspirata | ... | *kh* | .... | छ | .... | ... | ... | ... | ... | *kh* |
| 15 Media | ... | *g* | .... | ज | 𐬘 | [Pehlevi character] | ج | ج | ... | ... |
| 16 „ aspirata | ... | *gh* | .... | झ | .... | ... | غ | غ | ... | ... |
| 17 „ Nasalis | ... | *ñ* | .... | ञ | .... | ... | ... | ... | ... | ... |

| CONSONANTS (*continued*). | MISSIONARY ALPHABET. I Class. | II Class. | III Class. | Sanskrit. | Zend. | Pehlevi. | Persian. | Arabic. | Hebrew. | Chinese. |
|---|---|---|---|---|---|---|---|---|---|---|
| 18 Semivocalis . . . . . . . . . . | y | . . . | . . . . | य | [illegible]; [illegible] [illegible] init. | و | ي | ي | י | y |
| 19 Spiritus asper . . . . . . . . . | . . . | (*ẏ*) | . . . . | . . . | . . . . | . . . | . . . | . . . | . . . | . . . |
| 20 „ lenis . . . . . . . . | . . . | (*ẏ*) | . . . . | . . . | . . . . | . . . | . . . | . . . | . . . | . . . |
| 21 „ asper assibilatus . . | . . . | *s* | . . . . | श | [illegible] | [illegible] | ش | ش | . . . | . . . |
| 22 „ lenis assibilatus . . | . . . | *z* | . . . . | . . . | [illegible] | [illegible] | ژ | . . . | . . . | *z* |
| **Dentales.** | | | | | | | | | | |
| 23 Tenuis . . . . . . . . . . . . . | t | . . . | . . . . | त | [illegible] | [illegible] | ت | ت | תּ | t |
| 24 „ aspirata . . . . . . . . | th | . . . | . . . . | थ | [illegible] | . . . | . . . | . . . | ת | th |
| 25 „ assibilata . . . . . . . | . . . | . . . | TH | . . . | . . . . | . . . | ث | ث | . . . | . . . |
| 26 Media . . . . . . . . . . . . . | d | . . . | . . . . | द | [illegible] | و | د | د | דּ | . . . |
| 27 „ aspirata . . . . . . . . | dh | . . . | . . . . | ध | [illegible] | . . . | . . . | . . . | ד | . . . |
| 28 „ assibilata . . . . . . . | . . . | . . . | DH | . . . | . . . . | . . . | ذ | ذ | . . . | . . . |
| 29 Nasalis . . . . . . . . . . . . . | n | . . . | . . . . | न | [illegible] | [illegible] | ن | ن | נ | n |
| 30 Semivocalis . . . . . . . . . | l | . . . | . . . . | ल | . . . . | [illegible] | ل | ل | ל | l |
| 31 „ mollis 1 . . . . . | . . . | *l* | . . . . | ळ | . . . . | . . . | . . . | . . . | . . . | . . . |
| 32 „ mollis 2 . . . . . | . . . | . . . | L | . . . | . . . . | . . . | . . . | . . . | . . . | . . . |
| 33 Spiritus asper 1 . . . . . . . | s | . . . | . . . . | स | [illegible] | [illegible] | س (ث) | س | שׂ | s |
| 34 „ asper 2 . . . . . . . | . . . | . . . | s (ʃ) | . . . | . . . . | . . . | . . . | . . . | ס | . . . |
| 35 „ lenis . . . . . . . . | z | . . . | . . . . | . . . | [illegible] | [illegible] | ز (ذ) | ز | ז | z |
| 36 „ asperrimus 1 . . . . | . . . | . . . | z (ʒ) | . . . | . . . . | . . . | ص | ص | צ | ʒ, ʒh |
| 37 „ asperrimus 2 . . . . | . . . | . . . | ẓ (ʒ) | . . . | . . . . | . . . | ض | . . . | . . . | . . . |

| | | | | | | | | | | |
|---|---|---|---|---|---|---|---|---|---|---|
| **Dentales modificatae (linguales, &c.)** | | | | | | | | | | |
| 38 Tenuis | ... | *t* | .... | ट | .... | ... | ط | ط | ט | ... |
| 39 " aspirata | ... | *th* | .... | ठ | .... | ... | ظ | ظ | ... | ... |
| 40 Media | ... | *d* | .... | ड | [illegible] | [illegible] | ... | ... | ... | ... |
| 41 " aspirata | ... | *dh* | .... | ढ | .... | ... | ... | ض | ... | ... |
| 42 Nasalis | ... | *n* | .... | ण | 𐬣 | ... | ... | ... | ... | ... |
| 43 Semivocalis | r | ... | .... | र | 𐬭 | [illegible] | ر | ر | ר | ... |
| 44 " fricata | ... | *r* | .... | ... | .... | ... | ... | ... | ... | *r* |
| 45 " diacritica | ... | ... | R | ... | .... | ... | ... | ... | ... | ... |
| 46 Spiritus asper | sh | ... | .... | ष | 𐬴 | [illegible] | ... | ... | ... | sh |
| 47 " lenis | zh | ... | .... | ∘ | .... | ... | ... | ... | ... | ... |
| **Labiales.** | | | | | | | | | | |
| 48 Tenuis | p | ... | .... | प | 𐬞 | [illegible] | پ | ... | פּ | p |
| 49 " aspirata | ph | ... | .... | फ | .... | ... | ... | ... | פ | ph |
| 50 Media | b | ... | .... | ब | 𐬠 | [illegible] | ب | ب | בּ | ... |
| 51 " aspirata | bh | ... | .... | भ | .... | ... | ... | ... | ב | ... |
| 52 Tenuissima | ... | *p* | .... | ... | .... | ... | ... | ... | ... | ... |
| 53 Nasalis | m | ... | .... | म | 𐬨 | [illegible] | م | م | מ | m |
| 54 Semivocalis | w | ... | .... | ... | 𐬎 | ... | ... | ... | ... | w |
| 55 " aspirata | hw | ... | .... | ... | .... | ... | ... | ... | ... | ... |
| 56 Spiritus asper | f | ... | .... | ... | 𐬟 | [illegible] | ف | ف | ... | f |
| 57 " lenis | v | ... | .... | व | 𐬬 | [illegible] | و | و | ו | ... |
| 58 Anusvâra | ... | *m* | .... | अं | 𐬯 ã | ... | ... | ... | ... | ... |
| 59 Visarga | ... | *h* | .... | अः | .... | ... | ... | ... | ... | ... |

| VOWELS. | MISSIONARY ALPHABET. I Class. | II Class. | III Class. | Sanskrit. | Zend. | Pehlevi. | Persian. | Arabic. | Hebrew. | Chinese. |
|---|---|---|---|---|---|---|---|---|---|---|
| 1 Neutralis | 0 | ... | ... | ... | ... | ... | ... | ... | ֲ | ă |
| 2 Laryngo-palatalis | ĕ | ... | ... | ... | ... | ... | ... | ... | ... | ... |
| 3 „ labialis | ŏ | ... | ... | ... | ... | 𐭠 fin. | ... | ... | ... | ... |
| 4 Gutturalis brevis | a | ... | ... | अ | 𐬀 | 𐭠 init. | َ | َ | ַ | a |
| 5 „ longa | â | (*a*) | ... | आ | 𐬁 | 𐭠 | َا | َا | ָ | â |
| 6 Palatalis brevis | i | ... | ... | इ | 𐬌 | ... | ِ | ِ | ִ | i |
| 7 „ longa | î | (*î*) | ... | ई | 𐬍 | 𐭩 | ِي | ِي | ִי | î |
| 8 Dentalis brevis | *li* | ... | ... | ऌ | ... | ... | ... | ... | ... | ... |
| 9 „ longa | *lî* | ... | ... | ॡ | ... | ... | ... | ... | ... | ... |
| 10 Lingualis brevis | *ri* | ... | ... | ऋ | ... | ... | ... | ... | ... | ... |
| 11 „ longa | *rî* | ... | ... | ॠ | ... | ... | ... | ... | ... | ... |
| 12 Labialis brevis | u | ... | ... | उ | 𐬎 | ... | ُ | ُ | ֻ | u |
| 13 „ longa | û | (*u*) | ... | ऊ | 𐬏 | 𐭥 | ُو | ُو | וּ | û |
| 14 Gutturo-palatalis brevis | e | ... | ... | ... | 𐬆(e) 𐬈(*e*) | ... | ... | ... | ֶ | e |
| 15 „ longa | ê (ai) | (*e*) | ... | ए | 𐬉, 𐬊 | 𐭩 | ... | ... | ֵ | ê |
| 16 Diphthongus gutturo-palatalis | âi | (*ai*) | ... | ऐ | ... | ... | َيْ | َيْ | ... | âi |
| 17 „ „ | ei (ĕi) | ... | ... | ... | ... | ... | ... | ... | ... | ei, êi |
| 18 „ „ | oi (ŏu) | ... | ... | ... | ... | ... | ... | ... | ... | ... |
| 19 Gutturo-labialis brevis | o | ... | ... | ... | 𐬊 | ... | ... | ... | ָ | o |
| 20 „ longa | ô (au) | (*o*) | ... | ओ | 𐬋 | 𐭥 | ... | ... | ֹ | ... |
| 21 Diphthongus gutturo-labialis | âu | (*au*) | ... | औ | 𐬆𐬎 (*au*) | ... | َوْ | َوْ | ... | âu |
| 22 „ „ | eu (ĕu) | ... | ... | ... | ... | ... | ... | ... | ... | ... |
| 23 „ „ | ou (ŏu) | ... | ... | ... | ... | ... | ... | ... | ... | ... |
| 24 Gutturalis fracta | ä | ... | ... | ... | ... | ... | ... | ... | ... | ... |
| 25 Palatalis fracta | ï | ... | ... | ... | ... | ... | ... | ... | ... | ... |
| 26 Labialis fracta | ü | ... | ... | ... | ... | ... | ... | ... | ... | ü |